A Lexicon of Alchemy

By

Dr. Martin Rulandus

Translated by Arthur E. Waite

A Lexicon of Alchemy
or
Alchemical Dictionary

Containing a full and plain explanation of all obscure words, Hermetic subjects, and arcane phrases of Paracelsus.

By

Dr. Martin Rulandus

Philosopher, Doctor, and Private Physician to the August Person of the Emperor.

With the Privilege of
His majesty the Emperor
for the space of ten years

1612

© Theophania Publishing

All rights reserved. The use of any part of this publication reproduced, transmitted in any form or by any means, electronic, mechanical, photocopying, recording, telepathic, or otherwise, or stored in a retrieval system without the prior written consent of the publisher is an infringement of the copyright law.

Theophania Publishing
Calgary Alberta Canada

PREFACE

To the Most Reverend and Most Serene Prince and Lord, The Lord Henry JULIUS, Bishop of Halberstadt, Duke of Brunswick, and Burgrave of Luna; His Lordship's most devout and humble servant wishes Health and Peace.

In the deep considerations of the Hermetic and Paracelsian writings, that has well-nigh come to pass which of old overtook the Sons of Shem at the building of the Tower of Babel. For these, carried away by vainglory, with audacious foolhardiness to rear up a vast pile into heaven, so to secure unto themselves an immortal name, but, disordered by a confusion and multiplicity of barbarous tongues, were ingloriously forced. In like manner, the searchers of Hermetic works, deterred by the obscurity of the terms which are met with in so many places, and by the difficulty of interpreting the hieroglyphs, hold the most noble art in contempt; while others, desiring to penetrate by main force into the mysteries of the terms and subjects, endeavour to tear away the concealed truth from the folds of its coverings, but bestow all their trouble in vain, and have only the reward of the children of Shem for their incredible pain and labour. Unto both these classes I wish to come forward with help, that they may not only seek more diligently into the writings of the Hermetists, but that they may understand them better, and that in this manner the divine Art of Alchemy may be more successfully taken in hand. For which reason I have concluded to publish this Lexicon of Alchemy, formerly compiled, and enlarged and completed since by me. Which also I would dedicate to one who shines over all princes, not only in knowledge of the learned languages and more celebrated arts, but also daily shows himself, by his singular industry and skilful hand, most intelligent and studious in the Art of Chemistry. Whence I have justly brought this trivial work to be consecrated by your patronage, well knowing that it will receive no small increase of reputation from the greatness of your erudition and from your illustrious name; and as in some way a monument of most humble reverence, it shall stand forth to its own greater adornment and preservation in the future. Fare thou well, most serene and learned lord, and hold me and mine as committed unto thy care.

With humblest deference,
Your respectful Servant,
Martinus Rulandus, Doctor.

A LEXICON OF ALCHEMY
by
DR. MARTINUS RULANDUS,
PHILOSOPHER AND PHYSICIAN.

AABAM, ABARTAMEN, ACCIB, AIARAZAT ~ are all Hermetic equivalents for lead. See Plumbum and Saturn. Other equivalents in use were the Scape-Goat, the Dual Chibor, Draiccium, Elevator, Araxat, Alusa, Ruba, Alech, Allonoch, Alabrig, Alokot, Armic, Amioch, Amitich, Araxat, Azoro, Balamba, Cartistilium, Koal, Molybdos, Mosquet dei, Molibra, Mosider, Rasas, Rasasa, Rolos, Roe, Rocli. All these are technical terms, which in themselves have no meaning, but which were used to signify Lead.
ABACUS ~ A counting-board, table or tray, etc.
ABACUS MAJOR ~ A larger table, etc.
ABESAMUM ~ The mire or grease which accumulates on the axle of a wheel.
ABESUM ~ Unslaked lime.
ABESS ~ is the same as Rebis, to wit, the last matter of the nutriments which are absorbed by the body; that is to say, it is the excrement of the bowels.
ABESTUS ~ Albesten, Abesten, and Morago, are Hermetic names for Asbestos.
ABICUM ~ A cover.

ABLATIO ~ A separation by means of the superior part. It is performed after several manners. In the dry region, where there is less specific gravity, such cleansing can be effected by the hare's foot or like agents. Sometimes we accomplish separation with a feather, with small knives, spatulas, etc. At other times, we purge in a narrow bag, with twigs, and with wooden, iron, and bristly substances.

ABLUTION ~ is exaltation by means of successive lustrations, washing away the impure refuse, and reducing the matter to a pure state. It is also called Imbibition and Cohobation, or digestion.

ABLUVIEN ~ Cleansing.

ABNELEITEM ~ is Alum; also called Asfor.

ABOIT, or **ABIT** ~ is White Lead. The same thing is signified by Alkarad, Almachabar, and Alsiden.

ABRIC, KIBRIT, and **KIBUZ** ~ are names of Sulphur.

ACACIA FERREA ~ An iron spoon.

ACAHI ~ is Alum-water; called also Fefcol.

ACAID ~ is Vinegar, or sour substances.

ACALAI ~ is Salt; called also Alet.

ACAMECH, or **ACEMECH** ~ is the scoria or refuse of Silver.

ACARTUM ~ is Cinnabar or Red Lead; called also Azemasor.

ACATO ~ is Soot; called also Araxos.

ACAZDI ~ is Jupiter, or Tin; called also Alkain and Alomba.

ACCATU ~ is Tinsel; called also Aurichalcum, properly Orichalcum, which is the brass of the ancients. Accatem signifies the same.

ACCORDINA ~ is Indian tutty; called also Alcordine.

ACETABULUS ~ A vessel for vinegar, or a cup-shaped vessel, holding as much as would an eggshell.

ACETUM ~ Vinegar.

ACETUM AMINEUM — White vinegar. Acetum also signifies sour wine, and in this sense Acetum Amineum would be sour white wine, wine of Aminaea, which was distinguished for vine culture.

ACETUM PHILOSOPHORUM — is Philosophical Vinegar, that is, Virgin's Milk, or Mercurial Water, in which metals are dissolved. One of its Hermetic names was Sophic Hydor. According to Theophrastus, the Philosophical Vinegar is the Chemist's Vitriol-water, but the Turba states that it is the water of mercury which dissolves gold. Others affirm that Philosophical Vinegar is that which is made from fresh shells of tortoises by sublimation and distillation.

ACETUM RADICALE — is Radical Vinegar, or Vinegar distilled from its proper radix or matrix. It is also called dissolvent water.

ACETUM RADICATUM — or Radicated Vinegar signifies in some authors that most sharp liquor of vinegar which remains at the bottom of the retort, after the phlegmatic part has been evaporated. It is made by distillation in the retort out of the crystals of the dregs of vinegar. Or good vinegar, made from wine, may be placed in a retort, distilled gently by a moist heat, often poured back upon its caput mortuum, and dissolved in dung, after which it must be finally distilled, when that which is left may be taken and liquefied in a strong fire. The result is radicated vinegar.

ACHATES — The Agate, first found in Sicily, near the river of that name, and afterwards in other localities, as testifies Pliny, 1. 37 c. 10. There are various species, each bearing separate names: Jaspachates, Ceradhates, Sardachates, Haemachates, Leucachates, Dendrachates, the veins of which are like unto minute trees; Autachates, which, when burnt, gives forth fragrance of myrrh; Coralloachates, distinguished by a golden speckling, after the manner of the sapphire; this variety is found in Crete. Agates are a safeguard against the bite of the spider, and eagles carry them to their nests to defend their fledglings against venomous animals. They allay thirst and strengthen sight. Concerning the rest, consult Pliny in the place cited, who also relates that various impressions of figures appear in agates; in some, for example, may be seen rivers, woods, cattle, beasts of burden, herds, war-chariots, minute statues, and the furniture or ornaments of horses. In particular, he relates (1. 37, c. 1) how Pyrrhus had an agate gem in which could be seen Apollo and the nine Muses, with their insignias. I myself have beheld a gem belonging to a nobleman, which, however, was not a true agate, but when the blemishes had been dispersed, it exhibited a rustic and a complete plough. I found also another at Albion Silicem, near the gate of Tangra, wherein appeared the likeness of a wolf or a lion, near a half-rose, so clearly cut by nature as though the work had been done by a jeweller. Most credible truly are those things of Pliny when writing of the impressions upon this kind of stone.

ACIES ~ Steel.

ACORTINUS ~ A lupine, wolf's-bean, or horse-bean.

ACSUO ~ is Red Coral.

ACUREB ~ Glass.

ACUS ~ A needle.

ACUSTA ~ Saltpetre.

ADAMAS ~ in Arabic Subedhig, in Latin Adamas (Pliny, 1. 37, c. 4), the diamond, which is found both apart from gold and in gold, contrary to the opinion of the ancients, who knew it only as native in gold among the metals of Aethiopia. But for the better understanding of this subject, observe the ensuing scheme, which we have elaborated out of Pliny in part, and in part from other authorities.

Not found in gold, and of this there are two species.

The Indian diamond, not having its birth in gold, is known by its translucid crystal colour and sex-angular sides; it is either cone-shaped at one end or else it has the form of a lozenge; it is sometimes as large as a hazel. This species is said by Serapion to approximate to the colour of Sal Ammoniac.

The Arabian diamond, likewise not found in gold, is smaller than the preceding.

Native in the most Perfect Gold.

I. The Greek stone called Cenchron, because it is the size of a millet seed.

II. Macedonian; generated in gold of Philippi; like the seed of cucumber in size.

III. Cyprian; found in Cyprus; approaching brass in colour; most efficacious in healing.

IV. Having the splendour of iron sideritis (that is, according to Pliny, a precious stone; according to others it is loadstone ; and again it is the plant ironwort); surpassing the others in weight, but differing from them in nature; can be broken by blows, and pierced by another diamond.

The two last are degenerate, and scarcely deserve their name. The best diamonds are impervious to blows on an anvil, which they repel, so that even the anvil bursts asunder, while they themselves leap away invulnerable. And inasmuch as the diamond is indescribably hard, it contemns and conquers fire, nor has ever been consumed thereby. Whence, from its indomitable life and strength, it has the name *** among the Greeks.

That herb which is mentioned by Pliny (1. 24, c. 17), which cannot be torn up, was also called adamant. The stone, however, can be shattered by the flesh, or rather by the warm blood of a young goat; more especially when the goat has first drunk wine or eaten rock parsley and mountain skirwort. For the above reasons, diamonds are much in request among lapidaries for cutting and shaping gems and other substances, for which purpose they ought to be mounted only in iron. Other metals they will by no means tolerate, while by lead, wonderful to say, they are themselves dissolved.

Furthermore, the diamond is so hostile to the loadstone that it will not permit iron to be attracted in its neighbourhood, and if a magnet at close quarters should have attracted a piece of iron, the approach of a diamond will cause it to lose its hold.

In short, the diamond binds the magnet and strips it of its virtues. Oh, how wonderful is God in all His works! For the rest, the diamond irritates venomous animals, drives away frenzies, lemures, incubi, and succubi; it makes men strong and lively, and is for this reason called anachitis (that is, anancitis — from the Greek *** — to free from distress). It prevails against contentions and quarrels, and cures viscous fluxes. Consult Serapion and Evax. Some will have that the diamond is cold and dry in the fourth degree, others, on the contrary, that it is hot and dry, inasmuch as it is mixed with warming medicines. Did the matter receive investigation, doubtless diamonds would be found in our mines, as they have been found in times past: witness Pliny on the authority of Metrodorus Scepsius. In Bohemia stones of excellent quality are still seen, which surpass Oriental diamonds in shape and lustre. Consult Solinus, De Adamante, c. 55. The ancient astrologers referred the diamond to the Moon.

ADAMAS ACUMINATUS — A four-sided diamond point.
ADAMAS QUADRATUS PLANUS — A flat square diamond.
ADAMATUM — A kind of bright stone.
ADAMITA — A species of tartar; a kind of wine-stone or kidney-stone. (Wine-stone, Germ. = Tartar.)

ADARCES, ARTIS — According to some this is a marine flesh, a spongy growth, a froth or efflorescence, a congealed saliva having birth in sea-shallows, especially of Cappadocia and Galatia. The Indian species is found among reeds and cane-brakes on the shore. It has similar qualities to the substance called Halcyon. It was termed formerly Pericalamite and Calamoch. Some physicians make use of these ridiculous substances while they despise more noble things. They have even gone so far as to invent obscure names for it, which would be a puzzle to Oedipus himself. Some having written as follows: Take the fat of the deformed child and the tears of the vine of Dionysius. Who shall understand this save Oedipus? Who shall quickly interpret the deformed child to be the she-bear, and the gum of the vine of Dionysius to be the gum of the ivy? The Adarces here referred to must be distinguished from the true Adarces or Oysters. It is a sort of thick, salt scum which collects about reeds in marshy places. Its proper name is Adarca, but this Rulandus confuses with the oyster, and says that its power in diseases is declared by Dioscorides (1. 5, c. 84) and by Pliny (1. 32, c. 6), who represents it as coming into existence around tender reeds amidst the spume of fresh water and sea water, and accredits it with caustic virtues.
ADARNECH — is Orpiment.
ADARRIS — is the spume or foam of sea water.
ADDERE — To augment; but also used as an equivalent of temperare, to combine in due proportion, to keep within bounds.
ADDITAMENTA — Addition, increase.
ADEC — Sour milk.
ADER — Fresh skimmed milk.
ADECH — is our interior and invisible man, who raises up in our minds the image or archetypes of all those things

which our visible and exterior man copies and forms with his hands. Each works after his own nature, the invisible thin; unseen, the sensible, under form sensible, those things which are within the dominion of the senses.

ADEPS ~ A fluid in its final distillation.

ADHEMEST ~ with its equivalents Aiohenec and Altohonec, signifies a plate.

ADHEHE ~ Another term for sour milk.

ADHO or **ADHOC** ~ Milk.

ADIBAT ~ Mercury.

ADIBISI or **ADEBEZI** ~ The tortoise, also tortoise shell.

ADIDACHOS, ADIDE ALARCOS, ADIDA LARCHOS ~ Various terms for "mixed with lime", slaked.

ADIRIGE ~ Ammoniac.

ADMI SURAB ~ Earth.

ADOS ~ Water in which red-hot iron has been plunged.

ADOLESCENS ~ Young man.

ADORAT ~ A weight of four pounds.

ADRAM ~ Metallic salt, Cappadocian salt.

ADRARAGI ~ Garden Saffron.

ADRARIGES ~ is green atrament ; also blue sulphate of copper.

ADROP, AZAR, AZANE ~ A kind of stone.

ADSAMAR ~ Signifies urine, but also lotion, fountain, etc.

ADVERSA VENAE PARS ~ Against the grain, literally, against the direction of a current; hence, opposition in general.

AER ~ Equals breath, breeze, spirit, wind, weather.

AERIS ~ That is, verdigris.

AERIS SCOBS ~ Ordinary copper

AERIS FLOS ~ Metaphorically so called, was termed by the Greeks, Chalckou Anthos, and is misnamed Calcantum, that is, vitriol, the shoemakers' black of the Latins, the ignorant believed of old, being deceived by the similarity of the terms. But Flower of Copper differs among the ancients and moderns. For the ancients, as appears, denominated Flower of Copper those purple globules which rise suddenly when the melted copper runs from the furnace, and is purged from impurity by the sudden sprinkling of clear water. Of this kind of Flower of Copper Dioscorides speaks (1. 5, c. 43), and enumerates its medicinal powers and virtues. Among the moderns, however, the Flower of Copper signifies verdigris. This distinction should be remembered in comparing ancient and recent authors. It should also be borne in mind that formerly they intermingled copper scales and Flower of Copper, whence a new substance was developed which was called Lepis, as appears out of Pliny. At the present day Flos Aeris is not included in the Pharmacopia. Concerning its virtues Pliny says (1. 34. c 11): The Flower of Copper is useful to medicine; verily there is not a mineral throughout all the mines of so useful a nature as it is. It purgeth the stomach, strengthens the eyes, remedies hardness of hearing, stayeth bleeding at the nose.

There are two kinds of Copper Scales, namely, dense and light. Of the first Dioscorides treats (1. 5, c. 44). It is called Copper Slag by the Germans, but this, which is broad and thin, is produced from copper by hammering. Dioscorides (l. c.) avers that which is beaten from bars in the forges of Cyprus, and called Helitin, or Hammered, to be the best, but that which is beaten from poor and vulgar copper, or from white copper, is wholly to be condemned. He leaches further the virtues and the lustration of Aeris Squama. He makes mention in addition of Stomoma, the fine scales which fly off in hammering.

There is another stomoma which is the same as the lighter variety of Aeris Squama, and is mentioned, not by Dioscorides, but by Pliny. It is called Copperborn by the

Germans. And there is yet another stomoma which is, as it were, slack from the ore and is pierced easily. Yet again, there is that stomoma which is ferrum purgatum, purissimum, our chalybs, which is steel.

It was Pliny (1. 34, c. 2) who first taught that coarse copper scales differed from Flower of Copper, when he said: Now these scales come by being driven and smitten off from those bars which they use to forge of the said masses and lumps of copper, and all these most commonly are found in the Cyprian forges; herein only is the difference, that the aforesaid scales are driven forcibly from the masses of copper, whereas the flower of verdigris fails off by itself. And yet there is a second kind of these scales, more fine and subtle than any other, to wit, driven and smitten from the very outside and uppermost part of the bar, and this they call Stomoma. He adds that both the one and the other are calcined either over earthen or brazen vessels, and afterwards washed. Finally, he also avers that the scales made of the white metal are indefinitely less efficacious. But neither the scales nor the flower are used by our doctors as they were in the time of Pliny.

AERUGO AERIS — or Verdigris, which the moderns, as we have shown, contradictorily call Flower of Copper, is twofold, natural and artificial, the former being found in metallic Cypriot stones, having some proportion of copper; upon these the verdigris bursts out as in bloom, and this, though small in quantity, is the best, and is also found in our copper mines. Dioscorides (1. 5, c. 45) mentions its varieties, with their proportionate worth, and the manner in which they are sophisticated.

Concerning artificial verdigris, which is produced upon the surface of copper when the metal has become sufficiently green, this is of threefold kind, namely:

1. The smooth or scraped, whereof Dioscorides speaks firstly, and shows after what manner it is made.
2. The vermiculated, or worm-eaten verdigris, which is also duplex, that which is mineral and that which is made.
The former is the better, and is scraped by itself from the copperstone, upon which see Pliny (l. 34, c. 12), who disputes at great length as to whether it be a species of vitriol, or chalchitis itself. Great indeed is the knowledge of verdigris, of the natural above all, of Flower of Copper, of Chrysocolla, and of Vitriol, that is, true Chalchitis. Do thou, most excellent reader, well consider it, and judge the erudition of Pliny. Vermiculated verdigris, of the manufactured kind, and the way of making it, are taught by Dioscorides and by Pliny.
3. The third species of manufactured verdigris is goldsmiths' verdigris, which is also treated of by Dioscorides, and this is Santerna, which is used for alum. Some call it Tinckar or Arabian Borax. Goldsmiths' verdigris is nothing else but Chrysocolla, on which consult Pliny (1. 33, c. 5; also 1. 34, c. 11 and 12).

All these species answer to Burnt Copper; they are astringent, they reduce, and heat, which is the case with all kinds of copper rust.

After what manner the rest are burnt, consult Dioscorides. In our own day similar species of copper rust are largely manufactured in Spain.

The Arabians, if I mistake not, call all the above enumerated species by the name Zinckar; and these are the species according to Pliny, Dioscorides, and others. But if we consider deeply, there are some which have not been distinguished by them, and are set forth in the following tabulation:

Verdigris or Copper Rust is:

Scraped: Natural / Manufactured (1. Scraped; 2. Vermiculate — Mined / Manufactured; 3. Goldsmiths'. Scissile: Natural, i.e., copper-green. Gold-gluten / Manufactured, goldsmiths' green, scraped, manufactured copper, green.

The remaining species are distinguished thus:

1. Verdigris, colour of green copper; things dyed with green copper rust are so named by Martial.
2. Natural verdigris found on copper quartz.
3. A variety from Satberg, of leaden colour, found in rude copper ore.
4. Verdigris found on pure solid copper.
5. Manufactured verdigris.
6. Sublimed or distilled verdigris, used by painters.

AERARII LAPIDES — Natural copper stones.

1. Black scissile copper ore in which are natural plates of copper.
2. Ore containing natural green chrysocolla.
3. Ore containing natural blue chrysocolla.
4. Scissile ores in which is interspersed copper of a golden, ruddy, blue, purple, violet, or black colour.
5. Scissile ore, having seams of gold-coloured copper.
6. Ore containing seams of copper like the purest lead ore.
7. Cuprine scissile slate, burnt in the open air.
8. Burnt.
9. Burnt in the open air, afterwards melted out, and the dross separated.
10. Small globular slate-stones, perfectly circular, hard and heavy, of different sizes. Also found among copper quartz, with an ashy surface, as if composed of fine sand; if broken with a hammer, they are like silver or ash-coloured pyrites inside. Sometimes copper and some times silver is melted out of them.

11. Very hard, small pebbles, showing ruddy in black; found in scissile copper ore, like the kidneys of animals; when broken, they are of a deceptive colour, showing rich cuprine hues, but if searched with fire they possess no metallic quality.
12. Sterile ore, found beneath copper ore, showing white in ash-colour.
13. Primary masses melted out of rude copper.
14. Secondary, in which silver or gold are still present, which are sold to masters of laboratories for the separation of the silver and copper.
15. Crumbling or spongy masses, out of which, when lead is added, silver can be extracted.
16. Masses of silver and lead from which copper has been separated.
17. Copper containing silver combined with lead.
18. Copper, of fine quality, free from torrefied, crumbling, or cloven masses.
19. Copper masses free from all other metal.
20. Sharp-pointed ore stones produced in torrefying masses of crumbling ore.
21. Copper nuggets full of sharp points. Also layers of sharp-pointed copper.
22. Sharp-pointed nuggets of copper and lead, produced in the fusion of masses of ore.
23. Sharp-pointed pieces from nuggets which have been once subject to fusion.
24. Fused copper, containing gold.
25. Fused copper, containing silver. .
26. Fused copper, containing both gold and silver.
27. Tinged with magnesia. White copper.
28. Tinged with metallic cadmia. Yellow copper.
29. Gold-coloured copper.

30. Flattened copper wire out of which garlands or wreaths are made.
31. Copper showing flaxen colour in red colour.
32. Copper showing swarthy in red.
33. Copper tinctures with gold-colour by chemical art. Alchemical gold.
34. Gilded copper.
35. Copper coloured silver by chemical art. Alchemical silver.
36. Copper mixed with white lead.
37. Cremated copper.
38. Copper fused with white lead. Manufactured bell-metal.
39. Copper alloy, containing equal parts of copper and silver. Cobalt.
40. Copper fused in iron pipes. Finger-shaped pieces of copper. Used in testing.
41. Copper reduced to granules; vulgarly called granulated copper.
42. Flower of copper, given off from incandescent masses of copper; in appearance like millet seed.
43. A more minute kind, given off from molten crucibles, like flying poppy seed.
44. True flower of copper, given off spontaneously from red-hot crucibles. Very fine Cyprian copper dust.
45. Baked copper, hardened with hammers.
46. Scales of copper, beaten out by the hammer.
47. Most pure scales of copper, with which potters colour their vases. Brown copper, found useful in all coppersmiths' work.
48. Copper melted into the form of globules. Coarsely granulated copper.
49. Copper filings.
50. Plates of Copper, called sometimes by an Italian name, batitura. Sheet copper.

51. Copper wire..
52. Gilt copper wire.
53. Silvered copper wire.
54. Copper wire overlaid with white lead.
55. Black refuse, separated in the first melting, from copper ore.
56. Metal extracted from copper ore which is once fused and separated from its refuse.
57. The same, but melted up to the sixth time, then finally baked, and separated from its first and second refuse.
58. Yellow copper thread. Copper wire.
59. The first recrement of red colour is the material of those pitchers out of which we usually drink must, or unfermented wine.
60. The second recrement, mixed with brass or lead, is called, in our vernacular, stone, and is again added to the metals in the second melting when they begin to flow rapidly.
61. The third recrement remains in the furnace, when the copper, in which silver is still present, flows out. Out of this recrement, when pounded and prepared for another melting down, iron is extracted.
62. Recrements separated from torrefied copper masses.
63. The first recrements of copper are light.
64. The second are heavier.
65. The third are heaviest of all, and black, blue, purple, and red in colour. On the surface of the Islebian mountains there is found a red earth, or red ore, with which the copper ore of the mines is mixed in digging out. Beneath this there are eleven other species of stone, before the object of mining is attained, i.e., before the copper veins are reached.
1. Granite. Hyalomite.
1A. A hard, rude stone, of earthy colour.
2. Another not so hard, and of ashen hue.

3. Smokestone. Smoky topaz.
3A. A third harder and rougher, and of colour similar to the first.
4. Zechstein, permian limestone.
4A. A fourth, showing swarthy in ash-colour, but more solid than the second.
5. Smoky topaz.
5A. A fifth, ashen, hard, and rough.
6. Fulgurite.
6A. Another, like to the fourth.
7. Another similar to the second, but softer.
8. Another blacker than the seventh, small, and harder.
9. A ninth kind, showing ashen in white, soft, and may be broken like marl with a penknife.
10. Another of ash-colour, hard and solid as marble.
11. A layer of black horny slate.
11. Showing more black in ash-colour than all the others.
12. Scissile Islebian stone, dark ash-colour, rich in copper. Slate-stone, rich in copper.

AES ~ or Copper is attributed to Venus by chemists. (N.B. ~ Aes signified any Ore; i.e., any metal as it is dug from the earth, but especially refined copper.)

It is a metallic body of a bluish colour with a dark ruddy tinge; it is igneous and fusible, and occupies a middle position between Sol and Luna, gold and silver. It is composed of quicksilver, but impure, unfixed, terrestrial, combustible, ruddy, and not clear; and, in like manner, of sulphur wanting in fixity, purity, and density. Bad and feeble sulphur, like a father of ill complexion and disposition, copulates with a noble mother, that is, with quicksilver, and generates copper of good quality, a son of bluish colour, tinged with dark red.

This copper is obtained from veins in the mines, where there is abundance of pyrites, or marcasite, which beget the various natural species of vitriol, copperstone, copperas, inkstone, tutty, etc. Out of copper ore when it is melted there are obtained the several varieties of artificial Cadmia, Pompholyx, and Spodos (Pliny, 1. 34, c. 10-13). In the operation of the furnace, burnt copper is obtained, and scales of copper indifferently by cooling the heated metal and by hammering. Finally, verdigris is deposited on the surface of the excocted metal.

There are, broadly, two species of copper, first, that which is found pure in copper and silver mines, and is in need of no purifying. Intertwined veins are sometimes met with, and again whole plates of thin metal which encompass the stone. Of this Albertus was ignorant. The second species is that which is melted out of pyrites or marcasite, and other substances; such as, slate, stone, as well as out of various earths and clays; also out of Chrysocolla and Azurite, like gold.

Aes, however, does not always denote copper, but sometimes gold or silver, as they exist in nature, without any mixture of other metal or stone-a pure, unmixed metal, out of which money was stamped sometimes, in the same way as from alloys artificially prepared. This substance was first found in Galilee, but in a small quantity. In our own day it is likewise seen, but rarely, and is only to be obtained by a miracle. (The German version says: Properly it is called copper, some call it simply gold or silver ore which has not yet been melted, but has been prepared by nature, and out of which coins have been occasionally struck.)

(The copper nuggets referred to by Pliny are identified with burnt copper by Rulandus, who also enumerates, Loaf-shaped copper masses, completely baked ; Aes Caldarium, a copper warming vessel; Aes abstractum, copper extracted from the ore; Aes residuum, refined copper; Aes liquefactum, copper melted in an iron pipe. There is no context to explain the object of these enumerations.)

AERUGINATIS ~ Copper rusting, is the gilding of the earths in the ferment; the red earth which is resolved and cooked, which is the second operation.

AES HERMETIS ~ is the same as Mercury. It is also Solar Dust, the Head of the Raven, our copper, citrine earth, the thing containing and the thing contained, our lead. Mirerius calls it Gold extracted out of Metals; it is also termed Venus; Vitriol; Orpiment; Arsenic; Money; the Soul; the Green Lion; Green Water, because it germinates; Permanent Water; Wine; Blood. But it is truly and properly an imperfect body, not yet prepared, and in its original state.

AES USTUM, or **CREMTUM** ~ Burnt copper according to Dioscorides (l. 5, c. 42) is obtained by arranging alternate layers of copper bars with salt and sulphur, or alum, in an earthen vessel. The same author enumerates other methods, and burnt copper is made in our own day out of copper, sulphur, and salt. Dioscorides praises the aes ustum of Memphis and Cyprus. It is astringent, desiccating, restrictive; it reduces, draws out, and cleanses; and it heals ulcers. It is serviceable in complaints of the eye; it is a good emetic, when mixed with honey. It is cleansed like Cadmia, and is regarded as hot and dry in the fourth degree. The scum or excrement of copper, prepared after the same manner, has the same virtues, in a weaker degree. Consult Dioscorides as above.

The other species of Copper Ore and Copper are as follows:
1. Pure native copper.
2. Native red copper, unalloyed with other metals, found, clean and solid, in its own mines, in the Duchy of Mansfield.
3. Mined copper, found in its own veins.
4. Pure copper mined from argentiferous veins at Scheberg.

5. Red Mansfield copper, which contains silver.
6. Red native copper of Suacensis in the Rhetian Alps, which contains gold within it.
7. Copper of a chestnut brown colour, which adheres like a thin plate to the hard stone. Solid copper.
8. Of the ordinary colour, in a violet fluor-spar.
9. Of the ordinary colour, intermixed with stony substance.
10. Of its own colour, cleaving to hard stone, which has the glow of hot
ashes.
11. Of its own colour, cleaving to a scissile stone. The German context speaks of a red copper mixed with sulphur on a slate bed; ruddy, solid copper.
12. Thin shavings of copper, in a white flint.
13. Veinlets or fibres of copper in a bright, ruddy stone; a preparation of a copper ore in a hard stone.
14. A rich vein of copper; a speedy process for pure copper.
15. Rough, native, impure copper.
16. Pure solid copper of Moravia.
17. Natural yellow copper, gold-coloured copper, cleaving to brittle Mansfield stone.
18. Blue copper, cleaving to brittle stone.
19. Copper, entirely blue.
20. Brownish or violet copper, cleaving to brittle stone.
21. White copper, similar to rude white silver, in a brittle stone; a rich white copper ore.
22. Black copper ore.
23. Copper ore so abundantly mixed with brittle stone that 100 lbs. contains 40 lbs. of copper.
24. A natural solid copper of several colours, distinguished into zones of gold, purple, saffron, flaxen, green, and blue.
25. Friberg copper, allied to black lead, of so many excellent colours that they shine as if they were transparent.

26. Copper native in white lead, having the brightness of polished gold. The German version reads, born in black lead, as crystallised tin-ore.

AETHNA — This name is given to a subterranean, invisible, and sulphureous fire which burns stones into coals similar to asphalt; they are full of resin and bitumen, and some nations use them instead of coals or wood, especially spurious sophisticators of metals. Formerly, these subterraneous fires were to be seen in several places, as, for example, that called Aetna in Sicily, and another in the Neapolitan Kingdom not far from Naples. In ancient times the men of those days, wonderstruck as to what could be the cause of these fires, and after great investigation being unable to assign it, became so desperate that one among the most celebrated philosophers, physicists, and doctors, Empedocles, cast himself headlong into the flames, choosing to be vanquished by shame rather than by ignorance. Again Caius Plinius delivered himself to suffocation from the smoke of this fire. Oh insane talents of men, who, whilst they will be ignorant of nothing, have attempted no labours, so that they can know nothing, and have nevertheless borne a shameful death, esteeming it better not to live than not to know that which at the same time they knew to be transitory! Housewives, when they have done cooking, shut up the fire in their grate, so that there may be no entrance of air, by which means the fire dies out, for it can live only in air. But if a draught be admitted before it is quite extinguished, the flame will revive. In the same way we must regard volcanoes, whose fires originate in the earth's centre, which holds them like a grate. They are the air-holes of the earth, by which the central fires have their nourishment from the atmosphere, and without which they would be extinguished like the fires in a grate. (An invisible sulphureous fire in mountains, which turns stones into coal.)

Item. All fused ores are understood by the name Aethna.

AETHNICI — are igneous spirits, or spirit-men, burning in the midst of flames. They appear in various modes and manners, like burning fires, live circular coals, or fiery globes; they are also seen amidst the sulphureous eruptions of volcanoes.

AETITES — are Eagle-stones, so called on account of their colour and their virtue, for without them can no eagle bring forth. For the Eagle-stone alleviates parturition. It is also called Lapis Erodialis and Lapis Aegreileius. It is a gem of several species. The first is the Pregnant-stone described by Dioscorides. When it is shaken another stone can be heard rattling in its stomach. It is of globular shape, is hollow, like the oak-apple, and bears another stone within it; this species is found in the vicinity of the Saale and the Elbe, and especially in that district which we now call Steuermarch. Very great virtues are possessed by this species; in particular, it relieves the sense of heaviness experienced by women before child-birth if the uterus be rubbed with it. The second species of Eagle-stone is that which is filled with earth, i.e., with white or saffron clay, and this is the Geodes (full of earth, earthy), a precious stone mentioned by Dioscorides. Varieties of this sort, containing earth or clay, are found at Dresden and in Saxony. I have myself seen a species, containing a saffron clay, on the banks of the Elbe, and another, full of white clay, is met with in the vicinity of the Saale. The third species is filled with water, and perspires in a warm place. It is called Enydros; hence those lines of the poet:

"The Enidros pours forth perpetual tears, Which spring like water from a fountain full ".

Pliny (1. 37, c. 11) and Solinus (c. 40) make special mention of this species. Says Pliny: The Enydros is always perfectly round; it is white, and of little weight, but when moved water is seen to flow within it like the liquid in eggs. And Solinus: The Enydros exudes moisture, as if a spring of water were contained within it. The fourth species of Eagle-stone is full of sand and tiny pebbles. The fifth is full of chelonitis, the sixth of a white lime; this is the variety which I discovered by the Elbe; it was of oblong shape, very hard, and honeycombed on its surface. I met also with another species separated from the matrix and of a peculiar shape similar to the variety described by Pliny (1. 10, c. 3), called Gagates by other writers, said to be found in the nests of eagles, especially in those of the bearded eagle, and termed the Pregnant-stone. When struck, or shaken, another stone can be heard rattling within it. It is not consumed by fire, a quality it possesses in common with the true Gagates (this is a species of bitumen), whence the identity of name. Those Eagle-stones, which are taken from the nests of eagles have the greatest medicinal virtue. Pliny also pretends (11. 36, c. 27) to distinguish two kinds of Eagle-stones which are found in the nests of these birds, a male and female, which are both necessary to the hatching of their eggs. After the same manner, the eagle places an agate under its unfledged young to protect them from poisonous reptiles. Pliny otherwise distinguishes four species of Eagle-stone.
1. The small soft African eagle-stone, containing soft white clay, as in a womb. It is easily crumbled to pieces, and has been regarded as feminine. It is found at the present day full of yellow clay, and is the Geodis of Dioscorides.
2. A variety from Cyprus, similar to the African, but larger and broader, globular in shape, soft on its surface, easily crumbled, and containing fine sand and pebbles. Varieties of this sort are also found pregnant with lime and conchylii.

3. Found near Leucadia, in the island of Taphus, whence it is called Taphinsius; it is met with in rivers, is white, and round in shape. In its womb it contains the stone called Callimus, and it is exceedingly soft.

4. A hard Eagle-stone like the oak-apple, found in Arabia, and believed to be masculine; it contains a reddish stone, also hard, and is much praised by Dioscorides. This also is familiar to us, and has been previously described.

All species of aetites assist parturition and prevent abortion, as also Pliny witnesses (1. 36, c. 21). They are to be distinguished from the Echite which is an herb of the clematis genus; from Echites, a stone spotted like a viper; and from Echitis, a variety of the last. Consult Pliny as above, Solinus, c. 40, Serapion, Albertus, Rhasis, and others. The eagle-stone is also classified as follows:

1. African male aetitis, very hard, black and red in colour, containing a white crumbling earth.
2. Feminine, from Hildesheimer, mud-coloured, with yellow ochre adhering to it. This species contains a hard, mud-coloured earth.
3. Another kind, with a loose stone inside it, which sounds when shaken.
4. Hard, ruddy aetites, having an iron-grey stone.
5. Another, from Motteschanus, shaped like the human head, round, and very hard, having quadrangular, crystalline fluors like adamant.
6. A concave, iron-grey stone, found in iron ore, and containing nothing but air. The German Druse.

AFFARX, or **AFFARIS** — is Atrament.

AFFRONITUM — is Froth of Nitre, in Arabic Baurach; or it is that pseudo-Froth of Nitre which is called Glass-gall by the Germans; or it is the metallic salt called Cappadocius and Gemma.

AFFENICUM — is Soul.

AFFEOS, or **AFROS** — is Froth or Spume.
AFFORMAS — is Glass.
AFRICUS — Mid south-west.
AFFRODINA — is Venus.
AFFROTON — is frothy, spumous, etc.
AFFRENGI — is Minium, Red Lead, Vermilion.
AFFIDRA, or **ALLMAT** — is White Lead.
AFRAGAR — is Verdigris.
AFROS — is our Lead, the unclean body.
AGABAR — is Prepared Calx.
AGAR, ALGIT, ALGERIT — Names of Calx.
AHENUM — is a metallic vase of copper, or iron, two feet high, and of about the same width. On the top there is a cover which fits it exactly, and is made in the following manner: A plate of copper is made in exact correspondence with the capacity of the ahenum (for the sake of convenience some affirm that a wooden cover may be substituted), and of circular shape, in the centre of which (when the ahenum is intended for the reception of only one cuppingglass) a little door is cut, of the exact size of the vase which is to be placed in the ahenum, and out of which at the same time it can project a certain distance. On one or the other side, and near the bottom of the ahenum, another door must be made, through which the heat can flow under, and more water be supplied to make up for evaporation. The use of this covered ahenum is manifold in the operations of the baths.
AHIUS — is Rock-Salt, or Muriate of Soda.
AHUSAL — is Arsenical Sulphur. Also the Eagle.
AIARAZATH, or **ALHENOT** — is Lead.
AKIBOT, ALCHIBIT, ALCHINIT — are names of Sulphur.
AKON — is a sharp-pointed stone. Hence aconite, an herb which grows on rocks, derives the name it bears. There is

another sharp-pointed stone, with which knives and other instruments are sharpened, and it is called Whetstone. Of this we have several species-black, white, yellow, and one which is of a very deep black. Dioscorides (1. 5, c. 93) signalises the uses of the Naxian Stone which is worn away by the sharpening of instruments thereon. The species under notice is also called Heraclean and Lydian Stone ; it is the German Touch-stone, which is known to our goldsmiths and is called Coticula by Pliny (1. 33, c. 8). That stone which is found in Misnia, and is now used by book-binders, is also a species of cos-stone. There is, moreover, a variety which is of green colour, and is called Eye-stone, or Oil-stone, because instruments of various kinds are sharpened upon it after it has been lubricated with oil. There are additional species which the reader himself will be able to recall to his mind without further enumeration — Lydian Stone, Grind-stone, Clinthy Slate, etc.

ALABASTRITES — Alabaster, from the town of that name in Upper Egypt, and also from Damascus of Syria. It is a species of marble, and is familiar to the Venetians. There are three kinds; the first is white and shining, and is that white alabaster of which in times gone by it was usual to make the images of saints and -the monuments of the departed. The second species has black spots. The third is white and ruddy, and is hence called Onyx, ruddy Alabaster, because it has the tint of human flesh. It is the species referred to by Dioscorides when he says: Alabaster, also called Onyx, when burnt with pitch or resin, removes indurations of the body. For the various uses of the onyx, and concerning the vessels and boxes for ointment which are made of it, consult Dioscorides (1. 2). At the present time there are two species found in Germany, in Cheruscis, not far from Northusia, and in Saxony, near Hildesheim. Pliny (1. 36, c. 7 and 8) says: Alabaster is used for vases containing unguents, and is medicinally valuable in plasters to be placed over burns and scalds. He also informs us that its native places are Thebes of Egypt and Damascus of Syria. There is, however, a useless and inferior species which comes from Cappadocia, a country of Asia between the Black Sea, or rather Pontus, and Cilicia. Consult also the same writer in the thirteenth chapter of his thirteenth book of the History of the World.

ALABONI, or ALOANACH ~ is Lead

ALAFOR, ALAFORT ~ Salt of Alkali.

ALACHASCHE ~ is a caltrop.

ALAFREG ~ is a species of white lead.

ALAHABAR, ALABARI, ALCHONOR, ALLARINOCH, ALHOHONOCH, ALRACHAS, ALASTROB, ALOMBA, ALOOC, ALLABOR, ALCAMOR ~ are all names of Lead. See Abam, etc.

ALAHATIB ~ is a ruddy stone.

ALAHIC ~ according to some is an oven of the alchemists; according to others, it is Charcoal.

ALARTAR ~ is burnt Copper Ore.

ALASALET ~ is Ammoniac.

ALATAN ~ is semi-vitrified protoxide of lead.

ALAURAT ~ is Nitric Salt.

ALBANUM ~ is Salt of Wine.

ALBANI ~ is a stone of salt of milk.

ALBARAS ~ is Arsenic.

ALBATIO ~ Whiteness; white ashes left by calcination.

ALBERICK ~ is White Copper or Metallic Ore.

ALBESTON ~ is Quicklime.

ALBETAD ~ is Galbanum, a disputed substance, supposed to be the resinous sap of an umbelliferous plant in Syria. It is referred to by Pliny and Suetonius.

ALBI ~ That is, Sublimated.

ALBIR ~ is Pitch from the bark of the yew. I believe it to be a substance from which ink is made.

ALBOR ~ is Urine.

ALBOT ~ is Goldsmith's Brick.

ALBOTAT, ALFIDAS, and **ASFIDE** ~ Names of White Lead.

ALBOTIM, or **ALBOTAI** ~ is Terebinth, Turpentine. It has other arbitrary names, such as, Albuhen, Altilibat, Albotra, Bora, Debutum, Helcabatan, Helkaboni, Helcalibat, Helcalidar, Kytram.

ALBUHAR ~ White Lead.

ALBULA ~ Pearl-white.

ALBUM ~ is White Copper.

ALCADP ~ is White Atrament; a contradictory designation because atramentum is essentially a black liquid.

ALCALI ~ Symbolical principle of the Chemists. It is the salt derived from the ashes of any substance without the limes of the bodies, and it inheres in all substances whether aqueous or fiery. It may be called Salt of Ashes, or Salt of Limestone.

ALCAOL ~ is Sour Milk, otherwise Mercury.

ALCAHEST ~ is prepared Mercury; some will have that it is tartar ; but the special meaning of any writer may be judged easily by the description of his preparation.

ALCAHESTI ~ Mercury prepared as a medicine for the liver.

ALCANNA, or **ALCONA** ~ according to Avicenna, are long slender plants, knotted like reeds, which are used as spears by the Arabs. Some also understand it to be the Guaiacum, or Tree of Life of America.

ALCEBRIS VIVUM, VIVIFIC ALCEBRIS ~ is Sulphur. Called also Alneric, Anerit, Aneric.

ALCHEMY ~ is the separation of the impure from the purer substance.

ALCHITRAM, or **ALCHIERAM** — is Oil of Juniper, Liquid Pitch, Arsenic purified by washing.

ALCHITRAN — is also Oil of Juniper, but especially the dregs left after distillation.

ALCIMAD — is Antimony ; called also Alcofol, Alfacio.

ALCOCL — is Sour Milk.

ALCOHOL — is a most subtle powder.

ALCOHOL — is Stybium or Antimony.

ALCOHOL OF WINE — (sometimes termed Distilled Wine) is thus called when every superfluity of wine has been so purged away that the whole is consumed and neither dregs nor moisture remain in the retort. The most subtle powder that can be made. If alcohol of wine be added, it is rectified, distilled wine.

ALCOLISMUS — is crushing or corrosion.

ALCOL — is Vinegar.

ALCONE — is Aurichalcum, i.e., Brass, Bronze.

ALCOOL — has been most incongruously interpreted by some writers to be a powder ground to extraordinary fineness by a brass or iron mortar; but their error is made sufficiently plain by the fact that Paracelsus speaks in many places of alcool of wine, which he uses for rectified Aqua fortis, and this has nothing in common with a powder. The alcool of any bodies whatever is therefore nothing else but the purer and cleaner part separated from the impure. As regards the Paracelsian Alcool of Antimony, it is nothing else, according to this author, than antimony not merely ground with pestle and mortar, but exalted into its volatile condition without change in the natural colour. And it is needful that this should be done by the exclusive conduct and guidance of fire and heat, in such a manner that after it has been ground in the vulgar fashion, it shall be disintegrated further by sublimations, which are the philosophical pestle and mortar. Paracelsus also teaches elsewhere that such sublimation is to be performed without a caput mortuum, i.e., without leaving a residuum. It is further certain that no refuse must be present before sublimation. This sublimation of stibium is wholly indispensable, or frustrated energy and vain labour will be spent upon the flowers of antimony. Most of those who have attempted to analyze the preparation of Paracelsian substances have failed over this arcanum. By vulgar trituration the substances evaporate into white smoke, and it is easier to ascend into heaven than to produce in this way the citrine or ruby flowers, as they have proved to their own cost. The operation is not vulgar and the philosophical artifice is known to few. But it is made known to the Sons of the Doctrine. The sublimation is performed by a carefully tempered fire, so that the powder of antimony may be liquefied as little as possible, but at the same time may ascend until the flower of the powder is seen sticking to the walls of the furnace.

ALCOR ~ is Copper, burnt till it is fine as powder.

ALCORE ~ is a kind of stone having spar like silver. Called also Altores.

ALCUBD ~ is Crude Butter. Called also Alumbair.

ALCUBRITH, ALCUR, and **ALUZAR** ~ are all names for Sulphur.

ALEC ~ is Vitriol.

ALECHARITH ~ is Mercury.

ALECHIL ~ is three-footed. Cf. Tripod.

ALECTORIA ~ is a gem mentioned by Pliny (1. 37, c. 10), which is like crystal or clear water; and he shows that this crystalline substance, which is as large as a horse bean, is found in the gizzard of poultry, or, as Albertus has it, of a castrated cock. It is found after the bird has attained the age of four years. It renders the possessor rich and of warlike aspect. And they report that Milo of Crotona was made invincible by such an Alectoria. It conciliates girls and quenches thirst. See also Solinus, etc.

ALEFANTES ~ is Flower of Salt.

ALEMBACI ~ is Burnt Lead.

ALEMBIC ~ is Mercury.

ALEMBICUS ~ or Capitellum (helmet) is a vessel set over the retort to receive and collect vapours. The Alembic is of two kinds, beaked or curved, and without beak. The first transmits the resolved vapours by a channel or neck to the receiving vessel. The second, which is without a beak or conduit, is used in sublimations, and in some cases is pierced at the top for the passage of the rising vapours.

ALEMBROTH ~ is Salt of Mercury, or Philosophical Salt, Salt of Art, and Key of Art.

ALEMBROTH DESSICATUM ~ Dessicated Alembroth, is by some called Salt of Tartar, the Magistery of Magisteries.

ALES ~ is compounded Salt, or manufactured Salt.

ALEXANTHI ~ or Altingat, is Flower of Copper.

ALEXIR ~ is a medicine alchemically prepared.

ALEZARAM ~ is the washing of lead.

ALFACTA ~ is Distillation.

ALFADIDAM ~ is Dross of Gold.

ALFAMADI ~ is ashen.

ALFATIDA ~ is Burnt Copper, or Plates of Venus-Copperplate.

ALFATIDE ~ is Sal Ammoniac. Among its other Hermetic names are Salmiax, Alacap, Alorap, Alfol, Alisteles, Alcob, Azonec, Anoxadic, Anacab, Andex,
Aquila, Butrum, Alizeles.

ALFASIT, or **ALVASIT** ~ is Brick, burnt Clay ; also Earthenware.

ALFUSA ~ is impure Protoxide of Zinc.

ALGA ~ is a reed, according to the German context, but it is properly sea-weed.
ALGALI ~ is Nitre, or Saltpetre.
ALGEMET ~ Coals.
ALGERIAE, ALGERIE ~ is Lime.
ALIGULUS ~ is Confection, Composition.
ALIM ~ is a sand found in auriferous metals, out of which lead is extracted.
ALINZADIR ~ is cold and dry earth. It is called in Arabic Boneza and Tinckar.
Arles calls it Salmiac.
ALIOCAB ~ is Sal Ammoniac.
ALKAES, or **ALCHOCHOS** ~ is fine powder.
ALKALIA ~ is the vase or vessel.
ALKALE ~ is Oil of a Hen.
ALKALID, ALKES, ALCOB ~ are Burnt Copper.
ALKALI ~ is Vitriol from the mines, or fluid Vitriol, calcinated in aludal. With others Alkali is a pebble of salt, derived from pounded limestones, extracted by moisture and coagulated by the dissipation of moisture. Above all alkali signifies the elaboration of the essential form of the said stone, freed from what is impure and separated from its body. The term is also ascribed to calcined and diffused substances when they are reduced to a solid consistency, as when common salt is dissolved by moisture and again coagulated. Also when pearls are calcined entire, are dissolved, and again coagulated, they are in themselves magisteria, and are called alkali symbolically.
ALKAMIS ~ Name of the philosopher.
ALKANTUM ~ Sometimes Burnt Copper, sometimes an aromatic substance, sometimes Arsenic.
ALKANT ~ is Mercury, or a species of inky matter.
ALKARA ~ is a gourd. In medicine it is a cupping-glass, and in alchemy a Cucurbite.

ALKARANUM — is green Duenech, or Antimony.
ALKASA or ALKAZOAL — is goldsmith's brick.
ALKASIAL — is Antimony.
**ALKIBRIC, ALKIBERT, ALGIBIC, ALKIBIC,
ALCHABRIC** — are names of Living Sulphur.
ALKIN — is Woad Ashes, or woad-colour Ashes.
ALKIR — is Smoke or Coals.
ALKITRAM — is Liquid Pitch.
ALKO — is Tartar. Theophrastus says that it is the purer substance of a thing separated from the impure. Thus Alcool of Wine is aqua ardens rectified and cleansed, the best and purest, the most subtle and celestial.
ALKOEL — is the finest Lead of the mines; Lapis Lazuli; Antimony.
ALKOSOR — is Camphor.
ALKY OF LEAD — is the soft substance of lead.
ALKYMIA — is the powder of the basilisk.
ALLABROT — is a certain species of manufactured salt.
ALMA — is Water.
ALMABRI — is a stone like amber.
ALMAGER — is Synopide, like red grains (cf. Synephites).
ALMAGRA — is a copper bolus, or laton, which see. A red soil or clay, used as a lubricant by wheelwrights. Also a lotion.
ALMAKIST, ALMAKANDA — That is Litharge.
ALMARCAB, or ALMARCHAZ — is Litharge.
ALMARCAT — is Dross of Gold and Cathmia of Gold, which see.
ALMARCAZIDA — is Litharge of Silver, or Argyritis.
ALMARCHAT and ALMARETH — signify Silver Litharge.
ALMARGEN, ARMALGOL, ALMARAGO — Names of Coral.
ALMARTACK — is Ash of Litharge.
ALMATATICA — is a Mine of Copper.

ALMATKASITA — is Mercury, the Mineral Stone.
ALMECHASIDE — is Copper.
ALMENE — is Solis Gemmae (Solis Gemmae is a kind of glittering precious stone, mentioned by Pliny. But the German version seems to refer to Sal Gemma, which see.).
ALMETAT — s Dross of Gold, or Refuse of Gold.
ALMISADIR — is prepared Sal Ammoniac; called also Asanon, Meradum, Almisadu, Amizadir; it is the German Salmiak.
ALMIZADIR — is Verdigris.
ALNEC, ALLENEC, ALKALAP, ALETH, ALMIBA, ASEREBRAN, ASEBUM — are names of Tin.
ALOE, EPATICUM ALOE — A medicine for the liver.
ALOFEL — is the cloth which covers the Vase.
ALOHAR, ALOHOC, ALOSOHOC, ALOSOT — are names of Quicksilver.
ALOS, ALO, ALIX, ALMELE, ALEC, ALKALAT, ALKALAC — are names of Salt.
ALOSANTHI — Flower of Salt, in use among dyers.
ALRAMUDI — Ashen.
ALSECH — is a species of Alum.
ALSELAT — is burnt Copper, or Calcecumenon, which is burnt Earth.
ALTAMBUS — is the Red Stone, to wit, blood from men's veins.
ALTANUS — is the South-west or South.
ALTARIS, ANTARIT, and **ALOZET** — are names of Quicksilver.
ALTHANACHA — is Orpiment. Called also Alernet and Albimec.
ALTIMAR, or **AYCAPHER** — Burnt Copper.
ALTIMIO — is Dross of Lead.
ALTINURAUM — is Vitriol.
ALTINGAT — is Flower of Copper.

ALUDEL, or **ALUTEL** ~ is a glass vessel used in sublimation.

ALUDIT, ANTARIC, AZOMSES, AZON ~ Names of Mercury.

ALUSIR ~ is redness.

ALUECH ~ is the pure body of Jove. Called also Aluach.

ALUEUS ~ is boatlike, otherwise a vessel shaped like a boat. Alueus minor is a vessel of like shape but smaller size.

ALUIS, or **ALAFOR** ~ Called also Vabs, is Salt of Alkali.

ALUMBOTI ~ is burnt lead.

ALUMEN ~ is known to all, and signifies Mercury, because it dissolves. It is the best of all crystals. Its species are various, of which some are called technically Jamenum, Roccum, Scissum, Rotundum, Zacharinum, Debelgamo, Genoese Nitre, Alum from the mines, Fusible Alum, Scaly Alum, Liquid Alum, Preserved Alum, Common Alum, Alum Placodes, Burnt Alum, Sodden Alum, Rock-Alum, and Native Alum.

Albertus distinguishes four broad species-Simple, or Common Alum; Black, White, and one which he describes fully in his book on Minerals. But here follow the several species of Alum.

1. Alum of the mines.
2. Liquid, clay-like, pale yellow Alum, from the Island of Elba in the Mediterranean. When handled it becomes so soft that it almost flows.
3. Natural liquid yellow Alum like a soft butter; it is found in the lead mines near Naples.
4. Grey liquid Alum from the same place.
5. White scaly Neapolitan Alum.
6. Very white scissile Neapolitan Alum.
7. Yellow Neapolitan Alum.
8. Scissile Alum, mixed with black dye, and redolent of sulphur when burnt. This also is from Naples.

9. Fibrous Neapolitan Alum.
10. Globular Neapolitan Alum.
11. A Neapolitan variety, found in layers, having wide crusts.
12. Manufactured saccharine Alum.
13. Square-shaped Alum of a violet colour.
14. Bright reddish Neapolitan Alum.
15. Manufactured Alum, having the appearance of fluorspar. It is produced by placing any igneous crux (untranslatable in this connection) into deep vessels, to which it adheres as if consubstantial with them, and crystallises in four-sided figures.
16. Pure bright digested Alum, found in Thuringia at Lobestein.
17. Venetian Alum which shows reddish in grinding, but is otherwise white.
18. Common Alum.
19. Burnt Alum.
20. Bright melted Alum of Dibanus, from which a sort of inky copperas exudes.
21. A variety of the above, combined with Atrament, and found in a moist clay.
22. Alum combined with Atrament excocted from Lye.
23. Pure white cocted Alum from Dibanus; this is pellucid and free from inky matter.
24. Bohemian Alum.
25. Alum of Misnense, mined in Burgos and Heringisdorf.
26. Alum of Tolpha, first mined in Italy during the pontificate of Pius the Second.
27. Veins of Alum mixed with Persulphate of Iron (misy).
28. An exceedingly white earth, out of which Neapolitan Alum is melted.
29. Rocca stone, from which Alum is derived.
30. Earth in the black ash of Dibanus, from which Alum is excocted.

31. A vein of globular Alum found on the top of the mountains near Naples.

32. A black Lobestenian vein, wherein there is a white natural Alum.

ALUMEN ~ A name of Antimony.

ALUMEN ALAP ~ Possibly Clay-like Alum.

ALUMEN ALAFRAN ~ Final State.

ALUMEN ALAFURI, or **ALAFOR** ~ Native Soda.

ALUMEN ALBEDANE ~ Zacharine Alum.

ALUMEN ALBUM ~ i.e., Learto (unexplained).

ALUMEN ALKORI, and **ALUMEN ALKALI** ~ Saltpetre.

ALUMEN ALEXANDRINUM ~ Soda, or Natron.

ALUMEN BULGANUM ~ The German Eyestone, a species of Varnish. It is red and transparent as mastic.

ALUMEN CALCILIEN ~ Arabian Azub, or Alum.

ALUMEN CREPUM ~ is tartar obtained from good wine.

ALUMEN DE ALEP ~ is Greek or Macedonian Salt.

ALUMEN DE BABYLONIA ~ is Zacharine Alum, and the same as globular alum.

ALUMEN DE CRYSTALLO ~ is Alumen roce, which is untranslatable.

ALUMEN DE PLUMA, or **ALUMEN SCARIOLA** ~ is Gipsum Or Gypsum.

ALUMEN FASCIOLI ~ is Alkali, and is identical with Cabia.

ALUMEN GLACIOSERO ~ is fixed, saline alum.

ALUMEN IONID ~ is Limpart.

ALUMEN LAMENUM ~ is laminated Alum.

ALUMEN LIQUIDUM ~ is Amonum, an aromatic Balsum, otherwise limpart

ALUMEN LOSE ~ is scaly Alum.

ALUMEN MARINUM ~ is a humid spirit.

ALUMEN ODIG ~ is Salmiac.

ALUMEN PHILOSOPHORUM ~ is Lime of Egg Shells.

ALUMEN ROSA, ROSE ALUM ~ That is, Burnt Alum, Baked Alum, and Alum consumed by fire.
ALUMEN ROTUNDUM ~ which is laminated Alum, is also called Zacharinus.
ALUMEN SCARIOLE ~ is Gipsum.
ALUMEN SCAROLUM ~ is split Alum.
ALUMEN SCISSUM ~ is laminated alum.
ALUMEN SYRACH, ALUMEN SYSARACH, ALUMEN ALKOKAR, ALUMEN ALURINT, ALUMEN LANIOSUM ~ are all names of Alumen combustum, which is Alum after it has been treated with fire.
ALUNIBUR ~ is Luna ~ Silver.
ALUNSEL ~ is a drop.
ALUSAR ~ is Manna.
ALUSEN ~ is sulphurated.
ALZEGI ~ is Atrament.
ALZEMAFOR ~ is Cinnabar.
ALZILAT ~ is a weight of three grains.
ALZIMAX ~ is green.
ALZOFAR ~ is burnt Copper.
AMALGAMA ~ is a composition of Gold or Silver and Quick Silver.
AMALGAMATION ~ is a calcination of the familiar metals by means of artificial Quicksilver. At the same time, the operation of calcining is not carried out invariably to its utmost limit, and it is enough for the metal to be sufficiently melted to assume the consistency of the pulp or amalgam of the goldsmiths. The disintegration into a most fine powder which takes place under this process is also called a calcining. Further, amalgamation is calcination of a metal by Quicksilver; and it is performed when a metal, after being reduced into fine filing, thin plates, or lamina, is blended and mixed with six, nine, or twelve parts of Quicksilver, so that it becomes a homogeneous mass; and in this way also is

the metal calcined and disintegrated. For the metal is reduced into the condition of a fine ash by evaporation with Quicksilver over a gentle fire.

AMANDINUS ~ is a stone of various colours. It destroys and binds all venomous animals, and is in no way contemptible; for which see Albertus.

AMASSA ~ means confect, got together; hence, to amass.

AMBRA ~ is Spermaceti.

AMENE ~ is Common Salt, called Apostolus.

AMENTUM ~ is Powdered Alum.

AMETHYST ~ is a gem of violet colour, which Pliny says (l. 37, c. 9) approaches the hue of wine, yet, before it thoroughly taste thereof, it turns into a March violet colour, and its purple lustre is not fiery altogether, but declines in the end to the colour of wine. India is the native place of the amethyst, as Pliny also testifies. Thence the finest are brought; their colour is an absolute purple, and indeed the dyers would give anything to reproduce it. There is, however, another species which approaches hyacinth, which colour the Indians term Sacon, and the gem itself they call Socondion. There is a third species which is paler, and is called Sapenos and Paranites. A fourth species is wine-colour; a fifth approaches crystal, having a whitish purple tinge; and by some this species is termed Anterotis, by others Pcederotos, and by yet others the jewel of Venus. Amethysts are also found in Arabia Petrea, Armenia, Egypt, Galatia, Tarsus, and Cyprus. But these are of a miserable and worthless quality. The superstition of the Magi declares amethysts to have power over drunkenness and evil thoughts, to protect against poisons, to hive access to the persons of kings, and to avert hail. Upon the colours of the amethyst, consult Pliny (1. 20, c. 8, and 1. 9, c. 38). Inferior amethysts are found in many parts of Bohemia, and in its mines are fluorspars similar to these. The following varieties are inferior to Oriental:

1. Amethysts of Misnia, from the mines of Bergenbricht.
2. Amethysts from the waters of Misnia, and from the river Trebisa near Misena.
3. Amethysts found in the Bohemian mountains.
4. Amethysts which have the appearance of crystal.
5. Amethysts having crystalline lines.
6. Quadrangular and sexangular amethysts, brown and pointed.

AMIANTHUS, or **AMIANTUS** — On the testimony of Dioscorides, is a stone of Cyprus, not unlike certain species of alum. It is impervious to fire, from which it issues more brilliant. It is fabled by the Germans to be produced from the hairs of a Salamander, which is accounted for by its fireproof nature. It is a kind of stone which may be split into threads and spun. It is without doubt a scaled or feathered Alum, which can burn for ever (i.e. to say, it is Asbestos). In other respects, the Amianth is not of great virtue; however, it absorbs moisture. Pliny (l. 36, c. 19) says that it is similar to alum, losing nothing in the fire, and especially defying all the witchcraft of sorcerers. If we consider well, we (Germans) ourselves are possessed of a species of Amianth, which is found in our mines, and which we call Micah. It is of a silver colour. It is called Cat's Silver, by similitude, because cats' eyes shine like the Amianth at night, or because it is useless and thought only fit for burning. But if we consider deeply, it cannot be burned like the true Amianth; but is rather purged, and assumes another colour; a thing of no moment. What is more important to know is the power which resides in a certain stone called Asbestos, which is found in the mountains of Arcadia, as Pliny assures us (l. 37, c. 10). It is of an iron colour, and Albertus tells us that it exists also in Arabia. When this stone is set on fire there is scarcely anything that will extinguish it. Its nature is humid and unctuous. There is also the vitreous, ruddy-veined Absinth or Wormwood Stone, which will burn for days at a time, and is said to make blood, or to cause blood to flow, and is the opposite to Hematite, which congeals or checks blood. Pliny (1. 37, c. 16) calls this stone Apiston. There is again the stone called Iscultos by Albertus, and you shall judge by his own words whether it is the same as the Amianth, or a stone of other species. It is similar to the flower Saffron, he tells us; it is found in the farthest parts of Spain and in the vicinity of Cadiz; it is of a crumbling nature, on account of its dried up viscousness. If garments be spun from it they may be cleaned and made white by fire without burning. It is this perchance which is called the Salamander's hell, a wool, spun, as it were, from a humid stone.

AMIDUM, or **AMYLUM** ~ is a most white meal.

AMMONIS ~ A precious stone of an ashen colour, representing a ram's head. It was held sacred in Ethiopia. Otherwise, a horn-shaped stone, without polish, about eight fingers wide, and over two pounds in weight. There is a variety from Hildesheimer, also without polish. There is a third or polished form which has an iron-coloured surface. A fourth is overlaid with aurichalcum, a metallic substance resembling gold, and usually regarded as mythical. There are also the following varieties:

1. Ammonites minor, like ova of fish, the lesser Rainstone.
2. Ammonites major, or greater Rainstone.
3. Lepidotus, or multi-coloured, like the scales of fish.
4. Strombites longus, the Snailstone, like the marine snail because it tapers off even as, for example, the whorl of a univalve, in a high and elevated spire.
5. Strombites brevis, a smaller variety of the same.
6. Ctenites parvus, Musselstone, ashen-coloured, striated, comb-shaped.

7. A shining sandy stone, in which Musselstones are imbedded.
8. A hard ashen stone, found in Lusatia, and containing Musselstone.
9. A polished ashen stone, overlaid with gold colour, and in which a stone like the Chama is found.
10. Onychites, having the appearance of talons.
11. Ostreites, oyster-shaped Ammonites.
12. Ostreites, another species, consisting of six of the above kind joined together.
13. Tellinites, precisely similar to the molluscs, called Tellina, overlaid with a gold-coloured covering.
14. Chemites, ashen, similar to Chama. See above, species 9.
15. Conchites, similar to a bivalve shell, with a gold-coloured armature. Another variety of the Snailstone.

AMNIS ALCALISATUS — is water filtered through limestones. Alkalis are waters filtered through the stones of the earth.

AMONGABRIEL — is Zynobrium.

AMPULLA VITREA — is a retort. There is another Ampulla Vitrea, which is a vessel of glass.

AMYGDALAE (Almonds) — Signifies among surgeons a certain fleshy excrescence which forms at the root of the tongue. The German version calls it mouth-almond.

AN — Father, Sulphur.

ANATON, AMATRON — Native Soda.

ANATRON — Refuse of Vitrum (glass).

ANATRON — i.e., Baurac, which see.

ANATRON — i.e., Sagimen (salt) of Vitrum (glass), or Salt of Alkali.

ANATRON — Froth of Vitreum, Gall of Vitreum. The German context terms it Sandiber, Gall of Glass.

ANATRIS, or **ANTARIS** — is Mercury.

ANATOMIA ESSATA — is the parent of diseases.

ANATRUM — is Vitreum melted into various colours. Called vulgarly Smaltum or Saracenic earth. The species are numerous-black, red, blue. It is also a substance which grows in stones, and is itself of a white and stone-like character; by some it is called Native Soda. The ancients erroneously called it Gall of Vitreum, whereas it is Gall of Stone.
ANCORA — is calx.
ANCOSA — is lacka.
ANDARAC — is red orpiment.
ANDENA — is Chalybs, i.e., Steel, brought from Oriental places. It melts in flame, in the same way as other metals, and can be poured into moulds.
ANFAXA — is a congealed substance.
ANHELITUS — is smoke, otherwise horse-dung.
ANIADA — are the fruits and powers of Paradise and of Heaven; they are also the Christian Sacraments. In things physical they signify the astral potencies, and the celestial potencies, and they are those things which, by thought, judgment, and imagination, promote longevity in us. But these things are the gift of God, and make for life eternal.
ANIADUS — is the efficacy or virtue of things.
ANIADUM — is the archnatural body which in us Christians is implanted by the Holy
Ghost working through the most holy Sacraments. Or it is the spiritual man reborn in us.
ANIMA — As the philosophers conceive three principles, Salt, Sulphur, and Mercury, so also they conceive three other divisions-Soul, Spirit, and Body, not that the Soul and the Spirit are to be distinguished as cattle from men, but by way of similitude. The Soul is nothing else but a living, formed Body, that is turned into Mercury, and when this is done to the dead Body and Spirit, then the whole is made living Elixir. Therefore, do not make a mistake, when the philosophers speak of one Soul instead of two Souls, for it is

all one thing. The Mercury has in itself the Soul, and is called our Mercury, which is the house and dwelling of the Soul. Also the Soul is called Spirit, and the Spirit is called Soul. The Spirit produces the Soul from the Body, and returns it when it is white. Therefore, it is called the Life of the Soul — Vita Anima. Should the Spirit depart from the Soul it could not give the life. The Soul unites and conjoins the married, Body and Spirit; so the Spirit unites the Soul with the Body, so that it is all one thing. There are two Souls — one of gold, the other of silver. The Soul of the gold must remain, and cannot do so without the Spirit, nor yet the Spirit remain without the Soul. There must be fixed, abiding, undying Souls. At first the Soul lies hidden under the Spirit; finally, the Soul and Spirit remain hidden under the Body. Then dost thou first behold pure Mercury. Through the crude Spirit is the mature Mercury taken away from the released Body, which is a fixed ash remaining behind to be dissolved further. Out of this is extracted a petrine, incombustible Olitet or Gum, which vivifies, unites, and welds the natures together, and as they separated the natures through the Spirit, accordingly through the Soul they unite them again. This Olitet preserves the colour of the Spirit even to thickening. Then is it fit for the production of royal weapons and metallic figures. It manifests itself as golden in golden and as argentine in silver. The Soul's ascent is when the Body becomes white, clear, and fluid. Immediately they are one and living. Then is there danger. If the Soul escapes or burns it is lost. So is the Soul quickly given to the Body and takes shape. The Soul proceeds out of the unified Body; she is herself the living body, and is called REBIS, Putrid Water, Corruption of the Dead, Blood and Blood Water, Lymph, the Animal Stone, Blessed, Blood, Sulphur, Olitet. The Soul is a simple thing, which sometimes has power to bring the Body with it.*

[* It is the tincture withdrawn from the body. Soul also is said to be in Arsenic.]

ANIMA SATURNI, or **ALTHEA** — (Literally, Marshmallows) of Saturn, is a most mellifluous sweetness which is extracted from Lead by vinegar. (A right noble sweetness, according to the German.)

ANNORA — is Calx of Eggs, or living Calx, or Quicklime.

ANNUS PHILOSOPHICUS — The philosophical year, is the vulgar month.

ANODUS — is the nutriment which is separated in the veins.

ANONTAGIUS — is the Philosophical Stone, the gift of God, Sulphur fixed by Nature.

ANORA — is Quicklime.

ANOTASIER, ALIOCAB, ALEMZADAT — are names of Sal Ammoniac.

ANSIR — Son, Mercury.

ANSIRARTO — Spirit, Salt.

ANTAL — is a pure lotion.

ANTERIT — is Mercury.

ANTHERA — is extract of the medicinal properties of the Hyacinth. It is also the yellow centre which is found in such flowers as the Lily.

ANTHONOR, ATHONOR — That is, Oven.

ANTHOUS — is properly ROSEMARY, but in the terminology of metals it signifies Quintessence, or Elixir of Gold. It means further the extracted medicine.

ANTICAR — is Borax.

ANTIFIDES — is Calx of Metals.

ANTIMONIUM, or **ALKOFOL** — A stone from a lead vein, or vein of Othi. It is also Marchasite, a kind of Saturn, a kind of Antistinus (unknown), and Stybium. It is a muddy

Marchasite, having a fixed Sulphur, and is insoluble. It is of two kinds. One is the ordinary black species of Saturn, and is called Magnesia, Bismuth, Contersin. It is of the race of Jupiter, an immature, ill-favoured product. It is Dross of Lead and has the virtues of burnt Lead, being of similar substance. It is cold, dry, and astringent.

ANUCAR, ANCINAR — is Borax.

ANYADEI — Eternal Spring, the new world, the Paradise to come.

APENSALUS — A utensil with a narrow mouth, used in manufacturing oil.

APHEBRIOCK — is Sulphur.

APHRODISIA — is the venereal state.

APHRONITRUM — Froth of Saltpetre, Wall-salt. As salt and froth of salt have great affinity for each other, so also have Nitre and Froth of Nitre in like manner. For the rest, Aphronitum, Froth of Nitre, Flower of Stone, or Wallflower (like froth of salt) is excessively light, lumpy, crumbling, frothy, pungent, and that which approaches a purple colour is the best kind. We term Froth of Nitre both Aphronitum and Frothy Aphronitrum which grows on walls and stones; in many places it is known by the German name of Mergell. Froth of Nitre varies in its species according to the stones and walls where it grows. Its virtue is similar to burnt salt. Froth of Nitre, Flower of Stone, and Flower of Stone of Asia are very nearly the same, differing slightly in substance. If it melts in fire, it is Flower of Stone of Asia; if not, it is our own Froth of Nitre.

At Iena, in Thuringia, which is rich in simples, a very beautiful species of Aphronitum is found, which corresponds in the main to the Flower of Stone of Asia, described by Dioscorides.

AQUA — i.e., Liquid; the elemental matter from which water can always be obtained. It is not water from the clouds, but a dry mineral first substance, a catholic water, which dissolves all metals, and can be reduced to water even as ice is reduced. It is almost like a blackish gum, according to R. W. This water cleans, washes and expands, it renders substances spongy and liquid, and afterwards dries and fixes them, making them white and red. Therefore Gebir says: Burn it in water and wash it in fire. The end of the Epistle to Thomas of Bonona describes this water. As ordinary water in which vegetables are boiled partakes of their nature and virtue, so also is it with the mercury which is boiled with metals. Out of this water all things grow and have their nourishment. It unites itself with metals, which can be performed by no common water without aqua fortis.

The fruit shall not be disturbed for the intercourse of the bridegroom and the bride, but no ordinary water shall be extracted from the mercury, for if the mercury be changed from its first nature, it is useless for this purpose, because it has lost its spermatic and metallic character. Therefore our water is not clear and translucid, but dark, for the (philosophical) earth is beneath it.

There are two kinds of water; the first dissolves and makes its subject spongy ; the other completes the operation. This is truly fire, and even stronger than fire, for it is a universal solvent. One is simple, though evil, the other is composite; both are philosophical. The Water is Adam, the Earth is Eve, and these two are one flesh. They are also called Salt Urine, Salt Water, Vinegar, Sour Wine, Living Calx, Water, Sea Water, Ashen Water, Yeast, Alum, Nitric Water, Dog Bane, Dragon's Tail, Soul, Wind, Air, Life, the Illuminating Gift, Broad Daylight, Virginal Milk, Armenian Salt, Saltpetre, White Smoke, Red Sulphuric Water, Gummy Water, the Male, Tartar, Saffron Water, Burnt Ore, White Composition, Putrid Water, Putrefaction of Dead Bodies, Blood, Mercury, Cucurbit, Alembic, Vase of the

Philosophers, of which the upper part is called the Grand Man, or Head-piece, the middle is called Belly, the end is called Foot. When the vessel is put in the oven, a vapour rises into the funnel, and passes as water into the belly, immediately producing a soul. The water dissolves the rest and absorbs it upward. This takes place in a philosophical month of 40 days. It is called the Flying Dragon, heavenly natured, dividing the elements of bodies and again uniting them. At last it turns thick like honey, and of green colour. It is called the Green Bird.

AQUA ALMA — is Water produced from Wine by sublimation.

AQUA ALREGI — is Lime Water.

AQUA COELESTIS — Celestial Water, is rectified or sublimed Wine, partaking, in a certain way, of the nature and likeness of heaven, passing through many revolutions. It is the German Himinels Wasser.

AQUA CCELESTINA — is Mercurial Water.

AQUA CEREBRI — is Tartaric Water.

AQUA CORRODENS — is Vinegar, or any corrosive liquid.

AQUA ELSABON — is Water of Common Salt.

AQUA FIECUM VINI — Water of Wine Lees (in German Weinhesen Wasser) is made when the lees, having been evaporated, whitened, and calcined, are dissolved with water in a marble basin, after the manner of oil of tartar.

AQUA FOETIDA — is Mercurial Water.

AQUA FORTIS — is composed of corrosives combined in a certain proportion (that is to say, it is impure Nitric Acid), and distilled by a fierce fire; it has a most piercing corrosive power. The strongest is called Stygian, which rules Sal Ammoniac with the rest, as therein gold is dissolved. The other species have various qualities. Aqua Fortis, increased by careful mixture, to be suitable for certain purposes, is called Gradatoria, which is applied to the graduation of dyes. And they (the other kinds) become like Aqua Fortis of the same material, but this is done by the addition of colouring matter like cinnabar and alum. In which (operations) it should be noted that it dyes nothing unless there be cohibition over the feces at least eight or ten times, since otherwise they will not be fixed.

AQUA HOLSOBON — is common Salt Water.

AQUA LILII — is Orpiment.

AQUA LUBRICATA — or Mucilage, is Water combined with Sugar, julep, and similar substances, such as claret and spirituous liquors.

AQUA MARINA — is sea water.

AQUA MERCURII — Mercurial Water. Essential Water of the stone.

AQUA NITRI — is Salt of Alkali, or Aqua Fortis.

AQUA PERMANENS — Enduring Water, is that which is made by the philosophical solution out of two perfect metallic bodies. It is Sol and Luna dissolved in water, and likewise united. It is also called Celestial Water, and Mercury of the Philosophers. It is Incombustible Gum, the very best Vinegar; a sharp, penetrating Water, which dissolves bodies; and the Spiritual Virtue. Called Mercury because it has sharp and clear Mercurial power and property. Also Male, or Husband, and White Smoke, because it rises and goes up. Also Dragon's Tail, and Flying Bird.

AQUA PHILOSOPHICA — Philosophical Water, signifies, with some writers, Sublimed Vinegar; with others, Circulated Wine; with yet others, Perennial Water, which does not wet the hands.

AQUA PALIESTINA — Palestine Water, is Flower of Copper, or Verdigris.

AQUA PLUVIALIS — is Rain-water, Soft-water.

AQUA RUBICUNDA — Ruddy Water; Aqua Megi and Aqua Segi are Vitriol Water.

AQUA SALMATINA — is Water made from Salt.

AQUA SATURNIA — is Water generated from the first principles in the bowels of the earth, and resolved into small diaphanous stones. Radicated Vinegar Water. Chalybeate. Aqua Saturnia is also that which retains the nature of the three first principles through which it passes, such as thermal springs said to be naturally medicated.

AQUA STILLATITIA — Dropping Water, is a specific extract of aqueous consistence produced in the condensation of vapours after distillation. It is of two kinds, solvent and simple distilled water. Simple distilled waters are specific material arcana, distilled from substances in such a manner that, while retaining the arcane virtue, they are nevertheless softer and weaker than are solvent waters, and approach nearer to a phlegmatic element; more correctly, simple distilled waters, which are softer, and more diluted in strength and consistence, are produced by a more simple distilling. For the phlegmatic element is cruder, and differs little from common water in appearance. Simple distilled water has a more aqueous and less igneous character than solvent water, but is more igneous and less crude than phlegm. And although all the water is used up in distillation yet it is first named from its office, and in the end more properly receives the name of a solvent. It differs from simple distilled water by its penetrating and ardent sharpness, and laborious distillation, so that it has a minimum of aqueous element, but is more like a flowing fire, or a fiery water. By Gebir it is termed Aqua Acuta; by others, the Key of Philosophers. Quicksilver obtains in certain cases the whole strength of this water. Other substances have the same office, as lye, stalactite, and honey, also undefiled aqueous substances, like sour wine. It is the vulgar custom to distinguish between simple distilled water and corrosive water. True solvent water is the same as aqua fortis. (Solvent water is distilled vinegar; also called sea water, because in distillation there is more fluid than residue; and again cloud water, because of the brightness of rain-drops.

AQUA VALENS — is Aqua Fortis.

AQUA VITRI — is glass dissolved with water.

AQUA VITAE — is Mercury, but the term is sometimes used for distilled Wine, and for various Waters mixed with distilled Wine.

AQUARIUS — is iron colour.

AQUASTOR — is a simulaerum, which stands for a thing, but is not the thing itself.

AQUILA — The Eagle, queen of birds, signifies Sal Ammoniac, because of its lightness in sublimations. In many places Paracelsus, however, uses it for Precipitated Mercury.

AQUILA — is Birdlime, which appears reddish in the first coagulation. It is also the Spirit that is changed into Earth, i.e., the Spirit of Mercury, the stone itself. The Turba says: The perfection of every single thing is in its own order. Therefore the adept fixes ten Eagles, etc. It is also said to be Sal Ammoniac and Fixed Sulphur.

AQUILA — is Arsenic, or Sulphur.

AQUILA — is Aurum Guttendo (probably gold liquefied), also Fidelo, Edel, Sedalo, arbitrary terms not explained by Rulandus.

AQUILA PHILOSOPHORUM — The Eagle of Philosophers is the Mercury of Metals, i.e., a metallic nature reduced into its first matter.

AQUILLO — Wild Marjoram.

ARAGON — is Laton, i.e., Aurichalcum.

ARBOR MARIS — is a metalline substance which grows in the sea. That is, it is a coral, and its other names are

Corallia, Curallion, Gorgonion, Dendrites, and Lithodendron.

ARBORES — Same as Morphea (? Morphew); a scurfy eruption of the skin, at first without ulceration, which, however, follows in time.

ARCANUM — is a secret, incorporeal, and immortal thing, which no man can know save by experience. It is the interior virtue of any substance which can achieve a thousand more wonders than the thing itself. The unrevealed principle, undying essence.

ARCANUM MATERIALS — or Physical Secret, is a specific extract akin to the matter of a body. But when the matter of fixed bodies is composed of a duplex element, namely, humid and dry (note that air and fire are more properly formatives, and possess an efficient faculty), then does the Arcanum imitate a like condition: distilled water and coagulate specific.

ARCANUM SPECIFICUM — is an extract of the interior nature, related so intimately to the substance of any species that the same may be known therein. It must be educed with care lest the gross substance perish. For this reason is it called specific. And it differs from quintessence, which, by reason of its extreme subtlety and excellence, seems almost to have deserted its species, and gone over to the class of ethereal things. But the Specific Arcanum exhibits the substance, shape, and specific difference of composites as an extract more akin to the interior body. The Specific Arcanum is duplex. One is of the essential and substantial form, and is called Astral, the other is Material.

ARCHATES — as it were, the pillars of the earth, the Paracelsian foundation of the earth, which does not appear to be supported by its fellows, but by a great and secret power of God. Called also Archallem. The power which upholds the earth by itself, for the other elements do not hold it up.

ARCHAEUS ~ is the divider of the elements; he disposes them, and relegates everything to its place, genus, and species.

ARCHEUS ~ is a most high, exalted, and invisible spirit, which is separated from bodies, is exalted, and ascends; it is the occult virtue of Nature, universal in all things, the artificer, the healer. Also Archiatros ~ supreme physician of Nature, who to every substance and member dispenses in an occult manner, by means of the air, its own individual Archeus. Also the primal Archeus in Nature is a most secret virtue producing all things out of Master, doubtless certainly supported by divine virtue. Or, Archeos is an errant, invisible species, the power and virtue of Nature's healing, the artist and healer of Nature, separating itself from bodies, and ascending from them. Archeus signifies, in addition, the power which educes the One Substance from Iliaster, and is the dispenser and composer of all things. It individualizes in all things, including human nature.

ARCOS, AYCOPHES, AZAPHORA ~ are names for Burnt Copper.

ARCUS ~ is a small bow.

ARDENTIA ~ Ardent or fiery matters, which are not assimilated in food and drink and are by their nature obnoxious to operations, as, for example, Carabe, Therebinth, Bitumen, and similar substances. That which naturally burns, or gives forth fire.

AREA ~ Any flat or open surface, as, for example, a heath. In metals, a mass excavated from a mine. Tow.

AREAE ~ Clear spaces.

AREA CAPITIS ADVERSI TODINARUM ~ Shaft of a Mine. Mine where ore has been found.

AREA ROTUNDA ~ A sandy circle.

ARE MAROS ~ Cinnabar.

ARENA ~ Sand is the clear body of the stone.

The Species of Sand are as follow:

1. Common sand.
2. A beautiful white sand dug up in deep gulleys to the west of Misena.
3. Pestgrana, also from Misena.
4. Thirsty or absorbing sand, which is washed and sifted, and has the character of German blotting-paper.
5. Table sand, or Block sand. Sand which has not been washed.
6. Sand found at Groede, in the Netherlands.
7. Sand from the pits of Misena.
8. River sand, which is mixed with lime, and is made use of in building.
9. Metallic sand from gold mines, in which particles and grains of gold are found.
10. Metallic, out of which gold is washed in the Elbe.
11. Metallic sand of Misnense, in the district spoken of by fishermen, near Leisnic.
12. Sand of Misnense, from the bank near the bridge of Schellenberg, and in that wood.
13. Coarse sand which is strewn over roads-sand for pathways.
14. Coarse black sand, from which those small black pellets are obtained out of which white lead is extracted. Sand containing tin.
15. Coarse, barren Sand.
16. Red Sand of Thuringia.
17. Yellow Sand of Glogaw.
18. Sand of a golden colour, from which the Roman mountain derives its name ~ Golden Mountain, formerly called Janiculum.
19. Grey Sand.

20. Shining or Sparkling Sand
21. Sea Sand.
22. Sand out of pools and stagnant water. Muddy Sand.
23. Slimy metallic Sand.

ARENAMEN, or **ARENARMEI** ~ Armenian Bolus. See Bolus.

ARENAS RIVORUM FLUMINUMQUE LAVARE ~ A scouring, washing with lather. The cleansing of any sand from the foreign matters which are mixed with it.

ARES ~ Not to be confounded with the chemical Mars. It is the giver of seed, the occult dispenser of Nature in the three prime principles, and the bond of their union. It distributes to all things whatsoever its peculiar form, species, and substance, so that it may put on its proper and specific nature, and no other. Between these three there is therefore to be noted a difference in nature beautifully ordained by divine providence. Ares is the spirit in Nature which out of the three prime principles gives to everything its shape, genus, and substance. These three are Iliaster, Archeus, and Ares. Iliaster is a substance of most widely spread nature, consisting in the universal first matter of all things, which it first distributes into the three principles, Sulphur, Mercury and Salt. Iliaster is the substance, the First Matter of all things, out of the said three principles. Archeus is the first dispenser of Nature. He produces and creates, like an artificer, all things, after their own kinds, out of this Nature. Ares, or the Assigner, extends the peculiar nature to each species, and gives individual form, so that it is by him that, for example, in the vegetable world, plants are endowed with root, stalk, flowers, leaves, and sap.

ARFAR or **ARSAG** ~ is Arsenic.

ARGENTUM ~ The Luna of Chemists, to which also it is attributed, is the metal ranked next after gold, white with a pure whiteness, unspotted, hard, resonant; and the colour of its whiteness is due to pure, very fixed quicksilver, which is also white and clear. In like manner, it is composed of sulphur, clean, fixed, white, and clear, which has precipitated the substance of quicksilver, but is something deficient in fixation, colour, and weight. Silver is, as it were, a daughter of Nature most near unto gold, produced from the copulation of quick silver, and white, incombustible sulphur. Silver is found in our mines.

1. Pure, unmixed silver, needing no cleansing in the furnace; solid silver, wanting no fusing, generated in perfection, possessing a perfect colour, firmly encrusted with a species of rock or ore. At this present time such silver is still turned out from our mines. But of this species Pliny was ignorant when he said (1. 33, c. 6): It is never found but in pits sunk on purpose for it, nor is it ever found pure and solid, nor are there any bright sparkles, as in gold mines, to indicate its existence in the ore. The earth that engenders the vein is either reddish or of an ashen grey. So far Pliny. But this pure silver surrounds the stone in extremely thin plates; sometimes also it exhibits a species of small hairs upon its surface, or little curls of thread, also small twig-like filaments, either white or red, or like such fibres of red silk as are used in spinning. Again it bears impressions of trees, instruments, mountains, herbs, and other objects. I have myself beheld likenesses of fish; I have beheld the crucified Christ and our Lady; I have seen a serpent, a scorpion, etc., formed out of pure silver in the bowels of the earth.

2. Rude silver ore, of which various kinds are produced from our mines, namely, deep red, leaden, black, purple, ashen, and reddish in colour, of which we proceed to treat successively.

3. Silver melted out of other metals, such as leaden pyrite, mica, etc., concerning which see also below.

Rude silver of a ruby colour- — called red golden ore by the Germans. It seems to be a kind of carbuncle. The carbuncle has, however, an intenser ray, but this rude silver is of a paler ruby. It is found in mines, valleys, and other places variously deposited, but chiefly after three manners: Firstly, in a black-coloured ore ; secondly, like minute bright particles adhering to a certain species of rock; thirdly, in pure solid masses or nuggets cleaving to stones or rocks. It is sometimes found by itself, sometimes in combination with a foreign substance, which projects in a sharp-pointed pyramidal or top-like manner. Sometimes it assumes a square or quadrangular form, sometimes it is sexangular, like the Iris stone; frequently it consists of many unequal angles. Thus by a wonderful operation does Nature practice geometry in the bowels of the earth. Lastly, rude ruby-coloured silver is found beautifully aspersed with blue, so that Nature would seem to have exhausted her ingenuity over the formation of the metals, and to have diverted and amused herself with so many and such brilliant colours, that no art, however high, could possibly attempt to follow. This last species of silver was unknown to Dioscorides, to Pliny, indeed to all the ancients. Theophrastus was the first to make mention of it, when he said: There is another gem of a colour like unto plums, which loses a little of its weight in melting, as the smiths know". It should be noted, in fine, that a most admirable colour for painting is composed out of this species. It might also have a place in medicine did any one make the experiment. It has been erroneously confused with Sandarach, as will be shown under that head.

Rude silver of a lead colour. Nature, by hot and dry vapours exhausted in the bowels of the earth, tinges or dyes the sap or moisture whence silver is made, or joins it with various colours, as we find in these species of rude silver. The first of these is of red colour, sometimes aspersed with cerulean.

The second, with which we are here concerned, has the hue of lead, and is found in vale and mountain. It is conspicuously like the lead ore with which it is connected by name. But this is as regards colour, for in other points it differs, as the illustrious Georgius Agricola very plainly lays down in his Berinannus, or Metallic Nature. But to return to our subject. I have said that rude lead-coloured silver resembles lead ore, but it differs in this, that lead ore is of crumbling nature, and falls to pieces easily when struck with a knife. But the silver species cannot well be pounded; it can be cloven, it is true, with a knife, like lead, but when it has been bitten with the teeth it rebounds again, and lead ore will not do so to any appreciable extent. This species of silver is found in large lumps in its own veins, as if imbedded in a nest. It is also found in conglomerated masses, looking something like buds distributed on the branches of a tree, with perfectly circular nodules, cleaving to rocks, or imbedded therein. At other times it assumes the shape of little sticks, or other similar figures. Agricola testifies that he has seen perfect specimens of metallic instruments such as shovels and small hammers taken from the ore. I myself have beheld natural figures or images of small fish, lions, wolves, etc. Truly Nature is not idle in the darkness and the depths of the earth. Other varieties of this species adhere like thin plates to the rock.

Rude black silver, the black silver ore of the Germans, is the third species of rude silver. Occasionally it shines in the black ore, much like the lead-coloured species which has been already described. Again, it has little particles of the red-coloured variety, or particles at other times of white silver, and the more it abounds in these, the more metal does the ore yield when it is melted, which was unknown to Pliny and the ancients. Occasionally the ore is sterile, when it is simply termed black earth, and as such is treated in its proper place, s.v. Terra.

Rude purple silver, the fourth species of the rude metal, the Braun Erz of the Germans, was unknown to Pliny and the ancients, but it has no little percentage of silver in the ore. It is found chiefly in the mines of Tarcicus.

Rude reddish and ash-coloured silver, otherwise grey ore, is the fifth of the rude varieties, and yields more metal in melting because its proportion of silver exceeds the others. Thus we certainly see that the grey ore is frequently rich in silver, more especially when it is somewhat hard, so that it can be cut with a knife, or if it be soft, with very thin morsels of silver shining in the leaden ore. When it does not possess this colour, it is then of least value, having the smallest proportion of silver. With these two varieties Pliny seems to have been acquainted when he says (1. 33, c. 6.), One ore is ruddy, the other ashen; I find little of any other kind. And these were known to the ancients. These are the six species of rude silver ore which are known to German metallurgists. Perchance there are others also which might be discovered by a diligent examination of the mines, such as we ourselves may undertake at a future time when our leisure is greater than at present.

The refuse of silver, called also Scoria, Helcysma, Encauma, Silver Slack, :; that which is left after the metal has been melted out, or which is commonly removed from the furnaces where silver is subjected to the operation of fire. Dioscorides (l. 5, c. 51), affirms that the recrement of silver has the virtue of lead wort, or plumbago, which is an astringent, and draws out. It should, therefore, be an ingredient in plasters placed upon wounds. But do you, candid reader, consider how complicated with us is this matter of the recrement of silver? For silver is melted out of pyrites, that is, out of copper ore, and out of lead ore. Do

you judge whether this, which is our true recrement of silver, is that meant by Dioscorides, who was unacquainted with these same species, and how, therefore, could he know the true recrement of this precious metal? But we will set aside these considerations. Consult Pliny on the recrement of silver (1. 33, c. 6). It may be granted out of hand that silver cools and desiccates, and, therefore, its scoriae are of a drying nature, as .va may experience in our own recrement of rude silver, if we put faith in the recrements of medicine.
ARGENTI SPUMA — is Litharge, which still contains a certain percentage of silver; it used in plasters, and has otherwise a penetrating quality. It differs little from recrement of silver obtained from the leaden ore, and is very like lead spume. Dioscorides, who was well acquainted with the workshops where metals are melted, and little with the mines, enumerates (1. 5, c. 52), three species of silver litharge:
1. Molybditis, spume of lead, which is melted out of sand in furnaces, until it burns with a perfect flame.
2. From lead, which is made from leaden plates; Dioscorides praises the Attic and Spanish, and afterwards that which comes from the warm wells of Puzzoli, Baia, the Campania, and from Sicily.
3. Litharge of silver, which is of two kinds, Argyritis, German silver litharge, from silver-coloured silver, which at the present day is used in a crude and not a prepared state. Chrysitis, which is of gold colour, and is the gold litharge of the Germans, not that it is made from gold; it is derived from silver, and the reference is to the colour only. The virtue of these varieties, according to Dioscorides, is astringent, mollifying, restoring, restraining, and cooling. Consult also Dioscorides upon the methods of burning and cleansing litharge of silver, how colouring matter is added to

it, how its mature state is ascertained, and what its virtues are. Pliny (1. 33, c. 6), makes three species of silver litharge:
1. The best, which he calls Chrysitis.
2. Argyritis, made from silver.
3. Molybditis, fused out of lead, whence its name is derived. Hence it would appear that Pliny represents Molybditis to be fused out of lead, while, according to Dioscorides, it is obtained out of sand, unless the species derived from leaden plates was formerly called Molybditis. Pliny, who, according to his custom, transfers all the information of Dioscorides concerning litharge of silver to his own pages, notes also that litharge from scoria differs as much as possible from litharge obtained from recrement. There are others who regard Sterelite and Pneumenis as species of litharge. When litharge of silver is drunk, it is said to be a potent and speedy acting poison, which also Dioscorides affirms (1. 6, c. 27). And Nicander, to whom Dioscorides is in this place considerably indebted, in the twenty-second recipe of his Alexipharmaca, which may be consulted concerning symptoms and antidotes. On this point, see also Serapion, his book of Aggregation, in the chapter on Marechet. See also Paulus on the virtues of Litharge of Silver, s.v. Galenum.
Silver is otherwise thus divided.
1. Rude white lumpy silver from Schneberg, which can be cut with a knife and beaten out with a hammer. Snow-white solid silver; thick silver.
2. Nuggets of solid silver in a very white metallic spar.
Capillary.
1. Silver of Anneberg, solid, white, capillary silver.
2. Solid capillary silver, having a multitude of wiry fibres bundled confusedly together.
3. Very white silver, like a ball of minute silver threads ; twisted silver.

4. Like a silver curling iron, in a crumbling earth of a nut-brown colour.

5. In a shiny loam-coloured earth.

6. Silver of Marieberg, in a gray, metallic, fluid cobalt.

7. In a very white horn stone.

8. In a red quadrangular translucid fluor spar.

9. Silver of Marieberg, in a hard grey stone.

10. Capillary silver of Anneberg, in a mass of lead-coloured silver.

11. Capillary silver of Anneberg, with silver of a lead-colour in a very white spar, combined with a red-coloured pyrites.

12. Capillary silver, combined with lead-coloured silver in white fluor spars. 13- Capillary silver found in the valley of Joachimica, in a forest of fir-trees. 14- White ore of Anneberg, containing rude, ruby-coloured capillary silver, of transparent appearance. Also rude lead coloured silver clearly distinguished in the same stone. Golden ore and vitreous ore combined, yet clearly distinguished.

Compounded in other Forms.

1. Deposited in the form of little trees.

2. A flame-shaped ore to which little masses of lead-coloured silver are found adhering.

White.

1. Pure, solid, white plates of silver in a fatty stone.

2. Thin solid plates of white silver in hard grey ore of Marieberg.

3. Pure white silver in iron pyrites.

4. A clear, solid silver in a clear mountain Chrysocolla, from the Alps of
Suacia.

Lead-coloured.

1. Lead-coloured silver, easily cut and made into coins, and easily hammered into plates.

2. In hard and very white pyrites.

3. In sexangular white fluors.
4. Impressed, or stamped, vitreous ore, which has not been tried by fire. Soft, and therefore easily broken.
5. A pure, quadrangular, vitreous ore, of conical or pyramidal form.
6. In transparent, purple, quadrangular fluors, blunt-pointed.
7. Rude ruby-coloured silver in the centre of a solid vitreous ore of lead colour.

Grey or Ashen.
1. Grey solid silver, in shape like tongues of flame, found in the hard cobalt of Anneberg.
2. A specimen of solid grey ore.
3. Grey silver in a very white flint.

Black-coloured.
1. Black solid ore in a sheer hornstone, or flint.
2. In grey pyrites.
3. Shaped like a branch of the cypress tree.

Transparent and Ruby-coloured.
1. A small nugget, like a carbuncle or amethyst. Fine ruby-red, gold-red ore.
2. Like a carbuncle, with six, seven, or eight angles. Of the shape of an upright beam, in grey pyrites, and natural yellow sulphur.
3. Like the bristles of the hedgehog in a black metallic cobalt; shaped like a head.
4. Little masses seeming to be compacted of red garnet.
5. Larger nuggets compacted like transparent red garnet.

Non-transparent Ruby-coloured.
1. Blood-red, seven-angled, gold-red ore.
2. A nugget in a white metallic spar.
3. A nugget in a gold-coloured pyrites, similar to natural cinnabar.

4. In white sexangular fluorspar, like the exterior cortex of the chestnut rough and sharp and prickly.
5. In an ashen flint.
6. Beaten, golden-red ore, cleaving to a grey hornstone.
7. Showing white in a very golden-red ore.
8. White, red, and gold in a soft white stone.
9. In ashen pyrites.
10. In a worthless sulphuret of lead.
11. Silver containing gold; golden silver.
12. Dark golden red.
13. Liver-coloured, golden red.

Yellow-coloured.
1. A yellow capillary silver in a yellow earth.
2. Like copper pyrites, to which lead-coloured particles adhere.
3. A transparent horn-coloured pure silver of Marieberg, scintillating with light.
4. Solid dark silver, like an ordinary grey earth. It is heavy, and if struck with a hammer, will sparkle. Many experienced miners are unacquainted with it.

Blue-coloured.
1. Containing in its centre, like a kernel, a rude red silver.
2. Mixed with lead-coloured silver and pure white nuggets.
3. Green silver of Anneberg, mined in celestial blue veins.
4. Purple or brown-coloured silver mined in the same place.
5. Silverine stone.
6. Veins of silver in a hard gravel-stone.
7. A rich silver ore from which the recrement has not been removed.
8. Silver mixed with lead, separated from copper. Mixed with lead, i.e., tin, black lead.
9. Rich ore mixed with lead.
10. Lead or pig of workable lead, rich in silver.
11. Mediocre, a thin line in the vein.

12. Poor, a freshly deposited layer.
13. Hard layers, rich in metal.
14. Soft and dry, with a large proportion of black lead.
15. A small specimen of silver nuggets.
16. Refined silver.
17. Grey recrement of gold; grey silver slag.
18. Black silver slag.
19. Silver litharge.
20. Prepared silver, rich in lead.
21. Refined silver, purged from other metals.
22. Burnt silver.
23. Fine, prepared silver.
24. Pressed or stamped silver.
25. Gilt silver.
26. Silver drawn into wire.
27. Silver plates.
28. Silver separated by washing from copper.
29. Silver dissolved into grains.

ARGENTUM POPULI ~ Alkali or nitre.

ARGENTUM VIVUM ~ is the chemical term for Mercury. It is simply a viscous water, in the bowels of the earth, of a subtle substance, having the nature of white earth, made one with a perfect union, up to the last point and particle, until that which is humid is modified by that which is dry, and the dry again by the humid, until the whole is absolutely homogeneous. Also Vivific Silver, i.e., the philosophical substance which is to be distinguished from common quicksilver, is the complementary part of the stone of the philosophers, as the chemists tell us; the second principle, the mother of all the metals, and in proportion as it copulates with their father, the male sulphur, it engenders perfection and imperfection in metals, and when it predominates the metals (like a foetus) derive more from the mother than the father. Into that also from which they most originate are they most resolved. Now quicksilver is twofold-natural and artificial.

Natural, possessing without excoction its own inherent colour, in which state it is found among metals in the smith's troughs, commonly in the form of filaments. True, Native Quicksilver, the mother and element of metals. This species was known to Pliny, 1. 33, c. 6, who says: Within these veins and mines there is a certain stone found which yields from it a humour continually, and the same continues always liquid; men call it Quicksilver. It may not have been seen by Dioscorides when he said: Quicksilver is also met with among the debris of silver mines, exuded in drops; others testify to having found it by itself among metals.

Artificial, which is made out of the minium secundarium of Pliny (l. 33, c. 7), or out of veins of minium, or cinnabar, which is found in our mines. The first was known to Dioscorides (l. 5, c. 60). He describes the method of its preservation, its use, its poisonous nature, and the antidotes thereto. Consult also Pliny, 1. 20, c. 5, and 1. 28, c, 9, 10, as well as other places and authors.

For the rest, it may be noted that the Greeks called both native and artificial Quicksilver by the name Hudrargyron. But Pliny only distinguishes the natural species, as appears by our former quotation, by the name of Quicksilver, and that which is artificially produced from cinnabar, or derived from its ore, he distinguishes, if I err not, by the name Hydrargyron — a classification which is also observed by the most learned Leonicenus. It may be finally noted that Quicksilver, while in its liquid state, is called crude in our workshops; when mortified, it is called concreted, or by some sublimated. It is warm and moist in the fourth degree. Some say that it is cold in the fourth degree. The chemists consider it both cold and moist in the fourth degree, liquid in the third, white in the second, and dark in the first degree. There are, moreover, other opinions.

The following species of Quicksilver are also enumerated:

1. Vivific Silver (Philosophical Quicksilver), i.e., Spirit, or Mercury, which is also the Fugitive Servant, Asoc, Ydrogiros, Sanlarum, Anzatig, Asoc, Zaylat, Azehoc, Kyregiros, White Smoke, Alsohoc, Asob, Ayor, Azec, Alozet, Azoar, Aurarid, the Dragon.
2. That which is obtained without smelting, pure among metals. Pure Quicksilver.
3. Quicksilver smelted from veins of cinnabar.
4. That which is called Sublimated Quicksilver.
5. Precipitated.
6. Mortified, or killed.
7. Quicksilver solidified, or fixed by art.
8. Native Minium.
9. A hard round nugget which the Arabs call Cinnabar.
10. Fragile Cinnabar.
11. Artificial Cinnabar.
12. Natural Cinnabar, or Red Lead. The vein from which it comes.
13. A vein of Cinnabar in which Quicksilver exists, and which exudes in drops when the ore is broken up.
14. Solid Quicksilver from the valley of Joachimica, similar in colour to rude ruby coloured silver ore.
15. Similar to coccolite, with pyrites of gold.
16. Similar to coccolite in a white fissile stone.
17. A variety in a grey fissile stone.
18. Liver-coloured ore, rich in Quicksilver.
19. Similar to rude golden-red silver in silver coloured loadstone.
20. A swarthy-red Quicksilver ore from Hydrensis, which exudes drops of Quicksilver when broken with a hammer.
21. Liver-coloured Quicksilver ore from Hydrensis.

22. Tawny-coloured Quicksilver ore in which there are layers of gold
coloured pyrites.
23. Recrement of Quicksilver.
ARGILLE — are so called because they are similar to the clays used by potters. Potters' Earth. There are numerous species of these clays, which are distinguished by their colours, and are found in our mines, distributed through many places.
1. White Seburg clay.
2. White clay of Anneberg.
3. White Islebian clay, sparkling with silver particles.
4. In white ashen Islebian deposit, which is found in copper mines under a red sandy earth.
5. Fine grey ash-like clay of Misnense.
6. Light green ashy clay of Misnense, near Risa and the Elbe.
7. Cinereous clay from Herlesberg, which the people of Nuremberg combine with a sandy earth to make those melting pots in which brass is manufactured.
8. Combined with a sandy earth ; clay for the melting-pot.
9. Slime of Misnensis, of beautiful yellow hue.
10. Yellow clay of Anneberg, or silver clay.
11. Like red earth from the district of Okroll.
12. Red Islebian clay, in which silver particles are sparkling.
13. Iron-coloured Bavarian clay, with which those furnaces are coloured
wherein iron is treated. An iron-grey sand.
14. Purple clay, which much abounds in my own country. When the spade
is removed it appears quite red. 15. Ash-coloured.
15. Bohemian, crumbling, loamy, rich in ore, abounding in garnet.
Colours may be manufactured from all these species, provided they are not over-moist. The best jars and pots are

made from them, if the clays be treated rightly by the potters in moulds shaped according to the prescribed rule. But this I leave to the potters.

ARGISTATA is engrafted.

ARGYROS is Silver ; hence lithargyros, argentiferous-stone. For lithos signifies a stone.

1. Aridura is the wasting of any bodies, or menstrua, in what manner soever. It is especially the shrinkage of metals, dissolution, dying. It is also called Sideratio, Numbness, Sphacelus, Sphacelismus, Telia, Necrosis.

2. Aristolochia has a white flower, red inside, like a stone itself.

3. Arles Crudum ~ not translatable; the Germa context menas soimpletpons or ninny, which seems irrelevant. What are refered to, however, are drops of water falliong in June as the dew in May. Caled also Hydatis (a precious stone of te colour of water), Stalagmi (consisting of drops; also a species of vitriol, Stagen and Straax.

4. Armoniac Sal, i.e., star. Called also Genzir.

5. Arohot ~ Quicksilver.

AROLPH ~ Mandragora.

ARSALTOS, ASPALTUM ~ Asphalt.

ARSENICUM ~ is the Greek Nitre, Effulgence of Metals; Salt of Metals, and of Saturn Called also Artanek, or Artanech. Found in many places. It is also Luna, and our Venus. According to Gebir, it is Sulphur's companion. It is the soul, the hermaphrodite, the means whereby Sulphur and Mercury are united. It has community with both natures, and is, therefore, called Sun and Moon.

ARSENII ~ is Lacten, (?) milky.

ARTAVECK, ARTANECK ~ **ARSENIC**, of which there are three species: White, Yellow and Citrine. Yellow orpiment, golden dye; crystalline arsenic. Item: Red Greek Sandaraca which is of two kinds, rough and manufactured;

the former was a red arsenic mixed with brimstone, the latter a kind of vermilion.

ARTEFICIUS ~ Deficiency of some member.

ARTHOICUM or **PANNONIUM** ~ A red oil from the roots of certain herbs obtained by their digestion with bread in horse-dung.

ARTIFEX ~ Refiner, one versed in ores and metals; an assayer.

ASABON ~ Soap.

ASAFOETIDA ~ Fetid inspissated Sap from an Indian tree.

ASAGEN ~ Blood of the Dragon.

ASAGI, or **AZEGI** ~ Vitriol or Red Atrament.

ASAMAZ ~ Verdigris.

ASAPHATUM ~ Impetigo, a cutaneous disease, and Serpigo, twisted ringworm. Ulcers and blemishes of the skin are of cognate character.

ASEB, or **ASEP** ~ is the German Alaun, Alum. It is a metallic substance or vein of earth, which occupies a middle position between vitriol, or copperas, and salt, and is found in mines. It is like a salt substance, or liquor, issuing out of the earth (see Pliny, 1. 35, c. 15). It is composed of water and slime; whence its nature is that of an earthy efflux. It is drawn off in streams during winter, and it is perfected by fermentation under the summer suns. It is like a vein of earth which is transmuted into a white colour by excessive heat. Every species of chalcantum contains alum. Now the name alum signifies something manufactured (in this place the sense of the text is obscure); we may admit several species of alum on the authority of the learned, and most certainly that alum is made in hot places, and above all in those which are sulphureous and igneous. But as there are indeed many kinds of alum, we proceed to tabulate them for the sake of those who are interested in this matter.

ASEB, SEBEL, ALPAR, ALUMAIC (in Arabic; Scipterea ; in Greek, **ALUMEN, ALAUM**) — is hot and dry in the fourth grade, according to Avicenna. Others say that it is hot and dry in the third degree. It is found native in mines; it is composed of water and slime, and is like a salt of earth. It is either white or black in Cyprus, and there gold is purged with it.

The white is thick or concreted, and liquid; it is called Alumen de Rocha, or Rocca, otherwise Liparine (? from the island of that name in the Etruscan Sea, but Lipara was also a precious stone).

The Scissile is three-fold: Cloddy, Round, Scissile.

1. The cloddy again is two-fold-mined and manufactured. That which is manufactured is, further, of two kinds-that which is obtained by melting (generally of natural mined alum), and that which is coagulated. Of all these species we have the cloddy alone at the present day.

2. The round Zuccarine Alum, so called on account of its likeness to Zuccar (unknown), is again two-fold : Mined, and Manufactured.

The mined is, if I mistake not, called Strongylos. Round Alum from the mines is also two-fold: Spongy, and Porous. The spongy variety is easily dissolved in the mouth, and is wholly worthless.

The porous is better, and is full of hollow pipes, like the sponge. It more nearly approaches white, with a certain fattiness, is devoid of sand or grit, and is easily crumbled. It is neither as black as that of Egypt nor as white as the celebrated White Alum of Melos.

Manufactured Alum is that prepared by hand, and is worthless.

3. Scissile Alum is thick, hard, and massive. It is called Schistos by Pliny (1. 35, c. 15). It distributes itself into small threads, and is termed Trichitis, or Capillary. It is also made

and falsified out of Scissile Stone, and is now called Scaly Alum, or Feathery Alum, and by the vulgar Scaiola ; without doubt also the Amianthus of which we have before treated is our Scaly Alum. What they call Chalcitis and Trichytis is also alum, or rather the exudition of the stone thereof when it is coagulated into spume. Some" term alum Copperine because it occurs in pyrites. Hence Chalcitis is frequently called Concrete Alum. But this alum does not possess astringent virtue, only a dry quality. It is also called Scipterion, Alumen Jamenum, and Broken Alum. When alum is generically spoken of, this species is understood. Alumen Jamenum is brought from Babylon ; and because it is not astringent, but of drying quality, it is therefore not alum, much less broken alum, and has only the appearance of alum. Take notice of this error of learning.

Liquid Alum, called Alumen de Rocha, or Rocca, or Liparine, is two-fold (r) Soft, fatty, limpid, milky, called Phormion, the falsification of which with the sap of the pomegranate we are taught to detect by Pliny. (2) Rough, pale alum, which stains like the gall-nut, and is called Paraphoron. It is astringent, hardens, and eats away. It is found in Spain, Egypt, Armenia, Macedonia, the Pontus, Africa, the islands of Sardinia, Melos, Lipara, and Aeolian Strongylos. The virtues of these varieties are astringent, heating, purging out, and lessening. They are burnt like Chalchitis. For the rest, consult Dioscorides, Pliny, Serapion, Avicenna, etc., on the medical virtues, native places, and appearances of these kinds.

Alumen. The round, scissile, and liquid species are of use in medicine. There is another kind, which is called Alumen Affar; or in Arabic Usnen; and in Latin, Sparrow's Dung, several varieties of which are enumerated by Serapion and Avicenna. Some call it Salt of Alkali, and indeed it is not alum, but a sort of salt.

ASED ~ is the Lion.
ASEDENIGI ~ Haematites.
ASEGEN or **AZOGEN** ~ Blood of the Dragon.
ASENEC ~ is Sol.
ASEPH ~ is Broken Alum.
ASMAGA ~ is the permixture or commixture of any metals with each other.
ASOPER ~ is Soot.
ASPALTUM or **ASPHALTUM** ~ Flower of Copper, Red Bitumen, or Indian Bitumen.
ASSALA ~ is Nutmeg.
ASSALIAE ~ are worms which eat into boards, wood fretters, formed between the boards.
ASSANEGI, ASANIRGI, ASARAGI ~ A powder which falls from walls of salt.
ASSATIO ~ A species of hard and dry Ash.
ASSINGAR, ASUGAR, ASMIAR, ASIM ~ Names of verdigris.
ASSER TRIANGULARIS ~ Hand-barrow.
ASSERCULI or **PALI** ~ Small Planks, or Poles, on which miners sit for working the mine.
ASSERES ~ Boards joined by their sides.
ASSERES ~ An outside plank or slab.
ASSOS ~ An artificial alum of the appearance of the stone, i.e., white. See Morien.
ASTERITES ~ Quartz.
1. Astroites Mas, male Astroites, shaped like half a globe. An asterite full of stars.
2. The female variety, without the stars of the male, but having representations of caterpillars, in which way the stars are thickly compacted by nature.
3. Little Globules of Asterite, on which prayers, like the Lord's Prayer, were told formerly (Rosary Beads).

ASTRUM SYNUS ~ The Sidereal Celestial Star. Here star signifies the virtue and potency of things, obtained by preparations, as for example, the star of sulphur is the augmentation of sulphur, whereby it is changed into a most notable oil. Note. The star of salt is its resolution into a water or oil, by which it is endowed with more than its normal virtues. In like manner, the star of mercury is its sublimation, by which it acquires a wonderful increase of virtue and power, far exceeding, and far more subtle than, what it naturally possesses. (German version : Astrum.) But in our chemical art, it signifies the nature and power of a thing, which it receives from preparation, as when mercury is sublimed, sulphur lighted with a spark of fire, salt dissolved, and dissipated by itself. Then they become astral, starry, and are called the Star of Mercury, Sulphur, or Salt. The Star is the Alkol or Quintessence, the sheer and clear power, the extract, the cream, and the property of the thing, says Bacchus.
ASUB ~ is Galaxia, Constellation.
ASUBEVEGI ~ is a stone which cuts other stones.
ASULCI, or **LASURD** ~ is Azulite.
ASUOLI ~ is Atrament. Called also Soot.
ATACK ~ is Talc or Nitre.
ATANOR ~ is a perforated vessel.
ATEBRAS ~ A hook (literally); Uncus Aquinus, is a vessel for sublimation.
ATHANOR ~ Called both philosophical and arcane, is an oven adapted for composing the stone of the philosophers. The fire does not touch the base, and the required heat is suitably and uniformly imparted. Many vain things have been imagined by many persons concerning the method of constructing this oven. But the one of our invention, even as it exceeds all the other ovens which have been described by its superiority over all, requires to be minutely treated of in

this place, as much on account of the contiguity of the fire as of the equable nature of the same. A circular wall is erected of the height of one foot. On either side of this wall a vacant space, with a small door, is left. This is for the removal of the ashes. Above this structure there is placed a small iron gridiron, and above the said gridiron we erect another small door, which is broader at the bottom than at the top, and is an aperture through which the coals can be stirred with a poker. When this turret has been set in an upright position in the manner described, and has been filled with coals to the top we cover it with a covering of clay. But at the same time, in the hindmost part of the wall, and in that portion of it which is nearest to the gridiron, we leave a small hole open, through which the heat may be able to approach the Athanor, and we stop this aperture with a spatula (a long instrument for stirring), or with an iron bar (some term it a register), which can be raised and lowered. We make also at the top of the turret, of the breadth of five inches, beneath the cover, a small aperture, through which the index finger shall just be able to pass, by which the fire may draw the air, as if a fuel, to itself. Over against the turret constructed in the manner described, there is set another oven, which is the Athanor itself.

After the same manner, a circular wall, one foot and a half in height, is constructed, which completely fits with its sides the posterior opening of the first turret. On this wall we erect an oven, leaving on the top of the furnace a small aperture, like an imperial thaler, whereby the heat in this part, to some extent pressing upon the furnace, can pass upward to the next nearest furnace. Then we again build an eighteen-inch wall by the place where we commenced the furnace ; we cover the same with a lid, again leaving a small aperture at the top, as in the case of the lower one. However, it is necessary that in one side of this part there should be left a clear space where the matter can be put in and taken out. For in this middle part is the workshop where the matter is prepared in its proper vessel, placed over a tripod. In order to fill up the clear space, and close it up lest any air should be produced, a wellfitting lid is made to.cover it. Finally, with a third lid, we cover the whole of this second furnace, leaving, however, at the base four air-holes, which also have covers, whereby the heat may be increased or diminished. This is the philosophical distillatory oven, the Turba Clibanus, or Reverberatory Oven of the Philosophers.

ATINCAR, or **ATINKAR** ~ is Rock Borax.

ATRAMENTUM ALBUM ~ is White Vitriol.

ATRAMENTUM CITRINUM ~ is fixed Vitriol.

ATRAMENTUM HISPANICUM ~ is, I believe, Vitriol.

ATRAMENTUM RUBEUM ~ Red Atrament, is called Asaric or Asagi.

ATRAMENTARUM ~ is Akata; another variety is Alfrein; another, Kalkadis; another, Chalcanthum, is Egythian Atrament.

ATRAMENT ~ is variously classified.

1. Scrivener's Atrament, Writing Ink.
2. Printers' Ink, Oily Atrament.
3. Shoemakers' Ink, or Tanners' Atrament, Shoemakers' Wax, Chalcanthum, Hydride of Copper, Cobblers' Black, Copper Ore, or Vitriol, red inside and having red stripes.
4. Atramentum Rubeum, Red Burnt Vitriol.
5. Atramentum Tectorium, Vel Pictorium, Soot, Painters' Black.
6. Atramentum Album Tenue, soft, white Atrament, Hydrate of Copper Flower.
7. Atramentum Fossile, Native Copper-stone (apparently from which the ore has been extracted).
8. Atramentum Candidum, Durum, Stalacticum, native Stalactical Vitriol.

9. Reddish and spongy native Hydride of Copper.
10. Red Stalactical Vitriol, of good quality, native in white earth.
11. Hard green Copper Stone washings, native in Goslaria.
12. Native porous Green Atrament.
13. Green hard Stalactical Atrament of Goslaria.
14. Grey Stalactical Atrament in a white earth, natural grey Copperas.
15. Grey hard native Copperas.
16. Green hard prepared Copperas or Vitriol of Goslar. Green hard native stalactical Vitriol.
17. Green hard porous prepared Copperas of Goslaria.
18. Grey native Neapolitan, with a pure yellow Sulphur.
19. Very beautiful cerulean prepared Copperas from Cyprus.
20. Green bluish prepared Copperas from Goslaria.
21. Blue Roman prepared Copperas.
22. Blue Hungarian prepared Copperas.
23. Blue Hungarian Copperas combined with a very white Alum.
24. Blue prepared Copperas from Radeberg, similar to Pannonian.
25. Radeberg Copperas combined with Sulphur.
26. Blue prepared Silesian Copperas combined with Alum.
27. White hard transparent sublimed Vitriol or Copperas.
28. Distilled Copperas or Oil of Vitriol.
29. Burnt Vitriol.
30. Burnt Cyprian Copperas.
31. Recrement of Atrament, Salt, Nitre, and Alum after distillation. The dead body of Aqua Fortis.
32. Recrement of Atrament from which Sulphur of Radeberg is afterwards melted out.

ATRAMENTUM — i.e., Duenec, Malagislaca, Black Chalk, Brittle Pitch.

ATRAMENTUM SUTORIUM — is nothing else but Vitriol, i.e., Chalcanthum, i.e., a sort of Flower of Copper. It is not however Kalkou Anthos, or true Flower of Copper, as we have before stated. Chalcanthus, or Vitriol, or Atramentum Sutorium, is one thing; the ancient Flower of Copper is another, and was obtained, among other ways, from the washings of copper ore, while Flower of Copper has in modern times been given as an alternative name of Verdigris, or Copper-Rust. Once again then Atramentum Sutorium is Vitriol formerly used in leather tanning. But because it is corrosive to shoes, another kind was devised by shoemakers, which is in fact our present Cobblers' Black. But with the ancients Atramentum meant Vitriol, that metallic substance which is simply a congealed water, having a quality of copper, but differing in its form and nature with the stone to which it adheres. In a discourse upon springs and rivers, Seneca tells us that the earth contains various humours, and a spirit like that of the human body where there are also various humours, of which some are vital, some corruptible, some more fatty, and some which in time become dried or hardened. Of this substance are all metals which are melted out of the moisture in stone. Such also, in like manner, are those metals which chemists have not inappropriately termed spirit, and which are different from things which flow. Dioscorides (1. 5, c. 64) says that soft and hard Atrament are both Sutorium, or Shoemaker's Atrament, but that there are three species:

i. That which is concreted from humours which are collected by droppingsin mines, and is called Stillatic Vitriol. The best quality is furnished by copperine metals. This species is also called Pinarion and Distillatic. It is the German native Distillatic Vitriol.

2. That which is termed Pecton, i.e., concreted and congealed Vitriol; which forms in caves and grottos, and

brought afterwards by a simple process into excavated trenches, assumes a concrete form.

Now, these two species are natural, and differ in shape and manner of formation. This is the German Copper-smoke, or Soot of Copper, or Pyrites, concreted or congelated in the mines. Both species have their medical uses; they are astringent, healing, and induce the formation of skin. Classified according to colour, there are three species of Shoemakers' Black or Vitriol. White Vitriol, not mentioned by Dioscorides, but which Pliny describes (1. 34, c. 12). On account of its white colour, or similitude of colour, he tells us that it was called Leucoion (white violet), and is used by fullers in their trade. Shoemakers' Wax and Sory are akin to this species. For the rest, the white violet Leucoion of Theophrastus and Dioscorides is well known in physics. (But this probably refers to the herb called Leucoion. Some editions of Pliny read Lonchoton, following Dioscorides, instead of Leucoion in the passage cited above).

The second species of Atrament is green. The third is blue, and is said by Dioscorides to be the best stillatic atrament; it is heavy, close-grained, and translucent. By others it is called Lonchoton (see above), because it forms in the figure of a javelin. The method of operating upon this species by fire is taught by Dioscorides: And a great thing verily is the knowledge of the virtues of Flower of Copper, i.e., of Verdigris, according to the moderns, and of Chrysocolla, and of the Vitriols.

Manufactured Atrament is made in Spain, and the mode of its manufacture will be also found in Dioscorides, who further informs us that it is of high service in dyeing and colouring. By the Germans it is called Hydride of Copper, which is manufactured either simple or in clusters; that is reputed to be the best which is of a blue colour.

Pliny (1. 94, c, 12) divides Chalcanthum, i.e., Vitriol and Shoemakers' Black, into Native Mined and into Manufactured. Of the first there are three varieties:
1. That which is dug up in trenches, or obtained from caves.
2. That which comes from mines in the rocks.
3. That which is obtained from sea-water, on admitting sweet water, and by means of violent heat.
The manufactured species is made from materials found in those pits and pools of Spain where there is the same kind of water from which native Atrament is derived.
The Metamorphosis, transmutation, or transfiguration of these Minerals by the Artifice of Nature alone.
Great is the Knowledge of Flower of Copper, the Verdigris of the moderns, of Chrysocol, of the Vitriols, and other species of Atrament.
I. Green Zeg, or Shoemakers' Black, or Vitriol, or Chalcanthum (native or changed or passes into:
1. Misy, very easily.
2. After a long time into Chalchitis, as regards outward appearance; internally it is still Shoemakers' Black.
3. Filaments, when it is old. Manufactured Chalchitis is then wrought from it. Also Chalcanthum changed into Chachitis can then be made into Misy.
II. Chalcitis, or honey-yellow Zeg, according to Pliny; brass colour, according to Diosorides (Zeg is the name given by the Arabs, who also call it Colcothar), has a middle position between marchasite (i.e., Black Zeg, or Pyrites, or Black Atrament), and Vitriol (i.e., Green Zeg, or Chalcanthum), and when old can be changed, and passes into:
Sory, very easily;
Sory and Melateria pass on the other hand into:
Chalcanthum Leucoion, i.e., White.
The Arabs call Atrament Zeg simply, and distinguish these species thereof:

1. Black Zeg, i.e., Black Atrament, i.e., Marchasite, i.e., Pyrites. For Marchasite, or dissolved Pyrites, makes Ink, which Serapion calls Black Zeg, which mixed with wine and vine garis resolved into a black colour; Avicenna calls it (*De Atramento*, 1. 2) White Atrament, because before it is dissolved it is white.

2. Zeg Colcotar, or Chalcitis, or Zegi, of a citron hue, or copper colour, according to Dioscorides. Also called Citrine Atrament. There are in all four varieties: Red Zeg, or Ruby Zeg, or Ruby Atrament, or Red Atrament. It is called Asuria.

3. Green Zeg, or Green Atrament, which is Chalcanthum or Vitriol, already described. And this is Shoemakers' Black. Serapion in his chapter on Zeg affirms that he has himself seen in the mines Black Zeg, i.e., Marcasite, i.e., Pyrites, and afterwards Colcotar, i.e., Chalcitis, and Green Zeg, i.e., Vitriol, or Chalcanthum, in combination.

And he says that these three species differ in subtlety, and grossness. For out of them is derived the grosser kind, i.e., Black Zeg, i.e., Pyrites ; and also the finer, i.e., Green Zeg, i.e., Chalcanthum, or Shoemakers' Black. But Colcotar is a middle species between the two others. This is also called Chalcitis. Moreover, Green Zeg and Colcotar are liquefied by fire, but Black Zeg is not easily melted.

Green Zeg, Chalcanthum, or Shoemakers' Black, more especially the Cyprian kind, is solid, though it is the finer species of Atrament, and it is easily changed into Misy. Outwardly also it becomes Chalcitis, though inwardly it is still Shoemakers' Black. This transformation is very beautiful. All these are natural metals, namely, white, green, or blue Chalcanthum ; also Chalcitis, which is copper-colour ; also Misy, which is gold-colour ; also Sory, which is almost the hue of Melanteria (Shoemakers' wax) ; and they all are mentioned by Galenus, and were used by him in plasters; nor were they less valued by others of the ancients, for they were held in high respect of old, and were used universally in Cyprus. I do not know whether they are found in our silver mines, but I do not deny that they might be, if they were diligently sought. They are met with in the copper mines of Goslaria and in other places, though but rarely, it must be allowed. It is a remarkable thing that wherever Marcasite, i.e., Pyrites, exists there also are all the others, namely, Chalcanthum, Chalcitis, Misy, Sory. All these species blacken, and hence are called Atramen.

Chalcanthum is hot and dry in the fourth degree, according to Paulus.

We have treated of Shoemakers' Black from the ancient and the modern standpoint.

We must now briefly consider with Dioscorides the subject of Scriveners' Black, or Writing Ink. The methods of its manufacture which are described by Dioscorides, are, however, quite obsolete. We now compound ink for writing in a very different way, namely, from Vitriol, Gall, Gum, and in other fashions, as our clerks have reason to know, seeing how inks vary with the ingredients that compose them. It would be permissible to classify writing ink into natural and manufactured. The first is an extract well known to all scriveners, namely, Sepia, derived from the Cuttle-fish, on which consult Dioscorides, Pliny, and Nicander. It is also obtained from Eruca, a kind of plant which some call white Mustard, on which also consult Dioscorides in his 1. 2. The manufactured species, according to the same writer, are these:

1. From the Resin of Pine Trees.
2. From the Soot of other Resins, and Corrosives of Painters.

But among us manufactured ink is obtained:

1. From Stone, which we shall treat of in the section De Paigite.

2. ? From burnt Bark (*ex carta combusta* — but there is no such word as Carta).
3. From the Seed of the Alder.
4. From Milk and Curds [? the text reads *cate*, but there is again no such word in Latin].
5. From the Soot of oily or fat substances.
6. From Vitriol, Gall, and Gum. Pliny (1.35. c. 6.) gives other methods — as from Sulphur-coloured Earth, from Coals, Soot, etc.

ATTAGAR — i.e., Stone.

ATTINGAT — i.e., Flower of Copper.

ATTINGIR — i.e., a small clay Coffer.

ATTRACTIVA — is a name given to some Medicaments, also called Magnetite, which have an attractive power.

ATUREB, or **AZAZEZE** — is Glass.

AURANCUM, or **AURANTUM** — Signifies Egg-shells.

AURARIC, or **AZOCH, AZOG, AZET, BESECH, BESEC** — are names of Mercury.

AURUM COCTUM — is Gold-leaf.

AURUM COTICULA EXPERIRI — To test gold with touchstone.

AVIS HERMETIS — is that Red Lead in the middle of the egg which rises above itself, which flies on high, and again descends to earth for its nourishment, for earth gives nourishment to all things. It is also the Soil in the Matrix, and is called otherwise the Goose.

AURIPIGMENTUM — is Orpiment, Arsenical Earth, the Operment, Yellow Gold, of the Germans, and is used by painters. It is a native metallic substance, and is found in combination with Sandarac (Dioscorides, 1. 5, c. 70). It is covered with a crust, and glitters with a gold colour. In its fundamental nature it is a certain kind of sulphur, and is, so to speak, a terrestrial excrement in the caverns of the earth, which in the long process of time is turned into Orpiment.

There is also a fissile species, of scaly character, found in Mysia Minor on the Hellespont. Another variety is pallid, cloddy and granular, having the colour of Sandarac; it comes from Pontus and Cappadocia. The Arabs say that Orpiment is similar to Lapis Specularis (which see), but the latter has no unguent quality. The Arabs, however, confound Sandarac with Arsenic, and, in fact, give the name of Arsenic indiscriminately both to Sandarac and Orpiment, distinguishing only their variety according to colour. Chemists as well as physicians call our Sandarac Red Arsenic; and Arsenical Earth what we call Orpiment. Avicenna speaks of White Arsenic, but true White Arsenic is never found in mines, and his description may possibly refer to certain manufactured species, one of which is mud-colour and the other white, which are manufactured chemically, and are both at the present day known only by the general name of Arsenic.

Concerning all these species see Serapion (lib. Agg. cap. Harmech) and Avicenna (cap. on Arsenic), who treat of its good and evil qualities. Sublimed Arsenic, or Arsenical Salt, destroys life, and White Arsenic in its natural state is also fatal. They are all poisonous. (See Diosc., 1. 6.)

Orpiment is also the Blood of the Stone. The Turba calls it the female which we use to colour the Sun and to cook with Mercury. It is, however, genuine Sulphur. Quicksilver Orpiment is Sulphur which rises from the composition. There is also Auripigmentum Lempinas, which is Lily-water, Crusty Orpiment, Cloddy Orpiment, dry Yellow, Cloddy Orpiment, mixed with Sandarac, Ruby Orpiment, or Realgar, white Sublimated Orpiment, differing from that of the mines, and Sublimed Orpiment from black, ruddy, and mud-coloured veins of ore.

AURUM — Gold, called Sol by chemists, and dedicated to the Sun, is the most tempered of all the metals; it is said to be warm and dry in the second grade, and red in the third grade. It is a metallic body, of citrine colour, effulgent, heavy, equably digested in the womb of earth, washed with mineral water during a very long time. It is composed of pure living Silver, fixed, and of a clear red; also of a clean, fixed, red, incombustible Sulphur. In fine, it is the most subtle substance of Quicksilver. Truly we have beheld Quicksilver absorbing gold which it receives most willingly, even as a mother receives her son. Further, Gold consists of a small quantity of clean Sulphur and of a pure redness; the greater the quantity of Vivific Silver, the more does it derive from the mother than from the father. Purest Sulphur copulating as father with Quicksilver as mother, generates finest Gold as a son. Briefly, coagulate Quicksilver, together with Sulphur, like a pure fire, yet not burning, produces Gold. This is that beloved son which Nature ever intends to beget, after which she ever strives ; but various accidents intervene and procreate the other metals. Now Gold is duplex-native and prepared by fire.

Pure Native Gold, which is naturally pure, whose lumps or masses are called in Spain Palacrae (ingots), and by the Germans Solid Gold, this is found

1. In rivers, such as the Tagus, Elbe, Saale, Schwartza, etc., as you may learn from the gold washers.

2. In Arabian mountains, in mines, and wells; in part pure, in part with its grains cleaving to a certain species of white stone which the Germans call Quartz. Found plentifully at Cottenheyd.

3. In the heads of fish which we call trout.

Gold prepared by fire or by melting:

1. Out of Pyrites, of the colour of ashes and leaden ore or dross.

2. Out of a certain purple Earth, so tempered and effected by the vapour and breath of the earth, that it is fruitful of

gold, and in many places gold is melted out of it in the furnace.

3. Out of Borax, or Antiphane. Out of Cerulean (Jasulis), of which we shall speak in its proper place. Situation, however, as we have frequently had reason to see, is serviceable to the quality of gold. There are differences in distinct grades between Arabian, Spanish, Hungarian, and German gold. Gold is the substance and ferment in the philosophical gold which doth ascend into the height. For the Mercury of the Sun is a seed, according to Bernard. It is the Soul and the Red Knight who takes the White Lady in marriage. It is then he is robed in his kingly apparel, even the white gold, wherein is no metal but only gold. It must, however, be purified by means of Cement, through the repository of ashes, and very carefully cleansed by means of Salt and Brickdust. When it is dissolved with water, it is made into a spirit by the intervention of Chrysolite. Mix Gold with Gold, then Gold cannot become Silver unless it be corrupted, adulterated, and black; and when even it becomes Silver, then does it become Gold. But then we must apply processes. Says the adept Senior: The Sun rises when the Moon increases, and is hidden in the same; it is next drawn out from thence. The Body of the Sun and Water of the Sun is Mercury of the Philosophers. Yes, it is threefold, being black, white, and red. It is called the imperishable, because it cannot be destroyed. The Moon makes the Sun soft, spongy, and fluid, and it refines it from impurity. It is the Mother and the Field wherein Gold should be sown. Otherwise we need it not, except in Sun and Moon. Says Theophrastus in his ninth book of Archidoxes : The essential being of Gold is devoid of Salt that congeals, therefore it penetrates and dyes the metals. The ordinary Gold is dead, but the philosophical is alive, and is a true nutriment. The common Gold goes out of men

as it enters them. These are the words of Rupecissa in his third chapter. But Paracelsus in his book on Minerals has this concerning the Generation of Gold. Know that there is a Sulphur which is in the highest degree sublimated by Nature, and cleansed from all its blackness and refuse, and so highly diaphanised that there can be nothing among metals which is, or could be, higher in the bodily order. This also is the Sulphur which is the first matter of Gold, one of the three principles. If the alchemists might find it — (it is a gold tree and it is possible to discover it by its roots) — then would they have cause to rejoice. For it is the Mercury of the Philosophers, which is produced from Gold, not that other which is made from Mars and Venus; it is the Scrupulus (i.e., the Rough Stone), the Universal Substance. Now the Mercury, by a metallic art, is separated to the greatest possible extent from all terrestrial matters and accidents; it is transformed only into a pure mineral body, in every respect transparent. This is the Mercury of the Philosophers, which generates Gold, and is the second part of the First Matter. Afterwards comes the Salt, which is the third of the prime principles of Sol and of the Tree out of which Gold grows; it is crystallized to the greatest possible extent, and so perfectly separated and purified from all its sharpness, acidity, and flavour of alum and vitriol, that it is said to have no beginning, but is free in itself, to the greatest extent disengaged, and in the highest degree diaphanised. Now are the three together.

Gold is the Microcosmos, a small world. It has three principles and four elements; it is a heavenly substance, heaven, and the rays of the Sun. Therefore it withstands fire, and is the most eminent medicine. It has in itself all the stars of heaven and all the fruits of earth. It is called Incombustible Sulphur, Italian Antimony, Metallic Glass, Loadstone, Vegetable Iron (? the labiate plant called

Siderite), Marcasite, Cercilium Auri, Gold-Spiral, Purple Gold (i.e., Powder of Cassius), Chrysocolla (Borax, also a precious stone), Gold Stone, i.e., Chrysites, a precious stone of the colour of gold, the Green Mountain, Borax, Chrysocome (another name of Chrysites, but it may also mean Flax-Weed, or Beard of Jupiter), Gold Grain, Chalcedony. There are, however, several species of Gold:

1. Pure gold, which has not been tried by fire, such as is washed out from sand in the Elbe, and in many rivers of Misena. Solid washed gold, liquid gold, gold grains, etc.
2. Gold in an unmixed state, mined in a mountain of Carpathos. Solid gold.
3. Gold obtained in a small quantity from a ferraceous ore in the same mountain.
4. Solid gold in a hard white flint, from the same mountain.
5. Solid gold from the same mountain, found in a stone called Armenian. Solid gold in pot-stone.
6. Thin plates and dust of purest gold, in a hard white flint, from the borders of the province of Pannonia in Hungary.
7. Yellow, argentiferous gold in an ore containing Quicksilver.
8. Gold mixed with silver in an ashen flint, obtained from Noricum, between the Danube and the Alps, or from Styria, and called Electrum, which is gold with a fifth part of silver.
9. Gold combined with silver after purification by fire.
10. Gold prepared by fire and separated from other metals. Fine gold, called by the Greeks, Obrussa, Assayed Gold.
11. Gold which is combined with silver, equal or clean gold.
12. Gold coloured by copper.
13. Gold beaten into wire.
14. Gold beaten into plates.
15. Pellets, found in streams, near the bridge of Honstein, and out of which gold is extracted.

16. Pellets or shavings of gold from the same place. Solid gold strips or granules.
17. Veins rich in gold, found in the mountain of Carpathos.
18. Light pellets of gold from the same place.
19. Gold filings, collected, cleansed, and made into pellets.
20. Froth of gold.
21. Refuse of gold.

AURIGA ~ Fuse-Mallet.
AURIA MASSULA ~ Small mass of Gold. Queen.
AURICHALCUM ~ Brass, or Ore. Copper Ore, etc.
AURUM LATUS ~ is gold in a weak tincture or colouring, which dyes those substances with which it is combined.
AURUM OBRIZUM ~ is Gold Filings.
AURUM PHILOSOPHORUM ~ Gold of the Philosophers, i.e., Lead.
AURUM POTABILE ~ Potable Gold, devoid of corrosive quality, known to very few, and, among these, they who prepare it at the present day do so rather to the destruction than salvation of men.
AURUM VITAE ~ Gold of Life, is Precipitated Gold, or Mercury precipitated with Gold, and reverberated to a deep red. A precipitate made with gold, and brought by means of fire to an intense redness.
AURUM VIVUM ~ Living Gold is Quicksilver.
AUSTROMANTIA ~ is another superstition which some have devised from observation of the winds, in such fashion that when the stars which govern the winds cause more violence in them than is common, thence men, more idle than curious, draw an omen of the future.
AUVER ~ is Pure or Limpid Water.
AXICULUS ~ a small axle-tree, beam, pole, or roller.
AXICULUS FERREUS ~ Axle-pin.
AXUNGIA DE MUMIA ~ Fat of a dead body, sometimes written Mummy of Marrow, is the marrow of bones.

AYCOPHOS, or **ALECOFOC** ~ is Burnt Copper.
AZAA, or **MAGRA** ~ is Red Earth.
AZAGOR, or **AZRAGAR** ~ is Verdigris.
AZAMO, CALOR INDUS ~ Unknown.
AZANEC ~ Ammoniac.
AZARNET ~ Orpiment.
AZCI ~ Atrament.
AZEC ~ Green Atramant.
AZEFF ~ Broken Alum.
AZEDEGIM ~ Hematite.
AZEG, AZEZI, AZEGI ~ Names of Vitriol.
AZEGI AREC ~ Water of Atrament, Ink, Blacking Water.
AZEM ~ is melted butter.
AZEMASOR ~ is Red Lead, or Cinnabar.
AZENSALI ~ is a black stone found in gold ore. It is also moss which grows on the
rocks.
AZERNEC ~ is Burnt Copper, or Plates of Copper.
AZIUS ~ is a stone on which Salt is encrusted.
AZIMAR ~ is Flower of Copper, or Burnt Copper.
AZOCH ~ is our Mercury. It is a double Mercury of the Material Stone. Therefore they say: Azoch and fire are enough to whiten the Laton, and to prepare the whole work. In the first work it appears white. Then the woman overcomes the man, who thereupon becomes black. According to Braccesca, when Azoch turns into Salt, then it washes the Laton, or the metallic Sulphur. When it does not part with the red and become white, then it is useless. This Sulphur is called the Male. At first it is red, and when this red, or the sap which causes the redness, departs, then it is said that the Sulphur has departed.
AZOG ~ is Sweet Alum.
AZOTH ~ is Quicksilver, drawn out of any metallic body, and properly the corporeal Mercury, the Mercury of the

metallic body. With Paracelsus especially, it is the universal medicine, to which all things are alike, uncovering every species of substance, and imparting an immense strength, and catholic central virtue. It includes in itself all other medicines as well as the first principle of all other substances, their accidents excluded. Enclosed in the pommel of a sword, great exploits shall be performed by the wearer into whatever place he goes. For the rest, Quicksilver is extracted out of metal. But Theophrastus celebrates one Azoth for its eminent medicinal virtue. Some think it to be the philosophical stone. Azoth is drawn from bodies by means of Mercury, and is called a living spirit, a spirit endowed with a soul, our Water, Vinegar. Mary of Egypt says: When the Laton is whitened, it is called Azoth. Therefore men say Azoth whitens the Laton, then the Laton again whitens other things, and when again red, it reassumes the name of Laton. Gebir says Azoth is the Mercury which is drawn from substances through the Mercury of the Philosophers. Therefore it is, and it becomes, an elixir, i.e., a substance dissolved in Mercurial Water. It is called in Arabic Azoth, a dissolved silver; it is also the metallic earth in the mines, and is called Vitrefied or Vitre-coloured Azoth. It is white and shining, but red internally; also it is black and green to look at, and it has a colour like a poisonous earth. It is nearly related to the metals.

AZUBAR, or **BEDIGAR** — is the chemical vase.

AZUC — is Red Coral.

AZUMEN — is weight; also berry-covered, pearl-covered.

AZUR — See *Turba*, fol. 30.

AZURIC — is Red Vitriol.

AZUS — is the Arabic for Alum. Called also Azel.

AZYMAR, or **AZAMAR** — is Vermilion or Red Lead.

BACAR ~ Weight, ponderosity.
BACILLUM ~ A short stick.
BACILLUM FERREUM FOSSORUM TERES ~ Iron rod, with which a passage is forced.
BACILLA EX ACIE FACTA ~ A punch; otherwise, spike.
BACILLA FERREA SUCULA INCLUSA ~ A rod used in raising a winch, windlass, or capstan.
BACILLUM FERREUM ~ A nail, or push-pick.
BACILLA FERREA ~ Merchant-iron.
BACULUS FERREUS ~ is an iron instrument for the support of a super-imposed vessel.
BACILLA MAJORA FERREA UNCINATA ~ The same, but larger, and furnished with iron hooks.
BACILLUS TERES STRIATUS ~ A long hollow stick.
BAGEDIA ~ A pound of 12 ounces.
BAIAC ~ is Wax.
BALZIAM ~ is a kind of pulse.

BALASIUS — Burns and glows with a red colour, and is by some called Placidus. Some think it to be the Carbuncle diminished in colour and virtue, in the same proportion that the strength of the female differs from that of the male. Some have ascertained that the outer portion of one and the same stone belongs to the Balasius, the interior to the Carbuncle, and thus the Balasius is said to be the house of the Carbuncle. The potency of the Balasius consists in arresting and restraining impurity and evil thoughts, conciliating differences between friends, and conducing to the health of the human body. When preserved and drunk with water, it assists weakness of the eyes, is serviceable in diseases of the liver, and, what I conceive to be more wonderful, if the four angles of a house, garden, or vineyard, be touched with a Balasius, it will enjoy immunity from lightning, storms, and worms.
BALITISTERA — Red Earth.
BALNEUM MARIAE — Warm Water.
BALNEUM, ALUID MARIS, ALUID RORIS — A bath of sea water, or dew.
BALNEUM MARIS or MARIAE — is the dissolution of a substance in a suitable vessel of warm water, after which it is placed in the copper vessel belonging to it, and therein the operation is completed.
BALNEUM RORIS — is so called when a vessel does not touch the water, but is heated by the ascending vapour of hot water, and the matter in the vessel is dissolved thereby.
BALNEUM MARIAE, and **BALNEUM MARIS** — As it is called by many, is a distillatory furnace containing water, into which, when hot, a chemical vessel is placed for the putrefaction of the substance contained in it, for the separation of its component parts, and completing the process of that kind of humid evaporation.

BALNEUM RORIS or **RORITUM** — Bath of Dew or Dewy Bath is a furnace in which the distillatory vase is suspended only over the steam of water, in such a manner that the waters do not touch the body. We call this bath also by the name of Vapour Bath — Balneum vaporosum or vaporarium.
BALSAM — Pitch, the moisture which remains.
BALSAMUM — Balsam is a substance which preserves bodies from putrefaction. It is internal and external. In man the internal is a certain very moderating substance neither bitter nor sweet, neither acid nor mineral salt, but a fluidic salt which most effectually prevents putrefaction. It is also called a most tempered gluten of the nature of any body to which it belongs. Briefly, it is the liquor of an interior salt most carefully and naturally preserving its body from corruption. The external is Terebinth, which, according to Paracelsus, suffers nothing but digestion from the operation of fire.
In German, the term Baldzamen, i.e., quickly joined, is applied in chirurgery to anything which effects a speedy cure. It is also a distilled oil of the highest purity, and any principle which preserves a body, whether dead or alive, from putrefaction. (A preserver of all bodies from destruction and putrefaction. Of two kindsinternal and external. The internal is tempered or moderate, neither sour nor sweet ; a resolved salt or juice of the salt in man. Externally a balsam which prevents decay.)
BALSUM OF MUMMIES — is Balsam extracted from flesh.
BALSAMUS ELEMENTORUM EXTERNUS — External Balsam of the Elements is Liquor of External Mercury, i.e., Mummy of the Exterior Elements, one of the three Principles of all Things, the Firmamental Essence of Existences, the Quintessence.
BARACH PANIS — Saltpetre.
BARCATA — The Way of Fire.

BARDADIA ~ A Pound.
BARNABUS, BARNAAS ~ Wine of Saltpetre is a very acid vinegar.
BASILICUS MINOR ~ A kind of Lizard, Newt, or Eft.
BARURAC ~ Glass.
BASURA ~ Semen.
BASED, or **BESED** ~ is Coral.
BATITURA AERIS ~ Cubelatas. See Infra.
BATILLUM ~ A Shovel or Chafing-dish.
BATTITURA RAMI ~ is Copper Slag.
BATTITURA AERIS ~ is Metallic Slag; in Greek, Lepidos; in Arabic, Cubel, or Tubel, or Fuligo (smoke, soot); in German, Haneerschlag.
BAUL ~ is Urine.
BAURACH ~ is Conglomerate Salt.
BAURAC ~ A substance obtained from the scum of glass, or nitre ~ is Bores (untranslatable) ~ is Metallic Salt; also a blemish in gems ~ is bleached Litharge of Sapphires, white Litharge Composition ~ is a kind of Salt, Sal Abzedi; and Diabesis, i.e., covering of Quicksilver ~ is Vitreous Salt, Vitreous Refuse, Vitreous Spume, Vitreous Gall ~ is Attinckar, i.e., Rock Borax ~ is a certain species of Brine ~ Acurum is Baurac prepared by fire ~ is a Plaster with which fissures are covered. Also Goldsmith's Meal ~ is also Saltpetre, Armenian and Sulphureous.
BAYDA ~ is a vessel over which distillation takes place.
BELESON ~ is Balsam.
BERCOS ~ is Circular.
BERNA, or **BIRMINA** ~ is a Transparent Vessel.
BERILLISTICA ~ is the art of perceiving visions in the Berillus.
BERILLUS ~ is a Crystal Mirror superstitiously consecrated to auguries.

BERRIONIS, or **COLOPHONIA** — A dark-coloured Resin obtained from Turpentine. The Gum of the Juniper. Called also Bernix. Also a preparation of Linseed Oil.

BERYLLUS — This stone has much the same nature as the emerald; Beryls are indigenous to India and are rarely found elsewhere. They are all embellished with six angles, and their colour does not change, but is increased when the angles are struck. The varieties of Beryl are as follow:

1. The best and most esteemed are those which excel the green of the deep sea, or are otherwise of a middle colour between sea-green and cerulean.
2. Next to this species are the Chrysoberylli, a little paler, exhibiting an effulgence in a gold colour. They glitter more faintly, and are surrounded by a cloudy golden.
3. Chrysoprasus, more pallid than the last. They have a composite lustre of gold and leek-green. They are regarded as a species of Prasius on account of their gold-coloured spots, which seem, as it were, coagulated in the sap of a leek, as before stated.
4. Hyacinthizontes, which properly should be classified with the Hyacinthus, as their appearance demonstrates.
5. Heroides.
6. Cerini, i.e., wax-coloured Beryls.
7. Oleagini, i.e., of the colour of oil.
8. Similar to crystals. These have blemishes, cloudy spots, speckles, filaments, etc.

Beryls are found about the Pontus. The Indians who, more than any other nation, delight in Beryls, have falsified them by operating on crystals. For the rest, the Beryl is supposed to compel love, to cure complaints of the eye and liver, and to diminish the violence of vomiting ; exposed to the sun, it is said that it will kindle a fire. See Pliny, 1. 37, c. 5; Solinus (Polychist, c. 55) and Albertus (Lapid.)

BESACHAR — Fungus, Sponge.

BESONNA, BEZONNAR ~ Toadstool.
BEZAAR or **BESAR** ~ Green Stone, Diabase.
BIARCHETUNSIM, PYTHIUM ~ Names of White Lead.
BILADEN ~ is Calips, Calybs, or Steel.
BISEMATUM ~ is the lightest, palest, and poorest species of Lead.
BITRINATI ~ Coeruleum Montanum. Glazed.
BITUMEN ~ Jews' Pitch, Fossil Tar, Dry Coal.
BITUMEN ~ Called by the Greeks Asphalt, possibly on account of the asphalt lake in Judea, which is now called the Red Sea, where once stood Sodom and Gomorrah. Out of this lake a viscous asphalt is obtained which is useful to man when everything else near it is utterly barren. Bitumen is also said to exist in large quantities in Assyria and Chaldea, where it was used as mortar for walls. Indeed Semiramis is said to have built the walls of Babylon entirely with bitumen. Bitumen is said to be plentiful in Babylon because lightning is so frequent in that place. Bitumen is nothing but a lime of water, very slowly extracted, similar to pitch, and, as it were, an earthy pitch. On this account Dioscorides, in his first book, makes mention of Bitumen immediately after treating of pitch, and enumerates the species which are brought from Xtolia, Babylon, Zacynthos, and Sicily. He states that it is of good quality when it is of purple colour, or has a purplish brilliancy ; it is, on the contrary, bad and corrupt when it is black. For the rest, as to its nature, Bitumen is twofold, viscous, hard, earthy, and fluidic; in water also and in springs, as Curtius testifies, in which state some use it instead of oil, calling it erroneously Sicilian Oil. Pliny affirms that Bitumen is either Lime or an Earth; it is obtained in the form of lime from the Judean lake. In Babylon it is found both white and liquid, and this is Pissasphaltus (a mixture of pitch and resin), more liquid and nearer to the nature of pitch. A beautiful passage in the

ninth metamorphosis of Ovid refers to the Bitumen derived from the earth: "As the tenacious bitumen flows on the bountiful earth ". The best quality is that, however, which comes from Judea. It is undoubtedly a species of naphtha, but not naphtha proper, as some will have it. See Serapion in his chapter of Brafalendus.

Naphtha is Petroleum, and a liquid oil. But Bitumen is Asphalt-hard, tenacious; can be often reduced to powder, but is not soluble, and has the offensive smell of naphtha. I am surprised that it should at times be found in water, and is thus occasionally a substance in an element which is hostile to fire, and again in an element which is friendly to fire; it burns more fiercely when cast into running waters. Nicander, in his Antidotes against Poison, affirms that Bitumen drives away venomous animals. When drunk with wine, it certainly cures epilepsy. Its vehement and sharp spirit expels the quartan ague. It is not incredible, therefore, that it drives away venomous animals. It was used formerly in colouring statues and hardening iron. See the Arabian writers on this subject, also Dioscorides, Pliny, Solinus, Strabo, and others. A word may be added concerning Pissasphalt. It is lighter than bitumen, and has its name from picth and bitumen ; perhaps it exhales a mixed odour of both. It is of two kinds ~ that which is produced naturally, and that which is manufactured by art from pitch and bitumen. The one is described by Dioscorides (1. 1, c. 18), the other by Pliny (1. 24 c. 7), (when bitumen and pitch are melted together). That passage in the Third Georgics about the pitch of Ida and black bitumen must be understood as referring to a cure for scab in sheep, unless we are to understand the sordid and evil black Bitumen, or liquid Sicilian Bitumen. For the rest, natural Pissasphalton is obtained from the neighbourhood of Epidaurus. Other varieties of Bitumen are considered below.

BITUMEN PERVERSUM — is a liquid of uncertain nature, a kind of lime, or juice.
BITUMEN SULPHUREA TERRA — is a fatty sap or exudition; Brimstone, Copper Ore containing Quartz, etc. There are many species of Bitumen: Liquid, like oil in appearance, and petroleum. There is the odorous liquid Bitumen of Saxony, cleansing, and with a smell of natural camphor. There is the gross, black Bitumen, which takes its name from the Lake of Sodom; with this the Moors embalm dead bodies. There is the black, gross Palestine Bitumen, which is dug up like coal from the earth.
BLANCA MULIERUM, and **BLACTARA MULIERUM** — are names of White Lead.
BLICARE — is prepared Presil (unknown).
BLINCTA — Red Earth.
BODAGI — is a kind of vessel.
BODID, OVUM — Egg.
BOF — Living Calx.
BOLESIS — Coral:
BOLUS — Slime, clay, devoid of any mineral substance.
BOLUS — is, in metallurgy, ore decayed by the weather; in mineralogy, a substance formed in small crystals on the surface of a stone.
BOLUS — is a specific coagulate, which is essential and chemical, a certain essence freed from impurities and foreign matters by coagulation, which is necessarily preceded by solution; it is a separation and solidification such as that which is seen in boli, to give them a fixity and homogeneous shape like the Bolaris, but it makes little difference to the essence. [N.B. — This passage almost defies translation.]
1. The white Julian Bolus, made of the yoke of eggs, approaching red in colour. The Armenian variety is not dissimilar.
2. The true Pannonian Bolus.

3. The Yolk of Theophrastus.
4. The Bohemian Bolus, white or red, invented by Paracelsus.
5. Bolus of Anneberg; mountain Bolus.
6. The true Armenian Bolus, prized by the Turkish Sultan, and used by the Turks against fever, plague, and quinsy.
The Armenian Bolus, Cartwrights' Earth.
The Armenian Bolus, found in abundance at Villacum and Halberstadt; it is hard and like Pumice Stone in colour when first removed from the earth. Some term it Hematite, Bloodstone, Red Earth, or Chalk.

BOLUS INDIACUS ~ is Al (unknown).

BONATI ~ That is pellucid.

BORADES ~ Fit for polishing.

BORAX ~ is Chrysocolla (Borax), or Ranunculus.

BORAX ~ is a gum with which gold and silver are combined. And it is called natural Attinckar.

BORACO ~ is also called a band of gold.

BORERS, or **CARBAS** ~ East by North.

BORITIS ~ is the White Stone after the Black Slate. It reduces earth to water.

BOTAMUM ~ is votive lead.

BOTUS, BOTIA, BOTUS BARBATUS, or **BARBOTUS** ~ is a vessel called Cucurbite, which see.

BOTUS BARBATUS ~ is a vessel imposed on another vessel into which gold is melted.

BONUS BARBOTUS ~ Vessel for melting ~ Vessel into which liquids are poured from above ~ Vessel for mixing ~ joined for the operation of fusion.

BOTIN, or **BUTIMO** ~ is Turpentine. Item. Balsam of Turpentine is the essence
concentrated therefrom, according to the law of balsamic influence, a state when it is thought to have drawn more virtues from the heavens.

BOTHOR ~ is a pimply, postulous, tuberculous eruption on the skin, generally white; abscesses. Called also Box, Cezesmata, Pyrhedones.

BOTIUM ~ An abscess without excrescence in the gullet, like a wen. Boxus-Misletoe.

BRACTIA ~ A thin plate or scale of metal.

BRACTEAE LAMINAE ~ Larger plates of metal; an instrument like the sole of a shoe.

BRACTEAE FERREAE ~ Plates of iron.

BRACTEAE SIMUL JUNCTAE ~ Plates locked together.

BRACIUM ~ Copper.

BRARICIA ~ Glass.

BRASATELLA, BRASADELLA, OPHIOGLOSSUM, LINGUAR SERPENTINA, LANCEOLA, LINGULACA, and **LANCER CHRISTI** ~ terms for the most part signifying sharp pointed instruments like lances ~ are found frequently near Strasburg, and are natural objects.

BRASE ~ Coals, charcoal.

BRELISIS ~ That is, Katanos (unexplained).

BRUMATI TERREUM ~ A transparent vessel.

BRUNUS, BRIMIS ~ St. Anthony's Fire, Erysipelas. Called also Erythopelas and
Pyragion.

BRUTA ~ is a certain virtue of the celestial influence which is manifested to reasonable beings through the brute creation, as in the Chelidonia by the swallow, and in Salt by the stork. (The celandine is said to be used by swallows to restore sight to their young). N.B.~ There is also a stone called Chelidonius, which was said to be found in the maws of young swallows.

BUCCELLARE ~ To feed, or fatten.

BUCCELLARE ~ To cut in small pieces.

BULBUS BULBI ~ Probably the Sea-Onion or Sea-Leek. Officinal Squill.

BUCCATUM ~ Transparent.

BUGA ~ Leathern bottle in which running water is poured through a pipe.

BULGARE SE HAURIENS AQUAS ~ A leathern bottle for drawing up water.

BULGARUM GUBERNATOR ~ Overseer of the workshops.

BURINA ~ Pitch.

BURAC ~ Any species of Salt, called also by other names, such as Baurac Barago, Borax, Uritar, Angar.

BUSTA ~ Oiled with poison.

BUTIGA ~ Red spots or swellings, is an eruption of the whole face.

BUTYRUM SATURNI ~ Cheese of Saturn, i.e., Altheus of Lead.

CABABUS ~ i.e., a vase holding three Chores (? cubic feet). Also a lid or cover of a pan.

CABALA, CABALIA ~ Cabalistic Art is a most secret science which is affirmed to have been made known in a divine manner to Moses at the same time as the written law; it reveals to us the doctrine of the Messiah of God; it constitutes a bond of friendship between angels and the men who have been instructed in it; and it gives knowledge of all natural things. It also illuminates the mind with a divine light, and drives all darkness therefrom. The name is of Hebrew origin; in Latin it is called a Reception. It is that more secret and true exposition, forbidden to be set down in writing, which Moses divinely received upon the Mount, together with that other law which was afterwards given in writing to the people of Israel. It was handed down from generation to generation under the seal of an oath lest the divine mysteries made known to the profane multitude might be degraded or misused. This science was diligently studied by the Persians, as appears by the name which was given to their wise men. For they called their priests and those men among them who were intrepid explorers of secret things by the name of Magi. Such were those three wise men who came from the East to Bethlehem that they might adore Christ. They were not kings, as it is imagined by the vulgar and ignorant. Much upon these matters has been written by our own Reuchlin, by the Italian Mirandula, and by Petrus Galatinus. Indeed, Galatinus asserts that by means of this Cabala the ancient Rabbins came to the knowledge of the Trinity, and of Christ the Son of God.

Therefore this art is not folly in the opinion of many persons, but a certain and heavenly science, through which Theophrastus, as he himself tells us, developed his own doctrine by God's mercy; nor has it anything in connection with evil spirits, though this has been calumniously ascribed to it by its envious enemies. At the same time, I grant that in the hands of a number of persons it has, like other arts, fallen into abuse. For Theophrastus says that the Jews have done nothing but degenerate, and as in the doctrine of God, so in this science. Whence the Cabala has come to be divided into a true science and a false art. In addition, there is the literal Cabala which must be numbered among deceptive subtleties, more especially when it does not proceed from a Hebrew source. The true Cabala has its foundation in the Holy Scriptures.

CABALA — is a secret art bestowed by God upon Moses, which he afterwards, not by means of writing, but orally, handed down to his posterity; and these by knowledge of the Divine Essence can know the properties of all creatures in a wonderful manner, and use it to their own profit and that of others.

CABALATER — is Nitric Salt.

CABEBI — i.e., Iron Filing.

CABEL — is Dung.

CABILLI, CABALES, or **LEMURES** — are the astral bodies of men, who die immaturely, and before they have accomplished their natural course of life. They are supposed to wander over the earth until they have reached the proper term of their existence, so that what they should have lived out corporeally, they now live out spiritually, if it be right in God's sight to believe so, and indeed it can be ascertained from the Holy Scriptures that such a view is not opposed to true Christian religion; now in those Scriptures is to be sought the touch-stone by which we are enabled to discern and condemn everything which is not of the true gold of the Gospel.

CACEDONIUM TARTARUM — Actually a species of Tartar, but used to signify an offending matter in the human body, which may apparently be either stone or sand in the bladder, or an alburninous concretion.

CACIA FERREA — is an iron screw.

CACHIMIA — is a white argentiferous Chalk.

CACHIMIEN — are, as it were, the refuse of flesh, of feeble power, the enemy and robber of metals ; nothing can be made of them. Like Marcasite, Red Sun and White Moon-Red Pyrites and White Cobalt-Tutty is the dross of copper Bell-Metal. Perfect and imperfect Arsenical Sulphur in the body of the Mercurial Talc; red, white, and yellow in the body of the Salt. Accordingly, Theophrastus on Minerals writes that Bismuth, Marcasite, etc., are spirits produced by mixture of Venus and Mercury. Bismuth has an earthly Sulphur of Mercurial nature. Marcasites are found in all grades, and are,as it were, a superfluity of metal. The material is too abundant, and cannot become metal when the Archaeus differentiates. Accordingly, the Cachimien are imperfect metals, sports, monstrosities. There is more Venus and Mercury in the Cachimiera; it is more salt, and is a more fixed and excellent digest than Marcasite.

CADARIA — is Tutty.

CADMIA — is of two kinds, native and manufactured. Native Cadmia is also of two kinds: one which is found in mountains and rivers, and sometimes in torrents. I saw Cadmia sometime since which was obtained from the torrents of Westphalia, of which possibly Galenus has written. Others maintain that it is the gem Iris, but I neither wish nor would venture to affirm anything hastily in this matter. The other native Cadmia is found in metallic mines, fossile and petrine, as may be seen at the mine called Verona. It is this stone which the Germans call Kobalt, from the name of the demon who formerly haunted houses, as we see in Saxony (? Kobolds, a house-dwelling spirit of German folk lore). Pliny calls it Copper-Stone. And this stone or native Cadmia, fossile Cobalt, does not much differ from Pyrites or Marcasite, and is indeed very similar. The liquids out of which Pyrites and Silver are obtained are found compactly joined together in one body, and it is the same with native Cadmia. There are some who consider it identical with Pyrites because where there is one usually there is the other also, or because of this similarity in deposition. There are also persons who distinguish them, because Cadmia is so powerfully corrosive that it eats away the feet and hands of the miners, while Pyrites has little corrosive power. Hence Pliny well remarks (l. 34, c. 10), that the stone Cobalt, from which Copper is obtained is of itself useless as medicine, but that it can be rendered useful by combination with Cadmia. As regards colour, Cobalt, or native fossile Cadmia, is found in three ways in the mines: 1. Black Cobalt, which seems to have been first known to the Germans, for so we call those black imps who are seen in houses, and especially in kitchens, and after these perhaps, on account of its colour, we have named this metal. If this etymology be rejected, I would say that it derives the identity of name from some fabulous coincidence.

2. Ashen-grey Cobalt. These two species are the most common.

3. Iron-grey. This is not so common. I met with it formerly in those ancient mines of Thuringia which are situated at the extreme north. Whatsoever substances may be obtained from this, it abounds much more in silver than does Pyrites. Dioscorides was unacquainted with this species, as appears from these words in his 1. 20, c. 40. There are not wanting persons who believe that Cadmia is found in stone quarries, but it is through a false knowledge of stones. He describes how Cadmia is extracted from a mountain in Cyprus, which is covered to its base with the burnt stone called Pyrites ; and after how it differs from the known stones which are falsely called Cadmia, namely, in weight, scent, and taste; in concreteness, in manner of combination, in mode of burning, and in colour. But this native fossil Cadmia, from the burnt Pyrites in Cyprus, is now unknown, so far as I can say, while, on the other hand, our own fossil Cadmias were unknown to him.

The stones which are known to us by the erroneous name of Cadmia, i.e., which we know of, but are falsely so called, are found in many places in our mines. They are sterile, and hence have no corrosive quality. Simple men, Ignorant in the matter, have taken them for true Cadmia, and have grievously erred. For the rest, it should be noted that there is another stone which must be distinguished from true Cadmia; it is by some called Cadmia earth, and the stone Calamine. In certain places, by reason of its weakness; in others, on account of weight, it is possible to take it for true Cadmia. True native Cadmia is at the present day generally unknown in our laboratories, as, indeed, is all manufactured

Cadmia, except Botryites, which the Arabs call Tutty, and that Alexandine Cadmia called hard or solid Tutty. True Botryites Cadmia (that is, clustering like grapes), is, however, different from Tutty, as the Arabs affirm with Serapion. For Tutty is Orpine (or Spodion), but it may be, I grant, used as a substitute for Tutty, if prepared, as Serapion witnesses. Spodion, and not Tutty, is mentioned by Dioscorides, lest he should record the same thing twice. In fine, that which the Arabs call Tutty, the Greeks call Pompholyx, and we Spodion. It is an error, not in qualities, but matters. For they differ with the locality in which they are made. When made in the mouths of the furnaces it is called Capnitis (a kind of jasper or chrysolite); when made on the top it is called Pompholyx. Pliny 1. 34, c. 1), says that copper is made from the cuprine stone called Cadmia, celebrated formerly in Asia and Campania. But he also says that it was found in his time in the country of Bergamus and in the German province. Here I judge that Pliny is simply speaking of our Cadmia, and galls it a cuprine stone. Hence it appears that in the time of Pliny, Cadmia was found in our country. Possibly it was at a still more distant period that the Germans began to work their mines. Their iron and brass mines are most ancient. It was afterwards, under Otho the Great, that the mines of black lead were opened up, and after a long interval those of silver. Cornelius Tacitus emphatically states that the Germans of old possessed neither gold nor silver, much less mines of those metals. And now it has come to pass that our alma mater has far surpassed other places in the abundance of all species of metals.
Praise to the good and great God for ever!
Manufactured Cadmia.
Manufactured Cadmia is the substance and finest ash of pyrites, or of another metallic ore very similar to pyrites, translated to or ejected upon the sides or topmost roofs of

the furnaces, as Dioscorides testifies (1. 5, c. 40) when he says that Cadmia is derived from copper burning in furnaces, ejected in casting together with soot, and collected on the sides and tops. Others define manufactured Cadmia after this manner: Manufactured Cadmia is a substance which is obtained when coherent corpuscules are rejected from copper by expulsion through the summits of the furnaces, and collect together in globular masses, one of which will sometimes contain either one, two, or a number of species. This is a true definition, and they who make it give Cadmia the name of Acestida. At the same time we would say that Cadmia is either ash of Copper or of some other metal. The best is obtained from copper. That which comes from other metals, and even from gold, is of no moment. It is also made from silver, and this quality is whiter and less heavy than the others, and it is not at all like the cuprine species. By copper we would in this place understand pyrites, of which the best quality produces Cadmia in coction.

The Cadmia of Goslaria is the finest, containing not only silver or lead, but all other metals. When the pyrites is pure it produces Placodis and Botryitis; when mixed with other substances, then Cadmia alone is obtained. Dioscorides praises the Cuprine and Botryitis. There are many species of manufactured Cadmia, some of which are treated of by Dioscorides and some by other writers; they differ with the places in which they are made, and they differ also in shape, as Dioscorides teaches, and his interpreter Pliny. As these species can be understood by a child, we subjoin them in order.

Species of Manufactured Cadmia.

1. Botryitis, like a cluster of grapes, dense in appearance, but not very heavy, and liable to decrease in weight, orpine in colour, ashen, and cuprine. This and onychitis, subsequently

described, are useful in medicaments for the eyes. There is also another botryitis, which was possibly unknown to Dioscorides, and is made either in round coals or spear-shaped; for when the little flames play round the furnace, then botryitis is deposited, and afterwards collected. This kind is called Alexandrian Cadmia, because in that place many seek to make it; it is also called solid Tutty, and it is very like the barks of certain trees. It is produced by sublimation in the manufacture of brass, and is of two kinds — Alexandrine and Arabian Tutty.

2. Onichitis, similar to the stone onyx, blue on the outside, white and veined within, like that which, according to Dioscorides, was mined out of old metallic ore. In which place, do not understand that the mines were old themselves, but that the metals had been long deposited by nature. The reference is to the vast ancient stags, now again being melted; it is found in these.

3. Placodis, i.e., covered with a crust or shell. Among this species is the variety called tinctured or zoned, which is adorned with many rings.

4. Ostracitis, thin, black, crusted with burnt earth.

5. Capnitis, i.e., of the furnace, or volatile; it is very like Spodion (orpine matter) or Pompholyx (arsenic). It is found in the mouths of furnaces, and there is little difference in its varieties ; they are materially the same. Capnitis, Cadmia, and Arsenic possess the same qualities, but they can be distinguished by the places where they are made. The species under notice is good for plasters, and all are hot and astringent, in the same way that pyrites is styptic, as Serapion affirms. It is their nature to heal open sores, to cleanse the unclean, to remove fleshy excrescences, to dry up superfluous humours of the body, to help in the formation of skin, etc. As these species of Cadmia are exceedingly hot and dry, they are operated on with fire and washed in special

ways set forth by Dioscorides, so that they may be useful in plasters and other medicaments. Would that our own physicians, more especially surgeons, did not ignore the virtues of Cadmia, but brought it once again into use! Concerning these manufactured Cadmias consult Pliny (1. 34, c. 10), where he says: Cadmia is begotten in furnaces, whence its name of Furnace Cadmia; it is carried up with the flames, and by a gentle breath or wind, being a substance disengaged from the matter in the furnace; it adheres to the top or sides, according to its lightness.

1. The lightest is deposited at the mouth of the furnace, and in its exceeding lightness is similar to ashes. It is called Capnitis.

2. Botryites, which is of better quality, is of two colours — ashen, the inferior of the two, and that approaching purple, which is the superior kind. This is found in the interior of the furnace-roof.

3. That which is deposited on the sides of the furnace and cannot ascend to the top on account of its heaviness; this is crusty Placitis, of which there are also two species-Onychitis, outwardly almost blue, and within spotted like the onyx — Ostracitis, which is wholly black, the most powerful of Cadmias, and useful for wounds. All Cadmia produced in the furnaces where Copper is smelted is the best kind. So far Pliny.

For the rest, how Cadmia is cleansed, and how treated with fire, may be learnt from the same place in Pliny. See also Galenus, Avicenna, and others. Certain writers who were utterly ignorant upon these subjects, confound all the varieties together in a chaotic heap, and in a way which I am ashamed to behold or read. This has come to pass through the neglect of the thing itself, and through barren disputes over words. The excellent Simon de Janua says that the name Cadmia may be applied to three substances:

1. To the fumes which arise from certain metals, such as gold, silver, and copper. And this is the true manufactured Cadmia of which we have been here treating.
2. To the stone Calamine, vulgarly called Marcasite. And here this most excellent writer is ignorant that Calamine is one thing, while Marcasite is another, and is that Pyrites from which copper is obtained — a species of native Cadmia which we call Cobalt. From this Pyrites also the best manufactured Cadmia is made.
3. That which is found in mines of metals, and especially in copper mines. And this is the native Cadmia of which we have treated. It will be seen how confused this classification is, and how the same thing is said twice over.

To sum up: our native fossil Cadmia is our Cobalt, with its several species. But the best manufactured Cadmia is made in furnaces from pyrites, that is marcasite; in other words, it is simply made from copper, as Dioscorides teaches. But its name varies with the place where it is manufactured, and with its form and its colour.

Cadmia is duplex:
1. Native: In mountains and rivers. Described by Galenus. Said to be the German Iris. Fossile, from mines. Otherwise, Cobalt. If this there are three kinds: 1. Black, 2. Grey-ashen, 3. Iron colour.
2. Manufactured: 1. Acestis; 2. Like ashes and exceedingly light. Derived from: 1. Copper, 2. Silver, 3. Other metals, such as gold. Of these there are also various species which differwith the locality where they are made, and are also distinguished by their appearance: 1. Btyrites, i.e., clustered like graes; now falsely called Tutty. This is also duplex — one of an orpine colour, the other (manufactured) like ashes. Alexandrine, which occurs by chance I coals, and is made by art in iron tubes; 2. Oninchitis; 3. Ostracitis; 4. Placodis and

Planitis; 5. Capnitis, which is made in the mouth of the furnace. Also Pompholyx, i.e., Arsenic.

Furnace Cadmia.

1. Furnace Cadmia, obtained from the shaft of the furnace, differs from native Cadmia, in the ways hereinafter to be shown.
2. White Cadmia is a poisonous matter which sticks to the walls of the furnace, being given off by metals when they are burnt or melted.
3. Yellow Cadmia.
4. Red Cadmia.
5. Grey Cadmia.
6. Finest Cadmia, made in copper furnaces from pyrites, or metallic Cadmia.
7. That which sticks to the walls of the furnace where copper ore is smelted.
8. That which sticks to the walls of the furnace where silver is smelted.
9. That which sticks to the walls of a furnace where gold ore is smelted.
10. That which is obtained from furnaces of White Lead.
11. Impure furnace Cadmia, or slag.
12. Containing silver.
13. Containing gold.
14. Cadmia of Copper, of which various species are found in our metals, to which also Dioscorides and other Greeks gave names borrowed from their shape.
15. Crusted Cadmia.
16. Zoned Cadmia, having bands or lines encircling it.
17. Onychitis, of various colours, similar to the veins of the onyx.
18. Ostracitis or Testacea, which scarcely sticks to the furnace wall.

19. Botryitis, in clusters like grapes, of a grey colour, hanging from the sides of the furnace, as grapes from a vine.
20. Black Botrytis, having thin copper-colored plates.
21. Stalactical Cadmia, or Cadmia concreted like icicles.
22. Alexandrine Cadmia, now used in our workshops
23. Cadmia which sticks to the roof of the furnace.
24. Sublimed Cadmia.
25. Atramental Cadmia.

Cadmia of Metals, or Mined Cadmia.
1. Metallic Cadmia is abundantly mined in the veins of Bohemia and Misnia. It is called by our metallurgists Cobalt, which name is also given to the imps of the mines, for what reason is beyond the scope of our inquiry.
2. Mined Cadmia, which the metallurgist digs up in Lower Germany, in Westphalia. By us it is called the Stone Calamine.
3. Mined Calamine, or Cadmia of red colour, which has not been subjected to fire.
4. Well-burnt Cadmia, melted fourteen times, and then used for tinging other metals.
5. Purest soft Cadmia or Calamine.
6. A naturally grey Cobalt.
7. Crusty Cadmia, shaped like a head.
8. A Sulphureous Cobalt which burns very readily.
9. Cadmia on which there is a rude, red transparent silver.
10. Black Cobalt, in the block.
11. Very hard grey Cadmia.
12. Crusty, iron-coloured Cadmia.
13. Heavy, brittle, grey Cadmia.
14. Hard, grey Cadmia.
15. Light, grey Cadmia.
16. Light Cadmia, similar to pure, native grey lead, easily broken into small pieces with a hammer. A brittle Cobalt, like a solid bismuth.

17. Hard Bismuth, like polished iron.
18. Combined with grey lead.
19. Mined Cadmia, found in grape-like clusters in the mountains and torrents of Westphalia.
20. Sulphureous.
21. Bituminous.
22. Containing gold.
23. Shaped like a bare head.
24. Concave, full of very fine dust
25. Fluidic Cobalt, from which a poisonous sap exudes continually.
26. Fluidic Cobalt, from which an acrid yellow sap continually exudes.
CADMIA ~ White Liquor.
CADMIA ACINOSA ~ i.e., Tutty.
CADMIA CYPRIA ~ Cuprine Calamine.
CAL ~ Green Arsenic. *Item,* Vinegar.
CALAMINA ~ i.e., the Stone Calamine.
CALAMUS, CANNA, CANNUTUM ~ A Reed.
CALCADINUM ~ Vitriol.
CALCADIS, AL, SAL ALKALI ~ Names of White Vitriol.
CALCANTHOS, or **CALCANTHUM** ~ Signifies: 1. Flower of Copper. 2. Calcitis, a kin of Vitriol. 3. Vitriol. 4. Burnt Copper. 5. Green Vitriol, generated and nourished in powder of Atrament. It melts in salt, and congeals in cold. If red, water prevails; if green, copper preponderates.
The Species of Chalcanthum are:
1. Chalcitis, i.e., Colcothar, Zeg, or Green Zeg.
2. Misy: Native, having affinity with gold. Manufactured, when Chalcanthum is changed into Chalcitis.
3. Melanteria, Shoemakers' Wax: 1. Mined, 2. Maltria or Melatria found in the tunnels of mines, 3. Bitria, found at the mouth of mines. The Arabs say that these are species of Colcothar, i.e., Chalcitis.

4. Sory: 1. Egyptian, 2. Lybian, 3. Spanish, 4. Cyprian.
5. Diphyrigis of two kinds: Native, of which we have two species. Manufactured: Dross of Copper. Burnt Pyrites.
CALCANTUM or **CALCADIS** — A kind of Atrament.
CALCATON — i.e., a Trochish of Arsenic.
CALCITHEOS — Copperust. Item, Marcasite.
CALCATA — i.e., Citrine Atrament.
CALCATAR, COLCOTAR — Ruby Atrament.
CALCITEOSA or **CALCITHEOS** — i.e., Litharge.
CALCITHOS — i.e., Green Copper.
CALCEUS SIPHONUM — Pump-handle.
CALCIDUM — An Arsenical Medicament.
CALCINATIO — When the matter is like snow-white calx, full of fire and thirst. And this is the Dragon, who drinks up the water therein. He dies and bursts. This is the division between body and soul, pale or white and dead. Then comes the resurrection and the life, through the Red.
Calcination of Bodies is Combustion, which takes place in a strong heat; or it is the solution of coagulated matters into Calx. It is of two kinds: that of Corrosion and of Ignition. Calcination by dry corrosion is when dry corroding substances are added, instead of moisture, to the calcining matters, and are calcined thereby. It is cementing and commingling.
Calcination by vaporous corrosion is when the metallic bodies, reduced into thin plates, are calcined by an acrid and corroding smoke. But the methods of this vaporous calcination are several. Sometimes the laminated bodies are suspended over aqua fonts, sometimes over the recrement of the wine-press. Sometimes, especially with the nobler metals, the fragile parts are reduced and brought to powder by the vapour of melted lead or quicksilver; sometimes other modes are used which it would be too long to recount. Note: To reduce Chalybs into a subtle condition by a vaporous

corrosion, I proceed thus. In the first place, I prepare a small quantity of aqua fonts out of rock salt and vitriol calcined to whiteness in equal parts, and melt it in a glass cucurbite. Then in the upper part of the vessel I suspend plates of steel, and I close up the mouth of the cucurbite with clay, lest the spirits of the aqua fonts should endeavour to escape at any point, and for twenty-four hours I permit it to steam in hot sand. Next, having opened the vessel, I take out the plates, to which a yellow and very fine powder will be adhering, which I purge with hare's foot. Subsequently, I replace the plates, and repeat the operation continually until no more yellow powder can be made to rise up from the spirits, or to deposit on the steel. So also lead is calcined into white lead or ceruse over vinegar; so again copper over the refuse of grapes; and thus, in like manner, are the other metals corroded by vapours.

Calcination, by moist immersion is, when the body is plunged into some liquid which corrodes, then Calcines, and finally perfects by amalgamation or precipitation. Reverberatory Calcination is solution into Calx. Calx, in its general signification, is any powder ground till it is impalpable, which we are accustomed to call Alcool. Thus, the term includes Calx, properly so called, Alcool, which is obtained by pulverisation, ash, and powder obtained by corrosion.

Reverberatory Calcination is of two kinds:
Calcination, specially so called, and reduction to ashes. Special Calcination is that by which is produced true Calx in a reverberatory combustion. In this truly philosophical process, there is accomplished, after a most searching manner, an object of much importance towards the completion of our work. Herein a substance is calcined by itself alone, or with other substances added thereto, which materially help combustion, such as Sulphur, Nitre, etc. We

make this addition in those cases where the solidity of the matter is great and indestructible. Nevertheless, things volatile are dissipated quicker than fixed things are conquered by flame. An airhole, or vent, is required for nitrous compounds, to insure the safety of the vessel.
Every so called greater Calcination is that which is made sweet by spagyric art and not by nature, and is serviceable to a speedy, marvellous healing, as the Sweet Vitriol of Mercury, Salt, and the like, which are very rapid in consolidating.
Every lesser Calcination is that which is by nature sweet, and has the virtue of quickly healing, such as Manna, Honey, Sugar, Nostoch, and the like.
CALCITARI — i.e., Alkaline Salt, Alkael.
CALCITIS, CALTICIS, CALCOTA — Names of Red Atrament.
CALCOCOS — i.e., Copper.
CALCUKEUMENOS — Burnt Copper; Scales which fly off from Copper when hammered.
CALDAR — Tin.
CALECAMENON, CALCUCEMENTUM CASTICUM — i.e., Burnt Copper; called also Calcutium, Costicium, Calcute, Endebastum.
CALENDULE — Saffron Yellow.
CALERUTH — is an endeavour to revert towards the first everlasting substance, as
when any matter seeks to return into its first matter, whence it originated,
CALI — Wood Ashes. Item, Jamen Alum
CALLENA — A species of Rock Salt.
CALLIETTE — are certain Yellow Fungi, found on the juniper.
CALMET, COSMEC, COSMET, CASMET — Names of Antimony.

CALOR ARTIFICIALIS — is that heat which can be administered, applied, and directed at the will of the artist. It is either simple or compound.

CALOR CINERUM — is when the more fixed parts of a matter are extracted by ashes. This is intermediate between the heat of the bath and of sand; by the help of this, not only are there extracted the more subtle substances approaching to the nature of water, but also colours and fixed parts.

CALOR DIGERENS — is when the matter to be dissolved is digested, which takes place i the athanor, or in dung.

CALOR FIMI — is when the vase is placed in dung, and the material therein is digested. This form of heat is much in use among artists in the operations of melting, digesting, and the putrefaction of substances. Sometimes horse-dung is substituted, the vessel being buried therein. Formerly, a wooden vessel was filled with hay or straw instead of dung.

CALOR FORTIS — is when the matters are separated by a fire very much increased intensified. It is either bound or free. In the first case, the matter or the vessel, is separated from the fire by another vessel. It is either a heat of sand or of iron-filings.

Sand-heat is intermediate between ashes and iron-filings. The vessel which contains the matter in a sand melting-box surrounded with sand, ejects a substance more fixed than the ashes can. Here it is to be noticed that fine sand does not furnish a more powerful heat than coarse.

The heat of iron-filings is of a higher intensity than that of sand; it approximates to the glow of an open fire, and expels the matter, or educes it.

CALOR LIBER — is that which is immediately contiguous to the matter or vessel. By this beat, those things which contain a persistent moisture are best treated, whether it be on account of an inherent aridity or paucity of the moisture in question, or because of its homogeneous and viscous character. I omit its use calcination, fusion, and other operations. It is either a heat of charcoal or of same.

Heat of coal or charcoal is when the matter, or vessel, is in contact with metals. It is useful in melting, joining, testing, calcining, and disintegrating.

Heat of flame is when the flames are caused to leap up and have contact with the matter or vessel, on the addition of fuel to the fire. This heat is called Living Flame, and hereby the operations of reverberation and calcination are performed upon all kinds of metals. By this also the spirit of a substance is educed.

CALOR NATURALIS — is that operation by which the solar rays cook the matter either of themselves, or collected in the focus of a concave glass. Artificers make use of this fire. We can dissolve and calcine thereby. Some state that it is to be used in the preparation of the philosopher's stone; while I leave this 'opinion to those who maintain it, I do not, on the other hand, think that it should be neglected altogether.

CALOR SIMPLEX — is that which serves for one operation, either of digestion or separation.

CALOR VESICA LEVIS — The heat of a thin bladder-is when the matter is placed in a bladder, then in the alembic, and the moist part is thus educed.

CALUFAX — i.e., Indian Oil.

CALUFA CYPTAS or **SPEDRES** — i.e., crystal.

CALX — in its chemical meaning is any powder reduced by the separation of superfluous moisture into the most fine and impalpable state.

CALX ASSATA — Roasted Calx, Alum of Fruits.

CALX EXSTINCTA — Extinguished Calx.

CALX FIXA — is a permanent and inconsumable matter.

CALX LIGNORUM ~ The Ashes of Wood, which are not converted into a vitreous nature and remain ashes.
CALX JOVIS ~ Calcined Tin, wherein is the spirit of tin.
CALX LUNE ~ Silver, Calcined Silver, or Blue Flower of Silver.
CALX MAJOR ~ Calx of Eggs.
CALX MANILA ALGA ~ is white Tartar, Calx Peregrinorum, or the Calx obtained from the bleached bones of certain fish or sea shells, especially mussels.
CALX MARTIS ~ The Yellowness, or Rust, of Steel or Iron. .
CALX MERCURII ~ Precipitated Mercury.
CALX NON EXSTINCTA ~ Living Calx, is Asbestos, and it is made in several ways. In some places it is made from certain stones or pebbles of the seashore, which are of the colour of cats' eyes, and otherwise grey or white, the stones being either dug up in fields by the shore, or simply collected. There are also regular asbestos mines, as at Sala, and in other places. It is also made from the shells of oysters, of the sea murex, and from egg-shells, as Dioscorides informs us (1. 5, c. 80), and Pliny (1. 36, c. 24, 29), etc, Living Calx is of two kinds: white and blue. It is of a hardening, igneous, biting, and encrusting nature. In a word, it removes and extracts. It has a natural antipathy for water, by which it is burnt; it has affinity for oil, with which it blends easily. Consult also Serapion.
CALX PEREGRINORUM ~ Tartar.
CALX PEREGRINORUM ~ Calx of Mussel Shells, or the Bones of Fish.
CALX SATURNI ~ Red Lead.
CALX SOLIS ~ Calcined Gold.
CALX VENERIS ~ Verdigris.
CAMET or **LAMES** ~ i.e., Silver.
CAMINUS ~ Furnace, Forge, etc.

CAMBILL — Red Earth.
CAMBUCA — i.e., Bubo, Abscess, etc.
CANALES CUNICULI — A Water-filter.
CANALES OCCLUDERE — to close the channels.
CANALES RECLUDERE — to open the channels.
CANALICULI — Apertures.
CANALICULUS — A kind of sieve.
CANALIS — A Channel for conducting water, Aqueduct; also Windmill.
CANALIS AQUARII — Water-pipes.
CANALIS, CAPSA BREVIS PATENS — Ashpan, or Sieve.
CANALIS CAPUT — Ash-pan or Sieve.
CANALIS ET CANALIS DEVEXUS — A forked or branched Channel.
CANALIS LONGUS — A long Channel.
CANALIS TRANSVERSUS — A transverse Channel.
CANALISCULUS — A small Channel.
CANCELLI — Grate or Lattice.
CANCIN PERICON — The heat of horse-dung.
CANFORA — The Gum of a Tree.
CANNA or SIPHUNCULUS — A small Tube.
CANTACON — Garden Saffron.
CAPILLUS — Lapis Rebis, which see.
CAPISTRUM AURI — Borax.
CAPITELLUM — Soapy Water, Water Saturated with Vegetable Salt.
CAPRICORNUS — Lead.
CAPSA — A deep Vessel, a kind of sieve.
CAPSA PATENS — A species of chest.
CAPSA PUTEALIS — A wide Basket.
CAPSAE — In which ore is placed before distribution.
CAPUT AREAE — The top of the stove.
CAPUT FODINARUM — The mouth of the pit or mine.

CAPUT FODINARUM ADVERSUM — The place where a mine is first opened up.
CAPUT FOLLIS — The mouth of the bellows.
CARBONES COELI — The Stars.
CARBUNCLE — is also the name of a precious stone, and is so called because of its dusky fire. When it is not sensible to fire it is called Apyrusta or Apyrotus. The Carbuncle is also undoubtedly the Pyropus, which was celebrated by Ovid in his second Metamorphosis as the house and dwelling-place in the sun. There are distinct species or kinds of Carbuncles. The first are those which are native to India and the African Garamas. These are called Cardedonius. The Indian are base and of a dead lustre. Among this species those which shine with a weaker and more livid light are termed Liviucias. These are much more numerous than the true Carchedonius. The second species is the Ethiopian Carbuncle, which does not radiate lustre, but is aglow with a secret fire. The third are the Scabri of Alabanda, which are darker than the rest. The fourth species is found, on the testimony of Theophrastus, both in Thracian Orchomenus of Arcadia, and a darker variety in Chios. The fifth species is the Traezenius, which has white spots or blemishes; of this there are many varieties. The sixth species has a pallid whiteness, is called Corithius. For the rest, all those Carbuncles which have a sharper and more liquescent brilliance, which are more black and more lucid than others, are termed masculine, while to all those which have a feebler light the name of feminine is applied. The best Carbuncles are called Methystisonte because their extreme glittering approaches the violet of the amethyst.
Very nearly allied to the Carbuncle is the Syrtites of Callistratus and Pliq which radiates a kind of broken or feathery light, and has been spoken of as a species of white Carbuncle. Moreover, that Anthracrite which is so similar

appearance and in qualities to coal, and is mined in Thesprotia, is classified by Pliny (1. 37, c. 8) as a species of Carbuncle. The Greeks would appear to have called many substances by the generic name of Anthracias (Anthrax), for example, natural cinnabar, red lead, vermilion, minium, hematite, and for Carbuncle itself, of which the Rubinus, or Lychnis, is undoubtedly also a species. The same Pliny describes a variety of Anthracite which is encircles by white lines, and which is reckoned to be superior from its colour. More over, it has the peculiarity that if it be cast into the fire, it perishes, losing all its lustre; but if sprinkled, on the contrary, with water, it seems to burst into flame. Related to this is the Garamantitis, or Sandastron of India, which also is found in Arabia, and in its translucent depths seems to be glittering; with golden drops. There is also a stone which has a purple or scarlet colon and radiance; when warmed by the friction of the fingers, or by the heat of the sun, it will attract straws; it is found in Caries and Orchosa, and ma probably in India; it belongs, according to Pliny, to the Lychnis species, be is also, as it were, a kind of deficient Carbuncle. Our own Rubinus is species of Lychnis. Albertus also bears witness that the Carbuncle was called Anthrax by the Greeks, and that it was made to shine like a live coal in the dark when it was placed in a glass vessel and sprinkled with clear water. The species varied according to the country of its origin, and the splendour, a the substance thereof. There are gems found in our own mines which, plunged in water, seem to dissolve by their own fire; and these are of the nature Carbuncles. It should also be noted that Albertus describes a gem, which calls Pelagia, possibly after that kind of shell-fish which produces a pure dye, and is mentioned by Pliny as the Purpura, or Pelagia. It is of a transparent ruby colour, and is either a feminine Carbuncle, or else is the house of a gem, because a Carbuncle is found in its matrix.

There are also stones which are partly Pelagia and partly Carbuncle. For other information concern the Carbuncle, consult Pliny, Solinus, and others. Other Carbuncles:
1. Garnet from Meissen.
2. Zeblicius, mined in the hill which is over against the stone-quarry whence Ophites are obtained; very plentiful in the neighbouring river.
3. Ethiopian, or Oriental Garnet.
4. A Bright Red Ruby.
5. Amethystizon, or Ruby.
6. Lychnis, or Yellowish Ruby.
7. Falsified Carbuncle, combined with Crystals, usually having a colour like the Amethyst.
8. Alabandicus, a precious Garnet from Asia.

CARBUNCULUS — A poisonous Ulcer, much the same as anthrax, which, however, is of a more cruel character; and from the thick black blood, of which it is adhering, it more quickly eats into the flesh.

CARDANUM — Garden Saffron.

CARDIS MARS — Iron.

CARDONIUM VINUM — i.e., Wine medicated with herbs.

CARENA — The twenty-fourth part of a drop.

CARIUM TERRAE — Lime.

CARMITI — i.e., Obulus, or Farthing.

CARNIT, CANNA, CUSANUM — Various kinds of vessels.

CARSI — i.e., Saline Water.

CAS — i.e., Gold.

CASA — A House inhabited by the Superintendent of the mine.

CASA CAMPHORA — Camphor.

CASEUS PREPARATUS — is the worthless residue remaining in the dregs of milk flowing from cheese.

CASPA — Mud Trough.

CASSATUM IN SPECIFICO DIAPHORETICO ~ is an unhealthy or dead blood in the veins, which prevents the motion and circulation of good blood.
CASSIDBOLT ~ i.e., Coriander.
CASTELLUM, or **LACUSCULUS** ~ A Chest, Chest of Water.
CATELLUS FICTILIS ~ Potsherd.
CATENA ~ a Chain.
CATTENA DUCTARIA ~ an Iron Rope or Chain.
CATHIMIA ~ is (1) a vein of the earth, out of which gold and silver are taken, according to the saying of some masters. 2. Cathmia grows in furnaces of gold or silver. 3. Gold. 4. Spume of silver, 5. The smoke given off in the process of burning copper, and which is deposited on the upper walls of the oven.
CATHMIA AFFIDIA ~ i.e., Cathmia of Silver, having the colour of Litharge, i.e., Burnt Lead.
CATHMIA ~ i.e., Scoria of Gold, Copper, or Siiver.
CATHMIA FERRI ~ Scoria of Iron.
CATILLUS ~ A Porringer.
CATILLUS CINEREUS ~ A Coppel.
CATILLUS CINEREUS ~ is a Melting Vessel with two parts of moistened cinders of light wood, purified from all ashes and other dirt; and with one part of cinders properly ground out of bones that have no marrow [let not these bones be taken from pigs because they are so expensive] which have been reduced into a paste or mass, and properly mixed together in a mortar. Let this mortar be filled with moistened cinders, and the pestle, which is commonly called monachus, is hammered into it with three blows of a wooden mallet, and let there be cinders put inside, by means of a hair sieve, from the head of a calf. One or two blows may be added with a stag's horn. Then let the matter be removed and dried.

CATILLUS FERREUS EX ACIE TEMPERATUS ~ A Porringer of tempered iron or steel.
CATINUS ~ A kind of dish or platter; a Crucible.
CATINUS AEREUS ~ A round Pan or Caldron.
CATINUS AREXARIUS ~ the common sand Coppel, an earthen Vessel, shaped like a round cap, with a rim of three or four fingers broad. Made of some hard earth.
CATINUS FERREUS ~ An Iron Caldron.
CATINI MEDIA PARS ~ the Inside of a Caldron.
CATMA ~ the polished Surface of Gold.
CATROBIL ~ i.e., Earth.
CATHOCITES ~ Like the Iron Magnet, a kind of Sagda which attracts straws. There is also the Catochites or Catochitis, mentioned by Pliny, a kind of precious stone, which, by means of its very soft gummy or glutinous nature, causes the hand to cleave to it. It is found in Corsica, as Solinus tells us (Polyhist, c. 9). See also Pliny, 1. 37, c. 10.
CAUDA FOLLIUM VECTIS ~ Handle of the Bellows.
CAUDA VULPIS RUBICUNDI ~ The Tail of the Red Wolf; is Minium, obtained from Lead.
CAVERNOSUM ~ Glandular.
CAURUS ~ The North-west Wind.
CAUTELA ~ Caution; in the Spagyric Art, is that industrious habit combined with wariness, by which the Professors of the art do more easily carry out and accomplish their operations.
CAUTERIUM, or **KAUTIR** ~ is a Surgeon's Instrument, by which they remove the skin for the cauterisation of ulcerous and putrescent gatherings on the body. It is also a simple corrosive Medicament, by which the skin is taken off without pain.
CAVA ~ A Hole, Cavity, etc.
CAVERNA ~ Council House.
CAVERNULE VENARUM ~ Ore decayed by the weather.

CAVUM LIGUORUM CONJUNCTORUM — A Rut, a Space between two parallel planks of wood.
CARDIR — i.e., Tin.
CEDRIA — The Gum from the Cedar Tree.
CEDUE — Air.
CELSA — Literally, a Hill, according to the German; according to the Latin, literally, the Muscle of Life. It is the Pulse which is the sign of life.
CEMENTARE, CEMENTIREN, STRATIFICIREN — To place any substances in alternate layers.
CEMENTATIO — is Gradation by Cementing.
CEMENTUM — is a sharp and penetrating Mineral Substance by which the metallic layers to be cemented or welded, are, chemically speaking, reverberated upon. It is either simple or mixed; in form, it is either a powder or paste.
CEMENTERIUM — A Welding Pot.
CENIFICATUM, CINIFICATUM, or CALCINATUM — is that which is Calcined.
CENIPLAM, or CENIPLOTAM — is an Instrument, used in Epilepsy, for opening the head.
CENTRUM OVI — i.e., the Yolk of an Egg.
CEPA PORCI — i.e., Squilla, i.e., Officinal Squill.
CEPINI — Vinegar.
CERATIO — This operation is defined by Gebir, in the first book, and the fifty-fourth chapter of his Sum of Perfection, to be the mollification or softening 7to a liquid state of a hard substance or infusible juice. It is called by this name, because it easily reduces the philosophical medicine into a liquescent substance, like wax melted by fire. When the philosophers desire to convert quicksilver into gold or silver, it is necessary that they should possess the medicine in a flowing state, which, in the words of Gebir, doth suddenly before the flight thereof adhere thereunto in the depth, and

thereunto is conjoined by those things which are least. And it doth thicken it, and conserve in fire by its fixity, until there cometh unto it the leniency of a larger fire, containing the humidity thereof, and converting it by this artifice in a moment, to a true moist and a true dry, according to that for which the medicine was prepared. Ceration is performed upon a body which is hard and of dry humour by continual imbibition until melting takes place. According to the second book, and the twenty-seventh chapter of the Grand Rosary of Arnoldus, the sign of perfect ceration is when the medicine, being most swiftly projected upon a burning plate, resolves itself, without smoke, into the consistency of molten wax. Ceration is a subtilisation or making subtle of the parts, in order that their virtue and power may be poured out and dispensed into the bodies. And the moisture which is necessary is the science of the complements or the completion. This ceration cannot take place without a disintegration or dispersion, so that the matter may become as a piece of wax, melting and softening under a temperate heat. Note that such ceration is altogether a discovery of the Masters.

CERARE — i.e., to combine or incorporate.

CERAUNIA — Under this head there appear to be two kinds of resplendent gems which are referred to by Pliny (l. 37, c. 9). One is a shining and gleaming stone; the other is said to fall during storms of rain and lightning. There is the Asteria and the Astrios, or Astrion. The first encloses light like the apple of the eye. It is found in India and Carmania. The Astrios belongs also to India and Macedonian Pallene. In the midst of it there shines, as it were, a star, with the light of the full moon. When exposed to the stars, it is said to attract lightning. The best Asteria: come from Carmania. The poorer species are what some call Ceraunia; the worst have a light which is similar to that of candles (or perhaps of

a certain fish mentioned by Pliny which shines in a calm night). There is also a kind of Astrios which has the phosphorescent light of a fish's eye. It glitters with radiance like a sun. There are white Ceraunia:, which seem to have stolen the splendour of the stars. Others gleam with a crystalline blue splendour. There are black and ruby-coloured varieties, found only in a place which has been struck by lightning. Consult Sotacus sad Zenothemis on the authority of Puny. These are the Thunderstones of the Germans, which fall from the clouds with a great noise. They are found in Grania, and there is a white variety from Spain; in Germany they are met with about the neighbourhood of the Elbe, where there are some specimens of Ceraunia, which are like crystal informed with cerulean blue, being also of divers forms, sometimes like a stick, sometimes like a pyramid, or sugar-loaf. They are never found perfect, perchance on account of the force with which they are propelled towards the earth. They are said to induce sweet sleep, to protect against thunderbolts, and to give victory in battle and in law cases. See also the twenty-third chapter of Solinus.
CERDAC — i.e., Mercury.
CEREBRUM — Water.
CEREBRUM ARIETIS — White of Egg.
CEREBRUM BOVIS — Burnt Tartar.
CERVICULAE SPIRITUS — is a bone of the heart of the stag.
CEROBER — i.e., Water.
CERUSA — i.e., Rust of Lead, White Lead, the Psimytim, Psimytion, or Aphidegi, of the Greeks, a Poisonous Body, according to Dioscorides and Nicander, which is cold and dry in the second degree. It is, however, well known to almost every one, and retains its name of White Lead in our pharmacopia. It is the powder, ash, rust, or ceruse of White

or Black Lead. If manufactured from White Lead, it is called Spanish, and this is the whitest kind. At the present day it is made at Venice and Nuremberg. That which came from Rhodes, Corinth, and Lacedaemon was formerly much celebrated. Dioscorides (1. 5, c. 53), teaches the method of its manufacture, and also after what manner it may be roasted until it is like Sandarac or Sandix, and becomes a manufactured species of Sandarac. Consult Vitruvius and Serapion. It should be noted that there is some confusion both of names and ideas in regard to this substance. Sandaracs, or Sandaracha, is a kind of red colour; there are two species, rough and manufactured; the former was a red arsenic mixed with brimstone, otherwise red orpiment; the second was a kind of vermilion, and Pliny says that the colour Sandyx was formed by mixing equal portions of this substance and rubrics. Sandix, or Sandyx, is thus a manufactured red colour, which is referred to in the fourth eclogue of Virgil (1. 45), where some without need, would understand an herb, because Pliny (1. 35, c. 6), in speaking of this colour says that Virgil considered it to be a herb; but the colour of the herb may be understood. Hesychius speaks of a shrub called Sandyx, of which the flowers are a scarlet red. But Pliny speaks of a metallic Sandix, and of our adulterated ceruse, artificially roasted, which is like Sandarac. Consult Dioscorides, Serapion, and Avicenna. The finest of all ceruse is used as a cosmetic by women, and is referred to in Ovid.

CHAMBAR — Poison, the fruit of Poison, or Magnesia. The *Turba* says: It is the White Stone, and calls it Orpiment, Zendrio, Abaemech, Chalul. But when it has become white and innocuous, then it is called Lead, Exobmich, Magnesia, Martech, White Copper.

CHACEF — A Potter's Vessel.

CHALCOS — Sulphur Water.

CHALCITIS — Under the sections Atramentum and Calcanthos, we have exhaustively handled the qualities and differences which characterise Chalcites, Chalcitis, and Chalcanthum. There is that Chalcites or Chalcitis out of which copper is malted. This is Copper-stone, Marcasite, Pyrites, Macer, Mesne, the Stellate stone, etc. There is Chalcitis, a kind of precious stone, resembling copper or brass. This is Trichitis, a kind of capillary alum, which grows in pyrites. It is also called concrete Alum and Schistos. And the Arabs make mention of Colcotar. Chalcanthum is vitriol or copper, and the Chalcitis to which we refer under this heading is a species of Chalcanthum, which is a kind of Flower of Copper, and has a middle nature between Vitriol and Marcasite, i.e., it is Pyrites. This true Chalcitis is of two kinds: native and manufactured. There are also two kinds of native: Cyprian and Babylonian. The first has the ruddiness of copper. This is Zeg, or Citrine Atrament, which has elsewhere been sufficiently treated. It is also Colcotar. It is properly Red Vitriol, but not Sory; the Arabs, however, call it Sory, by a pardonable slip, for Sory is made from red vitriol. I have never found it in silver mines, but it is to be found in those of copper, as, for example, at Goslar. The second native variety, or that of Babylon, is described by Serapion; it is hard, and when broken has white spots inside. Manufactured Chalcitis is made from old Chalcanthum which is passing into a threadlike condition. Among other species of Chalcitis we may mention
1. The hard, red Atrament.
2. Brittle, milky, red Atrament.
3. Hard, red Atrament, combined with Misy.
4. Hard, red Atrament, combined with Sory.
5. Hard Atrament mixed with Pyrites.
6. Red Cyprian Atrament.

CHALCOPYRITES — Lead, according to Synesius.

CHALCHOS ~ i.e., Copper.
CHALCHITOR ~ Marcasite.
CHALCUTE ~ Burnt Copper.
CHAMBELECH ~ Elixir.
CHANCHED ~ Steel.
CHAOMANTIA ~ is an Art by which Omens are found in the air when the stars of the air disclose and make things visible, so that men see and prognosticate by means of the air.
CHAOS ~ The Unformed Matter, and the Confused First State of all Things. According to Theophrastus, it is Air or Master.
CHARATRA ~ Waterspout.
CHEIZI ~ This is a term of Paracelsus. When it is applied to minerals, it refers to Quicksilver. When it is concerned with the vegetable world, it means the Flowers of Vegetables and Plants. When it occurs redundantly, or in repetition, as Flos Cheiri, from silver, it signifies the White Elixir, or its Quintessence, as Flos Anthos, Red Elixir of Gold. Others say it is Potable Gold; others again that it is Antimony.
CHELIE ~ Shears, or Scissors; it may also mean a Rock or Cliff in the sea.
CHELIDONIA ~ is Gold.
CHELIDONIUS ~ Several distinct things are liable to be confused under this name. There is the Chelidonius Lapillus of Pliny, a kind of stone which the ancients supposed to be found in the maws of young swallows. Reference has already been made to this belief. There is the Chelidonia, which is the herb Swallow Wort or Celandine. Swallows were said to make use of it to restore sight to their-young. There is the Chalidonia Ficus, a kind of fig which ripens towards the winter. There is the Chelidonia Gemma, so called because it resembles a swallow in colour. There is the Chelonia Gemma, a species of precious stone, properly, the eye of the

Indian tortoise. It is sometimes called Chelonites. Finally, there is the Chelonitis, a Precious Stone in the form of a tortoise, which was found formerly where the Tangra joins with the Elbe, and of which there are several species; some of large size, and some so small that they are scarcely visible to the eye; some bright or pale tawny, or gold colour; some with black lines, after the manner of the shell on the sea tortoise. There are also some which have an oblong shape, and the quality of the ostracias. Others shine like the onyx. There is also a stone which Pliny calls Chelonia, and which is said to be the eye of the Indian tortoise, as already stated, or by others to be found in the heart of the tortoise.

CHEMIA ~ Some linguists say that Chemia is, and is called, an Art of Melting or Fusing, an Art of Analysis, and that the prefix ali is an emphatic and expletive particle, much as in the word manack, to which al is also prefixed, and then we have almanack, wherein the whole year and every day is numbered, and many other things are reckoned. But others would derive our term from the Greek, so that it should mean Archimia or Archodunia, the prime wisdom and knowledge, since it, moreover, has in itself the highest and most miraculous secret, and he that attains thereto will be facile princeps in all the other arts. Theophrastus, in the Book of Nature, says that in former times it was called Usopus and Usopaica; it is an art of melting and fusing which the world cannot dispense with, since hence come all wealth and property, medicine and handicraft. It is also called the Spagyric Art, the Art of Separation, whereby we learn to recognize the genera and species of all minerals; their beginnings, causes and effects; how they may grow, and are subjected to cleansing, improvement, alteration, commingling, union, augmentation and diminution. The ordinary definition runs as follows: Chemia is the Art of Separating Essences from any mixed substance whatsoever,

and of suitably preparing the magisteries of artifices. It teaches the method of removing that which diminishes the grade, which detains or impedes. It teaches how to separate the false from the true, and to reduce things to perfection. Theophrastus also says: The third foundation of medicine is Alchemy. Nature never produces that which is perfect, or that which is complete in its condition, but man has to complete. This completing art is called alchemical. For the baker is an alchemist up to the point of baking bread; the tender of wines in that he cools wines is an alchemist; so also the weaver up to the point of making cloth. Therefore concerning that which is produced by Nature becoming useful to mankind, whosoever brings it into that condition which was ordained by Nature is an alchemist, however dull and unskilled otherwise he may be, even he who turns a raw sheep skin into a fur cloak. Therefore there is no art without alchemy. Again Theophrastus writes thus: Alchemy is an art which teaches how to distinguish the stars from the bodies, in order to direct the stars following the constellation in obedience. For direction is not in the bodies, but in the firmament. Hence it follows that what the brain assimilates is implied in the course of the Moon; what the milk assimilates produces Saturn; what the heart assimilates produces the Sun. Therefore the external firmaments are the directors of the Balm for a long time. Melissa will not wait upon the mother, unless she takes Venus away. Some derive Chemia from the Greek word which signifies to melt.
CHRISTI PABULUM — i.e., Virgin's Urine.
CHROMA — i.e., Colour.
CHRYSOCALCOS — i.e., Brass.
CHRYSOCOLLA — It is necessary here to distinguish between the Chrysocolla, which is another name for Borax, and that which is another name for a precious stone called Amphitane by Pliny (1. 37, c. 10). Distinction must also be

made between both these, and the imitation Borax, which was used by painters of old, and also passed under the name of Chrysocolla. The Chrysocolla here mainly treated is not Borax of the common sort. It is, as it were, a gluten of gold; it is the German mountain-green, and that viridity which is sometimes found on slate. There is a native and there is a manufactured kind. Dioscorides treats of native Chrysocolla (1. 5, c. 54). There are varieties from Armenia, Macedonia, and Cyprus, and some excellent species of German origin. It is obtained from gold mines and copper mines, and up to the present time has been unknown to our physicians. It is also mined in Hungary, Burgundy, and Silesia, and gold is extracted from it by smelting. It is a sort of species of nitre. It may also be called a scissile green, as verdigris, or green of copper, is a rasile green. Pliny (1. 33, c. 5) calls it a putrid vein of humour congealed into a sort of slime in pits, and describes it as obtained from copper, gold, and silver mines. The manufactured Chrysocolla may be distinguished into hard, medium, and herbaceous, slimy, etc. But Dioscorides classifies them all among the species of verdigris, which are now used by goldsmiths, and were used formerly by doctors. He speaks of native Chrysocolla as formed of the urine of infants. And this is also called Tinckar and Borax. Native Chrysocolla has a dispersing and consuming quality. Pliny enumerates it among painters' colours. There is a distinct difference between manufactured and native Chrysocolla. Out of native Chrysocolla and azure blue, the best gold is made. Mica or Catsilver, of which we have already treated, is a species of Chrysocolla, concerning which consult Serapion, s.v., Tincar, who says that Chrysocolla is found on the shores of the sea, and is a species of salt which is hot and dry in the fourth degree. As to its medical uses, and how it is cleansed, see Dioscorides. Note that an over-dose is

poisonous. Chrysocolla is also called Azot, Rebis, Water of Sulphur, Flower, Soul, Ghost.
1. Pure native Chrysocolla from Carpathos.
2. Chrysocolla from Misnia in a metallic Copper Stone-pure mountain green.
3. Native Chrysocolla from the Rhetian Alps, combined with Molochites, or Malachite.
4. Chrysocolla from the Slate Stone of Islebia.
5. The greenness which appears on slates.
6. Artificial Chrysocolla.

CHRYSOLITHUM ~ The precious stone called Chrysolite, which, like the Hyacinth, comes from Ethiopia, and is translucent with a gold light, whence it receives its name. Consult Pliny (1. 33, c. 9 and 12). Solinus calls it Chrysolampin, and Pliny says that its colour grows pallid by day, but shines like fire in the night. Albertus speaks of it as a gem which is very beautiful in the morning; but, as the day waxes, it loses the charm of its lustre, and seems altogether to deteriorate. It has antipathy for fire, which causes combustion in it. The same writer regards Marcasite as a gold-coloured species of Chrysolite, and calls it a blue and red stone. The virtue of Chrysolite is to raise melancholy spirits, to cure scabbiness and ulcers, and to mitigate the heat of fever. In the second Metamorphosis of Ovid, we find that it enters into the composition of the chariot of the Sun, the axis of the wheel being gold, the spokes silver, and the yokes of Chrysolite.

CHRYSOCOLITE ~ also signifies Arsenic, and the unknown stone Achesium.

CHRYSOS, or **CHRYSION** ~ i.e., Gold.

CHYMIA ~ is derived from a Greek term which signifies the process of melting. Whence we have sap, or juice, and chemistry becomes the art of making or extracting sap. But among the ancient chemists the idea of coagulation was included under that of solution, and hence we have the term Chymia as the science of solution and coagulation. The prefix al is of Arabic origin, and with the Arabs the term signified the Spagyric Art, the art of extracting and condensing, also of separating and cleansing. Thus, chemistry is the science of dividing the pure from the impure for the confection of medicines, not alone for the healing of human bodies, but also, by another adjustment, for educing metals to the highest state of perfection.

CHYMUS — i.e., Mass. Also, refuse.

CIANUM — Whetstone.

CIBATIO — Corporation.

CIBUR, or **CHYBUR** — i.e., Sulphur.

CICATRISANS — What burns leaves.

CICINUM OLEUM — The Oil of an Egyptian tree, called also Croton.

CIMENTARE — To Unite.

CINEFACTIO — is that process by which substances are reduced to ashes. But alkalis and metallic soot are sometimes called ashes. The name applies properly to substances that have been reduced by fire. Its administration is twofold close and open.

CINIS — The Impure Body. When the Mercury kills the bodies, there remains a precious ash, and it is called Calcination, Cibation. The ash is a white powder.

CINIS HEDERAE — Ash of Ivy, or Clavellated Ash.

CINIS CLAVELLATUS — i.e., Alkali.

CINIS EX CINERE — is Salt, Extracted Water. The ash is fixed therein. It is a cinder of a cinder; it is called Congealed Coagulate, for it coagulates water into earth ; it is also called the Ferment of Ferment, i.e., it ferments gold, as Rosinus states. Senior says: The purified Ash becomes an incrustation, and it is called Lime, Glass, Silver Litharge,

Pure Water, Ashes. Then the bad earthly nature is removed, and that is their leaves and flowers-spirit and soul.

CINIS FARMENTITIUS — is called by the Germans Ashes of Vine Twigs. It is useful not only to physicians and surgeons, but to chemists. Pliny and Dioscorides enumerate its more secret virtues. It contains the potency of salt in a milder form. It removes fleshy execrescences. But its virtue differs according to the difference and quality of the material which is burnt. See Serapion and Galenus.

CINIFICATUM — i.e., Calcined.

CINERICIUM — A Goldsmith's Basket wherein gold or silver is totally burnt.

CINERIS VENA — Ash.

CINERITIUM — is an Amalgam of Gold or Silver, by some called Regale.

CINNABARIS — There is very great doubt among doctors as to what is actually signified by Cinnabar, for the term is applied by different authorities to very diverse substances. For the better distinction of true, fictitious, and manufactured Cinnabar, observe the following tabulation: Cinnabar is of two kinds. True, Cinnabar, of which we here treat, which was called by the ancients the Blood of the Dragon, a name it still retains. It is also twofold, namely, Metallic, of which we treat below.

1. Red, like Sandarac and red lead. It is found in the form of small lumps. It was used by Venetian painters, because it is blood-colour. It is an antidote in medicine.

2. Black, and of globular shape; but this is an adulterated kind, which is shown by its excessive toughness. It is sometimes sophisticated with gum, and in this state is sold by apothecaries as genuine.

Pliny (l. 33, c. 7) speaks of Indian Cinnabar, which differs from the other varieties, and calls it the corrupted blood, or gore, of the dragon, when that animal has been crushed by the weight of an elephant which it has destroyed, and Cinnabar is really a combination of the blood of them both. To this Solinus assents. Other writers regard it as a metallic substance, and Dioscorides places it among metals. The Arabians classify it as a sap. Serapion says it is the sap of the plant ironwort, but when Dioscorides very exhaustively describes this herb, he does not mention its sap. Those who consider that Cinnabar is the exudation of a plant, or rather of a tree, say that the fact is indicated by its taste and flavour. They affirm that the tree comes from Lybia and the neighbouring regions, and that in our own parts it is obtained from the pitch or resin of the pine, which the apothecaries of Italy sell for the resin of the terebinth, to which it is similar in colour. So also Platearius affirms the blood of the dragon to be the sap of an herb or tree in India or Persia.

There is also metallic Cinnabar, called Nulton and Minium, or Red Lead. It is of two kinds, native and manufactured. The first is red in colour, like Sandarac, and when melted it makes quicksilver and sulphur. It is otherwise called Minium, and is of red colour, like Sandarac. It is found in silver mines, according to Pliny. Cordus says that it exists also in the vicinity of the Rhine, and in very large quantities at Schonbach. There is a vein of it in the mines of Misnensia, and the Germans call it Quicksilver Earth or Ore. It was held precious by the Romans, as Pliny informs us (1. 33, c. 7), and is referred to in the tenth Eclogue of Virgil. The former writer speaks of it sometimes as a vein of Minium and the stone Minium, and we find that it commonly adheres to a species of fissile-stone. The continual exudation of the stone in these veins is called quicksilver. According to Vitruvius, Anthracite was regarded as a kind of Minium, and at any rate the concrete Anthracite is found in close proximity to metallic Cinnabar, and when the latter is dug up the spade of the miner causes quicksilver to exude visibly, and it is straightway collected by the delver. It is to be noted that the term Anthrax was applied to many substances by the Greeks, and among these:

1. To the veins of Red Lead, as appears from the words of Vitruvius already
referred to.
2. To the precious stone called Hematite, which see.
3. To that most noble gem which Pliny calls Carbuncle.
4. To a species of earth, which is mentioned by writers on husbandry, and I believe it to be that which is dug up in some parts of Saxony, is dried in the sun, and is then used for wood, and for fires; it is undoubtedly a species of bitumen. And bitumen dried on the surface of the earth by the heat of the sun is the mother of that coal which is bitumen hardened by heat inside the earth.
5. There is also that substance which Theophrastus describes as like coal yet hardly coal, and nevertheless used in fires, as if it were coal. But it is lighter; a variety of this substance is found in our mines, and is called Pit Coal. It is not mentioned by Pliny. That also should not pass without a reference which Theophrastus terms true Minium, not using the Greek word which signifies Cinnabar in its sandy state, but which he calls also Cinnabar, not that it is that substance, but because it is like it in appearance. There is one important difference between native Minium and Sandarac. From Minium frequently, both the adapted and the rude kinds, Quicksilver may be obtained, which in the case of Sandarac is scarcely possible. Again when the ore containing Minium is cleansed previous to roasting, a part of it changes into quicksilver, and when it has been dried and pounded returns to its original colour. It is named either after the nation which uses it or the purpose to which it is applied — either Sinopia or Rubrica, or Artisan's Milton.

Manufactured Cinnabar is composed by chemists of quicksilver and sulphur. There is also an adulterated Minium which is called Cinnabar, and is made from lead. Finally, there is a false Minium in argentiferous and saturnian alloys which is burnt out of a stone found in veins, and of this Pliny writes (1. 33, c. 7). The same author's account of the method used in the confection of minium is borrowed from Theophrastus.

CIRCIUS — North West.

CIRCULATIO — is the Exaltation by the agency of Heat of a Pure Liquid through a circular solution and coagulation in the Pelican. It is only for those liquid substances which are to be resolved or attenuated into air, and can thence in return be brought back into a liquid state; it most frequently follows those extractions by which essences are made. Not uncommonly it discharges the office of rectification, since liquids when they come out of it are not any weaker, but purer, more potent, and more translucid. Several operations concur in its administration, such as digestion, sublimation, vicarious distillation, etc. For example, much trouble and care are required for the proper extraction of spirit of wine, so that it may be obtained without any phlegmatic part. For as often as it is elevated, it always takes some moisture with it. Next, we will show by an experiment the manner of this circulation. The very best wine that can be obtained is taken, and it is poured in a capacious circulating vessel. When the aperture has been sealed up, it is left in the water bath for fourteen days, so that it may continually boil in water. Then it is taken out and put in a phial, and is in winter time placed still hot into cold snow water, an alembic being at hand with a receiver. But in summer it is placed in a cellar, in a refrigerating vessel, and the spirit being pure and free from all moisture, passes from the alembic and is discharged into the receiver. When no further ascension takes place the receiver is removed, and the phial is taken away with the wine, which now contains no true spirit but what Theophrastus terms vinum adustum. The spirit of wine is caused to revolve in the circulating vessel until no further liquefaction can take place; it is then dealt with by a humid elevation. When the material on which it is to operate is placed in the receptacle, it absorbs it readily, and relinquishes flight.

CIRCULATORIUM ~ is a Glass Vessel in which the liquor there placed is rotated, as in a circle, by alternate ascending and descending. It is used chiefly in rarefactions and circulations. There are many varieties in the conformation of this vessel, of which the two most important are the Pelican and the Diota.

CIRCULUS ~ is a round Iron Utensil for cutting glasses, the iron being heated and passed lightly round the glass, until that also is hot, when in this state it is aspersed with cold water, or subjected to a cold air, and so severed.

CISIA BIROTA ~ The Stand for the Whetstone.

CISSUM ~ A Tub for measuring.

CIST or **KIST** ~ is a Measure and a half of a Measure, according to the measuring of wine-about four pounds.

CITRINATION ~ is the Resurrection.

CITRINULORUM, PHARMACUM EX COLCHOTARE ~ i.e., Calcined Vitriol, reduced to an Alkali. It has much of the transparency which characterizes crystal.

CITRINULA ~ i.e., Flammula, an Herb mentioned by Paracelsus.

CITRINULUS ~ Crystal.

CLARETA, LEUCON, or **LEUCOMA** ~ White of Egg.

CLARUM ~ That which is made out of Crystal.

CLAVI CORNUTI ~ The curved Peg to hold the Leather of the Bellows.

CLEPSYDRIA — is the subduction of the liquor through the eye of a solid vessel perforated underneath. This was formerly performed in horological instruments, i.e., in instruments which registered the time taken over the work. Hence the name. Water, oil, and mineral solutions were treated in this way.

The term eye signifies the door by which the subduction took place, although for this purpose other names are used, such as channel, funnel, the top of the tube, lid, etc.

The method varied, as in other cases.

CLIMIA ERIPS — i.e., Cathimia of Orpiment. It has also a brilliant colour ; it resembles Cathmia of Silver, or Cathimia. Taken by itself, it signifies Chalk of Silver, or Silver Chalk.

CLISSUS — is the secret virtue of things going from and returning whence it first started. It displays itself first in shoots, then in leaves, then in flowers, and seeds, and then again in taking root.

CLYSSUS — is a composite species made of the several varieties of any matter, separately elaborated. Thus, Clyssus may embrace the entire essence of a substance, when, all impurities and refuse having been separated, the essential parts of the species are amalgamated into one composition. Or, it is the extraction of the subtlety of all portions of a plant, commonly conjoined. The unification is accomplished in two ways. All the extracted virtues of the various members are conjoined and incorporated, or, otherwise, the oil is obtained in one cucurbit, the salt in another, the aqueous liquor in a third, and then the three are distilled through a common channel communicating with each cucurbit into one alembic, and there united. But this process does not easily succeed. For oil and water do not rise up equally. But the oils and the waters may be united separately.

COADUNATIO — is Elaboration, by which things that are separated may be united. It is sometimes called Coagulation, and hence that dogma of the philosophers, that chemistry consists in solution and coagulation, which, nevertheless, refers chiefly to the mystery of the stone. Thus Coadunation is the reduction of a solution into a coagulated state, when it is possible for the substances operated on to assume that state. There are two kinds: Composition and Coagulation.

COAGULATION — is the condensation from a tenuous and fluid consistency of things of the same nature, and their reduction into a solid state. Thus, those substances which have been attenuated by an aqueous, aerial, or fiery resolution, are hereby reduced into a homogeneous body. And thus Coagulation is co-ordinated by many other operations-divaporation, exaltation, sublimation, distillation, etc. It is performed in two ways : by Segregation and Comprehension. And it is either cold or hot.

Cold Coagulation is when the substance dissolved by heat is coagulated by cold.

Hot Coagulation is when by means of a suitable heat the dissolved matter is coagulated.

Coagulation by Segregation is when, certain portions being segregated, the rest are concreted. The operation may he termed Concretion. It is performed with heat, whereby the humour is evaporated, or exhaled, and thus the cause of fluidity is removed.

COAGULUM — A coagulating or macerating mixture, planter of Paris ; it is produced from milk, and causes milk to coagulate; it is also a ferment. Mercury is the milk. Our Mercury is the coagulator of its Sulphur. Mary the prophetess calls the Sulphur of the Philosophers Coagulating Coagulate, the Soul of the First Matter, and our Gold, because the Sulphur coagulates Mercury. It is also Ash Out of Ashes.

COAGULUM ~ i.e., Mercury.
COAGULUM SPECIFICUM ~ is the material earthly essence congealed into a dry consistency by Coagulation.
COAGULATION ~ by Comprehension is performed when the whole matter, comprehended together and remixed, is coagulated into a uniform substance.
COATETZ ~ is Half a Drop.
COBASTOLI ~ i.e., Ash.
COSATIORUM FUMUS ~ Cobalt.
COCHLEA ~ A Screw.
COCHLEARE ~ A Ladle, or Trowel.
COCHLEARE ALBUM ~ A white Ladle.
COCILIO ~ i.e., A Weight of two ounces.
CODAX ~ Uvula.
COELI PLANETARUM ~ signify with Paracelsus the proper orbs, or the spheres themselves, not imaginary ones, to which certain motions are attributed by the heathens, Pliny and Empedocles, of which motions they knew as much as of the cause of volcanoes. If ignorant as to things that are upon earth, how could they judge of things at an immense distance except by deceptive conjectures? It is just that, on account of their infidelity, they should, amid their speculations and imaginations, receive no truth, whereas true visions are reserved by God for the faithful. False visions proceed from the enemy of the truth, and hence result the speculations of the infidels.
COELUM PHILOSOPHORUM ~ is some matter which far transcends the nature of the vulgar elements, such as the Stone of the Philosophers, the Universal Medicine, etc.
COELUNA ~ is a Heavenly Spirit which makes its way into the essential forms of things, and thereby solidifies and purifies them. It is the purest of all things, the quintessence, complete and abiding, and conducts with it all the stars of the circle of the underworld. This is Microcosmos, the

smaller world. Their proper spheres are in the planets. This under-heaven has earth and water, which must be separated and purified, and again conjoined to produce life and motion,

COEMENTUM — is dry Corrosion, by which any metallic body is arranged in layers with corrosive salts and other dessicating substances, and is so calcined and broken up. Calcination is performed in the following manner: The body to be cemented is reduced into thin plates, and cut up with forceps into small pieces. The corrosive substances are pounded into powder and steeped in vinegar, wine, or aqua fortis, till they are like a pulp, or poultice (some go to work with dry corrosives). The poultice or powder, or rather a part thereof, is placed in the box of the cementing vessel, a layer of the metal to be treated is deposited over it, then another portion of the corrosives, and so in succession, until the receptacle is full, or until all the metal has been exhausted, when it is covered with a final layer of corrosives, and the whole sealed up with pitch or some tenacious substance, and the operation of cementing is then performed with fire, or over a furnace, which must continue, according to the grade of cementing required, for four, six, eight, twelve, or twenty-four hours. N.B.-Let us suppose that it is my intention to prepare the Flower of Mars, or Chalybs, and that by cementation. I take a proper quantity of living calx, and compose it into a paste by means of an adult's urine. I place so much of this pulp in the bottom of the box of the cementing vessel as will be a finger's breadth deep. Over this I arrange plates of Chalybs, and seal the vessel as above. Everything being otherwise made ready, I place the box in a cementing furnace, and keep up for twenty-four hours a continuous fire rising from the third to the fourth grade. Then taking the matter from the vessel, I operate upon it in the mortar till it is reduced to a very fine powder; I separate the calx from the chalybs by heat; I dry the residuum; and the result is the best quality of Crocus Martis. Crocus Veneris is obtained in the same way, and is useful in many operations.

COENUM — i.e., excrement.

COERULEUM — so called on account of its colour, is Lapis Lazuli. The varieties are these:

1 Very beautiful Ultra Marine, or Cyprian, Coeruleum, similar to the best manufactured kind.

2. Native Coeruleum, in little clods, concave within, and removed from a very white earth. Beautiful blue, azure lumps which are internally hollow, and are found in a whitish grey earth.

3. Paduan, which is found in light grey earth. A blue and dark grey clod.

4. Native Thuringian, dug up in large quantities near Muchella. Ordinary blue, found in Thuringia.

5. Native, found abundantly, cleaving to hard, ash-coloured earth.

6. A fine Polish Lazuli.

7. A native Polish Lazuli, mixed with a hard, greyish earth.

8. Impure Lazuli on a white stone.

9. Spanish Lazuli, containing fine gold.

10. Native Snebergensian, cleaving to a rough stone.

11. Islebian mountain Lazuli, in a slate stone.

12. A beautiful mountain Lazuli, with mountain green in an iron ore and white quartz.

13. Native Snebergensian, together with a pure Chrysocolla on a hard and white flint, distinctly cleaving to it.

14. Native Gieshubelian, in a pyrites from which silver is excocted, and this is mixed with a congealed green sap, and is arranged in rings or zones, and the sap in question flows freely and plentifully outside the vein. A Mountain Lapis

Lazuli in an extremely beautiful copper ore, out of which there is daily produced a grey colour or sappy exudation.
15. Manufactured Lapis Lazuli.
16. Manufactured Ultramine, which is affirmed to be brought out of Spain and from Thrace.
17. Blue green, which appears in a slate.

Native mined Coeruleum, or Lazuli, is of two kinds. It is found in the mines of Cyprus, according to Dioscorides (1. 5, c. 56), among cuprine alloys, and a most excellent quality in our own gold and copper mines, as, for example, those of Saxony and Silesia. It is also found in Hungary and Lotharingia. It is like a little pebble or stone under the earth, and adheres, like Chrysocolla, a scissile stone. Gold is extracted from it in Silesia. Its medicinal virtue astringent and dispersing. It is burnt like Chalcitis and washed like Cadmia. Pliny gives warning against its use in a crude form. He enumerates three species, Egyptian, Scythian, Cyprian, and to these may be added Campanian and Spanish. The right understanding of Coeruleum is as important as that of Chrysocolla. It is hard and yields little in this to iron. There is a brittle species which is beautiful in colour, but is impure and of scant use. For the rest, consult Serapion (lib. Agg., c. Hager), Alzanard, etc. Some will have it that Coeruleum is hot and dry in the third degree ; others that it is hot in the second and dry in the third. It has affinity with Armenian-stone, which is blue according to Dioscorides and green according to Pliny: it is not so hard as the emerald, but is sometimes used as its substitute: The second kind of Coeruleum is found in hollows under caverns of the sea, among the sea sand.

Manufactured Coeruleum. Of this there are many species, some prized by chemists. Pills are occasionally made from it by a grave error, as they should be prepared from the native kind and from the Armenian, the purging virtue of which has been described by Aetius.

COHOB — is Sand, or Dust.

COHOBATIO — is the frequent abstraction of the moisture of a body by continual effusion.

COHOPH — is a Paracelsian term very often made use of in the sense of Cohobation. It is that operation by which the matter is frequently soaked in liquid, and the moisture subsequently removed by distillation. It is that also by which the vegetables are steeped in their own sap, and then are left, or caused to putrefy and corrupt in a glass or in the Balneum Marie, or else in dung, until it is possible to separate the pure from the impure. Also the separation of the sap from the substance.

COHOS — is whatsoever the skin covers in the whole body; and the allusion is to the chaos reduced into order by the divine power which comprehends and spreads over all created things, issued from the primeval chaos, even as the skin comprehends and spreads over the whole mechanism of humanity.

COLCOTAR — with Paracelsus, is properly fixed Vitriol, from which the phlegmatic part has been extracted by distillation until no moisture remains therein. It is also the serpent or green lizard, which devours its own tail. It very often signifies Caput Mortuum. Vitriol is made red in a simple way without cohobation. It is also called red or citrine Atrament. It is made red until it calcines. It is ironically called Red Henry, to satirise certain lying surgeons, etc., who pretend to treat all kinds of sores and wounds by means of this one medicament, and destroy rather than cure the sick.

COLERITIUM — is a Liquid composed of Corrosives which are destructive to metals. Gold is the only metal which can withstand it, and, accordingly, it is assayed therewith. It will demonstrate the existence of the minutest alloy of inferior metals.

COLICA ~ is a Pain in the Womb or Bowels, and is caused by tartar dissolved in the stomach.

COLIS ASSURGENS CIRCA MACHINAE CASAM ~ Heap of Rubbish.

COLLECTA, SYMBOLUM ~ Contributions to any expenditure.

COLLECTAM EXIGERE A DODLINIA ~ to ask contributions from the masters.

COLLIQUATIO, or **COLLIQUEFACTIO** ~ is the conjunction by an igneous melting of several fusible substances, molten into one composition.

COLOFONIA ~ i.e., Greek Pitch, Resin, or Gum at the Pine.

COLORATIO ~ or Colouring, by means of a Liquid Ingredient, is a method frequently resorted to. It is the liquid tinging. The substance to be coloured is made to drink, or to imbibe the colouring matter. It is performed in various ways, according to the quality of the subject, its texture, hard or soft, its degree of moisture or dryness, etc. Then also regulate the number of times that the operation must be repeated. It should be noted that there is a colouring of two kinds ~ when the whole substance of a thing is to be dyed, and when only an external coating is required.

External colouring concerns only the surface of a material, and is performed in many ways, the sides of the object being successively turned to the light when it is only required to tone down, or cause a fading in the actual hue.

Colouring by the heat of the sun is another method, made use of when it is required to educe a latent colour from potentiality into activity, or from the unseen into the manifest. It is serviceable also in arcane tinctures, such as invisible ink on paper.

Colouring by ablution is when dull, dusk, or obscure colours are washed with acid waters, and the colour is thus heightened and refurbished.

COLORITIUM ~ is a gradation of colour by means of a penetrating paste. It is a process for tinging, used principally with metals. It will not enter far below the surface, because of its grossness, unless, indeed, it be plentifully mixed with moisture, and thus formed into a thin slime.

COMBUSTIO ~ is Ignition, the reduction of bodies into Calx by burning. It is either
incineration or vitrification.

COMISDI ~ Gum Arabic.

COMFLEXIO ~ is the Nature of a Thing. It is the quality of Heat or Cold. According to Paracelaus the latter has a humid nature, the former a dry nature. There are therefore two complexions, not four. For the proper nature of things hot, when simple and unmixed, is always dry, and if such a substance should absorb humidity, it will be changed by the cold nature, and the latter will receive a dry quality from the former.

COMMINUTIO ~ The reduction of a matter into minute parts by the application of some kind of force, such as grinding, pounding, hammering, etc., The dessication or cribation of the substance will sometimes facilitate the process.

COMPOSITIO ~ is the Conjunction of Substances that differ. It is either mixture or conglutination.

COMMISSURIE SAXORUM ~ Fissures in the Stones.

COMPAS, INSTRUMENTUM ~ ? An Instrument with an Index.

CONCHA ~ A Glass Vessel in the shape of a trough or tub, with a mouth and a handle.

CONDER ~ i.e., Frankincense.

CONFIRMAMENTUM ~ The Stellar Body, or Astral Body of Man.

CONFORTATIVA ~ Tonics are Medicaments which strengthen the hearts and natures of man, and fortify the system so that what is hurtful cannot enter therein. This in a very eminent way is the method of all medicine, and herein consists the whole spagyric art. For nature is her own doctor : the man who bears the name of physician is only the minister of nature, and the servant of the true physician. If any one presume beyond this point, he is a molester of nature, and her destroyer. A tonic is that which strengthens man's nature and enables it to throw off accidental malady.

CONFUSIO ~ which is a pouring together, is a process for the commingling of liquids, which are naturally fluidic. Whether of the parts or of the whole, the consistency is aqueous, or fluidic. At the same time, there are many liquid substances which will unite readily without any methodical process.

CONGELATION ~ When the matter becomes thick and flows no more, but is instead tenacious, and stands firm, like ice upon water, then is the hard part broken, that all may become fluid and aqueous.

CONGELATIVA ~ are Medicaments which repress fluxes, and are of restraining and drying quality.

CONGLUTEN, or **CONGLUTINATUM** ~ That which by putrefaction turns into a lime or glue.

CONGLUTINATIO ~ is Composition by glueing or sticking together, the nature of the substances remaining the same. So also this is reduction, or integral restitution. Now, the nature of gluten varies, and the name is applied to any substance which by virtue of a tenacious viscidity joins one thing to another, or holds things together.

CONJUGIUM ~ is Copulation ~ the union of the man and wife. Some say that there are three kinds of it: the first of the spirit and the earth, the second of the ferment and the stone, the third of the medicine and of the subject. But here we speak at the commencement, when the red man approaches the white woman by means of the water. The conjunction is the copulation of the congealed spirit with the dissolved body, as Theophrastus states. When the blood of the Red Lion and the blood of the White Eagle are united, the Red Lion can become the White Eagle, and be one with it. The Red Lion becomes white in order that the white may become red. Secondly, they must be married alive; then the woman approaches the man; the man renders her fruitful; then they must be placed in the sealed bed, in order that the woman may not flee away, and, lastly, into the bath of the sea ~ that is, the black solution of conception. The matter suffers, the form works itself, making the matter like it; the matter desires after the form, as the woman after the man. The commencement of the union is the calcination; then the Mercury calcines and triturates the bodies; coition takes place when the matter begins to become white ; then the feminine seed coagulates ; and there arises from both a third substance. Then this loses its individuality, and commences anew.

Aristotle tells us that the true seed is a celestial and heavenly thing; it is possible to separate it, although it be indeed a separate and distinct power of life; for, when the matter of the seed enters, a living spirit doth also find s way therein. But the matter of the seed comes out, and then indeed a living spirit doth most assuredly find its way therein.

CONSOLIDATIVUM ~ is a Medicament which assists the formation of new flesh over wounds and ulcers.

CONSERVANTIATIA PHRYSICORUM ~ are especially Medicaments which preserve life and the body from corruption. They are to be sought for the most part in those things which naturally possess a persistent and long-living quality, which also have a tendency towards corruption ~ as perennial and evergreen plants in the vegetable world; in the mineral world, substances which possess an abundance of essential liquid; among metals, those which are least subject to rust and verdigris. That which sustains the health of men, and therefore wards off sicknesses.

CONSOLIDA AUREA SOPHIA ~ An Herb having leaves similar to hyssop, and circular ewers, like the Flammula of Paracelsus. It is also called Milkwort and golden Thalictrum. It is somewhat obscure and humble, it is not much down; but its virtues were familiar to Paracelsus. It is found in Carinthia and about the Danube, in Argentoria and other places, including parts of Alsatia. Note that this plant seems to be the same as wild honeysuckle.

CONSTELLATIO ~ *Supernorum astrorum in inferna virium et virtutum impressio operatio.* The influence of the superior stars upon things below, and the operation and infusion of virtues according to a natural and harmonic law. This doctrine is a combination of hermetic principles with the arcane theorems of Paracelsus, and is concerned with the impressions produced and the operations performed by the constellations of the superior stars acting on inferior things. It embodies a most excellent physical science concerning the signatures of natural objects and the sympathies and influences interacting between that which is above and that which is below.

CONSTRICTIVA ~ are surgical Styptic Medicaments which close up the mouths of wounds.

CONTERFEHE ~ Iliac Passion, bursting of the guts, a painful form of gripes.

CONTORSIO — Iliac Passion, burstig of the guts, a painful form of gripes.
CONTRACTIO — is Impotence, or deficiency of the virile members.
CONTUS — An Iron Tool.
CONTUS FERREUS — Pushpick.
CONTUS FOSSORUM — Crowbar.
CONTUS TERTIUS — A Trial Rod.
CONTUS UNCINATUS — A Tapping Bar or Matlock.
CONUM — i.e., the top of the alembic.
COOSTRUM — The middle of the Diaphragm.
COQUERE — To steep.
COR — Fire, or any great Heat. Among metals it signifies Gold.
COR FUFFLA — is the impurity of bodies.
CORALLUS, CORALLIUM, BASSAD, BESED, BASSATH, the Arabic **BELISIS** — are all names for Coral, and it was known to the Greeks as Gorgian, among other significations, on account of the fable that the substance originated from the head of Medusa. See Pliny, 1. 32, c. 2. It is also called CEeralium, Ciralium, and Curalium. It is to be distinguished from Coralloachates, a kind of precious stone or agate, which from its gold-coloured spots resembles Coral. See Pliny, l. 37, c. 10. True Coral is nothing else but a marine shrub, of which the nature is well-known, though many fables have been coined to account for its origin; among others that in the Fourth Metamorphosis of Ovid, where the legend of Perseus and Medusa is very prettily introduced to account for it. When Perseus concealed the head which he had severed from the Gorgon under twigs and leaves on the sea shore, it was found that the plants in question became hardened or petrified. In this state they were found by the sea nymphs, who scattered the twigs over the sea; and from their seeds we have Coral, which still

possesses the stony quality imparted to it by the head of Medusa.

According to Pliny and Solinus the stone Lyncurium, Lyncorion, or Lyncurinus, a precious stone, or, as some say, Amber, which some of the ancients believed to be formed from the urine of a lynx, congealed in the air, changes adorning themselves with gold. Solinus, in his eighth chapter, cites Methrodus and Zoroaster as his authorities, for I know not what fables about the virtues and potencies of Coral-how it protects against lightning, and those whirlwinds mixed with fire which are mentioned by Valerius Flaccus. Those who will may consult Serapion in his Lib. Agg., where it will be found that the root of Coral is called Nigem and Mergem, whereas the branches pass under the name of Bassath. Avicenna also treats of Coral, and both writers say that it is good for epilepsy, that it improves the blood, prevents bad dreams, and is generally a useful medicament. Other authorities signify other virtues, and experience itself teaches that red Coral has a whitening quality, and is most powerful in dispersing stone in the bladder. Pliny (1. 36, c. 19) says that Coral is called Pyrites, but it is not pyrites, nor any species of marcasite, but he seems to understand by the term any stone from which fire can be struck. Coral actually is a glutinous and humid viscosity of the earth which by its own heat and that of the sea is transmuted into a stony substance-that which has more aquosity being white-and that it is fashioned by nature after the manner of branches of trees. I have seen Coral specimens of immense size, and also true white Coral near the port of Tangra, which was undoubtedly formed of the viscosity of the earth, hardened by its own heat and by water. I have seen flints in the same place. As it is certainly true that the same things are at times made after different ways, so it is possible that coral may be produced not only by the induration or petrefaction of a marine plant, but also by a viscosity of the earth. We frequently find that lampreys, eels, and so on, are generated out of a viscous slime. They breed also by rubbing together, and so producing a sort of soft spume or froth. Finally, they breed by the ordinary fashion of depositing eggs. But enough of this matter. To return to our subject, Coral is made by art in imitation of Nature, and we find manufactured specimens which seem almost to equal, so closely do they resemble, the genuine kind. On this point the practical chemists may be consulted, and also as to the composition of counterfeit coral.

CORIUM TERRAE ~ Earth.

CORNELIUS ~ or more properly Corneolus, is a gem or stone found on the sea shore in Italy, and now also in Germany, where it is well known, as it is frequently set in rings. It appears to me to be, and so far as my knowledge extends, it is a species of jasper. But there are two kinds of Cornelian, one which is bright red, and another which is paler in its colour, for it approaches flesh tint, whence some say that it has its name of Corneolus. There is also a Cornelian with small white spots, another with white lines, yet another which is spread all over with a dusky redness, while some specimens are brilliant like vermilion. Its medicinal quality is to stop bleeding, to check menstruation, and hemorrhage. It is also said to assuage passion, and is a cleansing dentifrice for the mouth.

CORNU CERVI ~ is in chemistry the Beak of the Alembic. In Paracelsian medicine it is a healing herb for wounds, having leaves like the horns of a stag, with which it is connected by the doctrine of signatures.

COROCRUM ~ i.e., Ferment.

CORPUS ~ (1) The body is a metallic entity, wherein the virtue' of the Universal Spirit resides and fixes the spirits. That which is fixed is called a body. It is also called substance and ashes, because it is fixed. It also has a fixed Sulphur. It is, moreover, called Earth, Magnesia, Caba, Matrix, Key, Holy Virgin, the King's Crown, Talc, Glass, Spirit of Glass, Alum, Gum of Scotland, Sulphur Water, Lunar Froth, White Gum. For there are four bodies. (2) The bodies are not naturally dark, gloomy and black. When living they are bright, white and clear. A perfect body is ferment and tincture. The white is imperfect, the red is perfect. (3) The body is the earth which remains on the floor as dead. For the virtue ascends with the spirit. (4) The soul is the virtue of the body, which, being sublimated with the spirit, is the oil of the body. The spirit is the mercurial water which extracts and sublimates the soul.

CORPUS INVISIBILE ～ is the soul, so called because it holds a middle position between the visible body and the spirit. It is called a body because it participates in the qualities of a body, and invisible because it participates in the nature of an invisible spirit. These are physical and not theological definitions.

CORPUS PHYSICUM ～ is the subject of Nature.

CORPORA SUPERCOELESTIA ～ are those bodies which are known to the mind only by means of imagination, and not to the eyes of flesh. They are the subjects of wonderful spagyric operations.

CORROSIO ～ is a Calcination, reducing coagulated substances by means of corrosive spirits into Calx. It is either vaporous or immersive.

Corrosion by Stratification is performed by Calcination, when that substance which is to be corroded is arranged in any vessel, in alternate layers with corrosive powders. The matter is either cut into thin plates, or broken into conveniently small pieces.

Corrosion by Paste is performed when the thin metallic plates or fragments of stone, etc., are made into a kind of pottage or plaster. Hence this operation might be called a plastering.

The plates are set aside somewhere until the corrosion takes place. It is requisite that the pottage should consist of separate materials, such as salts or sour chalcanthum.

CORROSIVES ~ are Surgical Medicaments, by which callous and superfluous flesh is removed. They are also called Catharetica, Nemomena, Septica.

CORTEX AERIS ~ Flower of Copper.

CORTEX MARIS ~ Philosophical Vinegar.

CORUSCUS ~ The Ear of a Mouse.

COTICULA EXPERIRI AURUM ~ to assay Gold.

CRATER ~ A Kettle which is wide above and narrow beneath.

CRATICULA ~ A Grate, is an iron instrument consisting of four iron bars, about the thickness of a finger, with a breadth of about half a finger between them ; it contains the fire beneath the chemical oven.

CRETA ARGENTARIA ~ is Argentiferous Earth, in which the presence of the precious metal is denoted by small silver sparkles.

1. Silver Chalk-stone.
2. Good Drawing Chalk.
3. Hard Chalk-stone.
4. Soft Waldenburg Clay.
5. Tophacea.
6. In a hard violet-coloured Ash.
7. Blue, mined in Thuringia, used in colouring walls.
8. Hard Green.
9. Semi-green.
10. Soft Black.
11. Soft Black, with Argentiferous Sparkles.
12. Hard Black Chalk.

13. White Artificer's, of which the walls of Matrona in Catalan are built, and of which the port of Algiers is also said to be constructed.

CRETA NIGRA — i.e., is Black Sulphur.

CRIBRATORIUM — A kind of sieve, colander, or strainer. It is also Mercury. Senior (an adept) says: Strain it with the strainer, that is, with the top of the retort or cucurbit. Let it, otherwise, be threaded, for it cometh out like a thread. Also a Barrel.

CIBRUM — A Sieve.

CIBRUM ROTUNDATUM — A Copper-lined colander, having an iron bottom.

CROCUS AURICHALCUM — Yellow Bronze. Also Fire, with its companions, dried.

CRUCUS FLOS — Saffron Flower.

CRUCIBULUM — is a Melting Vessel, made of some earth which can absolutely withstand fire; it has a narrow base, and widens out into a round or triangular body; it is used for melting and liquefying metals. There is also a species of crucible which is vulgarly called a Cupel, and is adapted for melting metals.

CRUOR SALIS — The superfluous Saline Matter, separated from natural Salt in digestion.

CRUSTAE — Scales.

CRYSTALLUS — is a Stone congealed out of snow by the intensity of frost. It is certainly ice, because it cannot tolerate heat. Hence also its name. It is brought from the East, India, Asia, Cyprus, and the Alpine range. This is on the authority of Pliny (1. 37, c. 2), where he also cites the opinions of various authors as to its country, size, etc., also as to whether it is found in the earth, in pits, between rocks, and whether it is brought down by torrents. Certainly the white fluor which is found in our mines, and of which we have before treated, is, in all respects, similar to crystal. In the impassable

Alpine crags, where no ray of sunlight ever penetrates, it becomes of immense size. Nor is this wonderful. For the snow never melts, and it increases daily. Pliny says that six-sided crystals grow spontaneously. I have seen smooth and triangular crystals which have, perhaps, been so shaped by art. For as with electrum, so also with crystal, it is possible to prepare and cleanse it True crystals have many flaws. They are sometimes rough, sometimes have ruddy stains, sometimes there is a cloud in them, sometimes an internal abscess or tumour, etc. The pure and limpid specimens are called Acentala, that is, unblemished, by Pliny. Of these the best vessels and drinking cups are made, and it is a pride of luxury to make use of what perishes so quickly. When broken, there is no way of repairing or piecing together the fragments. For the rest, crystal has a medicinal use in consuming bodies. Placed under the tongue, it is said to quench thirst. Ground and mixed with honey, it increases the milk of mothers. It has other powers and uses. Consult Solinus on the crystal in, the twentieth chapter of his Polyhistory. It was referred by the old astrologers to the Moon. Chemically speaking, the crystal is a fragile stone made by a chemical congelation. The congelation takes place in such a manner that the aqueous humour is withdrawn, and the sap congealed, so that a stone forms, without any operation of manifest heat. If, however, a part of the moisture be evaporated, the work proceeds more quickly. There are many species of crystal.
1. The most pure Alpine Sexangular Crystal.
2. Translucid Sexangular Crystal of Bohemia, combined with Pyrites.
3. Mined in Misnia at the mountain of Cribenstein.
4. Impure Sexangular Crystal, of the colour of whey.
5. Shining with a yellowish colour.
6. Polished and shaped into various figures.

7. Combined and coloured with Cinnabar.
CUBIL ~ i.e., Red Earth.
CUCULATUM ~ i.e., Brandy.
CUCURBITA ~ is a Vessel shaped for the most part like an inverted cone. One form is globe-shaped at the bottom; another is flat.
CUCURBITA AGRESTIS ~ The Potato.
CUCURBITA COECA ~ A Vessel in which dissolutions of salts and other substances are thoroughly filtrated by vapour.
CULATUM ~ i.e., Calcined.
CULTELLUS ~ A small Knife.
CULTELLUS UTRINQUE ACUTUS ~ A two-edged Knife.
CUNEUS ~ A Wedge of Ore, cut into pieces.
CUNEUS FERREUS ~ An Iron Wedge.
CUNEUS SUSSCUS ~ Another species of Wedge.
CUNICULUS HABENS JUS POSSESSIONIS ~ A smaller species of Wedge.
CUNICULUM AGERE ~ To extract the live lode for working.
CUPEROSA ~ i.e., Burnt Copper.
CUPEROSUM ~ A Vein of Cuprine Ore.
CUPPA and **CUPPA PARVA** ~ A kind of round knob.
CUPRUM ~ i.e., Copper, Venus, Cancer.
CUPRUM KUBEUM INCOMPLETUM ~ Red Copper.
CURCUMA ~ is a yellow substance called Siradonia, in use among dyers.
CURTUMA, or **CURSUMIA** ~ i.e., Gold.
CURYATURA ROVE ~ Wooden Twist, Block.
CUTIS ~ Skin.
CYCIMA ~ Lithargyrum, Silver Litharge.
CYMOLEA, or **CHYMOLEA** ~ Sedge or Reeds.
CYMOLIA ~ White washed Ore, White Silver Litharge, Marl, or Fuller's Earth.

CYNNIA, CYMIA, CARORA ~ A Vessel shaped like an urinal.
CYNNABAR, ZINGIFUR ~ i.e., Cinnabar.
CYROENIA, CROCOMMA ~ i.e., Refuse of Oil and of Saffron.

DACH ~ A species of Rock.
DACTILETUS ~ is Meadow-Saffron, or Daisy. Also the timeless.
DAIB, DEHEB, DEHEHEB, DEAD ~ Names of Gold.
DANITI ~ A Weight of six barleycorns.
DANK ~ A Weight of six grains.
DANSIR, or **DENSIR** ~ is Sand.
DARAM ~ is Gem, jewel, etc.
DARAN, or **DAMATAN** ~ is Gama. [Unknown.]
DASAT ~ That is Lime, Birdlime, or Misletoe.
DAURA, HELLEBORE ~ Winter Aconite. Others say that it is Gold-leaf.
DEBESSIS ~ i.e., Tortoise-shell.
DECIMAR ~ is Lead, used for paying taxes.
DECUMA ~ Decade.
DECUMANUS ~ A tenth part.
DEGEGI ~ i.e., a Hen.

DEHEN – in Arabic, Zaic, or Zaich, is called Oil by every one, i.e., it is oil extracted from olives.
DEHENE – i.e., Blood.
DEHENES, or **DUENES** – i.e., Atrament.
DEHENEZ, DUENEC, DUHENEC – Names of Roman Vitriol.
DELIQUIUM – A melting or flowing down, is the cold bath or solution of the chemists. Any coagulated substances are exposed upon glass or marble slabs either in a cold chamber, a well, or in a chamber of frigid air, when the same bodies, by reason of the surrounding temperature, and by the aid of the external moisture, are resolved into liquid, and flow and distil into a vase beneath. Calcined Ashes, Salts, and bodies which are largely composed of Saline matter, are the most easily operated on in this way. But all bodies which melt in the cold can again be coagulated by heat.
DELIQUIUM IN AERE – Melting in air, is the Liquefaction of a concrete substance, which is accomplished by impregnating it with external humidity, dissolving its dry nature, so that the whole flows. The resolved matter is called liquor, and has an aqueous consistence. (Albeit, when, as sometimes occurs, limestones are dissipated by atmospheric or aqueous heat, this process is not called Equation, nor is that which results from it liquor.) Melting, or Deliquium, is of two kinds: Vaporous and Embaptic.
The Vaporous Process is that whereby the matter, having been educed into a subtle powder, is exposed to the decomposing action of the air, and is dissolved by humectation into liquor. This corrupting air is warmer or colder, according to the nature of the subterranean waters. And unless the thing is capable of being dissolved by itself, it is laboriously reduced to the nature of a Salt, or something of that kind, this being principally effected by calcination, or

by restoration to a dry state, which absorbs the external moisture with avidity, and is soon saturated. It is necessary to overcome the coherent tenacity, and to induce the crumbling quality of Salt.

The Embaptic Process is that by which the matter is immersed in moisture and kept there till it is melted. This is done in two ways. For the matter is either placed first in a vase, which is then immersed in the moisture in such a way that the moisture does not itself touch the matter, or it is gradually permeated by a very subtle sweat, such as would work through a vessel of wax, or an ox bladder, and is taken out when the melting is completed. This process, if the moisture be warm, as is frequently the case, serves the purpose of a bath. In the second method, the matter is wrapped in a linen cloth, or else, without any covering, is immersed in the same moisture. The liquid may be either cold, which answers for the dissolution of saccharine matter, sap, etc. In other cases, it is in need of heating, as is the case with manna, and those substances which have a tenacious, sticky fattiness or sap. The humour, which is the medium of the solution, should be of such nature that, if requisite, it can be easily separated again, and it should add nothing to what it dissolves, unless it is necessary that it should do so.

DEM, or **DEHIN** — is Blood of Man.
DEMENSUM — Slacking of Lime.
DEMENSUM DUPLICATUM — is Double Measure. Might be also a Two-edged Tool.
DEMETIRI — To Measure out.
DEMOTIVUS LAPSUS — is Sudden Death.
DENEQUAT — i.e., Borax.
DENODATIO — i.e., Dissolution.
DENS PILI — A small Vein. (In Mining.)
DENSES — Wedges.
DENTES AXIS — A Knob, Lift, or Tappet.

DENTES PILI ~ The Boundary of a Gorge.
DERSES ~ is the Secret Smoke or Vapour of the Earth, out of which every tree is born and grows.
DERUET ~ i.e., Vernix.
DESCENSIO ~ Distilling. Or ~
DESCENSIO ~ is the name of a process whereby a thing becomes less noble, as when the sun becomes Mercury. Afterwards we call it falling and refining, when the vapour again descends, so that the water drawn from the earth is again poured upon it. The sediment remains in the glass.
DESCENSIO, DESCENSION ~ is a process by which the subtler parts of any matter are caused to settle, or go down. It is warm or cold.
The Warm Descension (vulgarly, Distillation by Descension) is the distillation in an inverted vase of the liquor dissolved out of bodies. It is in this way especially that all kinds of trees, bones, and other substances, the liquor of which is too heavy to ascend, are dissolved. And it is done in this manner. I take a clay cucurbit, and place therein certain portions of the substances that are to be dissolved; and these, lest they fall out when the cucurbit is inverted, I cover with some bigger pieces, or sticks, transversely arranged. The preliminaries being thus dealt with, I fit another cucurbit, in which there is a little water, to the inverted one, in such a way that the upper one shall be exactly suited to the orifice of the lower; but, at the same time, between them I arrange a strong plate of iron of concave shape, pierced with holes, to receive the falling fragments, and prevent them from getting into the vessel below. Lastly, I encrust the firm structure with the best clay; I place the vessel in its furnace; and set the receiving vase in sand or ashes, so that, safe from the fierceness of the fire, it may receive most easily the deposited moisture.

DESCENSIO FRIGIDA — the Cold Descension is that process by which the liquor descends, being resolved in cold. This is Deliquefaction or Filtration.
DESCENDUM, or **DESCENSORIUM** — An Oven Or Chemical Furnace into which liquid goes down when separated from the gross matter.
DESCENDERE — is to Liquefy, or to Melt together.
DESCENDERE GRADIBUS SAXO INCISIS — To go down Steps cut out of a Rock.
DESERERE FODINAM — To Abandon a Mine.
DESTILLATIO — is Purging or Clarifying.
DESTILLATIO, DISTILLATION — is a process in which the essence is extracted in the form of a liquid, and is brought away condensed in the form of drops, from the vessel containing the matter, into a receptacle placed underneath. It is necessary that the matter to be distilled shall be resolvable into a moist condition, whether such moisture be added from without, or be inherent in it. Some matters are exceedingly vapourous, and some have oleaginous spirits. Hence if they are not naturally capable of distillation, they must be rendered so by art. Distillation has been invented chiefly for extracting essence, yet, at the same time, it serves for abstractions, purgations, and similar processes.
Distillation by Ascension is performed when the extract, before it is distilled, is sublimed into a kind of vapour. The operation should be continuous, from beginning to end, for if broken off at any point, that which is left can with difficulty be induced to ascend.
Distillation by Descension is performed when the moisture is drawn forth and distilled downwards without elevation.
Distillation by Inclination is when the vase containing the matter is inclined on one side, with the mouth downward. When the vessel used is a retort, as occurs often, the process

is called distillation by the retort. Sometimes also it is called distillation by descension, because there is a slight elevation, and afterwards a very strong reflux downward, or because the spirit is most urgently brought down again, and, without an alembic, descends coagulating in the bending.

DEVEXUM VEL DECLIVE MONTIS ~ The Declivity of the Mountain.

DIAMASCIEN, DYAMASSIEN, or **DELIATITEOS** ~ i.e., Flower of Copper.

DIAPENCIA ~ is the Plant Alchimilla.

DIAPHANUM ~ Any substance which shines transparently.

DIAPHORETICUM ~ Promoting Perspiration.

DIASATYRION ~ is a confection which excites venereal desire.

DIATAETIS ~ An Innate Art Or Nature.

DIATESSADELTON ~ is Precipitated Mercury.

DIENEZ ~ are Spiritual Essences which inhabit large stones.

DIKALEGI, DICALEGI, DITALEM ~ Names of Tin.

DILUTUM ~ Lye manufactured by means of Earth.

DIMIDIATAE ARMILAE FERREAE ~ Fang of a Windmill.

DIONYSIUS LAPIS ~ The Stone called Dionysius is a gem which takes its name from Bacchus, and is either black or dark ruddy, mixed or sprinkled with ruddy spots or blemishes. When rubbed, it has the flavour and smell of wine. It is said to check drunkenness, by dissolving and expelling the fumes which cause intoxication. A precious gem, concerning which consult Pliny (1. 37, c. 10), Solinus (Polyhist., c. 40), Albertus in his Lapid., and other writers.

DIPHRYGES or **TUTTY** ~ is divided by Dioscorides (1. 5, c. 69) into three chief species. The first is native mineral Tutty, which is found in Cyprus, and is extracted only in the form of mud or slime. A pit is made in the mud, and that which is taken out is allowed to dry in the sun, and is then burnt by means of lighted faggots placed round it. And it is hence called Diphryges, i.e., twice burnt. The native Tutty is in appearance not unlike Chalcanthis. It is a humour, like mud flowing through channels. It is believed that it is obtained only in Cyprus. However, a similar substance of yellow colour, approaching misy, is found in the caves of Goslaria. But it is not so shining, or so much like the colour of dry leaves. It comes from its own earth. It is occasionally utilised by surgeons. If it be Islebian Pyrites and not that fissile stone or slate which is called "Pig", it is certainly the first species of Tutty. There is also another species of native Tutty found in the pits of Islebia, and it is called Barleystone. So, if the matter be considered, we have two species of native Tutty.

The second species recognised by Dioscorides is manufactured Tutty, also of two kinds. The first is nothing but the dregs of Purified Copper, just as manufactured Molybdena (Lead Ore) is the dregs of Silver, as already shown. It is made at the same time as Flower of Copper, by the obfusion of water, and it is found sticking to the lower part of the furnace when the copper has been removed; it has the astringency and flavour of copper. For the rest, whether in our own day Tutty is produced at the same time as Flower of Copper, the coppersmiths may best be consulted. The other species of manufactured Tutty is obtained when pyrites is burnt in a furnace until it becomes red. Dioscorides relates that this species is by some affirmed to be derived only from copper ore which has been dried in the air and subsequently burnt in the pits. And this species is adulterated with burnt ochre. The adulterated and genuine kinds may, however, be distinguished by their taste. Tutty which has been burnt out of true pyrites or its substance, has the taste of copper and verdigris; it is astringent and drying to the tongue. On the other hand, burnt ochre has no such taste or virtue. Concerning these species of Tutty, consult Pliny (1. 34, c. 13). Serapion (lib. Agg. s. v. Diphrygis). Tutty is most useful in medicaments; it is astringent, purgative, eradicating, drying, consumes execrescences, and assists the healing of ulcers. But unfortunately nothing of the virtues of Tutty is known now to surgeons, nor is it included in the pharmacopia. To such a degree are things excellent contemned by the stupid. O that such like substances were again brought into use among our physicians! But I tell my tale to deaf ears.

The species of Tutty:

1. That which remains at the bottom of the furnace after the copper has flowed out.
2. That which is produced from consumed Pyrites. Slag from the furnace.
3. That which comes from burnt Copper Ore, otherwise from Cuprine Stone.
4. Mansfield Slate.
5. That which is deposited in deep vessels and furnaces.

DIGESTIO — A Change of any Substance into another by a process of natural coction.

DIGESTION — is simple Maturation, by which an uncooked matter is digested in a digestive heat. The true digestion is after the pattern of that process to which food is made subject in the stomach, a corresponding warmth which restores dissipated energy. So do things which are intractable become, by digestion, more apt and amenable to processes. And if there be anything present which is semicocted, it is brought to the condition of those which are perfectly digested, so that afterwards there may be more abundantly a harvest of essential virtue derived therefrom. This name Digestion is used sometimes for elaborations, and, in another terminology, it is called Maceration, also

Nutrition, as when slag was formerly said to be nourished, i.e., steeped (macerated) in vinegar. The coarse part or thick juice is, as it were, subdued, and made smooth; and not only does it increase in essence, but it can be easily separated from its inert dregs. For maceration has a certain penetrating, fortifying and cleansing power.

Digestion may also be described as a chemical operation, or process, by which any matter is ameliorated unto the separation of the pure from the impure. It sometimes stands for the glass vessel or furnace in which this magisterium is performed.

Digestion is, otherwise, Subtilisation, the dissolution of a crude matter in a digesting heat. It is also Putrefaction and Extraction.

Digestion is performed in the athanor by the filling of the turret of the athanor with coals to the top, kindling the fire in the furnace, and increasing the heat by the use of the poker, or the register, thus transmitting the warmth of the fire to the athanor. But after what rule this heat is to be conducted, when it should be diminished and when increased, the philosophers are not unanimous. Some contend that what they term the operation of nature should be imitated, and that it should be continuous and equable from first to last. Others would distribute it in grades, beginning with a white heat, passing to golden, and thence to a most deep red. To which view we ourselves incline, basing our opinion on numbers of authorities, and on many weighty reasons, and leaving its alternative to those who have originated it.

DISCESSUS ~ Discession, or Separation, is performed when the essential potencies of a substance are separated and disjoined by the action of solvent heat. This is done by exhalation and resolution of composites. Separation by the first process occurs when a component part is so attenuated that it passes into a spirit. And that is chiefly termed exhalation when a substance is liberated and set free into the air. When it is intercepted, the process is called Distillation, or Sublimation ; which operations serve sometimes in place of exhalation. There is exspiration, i.e., exhalation, from things moist and from things which steam.

DISCRETORES ~ Separaters of Ore.

DISCUS SOLIS ~ is Quicksilver extracted out of Gold.

DISPOLIARE ~ Dissolution of dead matter.

DISTILLATIO ~ Distilling, Humid Elevation, is that process by which the more subtle humid parts, elevated into an ethereal consistence, and collecting on the cold roof of the alembic, are condensed into moisture, and pass off in drops through a pipe, to be received in another vessel. It is performed after this manner The matter to be distilled is put into a cucurbit, of sufficient amplitude and not of less height (for the height occupies the artificers in vessels and the amplitude controls the height); thereupon is placed a great alembic, which easily receives the ascending spirit and resolves it into moisture. Afterwards, on account of the matter that is to be elevated, a fire is prepared, which shall be adequate to the business, and contiguous to the receptacle of the moisture which is to be treated. The latter, however, is to be well shielded at all points from the flame, which must be graduated until all the humidity has passed through the alembic. We may take an instance from vegetable substances. I fill a cucurbit a third part full of fresh roses, and place it in a cold water bath. Afterwards, I fill an alembic with the leaves of red roses, from which the useless thorns have been removed, and place it over the cucurbit; then I make a fire of the branches contiguous to the receptacle, and to the juncture of the vessels. The moisture ascending occupies the alembic; the tincture is extracted from the roses, and, condensed into water, distils rose-red into the receptacle. It is to be noted that, if the thorns are not removed, it is impossible for the water to have the pure rose-red tint. I keep up the continuous heat until no further moisture rises up, and the roses in the alembic have become white. I have cited this because of the artifice whereby the tincture is extracted from roses by their own moisture. This method of elevation is very much in use. For we avail ourselves thereof when we extract or elaborate anything by means of the bladder, as also when we elevate a substance by means of an alembic joined to a cucurbit.

Oblique Distillation and Elevation are performed when a moist substance is elevated in a vase inclined obliquely. This kind of distillation is also performed with a retort.

DISTRACTIO — is a Disintegration which takes place after two manners known as Separation and Calcination. The different constituents are separated, though each remains intact. It is a separation of things which naturally heterogeneous, and has nothing to do with disjoining substances possessing affinity for each other.

DISTRIBUTOR — A Divider.

DIVAPARATIO — is an Exhalation in the form of dry vapours, for the chemists have both a dry and humid spirit. The process is performed by various degrees of heat, and takes place in a vessel which may be like a boiling-pan, frying-pan, cucurbit, etc., according to the nature of the substance treated.

DIVERTALLUM — is Generation of the Elements-that which is produced from metals.

DIVINATION — is an uncertain Presage, or Prediction, which is interpreted by reflection after the judgment of a private light, as when it is said : My mind or heart for tells this and that to me; or : This the angel, my spirit, indicates.

DOAL — i.e., Sol. Called also Elemptis.

DOLET — i.e., Red Vitriol, or Red Atrament.

DOMICILIUM — is Brine, Salt held in Solution.

DRACATIUM — i.e., Saturn.

DRACO — is Mercury, also the Black Raven, or the Black on the Floor. It devours the tail, drinks the mercury. It is called Salt and Sulphur of the Dragons. It is the Earth from the body of the Sun. It is killed when it loses the soul [i.e., the earth is killed], and rises again when the soul returns. The Dragon devours the mercury, like a poison, and dies; again drinks it and is made living. If he puts off all impurities he becomes white and truly living. This is also called the Woman who kills her Husband, and is herself killed in return.

DRACONITES, DRACONTIAS, or **DRACHATES** — is a Precious Stone which Pliny represents (1. 37, c. 11), as also Solinus (c. 33), to be found in the brain of serpents, but unless it is removed while they are alive, it will never become a precious stone, by the inbred malice of the animal who, conscious of death approaching, destroys the virtue of the stone. Therefore the head is removed from dragons while asleep, and thus the gem is secured. The energy of the living soul is imparted to many things which the corruption of death in the humours impairs. The colour of the Draconite is white; it drives away all poisonous animals and cures envenomed bites. It is much affected by Eastern kings, for in the East there are many serpents. Our own Chelydrus and watersnake sometimes have gems in their heads, as I have myself seen; these may be called Draconites by analogy. Such stones may perchance grow from the brain, or, as others say, from the foam which these creatures make by rubbing one against the other in Spring-time; or again from the foam which they produce with their hissing, and which is hardened by the sun. I have seen pyramidal Draconites of this kind, both black and cerulean in colour. Albertus testifies that he beheld a Draconite taken from a serpent like our Chelydrus, which was of an opaque black, surrounded by a pale ring, and having a very beautiful outline of a serpent on the surface. These species also drive away venomous animals and heal poisoned wounds.

The Syphar, i.e., the Old Skin, or Slough, of our Chelydrus, has medicinal virtues. It wonderfully heals complaints of the posterior and falling of the womb, when these parts are fumigated therewith. Also the skin of the eft or lizard, which is very rarely found, because it is eaten by the animal itself (even as the peacock devours his own dung, which to man is so valuable), is good for the falling sickness.

DRACUNCULUS, CRASSATELLA, OPHIOGLUSSUM — are names of wild adder's tongue.

DRAGANTUM — the vulgar Zeg, is Vitriol.

DRAGANTUM, or DRAGANTIUM — is Spanish Vitriol.

DRAGANTUM — is a Gum; some say it is Vitriol. There are four kinds-Indian and Arabian, which are yellow, Cyprian, which is green. The fourth (terra Francisca), is black Atrament.

DUAMIR — A Medical Preparation, good against the bite of serpents.

DUBELECH — is a concave Abscess, generally running with matter.

DUBEL COLEPH — is a Composition of White Coral and Amber.

DUCTARII FUNES — Leading Strings.

DUELECH — is a species of Tartar in the human body, a Porous Stone, dangerous and very painful.

DUENECH — Azoth of the Stone; Green; then he begins to grow.

DUENECH — is Antimony.

DUENEGE — Green Vitriol.

DUENEZ, or DAENECK — i.e., Iron Filing.

DULCEDO SATURNI — is Altey, or Ceruse. White Lead.

DUNEQUER ~ Borax.

DURDALES ~ are Corporeal Spirits which inhabit trees.

DUO FRATRES ~ The two brothers, Saturn and Jupiter ~ Venus and Mars ~ Gold and Silver ~ Edar and Michati.

DUUMVIRI JURATI ~ Guards of mountain mines.

DYOTA ~ is a circulatory Vessel, having two ears or arms. The lower part is like a cucurbit, whereupon is placed an alembic, having a channel at the top, through which water can be poured. In a convenient place, there are curved beaks, conveying the condensed moisture from the top into the cucurbit. See sections which treat of the alembic and cucurbit. (It is to be noted that as in the ancient writings of Gebir, so here, these descriptions are hard to understand.)

DYOTRA ~ is a small perforated lath, or small wooden tablet, furnished with a handle, and pierced through the side, so that we can examine the condition of the work and of the fire, without injuring the eyes, by simply looking at them through this object.

EBEL — i.e., SALVIAS, i.e., juniper Seed.
ECHIDNA — i.e., Female Viper.
ECHIES CATULI — Viper's Whelps. The viper is a serpent which is known to us as the adder. It inhabits the neighbourhood of houses, and especially thickets near water. It is very accurately described by Nicander. Some things have been fabricated concerning the manner of its copulation. At the time of pairing the male viper puts its head into the mouth of the female, and so injects the seed. The female, whether conscious of her coming trouble, or moved by the pleasure which she experiences, or aware that the male is in the habit of committing adultery with eels, immediately bites off the head of her husband. Furthermore, the young, thus conceived, when they are conscious that the moment for their birth has come, tear their way through the womb of the mother, and enter the world by matricide. The viper is the only member of the serpent-tribe who carries the ova in the womb; the rest all lay their eggs in nests after the manner of

birds. Nor are these vain fables which we have just related. I have myself beheld a female viper which had been thus gnawed through by its offspring, and the young were lying about like earthworms in the open air. From this name of the viper is derived that of the echitis, or adder-stone, so called, either on account of its colour, or because its marks are not unlike the form of the adder. On this subject, see Pliny, 1. 37, c. 11 and Solinus, c. 40. The stone is a preservative against venomous animals, and the same virtue is possessed by the forked tongue torn from the living reptile. Also by the head when cut off and dried. So Nicander testifies in his Antidotes.

ECHIS — i.e., Male Viper.

ECLIPSIS — i.e., the Head of the Raven.

EDELPHUS — One who prognosticates by means of the Elements.

EDES — i.e., Gold of Elempius.

EDIR — i.e., Iron or Steel.

EFFIDES — i.e., Ash of Lead, White Lead.

EFFILA — Freckles, Spots caused by the sun upon the face, or other parts of the skin.

EGILOPS — i.e., Wild Oats, Straw, etc.

ELABORATION — is a Manual Operation by which the vital, inmost, and essential substance, or quality, of a matter is developed, and the whole nature is changed. Now-a-days, we term Elaboration that process by which we separate the ignoble, or worthless, portions of any substance, and most powerfully draw out whatever belongs to its essential part. Thus the separation of the pure from the impure proceeds quickly. Elaboration is either Solution or Coadunation.

ELANULA — is hard Alum, like Iron.

ELAQUIR — i.e., Green Vitriol.

ELECTRUM — is Amber, a Gum from a Tree.

ELECTRUM — is Gold, according to Pliny. It is Gold containing one part of Silver to five of Gold. It is called Electrum because it shines in the sun like the pure metal. It is found in mines, but is also manufactured.

ELECTRUM — according to Theophrastus, is a Metallic Composition containing all the metals attributed to the seven planets. Of this substance were made those bells of the ancients which were used to give the signal for the execution of male or female adulterers. Also it was used for the manufacture of drinking cups, which had the signal virtue that no poison could be placed in them. For the moment it was put there, a great bubbling or spluttering would ensue, as if nitre were thrown on live coals. Paracelsus relates that he was acquainted with a Spaniard who had a bell made of this metallic composition, and inscribed with strange signs and words. With this instrument the Spaniard could at will produce the apparition of spectres and kindred prodigies. Paracelsus makes out that the virtue mainly resided in the magical signs and characters, but supposing there was virtue in the characters, there was, doubtless, much more in the metal.

ELEMENTA — The Elements are the Matrices of Substances, and in and out of these are all things generated. For Fire, Air, Water, and Earth are the four Universal Matrices. Each of the four elements individually contains all the others. The more simple a thing is in its occult nature, the more general is it found to be by the adepts and spagyric philosophers, and by so much as it is particular is it found to be composite and material. For example: by so much the more that a species is removed from its essence, so does its substance approach the simple elements, and in like manner the form approaches the most simple, general, and universal influx or influence. It is not so in manifest nature, wherein special parts deteriorate and are inferior, by so much as they are removed from the universal part. This takes place because the principles of natural things contain all things potentially in themselves. Most true therefore is the judgment of the spagyric philosophers concerning the difference of occult nature from manifest nature, and vice versa.

ELEMENTUM ~ That which proceeds from the Matrices of the Elements.

ELEMENTUM PARACELSI ~ is the corruptible and transitory Essence of the World and all therein, which all suffer mutation and are a prey to anxiety and necessity, even until the last day and final consummation of the world. There is also the Essence of Spirits subsisting in a concealed manner in the elements; and these are the stars thereof.

ELEMPTIS or **EZEPH** ~ i.e., Sol.

ELEPHAS ~ is Aqua Fortis; it also stands for Leprosy, Elephantiasis, and the varieties of these diseases.

ELEPODATUM ~ i.e., polished, refined.

ELERSNA ~ The Manipulation of Silver, Silver Vein, Lead Vein, and this also is Molybdena.

ELESMATIS ~ Burnt Lead.

ELEVATIO ~ Elevation, is Rarefaction, when the spiritual portions of a substance are elevated from the corporeal portions, the subtle raised from the gross, the volatile from the fixed, in the form of a vapour, by the power of fire, and are condensed at the top of the vessel. It is either dry or humid.

Dry Elevation (vulgarly, Sublimation) is a process by which the subtler dry parts are elevated, with adherence to their proper vase. It is performed in the following manner: I take any material which is to be sublimated, whether by itself, or combined with other substances, and place it in any vessel of glass or clay which has a broad or round base, in such a way that the vessel is one-third full and two-thirds empty. Over this vessel, or cucurbit, I impose a blind alembic, perforated at the top by a small aperture. I make it fast, and cover it with clay, to prevent any escape of the spirit or sublimed parts. Afterwards I place it in a deep vessel, with three fingers' depth of sand at the bottom, and round the sides, or in an open fire, and increase the heat by degrees. In the first degree, it is necessary to remove all the moisture. I discover if this has been accomplished by placing over it a smooth iron plate. When any moisture remains it appears upon this plate, but when it has all been absorbed then the dry spirits rise up, and, on this account, I seal the mouth of the alembic with a sufficient quantity of good clay, and continue to graduate the fire, until all the matter which has to be sublimed is elevated. In place of a cucurbit some operators make use of a scutella (a square salver or waiter), or otherwise of a shell-shaped clay vessel, which contains the material, and over which a tight-fitting glass cone or helmet is imposed. Additional note: I take two pounds of the best purified green sulphur, five pounds of common salt, and five of Hungarian vitriol, which has been partly calcined; I pound them severally, place them in a cucurbit, and impose over it a blind alembic, perforated at the top; I kindle a fire of the first grade, until the moisture has disappeared, then, closing the orifice, I proceed by degrees until all the sulphur has ascended in a subtilised form. This sulphur (called flowers of sulphur by the chemists), taken out of the alembic in the second or third alternation, I rectify by adding a fourth part of salt and of vitriol, restored by sublimation, and obtain the finest flowers of sulphur, of use in many complaints.

The Humid Elevation (vulgarly known as Distillation) is the rarified sepa. ration of the moist parts into vapour away from the dry and crude parts. It is either direct or oblique.

The Oblique Operation is when the moisture is drawn out of a vessel which is bent on one side.

The Direct Operation is when the moisture is drawn out of a retort; either of these ways are useful in dealing with substances that give up their spirit reluctantly.

ELIDRION ~ is Mercury, like to Rha.

ELIDRIUM ~ is Gum Mastic.

ELIDRIUM ~ is a Preparation of Gold or Silver, which is produced from two parts of
silver and one of gold, together with one of copper.

ELIXIR, or **ELEI** ~ i.e., the Medicine. Elixir is an incomparable Medicine for conserving life and eradicating diseases. Or:

Elixir is a Ferment of which the smallest quantity will amalgamate a large mass of any generic substance, or substance with which it has affinity, into a confection like unto itself. Here the confection signifies the spirit of the life of man, and the internal balsam of life. It is that internal conserver which preserves the body in a fitting condition. Elixir is also an external balsam, extracted and prepared from external things into a Spagyric ferment. Or:

Elixir is a Medicine fermented either out of gold alone, or out of the seven metals. (A medicine made of gold or all the seven metals. It is like a leaven, of which a little lasts a whole day.)

Elixir is a species of diverse nature, composed of many species of simple substances, as, for example, when oil of terebinth is compounded with flowers of sulphur and oil of myrrh; when the quintessence of wine is mixed with tincture of saffron, etc. It is also called Elixir when the magisteria of vegetables are combined with mineral magisteria, essences, or other extracts, and composed into a homogeneous medicinal compound. Liquid Elixirs are, however, the most preferable, those especially which have the appearance of

Bezoardic waters, and other distilled compounds. It is to these also that the term is chiefly applied. Some writers distinguish Elixir from all other essences, because it is compounded of many substances, and is used for the preservation of normal health, for curing or preventing diseases, and for preserving bodies from putrefaction. Or: Elixir is the Ferment, the Leaven, the Dough, which is produced from Water. It is a Coloured Water, mingled with Bodies; it is also the White Stone, Olitet and Powder, for it is all one thing. It is also called the Treasure, First Matter; this is an imperfect Elixir. When it is perfect and ready, it is then truly a treasure. Lacinius says: Elixir is made of three things-Sol, Luna, and Mercury. But it must be of a moderate quality, between hard and soft — softer and more subtle than Mercury. Otherwise the gold that is made of it cannot be hammered. Out of the Elixir comes Azoth, and is the first part of the work. Therefore is the Elixir of two kinds-white and red. When it is red, one adds the ferment to it, and it is multiplied. Or:

Elixir, otherwise Xir: It is a subtle and penetrating Medicine, which is made and derived from things of vegetable nature- that is to say, from four spiritual essences, by the mediation of a certain body, and this body is the ferment of a medicine, or, more tersely, it may be termed a medicinal ferment.

ELOANX — is Orpiment.

ELOME — is Orpiment.

ELOPITINUM, or **DRAGANTUM** — Vitriol.

ELOS MARIA — i.e., Burnt Lead.

ELPIS — i.e., Recrement of Silver.

ELTZ — i.e., Flower of Copper.

ELZIMAR — i.e., Flower of Copper.

EMA — i.e., Blood.

EMATITES — i.e., Bloodstone.

EMBULA — i.e., is a Vessel like a reed.

EMUNCTORIUM — is the place through which the expurgation of corrupt matter or disease takes place. An outlet for corrupt matter.

ENDICA — is the Impurity, the Excrement on the floor. Morien says : Seek Endica in glass vessels, and shut it up till it begins to taste like vinegar, for you can do nothing while it is sweet. When this is applied to bodies and turned to earth, keep it that it may not burn, for when bodies lose their soul, then they burn easily. Endica is serviceable to all bodies, makes them vital and valuable, and prevents their destruction by fire. It is called also Mose Hazuania.

ENS — is the First Extract of Mineral Natures which have not yet attained their final perfection, and are richer in seminal virtue. Hence it is also termed First Matter, which is that principle of every genus out of which the first natural life-impulse derives to the substance of that genus, and possesses potency like unto it. The primum ens is to be sought above all things in the mineral world. For in this world there is a rich potentiality, not developed by Nature. In the vegetable world it is to be sought among plants which are still in the blade, i.e., still sprouting, and among unripe fruits. In the animal world, there is not much profit in seeking it, unless it be in the blood, or in the ova. The spawn of frogs and similar organisms are utilised for this purpose.

ENTALE — i.e., Vessel.

ENTALI — is Broken Alum, White Lead (Ger. Federweiss, a name given to several mineral substances), when it is melted from Cappadocius by the Spagyric Art.

ENUR — is the Arcane Vapour of Water, out of which stones are generated.

EPAR — i.e., Air, or Ether.

EPATUM — i.e., The Hepatic Aloe.

EPIPOLASIS — when a sublimed matter rises as far as the surface and settles thereon. Indeed, essences are drawn up first of all from the centre to the surface. But sometimes the same operation serves for repurgation. The process is of two kinds: Dry and Moist.

Moist Epipolasis is performed when the sublimed substance floats from the matter in the form of moisture, and emerges visibly at the top. It may be called Sublimation by Floating, or Emerging. It is assisted by the natural upward tendency of a light body, and by the disagreement of diverse natures. It is procured by actual and potential heat.

Dry Epipolasis is performed when the sublimed matter rises immediately from the thing itself, and coheres to it intimately in a dry state. It is performed in many ways, which are variations of heat-elevation, allowing an egress through the doors of the vessel.

EPOSILINGA — i.e., Iron Filing.

ERODINIUM — is an Omen of any thing or occurrence to come, which meanwhile is
hidden from man until it takes place. Afterwards, it is a certain Presage which signifies the recurrence of the event.

ERYSIPELAS — The Beautiful, the Clouds.

ESSARE — are small scabby Pustules, like bubbles, unless they have a fleshy swelling caused by burning.

ESSATUM POTENTIALE — The strength, power, and virtue which dwell in vegetable and mineral things.

ESSATUM VINUM — Herbs steeped in rectified and distilled Wine, so that it may draw out their essences. Such is Honey Wine, useful in asthma, and Pulmonary Wine, which indeed is the same thing.

ESCIRA or **ESTPHARA** — is black, Dead, or Bruised Flesh, which by means of a cautery or of corrosive medicament is removed from healthy and living flesh.

ESEBON or **ALSABON** — i.e., Common Salt.

ESSENTIA — Essence, is a simple Extract which contains the whole nature and perfection of the substances from which it is derived. And it is called Essence because originating and comprehended in the elementary divisions of Nature; it is the perfect part of every composite substance, and is informed with their virtue, nature, and essential quality. It can be extracted from every species of mixed substance, mineral, vegetable, animal, with great success. Essence is of two kinds : Sap, or juice, and Mystery. Quintessence is the bodily matter of all things wherein there is life, separated from every impurity, and most subtilely purged from corruptibilities. Therein is all the potency and heating quality of substances.

Quintessence is so called because it is something higher than the elements, nor does it originate from these or from what is gross therein, but is divine in source and in effect.

ESSODINUM — is a certain Presage of a future thing by means of a sign.

ESTHIOMENUS — is the complete Corruption of a Member, which is entirely eaten away, as takes place in lupus, consuming ulcer, St. Anthony's fire, etc., etc.

ETESLE — West, North-west.

ETHEL — is the Black, also the Fire.

The *Turba* says : Ethelia is the Burnt Body, parched and dry, red and white, fire and sieve, or riddle, which holds together the water of the Mercury. It is the red Tincture. It is also the white Blossom of Gold. They call it the boiling when the black mounts to the top.

ETHESIUS LAPIS — i.e., Chrysolite. ETHEEs-Precious Gold.

EVENTILATIO LINTEAMINUM JACTATUO — The Purification of Linen by Shaking.

EVESTRUM — is the Eternal Substance of Heaven in the regions of the four elements. It is also the Prophetic Spirit which forecasts by the interpretation of those signs which go before events. It is also the Sidereal Body of Man whose apparition foretells to us our approaching death or some other evil.

EUXOXORUS — South-east wind, or S. by S.E.

EUXUS — Middle South-east, i.e., S.E. wind, or wind generally.

EYEB, EFFEBEB, FILON — Names of Gold.

EXALTATIO — i.e., Sublimation.

EXALTATION — is an Operation by which a Matter is Altered in its inclinations, and is elevated to a higher dignity of substance and virtue. It is twofold-Maturation and Gradation. Or:

EXALTATION — is rarefying, the gradual transmutation of a substance, by dissolving into a purer and higher degree of its own virtue. It is done by circulation or ablution.

EXCOQUERE — To Smelt.

EXCOCTOR — A Smelter.

EXCREMENTA — Excrements, are in general all Superfluities that are Ejected by Nature. The excrements of women are the menstrua.

EXHALATIO — Exhalation is performed when dry spirits are caused to depart upwards into the air by the operation of heat. It is accomplished chiefly in dry substances, which have been triturated, and placed upon iron tables, or in deep flat vessels, or at the bottom of ovens, etc. The matters are heated by a fire from below, around, or above, until the spirits are consumed, as happens in metallic veins.

EXSILERE — To spring out of.

EXITURA — Refers in general to all kinds of Abscesses which exude matter.

EXORCISTA — A Superstitious Operator who evokes shades and spirits by adjurations, and causes them to appear.
EXPERIRI VENAS — To Assay.
EXPRESSIO — is Extraction by means of a Press (e.g., wine-press) which causes the substance of a thing to flow out in the form of liquid. Its chief use is for extracting oils and juices.
EXTRA ORDINARIA OPERA — Work done in overtime.
EXTRACTIO — Extraction is Digestion, a process subsequent to the separation of the recrement, dissolving, by corporeal concretion, the subtler and purer parts of a given substance. Thus I take any quantity of rhubarb, and, having pulverised it, I pour thereon sufficient spirit to cover the substance and float over it to a height of four inches. I then seal up the vessel and for the space of four days digest the matter in a bath. At the end of that time, I open the vase, and separate the root from the tinged spirit by inclining the vessel on one side. I again pour spirit upon the matter; again seal and digest it, and repeat this process until the spirit is no longer tinged by the rhubarb, from which all the tincture and essence is now extracted. I combine the extractions together, and abstract their spirit in the Balneum Maria; the essential residue I reserve in a glass vial for future use; it is good in bilious complaints and in other affections. Or: Extraction is the Separation of the Essential Part from its body. It is really a similar operation to the disintegration of composite substances, and has affinity with calcination, melting, etc. Moreover, the essential nature of any matter cannot be extracted without a continuous dissolution. For the rest, extraction and its connected operations are often interchangeable.

Extractum, or the Substance Extracted, is that which is separated by corporeal concretion, the elemental grossness being left behind. It is a species of marrow, the most noble portion in the elements of an entire substance being educed, the seminal potency being conserved therein, and a still higher virtue being elaborated. There is a fourfold root of the elements, between which there is an intimate intercourse and a collateral nourishment continually interchanged; the chief sustaining power being at the same time derived from the power of the creating God, and the secret influence of heaven. This extract puts on the nature of ethereal and celestial things, and when it has been thoroughly and skilfully prepared, it can perform great works in medicine, which are very serviceable to the health of man, and for which God be blessed 1 When it is fully and perfectly liberated from its elements, or matrices, for the fourfold root is of unequal quality, and elaboration must be performed upon each, it differs in a special way from magisteries, wherein the elements still persist. When an extract is thus carefully educed, the subtlety of its essence endows it with a great power of penetration into the substance of bodies. It has received many appellations, which must all be understood as referring to this full and perfect extraction of elemental property. Such are the Soul, the Balsam of Life, the most Pure Essence, the Celestial Nature, and indeed it has a certain quality of heavenly being. It is also the Second Matter, which is produced in the separation of the celestial light, the pure Transcendant Ray of the Arcane Philosophy, from the obscure earth, which is reprobate and accursed. It is the Aethereum of Plato, and the active Manifestation of Heavenly Power and Virtue in the bodies of sublunary or inferior things.

EZEZICH — i.e., Salt.

FABA ~ The Third Part of a Scruple and Gram.
FABA AGRESTIS ~ i.e., Horse-Bean.
FABIOLA ~ Bean-Flower.
FACINUM ~ i.e., Metal, Ore.
FALCANOS ~ Otherwise Arsenic; vulgarly Orpiment.
FASCES VIRGULTORUM ~ Bundles of Twigs.
FASDIR, or **SASDIR** ~ i.e., Tin.
FASSIN ~ A Matter which flows out when Stones are Melted.
FATUM ~ The permanent imperceptible Influence of the Stars of Heaven, the Sun, and the Moon.
FAULEX ~ i.e., Steel.
FAVONIUS ~ The West Wind.
FECES ~ Capt Mortuum.
FECES CANDIDAE ~ i.e., Ruby and Saffron Waters.
FECLA ~ i.e., Dregs of Wine, or of Vinegar.
FEDUM ~ i.e., Saffron.
FEHLECH, or **FAULES** ~ i.e., Iron. Called also Falex.

FEL DRACONIS — is Living Silver extracted from Steel.
FEL VITRI — is Froth of Glass.
FELLA — is Sulphur Water.
FEMINA — i.e., Sulphur.
FERMENTATIO — The Exaltation of a Matter into its essential part by means of a ferment which penetrates the entire mass, and operates therein in a peculiar manner, acting immediately on the spiritual nature. Thus, it is found that out of an agent of medicinal fermentations which is of little symbolic value, the most noble substance is produced which nature suffers us to attain. But it exists much more abundantly in metals, the nature of which is more akin to it. It takes its name from its likeness to a fermented mass. Or: Fermentation is the incorporation of a fermenting substance with a substance which is to be fermented. For even as a small modicum of ferment, or yeast, can leaven a large mass of flour, so does the chemical ferment assimilate itself to the thing that is to be fermented. Whatsoever be the nature of the ferment, of such is the fermented matter. By ferment the philosophers understand a true body and a true matter, which, united to its proper Mercury, convert it into the nature thereof. Some will have that the stone itself is the ferment of a perfect body. For when the stone is so subtle, as the philosophers term it, that when it is projected over an imperfect body it floats after the manner of an oil, without combining therewith, we need some other body, which still retains traces of its former affinity therewith, which shall receive and introduce it into other bodies.
FERMENTUM — is Elixir, a Leaven, which makes the body spongy, which ascends, and the spirit finds place, so that it may be prepared to be baked, since now the meal is no leaven, and the meal and the water and the whole dough are thoroughly leavened, and indeed mere leaven, therefore also

is the stone itself the Ferment, yet are gold and mercury also called Ferment.

2. Hermes says: Ferment displays the work, otherwise nothing comes of it.

3. Gebir says (*L. Form.*, c. 19) : Resolve Sun and Moon into dry water; this is what is called Mercury. Also the twelfth part of the water holds a part of the perfect body. After forty days you will find the body resolved into water. The sign of the complete dissolution is the blackness which appears above, and is our Mercury, which we take for a Ferment.

4. The Paste which we wish to Ferment, which we extract from imperfect bodies, the white out of Saturn and Jove, the red out of Mars and Venus; but every body shall be dissolved in its own ferment.

5. The English Richard says: Take white Ferment, but for the red take red; nevertheless, the red can give white.

6. Gebir says: After the fermentation, it must be shut up; thus the material is brought to the white stage in forty days; to the red stage in ninety days; in one vessel and operation.

7. Lully says: The ordinary gold cannot be a Ferment, for it must have an actual, effectual, and working power, and be full of spirit; yet it is also called Ferment, and silver is called White Ferment. Or:

Ferment is a firm, and, as it were, a fixed matter, which prepares a substance after its own nature to become of its own fixed condition, which also before it was prepared had itself no greater fixity ; as, for example, Ferment of Bread is flour condensed into a paste which will also communicate the fermented state to other flour.

FERMENTUM ALBUM, or **FELDA** — is Silver.
FERRAMENTA — Plate of Hammered Iron.
FERRAMENTO EXPOSITA — Another Mining Instrument.
FERRAMENTUM PRIMUM — A Mining Instrument.

FERRAMENTUM QUARTUM ~ A Miner's Wedge.
FERRAMENTUM SECUNDUM ~ A Pitching Tool.
FERRI SCOBS ~ Iron Filings.
FERRUGO ~ Rust, Must, Iron Mould, or Scoria of Iron. Iron Refuse.
FERRUM ~ Iron, is a Metal, for the most part, of a livid colour, but having also a certain quality of redness and a kind of impure whiteness, while it is also hard in texture. If fixed, earthy sulphur be mixed with fixed, earthy quicksilver, neither being pure, but partaking of a livid whiteness, and if the sulphur predominate, then iron results. In fine, if the quicksilver be porous, terrene, and impure; and if the sulphur be also impure, fetid, and terrene, then their copulation produces iron. This metal is attributed to Mars by the chemists, and is so called, because of its many uses in war. By some the stone Sideritis is called Iron Filing, or Scale of Iron, and the magnet, which attracts iron, sometimes has the same name. Now, iron is of two kinds, native and melted, or excocted. The native is pure, and is found in mines, either in grains or nuggets. The second species is that which is produced in the forges of Germany after one of two manners: either from iron ore, as it is in a certain valley which takes its name from Kings, and in a number of other places. It is to be noted that the same veins which produce iron frequently produce loadstone, which has affinity with iron. Iron is also melted out of ruddy ferruginous earth, among other places, in Silesia, where I have myself witnessed the process in a foundry not far from Berlin, and am in a position to affirm that, even as some Pyrites is hard, solid, and close of grain, while other is brittle, and easily pounded, so also some iron ore is solid, and requires much melting, while some is brittle and like a rusty corroded earth, which can be operated on with little fire, as is the case with the rich ore of Silesia, and the earth of Marchia and Nicia. There are

also very ancient mines of iron which were worked, as Tacitus informs us, by the Goths of Gaul. In Germany the first mines worked were those of iron. For the rest, concerning what iron is good and what bad, I refer to the smiths. If I mistake not, in Thuringia the Dylmeratian species is commended, while that which is derived from a vitreous ore is condemned for its brittleness. On the varieties of iron and its metallic alloys, consult Pliny (l. 34, c. 14, 15, etc.), and Dioscorides (1. 5, c. 46), who treats of Iron Rust and its virtues. Iron rust has a powerful, restringent, medical quality, and is also binding and drying. It is warm and dry in the second degree. With it Hercules is said to have healed the wound of Telephus, to which occurrence an allusion is made by Ovid in his first elegy: " Either no one, or Achilles only, who inflicted the wounds, can heal me ". Dioscorides also (l.c.) treats of Recrement of Iron, or Iron Slag, which he also calls Scoria and Excrement of Iron, or the Stone Sideritis, the German Thunderstone (Arolite). For even as all the higher metals yield recrement when melted, so also does iron. Thus we have:

Recrement — of Copper:Copper Slag; of Silver: Silver Slag; of Iron: Iron Slag; of Lead: Lead Slag.

Recrement of Iron has the same kind of virtue as Rust of Iron, but it is of less efficacy. This will apply also to that broad and thin scaling of iron which is obtained by hammering. For the rest, on these subjects, consult the Arabian writers, Serapion, and also Nicander, who calls Scoria of Iron by the name of Iron Feces, and says that it is an antidote to Belladonna, which Dioscorides appropriates after his usual fashion.

1. Pure Iron of an iron colour, found in seams in a white flint.
2. Pure Naricum Iron, found in river sand.

3. Liver-coloured Iron-stone, mined in Franconia, and containing particles of purest Gold.
4. The same, from the same place, but containing particles of purest Silver in place of gold.
5. Combined with Loadstone.
6. Solid, pure, heavy, liver-coloured Iron, found in seams of Gishubelia.
7. Liver-coloured Iron in grape-like clusters.
8. Liver-coloured Iron in White Flint, so combined that it is like Leucostic Marble.
9. Cuprine seams of Iron.
10. Mixed with Cobalt.
11. Containing White Lead.
12. Spongy, liver-coloured Iron, from a rich iron ore.
13. Containing White Lead.
14. Seams of Iron in a fissile stone.
15. Best liver-coloured Iron.
16. Iron of Norica, extracted from ferruginous water.
17. Iron of Sagana, in Eastern Germany; when the iron is removed from the ore more metal is produced.
18. Black, hard, heavy Iron Nuggets, shaped like the human head.
19. Iron obtained from a mine in that district which lies between Hoenicha and Veterocella.
20. Iron combined with Ochre, mined between Francoberg and Chemnic.
21. Black, hard Iron, similar to Gagates, and as if composed of many fibres, originating from one clod, and being of a saffron tint, owing to a certain terrene exhalation.
22. Iron of a normal colour, with a black tinge derived from a hot vapour.
23. Cloddy Iron, of normal colour, similar to Gagates, covered with a black stratum. Light-grey Ironstone.
24. Ashy, similar to thin stalks.

25. Like Hematite.
26. Combined with mud or clay.
27. Botrytis, i.e., in clusters like grapes, black in an ashen deposit. Like pellets of Gagates, black in colour, and surrounded by white floors.
28. Containing a sterile Plumbago.
29. Containing Mica.
30. Containing gold-coloured Pyrites.
31. Combined with sterile Lead, similar to sterile Pitch.
32. Iron that has been melted out.
33. Living Iron of Pliny; Iron tinged with magnetic virtue.
34. Burnt Iron Ore.
35. Washed Iron Ore.
36. Best Iron of Norica, melted out from a coagulated slime in a ferruginous water.
37. Slimy Earth, from which Iron of Norica is melted out.
38. Ilmenanum Iron, melted from a chestnut brown earth.
39. That which is melted from a ruby-coloured ochre. Hepatic, Copper ore.
40. That which is melted from old mounds of Iron.
41. Melted from cuprine recrements, which remain at the bottom of the caldron.
42. Hard, the pure part which remains at the bottom of the vessel, and is extracted with difficulty.
43. Hard.
44. Tenacious Suevian Iron.
45. The best Iron-that which comes to the surface in smelting.
46. Full of fissures. Slatey Iron.
47. Iron changed into Steel by continual extinction.
48. Iron from which recrements are removed. Iron Ashes.
49. To which Steel is added. Iron made into Steel.
50. Ductile Iron.
51. Brittle Iron.

52. Small Sticks of Iron.
53. Plates or Shavings of Iron.
54. Iron Wire.
55. Iron Filings.
56. Iron Rust.
57. Polished and so prepared by art that it does not rust.
58. Polished Iron.
59. Gilt Iron.
60. Overlaid with White Lead.
61. Silvered Iron.
62. Coloured Iron. Atramental Water, coloured like copper.
63. Iron naturally changed into Brass in the Spring of Cepusius.

Black Recrements of Iron:
1. Ashen.
2. Cerulean.
3. Smith's Recrement.
4. Given off from a hot Iron mass, when it is compressed and kneaded into a mass by a mallet.
5. Shavings of Iron which are given off in the making of iron bars, shaped by large mallets.

FERRUM INDICUM ~ A species of Iron which most nearly approaches Steel.
FERRUM SIGNATORIUM ~ A Stanchion.
FERU, or ZEGI ~ is Tin.
FERVERE ~ To Boil.
FEUSTEL ~ A kind of hammer or mallet.
FEX VITRI ~ i.e., Vitreous Salt.
FEXA ~ is the Scum or Lees of the Germans. But we always understand it to be the Dregs of Wine, as Dioscorides teaches (1. 5, c. 79). He adds also Dregs of Vinegar, and describes how it is dried by fire and in other manners; he refers also to its medical potency, which is abstergent and heating, and the various properties of the crude, burnt and

washed species. Consult Serapion (*I. Agg.*, c. Haarim.). Concerning indurated wine dregs, consult Paulus, De Tartaro.

FIBULA FERREA — An Iron Buckle, a Cramp Iron. A Triple Band.

FIBULAE — Clasps, Braces, Buckles, Bands, etc.

FICUS CUTIS — Lichen of Pliny and Dioscorides, a Wart or Swelling on the knee of a horse, a good Medicament for the matrix.

FIDA — i.e., Gold or Silver.

FIDDA or **FIDHE** — i.e., Luna.

FIDER or **FIDEX** — i.e., White Lead, Ceruse.

FIDO — i.e., Quicksilver, sometimes Gold.

FIGERE — To make Fixed, so as to withstand Fire.

FIGURA DISCI — Eye. (The Centre of a Circle.)

FILLETIN — i.e., Plates of Iron.

FILIUS — i.e., the Son, the Child. According to Morien it has a father and mother, by whom it is nourished, and is one with them, yet where the chicken is not hatched and born it dies in the egg, just as bread which is sufficiently baked, and soap which is sufficiently melted.

2. When he is born, he wants food and nouruishment. The nourishment is the augment. When the material is nourished by means of the ferment, then the child becomes a seed again.

3. The Stone is at first the old man, then young; then the strength and working is like those of youths full of blood and fighting power. The aged are grey and white. At first the Egyptian is moist and white, afterwards red and dry. Therefore it is said: The son killed the father; the father must die; the son must be born; die with one another and so rise again, according to the saying: He who dies with me must live with me. The Sun kills the Mercury and hardens it.

4. His nourishment is first in the bath or in the matrix of the earth, which receives and nourishes until body and soul become one thing, and of a fixed nature. Bernard says: The feminine germ nourishes the Stone, not by dissolution but by addition, thereby it grows strong and great.

5. *Turba* (fol. 89): Take the white tree; build about it a round and gloomy house; surround it with a tower and put therein a centenarian. Then shut it up so that no wind or dust can get to him. Leave him there eight days. I say to you that the same man must not cease to eat of the fruit of the tree until he grows young again. O what a wonderful quality! Here is the father become a son, and born again.

FILIUS UNIUS OSTUM ~ is Vitriol or Orpiment. It is also the generated Stone which is eaten. It is, moreover, the Mercury which destroys the son or the father.

FILTUEN ~ To Clean through a Colander; to Strain.

FILUM ARSENICALE ~ i.e., Sublimed Arsenic.

FILUM EX ALUMINE PLUMOSO ~ Virgin Thread.

FILIUS UNIUS DIEI ~ Son of a Single Day, is the Philosophic Stone.

FILIUS UNIUS OSTUM ~ An Egg.

FILIUS VENERIS ~ i.e., Brass.

FILTRATION ~ is Subduction by Filtration in a Colander; but this process in the chymical filter may be also called Straining, or Percolation; it is performed chiefly in operation upon moist substances, from which the aqueous part passes through the colander, and those which are oily or thick are left behind. The practice is principally this. A sheet of commercial paper [carte emporetica], or a rough basket, is shaped into the form of a bag, or applied to the vessel, after the manner of a funnel, etc. The infused liquid passes out by degrees, to be distilled into its receptacle, whence this operation is called Distillation by the Colander. Or:

FILTRATION — is a Frigid Descension, the aqueous portions of the matter treated, passing through the colander, or filter, or funnel, etc., the refuse being left behind. But, in place of the filter, some employ other instruments, especially the chemical glove, woolen bag, flax bag, etc.
FIMUS EQUINUS — Horse Dung.
FIOLA — A Glass with a long neck.
FIREX — i.e., Oil.
FIRFIR — i.e., Ruby Colour.
FIRMAMENTUM — i.e., Lazurium.
FISARUM — i.e., Confection of Sal Ammoniac.
FISSURAS AGERE VEL ADIGERE — To dig Trenches.
FISTULA — i.e., either a Fistulous Ulcer, or a narrow reed-like Opening, Pipe, or Channel.
FIXATION — is an operation upon a volatile subject, after which it is no longer volatile, but remains permanent in the fire, to which it is gradually accustomed. It is performed by calcination, or by slow decoction, taking place daily, or by frequent sublimation and coagulation, or by the addition of a fixed matter.
FIXIO or **FIXATION** — To make Firm, to Solidify.
FIXIO — Making Firm or Tenacious.
FLAGIE — are Spirits who divine the Secrets of Men; invisible, and yet concealed among us; ever present in our words and works.
FLAMMULA — Crowsfoot.
FLEGMON — Common Abscess.
FLORIFICIREN — Flowers, or the production thereof.
FLOS — is **BOLUS** (which see), extracted by sublimation. It is also elevated and produced from the centre and inmost parts, that it may coagulate in a dry form at the top. The spirituous Flos, or Flower, is the substance of a thing. Every flower of a matter is in itself volatile and spirituous,

although it is possible to fix it by a masterly skill, and to bring it to the nature of Turbith (which see).

FLOS AERIS — Verdigris. Flos AEris is the coagulum, the spirit of the male essence which works upon the female essence; the masculine spirit which completes the work.

FLOS CHEIRI — i.e., Essence of Gold.

FLOS SALIS — is the Greek Alasanthos. Fine Salt.

FLOS SECTOREM CROE — Some say that this is Saffron Flowers. It is a substance mentioned by Paracelsus, and there is supposed to have been a mistake in his manuscript. For myself, I understand it to be the Flower of Moss-nut [? Florem muscatce nucis. Red Emuscata.] Others suppose it to be Flower Extract of Celandine.

FLOX — i.e., Flame.

FLUORES — are Stones similar to gems, but less hard. They are called Fluors by the metallurgists, because they melt and flow under the heat of a fire, even as ice does in the sun. But there are also species which dissolve under the influence of a spirit, and of the air. Theophrastus, if indeed he is referring to these things, calls them *** [Greek], because they are produced in a terrene flux. But I believe that they were unknown to all the ancients. In order that the various species may be better known, we subjoin them in the interest of the student. Fluors are the rudiments of gems, and like unto the same in appearance; they are found in mines and are:

1. Of red colour. At first sight this kind is like rude reddish silver, or carbuncle, but it is of less effulgence. Also the carbuncle withstands fire, whereas the Fluor melts immediately under its influence.

2. Of pale purple colour. This kind is at first sight like pale green amethysts, such as are found in Bohemia, and certainly are not very different from these. As uncritical persons are deluded by the similarity they are unable to

judge amethysts. They are unlawfully set in rings and sold as the genuine stone.
3. Of white colour, looking like crystal.
4. Of clay colour, looking like topaz.
5. Of ashen colour.
6. Of semi-black colour. But there are also Fluors of other colours, if we look closely into this matter. It is the custom, when metals are smelted, to treat them and cast them in. The material is restored in a more fluid state, even as with the kind of stone out of which pyrites is made. If the experiment were made, I consider that the best colours would be obtained from Fluors thus treated.

Red Fluors:
1. Showing ruddy in white, sexangular, and pellucid.
2. Long red Fluors, like an upright beam, whence are obtained those small black stones from which White Lead is obtained.
3. Pyramidal quadrangular and sexangular Fluors.
4. Sexangular Fluors, showing ruddy in white, like the sea-urchin.

White, transparent Fluors:
1. Long, white, pellucid, sexangular Fluors, like crystal.
2. Long, white, pellucid Fluors, in the middle of which is a small black stone, from which White Lead is made.
3. White, pellucid, sexanguar Fluors, like a straight beam, such as Misenian Bisalt.
4. White pellucid, quadrangular Fluors, like adamant, adhering to a red metallic marble.
5. White, pyramidal Fluors, transparent at the top, in a white metallic rock, which are overlaid with saccharine matter, like grains of coriander in appearance. They also contain bright particles, as it were, gold-coloured pyrites.
6. Long, white, pellucid, sexangular Fluors, in white, aqueous plumbago and pyrites.

7. White, pellucid, quinquiangular Fluors, in a hard metallic rock.
8. Long, white, pellucid, sexangular Fluors, in an argentine mica.
9. White, pellucid Fluors, as it were, composed of scales.

Ashen Fluors:
1. Long, ashen, sexangular, transparent Fluors, in a hard, ashen stone, like the sea urchin, interspersed with silver-coloured grains of pyrites.
2. Semi-ashen pyramidal Fluors.
3. Tessellated semi-ashen Fluors.

Black Fluors:
1. Square, and not transparent.
2. Very black and multiangular-not unlike the black stones out of which White Lead is excocted.
3. Cloddy, and like dark, glossy bitumen in appearance.

Blue Fluors:
1. Blue, pellucid, quadrangular Fluors, like sapphire.
2. Non-pellucid.

Purple Fluors:
1. Of the colour of amethyst, found in a stone at Trebisa.
2. From the Geodes (a kind of valuable stone), found at Motschen.
3. Showing red in white, and found in a metallic marble.
4. Quadrate Fluors, in a hard, white mica.
5. Quadrate, pellucid Fluors, covered with silver-coloured pyrites.
6. Non-pellucid, from which Chrysocolla (or Borax) is derived.
7. Purple Fluors, combined with green layers.
8. Blood-coloured Fluors of Aldenberg, white inside, outwardly coloured with metallic water.

Scarlet Fluors:
1. Of scarlet-colour, pointed and sexangular.

2. Long, non-pellucid, scarlet, sexangular Fluors, with white, cloddy Fluors, like the sea-urchin; adhering to it is a very beautiful native Ochre.

Yellow Fluors:

1. Long, whitish-yellow, sexangular, pellucid Fluors, in a metallic marble.
2. Yellow, transparent Fluors, with a grey metallic marble, in which there is a sexangular stone containing Lead.
3. Tesselate, transparent Fluors, with silver-coloured pyrites, in a simple grey stone.
4. Solid Fluors, white on the upper surface, and, as it were, sprinkled with large grains of salt.
5. Yellow, Hanoverian, pellucid, crusty Fluors, like the mirror stone.
6. Pellucid Fluors, like chrysolith.
7. Transparent Fluors, like topaz.
8. Square transparent Fluors, covered with white Fluors.
9. Triangular transparent Fluors, covered with gold-coloured pyrites.
10. Crocus-coloured, transparent, square Fluors.
11. Fluors in colour like falernian wine, similar to amber.
12. Non-transparent, pointed, sexangular yellow Fluors.
13. Altenburg Fluors, white inside, yellow outside, tinctured by metallic water.
14. Opaque, square Fluors, sprinkled right at the top with, as it were, gold-coloured sand.
15. The same, sprinkled at the top with magnesia.

Green Fluors:

1. Green, square, transparent prase-colour Fluors.
2. Transparent Fluors, like emerald.
3. Green, mixed with transparent slime in layers.
4. Square, tesselated Fluors, in which there is plumbago.
5. Solid Fluors, white on the upper surface, and, as it were, sprinkled with large grains of salt.

Opaque and imperfect Fluors.
1. White, imperfect opaque Fluors.
2. Long, white, opaque, sexangular.Fluors, like an erect beam, in a beautiful silver-coloured pyrites.
3. Long, white, pellucid, sexangular Fluors, which in one part are like a white metallic stone, covered as it were with coriander grains, and which are sprinkled with grains of gold-coloured pyrites.
4. Long, white, sexangular, opaque Fluors, like an upright beam in a tesselated lead ore.
5. White opaque Fluors, ornamented with beautiful grains of silver-coloured pyrites and purple Fluors.
6. White, opaque, sexangular Fluors, covered with gold-coloured pyrites.
7. White, opaque Fluors, native in soft coal.
8. Long, upright, sexangular white Fluors in a grey flint, partly covered with very small scales of different colour, mud-colour, ruby, ashen, black, and which are sprinkled with grains of gold-coloured pyrites.
9. White, crusted, opaque Fluors.
10. White, smooth Fluors, like mirror-stone.
11. Purple in white quadrangular and sexangular Fluors from the earth of Moteschano.
12. White Fluors in which there is pure white capillary silver.
13. White Fluors, concreted as in layers.
14. White Fluors, like thorns of the bramble, rising out of gold-coloured pyrites, and to which, as it were, numberless scales are affixed.
FOCUS, etc. — A Hearth on which Lead is purified.
FOCUS, etc. — A Hearth outside the house, on which masses of Lead are melted.
FOCUS EXCOCTORUM — The Hearth of the Furnace.

FODINA, CUNICULUS — A Pit, Mine, Underground Passage or Channel.
FODINARUM FRUCTUS EXSTANS E FORNACE — The Product of a Mine coming out of the Furnace.
FOEDULA — is a species of Mushroom.
FOENIX, or **PHOENIX** — The Son of One Day, the Philosophical Stone.
FOLIA — Leaves; that which is absolutely separated. When they say: Change gold into leaves, i.e., dissolve it in water, so that the soul may be extracted from it; which soul is sulphur, and it tinges.
FOLIA DATURAE QUASI OLIA AUREA — Leaves like Gold-leaf.
FOLLES SPIRITUALES — A five-fold Ventilator for a Mine.
FOLLIS — Bellows.
FOM — i.e., Sound or Voice.
FONS PHILOSOPHORUM — The Bath of Mary, which see.
FORAMEN FISTULARUM — The Opening of Channels or Fistulas. Item, of a trunk or chest.
FORAMEN SPIRITALE FOLLIUM — Contrivance for catching the wind.
FORAMEN SUPERIORIS TABULATI FOLLIUM — i.e., Bunghole.
FORAMINA SPIRITALIA — Airholes
FORCEPS — Pincers.
FORCEPS FERREUS — Iron Pincers.
FORES QUIBUS VECTIS INSUNT — Doors with Dampers.
FORFEX — An oblong instrument like tongs, which can be easily opened or shut, and is useful for stirring and moving coals under the vessel, or for taking hold of the vessel itself.

There is another kind, not unlike forceps, by which the vessel is generally lifted off the fire.

FORICULA — Small Doors for Ventilation.

FORMAE RERUM — The celestial influx which things below derive from things above; the secret potency, power, and virtue of a substance.

FORMICAE — Emmets, Ants; in skin diseases, Pimples, Warts, a kind of Abscess, Black Warts, Pimples raised by irritation, etc.

FORNACIS MAGISTER — Overseer of the furnace.

FORNACULA — Assaying Furnaces.

FORNAX — A Furnace or Oven.

FORNAX PRIMA VITRARIORUM, ET ETIAM EA, IN QUA EXCOQUUNTUR VENIE — A Smelting Oven.

FORNAX, etc. — A Refining Oven in which silver is separated from lead.

FORNAX, etc. — A Furnace or Oven in which iron ore is smelted.

FORNAX, etc. — An Oven in which copper nuggets are melted by baking.

FORNAX, etc. — An Oven in which copper nuggets are heated.

FORNAX, etc. — An Oven similar to a furnace.

FORNAX ANEMIA — is an Oven shaped after the manner of a tripod, with a conistery and a grate, divided into two parts by a gridiron. The conistery is made fast by an iron gate, by which air can enter. The grate is open and covered with coarse clay. The free space is called Ergastulum. The matters are frequently prepared, or treated, in a frying pan, baking dish, saucepan, triangular vessel, etc., so that they may be set upon the burning coals, or quickly removed therefrom. Frequently the fire is increased by a fan, or bellows, but usually a proper draught of air is sufficient. It should also be said that the gate of the conistery can be opened by the current of wind or air. The only other exit should be that of the shaft or chimney; more especially when a matter has to be melted or calcined by a great heat.

FORNIX — A Vaulted Place.

FORNICULAE — A kind of lancet.

FOSSA LATENS — A Cross-cut.

FOSSA LATENS JUXTA LACUNAM — A Cross-cut by a pool, ditch, etc.

FOSSA OCCULTA — The End of a Passage in a Mine.

FOSSAM LATENTEM SUBSTRUERE — To build a shed in which rubbish may be thrown.

FOSSAM PATENTEM DUCERE — To construct a Channel for getting rid of water in mines.

FOSSOR — A Miner.

FOSSORES, QUI COLLEGERUNT INTORTA — Miners who have to work in a stooping position.

FOSSOS DUCERE — To construct Channels.

FRONDES LAURI — Laurel leaves, or of the colour thereof.

FUGILE, PAROTIS, ABSCESSUS SECUS AURES — Literally an Ear-ring. In diseases, a Tumour of the Ear.

FULIGO — Painter's Black, Cream-soot, is made in several ways and of many materials; among us, out of pitch. Dioscorides says that it is obtained from glassblowers. Its medical virtue is astringent and consuming.

FULIGO METALLORUM — Properly Arsenic, but it often signifies Mercury.

FULMEN — In the present connection is the Flowers of Cupellated Silver, in the cleansing thereof with lead. Consequently, Metallic Fulmination is, especially with the higher metals, a process of purging.

FULMINATION — is a Metallic Gradation, with Excoction, educing the pure part, the perfection thereof being indicated by an irradiating splendour. Hence the name of the operation, because there is a coruscation accompanied, like lightning, with a reverberating noise. After the foreign substances have been separated, a kind of sulphureous cloud appears on the surface, followed by a purplish splendour, which is called the brightness, lightning, or flow. When this has passed away, the matter has already begun to grow cool.

FULTURAE NATIVE VEL FORNICES ~ Natural Supports or Arches.

FUMIGATIO ~ Fumigation is Calcination by an aerial and corroding smoke. It is performed in diverse manner, the nobler metals by an afflatus of fused lead or artificial quicksilver; the fragile parts are given up, and subsequently triturated by rubbing with salt.

FUMUS ~ is the Scoria, an incrustation on the floor, yet properly that which arises and brings the body with it. For there are two kinds of smoke, which mix with the earth, make the stars fall from heaven, make also comets and rainbows about the sun and moon. When the batia finds a mineral matter, then it is to the smallest extent mingled with it. It also becomes fixed and a metal, but should the batia not find any, then it becomes a mercury; but the mineral power which it ought to find is clear sulphur washed, and partially fixed, and it is found in the extracted stones, and in sand. It shines like silver, and because nothing can be produced without this, it is found in every place wherein metals are generated. Consequently, metal which contains much sulphur is called the lake of the generation of metals.

FUMUS ALBUS ~ is Mercury, the Soul and the Tincture, Heavenly Water, the Quintessence of Venus; this smoke conducts the colour of the gold by a dry process into the height. Then the snake climbs up into the tree, and finds the mother with two children, and devours them all. That is to say, the smoke rises over itself, and finds two sulphurs with the Mercury. It dissolves all, generates it in itself, becomes fixed, and is petrified. The white smoke is the soul of the dissolved bodies; it imparts life and whiteness.

FUMUS CITRINUS — is Yellow Sulphur.

FUMUS RUBEUS — is Orpiment. It is also called Gold because it is bright.

FUMUS VIRIOSUS, or **VIRUS** — is poisonous, pestilential Smoke.

FUMUS CASAE — Smoke from a house chimney.

FUNIS DUCTARIUS — A Rope.

FUNIS EX PHILYRIS, TILIAE FACTUS — Rope made from the Bark of the Linden Tree.

FUNICULUS CANAEINUS — String.

FURES CANDIDI — Red Water.

FUROGI — i.e., a Cock.

FURNI TECTI — Covered Furnaces; those which have a roof.

A Covered Furnace is either simple or compound.

A Simple Furnace is that which stands by itself, and has no connection with any other furnace. It may be either a calcinating or dissolving furnace.

A Calcining Furnace is one that is used for calcination. It may be a welding or reverberatory furnace.

A Welding Furnace is one in which the fire is conveniently arranged for welding substances. It would be possible to mention various kinds of furnaces for conducting this operation, but that which I am now about to describe is more satisfactory than all the rest, both on account of its continuous fire, and also because of the easy regulation of the degrees of the same. A square brick wall is built, having internal breadth of a cubit, and extending upwards to the first compartment a height of one foot, thus forming the ash-pan. It extends to the second compartment one foot, thus completing the Ergasterium. Next, the furnace should incline towards the tower a height of one foot. Next, from the top of this furnace we must erect a tower three feet in height, and having an internal capacity of one foot. The height of the furnace so constructed will be six feet or three cubits. But two doors must be left in the interior wall-one in the ash-pan being a third of a cubit in length and the sixth of a cubit in breadth, convenient for removing ashes and inducing currents of air; the other door in the oven must be nine inches. Between these doors an iron grate is placed, and over it we set an earthenware plate, which can be surmounted by an archshaped roof. Coals supplied through the upright tower burn upon this roof. Moreover, four apertures must be made in each wall, so that on any side the coals can be stirred by a poker. Also, let the tower have an aperture at the top about the breadth of a little finger, which in most cases is to be left open, so that the fire may draw the air which sustains it. The outer doors and apertures are duly closed by their lids, so that the furnace may sustain the fire for an uninterrupted space of twenty-four hours, according as the work requires.

The Reverberatory Furnace is that wherein the matter is calcined by bounding or resilient flame. It is constructed in the following fashion. Let a brick wall of oblong shape, and of the height of one foot, be erected to serve as an ash-pan, having an aperture of the breadth of four fingers, which will serve as a door for the removal of ashes. Place upon this wall a grate obliquely, and over that let there be a wall extending to the height of one foot, to serve as an oven. In the ash-pan there must be a door four fingers broad through which the ashes can be removed. Above it there must be another door in the wall of the grate, wherein wood can be put. After these arrangements have been completed, let a sort of gallery or terrace [solarium] be constructed of bricks, which shall not be in contact with the posterior wall, and shall be three fingers in breadth. Through the aperture thus left the flame will make its way, and being stopped at the arched roof, will reverberate upon the matter. We next leave a moderately sized door in the interior partition above the gallery, through which the matter to be reverberated upon may be put in and taken out. We cover the remaining portion of the furnace with an arched roof, which is a little lower down than the other part. We cover the anterior and posterior portions of the furnace, and strengthen them with walls of brick, after having left four ventilators, side by side, being of the space of two fingers, in the said upper door. By means of these ventilators it is possible to regulate the fire readily and conveniently, to increase and diminish the heat at will, as the operation requires. When everything has been constructed after this fashion, we make a lid to fit each down, and adjust it thereto. The furnace is then ready for use.

The Simple Dissolving Furnace, dissolves matter by its power of resolving the coarse into the refined. It may be either an ascending or descending furnace.

An Ascending Furnace is that which dissolves by ascending. It is either dry or humid.

The Dry Furnace is a vessel containing the matter, the vessel in question not being put into water. The dissolution is effected by means of an external moisture. It takes place in a bladder and sand melting box.

The Bladder Furnace is that which serves for dissolving the matter in a bladder. It is as follows: Four walls are erected in a square, being of the height of one foot (the breadth varying according to the capacity of the bladder), and this serves as an ash-pan. But from one side of the bottom two fragments are so placed at the corners as to leave in their midst a vacant space of six fingers' breadth and the same height for the ash-pan, which completely fills up the space designed for it. Over this structure we must place iron bars to form a grate, and then we shall have finished with the ash-pan. Above this an oven is to be constructed by means of similar walls, eighteen inches high, a door being left in the centre of the furnace by means of which the coals can be manipulated. Over this wall-structure we place an iron bar, which holds the bladder suspended. Having made this structure, the wall is continued to the height of the bladder. It is to be noted that the furnace is to be constructed with such a capacity that a space of at least two fingers' breadth shall exist between the furnace and the vessel, so that the latter may be properly encircled by the heat. Having put in the vessel we cover the furnace ; nevertheless, we allow the orifice of the bladder to protrude, and the four ventilators are also left open. Finally, we construct a lid for each hole and adjust it thereto.

The Sand Vessel Furnace is that which dissolves metals by means of a sand box. It is made after the manner of the furnace described above; there is no difference in the structure, except that instead of a bladder, we place therein a melting, or any other vessel containing the matter, and we keep a watch on the furnace. But if we wish to dissolve anything by an open fire, i.e., without a vessel of sand, and by inclining the other vessel which contains the matter upon its side, let the furnace have a vacant space in one of its walls, four or six fingers wide, according to circumstances, and of a suitable capacity. Such a furnace is of great use in all kinds of dissolutions, either when performed by ashes, by sand, or by iron, or even by naked fire.

FURNUS — A place wherein the fire for chemically operating upon a matter may be properly and conveniently placed. The furnace may be either open or closed. An Open Furnace is one which has the upper part open. This kind may be either a testing or blasting furnace.

A Testing or Assaying Furnace is a furnace wherein the nobler metals are refined and searched, or, to use a more correct and technical term, are fulminated. It is constructed of potter's earth, iron plates, or tiles. An iron or earthenware plate is taken, and a four-sided structure is built, in such a way that its base is eleven feet square, but its height is sixteen feet. After the first eight feet of its height it becomes narrower by four feet, yet must the mouth of the furnace be seven feet wide. It is correct also for the plates to have a thickness of one foot and a half, but the floor and the base should be potter's clay, half a foot thick. Having erected this building, we measure three feet upwards and four feet along. This constitutes the lower doorway. From the post of this doorway a wall is continued for two feet, which takes up the space between the first door and that next to be mentioned. Measuring three feet and a half above, and four feet along, we have a convenient door for taking things out and putting them in. We must next proceed to bore a certain small hole at a foot's distance in the centre a hole in which the little finger can be placed, this is convenient for the poker whereby the coals are stirred. Moreover, three-quarters of a foot away, and at the extremity of the door, partitions must be placed on the right and left, where the two holes are of the breadth of an ordinary finger. Into these holes, with which two others should correspond in the opposite wall, are placed iron rods, extending to the breadth of four fingers along the wall. Lids or stoppers must be fitted to either door, having a handle, so that they can be removed and replaced. The upper of these lids must have an oblong hole, so that when the door is closed the interior may yet be visible. Let the lower lid be provided with a circular and larger hole, so that the fire may attract the air which sustains it. Over the rods let an earthenware plate be placed, hollowed out on three sides, but intact on the fourth side, and fitting accurately to the anterior wall. Then the floor of the compartment must be fixed, and an arch-shaped roof placed above, which must be distant two feet and a half from the side and back. Further, let a circular hole-as it were, another door-be cut out, to provide air. When everything has been constructed on this model for the furnace, before it is baked, let the iron plates which constitute the furnace be properly fastened together and riveted. Let, finally, the whole construction be dried in a sunny place, and properly baked by a potter. This manner of making a furnace is the most convenient possible, both because it is not easily choked up with ashes, and because it is sufficient for all assaying purposes, far excelling all others in the facility with which the fire can be directed.

A Blasting Furnace, or Anemia, is an open furnace wherein, by means of a current of air which increases the flame, the minerals are liquefied and melted. Should the metals be exceptionally difficult to fuse, so that the blast cannot produce sufficient heat, or the worker desires to melt something very quickly, a bellows can be conveniently attached to the furnace, to increase the fire and accelerate the melting. The blasting furnace may be constructed with its own bellows in the following fashion. Erect four walls, a foot apart either way, and a cubit in height, to serve as an ash-pan. On either side of the ash-pan let there be a door, by which the fire can draw the air, and the ashes be removed. Moreover, above the ash-pan, let iron bars be arranged to form a grate, for holding the coals and the vessel placed therein. Let there be another hole of the breadth of a finger beneath the grate, through which the beak of the bellows can pass. Then let the furnace have an oven added thereto. When it is sufficiently dried by coal-dust, and washed over with mud mingled with water, the bellows may be affixed.

This furnace, in case of necessity, may also be used for calcination.

FURNUS BALNEI — is that in which we dissolve the matter when hot in the bronze vessel which contains it. This furnace is built in the same way as the two others, and instead of a bladder or sand box, a brazen box made for the purpose is substituted. But in the vapour bath another vessel of copper made in the following manner is fixed to the top. The vessel is round, and two or three feet in height, the base being comprised in the interior of the ahenum, and the whole arrangement is so exactly adjusted that no vapour can escape. From one side of this vessel a canal or pipe projects, the lower end of which is in contact with the ahenum, so that, if necessary, fresh water can be poured through it. In close proximity to the ahenum, this vessel has a kind of twist upon which a perforated plate something like a diaphragm is placed, containing the vessels. It sometimes happens that more things require to be digested than can be contained in one vessel, whence it is necessary, in order to supply this deficiency, that a second and even a third vessel should be added, according to the need of the moment, and the number of things to be digested. We fix on the top of the vessel a copper lid, which fits exactly, lest any vapour should escape. But when we wish to abstract anything by means of the vapour bath, we do not need this vessel. A cucurbit is placed in a deeper ahenum, care being taken that no water shall reach the glass. It is necessary, however, that the vapour should surround and heat it. As a further precaution, let the lid itself have a cover.

A Descending Furnace is that whereby we drive the moisture downward, and so dissolve the matter. Walls are erected for the ashpan, that the containing vessel may be sheltered from the violence of the fire. Upon the ashpan a grate is arranged with a circular aperture in the centre, through which the orifice of the upper vessel may pass. The walls are continued to form the oven, where also the ergasterium is constructed, and in this the vessel is put reversed. Then, a fire of the required temperature being sustained, dissolution takes place.

Composite Furnaces are those in which one fire is used for all. Such are the Athanor and Acediae (time-saving) Furnaces.

The Time-Saving Furnace is that where many furnaces are sustained by one fire with very little trouble. It takes its name from idleness, and is called "Idle Henry" by the Germans. A round or square tower is erected in the fashion before described, and we leave apertures over the grate which conduct the heat to the side furnaces. There may be three, four, or five of them. Iron stoppers must be provided, by which the heat can be cut off or communicated. By the means of these separate holes another furnace may be closely connected. Nevertheless, it is necessary that each furnace should have its own particular ash-pan and pyreterium, with a separate grate and chimney. By the help of these time-saving furnaces almost any purpose can be accomplished.

FURNUS PANIS ~ A Heated Oven.

FURNUS SABULI ~ A Heated Sand-furnace.

FUSI ~ Spindle, Windlass. Perhaps also a Pulley over which a rope runs.

FUSIO ~ is Liquation by Heat.

FUSION ~ by Antimony is that process by which we separate true gold not only from imperfect metals, but also from silver, and it is performed in this manner. I take gold combined with other metals, and mix with it three parts of pulverized antimony. I then place it inside a crucible which will withstand fire, and this vessel I place in a blasting furnace. Afterwards (if necessary, with the help of the bellows) I transfer the duly liquefied substance into a heated pyramid, then, having struck the sides with a mallet, the regulus containing the gold will settle itself at the top, and we strike off the top with a mallet. The residual antimony contained in the pyramid I again put to the fire and proceed as before, up to the third time, so that all the gold may be taken from the antimony. Each metal regulus thus obtained, having been put into an earthen vessel, and coals having been piled on the top, I set a light to them just like the fire of a furnace, and keep up the flame until all the antimony being evaporated, there is a residue of pure unalloyed gold, which instantly solidifies.

FYADA — i.e., Mercury, White Smoke.

GAGATES — is a Stone which is to be distinguished from the Gagites of Pliny (1. 10, c. 3). The latter is the Eagle-stone. True Gagates, with which we are here concerned, is the German Jetstone, Agatestone, etc. It is, in fact, a dark, glossy bitumen. It is native in the sea and in rivers, and is doubtless made from petroleum, i.e., a subtle naphtha, or natural liquid bitumen. The stone Thracius or Black Agate is a kind of Gagates, which is composed of black naphtha or bitumen. When bitumen or liquid naphtha flows in the sea or in rivers, that petroleum, I say, makes Gagates. The Germans confound Gagates with amber; the matter differs in the two cases, though it may be granted that they are allied, both having the power, when heated by friction, of attracting threads and straws, as the magnet does iron and the Sagda wood. Moreover, they are both of inflammable nature. But amber does not burn in water, whereas Gagates, which are composed of bitumen, burn very fiercely therein, and the water itself seems to be set on fire by the strength of the bitumen. Amber is not bitumen, but an exudation of the poplar tree or of the pine tree.

Gagas or Gagates:
Yellow: Jetstone, Agatestone, Wellstone, Amberstone, Pearstone, of the colour of the ion's coat, also very closely approaching green.

Black: This is the stone Thracius, Black Agatestone.

Yellow and Black Gagates are indurated stone of naptha or bitumen, i.e., petroleum from Cilicia and the river Gages in Lycia, where it falls into the sea.

Sunstone: A stone composed of indurated naptha or bitumen, indurated by a terrene heat. It is a species of Gagates.

Amber:
Wood Glessum Amber, yellow in colour; it is a gum or resin indurated in the sea; of the poplar according to Discorides. Also of the pine, or the wild pine.

Basthard Amber is whitish in colour. We shall treat subsequently of amber.

The name of the stone Gagates is derived from the place and river Gagas in Cicilia. This is on the authority of Dioscorides (1. 5, c. 92). But others say it is the city of Gangis in Lycia, where this stone is found on the shore, being of great size and green colour. This is supported by Nicander in his Theriaca, and he calls the stone Engangin, or Gangitis. He affirms also that the vapour which it gives off in the fire, by reason of its bituminous character, drives away serpents. It is, as I have already said, its nature to burn, to set fire to water, and to be quenched in oil, because it is composed of bitumen. And hence Nicander says it destroys the impetus of a strong and consuming fire. Also Dioscorides teaches that it must take rank before all things of like nature, because it burns with such facility and gives off the odour of bitumen. Pliny (1. 36, c. 29) says that its name is derived from the place and river of Gagas in Lycia, that it is cast up by the sea in Leucola, and is there collected. If I mistake not, Galenus declares that he is unacquainted with any river of the name in Lycia. But it is possible that the name may have changed, as occurs sometimes. Strabo and other geographers are in agreement with Dioscorides on the point, that the river is in Lycia. Is it not possible, moreover, that it is a small river, not generally known, which also is the case with some streams in our own country? The Orla, the Schwarza, and the Pangera are very celebrated streams, but because they are small and of no length, who really knows anything about them except those who live in their vicinity? For the rest, consult Dioscorides and Pliny in the places already cited, concerning the virtues of the Gagates. Its vapour in burning drives away serpents. It arrests dangerous disease when a fumigation is made of it, and eases contraction of the womb. Within my own experience it has an assuaging and dispersing virtue. Gagates were formerly a favourite ornament of matrons, wherewith they were wont to deck themselves as with corals. They are still worn as a favour, by those who desire to beget boys, in some places. Shields, swords, and helmets are also ornamented with them. I have myself seen a church near the port of Tangera which was built and enriched with many gems by the Emperor Charles IV, the windows of which were made of Gagates in a wonderful manner. I have also seen, in the same church, a dagger belonging to this emperor, the haft of which was made, with extraordinary skill, out of a single Gagates. Would that at this day our kings and princes had such care for religion as this good Charles! At the present day amber is preferred, as its smell is sweeter. For the rest, every species of Gagates has one thing in common with the eagle stone, because it is but little reduced by fire. Hence eagle stone is also called Gagites, but it is not the same as Gagates, which we affirmed at the beginning. Some make it out to be a species of Gagates, because of its colour, which is like lion-skin. The Gagates of this colour is our common Agate. There is a second species, which is black, with white veins; a third, which is black, with yellow veins; a fourth, which is spotted, as with blood, and is found in various parts of India, even as the third is of Cretan origin, while the fifth and last species is black like coral.

The stone Gagates is made of naphtha, that is, petroleum. The stone Thracius is another species of Gagates, and is made of black bitumen, or naphtha. Of this also there are two kinds: a certain scissile stone, and lithanthrax. Amber, however, is made of the resin of the poplar, according to Dioscorides, distilled in Eridanus, and hardened either by its own heat or by that of water. Among its other names may be mentioned Electrum, Glessum, Chrysophoros, Chrysolectrum, and it has received different appellations from different learned persons. We ourselves possess a true amber, as Tacitus commemorates. The islanders still collect Succinum as it is washed up by the waves on the shore. So also do the Britons. He is called the master of the shore who pays the wages to those who collect the amber.

True Amber is nothing but the sap of certain trees which falls into the sea, and there hardens. It can be set alight like pitch, and the flame is nourished by its oily substance. It is of two kinds-Electrum and Succinum. Electrum is opaque, white, almost like bone, and very valuable. It is commonly called Basthard. Succinum is yellow and transparent like glass. Because of its glass-like transparency, it was called Glessum by the ancients. Hence also we learn on the testimony of Pliny (1. 37, c. 3, and 1. 4, c. 26), that the poplar, whence amber is obtained, was itself termed Glessinga, Glessaria, etc. In the neighbourhood, about Borussia, and along the sea-coast of that part, Electrum would appear to be obtained not from poplars or alders, but from wild pines and fir-trees. Succinum can also be made from the resin of these trees, and its piney nature is known by the odour it emits when it is set alight. (See Pliny, 1. c., and Solinus, c. 23). Thus, Succinum is not made only from the alder or poplar at Eridanus, and what the poets have written on this subject is very fabulous. Consult Irenxus and Tacitus. For the rest, Succinum is an exudation or resin of trees, chiefly of the pine and the wild pine, which is shown by its odour, colour, and substance generally, when set alight. Thus it exists first in a liquid state, and it is for this reason that we find it to contain flies, particles of dust, spiders, worms, and such insects as gnats, which get into it when it is in its liquid state, and are still incorporated with it when it has become hard. See Tacitus and Pliny. Some writers, moved by I know not what considerations, will have it that it is the prolific seed of a viviparous fish, hard, and like a clod of earth, found in the sea, and floating to the shore. Others state that it is brought from the Caspian Sea. Benedictus Veronensis (*De Morbis*, 1. 13, c. 26) describes a kind of succinum of a combined black and white colour, having a smell which is at first disagreeable. I do not know what this can be, unless it is a species of impure Basthard. In fine, great has been, and still is, the division between authorities as to what amber is. I affirm that it is a resin of trees, and especially of pine and the wild pine. Pliny enumerates other species of electrum, besides the white, which is an extremely odorous Basthard. There is, moreover, the pale yellow, which is Glessum; and also a kind which has a softer brightness, and is called Falernian, because it is like Falernian Wine. Finally, there is that which is of a pleasing honey colour. And these species are found among our own ambers, if the subject be properly considered. Pure electrum is said to be obtained from the mines of Liguria, but I believe it to be simply Gagates from the bitumen of the earth, and not amber. Or perhaps it is another kind of stone, for there are many gems of kindred colours, such as the topaz and lyncurion. Formerly, amber and Gagates were both worn by matrons who wished to obtain children, now amber is worn only, and is supposed to induce the conception of male children. This stone is very potent against madness, and it is an amulet, which, on the authority of Pliny, is more available than anything against contraction of the womb, if the smoke or vapour, given off from it when burning, be applied to the nostrils. It prevails over disorders of the stomach, it sharpens the understanding, and is good for epilepsy. The logical position is as follows: Whatsoever emits a pleasant smell exhilarates the spirits: Electrum emits a pleasant smell, and indeed is of the best and sweetest fragrance. Thus it exhilarates the spirits, and by consequence is good for epilepsy. For the rest, consult Avicenna, Serapion, Paulus, Galenus, and others, s.v. *De Karabe*, i.e., Electrum, or Succinum. For the rest, amber, when rubbed till it becomes warm, attracts straws, threads, and dry leaves, like the Gagates, and even as the magnet draws iron, and the stone sagda draws wood. Consult Hesiod and Euripides on amber.

Apollonius, in the 4th Bk. of the *Argonautria*, says that it does not originate from the sap of poplars but from that of the laurel. Consult Solinus and Strabo, and the opinions of various writers recorded in Pliny, 1. 37, c. 2 and 3..

Gagates:
Jetstone, Agatestone, Wellstone, Pearstone, Burningstone, a tenuous liquid Bitumen which is found on the surface of springs (Bornstein, in Germany);
Silverine from White Naptha, i.e., petroleum, in Cilicia;

Black from Bitumen or Black Naptha in Thrace; an indurated stone, of which the species are carbonaceous stones and scissile stones.

Succinum Electrum is improperly confounded by the Germans with Gagates; it is a gum, resin, or indurated exudition.

1. Of poplars, according to Dioscorides, Ovid, and others; otherwise of the alder, though these writers seem to regard the alder and poplar as the same tree.
2. Of the pine.
3. Of the wild pine, whence comes the Basthard of the Germans-bright, transparent, yellow, like honey-water.

GALA — i.e., Milk.

GALACTITES, GALACTITIS, or **GALAXIAS** — is a precious stone of a milk-white colour, with white and red stripes. It exudes a milky sap of a greyish hue and a sweet taste, especially when mixed with water. I have seen it as it originates in Saxony earth, and while it was still increasing. Consult Dioscorides and Pliny (1. 37, c. 20), who says that it is like the medlar. Pliny also calls the Galactites the Leucogogxa, Leucographia, and Synephites. It increases the flow of saliva, and is said to be of very great use in developing the milk of women who are suckling infants. It also refreshes the memory. That variety of the Emerald which has white lines surrounding it is by some called Galactites. Consult Albertus, who attributes to Galactites I know not what magical virtues. Also Solinus (Polyhist., c. 13), who says that the black scrupulus is composed of white sap.

GALAXIA — Star-colouring, purification.

GALLICUS — North, North-East.

GAMATHEI — are certain Mysterious Stones wherein the celestial potencies and the superior constellations are imprinted, and take shape in wonderful characters, signs, and symbolic figures. They are found occasionally by miners on the mountains and on the banks of rivers.

GANGRIENA — Incipient Mortification of a Diseased Part.

GASAR — i.e., Lomus [unknown).

GATRINUM — i.e., Woad Ashes.

GAZA FUMI — i.e., Crystalline Arsenic.

GEBALUM — i.e., Reparation. Coagulare sometimes has the same meaning.

GECHARSUN, or DIFDAHA — i.e., a Frog.

GELION, FOLIUM, PHYLLON, COME, CHOETE — Names for a Leaf.

GELUTA — i.e., the herb Carlina.

GEMMA EX ARANEO — Stone from a Spider. In Germany, we have a species of domestic spider which is of immense size, which takes its name from the Cross, and is called the Cross-Spider — I know not why, unless from the shape of its web, or from the transverse colouring of its body — and it is considered wicked or unlucky to injure it. It is said to drive away every kind of poisonous reptiles from houses, and in times of pest it is seldom or rarely seen. A precious stone is found in the heads of these spiders, which is of singular value as a preservative against poison and sorcery. I have never seen it, as I have not had the courage to dissect such a spider. But there is no cause for surprise at the virtue of the gem when even the webs of these creatures are held by many in the highest estimation.

GEMMA BERYLLUS — The Stone Beryl.

1. The Beryl.
2. Chrysoberyl, or Yellowish Beryl.
3. Chrysopras, or Green Beryl.

GEMMA CERAUNLE — Shining Stone, Gleaming Stone, Lightning Stone. There are two varieties — round and long.

GEMMA IRIS — (1) Iris is a Sexangular Stone, of white colour, which, under the rays of the sun, radiates like a rainbow; (2) Manufactured Iris in imitation of the true stone. It is made of the stone called Brontia, which is white and polished. Item: Translucent Yellow Fluors such as I have seen at our jewellers.

GEMMA OPALUS, or **POEDEROS** — A kind of opal.

GEMMA PRASIUS — A Stone similar to the leek in colour.

GEMMAE RUBETARUM — The Frog, Toad, or Rubeta, an ugly animal, dwelling in holes, contains a certain gem. There is a species in Spain or Gaul, which has horns, and spots of yellow and livid black. It is called Borax, and has a stone in its head of the same name, i.e., rubeta. The colour is between white and brown. I have seen a specimen at the house of a nobleman. If the stone be extracted while the toad is alive, it will have a blue eye in the middle. Sometimes it is black, with little livid black spots, like our own toads, or toadstones. I have possessed a specimen, of round shape, about the size of a bean. Some are green, some variegated; such are found by the Borax-seekers. These stones are called commonly Cropodina. Sometimes they have the figure of a toad upon them. Rings set with these stones are worn by princes, for, when they are in the presence of poison, they change colour, and emit a sweat. They are greatly desired by our frogs, who endeavour to leap away with them, as I have myself seen. They gather round them when they are set upon the ground. For the rest, whether the Borax stone actually grows in the head of the toad, like Draconites and Echites, I leave to the reader. Others say that it is produced in a viscous spume, which toads blow upon the head of the special toad whom they desire to be their king. See Pliny. Nowadays our toads are hung up in the air till they are dried, when they are said to be a cure for every flux of blood.

GEMMA TARTAREA — Common Stone of Transparent Tartar.

GENULA EX TRANSPLANTATIONE PASTINACAE ~ A kind of monstrous Parsnip.
GEOGKAPHIA ~ The Art of the Knowledge of the Earth.
GEOMANTIA ~ is a notable Art and Science of Earthly Things. It is also the manifestation of the stars of earth to men, whence they obtain a prophecy or presage. It is called also Astronomy of Earth, and is operated in two ways, either by astronomical calculations, or by spots.
GEOMETRIA ~ A Measure in Land-surveying; length ten feet.
GEPHULLE ~ A species of Rock.
GERSA ~ i.e., White Lead.
GESOR ~ i.e., Galbanum, a strong-smelling Gum.
GI ~ i.e., Earth. Also a material in use among painters, which is obtained from glass ovens or chimneys.
GIBAR ~ i.e., the Medicine of Metals.
GIBUM ~ i.e., Cheese.
GICH, or **GEPSIN** ~ i.e., Gypsum.
GIGANTES ~ are long and tall (but what the text does not say), placed over the vessel. Also men who exceed the stature and laws of nature.
GILLA, or **GRILLUS** ~ is Vitriol, which resolves of itself into water. Some call Water of Sal Ammoniac by this name. It purges the stomach.
GILVUS, or **HELVUS** ~ is intermediate between white and brown. Called also Melinus, Cirron, Balion, Citrinus, Citrinon.
GIPSUM ~ i.e., Armenian Earth; Plaster of Paris.
GIR, GITH ~ i.e., Living Calx.
GIRLIES ~ i.e., White River-stones; also Perch.
GIRMER ~ i.e., Tartar.
GISISIM ~ i.e., of Gum.
GITENON ~ i.e., Common Lime.
GLACIES DURA ~ i.e., Crystal.

GLADIALIS — is that art by which swords and daggers are manufactured in correspondence with the course of the stars of heaven. Even the anvil cannot resist these swords. Hence the art is also called Incusina.

GLASSA — is a kind of Dry Varnish.

GLIMMER, MICAH, or **CAT SILVER** — has a certain appearance of silver, but is not silver. It is called Cat Silver by similitude, because cat's eyes shine at night in the same manner, or because it is vain and useless, bears no fruit, and is only fit for burning. But if we consider profoundly, it is not so much burned, or consumed, as purged, as I have observed elsewhere, and assumes another colour, being doubtless a species of amianth. Consult Serapion (Lib. Agg. c. Tincar), who says that native chrysocolla is found on the sea shore, and has a saline nature. It is hot and dry in the fourth degree. As to its medicinal qualities see Discorides. Note that chrysocolla is poison if an overdose be taken.

GLISOMARGA — is a White Clay or Chalk.

GLOMER — i.e., Round.

GLUTEN — i.e., Oxgall.

GLUTEN — is Glue or Blood. Also Lime.

GLUTEN, SIMONIA, or **SINOVIA** — is the most noble part of the body, subtle, pure, white, transparent, a sweet resolved salt, and natural humour, or liquid, in all the joints of the members, like the albumen of eggs. When tartar is generated in this matter the result is gout.

GLUTINIS TENACITAS — is a Mineral Resin, as the resin of the terebinth tree.

GLUTA — The virtue and efficacy of Pitch.

GNI — A species of rock.

GNOMI, HOMUNCULI — Corporeal Spirits who dwell in the Earth. They are scarcely a foot high. Called also Pygmies.

GOBEIRA, MESPILA, AGABOR — Dust.

GOSEL — A beast with horns.

GRADATIO — is the gradual Exaltation of Metallic Qualities by which their weight, colour and fixity are excellently increased. It accomplishes the transmutation of a matter into its essential substance, provided it is performed gradually. It also manifests concealed potency without changing the original species. For example, if nature produces white gold, gradation makes it red; if nature produces what is volatile, gradation fixes, purifies what is impure, etc.

GRAECA MAGIA — A Superstitious Art invented by the Greeks, or a form of worship, by which useless visions are obtained, so that things which are not real appear, and whereby wise men captivate the imagination of the vulgar. It is nothing but a troubling of the sight, and a deceptive, mendacious machination which is represented in the likeness of the thing itself.

GRANATUS — The Garnet perhaps takes its name from the pomegranate. It is undoubtedly a species of carbuncle. It is a transparent, ruby-coloured gem, like the blossom of the pomegranate, and is more dusky than the carbuncle. There is one species which is between ruby and violet, and is called the violet garnet. It is very similar to the amethyst-coloured carbuncle. It is native in Ethiopia, and the sand of the sea. The garnet raises the spirits, and drives melancholy away. It is called the feminine Paeantis, which garnet is also termed Michedon. And they say that at certain times this gem conceives and bears a stone. See Pliny and Solinus. The Pxantis is the German Gemmaho, which also Pliny calls gelnonida, and it is said to conceive, bear, and undergo parturition. It is found in Macedonia, and is a species of congealed white water.

GRANULATIO — is the Process of Reduction into Powder. It is sometimes subsequent to fusion. It is special to metals, and is performed in several ways, such as by the pouring of

molten metal into water. The melting should be done in an iron vessel. Sometimes small brushes of dry twigs are introduced into the water to assist granulation. Sometimes, instead, a perforated tablet or very narrow sieve is used.
GRANULIREN — Reduced to Powder.
GRANUM — is Indian Seed.
GRANUM VIRIDE — is the Fruit of the Terebinth Tree.
GRASSA — i.e., Attinckar or Borax.
GRATIOLA — An Herb, formerly imported at great expense, and since found native in the vicinity of Norimberg. Abundant at Argentora.
GRAVUS — Marble, Porphyry, Porphyretic Stone, of reddish purple colour, useful in spontaneous solution of substances.
GRUMA — is Tartar.
GRUS — An ancient Elevating Apparatus, a Crane.
GUARIL — i.e., Newt or Eft.
GUARINI — are Men who Derive Life from the Influence of Heaven.
GUMA — i.e., Quicksilver, Mercury, Dual Quicksilver.
GUMA or **GUMI** — Olitet Sulphur and Coagulum. It is a Ferment, and may be dissolved by milk.
GUMA CUPRI — Verdigris, or Vitriol. Also called Gypsum, Stucco, Plaster of Paris.
GUMA PARADISI — Orpiment.
GUMICULA — The herb Valerian, Limicula, Phu, Baldrian.
GUMMI ASIMAR — i.e., Almond Gum.
GUMMI ARBORIS NUCUM — A sappy Exudition from the nuts of certain trees, also Catkins [*tremulae arboris*].
GUMMI CEDRI — The Gum of the Cedar called also Cedrina, Kedria, Kydria, Kitran, Alkitran, Xerbin.
GUTTA ROSACEA — Is a red Breaking Out on the Face, Incipient Leprosy. A Scabby Disease.
GUTTEO — A Gum found in the Sea.

GYPSUM — Probably the derivative of a spar. It is cognate to calx, but not so hot in its nature. It differs also in this, that when calx is extinguished by any moisture, it acquires heat, but Gypsum when thus extinguished does not acquire heat. Its virtue is in its astringent quality; it restrains and it destroys. Its use is chiefly in external application, on account of its extremely drying and destroying nature. Gypsum is of two kinds. The one is native mined Gypsum obtained from the earth, and especially from clay. It is a substance very similar to nitre, and occurs sometimes in broad layers. It was known to Theophrastus and to Pliny, who borrows from Theophrastus. Its name is retained by the Germans who call it Gyps. It is found in several places, including the vicinity of the Elbe. Spar and Gypsum, are always deposited during the inundation of that river. The other Gypsum is manufactured, and is made, or melted out, from a white stone similar to alabaster, which stone is found in the seams of Jena, in the wood of Hyrcinia, in the mines of Salveldia, and in the rivers of Saxony. It seems to me that it is, as it were, a hardened marrow of stone or otherwise a species of aphronitum, true Gypsum, or the Stone Calminar. So also the people of Saxony call this stone Our Dear Lady's Ice. There is a second kind of manufactured Gypsum made of a scissile spar called Mary's Icicle, because it has the appearance of an icicle. This is the best Gypsum, as Pliny testifies (1. 36, c. 2c}). Concerning true spar, see infra, s.v. De Lapide Arabico et Selinite. Albertus says that the extremity of Gypsum is spar, i.e., of native Gypsum. For the rest consult Pliny in 1. c., also 1. 35, c. 12 and 17, and Serapion, 1. Agg. s.v. Gypsen.

Gypsum:
1. Very white, solid, Cyprian Gypsum from which drinking cups and vessels for holding scents are made.

2. Another very white Cyprian Gypsum distinguished by grey veins.
3. A very white Gypsum from Hildesheim, not unlike ebony.
4. A very white Gypsum of Narthusia from which also drinking cups are made.
5. Another kind from the same place adorned with greyish lines, from which also drinking cups are made.
6. Block Gypsum, which glitters and sparkles after the manner of marble.
7. Soft block Gypsum, like sugar in appearance.
8. Capillary Isfeldian Gypsum.
9. White Scissile Isfeldian Gypsum.
10. White Gypsum of Ienum, found in contiguity to a grey, calcareous stone.
11. Greyish Gypsum of Hildesheim, found in the block.
12. Grey Gypsum from the same place, consisting of many layers.
13. Transparent and honey-coloured Gypsum.
14. A reddish Gypsum of Misena.
15. Burnt Gypsum of Thuringia which is utilized in place of calx.
16. Another burnt Gypsum of which many images are made by the modellers.

HADID — is Iron.

HAEMATITES — In Arabic Sedeneg, in German Blutstein, Bloodstone, on account of the blood colour with which it is tinged, and which it is also seen to have, which is dug up in mines, and on account of its effect in stopping the flow of blood in all kinds of bloody fluxes. Pliny distinguishes between several species according to the places in which they are found, as Lybia, Egypt, Spain, and between the Weser and Elbe in Germany; also in Saxony and Anneberg, at Sala, Goslaria, Geuro, Salfeldia, Salburg, Iona, many species occur.

Hematites may also be classified according to their degrees of hardness and softness. I am acquainted with the following species:

1. Those which are described by Dioscorides (1. 5, c. 90), and which are mined in Egypt. They have a black ground, are full of colour, and are hard, crumbling, smooth in quality, unmixed with any dross, and not encircled by zones.

This species is found among the Hematites obtained from our mines, but very rarely; I have barely met with a couple, and to the vulgar they are wholly unknown.

2. A black species, found at Gossaria, which exudes a yellow fluid; very hard and unknown to jewellers. It is found, but that rarely, in the portion of the ancient Hercynian forest which filled the country between the Weser and Elbe. It is undoubtedly the black stone Medus of Albertus, which also when broken exuded a yellow fluid. There is another species of a green colour. The name Medus refers to Media whence it is brought, and it is also found near the Phasis, a river of Colchis.

3. The scissile, purple Hematite, found in many places, notably in the mines of Hassia.

4. A very beautiful variety which is dug up in Geuro, Anneberg, and Salfeld. It is much praised by goldsmiths, because it is extremely hard at the side, and is useful for polishing gems. This also is black and is like a top in shape.

5. A variety from the same places, black, but exhibiting three colours at the sides, and is probably the Trichrus of Pliny (1. 37, c. 10), an African stone which he describes as black and exuding three kinds of moisture — at the bottom, black; in the middle, blood-red; at the top, white. This also is top-shaped and hard.

6. There is a sixth species found between the Weser and the Elbe, in Cherusca, and in certain mountains, which generally has the shape of a bare head. This is the most beautiful of all, and its shape cannot be sufficiently admired. I have experienced its wonderful virtue in stopping bleeding at the nose. Pliny distinguishes between the Hematite and Schistos (1. 36, c. 20), and between the red-veined Hematite and the crumbling species. He also calls Hematite by the term Anthracite, a word which the Greeks gave to many

things, including the carbuncle. Sotacus distinguishes five species, besides the stone Magnesia.

The Haematites of Pliny are as follows:

1. Ethiopian, good for the eyes, classed among the Panchresti, as universally useful objects. This is the grand Hematite of Pliny. It is found in Ethiopia, whence also comes the Ethiopian Magnesia, or loadstone, to which it is closely allied, even to the ruddiness of its colour. If broken, it gives forth a red and yellow fluid, but it does not attract iron like the loadstone. Great indeed is the knowledge both of loadstone and Hematite. Hematite can be made from loadstone when it has been burnt by a fiery heat.

2. Androdamanta, or Atrodamanta, of extraordinary weight and hardness, whence its name. This also is black, and exudes a blood-red fluid; it is found chiefly in Africa, and it attracts iron. To this our own Hematite from Geuro very closely corresponds, being very hard at the side, which is tri-coloured.

3. Arabian Hematite, hard, and scarcely exuding moisture on its aqueous side, sometimes similar to saffron. This answers to ours which is found at Goslar, and in the Hercynian wood.

4. Elatites, Bloodstone in the rough state; in its finished condition it is called Miles. It is useful for burns, and more so for all species of red eruptions.

5. Schistos, of which Schistos Nigrum, or Schiston, another species, is found in Africa. When broken on the aqueous sides a black-coloured moisture exudes from the root, and a yellow from the other portion. For the rest, consult Pliny and Dioscorides on the virtues and efficacies of these species; where is also to be found the method of burning and corrupting Hematite ; also where Hematite is chiefly found, namely, in red Sinopis, and how it may be made from loadstone fiercely burnt by an artificial fire, or by the

heat of the earth. Where loadstone exists it is most likely that Hematite will be also found, and vice versa, which is the case in iron mines where loadstone is found. Dioscorides also states in the same place that Hematite is produced naturally among metals in Egypt, which is found to take place also in the mines of the Bohemian mountains. For the rest, consult Serapion on the Hematite, s.v. Sedeneg. The ancients consecrated the Hematite to Mars.

HAEMORRHOIDES — A flux of Blood from the Anus.

HAGS — is Stone.

HAL — is Salt.

HAL, or **HOL** — is Vinegar.

HALCYON, ALCION, ALCEDO, ORNIS ACTAE — Sea-fowl, Cerylus, Ice-bird.

HALCYONIUM — The Halcyon Birds, beloved by the goddess Tethaeos. See Pliny (1. 10, c. 32; 1. 2, c. 49; 1. 18, c. 26) as to the manner of their pregnancy, the mode in which they prepare their nests, and their appearance. Compare the very elegant fable in the eleventh metamorphosis of Ovid, and other writers who have treated concerning these birds. Deservedly indeed did these most beautiful Halcyon birds partake of the pleasures of the Nereides, as our Virgil and Theocritus tell us. From these same Halcyons we derive the name Halcyonium Ceycum from Ceyce, Kingfisher. It is simply congealed seafoam, internally brittle, stimulating to throat and eyes. It is at this day called Spuma Maris, Sea-foam, in the workshops. But it is not the Spuma Salis, or Maris, of which we have before spoken, though it is related thereto. Spuma Salis, or Froth of Salt, is a wool or fibre of sea-foam congealed into stones. But Halcyonium is a concrete, scissile, and spongy Sea Spume. It is so called because the Halcyons make their nests floating on a calm sea from this spongy and spumous substance, as the poet says; and Dioscorides (1. 5, c. 8) enumerates five species. Today we have barely two. There is the Halcyonium Spissum, thick, and of astringent taste, with a spongy surface, and a foul, fishy smell. It is found upon the seashore and at Havel, where there are Halcyons, called by the inhabitants Spur-winged Water-hen, but improperly, and also more correctly, Kingfisher, because it builds its nest in the cold winter, and also hatches its young. By the latter name also another bird is signified. The second species of Halcyon is like the lashes of the eye, spongy, full of holes like pipes, light, and smelling like sea-weed. These two first species are included as ingredients in the purifying medicine of women. In De Medusa Facie, Ovid tells us: Add medicines taken from the nests of quarrelsome birds. These banish pimples; they are called Halcyons. The third species is similar to a worm in shape; it approaches purple in colour, and is called Milesius. It promotes the flow of urine. The fourth species is not unlike the wool shorn from a sheep, but still hanging together. It is light, and honeycombed like a sponge. The fifth species has the appearance of a fungus, without any repellant odour; it is found in the Sea of Marmora, near the island of Besbica, and on account of its place of origin, because it is salt and bitter, they call it Halosachnem. It is useful for cleansing the teeth, and is used in purifying medicine and depilatory unguent. For the rest, after what manner Halcyonium is prepared by fire and cleaned, consult Dioscorides and Bulkasis. Pliny (l. 32, c. 5) affirms that Halcyonium is made from the nests of the Halcyon or Kingfisher, or from a gross spumous refuse, or from lime, or from sea-wool. He enumerates four species: (1) thick, ashen, and coarse smelling; (2) soft, lighter, and with an odour of sea-weed; (3) whiter and worm-shaped ; (4) that which is called Milesius, and is the best kind; it is porous, like rotten sponge, and approaches purple in colour. Consult Pliny and Serapion on the virtues of these various species. Also the third tractatus of Almansor in the chapter on Sea Spume. All these species are said to be hot and dry. Later authorities have affirmed that Halcyonium is not Sea Spume, but the manufactured substance which is called Adarca and Sea Flesh.

HALIMAR ~ is Copper.

HALINITRUM ~ is Saltpetre.

HARA ~ is juniper.

HARMAT ~ is the Berry of the Juniper.

HARMEL ~ is Seed of the herb Rue. Also Grains of Silver remaining on the hearth.

HARO ~ is a Fern like the Polypody, or Wall-fern.

HARPAGO ~ A Hooked or Crooked Instrument.

HARPAGO PRAEGRANDIS ~ A Hooked Or Crooked Instrument of large size.

HARTWERCH ~ A kind of copper or Brazen Loaves.

HASACIUM ~ Sal Ammoniac.

HEINRICUS RUBEUS ~ Vitriol calcined to the Red.

HEL ~ is Honey.

HELEBRIA ~ is a species of black Verarrius (? Weratrum, Hellebore), putting forth red flowers.

HELLE ~ Viscidity.

HELIOTROPIUM ~ is the Melissa (Bee) of Paracelsus; the Root of the Sun; the Dandelion; the Balm of Paracelsus.

HELIOTROPIUM ~ is a Gem found in Ethiopia, Africa, and Cyprus, of a leek-green colour, similar to the emerald, but distinguished by its red speckles. It is called Heliotrope because, if thrown into a vessel of water and exposed to the sun, it changes to blood colour, and this is especially the case with the Ethiopian variety. Concerning the Heliotrope, the impudence of sorcerers affirms that the unguent made from the sap of an herb so named will make the person using it invisible. The Heliotrope is also said to bring riches and good name; it is a safeguard against poisonous reptiles and bloody fluxes. (See Albertus Magnus and Pliny, 1. 37, c. 10).

HELNESED ~ is Coral.

HELUNHAT ~ is the Ring of Solomon which figures in Necromantic Art.

HEMICYCMUM, HADE ~ A mining term.

HESMIC ~ The fourth part of a pound.

HIDUS ~ Flower of Copper.

HINNICULA, GENICULA, GUMICULA ~ The medicinal root, Valerian. The variations I conclude to be mistakes of transcribers.

HISMAT ~ is Froth Or Scum of Silver.

HISPANICUM VIRIDE, or HYSPALENSIS ~ is Verdigris.

HOLSEBON, HELSATON, HELSEBON ~ Names for prepared Common Salt.

HOMO FUNEM IN BRACHIUM VEL PECTUS INVOLENS ~ A man carrying a rope twined round his arm or waist.

HOMUNCULI IMAGUNCULAE ~ The Minute Image of a Man or Homunculus, the invisible sidereal man made in the likeness of man. Diminutive men who have within them the invisible, sidereal man.

HORIZON ~ Mercury or Quicksilver of Gold.

HUNC, or HUCCI ~ is Jupiter, or Tin.

HUMOR VITAE ~ Vital Moisture, which prevents all living things from becoming dry, the Radical Humour, the Food and Nourishment of the Natural Heat.

HUMORIS RECEPTACULUM ~ A Receptacle of Moisture.

HYACINTHUS ~ A Gem which differs from the amethyst, the violet which is so conspicuous in the latter being paler in the former, pleasing at first sight, but seeming to grow pale before the eye is satisfied, fading more quickly than the flower which bears its name (see Pliny, 1. 37, c. 9, and

Solinus, c. 33). Hyacinthus and Chrysolites are brought from Ethiopia, India and Arabia. The Arabians distinguish three species-of a, red, citrine and antimony-colour, i.e., silver-white. Albertus makes two species of this class, the first showing white in saffron, watery in red, which he calls humid; the second sapphiric, which is very yellow and translucid, and is called the Ethiopian Sapphire Hyacinth. The Hyacinth has the virtue of promoting sleep; it preserves against poisoned arrows; it raises the spirits of men; and it fortifies the heart. I omit other qualities which seem to me magical. In conclusion, the ancients dedicated the Hyacinth to Jupiter.

1. Hyacinth showing reddish in golden.
2. Golden.
3. Approaching amber.
4. Rough.
5. Manufactured and falsified.

HYARITH ~ is Luna.

HYDROMANTIA ~ is an Art of Divination derived from the astrology of water or from the stars which rule the water and which make known to men the approach of unusual inundations, high floods, and other phenomena.

HYDROPHOBIA ~ Dread of water, a stye in the eye.

HYDROPIPER ~ Red Water-pepper, or Persicaria.

HYPOGLOSSUM ~ Hippoglossum, Epiglossum, Epiphyllocarpon, Uvularia, Boni facia, Lingua Pagana, Bis Lingua ~ Names of plants, the Laurel, the Campanula, the Uvulum, the Gypsophila.

ICTERITIA RUBEA ~ Erysipelas.
IDAM ~ Victuals, Food.
IDIOTAE ~ are the Despisers of the True Arts, although they may be most able professors of false ones.
IDROAGIRA ~ Alkaline Water.
IDRAOGIROS ~ A Dung-hill used as a Furnace.
IFFIDES ~ White Lead, Ashes of Lead.
IGNIS ~ is, according to some opinions, the Oil which comes to the surface in distillation.
IGNIS ~ Fire for the Stone of the Philosophers.
1. Bernhard says he would have preferred to reveal it; they say it should be made with dung, lamps, or coals. The first degree takes place in water, the second in ashes, the third in sand, the fourth in iron, or in the flame.
2. *Rosarius* says: The heat of dung operates in digestion; the bath is useless. Some will have it that ashes should be put into the bath, and if the fire is to be increased, sand must be put therein.

3. They compare the rule of the fire to the four seasons of the year. *Aurora* says: Make a dampish fire; digest and coct it steadily, without letting it flicker or boil over; skilfully enclose all round with air, so that nothing may burn, alter, or penetrate. So also says Trevisan.

4. The first grade of the fire lasts until the white appears, and takes place with one lamp in three months. The next takes place until the white breaks up, with two wicks in the space of three months. The third until the white is fixed; the fourth until the end of three months.

5. The flame must not touch the cask.

6. The glass must not be taken out until all is ready. Let not others deceive you.

7. When you have decided to put in the matter, the glass and the matter must he warm; then shake the whole effectually together, so that it may sink to the bottom; then seal it.

8. In the distillation the alembic must be of glass, and covered at all joints.

9. Trevisan says: Cook it so that the elements may remain, and regulate it so that the water may not be destroyed. Regulate the earth 5o that the air may not be destroyed. The ash is a dead thing and cannot be raised up. But the calx can be raised up.

IGNIS ALGIR ~ is a very powerful Fire.

IGNIS CALOR ~ Caloric is either natural or artificial.

IGNIS CLARE ARDENS ~ Clear burning Fire, is Sulphur.

IGNIS ELEMENTARIS ~ is Sulphur, but not vulgar sulphur.

IGNIS EXSTINCTUS ~ Extinguished Fire, is Sulphur deprived of its virtue.

IGNIS PERSICUS ~ Persian Fire, is an Ulcer torturing with a fiery heat.

IGNIS PRUINUS ADEPTUS — Adeptic Frozen Fire, is Quintessence of Wine, Spirit of Wine, rectified with Tartar.
IGNIS LEONIS — Fire of the Lion, Elemental Fire, Aether, called also Pyr, Ethos, Jupiter Argos, names for the element of fire.

The four grades of fire must be studied by operators, for so is fire distributed, there being not one grade merely at the crowd conceive ; so also the beginning, middle, and end of these stages must be considered, as they were observed by the primeval philosophers. They must be appreciated, however, not by the senses only, but by their effect in their proper subjects, and by judgment joined to the perceptions of sense, and chiefly of sight and touch. The first grade is very slow, and is like an inactive lukewarmness; it is called the heat of a tepid bath, of excrement, of digestion, of circulation, etc. This grade is shown to the touch when the finger of a sensitive man can stand it without begetting any acute feeling of heat. Of this nature is the vapourous fire of the philosophers which is likened to the warmth generated by a fowl when hatching its young, or of a man rightly constituted by nature. It is generally as follows: such as is yielded by a furnace of a gently kindled vapour-bath, or such as is that of an earthenware melting-pot placed on a furnace, or of a vapour-bath placed in a sound vessel over a moderate heat. The second grade is fiercer, yet such that it is safe to touch, nor does it injure the hand. They call it the heat of the ashes, because it is produced by a fire kindled under a cinder-pan. Cinders on account of their fineness do not produce much air. The third grade will burn the hand, and is compared to boiling sand or iron filings; it is called the fire of sand or of iron plates. The fourth is the highest grade, and is generally the most destructive. It is the reverberatory fire, and a living flame is produced from wood or coals easily influenced by the bellows. These grades when we refer to their effects in certain cases differ very much. The grade which is last in that of vegetables is first in antimony; but the first grade may be understood as the heat of a bath. Nevertheless, in the operation of the bath, there may be all four grades; the first when heat is produced with a little water, the second when it is very fierce, the third when it rages, the fourth when it destroys by extreme ebullition.

IGNIS SAPIENTUM — Fire of the Wise, is warm Horse Dung.

IGNITIO — is Calcination, the Reduction of Bodies by the powerful action of fire into Calx. It is also Combustion and Reverberation.

ILECH CRUDUM — Crude Ilech, is a composition of the first matter of the three prime principles — Mercury, Salt and Sulphur — whereof all things are composed.

ILECH MAGNUM — is the Ascendant or Star of Medicine, which we receive with the medicine, wherein it is concealed ; as the superior stars in the firmament, so the inferior in man. It is given in medicine, but it is also implanted in man.

ILECH PRIMUM — is Principle or Beginning. Called also Ileias and Ileadus.

ILECH SUPRA NATURALE — Supernatural Ilech, or Primal Ilech of the Stars, is a supercelestial conjunction and union of the stars of the firmament with the stars of inferior things.

ILEIDOS — is Elemental Air, the Firmament, Heaven. In man, it is the Spirit which permeates every member.

ILIASTER — signifies in general the Occult Virtue of Nature, by which all thing increase, are nourished, multiply and quicken, concerning which consult Paracelsus in his book of Meteoric Generation. But it is understood variously concerning the elements and concerning man. In the elements it is the Vegetative Essences of Nature, which are fourfold, according to the number of the elements, and it is called Chaos.

ILIASTER, ELIASTER, or **ILIADUM** ~ is the first chaos of the matter of all things, constituted of Sulphur, Salt and Mercury. There is nothing in the wide nature of things which does not consist of this triplicity, and these are the three principles of Theophrastus which are discovered by spagyric analysis. We find nothing outside this triad which exists in each of its three components in each element. Fernelius comments on them in his Medicine of Inherent Moisture. Of these also the ancients treated, and they were not therefore discovered by Theophrastus, but he recalled them when they were forgotten from darkness into light. It is quadruple, we have seen, in the four elements. There is the chaos of earth, the chaos of water, the chaos of air, and the chaos of fire. There are also four Iliastri of men, constituting long life. The first, or implanted, is the span of life, even life itself or its balsam in man.

The second Iliaster, prepared Iliaster, is the span of life, and the life itself, which we derive from the elements or from elementary things.

The third Iliaster is the prepared span of the balsam which we derive from the quintessence of things.

The fourth, or great, Iliaster is the passage of the mind or soul into the other world, as took place with Enoch, Elias, and others.

IMAGINATIO ~ is the Star in Man, the Celestial or Supercelestial Body.

IMAGINES ~ Images, are Effigies in Wax or Metal, wherein the celestial virtues operate.

IMBIBERE ~ To Imbibe, is to thicken by rubbing, polishing, etc.

IMBIBITIO ~ is Ablution, when a liquid joined to a body is made light, and, finding no exit retreats into the body, and washes it so long with frequent lustrations, until it is wholly coagulate therewith, and is unable to rise further, but the whole remains fixed. This assuredly is a philosophical operation, nor does it yield its secret to the vulgar.

IMMERSIVA CORROSIO — takes place when bodies are plunged in other substances, and reduced to a calx. It is either humid or dry.

IMPRESSIONES — Impressions, Seals, or Signatures are invisible fruits of the stars of inferiors, not of sun and moots.

IMPURUM ALCALI — is Froth of Alcali, which is carried off in repurging after building up.

IMPURUM TARTARI — A Rough Salt, Dregs of Tartar.

IN GLOBULOS DISSOLVERE — To Melt into Globules.

IN MARMORE VEL IN MARMARIO TERERE — To Rub upon a Marble Slab.

INANIMATI — are the Pygmies.

INCARNATIVA — of Surgeons are Medicaments for contracting the skin over wounds, or Flesh Astringents.

INCERATIO — is the combination of moisture with a dry matter to the consistence of soft wax by a gradual blending. It is hence called a waxing over. There is also an imbibition performed by irrigation, the dry substance absorbing the moist. This is also the nutrition of physicians, in which the gum sarcocolla, litharge, and other things are absorbed by moisture, and become suitable for use.

INCIBIA — Graves walled over or covered with stones.

INCINERATIO — is an Ignition converting bodies into ashes by means of a powerful fire. We speak of vegetables or animals as incinerated, but the same operation performed on minerals we describe (in chemical language) as reduction to a calx.

INCINERATIO and **SCOURING** — When the black begins to yield, and the matter to whiten like ashes, then fire and water, or earth and water, combine; the water disappears, earth increases, till all is parched, dry, and like powder.

INCLINATIO — Inclination is the bent of Nature, or the disposition which indicates the nature of a man.

INCORPORATIO — Incorporation is Commingling, in which things moist are immediately blended with things dry into a conglomerate mass. But this is not done by a slow imbibing, but the whole fluid is at once poured on in sufficient quantity to produce a paste, whence the operation is called impacting, or kneading, or by others subaction and pounding. Incorporated substances are, however, left for digestion by means of heat, so that by mutual action and passion a common mingling may obtain.

INCUBA — is the Bride of the Sun.

INCUBUS — is a Nocturnal Demon which tempts and deceives women in sleep, as if they had carnal intercourse therewith.

INDICUM SAL, SAL GEMMAE — is Cappadocia Gemma, a Precious Stone found in Phrygia and polished in Cappadocia.

INDICUM — Indigo, is a Spume of two species, namely, Native Indigo, which is found to exist spontaneously in certain Indian reeds. It is called Indigo Stone by painters, but erroneously, for it is not a stone. Adarca, a thick salt scum which collects about reeds in marshy places, is very similar to indigo, but it is afterwards treated by art, whereas indigo is natural. There is, however, a second species made by dyers ; it is of purple colour, and is manufactured in caldrons. This is the better kind. It has a blue appearance, and is called by the Germans Woadflower, or Indian colour. It i slightly astringent, bursts, purges, and reduces ulcers. Pliny (1. 35, c. 6) remarks that natural indigo is as to its nature and constituents undetermined. The manufactured is produced from the black scum which adheres to brazen or copper caldrons. Others affirm that it is simply the sap of herbs, with which clothes are dyed, that they call indigo, that is woad, which is otherwise domestically familiar in Thuringia, where it is much used in dyes. This is properly a manufactured indigo, but there is also a wild woad. Consult Dioscorides, 1. 2.

INDICUS COLOR ~ Indigo Blue.

INFLUENTIA ~ Influx; when by thought and imagination we attract to us the virtues and natures of the planets and superior stars. It is two-fold, that which derives to us through the medium of created things, such as the influx of heaven through the firmament, and that which is given to us immediately, that is, by God alone ; the second is supernatural as the first is artificial, natural, and moral.

INFLUENTIA NATURALIS, or **NATURAL INFLUX** ~ is that which is poured down by the superior stars of the firmament, in accordance with natural law, into or upon inferior things, whereby they govern and rule through inclination in men, animals, etc., and through potencies and efficacies in insentient things. Hence we learn that this inclination is a certain brute force and magnetic attraction, which i easy to resist and withstand by moral influence; being assisted by the divine inspiration in any cases of special difficulty.

INFUNDIBULUM, or **FUNNEL** ~ is a Metallic Vessel of oblong shape, having a handle, hollow within, for the reception of molten metal, Its configuration is like that of a staff or rod. The Germans call it a Gutter or Dunghill.

INFUNDIRIN ~ To Soak or Moisten.

INGESTORES ~ A Carrier on the Mountains.

INHUMATIO ~ Humectation in a Dung-bath.

INHUMARE ~ To Bury under the Earth, to Putrefy, or also to Reduce into Earth. When the solution takes place, the old man is buried in a bath; then he is covered with blackness, and remains hidden without any lustre. The sun has entered a gloomy grave.

INSIDERE IN BACILLO ~ To Set on a Cross-beam secured by a rope.

INSIDERE IN CORIO ~ To Sit down on Leather.

INSTRUMENTUM CUM INDICE MENSORUM ALPINORUM ~ An Indicating Compass.

INSTRUMENTUM FERREUM, QUOD MACHINE FOLLES COMPRIMIT ~ An Iron Instrument which works the bellows.

INSTRUMENTUM FERREUM, QUO TERRA VERBATUR ~ An Iron Instrument with which the earth is beaten.

INSTRUMENTUM METALLICUM, SIGNIFICANS MUNDI PARTES ~ The Metallic Instrument which shows the quarters of the world, i.e., the Compass.

INTERIOR MURUS FORNACIS ~ The Inner Wall of the Furnace; Lining.

INTER VENIUM ~ A Wedge-shaped Rock.

IOS ~ is a Poison, or Drug.

IOTA, or **IORA** ~ is a Green Branch.

IPACEDES ~ Hairy Beard.

IRIS ~ is a Stone similar to crystal, and according to some is the Root or Foundation of Crystal; the hexagonal Iris is found frequently in Arabia, and, according to Pliny (1. 37, c. 9), in a certain island of the Red Sea. It is found in our own country in the mountains and rivers of Westphalia between Treves and the Rhine. It is maintained to be the native Cadmia of Galen, which we have treated under its proper head. They also say that the latter is hexagonal, although a round one is sometimes found, even as the holes in the centre of a honeycomb are hexagonal, and at the edges round. It is an exceedingly dry stone and very fine in constitution. Some say that it is composed of the essential moisture of water, which laves the matter of the stone, the same being generated in a red slime. It is called Iris because in the middle there are defined, rainbow-like lines; or because when shone upon by the sun indoors, it sends forth the colours and appearance of the rainbow upon the nearest walls. So testifies Pliny, and he adds that there are certain rough sides and unequal corners, which, when exposed out of doors to the sun, send forth rays which are reflected upon each other, but some also illuminate surrounding objects. He says also that an Iris like wax, but very hard, is found in Persia, but it has not the quality of the gem which he calls Zeros, a crystal encircled by a line. Compare the Demon Stone of Albertus, which was of two colours like the Iris, was good in fevers, and an antidote to poison.

IVA ARTHETICA VEL MUSCATA — A Medicine for Lame Limbs.

IVA POTABILIS — A Draught that restores Soundness to Lame Limbs.

JACENS ~ Base of the Mountain. Bottom of the Mountain.
JASPIS ~ Hematite, Bloodstone. There is a green variety.
The Jasp of the Germans is a stone of many species.
Dioscorides enumerates seven:
1. Green jasper, like the emerald.
2. Jasper like crystal, similar to phlegm in colour.
3. Jasper not unlike copper.
4. Smoky jasper, called Capnias.
5. Assyrian jasper, encircled by white and lustrous lines.
6. Jasper like terebinth, called Terebinthizusa, being of the colour of turpentine.
7. Jasper, similar to the stone Callais.
All these species are amulets, and, according to Dioscorides, hasten parturition when applied to the thighs. Pliny (1. 37, c. 8 and 9) enumerates several species, according to colour, country, and quality, some of which may be added in this place:

1. Translucent green Jaspar, like the Indian emerald, worn by many people. It is regarded as an amulet in all the East, and when surrounded by a transverse white line it is called grammatias and polygrammos.
2. Green or grey-coated Cyprian jasper.
3. Persian Jasper like copper, and hence called aerizusa.
4. Cerulean jasper from the vicinity of Thermodon, a river of Pontus.
5. Purple Jasper of Phrygia.
6. Dull purple or cerulean Jasper of Cappodocia.
7. Thracian Jasper similar to Indian.
8. Dark Jasper of Chalcis.
9. Violet Jasper of Sardis.
10. Crystalline or phlegmatic Jasper.

But the best, according to Pliny, is purple, rose-coloured, or emerald. He also notes an onyx called Jasponyx, which is a spotted stone, clouded as with snow, and dotted as with bright sparkling stars, similar to Salt of Megara, and as if discoloured by smoke. This he calls Capnias, but it is included by Dioscorides among the varieties of jasper. Pliny, Theophrastus, and Dioscorides, do seem in a measure to disagree. But this we leave to be threshed out by more learned persons. The stone which we now call Turquoise is beyond doubt a species of jasper. Its hue inclines to cerulean, yet it is sometimes flaxen, glittering, white, shining, and as if milk had mingled in a yellow colour. It is supposed to have the virtue of strengthening sight, and preserving from many mischances. We also in Germany possess a most beautiful species of jasper, which has great efficacy. It is found in Bohemia, and is of green colour, glittering with red lines and spots, or otherwise of a brown colour, or chestnut. It is found in Thuringia, Misnia, and other places. I have found jasper highly efficacious against excessive menstruation. It helps parturition and protects the foetus.

1. Jasper, on the one hand, similar to emerald, on the other, cerulean, obtained by mining.
2. Similar to emerald, ornamented with lines. Having blue bands.
3. Blue in green; bluish jasper.
4. Black in green; blackish green jasper.
5. Green, milky jasper. Whitish green jasper.
6. Jasper, called Borea, like a serene blue sky. Oriental Turquoise.
7. A variety of the former, but part green.
8. Another, shining white on blue.
9. Manufactured Borea jasper.
10. Jasponyx, part jasper, part Onyx, or Chalcedony.
11. Purple jasper, mixed with Chalcedony, and having white spots.
12. Purple jasper, full of spots and white blemishes. Also a similar species of flaxen colour.
13. Purple jasper, very strangely composed of Chalcedony and red and yellow jasper, in spots and lines.
14. Pure Purple jasper.
15. Corensian jasper, from Misnia; colour of red blood.
16. Black in red.
17. Pale yellow.
18. Beautiful reddish yellow jasper.
19. Yellow, with red spots.
20. Liver-coloured.
21. Dark liver-coloured jasper.
22. Islebian jasper, red in colour, with white, pellucid, sexangular fluors, like the stone geodes.

JASSA — Herb of the Trinity, Pansy, or Heartsease.
JUDEX METALLICUS — An Assaying Officer.
JUMNISUM, or **JUMNIZUM** — is Ferment.
JUPITER — is Tin.

JURATUS PARTIUM VENDITOR ~ A sworn broker of mining shares.
JUSSA ~ is Gyps; a kind of plaster.

KACHIMIA, or **KAKIMIA** ~ is the Immature Minera of any Metal, otherwise an Imperfect Metal, still in its first state, like the child hidden in the womb of his mother. Thirty species are known.
KAIB ~ Sour Milk.
KAL ~ is Salt from a torrent.
KALD ~ Vinegar.
KALI ~ is Clavellated Ashes, i.e., Potash, Woad-Ash, or Pearl-Ash. A Salt, Vegetable, or Plant. Its ashes, if burnt, combine into a heap. It is Soda from which Glass is made. The Salt which flows out in melting during the process of Glass-making is Sal Alkali.
KALI ~ The Arabian Usnen; Rhasis identifies it with Alumen Asfur.
KALNOS ~ is Smoke.
KAMAR, CAMAR, or **KYANA** ~ Names of Silver.
KAMIR ~ is Ferment.
KANSOR ~ is Tin.
KAPRILI ~ is Sulphur.

KAR ~ is a brilliant and fiery precious Stone.
KARABE ~ is a Gum, like amber.
KARLINA ~ is Dill or Anise.
KARTINA ~ Wild Spice.
KASAM ~ is Iron.
KATIMIA, GREEK CADMIA, LATIN CALAMINA, or **CALAMINE STONE** ~ is Ore of Zinc. But Calamine is a Root of Tutty, and indeed Tutty itself, in a raw state. It is the Stone, whereby the ore is dyed into brass-colour. True Tutty cleaves to the top of the oven.
KAYL ~ is Sour Milk.
KAYSIR ~ is Pumice Stone.
KAZDIR, KASDIR, KACIR, KASSICEROS ~ are names of Tin.
KIBRIC ~ is the Father and the First Matter of Mercury and all Fluids. That from which Mercury comes. The Stone is also called Kibric.
KIBRITH ~ is Sulphur.
KISES ~ Salt from a Spring.
KOBOLTUM, KOBALTUM, or **COLLETUM** ~ is a Metallic Substance, darker than lead or iron, sometimes of ashen hue, wanting in metallic tint or lustre. It can be melted and made into plates. It is not fixed, but takes away the higher metals with it in smoke. It is also Cadmia Stone, from which a useful medicine is made, Copperstone, Climia, Cathimia, Ore of Zinc. It is a pillaging Sulphur, which takes away the good ore in smoke.
KOMA or **KOMARTOS** ~ is living Calx.
KONIS ~ is Ash.
KOST ~ is the Beech Tree.
KUHUL ~ is Lead of the Philosophers. See Turba, Fol. 21.
KUMEN ~ is Unity.
KURIA or **KYMIA** ~ is Lump, Mass. The same art is called Alchimia, Alkymia.

KYBRIUS or **KEBRICK** ~ is Arsenic.
KYMIT ELEVATUM ~ is White Sublimed Cinnabar.
KYMUS ~ is Lump, Mass.
KYMUM or **KYMINUM** ~ is a joining or Uniting.
KYMIA ~ is the Instrument or Cucurbit used for Distillation.
KYMENNA ~ is a Vessel of Clay, narrow-necked and big-bellied.
KYMOLEA ~ is Slime which collects under the whetstone, on which weapons are sharpened.
KYRAM ~ is Snow.
KYVA ~ is Opoponax, Gum-resin of Parsnip-root.

LABOR SOPHIAE ~ i.e., Paradisus, the other world.
LABRUM ~ Fan, Winnowing Basket, Tub.
LAC PAPAVERIS ~ i.e., Opium.
LAC VIRGINIS ~ is Mercurial Water, the Dragon's Tail; it washes and coagulates without any manual labour; it is the Mercury of the Philosophers, Lunar and Solar Sap, out of catholic earth and water.
LACERTA CARNIS CORPORISQUE CAVITAS ~ A Skin Disease. Also a Fleshly Protuberance or Muscular Growth, a Cavity made by disease in the body.
LACERTA RUBRA or **COLCOTAR** ~ i.e., Red Vitriol, Hungarian Vitirol. The Alchemical Green Lizard.
LACUNA ~ A Marsh, Pit, or Cavity.
LACUNE ~ i.e., Embossed or Wrought Earth.
LACUSCULUS ~ A small Pit.
LACUS ~ Washing-tray, or Trough.
LAMAC ~ i.e., Gum Arabic.
LAMARE ~ is Sulphur.

LAMARE LAMPE — The same.
LAMINA — Plate.
LAMINA — i.e., Orpiment.
LAMINA CURVATA EXCOCTORUM — A Smelting Plate.
LAMINA FERREA, UTRINQUE CAVATA — An Iron Scraping Instrument.
LAMINA FERREA CRASSA — A Coarse Iron Plate.
LAMINA FERREX PARS — A Part of an Iron Plate.
LAMINAE AEREAE — A Pan of Brass or Copper.
LAMINAE FORAMINE PLENAE — Perforated Plates.
LAN — i.e., Dead Silver.
LANX — i.e., Bitter Almond. Item, a dish.
LAOS — i.e., Tin.
LAPIDES:
1. Dense, iron-coloured, masculine, Misnensian Magnet, mined at Swartzburg.
2. Female, black, from Suarceburg.
3. A species of Theamedes from the same place; on one side it attracts, and on the other repels, iron.
4. Theamedes, the Stone which repels iron.
5. Sterile or adulterated Magnet, which neither attracts nor repels iron. *Item:* tin ore dispersed throughout the rider.
6. White, the sixth species of Pliny.
7. A Burnt Magnet-stone.
8. Cloddy, iron-coloured Hematite of Misnensis.
9. Black, cloddy Stones of Hercynius.
10. A Black Bloodstone which exudes a black sap.
11. A black Stone from iron mines which exudes a yellowish black sap.
12. A black Stone of Hercynius, shaped like a head.
13. A Crustaceous Stone, like cinnabar or red lead.
14. A Bloodstone like burnt coal.
15. Burnt.

16. An iron-colour Schist or Bloodstone, easily divided into long sections.
17. Wedge-shaped, iron-coloured Bohemian Bloodstone.
18. A Stone of Hercynius, with an internal glittering like minium.
19. A species of Schist or Hematite from Anneberg, the size of a walnut, very hard, and when struck, causing the hammer to rebound.
20. Burnt.
21. A Red Rock containing Schist and Hematite.
22. A hard greyish Stone with an outer surface of iron-colour.
23. A red Earth like Rubrica, containing Hematite.

Stones that emit sap when struck:
1. Morochtus, or Leucogia, or Leucographia, a soft variety from Saxony.
2. The same, from the same place, but of hard texture.
3. A hard Galactite, exuding a milky sap when struck. From the copper mines of Hildesheimer.
4. Ash-coloured Galactite.
5. Black Hematite, emitting a yellowish black sap.

Other Stones of divers kinds:
1. Stelechites, found in a clay near Misena.
2. A Pentagonal Stone.
3. A Stone having thirteen angles; white; found at Hildesheimer.
4. Armenian Stone; slimy; found in true Armenian bolus, as the Samius is found in Saurian earth.
5. Emery, iron-coloured, and harder than iron.
6. A Stone found in flint, shaped like the almond nut.
7. The Stone Menoides, or Moonstone, or Pharmacite.
8. A white, heavy, cuprine Stone, composed of little pipes, like a honeycomb.

9. A yellowish Stone, light, like the gravel-stone Tofus; also of honeycomb nature; mined at Rabsich, above Misena. Sometimes its surface is smooth, sometimes excrescent.
10. A white, hard, round Stone, having on one side a number of small circles described round the same centre, and on the other side having the appearance of beams of ash.
11. Very hard black Zeblician stone, with a preponderance of granite.

Rough Stones:
1. A rude, green Stone, like unpolished jasper.
2. A rude Stone, like pyrites.
3. A sterile Stone, like lead.

Stones which are liquefied by fire. Of these there are three genera:
1. Similar to a translucid fluor.
2. Opaque, soft, as is the first also, and fire cannot be struck from it.
3. Hard; gives out sparks when struck ; it is a flint of which glass is made.

Watery or Aqueous Stones:
1. The lesser Ammonite, like the egg of a fish.
2. Greater Ammonite.
3. Lepidolite, like the scales of fish, having many hues.
4. Long Strombites, like the aquatic snail, whorl shaped.
5. The short Strombites.
6. Ctenites, greyish, striated, something like a comb; a scallop.
7. White, sandy, in which Ctenites is imbedded.
8. A hard, grey Stone, found in Lusatia, and containing Ctenites.
9. A grey Stone, covered with gold-coloured armature, containing a kind of lynx stone.
10. Onychites, like sweet-smelling nails.
11. Ostracites, like oysters.

12. Another, made up of six oyster shells.
13. Tellinite, in every way like Tellinus (unknown), covered with gold-coloured armature.
14. Hildesheimer Conchites, like a bivalve shell, with a gold-coloured armature.

Lightning Stones:
1. Black Ceraunea, i.e., Lightning Stone, large, heavy, almost wedge-shaped, perforated on its broad side. Its length is nine fingers, its breadth four, its weight three and a half pounds. In the year 1544 this stone was cast on a house in Vienna, and penetrated through the wine-cellar, being driven twelve cubits into the earth.
2. Another, hammer-shaped, bluish-black, perforated at the narrower end. In the year 1560, this stone fell at Torga with great force.
3. Another, greenish-black, quite wedge-shaped, perforated in the middle. About the size of the bluish-black one first mentioned.
4. A pointed ruddy Ceraunea, long, round, and somewhat smooth, driven into a tree at Torganus. About the size and density of the first one.
5. These Ceraunea are the product of lightning or thunderbolts, and stones of a similar kind are found at Epirus.

Glossopetrse, or precious Stones resembling the human tongue:
1. White, with blue lines on the surface.
2. White, and sharp as a saw on either side.
3. Prussian grey, like the tongue of the woodpecker.
4. Grey, like the tongue of the wren.
5. Dark brown.
6. Bluish grey, found at Tungros. Sometimes covered with iron, sometimes not.
7. Black, from Prussia.

Selenite Stones:

1. Selenite which shines like the moon, and hence its name, shaped like the specular stone, or Mary's ice,
2. Transparent and scissile, used for window glass in Thuringia, Saxony, etc.
3. Mesoselenus, greyish, small, striated, curved like a horn, having the appearance of a crescent moon.
4. Another, like the third, with a gold-coloured armature.

Stones formed of petrified wood:
1. Elatites of fir-trees.
2. Oaks turned into Stone.
3. Beeches turned into Stone.
4. Alders turned into Stone.
5. Sometimes these trees are found, on the other hand, to contain a white fluor, and sometimes a yellow pyrites.
6. A Stone is made of the alder-wood as follows: A piece of that wood is selected of the size required, and is placed in the vessel of brass in which hops are boiled to make beer. When the hops have been well boiled, the alder-wood is taken out along with them, and is then placed in the hop cellars, or beer cellars, and is covered with sand or gravel for the space of three years. After this time, it is taken up, and is found to have become Stone, and can be used for sharpening knives.

Stones called from living things-heavy and pointed:
1. Hieraclites, in colour like the wings of the hawk.
2. Perdicites, coloured like the breast of the partridge.

Thunder Stones:
1. Brownish, hemispherical, with ten lines on the surface, not radiating from a single point. A grey Thunder Stone, marked with ten lines distributed in pairs. Full of small holes.
2. Another, mud-coloured, twice the size of an egg, with twenty lines, grouped by fours. Full of small holes.
3. Of the same colour, having ten lines without holes.

4. Reddish, hemispherical, having ten unpunctured lines.
5. Brownish, with semi-circular lines, unpunctured.
6. Yellow and smooth on the surface, the lower part being perforated.

Heavy Stones:
1. Belemnites Major, ash-coloured, has a white earth, and when rubbed smells like burnt horn of oxen.
2. A smaller species, of the same colour, containing grey earth.
3. A large Stone, containing sand, without smell when rubbed.
4. A small Stone, containing sand, without smell. All these are found at Hildesheimer.
5. A Prussian Stone, reddish black, transparent, containing earth.
6. Another, but wax-colour, also transparent, and containing earth.
7. White, as if burnt, found in Hildesheimer earth. Contains a black hard stone. The best colour. Does not much differ from the smell of white sap.

LAPIDES, etc. — Stones like bones and shells, called Osteodes and Ostracodes :
1. Enosteos, a Stony Concretion found on fallen trees.
2. Osteocollus, white or grey, porous ; when taken into the body it joins broken bones in a wonderful manner.
3. A variety from Misnia, found in a clay, clay-coloured, hard and solid.
4. Lithostracus, a shell-coloured stalactite.

LAPIDES AB ANIMALIBUS, etc.:
1. Thuringian Myites, superficially full and round, and like a seated mouse in appearance. There is another mentioned by Georgius Agricola, which is like a mussel shell.
2. Grey, oblong Hessian Myites.
3. Onyx, or Onydrite, like the human nail.

4. The Stone Enorchis, like testicles.
5. Triorchis, like three testicles, found in rivers.

LAPIDES COLORATI:
1. Ashen, Violet, Aldeberg Iolite.
2. Red Aldenberg Iolite.
3. Laurenstein, found by chance; when moistened and exposed to the sun it exhales a smell of violets.
4. Marieberg Iolite; when struck with a mallet it gives forth an odour of musk.
5. Thuringian Iolite, which exhales an odour of wild thyme.
6. Zeblicius Ophites, of which some have no smell, and others a musty scent.
7. Solinum Echites, having a fragrance of wine, and therefore a kind of wine stone (Tartar).
8. Hildesheimer Iolite ; when struck with another stone, or with a mallet, it smells like horn.

LAPIDES GEODES — A Stone containing Earth, of oblong shape, filled with a hard ochrine sand, and rattling when shaken; the Stone Chemnicensis, of a ruddy colour, like iron-stone, and containing a moist clay.

LAPIDES JUDAICI :
1. Like the stone of an olive, striated, and still called Olive Stones in Palestine.
2. Another, also striate.

LAPIDES TROCHITIAE ET ENTROCHI:
1. White Spangeberg Trochites, called by us Wheel Stone.
2. Grey Wheel Stone.
3. Subashen Wheel Stone.
4. Slimy.
5. Equally long, White Hildesheimer Entrochus, consisting of fourteen Trochites.
6. Another of slimy quality, consisting of ten Trochites.
7. Grey, consisting of three Trochites.

8. A smooth Trochite, puffed up in the middle, and having zones, or encircling lines.

9. A rude Grey Stone of Spangenberg, in which there are Trochites. Found on a lofty mountain, mountain and citadel thereof being perhaps named after it.

LAPILLI ~ Pebbles:

1. Alectorius, said to be found in the gizzard of a cock.
2. Chelidonia, said to be taken from the swallow.
3. Crabstone.
4. Perch Stone.
5. Impure Pearls.
6. Indian Pearl.
7. Adulterated Pearl, made of very white glass.
8. Another, made of bone, tinged with spume of silver.
9. Another, round, and of Oriental origin.

LAPILLI COLLECTI EX MATERIA, QUAE LAVATUR ~ i.e., Soapstone.

LAPILLI MINUTI, etc. ~ Pebbles washed up by waves.

LAPILLI NIGRI MAGNI ~ Very large black Stones.

LAPILLI NIGRI MAJUSCULI ~ Small fragments of Ore.

LAPILLI NIGRI MEDIOCRES ~ A Bed of Hardened Mud over a vein containing ore.

LAPILLI NIGRI PARVI ~ Small black Stones.

LAPILLUS ~ is a Coagulation of Extracted Humour, which is crumbling and vitreous. The humour is of a middle quality. The lapillus also coagulates into moisture. Sometimes it is thicker and like slime, sometimes thinner. It is not often as large as hailstones, but it is frequently like grains of salt or particles of snow.

LAPILLUS FISSILI AEROSUS ~ i.e., Slate.

LAPIS ~ Stone, in chemistry is any fixed substance which does not evaporate.

LAPIS ~ or Stone, from which black lead is obtained.

LAPIS ADIZ ~ i.e., Sal Ammoniac.

LAPIS ANIMALIS ~ The Animal Stone, is Human Blood. Item, Curenta, the turtle, who carries his house on his back.
LAPIS ARABICUS ~ is similar to masculine ivory on the authority of Dioscorides and Pliny. It is chiefly useful in dentistry and in stopping hemorrhage. But such is the quality of this stone that many learned men have disputed about it and still do so. But if the subject be properly considered, Arabian Stone is nothing but the Moonstone or Mary's Ice, or Spar. Windows were formerly made of it, with thin wooden frames instead of lead. The best Gypsum is also made from it, as Pliny witnesses. It is according to Albertus the extreme part of Gypsum, and he calls it Aphroselinum, because at night it reflects the likeness of the moon, or because it is made from dew by the foam of the moon. Some dispute whether Selenite is the Moonstone which Dioscordes calls Aphroselinum. But of this elsewhere. This true Moonstone is called Lapis Arabicus, because first found in Arabia, though Albertus affirms that it was at first discovered at Saguntia in Spain, and that more abundantly than elsewhere; afterwards in many places in Germany. If the subject be considered, there are many species of this stone. There is first the small stone, of spotted appearance, found at Bononia in Italy, according to Pliny; it is like a blemished ebony, and Dioscorides calls it Lapis Arabicus. A second is found among us; it is blackish, and deficient in brightness. We have also one which is very transparent, and was formerly used as windowglass. This is the Selenite mentioned in Scripture. There is a fourth in Saxony, which is like ebony, and is the Arabicus of Pliny. There is a fifth with black or red blemishes, which may also be the Lapis Arabicus of Dioscorides. Albertus distinguishes three species of Moonstone-one clear as glass, of which windows are made; another black like atrament; a third of citrine colour, which he calls Orpiment or Arsenic. It should be noted that

the Arabians speak of arsenic or native Orpiment as similar to Moonstone, having regard to its outward crust. But although the Moonstone is citrine it is not merely orpiment, and Albertus errs. It has not the same fatty nature, and a comparison which is founded only on the outward crust is exceedingly foolish. The Moonstone is a precious gem, and, as it were, a concreted humour of the earth, petrified or congealed into a crystal and hardened stone, and is hence called Mary's Ice. Some say that it is the dew of heaven coagulated under the rays of the moon into a species of stone, especially the clearest kind, called Aphroselinum. The Moonstone is found in our mines, and in many other places. The Elbe brings this stone down with it as well as gypsum when inundations occur. For a more perfect knowledge of the subject consult Pliny (l, 36, c. 22), as we omit much on account of brevity. Finally, this should be noted :
Whatsoever may be the affinity between Moonstone and gypsum, it is certain that the former has great use in healing, while the latter is poisonous. A piece of Moonstone the size of a filbert is often used for dysentery. It also stops hemorrhage, and is a good dentifrice. Consult Dioscorides and Avicenna.

LAPIS ASIUS — The best kind is, according to Dioscorides, that which is like pumice stone in colour, fungous, crumbling, scissile, and with mud-coloured lines inside. It is called a Stone because of its colour and nature, but its texture is ot that of a stone, for it is light and fungous. It has been called the Asian Stone because it comes from Mount Troas of Asios, and not alone in Asia. Its virtue is astringent, removing, and slightly corrosive. It is also called sarcophagus. Pliny says that sucking this stone is a speedy cure for gout and all kinds of shin complaints, which indeed is a quality of all metallic substances. When placed in coffins containing the bodies of the dead, it will consume them all except the teeth in the space of forty days. What this stone actually is, few now know. Yet it exists in Germany on the surface of the earth. Underneath and around it an efflorescence appears, a kind of false flower of nitre, which is called flower of Asian rock, which according to Dioscorides is sometimes of yellowish colour, sometimes white, sometimes like pumice stone. It approaches the consistency of slime, is harsh to the tongue, has stronger qualities than the stone it comes from, is drying and cleansing, and has many medical uses. It will be seen that Aphronitrum, or Spume of Nitre, Flower of Rock, and Flower of Asian Rock, are very similar to one another. They differ somewhat in substance, for Flower of Asian Rock is melted by fire, and is therefore not burnt, whereas Spume of Nitre is not so melted. A very beautiful species of Aphronitrum is found at Jena, which in many ways corresponds to the Flower of Asian Rock described by Dioscorides. And the latter is no doubt a species of Flower of Asian Rock. Adarca, already described (see A), is similar in colour to the Flower of Asian Rock. For the rest, consult Pliny, who says that Flower of Asian Rock is like red pumice stone. Consult Serapion, who calls it a Sap, or juice, and distinguishes several species, some being white like that of Jena, some red or ruddy, and some approaching yellow. Others say that this substance originates from marine dew.

LAPIS AUREUS — Urine itself; otherwise the Golden Stone. Also Hair, and the Blood of Beasts.

LAPIS BEZAAR — According to Serapion, the term Hagar Bezaar signifies, in the first place, every Medicament which is an Antidote to Poison, and, secondly, that Stone which forms in the eyes of stags, just as the eye of the hyena is said to petrify, and the stone so produced is called Hyxnia by Pliny. It is said to be a solidification of the tears of the stag after it has contracted snake poison. The poison passes from the animal through its tears, and although its foundation is venom, it is a great antidote to poison. There are species of various colours-citrine, dust-colour, pale green, and white. Some say that they are found in Syria, India, and the East. But we also have a substance of the same nature, which is an ossification of the eyes of our stags, and is collected by stag hunters as an antidote to poison, a good stomachic, and an enlivener of the spirits. In appearance like a bone found in the head of the pike, is that species of bezaar which is in reality a bone from the heart of the stag. It is good in parturition, and quickens pregnancy. The same virtue is attributed to a stone found in the intestines of the same animal. While speaking of the stag, it may be said that its marrow is serviceable in all inflammations, especially those of the womb. Its genital part is good for nervous afliictions; its blood strengthens the womb. Its horns promote good fellowship at festivals. Its lungs are excellent for consumption.

LAPIS CALAMINARIS — i.e., Tutia.

LAPIS CALCIS — i.e., Recrement of Copper, Copper Filing, or Slag.

LAPIS CARPIONIS — A Triangular Bone, found in the hinder part of a carp's jowl, and said to be a Gem, or Stone. Its size varies with that of the fish ; it is white outside, and yellow inside. It is good for the gravel and biliousness. It is also a safeguard against colic.

LAPIS DE MONTANIS — i.e., Rebis, Tortoise.

LAPIS EX CANCRO — is the Stone called Crab's Eye, which is white and round. It is said to be found in the stomach and intestines of hares, and is supposed to break up stone in the bladder. Some say that it is of a frigid and humid nature, others that it is dry.

LAPIS EX PERCA — A Gem or Stone of the Perch. It is found in the head. There re generally two in one fish, and they are really very white Bones. Nothing is better for breaking up stone in the bladder, and it is therefore eagerly collected by fishermen. A certain part of the gut of the same fish possesses similar virtue.

LAPIS FACILE IGNI LIQUESCENS ~ i.e., Flux.

LAPIS FAMOSUS ~ Salt of Urine.

LAPIS FOSSILIS AEROSUS ~ Cuprine Slate.

LAPIS JUDAICUS ~ Hornstone, the stone Agapis.

LAPIS JUDAICUS ~ This is a name of the stone Thecolithos, because it is found in Palestine and Judea. There are two species, of which the larger is like the Phenicite stone of Dioscorides, and the acorn stone of Pliny. It has a variety of names, a fact which deceived the author last cited, who imagined that there were as many species. The stone in question is found in Germany, near Tangra on the Elbe. The smaller species, which is cylindrical (whereas the other is round), sparkles when broken. It was evidently unknown to Dioscorides. It is found in Saxony, and at Tangra on the banks of the Elbe; it has wonderful virtue in all difficulties of passing urine, and in stone in the bladder. Consult Dioscorides and Serapion.

LAPIS MAGNETIS:

1. The Livonian, silver-coloured, sparkling magnetic Stone, which can be broken into thin scales.
2. Misnenian in a scissile Stone.
3. Opaque, lead-coloured, in which there are many hard, round, heavy pebbles.
4. Cloddy, like impure carbuncles. A beautiful silver white Stone containing pebbles.
5. Onolsbach, crustaceous, iron-coloured, of which leaves of tables are made.
6. Bohemian, iron-coloured, mixed with brass, which appears like minute scales.

7. Pitch-coloured, in a metallic flint, full of fissures both on the surface and within.
8. Dust-colour, embedded in rock, which is heavy as lead. It is sometimes, but rarely, like that sterile metallic matter which we call our excrement of geese.
9. Round red Stones, found in a silver-coloured magnetic clod.
10. White Mica on the surface of the rocks.
11. Black Mica, like a block of white lead, but scarcer and softer.
12. Cloddy, silver-coloured, Marieberg Mica, in crustaceous flints, i.e., Hornstone.
13. Soft or crumbling Ammochrysos, out of which a dust like gold is made; used by clerks instead of sand. The Roman Janiculensis is called mountain of gold because it abounds in this sand.
14. The stone Hoplites, called Armature by the metallurgists.
15. Shining Armature, like polished iron.
16. Another, like brass.
17. Another, with which Hildesheimer conchites is covered, as with a single layer.
18. Armature, like scales over a pyrites.

LAPIS MAJOR — is composed out of the four elements, and is called the Sun of One Day. According to some opinions, the Calcined and Purified Body.

LAPIS MAJOR — i.e., the spirit extracted from the four bodies.

LAPIS NIGRI MEDIOCRES — Medium-Sized Pebbles.

LAPIS NON LAPIS — The Stone which is not a stone is a substance which is petrine as regards its efficacy and virtue but not as regards its substance. According, however, to Avicenna and Kodar, the Stone which is not a stone is the Elixir, and is called the Stone because it is tinged 6r coloured, and not a stone for the reason that it is melted.

LAPIS OCCULTUS — i.e., Blessed, i.e., Egg.
LAPIS PHILOSOPHICUS — Elixir.
LAPIS PHILOSOPHICUS — is the most potent virtue concentrated by art in the centre. Outwardly, it is a Tincture. Or it is that Universal Medicine by which age is renewed in youth, metals are transmuted, and all diseases cured. It was made by Theophrastus. It is the Stone of the Wise whereby the imperfect metals are improved.
The augmentation of the Philosophical Stone takes place in two ways: firstly, by repeating solution and coagulation; secondly, by projection upon the white or red body in such a way that itself becomes elixir. They must then be laid each in its menstruum and water to dissolve. Thus the first elixir is produced in the ferment of the tincture.
Grind the medicine, and dissolve it again into its mercury; coagulate it gently, and liquefy it again like wax, whereby the body will be doubled. If you dissolve and cook it again, then you will have multiplied it one hundredfold, and so on, the oftener the better. Take care how much gravity is obtained by your medicine; for the more powerful it is, the more mercury must you add to it in augmentation. When it has doubled the power that it had at the first multiplication, then add double the amount of mercury. But if the power have tripled, and you desire to increase the potency and strength still further, then take water. If, on the other hand, you wish to increase the substance and the quantity, then take sulphur, or the first matter of the stone, and cook it with the elixir. Thomas Tolet says: To twenty parts of the elixir allow four parts of mercury; seal it, and cook it for eighteen days in a fire of the first grade; in the second grade for twelve days; then put it again into the mercury, and cook it as before. You will complete the process in thirty days. Then take as much as a third or even a seventh part of the elixir of Thomas Aquinas; mix it with virgin's milk; add

thereto seven parts of purifying mercury ; mix it, and wash it as before. Dry it by means of a cloth or leather, so that only the seventh part of it shall be fixed. Thus you will have increased its virtue sevenfold. Take a part of this second powder; add thereto a seventh part of mercury; wash it and dry it thoroughly, and fix it. Make it seven times more, and so forth.

The solution of the Philosopher's Stone is a revelation of the hidden; it makes that which is coarse to be clean and fine, the hard and dry to be fluid. Then if the matters are to be united by their least parts, they must become water. Calcination takes place by means of the first water, but solution does not take place with violence; it is better in its raw state than cooked; it is better moist than dry, mild, bright, clear ; it alters nature, breaks and divides; is better black than red.

All ordinary solution and sublimation are of no use; everything must take place by means of water and without hands. This is called the acute vegetable water; it is the mortar and the stone for grinding with.

Roger Bacon says: The first destruction of the world took place by means of water ; the second will take place by means of fire ; therefore it is already here. The Turba says: Take iron; beat it into thin plates ; sprinkle it with poison ; put it into the vessel ; stop it well ; by means of this cooking the third part of the water is destroyed; the rest turns into air, which carries the Chambar (unknown) in its own body. The Senior says: At first it is dissolved with its water, but ultimately with fire, even as fruit in spring requires moisture, and afterwards warmth to mature it. The first solution is recognised when the body, together with the water, becomes completely yellow, or an intermediate colour between yellow and white.

The time of the Philosophic Stone: The times which belong to the greatly desired stone. Kalid says: Prepare the stone into the white stage for 130 or 140 days.
Trevisan says: Macerate unto the red stage for nine and a half months; and, says the King, look at yourself in the fountain after 130 days. Go out again after 282 days. *Clanga Buccinarum* [*Clangor Buccinae*] says: It requires 280 days, that is, forty days, until the white stage, ninety till the red, and 150 till the ferment appears. Lilium says: Some have prepared it in nine months, some in twelve, some in three, some even in eight days. Maria the prophetess is said to have "dissolved" in three days. This is the three labours. Night follows day, and the imperfect work must reach its perfection. On the sixth day a solution appears ; it is afterwards like an island when it is properly regulated. For the black there are twenty-one days, and the half of the work. Should you find that twenty-one weeks have now already gone by, do not make a mistake, for to them a day, a night, and a month are alike. The different length of the time counteracts the differences of weight, for he that takes much water must cook it all the longer. When it will not get black in forty or fifty days then increase the fire, wherein the metal shows itself as a hyacinthine liquid.
1. Grade Fire. Saturn clothes the King in black in forty days, and Jupiter with a grey coat in twenty or twenty-four days.
2. Grade Fire. Luna clothes in white linen in forty days. Venus clothes with yellow in twenty days.
3. Grade Fire. Mars clothes him in red in forty days.
4. Grade Fire. The Sun completes it in forty days. Then he perspires for three days in a potter's oven, and is perfected.
Compendium of the Confection of the Stone. Rosaries says: Take gold-coloured Olitet, and therewith dissolve your Stone after the first fixation two or three times three or four days,

in order that we may excuse you much solution and coagulation, so that you may have done in thirty days.

2. Cook the white Magnesia with a strong fire, until it is blood-red; then take the King out, and to his three parts, add one part of polished gold, and gold water two parts; mix it until the body is concealed, and cook it equably until it is red. Then increase it with gold water.

Corruption Stone: It belongs to the digestion as a chief part of the work, whereof all chemical books are full. It is a true dissolution of natures, and of that which connects them, both as to the form and the substance, in order that a new form may be introduced, for without putrefaction nothing can grow. It takes place therefore in the shade of the purifying fire in forty or forty-six nights. Then takes place the union by those things which are least, and lasts about five months, or 156 days, etc. That which is coarse perishes in the fruits, and makes the black, shutting the door on the volatilised. Then he goes out of the purifying fire into Paradise. There is life, light, and glory.

The Weight for making the Stone:
1. Some take 10 parts of the water and 1 part of the body.
2. Of the water 12 parts. Sol 1 part.
3. Of the water 4 parts. Sol 3 parts.
4. Lully takes equal proportions of each.
5. Water 4 parts. Sol 1 part.
6. Termis. takes 12 parts with X 1 part.
7. Theophrastus 2 parts with 7 parts.
8. Zenon takes 1 part and 3, saying that it does not much matter about the weight, so that the cooking takes places in such a manner as the instructions direct.
9. Of salt, 3 parts; of mercury, 2 parts; of sulphur, 1 part.

The Fermentation, Libation, or Nourishment of the Stone: Then is the Sun caught in the plated white earth, and is called our gold. They feed the moist at first with very little water or milk, and it gradually gets stronger and stronger. At first divide the water into two parts, in accordance with the process. Afterwards imbibe the dry parts, or ashes, earth, and rust, with another part, not once, but seven times, so that the matter may not be drowned. This takes place in fifty days; thereby it becomes sweet and large; treat everything with mild fire, so that the soul may not depart until it fixes itself. Then roast it.

The Scale of the Stone: The ash is the ferment of the gold, and the gold is its water. Body and ferment shall afterwards be a clean powder; dissolve them both in water before they are united. The ferment shall be the fourth part of our ore, i.e., four parts of ore and one part of ferment. But Rhasis speaks of 19 parts, another of 3 parts of gold and 7 of water, because the ferment is manifold, so also is the process. Sometimes the ferment is the Stone, and sometimes gold and silver, alone or both together.

Ablution of the Stone: Ablution is used to increase it in power.
1. It cannot take place in one process, although it is one operation and one matter.
2. It is first called Ablution of Water, because the matter, in comparison with its future perfection, is still moist and cold.
3. Ablution of Earth, because it is dry and stiff, or almost reaching the white stage.
4. Washing of the Fire is the Red Medicine, is the Golden Fiery Nature which penetrates; some call it Separation of the Elements, also the Washing.

The nature comes out of it, calcines, etc.

The Calcination of the Philosophic Stone is the highest purification; it receives the inherent moisture, restores the natural warmth, and introduces dissolution.

Floresc. Angl. (unknown work) says: The unlearned confuse the bodies which are calcined with the ordinary species of calcination, and they err therein. For our calcination is not ordinary, but Sol and Luna are calcined, together with the first water, so that they may expand, become spongy and subtle; so that the other may begin to work. This is our true calcination.

It is turned into a fixed earth, and is called Coagulation and Incineration, Division of the Elements, Extraction and Quintessence. Then the body becomes ghostly, light, white, and dry. It is called Sublimation, Incineration, Solution. Then the refuse becomes sublimated, so that the Olitet may be obtained. It is also called the White Death, Understanding, Putrefaction, Disintegration, Cooking, etc.

The Sublimation of the Stone: Arnoldus says: Our Sun must be raised from the earth on to the cross in the air, so that he through suffering may become glorious. *L. V. Venet.* (unknown) says: Through one single Sublimation the whole work is accomplished and completed. *Turba* says: Sublimate Chambar of Mercury; thus Sulphur becomes mixed with Sulphur, and is called Ethelia, Orpiment, Zendrio, Chulul, Magnesium, and under many other names is his white nature set forth. In him is no shadow. Therefore it is called White Lead, Martech, White Ore, and is an improvement.

But there is a three-fold Sublimation:

1. When the body becomes volatilised and united with the Mercury, even though he does not ascend.
2. When the Mercury is united with living Calx, and becomes nobler and improved.
3. In the colour and fixing. Bacchus says: By means of Sublimation are Soul and Spirit dissolved and expanded in the dissolved body of the Sun. This is the Arcanum, the Mystery, and the Power.

The Red Spirit in the first Sublimation, purified by the salted minerals, is no use to us. This purification effects nothing.

The Redness of the Stone: The white is the colour of life, and the red of immortality. Now perfection comes. When it is yellow like the yolk of an egg, then it is elevated, thin, and subtle, and is called Air, red Olitet, and by all the names of birds and spirits. When it is red, it is called Heaven, Gold, Red Sulphur, Carbuncle, and has the names of everything that is red and costly between heaven and earth, such as Red Gold, our Gold, Tinging Poison, Body of Magnesium, Treacle, the Pure Body, Ashes, Olixir, Kibric, Incombustible Sulphur, red and fixed Sulphur, ferment of the Sun, Gold of Coral, Superfluity, the Red, red Orpiment of the Philosophers, Ore, green Vitriol, Almagra, Laton, etc.

The Whiteness of the Stone: When the water covers the earth, then the white is over the black; but when the air comes above it is crocus colour, and when the fire rules it becomes red; but when the air arises, and the earth sinks to the floor, they denominate this Death of the Sun. Then Mercury conducts the Soul of the Sun into the height, and the body lies in the grave as a dead person. Therefore it is called the White, Water of Life, Continual, Permanent, Spirit, Soul, and is a Dissolved Earth, or like a blackberry leaf. It is also called Lead, Exebmich, white Bismuth, Martech, white Ore, white Stone, white Gold, the Full Moon, white fruitful Earth, Living Sulphur, Living Earth, clean pure Earth, white Lime, the Calcined Body, Metallic Salt, and by the names of all things that are white — Salt, Alum, and Marble, Crystal, Ethelia Alba, white Silver Litharge, Arsenic, Nitre.

The Blackness of the Stone: Should you make the fire too strong the matter becomes red too soon, and perishes. It appears first a red, then a green colour, and afterwards assumes almost all colours before it becomes properly white. It coagulates and dissolves frequently; it twice becomes black and white. The blackness is a sign of corruption, consumption, or reception. Then there appears an island in the sea, which gradually becomes smaller, until the white prevails, and is called the Raven's Head, Pitch, Coals, Ethelia, black Ore, our Ore, Alkali Mortali, Penny, the Dragon who devours his tail; it is also called Earth, Lead, black Sulphur, the Husband, and by the name of every black thing upon earth.

The Digestion of the Stone, Cooking, Maturing, Dividing: Digestion renders the humours thin and spongy, matures them, and prepares them for their separation. They speak of it in an extraordinary manner.

Often, as in dealing with other things, the neglect to follow nature leads to error. They have four methods of separating the elements — that of Olitet, of the Spirit. Of the Earth, of the Soul. It is all true, and everything is one. Take heed, dear reader; it is reserved for the understanding, but it is misleading to the wayfaring man. When the mixture is completed, it is called fermented Philosophical Tincture, Cor Suffle, Colla Auri, Poison, Brilliance of the Sea, Ethelia, Orpiment, Kanderich, Mercury out of Chamber, Thickened Gold, Zendria, Absemech, Magnesia, Bismuth, Chulut, Rust that adheres to Ore, a Leech, Ore, Rust, Stone (see folio No. 67). It is also important not to separate the water from the body in the glass, as in that case they would burn, and would perish.

See folio 67. Be careful not to open the door unto him that will not flee. See folio, No. 63. The water is wonderfully transformed into powder, while, on the other hand, the body is transmuted into water. It is, therefore, for this reason that they denominate the water Sand. The powder they call Gold Water.

LAPIS PHILOSOPHORUM — Is the Hair of Men.

LAPIS PHRYGIUS — The best species is pallid in colour, moderately heavy, not of great density, and is grained with white, like Cadmia. Dioscorides treats of its native place, its virtue, and of the mode of burning and cleansing it. It is called Phrygian, because formerly the fullers of that country used it in dyeing. We have several species : one is the glutinous sap which we call Fuller's Earth. Another is a porous glutinous Saxony Earth also used by Fullers. Pliny says that another name for it was glebous Pumice-Stone.

LAPIS QUIRIS — The obscene hoopo is a bird with a folded crest extending the whole length of its head. In its nest there is found the stone called Quiris, which is said to betray secrets, and occasions dreams. The bird itself is one of omen and augury.

LAPIS REBIS — is the Hair of choleric or sanguine men.

LAPIS REBUS — i.e., Tortoise.

LAPIS SPECULARIS — Mirror Stone — a Transparent Stone that can be separated into thin leaves:
1. Thuringian, white, transparent.
2. Adulterated, white, flexible,, sexangular. Found at Hala in Saxony, and there called Salt without Savour.
3. Opaque.
4. White, Transparent Thuringian, with grey gypsum.
5. Mixed with gypsum, and also from Thuringia.
6. Burnt.

LAPIS THRACIAS, THRACIUS, or **THREICIUS** — as it is called by Nicander, is found in that river of Scythia which is called Pontus. It has the quality of gagates; it burns in water, and is extinguished in oil, like bitumen. It is simply another species of Gagates, Agate, or Amber. It is composed of black Naphtha, or liquid black bitumen, even as yellow Gagates from Petroleum, i.e., white liquid Naphtha when it drops or forms in the sea. It is indurated into a stone by its own heat and that of the water. Lithanthrax is one of its species-a carbonaceous stone of variable density. Another is the fissile stone, Slate. That the Thracian stone is bituminous is shown by its smell, its substance, and its black colour. It is squalid, crusty, and light. In fine, it is of the same genus as Gagates, of the same material, but differing in colour. The black variety is more crusty than the yellow, on account of the impurer quality of its Naphtha, which is more terrene than the diluted white Naphtha. Nicander, from whom Dioscorides borrows, very well describes this stone when he says that when aflame it will burn and shine very brilliantly if water be thrown on it, but that a very little oil will extinguish it. The scholiast on Nicander says that the river of Threicius whence it comes is in Media and India. There is no information of value in the Lapidary of Evax. All the information in Pliny evinces its close affinity with Gagates. The Thracian stone is found in Lybia and Britain, and on the shores of the German Ocean. The images of St. James were made from it, and it is very serviceable in statuary. The magicians also made use of it in axinomancy.

LAPSUS DEMENTINUS — is a Seizure more dangerous than apoplexy, and resulting in sudden death.

LATER LICTRO — Quicksilver.

LATERES — Iron Tiles.

LATERIUM, LIXIVIUM, or CAPITELLUM — i.e., Lie or Ley.

LATON — i.e., Brass.

LATON — An Impure Red Body, says the Clangor. It is the first blackness when it leaves off being red and then becomes red again. Then it is again called Laton, and is composed out of the Sun and Moon. So there are two Latons. And if it does not become white, it is of no use. However, it is whitened by means of sal anatron. By means of the salt its blackness is removed, If you wash him until he shines like fishes' eyes, then there is a possibility of it being useful. They also call it Amalgam. Maria says: When the Laton is burned with Alzebric it is changed into gold.

Laton is Copper tinctured with Gold by means of the Stone Calamine, which by senseless chemists is called Electrum. It is composed from one metal, whereas electrum is made from many. Calamine is not a metal but a mineral matter which has not attained perfection, a caco-mineral body, which destroys rather than improves metals, even when it augments. True Electrum is made only by nature from gold and silver, and nothing is more prized for its wonderful virtues. Mixture of copper and gold.
LEBETEN ~ A Trough, Frying-pan, etc.
LEFFA ~ i.e., the Predestination of Herbs, or the use to which each is ordained.
LEFFAS ~ is that Occult Vapour of the Earth by which plants are made to grow and flourish on the earth.
LEMPNIAS ~ Some call this Orpiment, but wrongly, for it is a Red Sigillated Earth.
LEMPNIAS CALCIS ~ i.e., Scale of Copper.
LEMPNIAS LEMPNIA ~ i.e., Orpiment.
LEMPNIA ~ A Soil wherein Gold Grows or Incrustates.
LEMURES ~ Spirits of the element of Air. The Ethnics understood them to be the Shades of the Dead.
LENTISCUS ARBOR ~ Ash Tree.
LEO VIRIDIS ~ is the Ore of Hermes, Glass, and Vitriol, also the Blood from Sulphur, the First Mercury of Gold, altered by means of the Lunar Body. It is also Green Water which dissolves the living lime. The green is that which is perfect upon the stone, and can easily be made into gold. All growing things are green, as also our stone. It is called a plant. The stone cannot be prepared without green.
LEO RUBEUS ~ The Red Lion, is Red Sulphur, which is dissolved in Mercury; Lion's Blood; Male Gold.
LEO VIRIDIS ~ Gold according to some opinions.
LEO VIRIDIS ~ Vitriol.
LEO CITRINUS FOLIATUS ~ Orpiment.

LEO — Gold.
LEPHANTE or **LEPHANTEUS** — is a First Species or Bolus of Tartar ; it has a middle place between stones and clay, and it can be cut or broken.
LEPI FERREI — Iron Scale.
LEPOS CALCIS — i.e., Dust of Copper.
LETA — A reddening or scorching Heat.
LEUCASIA — Living Calx.
LEUX, AMYGDALA — An Almond.
LEVIGATIO or **ALCOLISMUS** — is Calcination, which educes the matter into Alcool by pulverisation. And it is also the reduction of some substances by glutination, of others again by fusion or fulmination.
LIBRA, LIBRA PENSILIS — A Level.
LIBRA STATUTA — A Legal Pound.
LIBONOTUS — South-West.
LIGNEA BRACTEA ROTUNDATA — A Wooden Plate.
LIGNA STATUTA — A Small Door.
LIGNUNC FOSSUM — Tool for Hammering.
LIGNUM CRUCIS — Wood of the Cross.
LIGNA IN SARA — Wood found in Rock.
1. Branches, Leaves, Bark, Pieces of Wood, Coals, Bones, Shells, incorporated into Rock, which occurs at Viadrum, not far from Frankfort.
2. Branches, Leaves, Bark, Wood, etc., incorporated into Rocks at Misnia.
3. Beams of Wood changed into Rock, found near Torga on the Elbe.
4. Subterranean Ebony combined with Shoemaker's Wax.
5. Beechwood incorporated into Stone, but half remaining Wood.
6. Manufactured Rock.
7. Manufactured Bricks.
8. Cement which holds under water.

9. Lithocolla.
LIGO — Pick, Pickaxe.
LIGNEA — A Little Tongue.
LIMBOS — The Universal World, the Four Primal Elements of the World, and of all things, Seed and Matter.
LIMPIDUBI — Pure, Purged.
LIMOS — Mud.
LINTEA — Made of Linen.
LILIUM — Mercury and its Flowers. Also Tincture of the Philosophers, Quintessence of Sulphur, Fixed Flowers, Fixed Sulphur.
LIQUA MUMIA — Human Grease.
LIQUATIO — is when that which is solidified is melted by liquefying, so that it can flow.
LIQUATUM — is that which assumes a fluid consistency.
LIQUEFACTIO — is the Liquefying of a Mineral Body. It is either simple or testing. Simple Liquefaction is when a body is melted, and the process has no other object than to bring it into a flowing state.
Probatory Liquefaction is when the body is tested, and the imperfect part separated from the perfect, either by antimony or earth ashes.
LIQUATIO — Liquation is Fusion or Melting.
LIQUINUM RESOLUTUM — is the reduction of anything into its first matter by melting.
LIQUOR AQUILEGIUS — Distilled Wine.
LIQUOR ESSENTIALIS — is Essential Liquor extracted from the inward parts, and transmuted into Flesh and Blood.
LIQUOR HERBARUM — is made from Herbs by pounding them entire, shutting them up in a glass vessel, cooking them in the water-bath, and straining the sap through a colander, etc., when it has attained the consistency of honey.

LIQUOR ET MULTARUM RERUM OLEUM ~ The Liquor and Oil of many substances is obtained by the addition of the essence, which is their fundamental principle. The Liquor of Terebinth is the Oil of Terebinth.
LIQUOR MERCURII ~ is the Balsam of All Things, wherein consists the strength of health. This Mercury is very potent in Tereniabin and Nostoch, which see.
LIQUOR MUMIAE DEGUMMI ~ i.e., Oil of Gum.
LIQUOR SALIS ~ is Balsam of Nature, whereby bodies are nourished, and putrefaction averted.
LIRAMENTUM ~ Axle-tree.
LITHANTHRAX, PIT COAL, STONE COAL ~ A species of Gagates, and nothing but Bitumen indurated and excocted by heat under the surface of the earth. There are two species of this Coal, one of which is light and of little density, while the other is heavy. It is said that the former will sometimes float upon the surface of water, and it is referred to by Theophrastus as an earthy or stony pit coal. The second species was known to the Greeks, but it is not mentioned by Pliny, and was in all probability unknown to him. It seems to have been described by Theophrastus as a sort of Bituminous Stone, and has therefore an affinity with the fissile slate, which has also a bituminous nature.
LITHARGYRUM ~ These are the species of Litharge:
1. Argyrite, Silver Litharge, or Spume of Silver.
2. That which is made when Silver is separated from Lead.
3. Formed from the mixture of Silver and Lead.
4. From the mixture of Gold and Lead.
5. From the mixture of Gold and Silver.
6. From the mixture of Lead and Copper.
7. Potter's Slag, Blue Recrement of Litharge.
LITHARGYRUM, or **LITHARGYROS** ~ Scum collected from Silver.

LITHARGYRUM OF PARACELSUS ~ is Spume of Mercury, otherwise of Silver or Lead, otherwise Silver of Repurging.

LITHARGYRIUM, or **ALMARACH** ~ The Ashes of any Metal.

LITHARGYRUS ~ He who seeks and finds Ore.

LITIM ~ A fourfold or eightfold Thread, completely drawn.

LIXIVIUM ~ Lye.

LOCI DEVEXI ET CONCAVI ~ Defiles or Recesses. Also Manufactured Ashes.

LOCUSTA ~ signifies either a Locust or Grasshopper, namely, the well-known devastating Winged Insect, or else a species of Lobster, or else the Tops or Young Shoots on Trees and Herbs. It was these that were eaten by St. John in the desert, and not the poisonous winged insects as theologians once thought.

LORCHA ~ The Whole Sweetness of Locusts, even to the centre of their substance.

LORINDT ~ A Commotion of the Waters, accompanied by loud Sounds and Noises.

LORUS ~ i.e., Mercury.

LOT ~ Urine.

LOTIUM ~ Urine of Infants.

LOTORES ~ Washers, or Buddlers of Ore.

LOTORES ~ Washers.

LUBAN, or **LUBEN** ~ is Frankincense.

LUBRICUM ~ A Moist Substance, one which is not solid.

LUDUS LAPIS ~ A Stone Removed from the Bladder, a Remedy for all Species of Calculus.

LUMBRICI ~ Worms are also found in man, every member having its own species. There are long and short and round intestinal worms, and various kinds of Ascarides. Worms are also found in water.

LUMBRICI NITRI — Worms found either in the Earth or in Dung.
LUNA — i.e., Silver. Sometimes a Month of Four Weeks.
LUNA COMPACTA — Fixed Silver, or White Gold.
LUSTUM — Fat, Flower, Cream of Milk, the Lower Cream, Cream-soot.
LUTIREN — To plaster over.
LUTUM ARMENICUM — i.e., Bolus.
LUTUM MAGISTERII — Made of chalk, and of the burns of blisters.
LUTUM MAGRA — Ruddle, Red Earth, or Chalk.
LUTUM SIGILLATUM — Sealed or Stamped Earth.
LUTUM STELLAE — Gypsum.
LYNCURIUS, or the **STONE LYNCIS** — a precious Stone, or, as some suppose, Amber, which some of the ancients believed to be formed of the urine of the lynx, coagulated in woods and mountains. The yellow and bright shining variety is the product of the males. The white and pallid kind is produced by the females. It is to be noted that the opinion which identifies Lyncurius with amber is an error, albeit the male Lyncurius, it is true, will attract feathers. The gem is mentioned by Ovid, Solinus, Albertus, and Evax. It is said to be good for gravel, stone, some species of flux, and generally for pain in the stomach. Some would identify it with the Dactylus, or Dactylos, a kind of precious stone, called Idmus, because dug out of Mount Ida. For the rest it should be noted that the lynx is the only animal which has two little toes in the heel. From these talons are obtained which are of the greatest use in medicine. They are worn by children as a preservative against epilepsy, etc. It is not incredible that the urine of the lynx may be indurated into a stone by the heat of the earth. This is certainly the case with the wild boar, and also with the castrated domestic pig, whose urine is hardened into a stone which is itself a remedy for stone in

the bladder. Why should not the same thing occur in the case of the urine of the lynx?

MACHA ~ i.e., a Flying Beetle.
MACHAL ~ i.e., Fastened.
MACHINA ~ Axle-tree. Called also Axis and Axis Strata.
MACHINA AQUAS TRAHENTIUM OMNIUM MAXIMA ~ A Wheel that can be turned in any direction.
MACHINA QUA RES GRAVES DEMITTUNTUR IN POTEUM ~ A kind of Crane used for wells.
MACHINAE SPIRITALES ~ A Vent.
MACHINA TRACTORIA ~ A Windlass.
MACRA ~ Red Chalk.
MACULA OCULI ~ A Disease of the Eye, Cataract, etc. Called also Hyposchysis and Hyposchyma.
MADIC ~ i.e., Butter Milk.
MAGIA, or MAGIC ~ is a Persian word; in Latin it is Sapientia, i.e., Wisdom. It is twofold. The first is natural and permissible, the mother of true medicine, the secret lore of nature, hidden and concealed in the very centre, and compared with which all human reason is sheer foolishness.

It is truly the gift of God, displaying to us the knowledge of things supernatural, and not proceeding from the inspiration of demons, wherein is no perfection or instruction. The other magic is unlawful, superstitious, and forbidden by the whole Church of Christ. It has the name of Necromancy; it is accursed, and nowhere to be tolerated. Consequently Wisdom has hidden her head.

MAGIA METAPHYSICA ~ Metaphysical Magic is neither concerned with sorcery nor with superstition, but it is a supernatural art, by means of which any hidden secrets desired are revealed, just as a manual teaches a mechanical operation.

MAGISTER ~ A Handicraftsman. Clerk of the Kitchen.

MAGISTER EXCOQUENS FERRUM ~ A Smelter.

MAGISTERIUM ~ is a Chemical State which follows the process of extraction, and in which a matter is developed and exalted by the separation of its external impurities. In this manner are all the parts of natural and homogenous concretion preserved. But they are so exalted that they almost attain the nobility of essences. Whence also there is left almost the same mass or quantity which nature gave. It is, however, impossible to prevent at all times the loss of a certain proportion of the essential matter along with the foreign matter which is removed, and a small percentage of such loss may in certain cases be overlooked. From which you may understand that we find what the chemists call alteration is here of great use.

There is a Magisterium of Quality and a Magisterium of Substance.

The Magisterium of Consistency is when the essence being preserved the consistency is changed into a nobler kind, This is performed in various ways, not so much that the nobility of the matter is itself increased, but that it is made adaptable to more numerous and better purposes.

The Magisterium of Fixed Substances is when volatile and spiritual bodies are reduced to a fixed state. The fixed is opposed to the inconstant and the volatile, and fire is the standard of comparison. That which resists fire is fixed ; that which yields to it is volatile; indeed it flies from fire and escapes in the form of a spirit or a smoke. That which reduces matters from a soft to a hard state is a kindred process, and comes under the same name.

The Magisterium of Odour is when a matter is exalted by odour. And this artists preferably use in those operations in the course of which an offensive smell is developed, as in the treatment of oils and waters by fire, as also in those substances which have naturally an offensive odour, or no odour at all. Even when the smell is not offensive, it is capable of improvement.

The Magisterium of Paracelsus is that which is extracted from natural things, without separation of the elements, by means of addition of other substances, whereby that which is extracted is separated.

The Magisterium of Weight is when the substance is exalted in weight. This is chiefly required in gold and silver, and it is one of the notes of perfection, since among metals gold is heaviest, and the weight increases its value as a coin. If there be any deficiency, it is compensated by art. A mass of gold or silver which is lighter than it should be is excocted in urine with precipitated coral ; or artificial quicksilver is rubbed into a homogeneous mass with the gold or silver, until it becomes of a uniform colour; or, gold and silver are cooked in a paste formed of sulphur and living calx; or, they are cemented with sulphur, or with fixed precipitate; or again, mix half an ounce of pulverised salt of Saturn, or the same quantity of powdered brick dust, with three ounces of fixed vitriol. Smear thin shavings of gold with albumen, sprinkle calx of silver, which has been previously dried with powder.

Arrange them in layers one over the other, and cement them in a pyx, or between tiles. Then the gold begins generally to become white. Add colouring matter and hold with pincers in the fire, until red hot, afterwards extinguish in urine.

The Magisterium of Colour is when the colour of a substance is educed to the highest perfection in its own degree. The colour is simply brought out from potentiality into manifestation. Sometimes a foreign colour is given to it which is excellent in its own way. If the colour be at once fixed and constant, the magisterium is more noble.

The Magisterium of Powders is the reduction of matters into a uniform consistence by making them into a powder. It is chiefly performed by calcination, and is vulgarly called Calx or Alcool. The end in view is to overcome the tenacity of any given substance.

The Magisterium of Principles is when a composite substance is again resolved into its constituents.

The Magisterium of Quality is when the matter, elaborated by certain forms, is exalted. It is performed in two ways, either in accordance with the secret or the manifest qualities.

The Magisterium of an Occult Quality is concerned with that which permeates the nature of a given substance, and is known by the effects it produces and not by an outward appearance, as for example the perfect exaltation of an essence which may have no outward difference from the same essence in a lower state of exaltation. If such a quality be hurtful, it is altogether abolished, though some of the substance may be destroyed in this process. Thus the perfection of a substance consists not in the thing itself, but in the use of the thing. In things healthful there is perfection both in the matter and in the use of the matter. If it be impossible to abolish altogether what is hurtful, it is restricted or restrained, so that it can be used without any injury resulting.

The Magisterium of a Manifest Quality is when a substance is elaborated by means of its outward forms. There are as many magisteries of this kind as there are outward qualities appealing to the different senses, and chemistry is concerned with the exaltation of each of them. Some of them are connected with the nature of the body and some with the forms thereof.

The Magisterium of Savour is when there is an exaltation or increase of flavour. The process concerns both the kitchen and the apothecary's shop. Chemically, it is chiefly used in correcting acidities, and in toning down what is too pungent or highly spiced.

The Magisterium of Sensitives is when a substance is exalted in its own sensible qualities, as for example in those which appeal to the sense of touch, namely, heat, cold, moisture, dryness, etc., of which the magisterium is developed.

The Magisterium of Sound is that process in which the sound is corrected by the chemist. This takes place chiefly in minerals, the sound being regarded as a proof of excellence; or those things which are dangerous in fire by reason of their explosive nature, which is obviated by this process.

The Magisterium of Volatiles is when the volatile is produced from the fixed. It has affinity with that process by which a tractable, ductile, or even fluid quality is produced out of the hard, rigid, and inflexible. It is performed by extinctions, macerations, incerations, sublimations, solutions, etc. Commonly we seek here the restoration of the moisture which has been removed, or the increase of a deficient moisture, or the removal of an objectionable asperity, etc. The process concerns volatile substances; its end is that they should put on the nature of spirits.

MAGNA CAPSA LIGNEA ~ A Great Wooden Box.

MAGNALIA, OPERA DEI — God's Works.
MAGNES — i.e., Mercury.
MAGNES — The Magnet is so called after its discoverer. See Pliny, 1. 36, c. 16. It is also called the Herculean Stone. Hence the Greek proverb about Herculean stones. It is so called from the city of Heraclea in Lydia (or, as some say, in Magnesia) where there is a most admirable magnet. Lucretius says: The magnet which the Greeks name after its origin, because it originated in its native mountains of magnets. The magnet is also called the Sidereal Stone because it attracts iron. For the Greek word Sideris signifies iron, although Sideritis is different from iron scoria, and is a remarkable gem, mentioned by Pliny, 1. 37, c. 10. By the Germans the magnet is called, after the Latin, Magneth. By the Saxons it is termed the Sailor's Stone, because of its use in navigation, it being its nature always to turn to the north. According to the testimony of Dioscorides (1.5, c. 93), its colour inclines to dark blue. The best is always dark blue. It is thick, not heavy, and attracts iron by a congenital property, as it were, just as the gem Sagda attracts wood, or as amber and gagates attract straws and feathers. Even iron, which is most obstinate in its property of resistance, is overcome by the magnet; and, what is more, when iron is touched by the magnet it will draw along with it another piece of iron. Thus iron, the mistress of all things, is held and remains in the grasp of the magnet. On the other hand (whereat I greatly marvel), garlic and onion are quite contrary to the magnet, and if the magnet be smeared with their sap, it by no means attracts iron. However, it recovers its properties when dipped in the blood of a goat.
The magnetic gem is also found in veins of iron, and in our mines — for example, in the territories of Bohemia, by Schwartzberg; and certainly at Sualvedia in ancient iron mines; also at Goslaria, in an old mine half covered over by

rubbish, the magnet is to be seen in a vein of its own. This also is said to be the case in Spain and in other places. It is affirmed that the magnet possesses a great affinity with hematite. For hematite is called a magnet by Pliny, the reference being to an Ethiopian species of hematite, and a magnet burnt, whether by the heat of the earth or by artificial fire, becomes hematite, and is sold for it. Pliny also enumerates five genera, according to Sotacus, and states that it derives its name from Magnes Armentarius.

MAGNES, MAGNETH:
1. The Ethiopian, which is most praised, and is found in Ethiopia, in a sandy region, together with the Hematite Magnet, which is of a bloody colour, and of which more above. This Ethiopian Magnet not only attracts iron but also a magnet of another genus. Hence those lines of Sinesius: The Ethiopians, a people not unknown to the Nile, who cut the magnet: their only boast is the magnet. They attract uncooked stone.
2. The Red and Black Magnesiacus of Macedonia.
3. In Echium of Boeotia, which is more ruddy than black.
4. A Magnet found about Alexander and Troas. It is black, of the feminine sex, and totally useless.
5. In Asiatic Magnesia, white, useless, does not attract iron. The difference in the various kinds of magnet is according as they are male or female, and also in the matter of colour. Concerning the affinity which exists between iron and the magnet, consult Pliny (1. 34, c. 24), who describes the Cantabrian Magnet, found with freckled bubbles. He also informs us that in the same part of Ethiopia where the magnet abounds there is a stone called Themanides, which repels all pieces of iron, and rejects them, being of an antagonisticc nature to the magnet. He further testifies that the magnet has another property, namely, that of attracting to itself the liquor of glass. Just as the magnet by its natural

potency and power attracts iron and the liquor just named, and has affinity with them, so conversely it disagrees with garlic and onions, and has so little sympathy with adamant that in its neighbourhood it ceases to grasp or to attract iron. Consult also Serapion (lib. Agg. c. Hager Abnantes, or Almagritos). He refers to the abundance of the magnet on the shores of the Indian Ocean, and says that all ships in those parts are put together with wooden nails, as those of iron would be torn away by the force of the attraction. The Magi assert that the magnet having such great agreement with iron, has also the property of producing and maintaining peace among men. As to the further medicinal use of the magnet, consult Dioscorides, Pliny, and others already cited. Evax states that there is a kind of magnet which attracts flesh, especially human flesh. But possibly this statement is borrowed from Aristotle. Albertus states that the magnet is found in France, and there has the appearance of rusty iron, burnt with pitch. Would that the French would seek for these things! Doubtless it would be found in Thuringia, which borders on France, if any one were to look for it. Moreover, the same Albertus states that in his day a magnet was discovered which at one end attracted iron, and at the other repelled it. Aristotle, if I mistake not, also mentions this species. If this be the case, we can understand Pliny's statement concerning the stone Themanides. Thirdly, Albertus adds that the Emperor Frederick possessed a magnet which did not attract iron, but was attracted by the iron itself.

MAGNESIA — i.e., Seafoam Stone, or Sulphul. Also, Tortoise and Tortoiseshell. Magnesia generally stands for Marcasite. Artificial magnesia is melted tin when mercury has been injected into it, and the two have been mingled together until they form a brittle substance, and a white mass. It is also silver mixed with mercury, an extremely fusible metallic compound which is liquefied as easily as wax, is of a wonderful whiteness, and is called the magnesia of the philosophers. Magnesia is produced when silver and quicksilver are united together so as to form a heavy fluid metal. It is also the matter of the philosopher's stone. Magnesia is further the mixed water congealed in air which offers resistance to the fire, the earth of the stone, our mercury, mixtures of substances. The whole therein is mercury.

Magnesia is a Stone having the virtue of marcasite. Or, it is a Stone like hematite.

MAGNESIA ~ The Woman.
MAGNESIA ~ Bismuth, or Barren Earth.
MAGNETINUS TARTARUS ~ A very hard and Spongy Stone in Men.
MAGNUS CLAVUS FERREUS OSTUSUS ~ A Big Blunt Piece of Iron.
MAGRA ~ i.e., Red Earth.
MAGRA ~ i.e., Cornelian.
MALECK ~ The Arabic Term for Salt.
MALLEI SPECIES ~ A Hammer for Splitting.
MALLEO PERCUSSUM DILATARE ~ To Extend, to Flatten.
MALTHEORUM ~ i.e., Sal Gemmae, which see.
MANBRUCK ~ i.e., Silver.
MANDELLA ~ Black Hellebore.
MANDIBULARUM LIQUOR ~ Liquid from the jaws. Oil from the jaws or jaw Bone.
MANGONASIA ~ Art of lifting heavy things without difficulty.
MANNA, or **MAMMA** ~ That Substance with which Vessels are Annealed.
MANNA ~ i.e., Dew Fallen from Heaven. A Species of Balsam, the Product of the Air. Also a Sweetness Extracted

from many Substances. Otherwise, Honey Dew, Dosomeli, Pure Honey, Melligo, Saliva of the Constellations.

MANHEB ~ i.e., Scoria.

MARCASITA PLUMBEA ~ Leaden Marcasite, i.e., Antimony.

MARCASITA ALBA ~ White Marcasite, i.e., White Arsenical Pyrites.

MARCASITA ~ Marcasite, i.e., Incrustations of Ore, such as Climia ~ Incrustations of Gold and Antimony ~ Incrustations of Lead.

MARCASITE ~ is an Imperfect Metallic Substance of as many Species as there are Solid Metals. Thus, there is Golden, Silver, Tin, Iron, Leaden, and Copper Marcasite. The last mentioned is Pyrites, or Stone of Light, Fire-stone, a Brazen Stone abundant in Ruddy Sulphur, and sending forth many sparks. Pyrites contains much Red Sulphur, Flint-stone, Copper Ore, and Metal Regulus of Copper.

MARCELLUS ~ i.e., a big Mallet.

MARCHED ~ i.e., Litharge.

MARGARITA ~ The Indian Ocean yields us precious pearls, also the Red Sea, the Persian Gulf, about Arabia, and nowadays, the British waters. Now, a pearl is nothing else than the production and offspring of a pearl-oyster. For these shell-fish, at that particular time of the year when they are stimulated by the season to giving birth, expand, and, as it were, gape. They thirst for the dew, as if it were a husband; it is in consequence of desire that they gape, and long to be filled with a dew-developed foetus. When the lunar dews have melted away, they drink in the dew, absorbing the desired moisture as into a gaping womb. Thus impregnated, they bring forth pearls, according to the quality of the dew absorbed. Should pure dew have been imbibed, pearls of a marvellous whiteness are produced. But if, on the other hand, muddy dew has been drunk in, the foetus will also be

muddy. Moreover, pearls grow pale if the sky threatens tempest at the time of conception. If the shells obtain their desire by gaping at the seasonable moment, the pearls become large. If, at the time of conception, lightning flashes, the shells close up, and yield pearls only in a meager fashion. Should it thunder, the shells close in terror, and then those abortions are produced which are called Physemata. It is also alleged that if, subsequent to conception, many peals of thunder are heard, the shells cast forth the pearls into the rivers, where they are found in large quantities, as, for example, in the Moselle, among the sands. Should a ray of sunlight have fallen into the gaping shell, together with the dew, then the pearls are tinged with red, as we sometimes see them to be. For this reason, when the sun rises, the shells dive, for they feel, as it were, that they are going to produce ruddy offspring. Finally, the pearl is produced in a more magnificent manner if the shells receive the seed of the morning air, i.e., the dew, rather than the seed of the evening air. Thus there is a wonderful affinity between the pearl and the shell in its copulation with dew, the seed, so to speak, of the air. Not without reason are pearls ascribed to Venus, on account of their marvelous copulation. The pearl is also called unio, because two have never been found together. Its value consists in its whiteness, size, weight, rotundity and polish. In the water all pearls are soft like coral. When removed therefrom, they immediately harden and become stones. But Pliny (1. 9, c. 35) should be consulted concerning pearls and the nature of their shells. Serapion and Solinus assert that they are cold and dry. They are good for heartburn or stomach ache, for syncope, diarrhoea, preservation of sight, etc. They retain the menses, cleanse the teeth, purify the blood, etc.
MARICH ~ In German Shacken.
MARCKASITA ~ i.e., Calcithes.

MARMORA CANDIDA — White Marbles.
1. White Lunensian Marble in. Etruria.
2. White Cartariensian Marble.
3. Patavian Marble cut with iron.
4. Italian Marble with ashen veins.
5. Marble from Ratisbon, out of which the slabs of tables are made. From this the altar of Anneberg was constructed, consisting of one solid block of stone, and there is not a more elegant altar to be found in Italy.
6. Very white Marble, of which the Caroline baths are built.
7. Ivory-like Marble from Hildesheim.
8. Ivory-like Arabian Marble.
9. Annebergian Marble, found in a spar, or in mud.
10. Marble from Hildesheim, having ash-coloured markings upon white ground, and smelling like burnt horn.

MARMORA CINEREA — Marbles of ashen hue.
1. From Hildesheim, smelling like burnt horn.
2. Zeblician, with white lines and spots. Called by the natives Serpentine.
3. Zeblician, ingrained with Carbuncles, which show up admirably when the Marble is polished.
4. Rochlician, having black marks which resemble the claws of crows.
5. Rochlician, with muddy spots.
6. Italian, with black spots, resembling serpents.

MARMORA FLAVA — Marbles of yellow hue.
1. A yellow Spar, found among metals.
2. Dull, opaque Belgian.

MARMORA NIGRA — Marbles of black hue.
1. Belgian, from which was hewn the tomb of the most illustrious Duke Maurice the Elector, and especially those slabs upon which inscriptions are carved. Item: Black Netherland Marble.
2. Marble from Anneberg.

3. From Ratisbon.
4. Belgian, which smells of sulphur.
5. Another variety, quarried in the same place, and smelling like burnt horn.
6. Andegavensian, polished, very black, quarried near the city.
7. Stolpensian, having the colour and hardness of iron. Agricola calls it Bisalt, and we call it Basalt.
MARMORA RUBRA ~ Marbles of red colour:
1. Egyptian Porphyry, uniform.
2. A beautiful red Marble.
3. Red Marble from Ratisbon.
4. A brilliant Marble with white spots, from Ratisbon.
5. Bohemian Marble, black on red ground.
6. Belgian, white upon red ground, distinguished by various spots.
7. Annebergian, found among metals.
8. Red on white ground, found amongst all metals.
MARMORA VIRIDIA ~ Marbles of green colour.
1. Laconian, quarried by the Venetians.
2. Light green, with markings of brilliant green.
3. Another from Laconia, with black marks upon green.
MARMOREUS TARTARUS ~ A very hard Stone, found in man, like marble in hardness.
MARS ~ i.e., Iron.
MARTACH, or **MARTATH** ~ is Litharge, Silver Litharge.
MARTEGON ~ Silphium.
MARUCH ~ Oil.
MARUCH ~ Oli.
1. White, fatty, soft, fluid Targatta.
2. White Juliacensian.
3. White Crustaceous Marl.
4. White, stony, hard Hallensian Marl.

5. Light ash-coloured Marl, found between Dresden and Meissen.
6. Ash-coloured Stony Marl.
7. Ash-coloured Stony Marl from Hallee, used by artificers in producing pictures.
8. Yellow Crustaceous Marl from Radeberg, found in sandy earth.
9. Hard, yellow, sandy Belgian Marl, from a more elevated region, used by the natives, as in other places, for manuring fields. A kind of Marl from Mxstricht.
10. White sandy and crumbling Marl, from Hildesheim.
MASAREA, or **MYOSOTIS** ~ Mouse's Ear.
MASELLUM, MOSEL ~ i..e., Jupiter.
MASCULINUM ET FOEMINUM SEMEN ~ Masculine and Feminine Seed, the substance of Mercury and Sulphur. For the Mercury is transformed into Sulphur; it is a spirit which possesses both natures, and is called Mercury. Out of one pound of Matter, scarcely half an ounce can be extracted. It is also called Ore, Penny, Lead, Albor Aeris; Turba, folio 16, calls the Female Magnesia. The white is red Sulphur. When the two are again united, they are still called Magnesia, until the end of the cooking. It is the medium between fixed and not fixed.
MASCULUS ~ i.e., Quicksilver.
MASSA EX CANCELLIS FORMATA ~ (?) A Mass of Ore formed of transverse bars like a lattice.
MASSALIS, MOSEL, or **MASSERIUM** ~ The Mother, i.e., Mercury.
MATER METALLORUM ~ Mother of the Metals, i.e., Living Silver.
MATERIA DISPERSA ~ Ore distributed for treatment.
MATERIA LAPILLORUM EXPERS ~ Metallic Ore devoid of petrine matter.

MATERIA METALLICA — Metallic Ore. Also an alloy of Copper, Lead, and Silver.
MATERIAM METALLICAM DISCERNERE A TERRIS — To Separate the Ore.
MATERIA PRIMA ET HUJUS VOCABULA — The philosophers have so greatly admired the Creature of God which is called the Primal Matter, especially concerning its efficacy and mystery, that they have given to it many names, and almost every possible description, for they have not known how to sufficiently praise it.
1. They originally called it Microcosmos, a small world, wherein heaven, earth, fire, water, and all elements exist, also birth, sickness, death, and dissolution, the creation, the resurrection, etc.
2. Afterwards it was called the Philosophical Stone, because it was made of one thing. Even at first it is truly a Stone. Also because it is dry and hard, and can be triturated like a stone. But it is more capable of resistance and more solid. No fire or other element can destroy it. It is also no stone, because it is fluid, can be smelted and melted.
They further call it the Eagle Stone, because it has stone within it, according to Rosinus.
3. It is also called Water of Life, for it causes the King, who is dead, to awake into a better mode of being and life. It is the best and most excellent medicine for the life of mankind.
4. Venom, Poison, Chamber, because it kills and destroys the King, and there is no stronger poison in the world.
5. Spirit — because it flies heavenward, illuminates the bodies of the King, and of the metals, and gives them life.
6. Medicine — the one most excellent medicine, for it speedily and marvellously heals all the maladies and infirmities of mankind and of metals.

7. Heaven — for it is light and bright, indestructible, and is Heaven in operation.
8. Clouds — for it gives celestial water and rain upon its own earth.
9. Nebula, or Fog — for it ascends from the earth and makes the air dark.
10. Dew — for it falls from the air and stimulates the soil, together with that which grows upon it.
11. Shade — for it casts a shadow over the earth and the elements, and causes darkness.
12. Moon — for she is in her nature and quality cold and moist; her influence extends to the Under World; she receives her light from the Sun; hence she ministers to the time of darkness, by means of the shade of the earth.
13. Stella Signata and Lucifer — the pre-eminent and morning star, for she gives the sign in operations, she shines first, then comes the sun, both evening and morning, which is a marvel to behold.
14. Permanent Water — metallic water of life, leafy water. It remains in fire, air, and earth, and cannot be destroyed by any element.
15. Fiery and Burning Water — for it is exceeding hot, melts up all metals more quickly than fuel and flame, yea, melts that which resists fire.
16. Salt of Nitre and Saltpetre for it possesses their nature and kind. It also rises with greater strength and violence than any saltpetre whatever. It is, moreover, extracted from the earth.
17. Lye — for it washes and cleans the metals, and the garments of the King.
18. Bride, Spouse, Mother, Eve — from her royal children are born to the King.
19. Pure and Uncontaminated Virgin — for she remains pure and unimpregnated, notwithstanding that she bears

children. She is a most extraordinary mother, who slays her husband and offspring, and revivifies them by means of her breasts. Assiduous says: The Mother of our Stone, which is now perfected, is still a Virgin, never having reclined in the nuptial couch, because this hermaphrodite and universal matter of the Sun and Moon has intercourse only with itself, and is not yet impregnated in any special manner, such as the golden, silver, or mercurial process, etc. Consequently, it is a pure, virginal birth.

20. Milk of Virgin, or of the Fig — for it renders things sweet, white, delicious, and wholesome.

21. Boiling Milk — for it warms, cooks, whitens, and matures.

22. Honey — for it sweetens, confers a pleasant smell, and renders things delicious and wholesome.

23. A Spiritual Blood — for it is like blood, and so remains; it reddens, vivifies, and has the spirit therein.

24. Bath — for it washes and cleanses the King, and metals, and causes them to perspire.

25. A Syrup — for it is acid, and produces strength and courage.

26. Vinegar — for it macerates, makes spicy, pickles, renders savoury, strengthens, preserves, corrodes, and yields a tincture.

27. Lead, for it is heavy, and is at first impure; gives colour and weight.

28. Tin — on account of its whiteness.

29. Sulphur of Nature. Lime Alum — for it consumes and burns up.

30. Spittle of the Moon, incombustible saliva.

31. Burnt Copper, Black Copper, Flower of Copper, i.e., Ore — as also Ore of Hermes.

32. The Serpent, the Dragon — for he devours and destroys.

33. Marble, Crystal, Glass — which is all clear and intelligible.
34. Scottish gem.
35. Urine of boys, urine of the white calf — on account of its acrid nature.
36. White Magnesia, a Magnet — because it attracts gold, or the King, unto itself.
37. White Ethesia, a white Moisture.
38. Dung — for it manures the earth, which it renders moist, fat, and fruitful.
39. White Smoke — for it renders white and glistening.
40. Metallic Entity — for it is the true Essence and Quintessence of Metals.
41. The virtue of mineral Mercury.
42. The Soul and Heaven of the Elements.
43. The Matter of all Forms.
44. Tartar of the Philosophers.
45. Dissolved Refuse.
46. The Rainbow — on account of its colours.
47. Indian Gold, Heart of the Sun, Shade of the Sun, Heart and Shade of Gold — for it is stronger than gold; it holds the gold in its heart, and is itself Gold.
48. Chaos — as it is in the beginning.
49. Venus — On account of the fruitfulness of Nature.
50. Microcosmos — because it is a likeness of the great world, through heaven, the sea, and all elements.

Other Names, not mentioned by Rulandus:
1. Adarner.
2. A Drop.
3. Asrob.
4. Agnean.
5. Eagle.
6. Alartar.
7. Albar lEvis.

8. Alkaest.
9. Alcharit.
10. Alembroth.
11. Alinagra.
12. Almisada.
13. Aludel.
14. Alun.
15. Abzernad.
16. Amalgra.
17. Anatron.
18. Androgyne.
19. Antimony.
20. Aremaros.
21. Arnec.
22. Arsenic.
23. Asmarcech.
24. Azoth.
25. Borax.
26. Boritis.
27. Caduceus.
28. Cain.
27. Chyle.
28. Cock (The).
29. Dragon.
30. Ebisemeth.
31. Embryo.
32. Euphrates.
33. Eve.
34. Feces.
35. Flower of the Sun.
36. Hermaphrodite.
37. Hyle.
38. Infinite.
39. Isis.

40. Kibrish.
41. Laton.
42. Lion.
43. Magnes.
44. Magnesia.
45. Mars.
46. Menstruum.
47. Mother.
48. Orient.
49. Salamander.
50. Sonig.
51. Sulphur.
52. Tincture of Metals.
53. Vapour.
54. Lord of the Stones.
55. The Bull.
56. The Sea.
57. The West.
58. Bird of Hermes.
59. Shadow of the Sun.
60. Philosophical Stone.
61. Animal Stone.
62. Lead.
63. Spring.
64. Vegetable Liquor.
65. The Moon.
66. The Garden.
67. The Spouse.
68. Summer.
69. The Woman.
70. The Son of the Water of Life.
71. Water of Gold.
72. The Belly of the Ostrich.
73. Anger.

74. Butter.
75. May Blossom.
76. Golden Wood.
77. The Tree.
78. Silver.
79. Whiteness.
80. Soul of Saturn.
81. The Lamb.
82. Sun and the Moon.

The matter of the Magnum Opus is the subject on which the philosophers exercised their practical science. All who have written on the art have concealed the true name of this matter, as the chief key of chemistry. Having potentially all the qualities and properties of elementary things, they have given it the names of all kinds of things. It is a fifth element, a quintessence, the material beginning and end of all things. It is the matter of which the Heavens are composed, says the Hermetic author. It is the quintessence of our sublunary matter, the soul of the elements, which preserves all things sublunary from destruction, and from corruption. It is the bird of Hermes, which descends continually from heaven to earth, and as continually ascends and goes back from earth to heaven. It is even as the mysterious ladder of the vision of Jacob the prophet, whereon the angels of God forever came and went between earth and the world which is above the earth. It is also the seeds of bodies, even the seminal life of all things, whether vegetable, animal, or mineral, which do propagate and continue their species by means of seminal generation. Now the seed of bodies is the first matter of the chemists; and this matter is found only in the seed of bodies. But each seed is to be found after its own kind, in its own species. There is a seed of individuals according to the three Kingdoms of Nature, and this seed is diverse in each. In the mineral kingdom, it is called a Sperm, and this sperm is the

Sulphur of Metals — an unctuous, sulphureous and mecurial vapour, says Aristotle.

MATERIA SAPPHIREA — A Liquid wherein there is no noxious matter.

MATHEDORUM — i.e., Sal Gemmae.

MATHEMATICA — Consists of many Arts and Sciences- Arithmetic, Astronomy, Geometry, Geomancy, Physiognomy, Chiromancy — Perspective.

MATRICES RERUM OMNIUM — Matrices of all Things, i.e., the Elements.

MATURATIO — is the Elevation from a Coarse and Rough Condition to Maturity and Perfection. There are four kinds of Maturation, each of which is accomplished by a moderate heat of the first grade, or near it, it mud, in a bath, in scum of olive oil, in fine cut straw, in a dry stone, with damp hay, with grape stones, by sunshine, the moon, etc, The four kinds are called-Digestion, Circulation, Fermentation, and Projection.

MATURATIVA — Maturatives are Surgeons' Medicines, which bring any Abscesses or Ulcers to Maturity.

MECHANICAE ARTES — Mechanical Arts, Manual Operations.

MECHANO PEOTICA — Inventions for Managing Water, such as artificial fountains, drawing up water by means of syringes, by pipes, bellows, and the like.

MEDEAE GEMMA — Medea's Gem, from the black Median Stone, which is brought from the Land of the Medes. But the Medean Gem, or Medea, is so called, because it was first discovered by the poisoner Medea. It is black, having veins of a golden colour; it yields a saffron sap, with a vinous flavour, and is extremely efficacious against drunkenness, and useful in the cultivation of friendship, as the Magi assert. It is, without any doubt, a species of the

Median Stone, or Black Hematite, which yields a saffron sap. It is found in Cherussia, where there is also Black Hematite, although the veins are not of so golden a hue. Consult Pliny concerning Medea's gem.

MEDITATIO — The name of an Internal Talk of one person with another who is invisible, as in the invocation of the Deity, or communion with one's self, or with one's good angel.

MEDIUM COELI — Middle of the Heaven — the Mid Day — Noon — the Zenith — White, also Margesia.

MEDULLA CANDIDA — White Marrow of the Stones of Targensae, white soft Lithomarge.

2. White thick Marrow of Targensian Stones.

3. White and soft Marrow of Rochlicensian Stones.

4. White hard Marrow from the same.

5. White Metallic Marrow, growing in veins of silver, which, when first extracted, yield a liquid like cheese in colour. In the air this immediately hardens, and yet it will melt like butter in the mouth.

6. Extremely white Metallic Marrow, thick and soft. Found in veins of iron at Sachsenfeld. Its touch resembles that of saponaceous earth.

7. White Metallic Marrow from the same place. Found in iron stones.

8. Hard yellow Lithomarge.

9. Yellow friable Lithomarge, found at Meissen on the floor of storehouses.

10. Red soft Lithomarge which is medically used with great success in place of the Armenian Bolus.

11. Lithomarge, flesh-colour or white.

12. Black Pirnensian Lithomarge, resembling pitch.

13. Greenish Lithomarge, from Chemnitz, above Hilberdorf.

MEHELUM — A Glass with a long neck, a Retort.

MELA — i.e., Lead.

MELANTER — i.e., Opium.

MELANTERIA METALLICUM CHALCANTI — A species of Copperas Water, or maker's Black, a species of Vitriol. Its colour is blue and grey, depending upon the different earths in which it is produced. According to Dioscorides (1. 5, c. 67), it has a twofold origin. Some of it solidifies and accumulates like salt in the cavities of mines, whence copper is obtained. Sometimes the same species is found upon the copper itself, and (if I mistake not) is called Maltira by Serapion, and by others Melatria. Secondly, Melanteria is found on the surface of mines, like earth, salt, etc. The Arabs call it Bitriant. It is sometimes found by digging in Cilicia, and other districts. Dioscorides affirms that the mined species is the best, especially that which has the colour of sulphur, and is light, pure and equable. According to the Arabs, on contact with sufficient moisture to moisten the finger, it immediately hardens. It also possesses a caustic virtue. This quality is scarcely to be found in our mines, although we have two species of it, which the Arabs maintain to be a kind of Colcothar, i.e., Fixed Vitriol, because its properties are the same. Also Melanteria is the rust of old iron nails, or Shoemaker's Black, being almost the same as is now produced by our shoemakers.

MELAONES, or **MELONES** — Black Insects, sending forth a good odour when crushed. They are found during May in the meadows — a kind of Green Beetle, shining with a muddled yellow hue.

MELCELHON — i.e., Mulbra.

MELECH — i.e., Salt.

MELIBOCUM, MELIBCEUM — i.e., Copper.

MELISEA, MOTHERWORT, MELISION — Is used for Manna or Balsam, being obtained from the higher vegetables by means of the Magistery.

MELITITES ~ A Stone now almost unknown, especially in laboratories. Dioscorides asserts that it resembles Galactite, and possesses the same virtues and potencies, only that it has a sweeter sap. Pliny (1. 36, c. 19) states that Melitite, when pounded, yields a sweet and honey-like juice, or sap, and that when mixed with wax, it is a medicine for excessive phlegm, spots on the body, ulceration of the jaws, and the pain of wounds.
MELLISODIUM ~ Burnt Lead.
MELUSI ~ i.e., Mercury ~ Albach, Messalis.
MELUSINA and **MELIORA** ~ were Kings' daughters in France, snatched away by Satan because they were hopelessly sinful, and transformed into spectres horrible to behold, and monstrous ghosts. The preceding is not a fictitious account. They are thought to exist with a rational soul, but a merely brute-like body, of a visionary kind, nourished by the elements and, like them, destined to pass away at the last day unless they contract a marriage with a man. Then the man himself may, perish by a natural death, while they live naturally by this nuptial union.
MEMPHITES LAPIS ~ Memphite Stone, found near Memphis, in Egypt, and deriving its name from the locality, and the size of the pebbles. It is thick, of the colour of the worm, according to the description of Dioscorides and I'liny. In fact, however, its nature is now unknown.
MENFRICE ~ i.e., Mastich.
MENSIS PHILOSOPHICUS ~ The Philosophical Period of Digestion, a space of homy Days. It is the time of putrefaction, the period which follows, or imitates, the movements of the Moon, which is in some cases thirty, and in others forty days. The space occupied in the composition of the Philosopher's Stone is also known by this name, but fewer days compose this month, which must be determined

solely by the nature of the matter, and by the completion of the work.

MENSOR — A Measurer, a Mathematician. A Measurer of Mines, a Surveyor.

MENSTRUUM — is that from which all metals are derived. It is of two kinds. One is like unto whey, and this is useless. The other is mercurial, and this is of good account. It is the Mercury wherein gold is dissolved. The whey is the superfluous moisture which comes from the matrix and cannot be dried. Consequently, when the solution is obtained it appears in the form of a menstruous blood. Our Water is a Fire, a Salt, Fire, the true universal Menstruum of Vegetables, stronger than the fire of wood, since it transmutes the physical gold into a spirit, the Fontin Vinum Aminaeum, Vinegar, the Water of the King of the Philosophers, the Genuine Extracting Solvent and Universal Vegetative Menstruum, without which the Sun and the Moon cannot be prepared, neither black nor white.

MERCURIUS — i.e., Sulphur.

MERCURY — is mentioned everywhere, in every alchemical work, and is supposed to perform everything. Everybody wastes his brain and his money in endeavouring to produce a quantity of it. Now, Mercury is a thick gluey liquid, yet it does not stick, for it is of a dry nature, Moist and Warm Water, almost inseparably mixed with Earth, so that they either remain together, or depart together.

2. *Speculum Alchimiae* states that Mercury is Living Gold, and kills or makes alive, moistens and drys, warms and cools, becoming opposite things according to the measure of its regimen.

3. It is also called Vinegar, Oli, a Father of all Wonders, and the Chief Medicine; also Living Silver because it possesses a soul; also Bath, a continually Stagnant Water, Water of Sulphur, Burning Water, Water of Life, of Gold, of

Saltpetre, Pure Water, White Karo, Vapour, Seed, Shade, Fiery, Poison, Fire, Ore, Lime, Azot, Gold, Orpiment, Lunar Saliva, Strftarna Boletorunr, Citronat, Juice, Wine of Souls, Brightness of the Sea, Heart of Salt, Kanderich, Colla Auriborites, Alum from Apples, Kuhul, Esbuit, Stomach, juice from Metallic Roots.

4. An essential of all metals, as it is in itself a poison to them all. It cleanses gold.

5. It is of the nature of silver, and of the spirit of the same, the White Stone, the Disappearing Water, Virgin's Milk, the Proud Lady.

6. When he conquers, he is white; when overcome, he is red; he is a Powerful Water.

7. Mercury of the Body is White Earth.

8. Exuberatus is Earth of the Body, which, along with the Menstruum, has arisen over the bright part of the body.

9. Mercury of Mars is red yellow, even as Mercury of Venus.

10. Crude Mercury dissolves the bodies, but Mercury of the bodies effects nothing.

11. The Earth wherein to sow the grain. It is incombustible, whether it sustains the brightness of the fire, or whether it flows right away. It is an index of perfection that nothing should remain in the fire.

12. Trenes — Mercury is the Subject and Matter of the Stone. When you have amalgamated with it the calx of the perfected body, press it through a linen cloth, and again through a hare's bladder. If it passes clean through, then all is well.

13. Rosin. Our Stone consists of fixed Mercury, which possesses in itself Soul, Spirit, and Body.

14. Lully says: Ordinary Mercury cannot be the Mercury of the Philosophers, no matter however prepared.

15. Bernard states that Mercury is in some fashion reckoned among the Metals, but it is the Medium for Uniting the

Tincture; it is not itself the medicine, but an aid thereto; it is purified through sublimation, washed with salt and vinegar.

16. Mercury is the bane of all metals, even of all things, for he eats away and devours the vessels; all things immersed in him swim to the surface, except gold which, however, he attracts to himself and purifies. He conducts the feces with himself through the strainer, and leaves the gold pure.

17. Adam of Mercury is the Essence of Sulphur and Earth.

18. Theophrastic Mercury is hardened by the Sulphur of Metals, and is transformed into the nature of the sulphur of that metal with which it is hardened.

19. Mercury is extracted from the body by means of solution, distillation, sublimation, and subtilisation: it becomes a Tincture of Mercury of the Sun; it is volatile, nevertheless, has the property of fixing, and does not blacken like the ordinary Mercury.

20. You must always be careful to distinguish what is generally and particularly stated concerning Mercury, as to whether it be about ordinary Mercury, or about our Mercury. Do not make a mistake; otherwise, the information will be useless.

MERCURIUS — Mercury naturally coagulated is a solid Metal, but we coagulate it artificially either with Metals or with Minerals; or without the aid of these either by itself or by other substances, not Minerals.

MERCURIUS — Mercury is the material principle, gaseous, of a watery nature, subject to generation; by its virtue shape is formed or impressed upon all things, and all things receive their perfection.

MERCURIUS — Mercury is one of the three principles in which the property of things is contained.

MERCURIUS — Quicksilver, C.C., S.Z.

MERCURIUS ARGENTIPIGMENTUM ~ Mercury of Silver Pigment is Sulphur, Vitriol, Alum, Salt, because it dissolves bodies.

MERCURIUS CHAMBAR ~ Magnesia, Fluid Body and Water.

MERCURIUS CORALLINUS ~ Mercury reduced to Red Coral by passing through the oil of eggs and other liquids.

MERCURIUS CRUDUS ~ Mercury which is crude remains unseparated from the oil.

MERCURIUS CRYSTALLINUS ~ is often sublimated into the form of Crystal until it assumes the transparency of the latter.

MERCURIUM EXSUPERANTEM, etc. ~ Mercury Triumphant is, according to Lully, when they bring to the King a white banner, with a picture of the moon on the increase, out of which pearls are made.

MERCURIUS LAXUS ~ is Mineral Turbith.

MERCURIUS METALLORUM ~ Mercury of Metals is that from which the nature of the bodies is derived, the Quintessence and Permanent Water, Spirit, Seed of Passive Female, the Bath and Mother of the King, who draws the King to herself because they are one and love each other.

MERCURIUS METALLORIUM ~ Mercury of Metals is precipitated Mercury of the body, physical Mercury, when metals are reduced to their first matter and precipitated into Mercury.

MERCURIUS MINERALIUM ~ Mercury of Minerals, the Oil or Grease extracted from Minerals, Gold and Silver, or Gold and Silver Ore.

MERCURIUS REGENERATUS ~ The First Entity of Mercury.

MERCURIALIS SIEVA, MERCURIAL CRUDENESS ~ Water of Alum Wherein Mercury is generated. It is also a Purging Salt of a golden colour, found in salt caves, best

known to diggers. It is often drunk for pneumonia, a disease of the lungs.
MERDASENGI ～ i.e., Powder from Burnt Lead.
MERGEN BASSEC ～ i.e., Coral.
MESBRA ～ i.e., Alexandrine Tutty.
MESEL, MOSEL ～ i.e., Tin.
MEST, MISAL, MASAL ～ i.e., Sour Milk.
METALLUM ～ i.e., Vein, Ore.
METALLUM ～ i.e., Melted Silver.
METALLUM CURRENS ～ i.e., Living Mercury.
METALLUM RUDE, A TERRIS ET SAXIS SECERNERE ～ Separation of Metal from Earth and Stones.
METALLUM FERRAMENTO FORFICIS SIMILI CONCIDERE ～ The Cutting of Metallic Substances by means of Shears.
METALLUM MALLEO PERCUSSUMM DILATARE ～ Extension and Flattening of Metallic Substance by means of a Hammer.
METAS, MECAL, MEKAL ～ i.e., Weight.
MEZ ～ The Son of the Servant of Red Copper.
MICHA ～ i.e., Venus. Passive Female, the Bath and Mother of the King, who draws the King to herself because they are one and love each other.
MICHACH ～ i.e., Copper.
MICROCOSMUS ～ A Small and Intermediate World placed between the Firmamental World and that of the Elements, as is only natural, since it, namely man, participates in both. Whatsoever is actually and visibly contained in them is in like manner spiritually and potentially held in man. Hence it results that thence there can and ought to be one philosophical classification, living, not dead as of a corpse, true, equally essential, and manifest.
MIFRES ～ i.e., Asphalt.

MINERA — i.e., Iron.
MINERA, VENA TERRA — i.e., Vein of Ore.
MINERA — An Iron Hooked Stick, or Pick.
MINERALE VAS — A Vessel of Mineral Substance, either Metallic or Earthenware.
MINERALIA — The Place of Minerals.
MINISTER — An Assistant, a Servant who brings Coal or Ore.
MINIUM — Mercury of Saturn precipitated, or Saffron of Minium.
MINIUM — Ordinary Red Paint and Burnt Lead.
MISADIR or **MIXADIR** — i.e., Sal Ammoniac.
MISSADAN — i.e., Quicksilver.
MISSERASSI — i.e., Gypsum.
MISTIO — Composition. There are four kinds — Inceration, Incorporation, Smelting and Melting.
MISTURA — A Pallid Kind of Paint.
MISTURA EX AERE ET ARGENTO EQUALIS — Cobalt.
MISY — According to some writers, is a Genus of Myrrh. Otherwise it is something derived from swellings (See Pliny, 1. 19, c. 3). But in this place, according to our judgment, it is a metallic substance like Rock Alum, being a coagulated moisture out of a species of Copperas. Now, Misy and Sory have an affinity with the genus Chalcitis, being produced from the same source. Misy is the more delicate, Sory the coarser substance. Nowadays, Misy is altogether unknown, and has fallen out of use for many centuries. Misy, like Rock Alum, is of two kinds, native and manufactured. Native Misy, produced spontaneously in mines, is coagulated with water. It is found in the copper mines of Goslaria, and resembles gold according to the descriptions of Dioscorides (1. 5, c. 66). It is hard and when polished assumes a golden hue, shining like a star. Some imagine that it is dyed by

water which flows from ochre. Pliny, however, states that it is accumulated and collected by the stone itself, and that the best quality is found in the laboratories of the Cypriotes. Some call it Red Vitriol or Red Zegi. The metallurgists themselves are ignorant of the German name; the wisest of them think that Misy is Mountain Vitriol. This name, however, seems properly to belong to Native Vitriol. Chalcanthum easily changes into Misy. But Misy, according to Dioscorides, is burnt like Rock Alum itself. Sporicon is made of it.

Manufactured Misy is produced when Chalcanthum is changed into Chalcitis, a fact mentioned by Galen.

Misy:
1. Misy that can be pulverised; Yellow Atrament.
2. Hard Yellow Atrament.
3. Yellow Atrament mixed with Red Atrament or Rock Alum.
4. Hard Yellow Atrament mixed with Black Atrament.
5. Yellow Atrament, having delicate White Atrament on the surface.
6. Yellow Atrament with Red Hard Atrament and a delicate White Atrament on the surface.

MITIGATIVA ~ Mitigating Medicants. Anodynes which soothe and diminish pain.
MODIOLUS ROTAE ~ Nave of a Wheel.
MODULUS ~ A Wooden Tub.
MOLA MATRICIS ~ Abortion in the Womb.
MOLE ~ Millstone.
MOLIBOTO, CHALCUM ~ Ore of Lead.
MOLERE ~ To Grind. There are several methods.
MOLIPDIDES ~ Stone of Lead, Leaden Stone.
MOLIPDINA ~ Incrustations of Silver and Gold. Pliny says it is the ordinary Vein of Silver or of Lead.

MOLOCHITES — An Opaque Gem of a Deeper Green than Emerald. It derives its name from the colour of the mallow. It is of great efficacy against all infantile disorders. It comes from Arabia. Molochites of moderate size may be seen in a church at the mouth of the Tangra. (Consult Pliny, 1. 37, c. 8. Also Solinus, Albertus, Evax, etc.).

MOLYBDENA — Hard Lead Incrustations found at the Bottom of the Furnace.

MOLYBDENA and **PLUMBAGO**:
1. Hard Lead, as above.
2. Produced from Lead and Copper.
3. From a Mixture of Lead and Gold.
4. From a Mixture of Lead and Silver.
5. Smelted from Plates of Lead.
6. Deposited in the Middle of the Vessel.
7. Ashes of Black Lead from the Incrustation of the Furnaces.

MONETARIORUM MAGISTER — Master of the Mint.

MONETARIUS — Minter, Coiner.

MONSTRA — Monsters are certain Animals which have been originated outside the order of nature, and which heaven hatches in the egg of their putrefaction. The fruit of an unlawful and accursed copulation. They generate nothing in their turn, because they were born from the copulation of diverse seeds, as of a man and a brute, or from empoisoned parents. Thus the giants of old originated, and other monstrous men, contrary to nature, whose sight provokes horror and cursing. They are not produced by any honourable means, but by the guile of men who force animals of diverse kind to come together, as the horse and the ass, in order to produce beasts of burden. Such is the wisdom of this world. These Monstrosities are impotent and useless for breeding purposes, since nature absolutely shrinks from them.

MONTES ~ Cucurbits, Retorts, Tops of Retorts, etc.

MORBILLI ~ Smallpox, Measles, Discharges of Phlegm, Cutaneous Eruptions.

MORO, MORUS ~ A Mulberry, an Abscess in the Flesh, a Swelling like Warts.

MOROCHTHUS ~ A Stone called Galaxia and Leucograph by Dioscorides. In Egypt it is produced in such a soft state that lines can be drawn upon it; it is extremely white, easily fusible, useful for whitening garments, even as Galactite. Hence we see that Pliny errs in confounding Morochthum, Galaxia, or Leucograph with Galactite. Elsewhere, Pliny, so far as I know, has nothing about Morochthus, unless (in 1. 37, C. 10), we prefer to read Morochthus for Merocte, which exudes a milk-like juice. Nor is this now found in laboratories. However, it is produced excellently in Saxony, especially at Hildesheim. As to its medical value, see Dioscorides, 1. 5, c. 93.

MORPHEA ~ A kind of Leprosy.

MORS ~ is called Death or Corruption. The body dies when the soul departs. The colour goes, the spirit or water is extracted. When it returns to it, it awakes, becomes living, bright, henceforth immortal.

MORTARIOLUM ~ is a small Model for forming Cinder Pans, generally constructed of Brass, in the shape of a wide circle or perforated pan. This model is furnished with a mortar, commonly called monachus, which is a pestle with a round protuberance, projecting from the centre of the broad base. The pit or hearth of the pan is constructed by means of this pestle. For larger pans, that is, for those which contain more matter for formation, we employ an iron circle and a proportionately large mortar.

MORTARIOLUM ~ Brazen Figures, which are engraved upon a Chemical Cupel.

MOS ~ i.e., Mycra.

MULCEDAR, or **MULCODAR** — i.e., the Dragon.
MULE — Blisters caused by Cold or Heat.
MUMIA — Not only the name of Human Flesh preserved with Balm, but also of other things, not dead naturally but killed, and possessing healing virtues.
MUMIA ELEMENTORUM — The Balsam of the External Elements.
MUMIA MEDULLE — The Marrow of Bones.
MUMIA TRANSMARINA — i.e., Manna.
MUMIA VERSA — Liquor of Mummy.
MUNDIFICATIVA — Medicines for Purifying Weak and Putrid Flesh, and separating it from the healthy and live flesh. Also Aperients, External Medicines, Cathartic Drugs.
MURIA — Salt Liquor, has the efficacy of Salt and Marine Water. There are two kinds — native, whence comes our ordinary salt; manufactured, when a little salt is mixed with rain from heaven. When the salt liquefies, we call it light salt; when it does not melt we call it hard salt. Note that garum is a salt liquor in which flesh and fish have been pickled. There is also sour brine, produced from vinegar and sea water. Pliny apppears to confound salt brine with garum.
MURIA — Salt Water, Stinking Menstruum.
MURMENTUM — Mountain Rat, Marmot.
MURUS — Mouse.
MURUS NIGER — Black Mouse; a Shrew.
MUSADI, MUZADIR, MISADIR, LIXANDRA — Names of Sal Ammoniac.
MUSCILAGO — Mucilage, a thick and slimy liquid of the consistence of Calamine.
MUSCULA SCIURUS — Hedgehog.
MUSTUM — Dark Blue Must.
MUSTUM IMMATURUM — Must not perfected.
MUSTUS — A White Lime of Urine; a kind of Fat; Water.
MYSI — Yellow Atrament.

MYSTERIUM ~ is the Essence of the Interior Nature, the sum of the whole substance in the subtle and withdrawn part of the given matter. Hence it differs greatly from sap, as much indeed as sap differs from the body. And because it is concealed in the most retired recesses of corporeal matter, and has an exceeding subtle nature, it is called a Mystery and an Arcanum. It is obtained immediately from the given thing, but after a certain necessary preparation. Also sometimes from a magistery and a sap. There are two varieties of this Mysterium or Essence, as it may be variously denominated. They are, namely, Quintessence and Specific Arcanum.
MYSTERIUM MAGNUM ~ The First Matter of all Things, the Principle and Mother of all the Corruptible Creatures of God, the Chaos, dark and rude.

NACTA ~ An Abscess of the Breast.
NAFDA, or **SINAPTA** ~ i.e., Petroleum, or Asphalt.
NAPELLUS ~ Wolf's bane.
NACDA, or **NATTA GIBBUS** ~ A Hunchback, or Dwarf.
NAPTA ~ i.e., Gum.
NAPTA ALBA ~ i.e., is White Petroleum.
NAPHTHA ~ We have said that the Bitumen of Judea is a species of Naphtha, but is not true Naphtha. For Naphtha is nothing else but Petroleum, that liquid oil which, although in an impure form, is manufactured in our own land. Dioscorides (1. 1, c. 84) says that Naphtha was called Bitumen by the Babylonians, or Colamen of Bitumen, and that there were black and white varieties. White Naphtha is our Petroleum. Black is perhaps that pitchy and glutinous matter of Amiantus, Asbestos, or Earth-flax, which is not dissimilar from Bitumen, and which when it has once been set on fire can be extinguished by nothing but dust being heaped over it, like that slime from the lake of Comagenes

mentioned by Pliny. By some among the ancients this black Naphtha was believed to be the Excrement of Demons, concerning which I venture to affirm nothing; but we also have an excrement of demons, namely, the plant silphium, which produces the juice called laser. Many stinking substances were held precious by the ancients. Naphtha is a violent potency of fire, as Dioscorides teaches, and there is no substance which can compare with it for sustaining and nourishing fire. Pliny cites an example which occurred in Media at the execution of an adulteress, who had a crown of naphtha placed on her, and when this crown was set on fire the woman was consumed. Pliny also bears witness that there is a naphtha which is found in Babylon and Parthia which is like Liquid Bitumen. Thus Naphtha is twofold- natural, dealt with by Pliny, and properly Petroleum- manufactured, which is Colamen of Bitumen, as Dioscorides terms it. And of this there is one kind which is white, and may be a species of Petroleum, but is inferior to the native. And there is another kind which is black, and which may be the Excrement of Demons, so called by the ancients. I affirm that it is from a subtle Bitumen, i.e., from Naphtha (which is true Petroleum) indurated by the operation of the sun, as Ovid says of amber, that gagates is made in the sea, and not from manufactured White Naphtha. Thus Bitumen is twofold, in the sea, and in the earth, liquid, and hard, or glutinous. Pissasphaltus is also twofold-native and manufactured. Naphtha is twofold-native and manufactured. Thus Bitumen, Pissasphaltus, and Naphtha are almost various species of one thing, and so is the stone Gagates, which is formed of natural Naphtha, i.e., true Petroleum, as its smell indicates. The Thracian Stone, another species of Gagates, may be formed of black Bitumen or black Naphtha. This also burns in water, and is put out by oil. Succinum, or amber, on the contrary, is made of the resin of trees, though both have the power of attracting hairs and straws. Succinum does not burn in water, because of the poorness of its resin. Gagates burns fiercely, and its flame is increased by water, because of the strength of the Naphtha or Bitumen of which it consists. So also those coals which are found in our mines, and which we call Pit Coal, are a kind of Gagates, and nothing else but Bitumen hardened under the earth, or excocted by heat. This stone also is put out by oil, and burns fiercely when sprinkled with water, as is the nature of Bitumen. And those coals also are bituminous with which the mountains Etna and Vesuvius are burning, as Pliny sets forth, and as we also see to be the case in many places of Germany, and especially in the night, because in the day the heat of the sun weakens them or overwhelms them; but in the night, which is cold and moist, the matter is excited by the moisture. That species of pyrites, called the Fissile Stone of Islebia, is evidently bituminous, because it burns quickly, gives forth a bituminous smell, and takes impressions very easily. For impressions are made upon a body of this bituminous quality, which is prepared to receive impressions with as much ease and celerity, as the chemists say, that a soul enters its body. But of this enough. Petroleum, i.e., Naphtha, which is manufactured by the Agyrtx, does not come from the tomb of some saint whom I forget, as is falsely represented. For the rest, there is another manufactured Naphtha, which is described in the antidotes of Nicander. There is also a Bituminous Peat which is dug up in Saxony.

NAR — i.e., Fire.
NARBASAPHAR — i.e., Brass.
NARCOTICA — A Soporific Medicament, which removes pain, or at least deadens its. keenness.
NARDINUM OLEUM — A kind of Oil, Spikenard.
NARIS — Nostril.

NATARON, or **NATRON** — i.e., Nitre.

NEBULGEA — is a Salt which is deposited by the moisture of a Mist, and is hardened by the Sun.

NECROCOMICA — are Portentous Presages, signifying something which is to come by signs falling from heaven upon earth; those crosses, for example, which fell in the days of Maximilian the First.

NECROLIA, or **NECROLICA** — are Medicaments which prevent death and preserve life.

NECROMANTIA — is a Forbidden Art, by which formerly divinations were obtained from the dead. But true Necromancy compels the dead to manifest, and extracts answers and speech from them, and compels them to perform wonders. Any operations connected with the death's head, bones, shroud needles, shrouds, or cerements, quivers, sepulchres, and such like, are comprehended under this cursed art, which is wholly superstitious, and avoided by Christians.

NENUFARENI — A name of those Spirits who inhabit the Elements.

NEUTHA — A Child's Caul, sometimes covering the eye, sometimes the ear, and sometimes the whole face of a new born child.

NIGELLA — A Rat.

NIGROMANTIA — Formerly a Natural Art, by which man, after a natural manner, sought to discover the secrets of minerals, metals, and things hidden in the earth.
Afterwards, by the suggestion of the devil, and through the perversity of wicked men, it fell into abuse, and became a diabolical art.

NITRUM, BAURACH, ROCK SALT, SALTPETRE, NITRE — is Hot and Dry in the Second Degree. It is a substance having affinity with Salt, and is a species of Salt. Hence, Transparent Salt, Alexandrine Salt, Salt of

Anderena, Salt of Nitre, are one and the same. But Nitre is formed from coagulated moisture. We do not know exactly what were the species of Nitre which are described by the ancients, but they differed from our own. They were used in food, and blended with wine, as we learn from Pliny 0. 14, C. 20, and 1. 18, c. 17), as well as from the Georgics of Virgil. Formerly, they seem to have been also of a rosy colour, bitter, light, spongy, and easily consumed by fire, whereas, ours in no way correspond to these descriptions, and are derived from the air, while the ancient Nitres were of terrene origin. Ours also are of greater medicinal virtues, provoking humours, and possessing laxative qualities. It should be noted that there are several species of manufactured Nitre, which are mentioned by Pliny (1. 31, c. 10). By us, Nitre is manufactured in several ways — in stables, sheepcotes, ancient dormitories, in rocks, cellars, walls, and other such places, as well as in old and disused sand-pits. There is also that Nitre which is called Spumous, and is Aphronitum, Saltpetre, the Spume of Nitre, and a true species of Nitre. It has affinities with the flower of the Asian rock or stone, referred to by Dioscorides, and of which we have already treated (see Lapis Asius). If we consider rightly, Green Chrysocolla, the Scissile Copper-Stone is a species of Nitre, i.e., Native Nitre. Dioscorides (1. 5, c. 78), describes Spume of Nitre along with Nitre, both as regards the country of its origin, and its quality. He indicates their medical virtues, how they are to be treated by fire, and the uses of the crude mineral. Information upon the same subject will be found in Serapion, under the name of Baurach.

It will be seen that the species of Nitre may be classified broadly as follows: Native mined Nitre, similar to salt from the mines. Under the generic name of Burach the following varieties are included :

1. Armenian, and this is the best kind.
2. Nitre from Rabath, which is either white — very similar to salt from the mines, and having a medium flavour between salt and vinegar — or black.
3. African.
4. Egyptian.
5. Roman.
6. Babylonian.

Manufactured Nitre, like a petrine or saline efflorescence. It is derived by coction from salt or saline water. The first and the sixth species were alone known to the Arabians. The Babylonians also had two kinds, namely, Nitre (rock salt, purple, moderately bitter), and Baurach, with which, when dissolved in water, it was the custom to besmear loaves before baking, and thus produce a gloss upon the crust.

There is copious information in Pliny (1. 31, c. 10), on Nitre and spume of Nitre. Nicander also treats in his Antidotes of Nitre as prevailing against a poisonous potion compounded of bullock's blood. Nitre is also an ingredient in the powder of the tormentors, as is well known to the apothecaries of Satan who take their name from torments.

NITRUM — The Saline Stone, i.e., White Sulphur.
NITRUM ALEXANDRINUM — i.e., is Clavellated Ash.
NITRUM — is a kind of Salt. It is also Borax, and one kind of Armenian Salt — black, red, or sapphire.
NITRUM — is a certain Brine from combinations of Urines prepared in Salt.
NITRUM — i.e., Baurac.
NITRUM — Nitre.
NITRUM — Sago, Talc.
NITRUM, TINCAR, or TINCKAR — Which See.
NITRUM — i.e., White Salt, Baurac.
NITRON — Vitreous Refuse.

NITRIALES ~ Whatever Calcines and Burns, as Sulphur, Saltpetre, whereby one calcines Pearls, Precious Stones, and Corals into a Saltpetre.
NOAS ~ in Arabic; Calchos in Greek; Copper in Latin; Ore in German.
NOAS or **NOAC** ~ Brass or Copper.
NOBACH ~ A Necromantic Instrument.
NOCHAT, NUCHAT, or **NUCHOR** ~ i.e., Venus, Copper.
NOCASIT ~ i.e., a Perforated Vessel, Sieve, or Colander.
NODI ARTICULORUM ~ Indurated Tumours, Knots in the joints, as in gout.
NOERA ~ i.e., a Cover over a Distilling Apparatus.
NORA ~ i.e, Calx.
NORA ~ i.e., is Nitre.
NORA ~ Every kind of Salt.
NOSIDIDACH ~ (?) A joint (Artus).
NOSTOCH ~ A Ray or Radiation of a certain Star, or its off-scouring, superfluity, etc., cast on earth. It falls, chiefly during June, July, and August, upon broad fields or meadows, being like a large fungus or sponge in appearance, and of a yellow or dark tawny colour, like a coagulated juice, and to the touch like jelly. By Nostoch some understand Wax.
NUBA ~ i.e., Copper.
NUBA ~ is a second species of Manna, red in colour, such as falls in Ireland.
NUHAR ~ i.e., Venus, or Copper.
NUMUS ~ Lead, Black Lead.
NUSIADAT ~ i.e., Ammoniac.
NUTRIMENTUM ~ is Material changed by Putrefaction in the Stomach.
NYMPHAE ~ Spiritual Men and Women, or Corporeal Spirits, inhabiting water, such as was Melusine.

NYMPHIDICA ~ The Spirits obtained by heat artificially from water may be so called.
NYSADIR, NUSSIADAI, NESTUDAR ~ Sal Ammoniac.

OBELCHERA — i.e., Cucurbit.
OBELKARA — i.e., Cucurbit.
OBRIZUM AURUM — i.e., Pure Gold.
OBRIZUM AURUM PURUM — Gold Calcined to a Dark Red by means of Art.
OCOS, OCOP, OBAC, or **OCAB** — i.e., Sal Ammoniac.
OCRA — Yellow Earth; called Uger.
OCRA GRAECIS — A Slimy Earth, called Sil by the Latins. It is twofold-native and manufactured. Native Yellow Ochre, or Yellow Earth, is obtained in the mines of Germany. There is a variety like Chrysocolla, and another called Sander's Blue. Dacian and Hungarian Ochres are most in use among painters. Our own is somewhat despised. Dioscorides (1. 5, c. 58) praises that of Attics, which is very

light, brittle, slimy, aqueous, and free from grittiness. He also states that it can be burnt and cleansed like Cadmia, and that its medical quality is astringent, biting, and dispersing. There are various species of Ochre — some metallic; some hard, as is our own; some simply a yellow earth, and this also is found in our mines. Theophrastus merely describes it as Ochrine Earth. Pliny enumerates (1. 33, c, 12) divers kinds of Sil, or Ochre, and says that the best of these pigments-whether yellow or blue-are derived from Metallic Ores containing Gold and Silver, that Ochre is properly a slime, that the Attics is the best, and that its nature is like marble. There is also compressed Ochre from Cyrus; Achaica, Gaul, India, etc. In the thirteenth chapter of the same book he says that dyeing with Ochre was first invented by a Myconian. Ochre is also found in rivers, as the Elbe, and above all in the Ocra, which flows through Brunswick, whence the substance takes its name, and is called Ochre in Saxony. If the matter be rightly regarded, we have four species of Ochre.

1. From the mines, of a stony quality, and found also on the shore and banks of rivers.
2. A Dust, or Dry Earth, adhering to stones, like Chrysocolla, Blue, etc. This is obtained from the stone quarries of Salveldia.
3. Another Dry Earth, found on river banks.
4. Slimy and sticky, or tenacious, of the nature of marble, and obtained from mines. That Ochre which is found in mines and by rivers, being parched by the heat either of the earth or the sun, is changed into native toddle, and consequently into a kind of clay. Ochre which begins to be changed into ruddle, but is still partly Ochrine, receives its colour from the sun or earth. Artisan's ruddle is made from artificially burnt Ochre. Manufactured Ochre is made from Lead.

OCHRA ATTICA — Ochre which is yellow as the yolk of an egg.
OCCIDENS — i.e., Vinegar.
OCCIDENS STELLA — i.e., Sal Ammoniac.
OCCIDENS — Mercury, Saturn, Salt, Spice, Hermaphrodite, Living Water, Viscous Water, etc.
ODORIFERA MEDICAMENT — are Medicaments which infuse health by their fragrance, and so dispel also diseases.
OFFICINA — A Workshop in which Lead is separated from Silver.
OFFICINA — A Workshop in which Silver is Separated from Brass. Any Place for Refining and Roasting metals.
OLEA SOLUTA — Dissolved Oils, are those which separate by a melting of the subtle oleaginous parts. Accordingly, this is done in the same way as the magisteries of liquids, except that for the magistery all the matters are dissolved into a liquid, and in this case the internal essential parts are dissolved into a thick sap, the coarser parts being left. It is necessary that there should be a preparation in order that they may flow and yield oleaginous matter. Hence they are generally prepared like magisteries, by calcination, maceration, cooking, etc., unless the matter is so tenuous that it will flow with little trouble.
OLEUM — i.e., Fire, is extracted from a dry substance, but the water from a moist substance, for the oil and the water distil each other, and that which remains below is called earth.
OLEUM — is called the First Water, i.e., distilled from blood or hairs.
OLEUM BENEDICTUM — is made of bricks.
OLEUM FRUMENTI — Spring Barley Oil, prepared in two ways, on a glowing plate, and by an ascending distillation.
OLEUM SULPHURIS — A Vapour Extracted by Elevation from Prepared Sulphur.

OLEUM FIXUM — is that which is reduced to an oily consistency out of dissolved matters, purified by filtration, by means of frequent abstraction, chiefly of spirit of wine. And what we call fixing is causing that which is diffuse and of small density to become oily and firm by abstracting or digesting its aqueous part. Hence it is needful that it should be dissolved in water, so that the coarse parts being separated by filtration, the thin parts may be immersed in moisture, whence they may be reduced by means of such a fixation. It is a common practice to dissolve the matter in any liquid, applying maceration, cooking, or melting, either to the matter alone, or combined with other things, The refuse is purged off by filtration.

OLEUM — Oil is either Distilled or Secreted. Distilled Oil is that which is extracted by distillation, which is performed either by ascension, descension, or mixing, or combination, which is absorption. Every absorption is performed by distillation only, but mixing can be effected in other ways.

OLEUM PALESTINUM — Vinegar.

OLEUM STILLATITIUM DESCENSORIUM — is Oil Obtained by Distillation downwards.

OLEUM PER ELIXATIONEM EXTRACTUM — is that which is extracted by cocoon, which can be performed either by boiling in moisture, or by a dry flame.

OLEUM EX ASSATIONE — is Oil obtained by roasting at a dry flame, no menstruum being used. Sometimes the method of burning is substituted for that of roasting.

OLEUM ARDENS — is Oil of Tartar, consummately corrected.

OLEUM VITRIOLI AURIFICATUM — Aureated Oil of Vitriol is Vitriol sweetened by Gold.

OLEUM COLCOTHARINUM — is Red Oil of Vitriol.

OLEITAS RERUM — is the Sulphur which exists in all things.

OLYMPICUS SPIRITUS ~ The Star in Man, the Astral Body which sends forth doubles.

OLY ~ is the Moisture or Glue of Metals which flows upon the Menstruum when they are dissolved.

ONYX ~ is a Gem which, according to Pliny, 1. 37, c. 6, is shaped like a nail or talon. There are many species, some having the colour of Chrysolith, some of Sand, some of jasper. Those of India are black, full of fire, hard, encircled by white veins, which give the whole stone the appearance of an eye. There are Arabian Onyxes which are also black, and have white bands, but they thin from the Indian forms. (See Pliny, 1. c.) We call the gem Sardonyx, from Sarda, which name has affinity with Onyx, and some say that the one stone is found in conjunction with the other. It is said further that Onyx in an erudition of a tree which hardens into a stone. When fire is applied to it, it emits a smell and various figures and marks appear on it. Albertus distinguishes red, black, and white species of Onyx, all of which when they are rubbed resolve into a substance like the human nail. They also say that these gems cause sadness and apprehension. They act upon melancholy temperaments, and provoke turbulent dreams and contentions. They increase saliva in boys. In conjunction with Sard or Sardonyx, their power is softened, and they make men chaste and modest.

ONYX: ~
1. Pure, transparent, horn-coloured Onyx.
2. Horn-coloured Onyx, having distinct white and purple transverse bands.
3. Horn-coloured Onyx, having milky bands in the upper part, and transverse purple bands in the lower.
4. Horn-coloured Onyx, which is naturally ornamented with lines of red Jasper.

5. Horn-coloured Onyx in which there are lines of dark brown jasper.
6. Horn-coloured Onyx full of red spots.
7. White, transparent Onyx, on which escutcheons are inscribed.
8. Impure, whey-like Onyx.

OPALUS ~ India is properly the Land of the Opal. It is a Precious Gem, inasmuch as it has the fire of the carbuncle, but somewhat softened ; the purple effulgence of the amethyst ; and the sea greenness of the emerald. There are several kinds. Some Opals have the smooth and equable hues of orpiment, some the ardent glow of sulphur, some the splendour of burning oil. The size of the opal is that of a hazel-nut. Those are corrupt if the colour be of crystal or like hailstones, or if they have spots, eyes, or other blemishes. On account of its beauty, it is called Paederos after one of the Cupids or Loves. Opals are also said to be found in Egypt, Arabia, and the Pontus, but these are the poorest ; better qualities are from Galatia, Thrace, and Cyprus.

OPHITES ~ is a species of Marble, of which Dioscorides enumerates three species ~ one black and heavy, another of ash colour, with grey lines and spots, found in Germany, at Mount Joachim; a third, with white bands. It is called Ophites because of its serpent-like hue. It is not true Echites, which is spotted like a viper, though the latter may be a variety of Uphite; nor is it dracontias, nor our serpentine marble ; and, again, it is not to be confused with the stone which is said to be taken from the head of the dragon, or to be composed of the froth of the dragon. That species which has black and grey lines is exactly like our serpents in colour. At the port of Tangra, where once was the royal seat of Charles IV., in the citadel, the temple is adorned with gems, and the walls on all sides are enriched with this kind of Ophite ; the same is a species of adder-stone, which has marks like a viper. There is also another species of Ophite, more nearly approaching the form of a serpent, because it has scales like the serpent; it is, moreover, a crustaceous stone. It is found in many parts of Saxony, but is altogether disesteemed. There is also a third species of Ophite, found on the banks of the Elbe, near Tangra. It is a slender, oblong stone, in shape, like a serpent, as though a serpent had hardened into stone. Within it is black approaching blue; without it is white. Pliny says that its name is derived from its serpentlike spots. He distinguishes two classes-the soft and white, and the dark, which is hard. From the white, he tells us that vessels and caskets are made. Ophite is good for lethargy, headache, and snake-bites.

OPERARIUS ~ A Workman.

OPERCULUM ~ The Cover of a Refining Furnace.

OPERCULUM AMPULLAE ~ The Cover of an Alembic.

OPERCULUM SUPERTORIS FORAMINIS TABULATI FOLLIUM ~ A Door, Stopper, or Plug.

OPERIMETHIOLIN ~ A Mineral Spirit.

OPILARE ~ To Shut, Cover, or Conceal.

OPILATIVA ~ An Astringent, Constipating Medicine.

OPPODELTOCH ~ is the most excellent Sticking Plaster of Theophrastus.

OPS METALLUM ~ Quicksilver.

OPTOS ~ Patched, Sewed On.

ORALE ~ i.e., Vessel.

ORBIS ~ A Dish, or Circular piece of Leather.

ORBIS SAXEUS ~ A Round Stone.

ORBICULI ~ Precipitated Cryetals of Salt in the Salt Pan.

ORIENS ~ i.e., Urine.

ORIENS ~ A Solution of Iron in Muriatic Acid. The Ascent, Red Olitet, the Father, Red Vitriol, the Ruby, Husband, Salt of Urine, Sun, Gold and Sulphur, Summer, Tartar, Ashes, Ore, Wine.

ORDOLEUM ~ is a Small Ulcer in the Eyebrows, like Grains of Barley.
OREXIS ~ is Heart Burn, a Heat rising from the Stomach to the Throat.
ORGANOPEOTICA ~ The Art of Making Warlike Instruments.
ORICHALCEA FILA ~ Brazen Threads, or Brushes.
ORIZEUM ~ i.e., Gold.
ORIZEUM FOLIATUM ~ Gold Beaten into Thin Plates with a Mallet.
ORIZEUM PRAECIPITATUM ~ Gold Reduced to its Flowers by means of Flowers of Mercury.
ORIZA ~ i.e., Rice.
ORMS ~ i.e., a Hen.
ORNITHAE CECIAS ~ South-East.
OROBO ~ Metallic Glass.
OROGAMO ~ Gold.
OS ~ Month.
OS FORNACIS ~ The Eye of the Furnace.
OS SPIRITALE ~ A Damper for Current of Air.
OSTRACITES ~ is a kind of Stone, or Precious Stone, or a species of Calamine, so called after the Shell of the Oyster, for it can be separated into flakes after the same manner as the oyster-shell. Pliny seems to speak of one kind only. Nevertheless, it may be regarded as divisible into three species, of which the first is like mussel-shell, the second like oyster-shell, and the third like agate. The first has scissile veins, and is found in Saxony, as also is the second. On the authority of Dioscorides, Ostracites checks menstruation, is good for inflammation of the breasts, and for corroding sores, or swellings.
OSOROR ~ i.e., Opium.
OSSA PARALLELI ~ is a Medicament universally used in Gout.

OSTRUTIUM TRANSPLANTUM ~ i.e., the Herb Angelica.
OTHAN ~ The Mercury of the Philosophers. Ovum, i.e., the Blessed Stone.
OVUM PHILOSOPHICUM ~ The Philosophical or Hermetic Egg used in Alchemical Operations.
OXOS ~ Vinegar, or Oil of Palestine, which is Vinegar.
OXY ~ i.e., Pointed.
OZEMAN ~ White of Eggs.
OZO ~ i.e., Arsenic.

PALANTINA ET PERSINA ~ Were Queens like. Melusine and Melora.
PALOS IN TIGNA IMMITTERE ~ To Support Beams by Cross-pieces.
PALUS ~ A Stanchion.
PANES AERIS FATHISCENTES ~ Cake, Carcase.
PANES EX PYRITE VEL CADMIA CONFLATI ~ Stones made of Pyrites or Cadmia.
PANIS ARGENTEUS ~ Silver Plate.
PANNUS ~ A Mole or Birthmark.
PANUM AEREORUM SPECIES ~ Matte of Copper.
PANUM EX AERE FOSSILI SPECIES ~ Troughstone.
PANDALITIUM, PANERITIUM, PASSA, VERMIS ~ An Abscess at the End of the Fingers.
PARS CUM PARTE ~ A Composition of Equal Parts of Gold and Silver.
PARTHENION ~ is Roman Camomile. Some say it is Persicaria.

PARTES FODINAE VEL CUNILI — A Share in a Mine.
PARTES FODINARUM VEL CUNICULI — Shares in a Mine.
PARTICULAE EMINENTES — Trunion, Gudgeon, or Stud.
PARIES — Wall.
PASSUS METALLICUS — A Metallic Foot.
PATER — i.e., Sulphur.
PATER ANTE FILIUM — i.e., Patricide, i.e., Satyrion, the Herb Ragwort.
PATER ET MATER REGIS — The Father and Mother of the King. The old philosophers have had such wonder and admiration for the Stone, and so greatly rejoiced therein, that they have not known how to describe it sufficiently, or how to glory in it or praise it. They have called it the Microcosm, the Element, Heaven, Earth, Stars. Unto all things have they compared it. Also they have called it the State of Marriage and the Birth of Children, as the old proverb runs.
The Sun is its Father — Noha, Coelum.
The Moon is its Mother — Aretia, Nohae, Woman, Vesta.
The Wind carries him in its Bosom — Air, Spirit.
The Earth nourishes him, etc.
Then the Sun is, with its warmth and power, the Father of all Vegetation; the Moon, with its moisture, is the Mother; the Air must embrace and carry all things; and the Earth must nourish.
But there is something peculiar in this operation, for the Metallic Sun is a true Father, and gives the masculine seed. The Moon is a true Mother, and gives the feminine seed. The Wind and Air must raise it and conduct it, as Hermes says. Our Mercury rises in the glass; the Earth lies beneath and comprehends in itself soul and spirit, so that a perfect child and king may be born.

The father is our sulphur, the mother is our Mercury, which carries the sulphur within it. For the woman shall have a ruddy-coloured child. When it is born, the red again becomes visible, and the woman becomes changed into a red man. She becomes an androgyne. The man, says Senior, is without wings, is taken up and down. When it is coagulated, the moon is dark; therefore he is called a shade. The wife is bright, is called a ray, and shining of the sun; she draws the shadow out of the brilliance, which is coagulated.

The husband is called Lead, Mars. The wife is called Venus and Arsenic. The husband is also the wife, and the wife is also the husband, like Eve. The sleeping man lost his ribs. However, he is not glorified, because he does not die. After death, in the resurrection is he glorified. So also is it the case with our Adam. Even in his first sleep Eve is given him. Afterwards, in the second solution he dies, and he arises gloriously. Then Eve can never moree be torn from him (S. Ternesius). The father is the calcination ; the mother is the solution ; the fountain is its mother. And he is yet older than the fountain, because he is born perfect. For that which is perfect is before that which is imperfect. But there is in Mercury that which is desired by Philosophers.

PATIAS, or **LEPIDA** ~ Scaly, a Scale, Metallic Shavings.

PEDAGRA ~ Tartar.

PEGERNUS, or **PEREGRINUS** ~ Mercury.

PEGERNUS ~ Lime from the extremely White Ears of Marine Fish.

PELECANUS, or **PELICAN** ~ is a Circulating Vessel, in the shape of a Pelican pecking its own breast with its beak, and thus feeding its young. It has a full body, which narrows towards the neck, and the neck bends round and the mouth goes back into the body. This vessel has a channel at the bottom, by which the liquor is poured in, and then the entrance is hermetically sealed.

PELICIDE or **PELUDE** — is Boiled Honey.
PENATES — are Secret or Interior Spirits of the Element of Fire, or of Heaven, born with us. They are also called Penuarii, Lares Hercii, Ephestii, Etesii, and Meilichii.
PENETRATIO — i.e., Submersion.
PENTACULA — Called also Periamata, Periapta, Apotroptea, Parartemata, is an Amulet which is worn round the neck, and is supposed to preserve the wearer against evil spirits and sorcery.
PERDONIUM — Wine seasoned with Herbs.
PERDETTAE — Small Yellow Carrots or similar Vegetable.
PERIODUS — The Muscle of Life; the Pulse.
PERONES — Water, Fishing, or Jack Boots.
PERPURGARE — To Purify by Burning.
PERTICA — A Bar.
PERTICAE — Measuring Rods.
PES METALLICUS — A Measure of One Foot.
PES LUCUSTE — i.e., Jamen Alum.
PETRA SANGUINARIA — Hematite; Bloodstone.
PEUCEDANUM — The Herb Angelica.
PHANLEC — i.e., Iron.
PHANTASMATA — are Apparitions which haunt desert places and the seashore, and speak with imaginative people. They are not diabolical, though they frequently cause terror. They are born of imagination.
PHIALA — A Glass Vessel used frequently in coagulations and solutions. It has a globular body and a long slender neck or funnel.
PHIBIT — i.e., Violent; Rapacious; a Robber.
PHLOTRON — A Species of Flux caused by the Coostrum (unknown).
PHOENIX — The Quintessence of Fire, or the Illustrious Philosophic Stone.

PHIONITIDE ~ Things naturally hostile to one another, as the stork to the frog, cats to mice, spiders to flies.
PHRASIUM VIRIDE ~ i.e., Flower of Copper.
PHTHISIS ~ Atrophy; Consumption; the plague which parches up, cessation of nourishment, arising through fear or from excessive appetite.
PHYSIOGNOMIA ~ is the Art by which a Man's Nature is judged from his Bodily Appearance.
PILA ~ Post or Pillar.
PILAE ~ Brazen Vessels wherein Things are well pounded.
PILIZENII ~ White Hairs round the Tail and Neck of the Hare.
PILOSELLA ~ A Mouse's Ear.
PILOS ~ i.e., Clay, Slag, or "Fired Hearth"
PINGUEDINOSA ~ i.e., any Fatty Substance.
PILUM ~ Pump-handle.
PILUM, or **PISTILLUM** ~ Mlllet.
PILUM EXCOCTORUM ~ Bat Beater.
PILUM ~ A Beam.
PILUM DENTIBUS CARENS ~ A Smooth Pole.
PILUM, VEL CAPUT PILI ~ The Top of the Instrument with which Copper is pounded. Also Broken Pieces of Copper or Brass.
PIRSTEIN ~ A Kind of Copper-stone.
PISARE ~ To Strain anything through a Colander, to Filter.
PISTARE ~ i.e., to Beat, Crush, Pound.
PISTILLUM ~ Pestle, Mallet.
PIX LIQUINA ~ Terebinth.
PIXARI ~ Pitch.
PLANITIES MONTIS ~ The Hauling Gallery driven for the Dip of the Vein.
PLUMBUM, AFFROB ~ Our Brass, is the Husband, and Impure Bodies.
PLUMBUM ALKALI ~ The Hermaphrodite.

PLUMBUM, or LEAD — Is attributed to Saturn by chemists and is so called. It is a Livid, Terrene, Heavy, Metallic Body, with very little Whiteness and much of Earthy Nature. It is converted into Tin by cleansing. Thus Tin is more perfect than Lead. And Lead has more of the substance of Fixed Sulphur in its composition than Jupiter, i.e., Tin. Lead is an Impure Body, procreated from the copulation of Imperfect Living Silver, which is impure, unfixed, terrene, feculent, somewhat white on the exterior, but red inside, with a similar quality of Sulphur. It is wanting in purity, fixation, colour, and fire. In sum, Living Silver, which is of bad quality, gross, of bad taste, fetid, and of feeble power, like a menstruous mother, unites with a livid or leprous Sulphur, and frigid Saturn for a son is the result, and this is Lead. Note that pure solid Lead is not obtained from the mines. I have never read, heard, or seen that it has been so found. Three qualities of Lead are excocted — black (which is true Lead), grey, and white. Black Lead is excocted from Galena, or Lead Ore, or from Pyrites. As to its cleansing and burning, and its medicinal uses, consult Dioscorides (1. 5, c. 48). Purified Lead is still used medicinally for inflamed ulcers and cancers. True burnt Lead is more efficacious than washed or purified Lead. And potters use it to colour their vessels. Scoria or recrement of Lead is the same as burnt bead, and it abounds in the workshops of Misnia where Lead Ore is smelted.

PLUMBUM CINEREUM — Grey Lead is the German Bismuth. It differs from the black and white species, and is, as it were, a metal by itself. It is more noble than Lead, but inferior to Silver, and has a middle position between both. The Ore from which it is excocted is like that of Black Lead, with this difference, that unless it is solid, it blackens the hand. When solid, it is not brittle, like Galena. It is blacker than the variety of rude Silver which we term lead-coloured.

It often contains Silver, and where it is found there is generally Silver lower down, for which reason it is called the Roof of Silver. Many articles are now made from it, even as from Silver, such as drinking-cups, vases, etc. A species of blue is also obtained from it. The Arabs and many chemists were ignorant of this metal.

As Black Lead is called Lead simply by the Germans, or Black Lead, so White Lead is called Ceruse or Tin. But it is an error to term our White Lead Tin, for they are distinct things. White Lead is more pure and perfect than Black. Pliny calls it Cassiterion, from the Cassiterides Islands, where it was first found by Midacrytus. Like Black Lead, it is now melted out of Pyrites or out of Galena, Gravel or Coarse Sand, as well as out of those Black Pebbles which are mentioned by Pliny, who also says that White Lead is found in Britain, Galicia, and Lusitania. Caesar, De Bello Gallico, 1. 5, also affirms its existence in Britain.

PLUMBUM NIGRUM — Black Lead.
1. Native Black Lead in a black ore, but impure.
2. Black Lead in a vein of white ore like Opaque White Floors.
3. Black Lead in a white vein like Clear White Fluors. There is sixty percent of the metal.
4. Caldebornian Black Lead, like Grey Marl.
5. Like a white Sandy Stone.
6. Like a Metallic Flint, with veins of Living Sulphur.
7. From Polonia, mixed with Native Ochre.
8. Flowers of Black Lead, like White Corals.
9. Yellow, full of lines of Slimy Sulphur, hence called Lead Sulphur.
10. Smelted Black Lead from Villacense.
11. Very soft Palatine Black Lead.
12. Refined soft Lead.
13. Containing much Silver.

14. Raw Lead containing Gold.
15. Raw Lead containing Silver.
16. Raw Lead, mixed with Silver, Copper and Gold.
17. Purified Lead, which is used for testing purposes.
18. Hard Lead, composed of Spume of Silver and Lead Ore.
19. Lead smelted from Spume of Silver.
20. Added as a flux to metals in excoction.
21. Granulated Lead.
22. Reduced to the finest powder or granules, and so used by the Venetians.
23. Common Lead Ochre.
24. Best English Lead Ochre.
25. Ceruse.
26. Native Ceruse from Vincentinus.
27. Minium made from burnt ceruse.
28. Minium imperfectly burnt.
29. Minium obtained from a Lead Stone rich in Silver.
30. Recrement or Scum extracted from Lead.
31. White Tapping or Recrement of Gossarian Black Lead.
32. Impure White Tapping of Lead.
33. Lead reduced to ash by the power of fire.
34. Alchemistic Lead Pigment-Lead Ash of the chemists.
35. A poisonous, slimy Lead Smoke, generated in smelting lead from silver.
36. Cleansed or Washed Lead of Dioscorides.
37. Burnt Lead of Dioscorides.

PLUMBUM CANDIDUM:
1. Purest White Lead from the valley of Joachim.
2. Small White Granules obtained at the same place by washing.
3. Filaments of White Lead, collected in rivers.
4. Purest Native White Lead, mined at Slacchenvald.
5. Lead Crystals of Aldenberg, like Clear White Fluors.
6. Yellow Crystals, like Living Sulphur in Hegnist Metal.

7. Slimy.
8. Red-yellow Lead Crystal.
9. Purple.
10. Green Lead Crystals, found in the waters near Schreckenberg.
11. White Lead Crystals collected in rivers.
12. White, found on the riverbanks near Schneberg.
13. Minute Black Lead Crystals deposited by the rivers.
14. Small Black Stones containing Lead.
15. Moderate-sized Black Stones containing Lead.
16. Large Black Stones containing Lead.
17. A Black Pebble, pure and unique. A very Rich Calcareous Sheolite.
18. Black and Yellow Pebbles, combined, from Hegnist.
19. Small Black Stones, combined with Thin Plates of the Finest White Lead, in a Yellow Fluor.
20. Black Stones of Slacchenvald, in a White Metallic Stone.
21. Black Stones in a Grey Metallic Stone.
22. Moderate-sized Black Stones in a Metallic Marble.
23. In a White Sexangular Pellucid Fluor.
24. Bohemian, in a Ruddy Cuprine Stone.
25. In an Iron Stone.
26. In White Pellucid Mirror Stone of Slacchenvald.
27. With Pyrites.
28. Of a Greyish Black Colour.
29. Stone of White Lead in a Metallic Flint.
30. A Vein of White Lead, combined with Metallic Cadmia.
31. A Mined Substance similar to Mica Silver.
32. Best and Purest English White Lead.
33. Purest Cooked White Slacchenvald Lead.
34. Adulterated Lead, to which Black Lead is added.
35. Lead containing Silver.
36. Hard.
37. Soft.

38. Reduced to Powder.
39. Soft Cancellate Lead.
40. Lead formed in Hard Blocks.
41. Smelted out of Recrements.
42. Ceruse from White Lead.
43. Small Black Sterile Stones, similar in form and colour to Black Aerolites. When melted with White Lead Stones, that which remains becomes hard, and is marked with spots.
44. Anneberg Lead Stones; when struck with a hammer, they appear like clay. They are not suitable for combination, because they contain stony matter.
45. White Lead, Cooked, and to which Grey Lead is added.
46. Recrement of White Lead.

PLUMBUM CINEREUM — Grey Lead.
1. This is called Bismuth by our Metallurgists, and it is also usually termed the Roof of Silver, Silver being generally found beneath.
2. White Flower of Grey Lead.
3. Purple.
4. Red.
5. Pure Native Grey Lead, which is Solidified into Stone in the Mountains by Internal Heat, and takes the form of Indian Salt.
6. Aldeburg Lead in a Hard Grey Stone.
7. Crustaceous Lead from the Valley of Joachim.
8. Glebous Lead of Schneberg in a Black Friable Stone.
9. In a White Stone.
10. In a very Hard White Flint.
11. Tessellated in a Grey Stone.
12. Veins of Roasted Grey Lead, from which, by the potency of fire, granules like unto the Purest Silver are extracted.
13. Excocted Grey Lead.
14. Impure Blocks from Grey Lead.
15. Pure Blocks of Grey Lead.

16. Scarce Excocted Grey Lead.
17. Veins of Burnt Grey Lead, or Saffron-coloured Lead, used by Potters for Glazing.
18. Recrement of Grey Lead, of a Saffron Colour.
PLUMBUM IN GLOBULOS REDUCTUM ~ Lead reduced into Granules.
PLUMBUM DIVES ~ Rich Lead.
PLUMBUM IGNIS VI IN CINEREM RESOLUTUM ~ Lead reduced to Ashes by the power of Fire.
PLUMBUM DEPAUPERATUM ~Uncalcined Lead.
PLUMBI ARTIS IMPURA ~ Untranslatable. According to the German version, Black Lead of an Impure Kind.
PLUMBAGO, GALENA, and **BLACK LEAD** ~ are one and the same. We prove this statement in the following manner. First, Black Lead and Silver are prepared from our mined Plumbago, out of Glance and Lead Oil, at Friburg and Misnia, at Goslaria, and many other places, just as Pliny (1. 34, c. 18), treating of Molybdena and Galena, says. Therefore our Plumbago, our Glance, is Galena and Black Lead. Secondly, the mention of the word proves it to be one and the same; for what Pliny (1. 33, c. 6) or the Spaniards call Galena we now call Glance. But Marcellus, the interpreter of Dioscorides, a man on other points leaned enough, asserts that it is not called Galena, for Pliny denies that Black Lead is made in Galicia. It is nevertheless made from Galena. Thirdly, our Plumbago is chiefly of the colour of Lead, and for this reason is called by the Greeks Molybdena, and by the Romans Plumbago, or the Stone whence Lead is made. Thus it may either be called the Lead Stone, a vein of Lead Ore, or Lead Earth. Fourthly, Pliny says nothing about the stone Molybdos, of which, nevertheless, Dioscorides wrote, and was contented with the name of Galena. Then the Galena and the Molybdos of Dioscorides are one and the same. Fiftly, Galen says that he

has himself seen a kind of Native Molybdena lying along the banks of rivers; nor does he make mention of the Lead Stone, because he considered them one and the same. Therefore Molybdena and Lead Stone are the same. In the sixth place, Galen states, in his book concerning the composition of medicines, that out of Ceruse and White Litharge, and from Grey Molybdena, which is of an ashen colour, Hydrelagon is made, and this is our Galena, not indeed the yellow but the leaden. Therefore Galena and Molybdena are one and the same. Seventhly, according to Dioscorides, our Galena, which is of the colour of Lead, is called the Leaden Stone, because it is a species of Lead, and contains the matter of Lead in itself. Moreover, it has the same properties as Washed Lead and Lead Scoria. It is washed in the same manner. It differs from the Native Molybdena of Dioscorides in colour alone, not in matter, for he writes that his mined Yellow Molybdena is brilliant, but the colour can easily be changed in the case of Plumbago by means of different gases stirred up from the bowelss of the earth. Thus, with us, in our mines, Black, Blue, and Liver-coloured Galena are all found. Just as Yellow Galena can be certainly found in warm regions, also there is found a Galena in our mines which is covered with a yellow colour, possibly the Molybdena of Dioscorides, and this yellow with which the Galena is tinged is sometimes found in veins, and is sometimes tempered by the heat of the earth. It sparkles, especially when split up, so that it seems to contain a metal. The Arabs know nothing about Molybdena, or think it to be the same as Litharge. They are indeed the same in temperament. Molybdena, however, is slightly colder. Its parts are denser. It does not possess the power of cleansing. Serapion has little or nothing about the virtue of Molybdena. (See *lib. Agg.*, s.v. Hasas.) If indeed you wish to have any difference or distinction, call Molybdena the Lead

Stone when it contains Lead alone. On the contrary, when it contains Lead and Silver, call it Galena. Whereas, therefore, Molybdena, Plumbago, and Galena are one and the same, note that Galena or Molybdena is twofold, native and manufactured.

The native is again double, i.e., I. Fruitful, which is a Vein of Lead alone, and then it is called Lead Stone by Pliny and Galen. Pliny (1. 33, c. 6) calls Galena a Vein of Lead, found near Veins of Silver. Next, because the Vein contains both Silver and Black Lead, we smelt lead and silver from it, and then it is truly Galena. This fruitful Galena is again twofold- as respects colour, not substance. They are of the same matter, though the colour differs;

1. A kind of Brilliant Lead, and this is our Plumbago, Galena, or Molybdena of Pliny. By Dioscorides, however, it is called the Lead-like Stone.

2. A Yellow Lead also Brilliant, described by Dioscorides. It is found at Sebastia and Coricum.

It is also mentioned by Pliny, who says that Molybdena or Galena is better when it is of a more golden colour, when it is less leaden and brittle, and is slightly heavier. In warm regions it is possibly given this colour by parched gases from the bowels of the earth. For if you rightly consider our Plumbago, as to its colour, and how it received that colour in the bowels of the earth, you will find that Plumbago has received the following colours in our mines, owing to different vapours:

1. Black.
2. Blue.
3. Liver-coloured.
4. Covered with a Yellow Colour — possibly that of Dioscorides. By the Germans all these species are called simply Lead Ore, or Glance, on account of their brilliance.

II. Sterile Plumbago is of no account. Its colour is not unlike the fruitful species, but it is altogether barren, and is wholly consumed by fire.

Manufactured Plumbago, made in furnaces of Gold and Silver. It is called Metallic by Pliny (1. 34, c. 18). It is called by the Germans Graphite, or Compressed Galena. By some it is called Silver Litharge, because of its affinity with Scoria of Silver. This is not its proper name. Pliny also regards it as a species of Silver Litharge. Dioscorides states that manufactured Plumbago competes with Silver Litharge. Emplastrum is made from it as from native Galena. Note that this metallic substance liquefies when treated by fire. Moreover, when cooked in oil it assumes a liver colour, which is not the case with the native, as Pliny affirms, who in this place misinterprets Dioscorides. Native Plumbago, cooked in oil, has the colour of the liver. Note, finally, that Sylvaticus in his Pandectis calls Molybdena Burnt Lead, and the Refuse of Lead. Truly there is an agreement here! This Molybdena, or Black Lead, is by no means Lead, or the refuse, or the scoria, of Lead, but it is the residuum, so to speak, of Plumbago, which contains Silver and Lead, and which adheres to furnaces, and Pliny notwithstanding, again becomes cooked Lead. Sylvaticus, however, errs in this passage; concerning the properties and the methods of washing and burning it, consult Dioscorides and Pliny, as also concerning its excoction (1, 34, c. 16), where the latter says that the source of Black Lead is twofold, for it exists either in a vein of its own, or else in combination with Silver. It is melted from mixed veins. The first liquid that begins to flow in the furnace is Tin; the second, Silver ; that which remains in the furnace is called Galena, which is the third portion added to the vein. This, again smelted, yields Black Lead.

Metallic or Native Plumbago, in Spanish Galena, i.e., a Vein of Lead and Silver indifferently.
1. Glance.
2. Simple Plumbago, Pure Glance.
3. Rich Plumbago, containing Cobalt and Arsenic.
4. Mixed with White Pyrites.
5. Cubical Glance in White Lime-stone.
6. Tessellated, in Long, White, and Pellucid. Fluors.
7. Intermixed with Yellow Fluors in a White Stone, which Melts in Fire.
8. With White Pyrites in a White Flint.
9. Quadrangular, in Purple Fluors.
10. Octagonal in another Barren Plumbago, or a Sulphuret of Zinc.
11. Polish Plumbago, containing Yellow Ochre.
12. Cloddy, in alternate layers, with a Grey Crustaceous Pyrites.
13. Mixed with Flint.
14. With Yellow Transparent Fluors.
15. Tessellated in White Fluors.
16. Of a Red Colour, whence Lead is abundantly smelted.
17. Black Glance, so dyed by a Vein of Copper.
18. Of a Liver Colour, which is derived from other Metals. When the external colour is rubbed off, its proper colour remains.
19. Of a Yellow Colour, like Muddy Fluors.
20. Of a Red or Rusty Colour, like a Solid or Refined Copper.
21. Cloddy, from Friberg Glance, containing Cobalt and Arsenic.
22. Like Copper Glance.
23. From Islebia, in a Slate Stone.
24. Rich in Gold and Lead.
25. Abundant in Copper and Lead.

26. From Friberg, dyed various colours, a kind of Glance.
Barren Plumbago:
1. Resembling Barren Pitch.
2. Containing Cobalt and Arsenic.
3. Yellow and Brilliant, from Schurfenberg, near Meissen. A Light Yellow Pseudo-Galena.
4. A variety of the preceding.
5. Sterile, resembling Galena.

PNIGITIS — is a certain kind of earth, which Dioscorides says resembles Eretrian Earth in colour, for which also it is sold. It has, however, a larger clod, and is cold to the hand. We ourselves have a black earth, which is not Pnigitis, but it is very black. This earth sometimes contains Silver. It is then called Coarse Silver. Sometimes it is barren, and then it is called Black Earth, and is indeed the same as Dioscorides calls Melanteria. It is of a sulphureous hue, becoming black on contact with water. True Pnigitis is not found in our land. In the torrent of Garmendorf, as it passes to meet the Saale, a Black Friable Stone is met with, whence boys' ink is made. It seems to be Pnigitis hardened by heat, of great size, but light in proportion to the size. Or it is simply Ochre, which, being burnt by the heat of the sun or of the earth, turns into Rubrica, or Ruddle. It may be a kind of Ampelis. It can be reduced into an extremely delicate and well-digested soft powder. It is an extremely beautiful substance, although it may be despised by the inhabitants of those regions.

POCZUS — A Large Cask.

POPANAX — Gum.

POMPHOLIX — Concerning this substance and the varieties of the same, see Dioscorides, who seems to confound Pompholix, Spodon, and Antispodon. In the first place, Pompholix is the same as that which is called white nothing or nil by vendors of medicines. Hence the proverb

that nothing is good for the eyes. They also call it White Pompholigum, which is coarser. On the other hand, Spodicem is what the chemists call Black Poncplcolix. Avicenna, if I rightly remember, calls it Succudus, i.e., full of sap. Thirdly, Antispodiusc, which takes the place of Spodium in use, is produced from the leaves, flowers, and immature berries of the Astringent Myrtle, or from a branch of Olive Wood as Dioscorides and Pliny tell us. Note that neither Spodon nor Antispodon are found nowadays; we do not actually know what they are, or how made. To deal with the substances themselves: Pompholix is a Metallic Ash, which is produced upon the tops or walls of furnaces, or of huts where there are extinguished furnaces. This Ash varies with the metals and the place of production. Grey Pompholix is obtained from Pyrites rather than from Lead Stone. Hence that of Goslar is better than any from Meissen, and contains Silver, Lead, and Copper. So also Dioscorides says that the best quality comes from Cyprus. That which adheres to the tops and walls of furnaces is Spodion. On the other hand, that which hangs from the top is Pompholix, differing from the first in whiteness and polish. Dioscorides states that the difference is specific, not generic. Spodon is:
1. Black.
2. Heavy.
3. Full of Straws.
4. Swept from the floors of Laboratories.
Pompholix is White like a Bubble, or like that Greek-vessel of globular shape from which it obtains its name. It is fat, light, and pure, and is produced on the top of furnaces. There are, however, properly speaking, two kinds of Pompholix.
1. Somewhat thick, and of a copperish hue. Its proper name is grey nothing.

2. Exceeding white, of the highest polish. Produced either in perfecting Copper, when the Cadmic purposely strewn upon the surface is rubbed off; or from Cadmia melted by means of bellows. Dioscorides gives a lengthy description of the method. The thin and very light matter which finds its way to the top of the furnace and adheres to the walls and roof is Pompholix, but the heavier substance which betakes itself to the lower parts is Spodion.

Dioscorides gives us further information as to genuine and adulterated Pompholix, the method of washing it, its virtues as an astringent, cooling, purifying, obstructing, and drying agent. He describes its torrefaction or roasting, and tells us from what substances it is preferably obtained- • namely, Gold, Silver, Lead, and Brass. Next to Pompholix from Cyprian Ore comes Pompholix from Lead. Pliny endorses these statements. Galen ascribes more powerful virtues to Pompholix than to Spodion. Indeed, Pompholix has a combination of virtues. Under Cadmia we have mentioned that Cadmia Botryitis, or Grape-shaped Cadmia, is called Arabian Tutty.

Accordingly, that of Alexandria is called Dry or Solid. But Botryitis Cadmia is not the same substance as Cadmia, to which the Arabs and Serapion testify. For the Spodion here treated of is Tutty and a matter of importance. Botryitis is not Tutty. Dioscorides mentions Spodion and not Tutty. What is called Tutty by the Arabs and Pompholix by the Greeks is by us termed Spodion. Avicenna testifies to this fact. We can use Botryitis Cadmia instead of Tutty, that is, of Spodion, if it has been prepared. The difference between Botryitis and Capnitis Cadmic, and between Pompholix and Spodion, which are all made of the same material, depends upon the places where they are made. Cadmic Botryitis is made or deposited on the walls or the highest roofs of the furnaces. On the other hand, Capnitis is, properly speaking, obtained from the edges of the furnaces. Genuine Pompholix, or White Nothing, an exceedingly light Metallic Ash, is produced on the tops of furnaces, or even on the tops of the huts in which the furnaces are situated. If obtained from the mouth of the furnace, it is Cadmia Capnitis; if from the sides and roofs, it is Pompholix; that which adheres to the walls is Spodion. Young students should diligently observe these points. The Arabs distinguish two varieties of Tutty: Native Tutty — White, Green, or Citrine-found among minerals on the shores of the Indian Ocean; also Manufactured, of which we treat here. Observe also that besides the Sooty Spodion of Serapion, Dioscorides, Pliny, and Galen — who says: I have never used Spodion, because I have always found Pompholix in abundance — the Arabs distinguish two other species.

1. Spodion from a reed and the root of a reed, or a product of Burnt Ultramarine, as Avicenna has it, who describes Spodion, saying: Spodion is a Root of Burnt Reeds, being cold in the second and dry in the third degree. But it may also be obtained from Burnt Ivory.
2. Spodion derived from the Calcined Bones of Elephants, Dogs, and other
Animals.

Bone is still found to exist in Spodion, at any rate in the variety which is obtained from ivory. It should be noted that now-a-days we never see either Spodion or Antispodion in our laboratories, and nobody knows them by experience; we carefully collect foreign substances, but those close at home we neglect. It should be rescued by physicians from the furnaces, but I speak to dull ears. Moreover, some call Copper Rust Spodion. The statement of Pliny should be noted, that Pompholix and Spodion are found in copper mines, and that Pompholix differs from Spodion in the fact that the first is subjected to washing, while the second is not.

He also states that Pompholix is an extremely white and polished substance and is the smoke from Copper and Cadmia. Spodion, however, is blacker and heavier; it is rubbed from the walls of furnaces, and is frequently mixed with embers and coals. That from Cyprus is the best, and it is obtained by melting Cadmia and Copper Stone. The same author represents Red Mellea as a species of Spodion. Then there is another kind called Lauriotis, which is obtained from gold and silver smelting furnaces. Finally, he mentions Antispodion, and enumerates its medical virtues. He is also the authority for the statement that Spodion can be produced from Lead in the same way as from Cyprian Copper.

Spodion: From Cyprian Copper, as stated by Dioscorides and Pliny. Our Spodion Goslarian Spodos has similar qualities. From Lead, in the smelting houses of Misnia,

Pompholix:
1. The Soot which is collected in Compartments of Furnaces.
2. Pompholix from Silver.
3. Slimy, sticking to the walls where Silver is separated from bead. Yellow, Poisonous, Crystalline Arsenic.
4. From Mansfeld Copper.
5. That which is collected where Silver is separated from Copper.
6. Obtained from Furnaces where White Lead is smelted.
7. Purest White. Best Crystalline Arsenic.
8. That which is Solidified from Pieces of Stone roasted when Copper is
cooked.
9. White Pompholix, termed by the Metallurgists White Nothing.

POMPHOLIX, TUTTY, and **SPODIUS** — are one and the same.

POMPHOLIX LUTEA ~ Crystalline Arsenic.
POPONAC ~ A Gum so called.
PORFILIGON ~ Shavings from Hammered Iron.
PORFIRETICUM ~ A Rasp or Copper Mortar.
PORRUM ~ A Corn on the Foot.
POTAEILIA ~ That which can be Drunk in by the Mouth.
PRASIS or **GREEN PRASIMUM** ~ Flower of Copper.
PRESSORIUM ~ i.e., Press, Wine-press, etc,
PRECIPITATIO ~ is when bodies rusted by means of Corroding Waters and dissolved into Water are reduced to a sort of Lime by removal of the Corroding Water. Thus Silver is precipitated when it is dissolved in Aqua Fortis by the injection of Common Salt or Ammoniac. So also is Gold reduced by dissolution in Aqua Regis with the addition of a little Quicksilver. If to this we add a small quantity of Sulphur, and place it in the fire in a closed vessel, in such a manner that the Quicksilver and the Sulphur can evaporate and depart, a most subtle Lime will be left. But by so much the more that bodies are dissolved, by so much also can they be calcined into a more subtle condition.
PRAEFECTUS METALLORUM ~ Overseer of the Mines.
PRAESAGIUM ~ A Presage, is a Wonderful Sign of a Future Event, anticipating History. Thence Prophecies are sometimes made.
PRESERVATIVA ~ Medicaments which Preserve Life and Prevent Corruption.
PRESES SEU MAGISTER METALLICORUM ~ Head Or Overseer of the Mines.
PRAESES FODINAE ~ Master of the Mine.
PRAESES OFFICIME ~ Superintendent of the Laboratory, Chief Refiner.
PRAESES LABORIS LAVANDI ~ Superintendent of the Washing Process.

PRESMUCHUM or **PRESMUCKIS** — Ceruse, White Lead.

PRINCIPIA CHYMIA — The Principles of the Alchemists are three in number: Salt, Sulphur, and Mercury, i.e., Body, Soul, and Spirit. Thence spring all things which exist; they can be exhibited in all things, and into them all things can be resolved.

Salt gives consistency, colour, strength, hardness; it makes substances visible and tangible; without it, they could not be grasped. It is depicted as follows — [Sol], fiery and watery. Sulphur imparts warmth, light, and strength; it gives the tincture. It is represented by a [Venus] fiery, with the Cross and Labour.

Mercury gives sponginess, subtlety, and fusibility, also weight and malleable quality; it makes them capable of being hammered and forged; it gives also celestial efficacy; it is represented by [Mercury], which enters into many planetary characters, and is connected with the symbols of Gold and Silver.

PRINCIPIA — Principles are those things whence a substance is produced in any genus of composites. These primes, or principles, because of their immanence, have a certain basic substance, wherein they flourish, and whereby they are produced. They are not those of Aristotle, which are not primeval substances, but, as the types of every genus, have at the same time an analogy with our principles. The properties of principles are based sometimes in the elemental and sometimes in the celestial region. Accordingly, they sometimes resemble elements, and at other times essences. These principles are three — Mercury, Salt, Sulphur.

PRIMA TEMPERATURA — The First Flux.

PRIMALES or **PRUMALIA** — Illusory Bodies made visible by the agency of the Stars.

PROJECTIA ~ The exaltation of a substance by a Projecting Medicine -which is projected over the matter to be transformed, by a sudden egression. It corresponds to the process of fermentation, which changes a matter substantially by acting within it. It differs from it, however, in that it is not effected by means of a slow digestion, whereby the different parts undergo alteration and mixture; it is, on the contrary, performed by a violent interpenetration, which transforms at the moment of ingression. Moreover, the Medicine is not called a Ferment, but a Tincture.
PROPRIETARIUS ~ Landlord.
PROPRIETARII PARTES ~ The Owner's Share of the Profits.
PROS CRIPTIO ~ Demand for Subscription Due.
PROLECTATIO ~ An Extraction by means of a Thinning of the Subtle Parts, so that being rarefied by the change of their nature, and separated from their coarser parts, they assume a certain consistency. Accordingly, things employed in prolectation are called Attenuating Agents. Before the substance to be operated on assumes consistency, a free, gaseous, or watery matter is added; the prolectation takes place by the agency of the several elements, and the substance operated on may differ from a solid earth only by reason of its lightness and instability.
PRUINUM ~ A First Species of Tartar; a sort of Stone in the Stomach.
PRUINA, PRUNA ~ Persian Fire; the Disease called St. Anthony's Fire.
PSAMOS ~ i.e., Sand.
PSIMITHUM ~ White Lead.
PSINEUS or **PSINKIS** ~ Ceruse.
PSITHOS ~ Coldness.
PULSATILES ~ Temporal Artery; the Pulse; Arterial Veins.

PULPEZIA or **PULPELZIA** — A Profound Stupor; Apoplexy; Palsy; the Hand of God.

PUMEX — In Arabic Famechi or Fenec, i.e., Pumice Stone, or Stone of Vulcan. There are two kinds, black and white. The black is also called Tufa. The best quality is from Melos, Scyros, and the Aeolian Isles; it is very useful for polishing bodies, as Catullus tells us. Dioscorides describes the white variety as light, spongy, easily split, not sandy, capable of polish. He describes the method of burning it and its medicinal virtues, concerning which see also Pliny. Theophrastus, if I mistake not, says: We call it Pumice Stone on account of its hardness, not on account of its density; in this matter, it has scarcely the quality of a stone. It falls from the dignity of a stone, because it floats in water. Pumice Stone is found and produced in conjunction with Alum and Sulphur. I think it is earth completely burnt in the Isles, and to this waters are added. It is also called the Stone of Barche, and it is found on the seashore. Hence some imagine erroneously that it is the solidified foam of the sea. By the German rivers, especially the Elbe, and by the promontories of the old March, are found pale Stones, spongy and loose in texture, resembling Pumice Stone, but heavy, and which have been thought to be the foundation of Pumice Stone, or Pumice Stone not yet cooked by the sun. An experiment was made to see whether fire would diminish its weight, and it was found it did to a certain extent. Pliny states that seaweed and fungi are transformed into Pumice Stone by the action of the sun. See Serapion. Ovid, very elegantly describing the cavernous bath of Diana, represents it to be formed of Pumice Stone and Tuff Stone by Nature herself.

"In her furthest retreat is a woodland cavern not artificially elaborated; Nature by her own skill bath hollowed it out; she bath constructed it of living Pumice Stone and light Tufa".

PULVIS — Powder; Dust.

PURGARE, PURGATIO ~ To Purge; Purifying.
1. Some Things are Purified by Distillation, as Water.
2. Some by Distillation, as Spirit.
3. Some by Solution, as Salt.
4. Some by Washing, as Cloth.
5. Some by Burning, as Lime.
6. Some by Separation, as Metals.
7. Some by Filtration, as through Cloth.
PURGATOR ARGENTI ~ Silver Refiner.
PUTRIFICIREN ~ To Putrefy.
PUTRIFICIREN ~ Putrefaction takes place in Seven Ways.
1. Some Things are Cleansed by Distillation through the Alembic, as
Water.
2. Some by Sublimation, as Spirit.
3. Some by Solution, as Salt.
4. Some by Washing, as Cloth.
5. Some by Burning, as Lime.
6. Some by Separation, as Metals.
7. Some by Filtration, or Straining.
PULVERISIREN ~ Reduction to Powder.
PULVIS VALENS ~ A Potent Powder.
PUTEUS ~ A Shaft; a Ventilator; a Pit; a Well.
PUTEUS RECTUS ~ A Perpendicular Shaft.
PUTEUS QUI LACUNA LOCO EST ~ A Conduit for Water.
PUTRIS ~ Rotten, Loose, Friable.
PUTREFACTIO ~ Dissolution of a Composite Substance by Purification in Heated Moisture. It is necessary for the humidity to overcome the dryness by the agency of external heat. When this is done, the heat, being akin to its moist substance, is separated from the component parts, preserves its homogeneous nature, and solidifies apart. Accordingly, if the matter to be putrefied abounds in moisture, it is beaten

up as it is, and operated on by the warm digestion of dung, or of the bath, a moist heat being applied externally. If the matter originally possesses little or no moisture, it is ground, and then proportionally sprinkled with moisture.

Putrefaction is the Dissolution of Component Parts, which have opened out under the dissolving power of a moist heat. It is the key to the most brilliant alchemical operations. It separates not so much the elements as the celestial essences from their elementary composition. Accordingly, in such experiments we must be on our guard against a complete dissolution, using only one that shall be enough to permit the escape of the essences. Hence it becomes plain that in composite substances, unusually removed from elemental simplicity, there is something internal besides the element, and this something is regarded as incombustible. By a natural putrefaction it produces a new substance, and solidifies. This kind of dissolution is twofold-putrefaction and dissolution by medicine.

There is another kind of putrefaction which occupies a middle place between corrosive calcination and putrefaction. It is called Dry and Philosophical Putrefaction. Some, not without reason, name it Sublimation of Elements, Cooking, and Solution. It takes place in the dry water of the philosophers, or very sharp vinegar, and belongs only to the Sun and Moon.

Putrefaction is a Digestion, dissolving the substance of the matter by the application of external heat. It is the property of putrefaction to destroy the old, original nature of a thing, and to introduce a new nature. It has sometimes the same result as a second generation. Corrosive spirits become sweet and mild thereby, and all colours are changed into others. The pure is separated from the impure-the latter sinking to the bottom. But the matter must be placed in the vessel, the vessel must be put into dung, the heat of the dung being sustained for a fixed period. It is preferable, however, for the vessel to be put into a bath of dew.

Putrefaction or Corruption takes place when a body becomes black. Then it stinks like dung, and true solution follows. The elements are separated and destroyed. Many colours are afterwards developed, until the victory is obtained and everything is reunited.

Putrefaction is understood as a Corruption which changes one thing into another.

PUSTA DIGESTIO, etc. — An Internal Digestion of Iron.

PYGMAEI — Pygmies are Little Men or Subterranean Spirits. They are called also Torches and Sparks. They are said to have no parents, but are produced from the corruption of the earth, just as beetles are generated from putrid horsedung.

PYRITES and **MARCASITE** — are the same, for what the Romans and Greeks called Pyrites the Arabs term Marcasite and Black Zeg. Others call it the Stone of Light, on account of its effects; also Marcasite Capporosa, Copper Stone, Chalcitis, Rock Alum in its first signification, etc. All that the Greeks have written concerning Pyrites the Arabs ascribe to Marcasite in their own language.

It is called Pyrites because fire is often struck from it. Hence we give it the generic name of Flint or Fire Stone. Soldiers use it for lighting bombs. It has also this name on account of its fiery colour. Otherwise, the Germans simply call it Gravel and Copper Stone. But these names have too wide a meaning.

Various kinds of Pyrites are found in our mines-Silver Colour, almost Gold Colour, True Gold Colour like Galena, Ashen Colour, and Iron Colour.

Silver-coloured Pyrites, the White or Water Pyrites, or Gravel of the Metallurgists. Silver is smelted from it. Pliny mentions it, if I mistake not, but, like all the ancients, is ignorant of its argentiferous character. Copper is also smelted from it, as Serapion testifies of Marcasite. Dioscorides also plainly states this fact concerning Pyrites. Silver-coloured Pyrites sometimes contains Silver only, sometimes Copper only, sometimes both, and again it may contain Silver and Black Lead, or several metals. Occasionally it is barren. I consider that it usually has more Silver than any other substance.

Semi-gold-coloured Pyrites, called by the Germans Yellow Pyrites, Yellow Copper, Pyrites Copper, Metal Regulus or Copper Ore. Found often in our Silver, but more frequently in our Copper Mines. Copper can be smelted from it. It is Pyrites proper, with the appearance of Copper, as Pliny observes. It is the true Marcasite of the Arabs, whence Copper is smelted. Dioscorides prefers it before all others for its medicinal value, especially when it is solid and yields sparks readily. He also shows how it is washed and burnt. Yet the first species of Pyrites is not to be despised medicinally. When Dioscorides says the second kind is like Copper, he refers to its shape rather than its colour. Like the former, it contains sometimes Silver, sometimes Copper, sometimes both, sometimes other metals, and occasionally it is barren. Pliny testifies that both species were found in Cyprus and round Acarnania or Acamania. It exists in many of our own mines. Whether of Golden or Silver Colour, it is often found among argentiferous metals, and still more often in a sterile vein of its own. It is also found in brooks and rivers, such as the Elbe. When it exists in large quantities a kind of stone is obtained from it which is very useful in smelting. Sterile Pyrites is found abundantly at Havelburg, and is very beautiful.

True Gold-coloured Pyrites has a larger proportion of Sulphur. It is sometimes combined with the fourth species.

It is brilliant and pleasant to the sight. It abounds in Bohemia and Misnia.

Galena-coloured Pyrites-sparkling and brilliant. Agricola thinks that it may be neither Pyrites nor Galena, but a distinct genus. It is true that Pyrites possesses neither its colour nor hardness. It has the colour of Galena, but its substance is very different. Gold and Silver are smelted from it. It abounds near Reichstein and Ravrisum, but at the latter place contains more Silver than Gold, while at the former Gold preponderates, or is exclusive.

Grey Pyrites is found in an exceedingly subtle condition at Reichstein, and is combined with the fourth species, so that Gold can be smelted from it. It exists in a slightly different form in Silesia, and from this also Gold and Silver are smelted.

Iron-coloured Pyrites is mentioned by Avicenna. It is found in certain iron mines. The miners call it Iron Stone, not that it is actually such, but is like it. From most of these six species fire can be struck. Some of them are very heavy, and are more adapted for striking fire, as Pliny observes. Some distinguish a special genus of Pyrites, which abounds in fire, and is called Live Pyrites. We may, indeed, deny that there is any other genus. Those species which are dense and compact, as the first two, abound in fire. The looser the texture, the more subtle and the more broken up, the less fire can be elicited. Albertus, though a man wise in his time, makes extraordinary mistakes about Pyrites, yet he is said to have written very carefully concerning all the metals. He states that fire consumes every species of Pyrites, or, as he calls it, Marcasite. He denies that Metals are melted from Marcasite, whereas Avicenna says that there is a Marcasite of Gold, Silver, Copper, and Iron. Dioscorides teaches that Copper is melted from Pyrites, and Serapion, the Arab, confirms the same point. Had Albertus read these statements he would not have fallen into such an error. He probably accepted the statements of chemists too readily, without diligently examining mines or metals. Pyrites has remarkable medicinal virtue of an abstergent and removing kind. As to its burning and washing, see Dioscorides. Pliny states that Black Pyrites burns the hand when touched. Hence the ancient verses: " It requires to be touched gently, and held in a delicate hand, for too hard a pressure burns his fingers who handles it".

I have not come across Black Pyrites myself, and so have been unable to test the above statement. Possibly Pliny is referring to Black Cobalt, which possesses the quality in question. Solinus corroborates Pliny, who also terms Coral Pyrites, because fire can be derived from it. On the same ground he institutes a comparison with Chalcedony and common Flint, while others identify our Cuprine Slate with Pyrites. This Stone is very susceptible to impressions when under the earth. Sometimes it has representations of fishes, serpents, and tree-crickets; sometimes an elaborate picture of a cock with drooping feathers and double comb.

Silver-coloured Pyrites:
1. Covered with Yellow Fluor.
2. Mixed with Yellow Fluors.
3. In a Metallic Marble-easily split, Wedge-shaped, yielding no Fire.
4. Mixed with White Fluor and Metallic Marble.

Gold-coloured Pyrites:
1. Solid, True Gold-colour-called by its Spanish name of Marcasite.
2. Mansfeldian, with White Opaque Fluors. 3. Earthy, rich in Plumbago and Glance.

True Gold-coloured Pyrites:
1. Earthy, like Fine Gold.
2. Earthy, with many Angles and Points.

3. Mixed with White Hornstone.
4. Composed of Small Square Stones.
5. Full of Angles, with White, Pellucid, Cubical Fluors on the outside.
6. Spongy, full of Round or Angular Granules.

Gold-coloured Pyrites from which fire is not struck:
1. Angular, Gold-yellow, Copper Pyrites in a Water Pyrites.
2. Gishubelian, containing Tinsel.
3. Ditto, containing Barren Pitch-like Plumbago.
4. Containing a beautiful Yellow Earth.
5. Annebergian, easily Melting in Fire.

Grey Pyrites yielding no fire:
1. Spongy and Honey-combed.
2. Containing Sterile Plumbago.
3. Of Loose Texture, like Soft Sandstone.
4. Spongy, with White Fluors, Sprinkled with Purple, Red, and Green Grains.
5. Earthy, containing much Gold and Silver.
6. Grey-black Suacensian Pyrites, devoid of Copper or Silver.
7. Spongy, Dyed Black by a Warm Exhalation.
8. Grey, Long, like a Bundle of Twigs, and exuding Atrament or Green Vitriol.
9. Earthy, Grey Copper-stone from Hildesheim, whence Atrament flows abundantly, according to the weather.
10. Earthy, from Radeberg, yielding Sulphur. Fire-yielding Pyrites of other colours.
11. Black, Earthy, like Pit Coal.
12. Sterile, Melts in Fire, often combined with Infusible Ore instead of Metals.
13. Easily Melted.
14. Poisonous Water-Flint, combined with Veins of White Lead at Eberndorf. It is fatal to drink or wash in it.

Various-coloured Pyrites, yielding no fire:

1. Golden, Green, Blue, Violet, Purple, and Grey-Spongy. Also White Iron Pyrites.
2. Golden, Red, Purple, Blue, and Green, in White Fluors.
3. Rainbow-tinted, on a Grey Stone.
4. Multi-coloured, in Metallic Marble, which is White upon Red in Flesh coloured Spar.
5. Variegated Copper Pyrites in Orange-coloured Ironstone.
6. Like Polished Copper, a Red Copper Pyrites.
7. Fine Red Copper Pyrites, on a Grey Stone, resembling Small Granulated Copper.

Fire-yielding Red Pyrites:
1. Red, very Hard, Copper Pyrites, from Islebia, like Red jasper.
2. Grey-white, Spongy, Fire-yielding.
3. Containing Metallic Plumbago, or Glance.
4. Spongy, tinged with Pyrites Water till it assumes a Copper-red, and resembles Polished, Purified Copper.

Pyrites of other colours, yielding no fire:
1. Spongy, Blue Pyrites.
2. Violet Brown.
3. Purple.
4. Brown or Purple, containing Native Chrysocolla.
5. Brilliant or Sparkling, like Plumbago.

Pyrites yielding sap:
1. Yielding Chalcitis.
2. Yielding Sory or Black Atrament.
3. Yielding Melanteria, a kind of Vitriol.
4. Grey, yielding Vitriol abundantly.
5. Silver-coloured in a vein of Quicksilver.
6. From Cromena in Moravia, yielding Sap like Red, Pellucid Sulphur.

Pyrites containing various metals:
1. Containing Gold.
2. Containing Silver.

3. Aserosus (?).
4. Found in Lygia, containing much Gold and Silver.
5. Bohemian, rich in Gold and Silver.
6. Rich in Copper and Black Lead.
7. Containing Lead and Iron.
8. Earthy, white, hard, fragmentary, used in polishing.
9. Found in ponds, gold-colour, in a cluster of two or three.
10. Silver-coloured, dyed grey by a slimy or poisonous vapour.

Fire-yielding Pyrites:
1. Eight or twelve-sided, white, Iron Pyrites.
2. Cloddy, in hard, white, sandy earth.
3. Brightish yellow, like Wolfs-Foam.
4. Fribergian, mixed with White Plumbago.
5. From Marieburg, composed of small tessellated pieces like Native Lead.
6. Containing Native Yellow Sulphur.
7. Scaly, resembling the skin of a serpent, dyed grey by subterranean vapour.

Silver-coloured Pyrites:
1. White Water Pyrites, as if made of small, thin, polished, silver crusts.
2. Cubical White Iron Pyrites.
3. A White Iron Pyrites in a metallic red spar.
4. Ornamented with square, purple, or amethyst-coloured transparent Runs.
5. In a silver-white spar, which sparkles like Mica.
6. White Iron Pyrites, covered with round, white grains of Quartz, like Coriander.
7. Spongy and sparkling.
8. Like Pumice-stone, dyed black by a warm exhalation.

PYRITES — i.e, Lithos, in Greek, Marcasite.

PYROMANTIA — Art of prophesying by means of fire, when the stars of fire become visible to man, so that a true answer to a question is given without any hesitation. For instance, take the statements concerning the box-tree. When its leaves have been put in the fire, after writing severally upon them the names of suspected persons, that of the guilty individual is said to crackle and leap out. Pyromancy is the art of adapting fire to our purposes and of ruling it. In this art especially the diligence of the alchemist is manifested; great indeed is the praise of the artificer, although there is much more value in practice than in precept, and there are some things which require active eyes and hands, not words only. The external heat which the artificer employs as his primary instrument is a certain heat which we call fire. Yet is the operation of cold by no means to be excluded, nor moisture, nor dryness, which at times singly, and at times in combination, will much assist the master.

PYROTECHNIA — We only employ this term in the preparation of natural things by the aid of fire.

PYRAMIS — Otherwise, a Conical Pan-is a metallic vessel shaped like a pyramid internally, the upper part being broad. The lower part narrows down to a point. The interior is, therefore, like an inverted Cone. The lower part is useful for reducing molten metals to a regulus.

QUANDROS ~ is a Stone or jewel which is found in the brain and head of the Vulture, and is of a bright white colour. It fills the breasts with milk, and is said to be a safeguard against dangerous accidents.
QUANLI ~ Lead.
QUARS ~ Cat-stone. (?) the Quartz called Cat's Eye.
QUARTATIO ~ is a separation of Gold and Silver; it is the alloying of one part of Gold, with three of Silver.
QUARTURA, QUARTATION ~ is the most searching test of Gold. It is performed by adding nine parts of Silver to every one of Gold in melting by fire; both are afterwards resolved with Stygian Water, or Aqua Fortis. The Silver is entirely absorbed or held in solution by the water; the Gold settles at the bottom as a dark-red or black-coloured Powder.
QUADRATUM ~ A Fourth.
QUADRANGULA CONTIGNATIO ~ A Quadrangular Floor or Story.

QUADRANS FODINAE ~ Works done at the lateral angles of the Mine.

QUEBRICUM ~ is, according to some, Arsenic, but, according to Stephanus, it is Sulphur.

QUEBRIT or **QUIBRITH** ~ Sulphur.

QUI HARPAGONE LABORAT ~ One who Labours with a Crooked Instrument.

QUIANOS ~ Veins of Earth, Copperish.

QUINTA ESSENTIA ~ Quintessence, Nature, Potencies, Virtue, Tincture, Life, Spirit, the Medicine itself, and the quality of substances separated by Art from the body. If removed from its special form, it reverts to its general form, and progresses higher, until it rests in the centre.

QUINTUM ESSE ~ of any individual element is the living substance from which alone it is produced.

QUINTA ESSENTIA ~ Heaven; neither cold nor hot, neither moist nor dry, but temperate, tempers the soul. Burning Water.

QUINTA ESSENTIA ~ is the Mysterium, exalted to the purity of ethereal nature, and the highest virtues. So is it usually called the Heaven and Celestial Substance, in which the substantial root and the purest and most sincere contraction do remain, a flowing down of the ether, as it might be, or the ray of the firmament, which, by the voice of the Creator, was flashed through the soul of the world.

QUINTA ESSENTIA VEGETABILIUM ~ the Quintessence of Vegetable Substances, is that which is extracted from the components of vegetable things. It is most generally extracted from the Sap. Quintessence of Wine has the primacy. Lully calls it Vegetable Mercury; others, Water of Primal Being, Heaven, Key, etc.

QUINTA ESSENTIA ANIMALIUM ~ Quintessence of Animals, is that which is extracted from the components of Animals, by reason of the mixture of the natural and vegetable parts. In this case, the Praxis differs little from the vegetable preparation.

QUINTA ESSENTIA MINERALIUM ~ Quintessence of Minerals, is that which is extracted from Minerals. Chief among such Quintessences are those of precious Stones and Minerals.

RABEBOIA ~ The Roots of the larger Ranunculus.
RABIRA, or **RADIRA** ~ Tin.
RABIEL, or **ROLIEL** ~ i.e., Dragon's Blood.
RACHI, or **RACHO** ~ i.e., Mercury.
RADIX ~ Radish.
RARI, RAAN, or **RANAC** ~ Sal Ammoniac.
RADIUS ~ A Right Line.
RADIUS ROTE ~ Spoke of a Wheel.
RADIUS, RUTRUM LIGNEUM ~ Strickle.
RAGADAE NOTAE ~ Ulcers in the Hinder Parts, the Womb, Penis, etc.
RAINALE ~ A Stone from which Uzifer is made.
RAIBX RUS, or **RAEB** ~ Stone.
RAMIGIRI, or **RAMIGI** ~ i.e., Bolofonia, rel Rotigenig, Unknown.
RAMAG ~ i.e., Ash.
RAMENTA ~ Metal Waste.

RHAPONTICUM — The Body changed into Water and Blackness [sigil Mercury].
RAMA — An Abscess under the Tongue.
RANAC — Ten.
RASAR, or **RASTIS** — Tin.
RASTOL, or **RASOES** — Copper.
RASTUL — i.e., Salt.
RASAHETI, RATAGI, RUSANG, KOSANGE — Names of Copper.
RASTRUM — Kiln Rake.
RASTELLUM BIDEN — Shears.
REALGAR — Red Orpiment.
REALGAR — is properly a Mineral Smoke, which has something of the nature of Orpiment, or Arsenic. Metaphorically, it is that poison of the body which generally is the cause of Ulcers. It is of four kinds, corresponding to the four elements, so is there the Realgar on the Surface of Water, the Arsenical Realgar of the Earth, the Terebinthine Realgar of Air, and that Saturnine Conjunction which is the Realgar of Fire.
REBIS — Excrement of the Belly.
REBIS — The Stone Rebis, i.e., Hair.
REBISOLA — is the Arcanum of Urine, when Urine is cooked and skimmed. Allow it to stand three days. Then the Arcanum will be found in the form of pebbles.
REBUS — The Ultimate Substance of Things.
REBOLEA — Mummy, Burnt Menstruum or Ordure.
RECHA — i.e., Marble.
REBIS — Man and Wife, body and soul, the first stage of the operation; clean subtle Sand which adheres to Mercury; doubly-mingled Seed is called Rebis; it is also Ferment and Elixir, Medicine, Tincture; a twice-composed substance, says Senior.

RECEPTACLUM ~ is an ample globular Vessel for receiving distilling Humours, commonly called a Receiver. But this Receiver differs with the substance that is distilling. If things Vaporous, Spiritual, etc., are undergoing the operation, it should be very broad, as it is liable to be shattered by the distending force of a Vapour or Spirit. If, on the other hand, the matter be hot, the Receiver should have a long neck. If it be a substance of a middle nature, then the Receiver should be of medium capacity and length.
RECREMENTA ~ Slag, Cooked Slag.
RECREMENTA FERRI ~ Cinders.
RECTOR MACHINE ~ A Governor.
REDUX ~is Dust, by which Calcined Metals and Minerals are Liquefied, returning again into a Metallic Regulus.
REDUCIREN ~ A Drying Process. It restores Fatness like Butter, and flows like Wax. Pouring water on dry earth, they call giving to Eat and to Drink.
REL, REBUS ~ Sour Milk.
RELOLLIUM ~ A Secret Virtue, such as Common Wormwood. It is its first virtue that it drives away worms. The second virtue is that it is of a warm and healthy nature.
REMANERE, etc. ~ To remain as Block Sheaves.
REPERCUSSIVA ~ Medicaments which cause Purging by Stool.
RES EFFOSSAS ALVEIS SUBTRAHERE ET RETROFUNDERE ~ To take the Metal from the Ore, and throw back the refuse.
RES FOSSILIS ~ Like Spume of Silver in the second grade.
RESOLUTIO ~ Resolution by Medicine is when things that are mixed together are violently separated, a dissolving matter being applied, and segregation thus effected. We term it Medicine, from Gebir, but if the dissolving matter be a liquid it is also termed Solving Water. In milky substances, it is performed with vinegar or like acids. The operation may

also be called Empyriasis. In some cases it is akin to coagulation.

RESTIS ~ A Rope or Cord.

RESTINCTIO ~ is Gradation, by which a substance at white heat is quenched in an exalting liquid, and is thus brought into the highest degree of perfection which is possible to it in its own species. This is the first and sole end of the process.

RESINA ~ Yellow and Beautiful Pitch, Serapine Opopanax, Ammoniac, etc.

RESINA AURI ~ is the Saffron extracted from Gold.

RESINA PINI ~ i.e., Resin of the Pine or Fir.

RESINA TERRAE ~ Sulphur.

RESINA TERRE POTABILIS ~ Sulphur Sublimed and Reduced to a Liquid, Balsam, or Oil.

RETORTA ~ is a Globular Vessel, with a Small Neck issuing from the Body, and gradually bent round into an Oblong Pipe.

REVERBERATIO ~ is Ignition, reducing substances under the influence of a Potent Fire, and by means of reverberation and repercussion, into a fine Calx. It is either close or open.

REVERBERATIO CLAUSA ~ Close Reverberation takes place when Bodies are Calcined by Reverberation in a Sealed Reverberating Furnace. By this process, the fire can be graduated to a nicety, which is not possible in the vulgar way.

REVERBERATIO APERTA ~ Open Reverberation is when the Matter is Calcined in a Reverberating Furnace with all the Shafts and Doors open. This species of Reverberation is very powerful, and is used for hard bodies which are not easily dissolved.

REX ~ King, Soul, Spiritual Water which gives Moisture to the Female, and is restored to the Fountain whence it was derived. The Spirit in Water.

REVERBERATORUM FURNUS ~ The Reverberatory Furnace in which Matters are Calcined by Flame.

RINAR or **RION** ~i.e., Filings; Superfluities.

RILLUS ~ A Chemical Instrument, of Oblong Shape, through which Molten Metal is poured.

ROBES or **ROSCON** ~ Vinegar; some say, Saturn.

RON or **ROTULA** ~ A Pound Weight.

ROSA ~ i.e., Tartar.

ROSEA ~ i.e., Erysipelas.

ROTA or **ROTINGENIUS** ~ i.e., Colofonia.

RORER THECA ~ Round Case of a Wheel.

RORER ~ Wheels.

ROTUMHA ~ A Vessel resembling a Cucurbit.

RUS ~ Thick Sap, any juice Cooked till it is Thick.

RUBEDO DE NIGRO ~ The Red that is Extracted artificially from Black Lime.

RUBEUM AURUM FALSUM ~ Tinged Copper, Sophisticated Alchemical Gold.

RUBIGO ~ is called in another work Hirudo, a Sweet Gall, and is made from Gold.

RUBRICA SINOPICA ~ Sinopian Earth, or Rubrica, so called because it first came from Sinope, a town of Paphlagonia, on the Black Sea, as we learn on the authority of Dioscorides (1. 5, c. 51), and also of Pliny and Vitruvius. It is also called Lepnia, and by the Greeks, Magra, or Mogan. It is close-grained, ponderous, homogeneous, free from grit and stones. It was an important product of Sinope, where it was made and sold. There is also a Rubrica which is brought in small quantities from Byzantium to Venice. There is also a Byzantine liver-coloured Pastille, on which Turkish letters are inscribed, and it is called Sigillated Earth. There was also that Lemnian Earth, which Pliny tells us was sold under a seal, and was called Rubrica and Sphragida. It was mined annually in Lemnos, and used both in medicine and dyeing. The seal upon it represented a goat. The island of Lemnos is not far from Thrace, and is now under the rule of Turkey, so it is easily imported to Byzantium. If its colour scarcely corresponds to true Rubrica, it is because the Earth with which it is blended for manufacture into Pastilles causes some change in its substance. The Turks hold it in high estimation as a cure for the plague, and so also they regard Armenian Earth, as we may learn from Galen. This Armenian Earth is not unlike Sigillated Earth, only it is not sealed. Whether the Earth which is made into Pastilles, and is signed with Turkish characters, be Sinopian Rubrica, or Lemnian Earth, or Armenian Earth, is not of much importance, as all have the same virtues. Formerly, one Earth alone was sealed, but Turkish intolerance checks its exportation. For the rest, consult Pliny (1. 35, c. 6) concerning Sinopian Earth, of which he makes three species — that which is red, that which is very pale red, and a middle quality.

RUBRICA FABRILIS — Artificer's Rubrics is twofold, and is called Red Chalk and Ruddle by the Germans. It is either native or manufactured. Ruddle is the native kind. It is mined in the vicinity of the Elbe. Dioscorides (1. 5, c. 62) says that there is a Burnt Ochre, or Degenerate Rubrica, which is native in Western Iberia. Pliny also writes of it, and says that it is obtained from Metallic mines. There is also a variety which has affinity with Marble. Manufactured Rubrica is called Brown Ruddle by the Germans, and it is made of Burnt Ochre, as Theophrastus and Dioscorides testify. But Pliny (l. 35, c. 6) negligently reverses this order, and says that Burnt Ochre is made of Rubrica, against which Nature herself protests. For the rest, as to what manufactured Rubica is best, I refer to the Artificers therein. Dioscorides commends the crumbling quality, not the marmorous, or that which has affinity with Marble, nor yet the Egyptian or Carthaginian.

Rubrica:

(1) Native mined ~ Sinopian and Lemnian Earth. German Rubrica. Native in Mines, produced by the heat of the Sun, or of the Earth. Native in Rivers, produced by the heat of the Sun, or of the Earth. When burnt, Indurated Pnigitis is made from it. Ochre is not manufactured from Rubrica, as Pliny says, but Rubrica is obtained from Ochre;

(2) Manufactured Rubrica, made from Burnt Ochre, by Art, in new clay Vessels.

RUTABULUM or **MUCUS** ~ Rake Iron, a long Iron Rod, having a Spoon at one end and a Scraper at the other; it is useful for docimastic (?) operations.

RUTABULUM ~ A Spade for Digging.

RUTUM ~ A Paddle.

RUTRUM ~ Rake, Rabble, Stirring Rabble.

RUTRUM ~ A Mattock.

RUTRUM or **RUTELLUM** ~ Chest.

SABON or **SABENA** ~ Saponaceous Matter, Slime, or Alkali, from which soap is made.
SACCUS ~ A Bag of Leather.
SACTIM ~ Vitriol.
SADIR ~ i.e., Refuse.
SAFFRATUM ~ A species of Salt.
SAGANI ~ Spirits of the Four Elements.
SAGDA or **SAGDO** ~ A Gem of the colour of Chrysoprase, is mentioned by Albertus, Evax, and Solinus. It has the virtue possessed by Gagates, of attracting threads and straws, as the magnet does iron. It is found adhering strongly to the bottom of ships. I have seen a specimen, which was however devoid of virtue, and was not of true Chrysoprase colour. Solinus says that the gem was common in Chaldea. Pliny speaks of a variety from Samothrace, which was black, like wood in appearance, and of no weight.
SAGIMEN VITRI ~ Vitreous Salt, or Salt of Alkali.

SALAMANDRI or **SALDINI** — Fiery Men or Spirits, Beings sustained by the influence and nourished by the element of fire, as was the case with that gentle lady, by name Zifer, who when ill was made whole by casting herself upon the fire, and sitting thereon, enjoying it as though it were a bath.
SALEBROT or **SAL LAMBROT** — Acid Salt.
SALEFUR — i.e., Garden Saffron.
SALINAE — An Excavated Gallery in which Salt is made.
SALLENA — A kind of Rock Salt.
SALSA — Potters' Clay.
SALSEDO MUCRUM — Rock Salt.
SALTABARI — i.e., Sal Alembrot or Philosophical Salt.
SAL — In the Greek, Alas ; in the Arabic, Melech or Selenipum, is Brine or Muriate of Salt, from salt melted by cold or damp. Or it is the Terrene Principle, powerfully restricting, coagulating, and so also preserving. Thus it is closely related to Nature, and works well therewith. It is also Mercury.
The Salt of the Philosophers is the Stone of the Philosophers. Some would extract the Salt from all metals, and make the art to consist in doing so, which is wholly unnecessary, as Hermes says:
1. Every Salt is present in this art, that one alone excepted whereby the souls are extracted from the metals.
2. The First Matter is everywhere, and in all houses ; it grows in the sea and in all men.
3. There is another Salt of Vegetables, another of Animals, a third of Metals, which is the most acrid of all.
4. It is the best Balsam, purges, acts as an astringent, makes thin, cleanses, separates, alters, and stimulates the power of the seed. Therefore we say that Venus is born out of the sea.
5. Senior and Gratian state that Lime and Salt can be made out of all things-Salt out of Ashes, Water out of Ashes, Gold

out of Mercury. Therefore have they sought for Gold in all things.

6. Everything which you would elevate and alter you must reduce to Salt and Alum, and this is the secret of preparing the Calcined Salt.

7. Everything that is capable of dissolution absorbs the nature of Salt and Alum, and after corruption assumes the Stone.

8. Salt which is fixed is used for holding the body together, and is extracted from calcinated things by means of putrefaction, until the whole composition alters its nature and assumes another.

9. Reinmund says: The Art requires Lime, that is, its proper earth, which, of all Minerals, possesses the greatest power of hardening the Mercury.

10. The Salt of the Metals dissolves the Mercury into a clear water in dung, and the same is mixed up and coagulates till the perfect medium is produced. Therefore, he that understands the Salt and its solution possesses the wisdom of the ancients. Therefore, place your whole reliance on the Salt. Count nothing else of importance. For Salt by itself is the most important secret which all the Wise have thought proper to conceal. Gebir says: You must know that this is a Salt, although at first it has by no means the appearance of a Salt, but it becomes like it during operation. It is white, bright, clear, and excellent. Then it becomes impure, and then pure again; it dissolves and coagulates; also it expands and it contracts.

Paracelsus in Paramiro affirms as follows: Salt produces coagulation ; it causes the given matter to thicken and to coagulate, till it assumes such a consistency that it can be touched, for nothing can be tangible without the presence of Salt. Now, there are many species of Salt, just as there are many kinds of Sulphur, and many kinds of Mercury.

SAL ALABROT ~ Salt, Black Nitre, is made out of three Vegetable Juices. It is called the Master of all Things. It effects the following marvel, namely, it transmutes the Mercury into true Moon and Sun. It is also called Sal Boroch.
SAL ALBUS ~ i.e., Borax.
SAL ALLOCAPH ~ i.e., Sal Ammoniac.
SAL ALKALI ~ i.e., Glass Salt, made from the Ashes of Cali. Item, Salt of Bitterness, Menstruation of Bitterness, Oil of Philosophers, Salt of Wisdom, causing the Spirit to enter properly into Bodies and permeate them.
SAL ALUMINOSUM ~ Derived from Fibrous Gypsum.
SAL AMARUM ~ Bitter Salt, Alkali, Nitre.
SAL ANATHRON or **ANATRON** ~ i.e., Nitric Salt.
SAL ARMONIACUS ~ i.e., Sal Saparicius, i.e., Arabian Salt, is the Dissolved Stone.
SAL ATRUM or **SAL THABER** ~ Black Salt.
SAL COLCOTHARINUM or **COLCOTHACIUM** ~ The Salt from Vitriol.
SAL CONGELATUM ~ Congealed Salt, originates in Thermal Springs, Fountains, and Medicinal Waters.
SAL CRISTALLINUM ~ Derived from Human Urine.
SAL DE UNGARIA ~ i.e., Salt of Nitre.
SAL ENIXUM ~ Dissolved Salt.
SAL ENTALI ~ A kind of Fixed Saltpetre.
SAL EX HERBARUM SALSARUM CINERE FACTUS ~ i.e., Sal Alkali, made from the Ash of Salted Herbs.
SAL GEMMA ~ i.e., Cappadocius.
SAL GEMMA ~ i.e., Salt Adrom, Sendaro Sabachi, Metalline Salt, Hungarian Salt, Sparkling Salt.
SAL GRAECUM ~ Alum from Alap or from Lacaph.
SAL INDICUM ~ Called from the place of its origin; Red in Colour.
SAL I NDICUS ~ Mercury, Resolved and Coagulated.

SAL LOTII — Salt of Urine.
SAL MARINUS — Gem or Metalline Salt.
SAL MERCURII — Intoxicating Spirit of Wine.
SAL FACTITIUM — Salt Artificially Cooked or Produced. It is of two kinds.

1. Marine Salt, which Dioscorides mentions, and states that it is white, dense, and a native of Cyprus. It is deposited in ponds that have been dried up by heat; both rain water and sweet water enter into its composition. No Salt can be made without sweet water, as Pliny affirms.

Those who prepare Salt mix sweet or fresh water with it, so as to remove its intense acridity, and this is still done in certain localities of Spain and France, in the Tarentine Lake, and in Sicily by the Lake Cocanicus. (See Pliny, l. 31, c. 3.)

2. That which is artificially cooked from the Native Brine of Fountains, just as our Salt is at Halle in Saxony, and at some places in Thuringia. The quality varies according to the nature of the water; that which is made in Marchia is exceedingly variable.

In the districts adjoining what is now called the Sea of Lisbon there are extensive marshes in many places quite stagnant, and containing salt water. The sailors call them havens. This is the Pond Salt of the sea-shore; it is carried in by the tides, and dried by the sun, which cooks the sea water into Salt. The poverty-stricken inhabitants of the place construct boxes of somewhat ingenious make, and collect the Salt therein, lest it should be carried away again by the tide. They pile them in great heaps on the shore, where the cooking takes place gradually on the dry sand, and the Salt is congealed into lumps — as of Alum or Ice, except that they are of a pale green or black, and are not transparent. This Salt is then conveyed in ships to various nations on the coast, and is pounded till it becomes like fine sand. It is used for salting many kinds of fish, including whales, seals, sea-dogs, flat-fish, etc,

We have a long description of the properties of Salt in Dioscorides and Pliny, as also in the Book of Aggregations by Serapion, under the name of Malk. Dioscorides furnishes a description of the process for burning Salt, whether natural or artificial. He describes Salt as a sort of residue of Sea-foam, which coagulates on the low rocks of the seashore. Pliny includes this Spume of Salt among the native species, and says that it is thickened by dew. The interpreter of Nicander, in the Book of Antidotes, defines Spume of Salt to be produced by the artificial mixture of salt and fresh water, which removes the natural acridity. The product was called by the Greeks Halos Achne, the Froth of Salt. In this case, we may distinguish two kinds of Salt Spume-that mentioned by Dioscorides as produced from the sea, and which Pliny calls a native Salt; while the other is the manufactured Salt of Nicander's interpreter. Salt and Spume of Salt are evidently interchangeable terms, as Nitre and Spume of Nitre. It should also be observed that there are innumerable species of Salt; if their native place, locality, quality, and the mineral in which they are found were to be regarded, the catalogue would be longer than the Iliad. We will briefly treat of some species: Cappadocian Salt, Lump Salt, Rock Salt, Common Salt, are the same. There is also Salt of Sodom, which comes from the Dead Sea, where the water is very bitter. It looks like a species of Sea-spume, or Solidified Salt. There is also a kind of Salt called Sal Alkali or Alkal, which is manufactured, and is produced from the herb Kali, or by the calcination of a plant called Anthyllis in a pit. Then there is the bright Salt called Nitre, Alexandrine Salt, Salt of Anderena, Baurach, Salt of Nitre, Coarse Soda or Potassa, Aphronitum, etc., for Nitre is a species of Salt. There is Sacerdotal Salt, which is included in the list of powerful antidotes. There is Tragesian Salt, Arsenical Salt, or Sublimated Arsenic; Alebrach, or Alebroth Salt, which is the Salt of chemists, on which consult the chemists.

SALIS FLOS, ALOSANTHUS — Flower of Salt, a species of Zoophyte, which comes from the sea, and is an efflorescence of the sea. In the laboratories it is called Sperma, Seed of Whale or Sea Monster, Pale Amber, Spermaceti, or Cetine, possibly from its efficacy in certain diseases. The ancients did not call it Spermaceti, but Flower of Salt.

The same substance is found in the sea, as sailors and merchants have told me, and in the Nile, if their reports be true; also in marshes by the sea. In the Nile Dioscorides says that it assumes the colour of the crocus, and it is purged to replace the red with a white colour. It is redolent of rank poison, and is very unpleasant. It dissolves in oil, but not in water. Dioscorides states whence it comes, describes its qualities, also the adulterated variety. He enlightens us on its medicinal uses. See also Cassius Felix on Alosachne. Pliny regards it as a substance of divers natures, and says that it smells differently both from Salt and Sea-spume. It is found in Egypt, is carried by the Nile, and floated about thereon. It is so well known in Saxony that it enters into medicines for almost every disease. I know of a most excellent lady who perished by excessive use of it.

1. Very fine Yellow and White Salt.
2. Spermaceti or Cetine.

SAL NITRI — Saltpetre or Sal Nitri, smelted out of earth which has been drenched in urine — for example, such earth as forms the floors of stables.

Native Salt, in Arabic Malk, is a most excellent condiment or spice. It is of two kinds — native and artificial. Native, Mined, or Mineral Salt may either be dug up from the mines, or obtained from lakes, springs, or rivers, the surface of which hardens or thickens into Salt. (See Pliny, l. 31, c. 7.) There are four varieties of Mined Salt:

1. Sal Ammoniac or Sagaraic Salt, Scissile. Dioscorides says that it is white, free from pebbles, clear, like alum in colour, and called Schist. Ovid mentions it when treating of medicaments for the complexion, and calls it Ammoniac, which others write as Armoniac, because it is found in Armenia. Others again affirm that it is made from the herb Salmoniac, growing on the mountains of Spain, and resembling the Anethus mentioned by Avicenna. Serapion distinguishes red, white, black, dust-colour, and transparent kinds, and says that it is warm and dry in the fourth degree.

2. Rock Salt from India and Africa, also Cappadocian, like the Mirror Stone, or Sal Gemma.

3. Black, from the mines of Poland; also sometimes white and blue. It is dug up in blocks like mill-stones. It is called Naphthic, and is found in c9mbination with Naphtha. It is also called Black Salt, Indian Salt, the last on account of its colour.

4. A green, crystalline Salt is mined in Transylvania, which is Sal Gemmae, and is also called Cappadocian, Costum, Metalline, and Taburen. It is called Sal Gemmaa, because it is clear as a gem. It is a vein of Earth, and has the properties of Sal Ammoniac.

All these species are called by the Germans Rock Salt, and are akin to Alum. They are corrosive and desiccating.

SAL NAPTAE — Salt of Naptha, extracted from Petroleum.
SAL NOMINIS — Nominal Salt, i.e., Sal Gemma.
SAL PANIS — Common Salt.
SAL PETRAE — A product of Dissolved Lime or Spume of Salt.
SAL PETRAE — To sublimate is called Contracting Salt.
SAL PLUMOSUM — Shadow of Mercury.

SAL RESOLUTUM EXTERNUM ~ When a person deems what he eats to be Salt.
SAL RUBEUM INDIAE ~ Red Nitre.
SAL SAPIENTIUM ~ Salt of the Wise, Sal Ammoniac; a certain measure of Salt.
SAL SCISSUM or **SAL ENTALI** ~ Split Alum, Spar-like Gypsum.
SAL TABARZET ~ The whitest species of Tartar.
SAL TARTARI ~ White Calcined Tartar.
SAL TRIPOLLINUS ~ Syrian Salt, Salt of Tabor, Metallic Salt.
SAL TARTARI ~ White Calcinated Tartar.
SANDARACA, otherwise **ERYTHACE** ~ A Food for Bees. As to its production, see Pliny (1. 11, c. 7). But in this place we are dealing with a native metallic substance, which the Germans call Orpiment, Realgar, Arsenical Orpiment, Red Sulphur, Fire Sulphur, Red Orpiment. It is hot and dry in the second grade. It is not rude Red Silver, as some fancy. Sandarac is a Metal and a Purple Earth. It is found in the same metals as Native Orpiment, of which there is a species resembling this in smell, substance, and properties, though it differs in colour, corresponding therein to Cinnabar, which is red. Hence Pliny says that Arsenic is a compound of the same matter as Sandarach, meaning Orpiment by Arsenic. Alchemists try to establish a distinction between this Orpiment and Sandarac, but they are mistaken. They are one and the same, and are produced from naturally weak Sulphur and Quicksilver. Finally, Sandarac is a Metallic Earth, either red, purple, or fiery, and exhaling a sulphureous smell. Sometimes red or fiery Clods are found among Orpiment. And, when properly considered, true Sandarac may be discovered in Orpiment. Pliny says that Sandarac is found in mines of Gold and Silver; it is red and has a strong smell. It is also pure and friable. Such a

substance is frequently found in our mines; it is something like Fine Sand. Theophrastus writes that Orpiment and Sandarac are Sand and Powder. This substance of ours might be called Sandarac from the similarity of appearance and colour, in the same way that Vitruvius calls something made out of Ceruse Sandarac, while Dioscorides calls it Sandix. Sandix, according to Pliny, is differently produced. So also our adulterated Minium, made from Lead, is a kind of artificial Sandarac. Our Sandarac may be called the Sandarac of Pliny, which is found in Gold and Silver Mines. It may also be called that of Theophrastus, because it is a Fine Sand. Whether it has the same virtues, I do not know. Possibly an excellent pigment might be extracted from it, were experiment made. I doubt whether the strong-smelling Sandarac of Dioscorides exists in our mines. There is a wide gulf between ours and that of Dioscorides. Sometimes the unlearned imagine that Sandarac is a Medicinal Gum, and almost all the Laboratories identify it with the Resin of the Juniper Tree. Sandarac is a Metallic Substance. The confusion began with the Arabs, who call Sandarac Varnish Resin, or juniper Resin, while Sandaraca they called Red Metallic Orpiment. Some have even gone so far as to believe that common Painters' Varnish was true Metallic Sandarac. Metallic Sandarac is not found in our Laboratories. Concerning it, or concerning Red Orpiment, which is the same, see Serapion and Avicenna. Pliny states that Native Sandarac is produced in the Island of Topazo in the Red Sea, but that it is not exported.
SAL VITRI ~ Sagimen of Glass.
SAL UXUM ~ Salt is one of the three principles which form the bodies of all things and unite them together.
SAL USUALE or **SAL MASSAE** ~ Block Salt.
SAMECH ~ Salt of Tartar, or Tartar itself ~ a remedy for all wounds.

SAMEN ~ Barley.
SAN ~ Same as Solatium [no reference].
SANDARACHA ~ Orpiment, Crystalline Arsenic, Yellow Orpiment.. There are four species.
1. Native Sandarac, Yellow Orpiment.
2. The artificial product named by Vitruvius, the Sandix of the Greeks,
Minium, Red Lead.
3. Imperfectly Cooked, Pale Minium.
4. Native, mixed with Orpiment ~ Realgar, mixed with Orpiment.
SANDARACH, SANDARACA in Arabic ~ Resin, Sap, Resin of Sandaros.
SANDERICH ~ Lunar Spittle, White Ore, White Magnet which attracts Iron, Yellow Orpiment ~ the thing we seek ~ Realgar, Minium, Spirit which makes Red, also a White Sandarach.
SANDIX ~ A Wild Herb, Red Earth, Philosophical Paul, Red Orpiment.
SANGUIS ~ Blood is Orpiment, that is, the Stone which is not yet perfect, the Philosophical Water which gives life and unites, according to Morien. It has great strength, which must be sapped by means of stinking water to render it innocuous, but this is after dealbation.
SANGUINEA ~ Saltpetre.
SANGUIFUCA ~ Slimy, Muddy Ore.
SANGUIS CALCETUS ~ Sharp, Acrid, White Blood.
SANGUIS DUORUM FRATRUM ~ Dragon's Blood ~ a Vein of Earth.
SANGUIS HOMINIS ~ The Red Man's Blood, Sulphur out of a Gold Pyrites, Mercury of the Sun, and its precipitate, for blood is not always fluid, but coagulates and
thickens.

SAPHIRUS — The Gem Sapphire, closely allied to jasper (see Dioscorides and Pliny). It is a stone glistening with Gold points. Some species are blue, some mixed with purple. The best are those of the Medes. Some are useless by reason of their crystalline spots. Some are dark blue, and these are thought to be the male kind. Albertus states that the Sapphire is called Sirites. He considers the Indian and Oriental varieties to be the best, and says there is a variety of a colour like the bright and cloudless sky, with yet a prevalent ruddy hue. Another sort has dark blue markings. The virtue of the Sapphire is to render men chaste, dutiful, and stable-minded. It is even now used for soothing the heart and cooling the interior of the body. Hence the old lines: The Sapphire cools the internal heat of the body, and abates the strength of the desires of love..
SAPO SAPIENTIAE — Common Salt, Soaked in Water.
SARAFFI — Gypsum.
SARCA, SAYRSA, or **SARRA** — Iron.
SARDA — A gem from Sardes, which is also called the Sardian Stone, and Darneolus, as Pliny states.. At one time it was used for drinking-vessels, and the gem changed names with Sardonyx. Its name is derived from Sardes, where it was first found. The best quality is at the heart of the stone in Babylon, Epirus, and Assus. There are three kinds in India. Albertus states that Sard sharpens the intellect, and makes men cheerful, because it purifies the blood, and imparts thus good spirits. Consult Solinus concerning Sardonyx. The various species of Sard are enumerated as follows:
1. Transparent Indian Sard, pellucid Cornelian, the male kind.
2. Pellucid, not so ruddy.
3. Pellucid, like human flesh in colour.
4. Pellucid, like human flesh in colour, full of red spots.
5. Opaque, flesh-coloured.

6. Opaque, with lines of brown, red, yellow, or white colour.
7. Opaque, on one side brown, on the other flesh-colour.
8. Flesh-colour, relieved by brown lines and circles.
9. Transparent, flesh-colour.
10. Opaque, flesh-colour.
11. Flesh-colour, with red, yellow, and white parallel lines and circles.
12. Transparent, showing somewhat ruddy in white.
13. Red, varied by white lines.
14. Red, varied by brown lines.
15. Transparent, ruddy gold-colour.
16. Transparent, honey-colour.
17. Transparent, yellow, like amber.
18. Opaque, ruddy.
19. Opaque, brown.
20. Opaque, brown, full of yellow lines.
21. Brown, with black and red spots and lines.

SARDONYX RUBER PELLUCIDUS ~ Red, Transparent Sardonyx, shaped like a
Human Nail; one side is like Onyx, the other like Sard.

SARNICUM, SECCHIEN, SACEN ~ Of the Dragon.

SARFAR ~ Iron.

SATURNUS ~ Lead.

SAURA ~ The Lacertus of the Latins, the Lizard of the Germans. We have many species. One has a brilliant belly, and is otherwise green. It dwells in thickets and hedges. If its belly be opened with a reed, the gem Saurites is discovered, which is said to be potent against poisons.. The bones of the Green Lizard are useful in epilepsy and falling sickness, if collected as follows. Place a Green Lizard, just caught alive, in a closed vessel, filled with the best quality of Salt, which in a few days will consume flesh and entrails, and then the bones will be easily collected.

SAXA — The following species of Rocks are dug up from the earth:
1. Fissile, of Bluish Colour, a species of Pyrites and Lythanthtax.
2. A very White Rock, with sparkles of Gold, sometimes of a soft and slimy
character.
3. The German Spath, denser and more polished than the rest.
4. Flint, of a Horn Colour, very hard.
5. Sandy, Concreted from Salt. When it is of great size it is used for Millstones. There are several specimens — White, Blue, Ruddy, Yellow, and approaching Black.

SAXA ARENARIA — Sandy Rocks:
1. Pirnensian Sandstone.
2. Clayey Fribergian.
3. Red Rochlician.
4. Grey Querfurdian.
5. Saxony Black in Red.

SAXA CALCARIA — Calcareous Rocks.
1. White Pirnesian.
2. Blue Pirnesian.
3. Grey Pirnsian.
4. Grey Pirnesian with White Veins.
5. Black, containing Granite, mined at Jeblicus.
6. Dyed with a Red Colour by a Metallic Moisture, not far from Friberg; it is combined wit Veins of Stibium and Schist.

SAXA FISSILIA — Fissile Rocks:
1. Black, Sterile, easily split up.
2. Hard, Sterile, can only be broken by the skill of a good artificer.
3. White in Grey.
4. Grey.

5. White.
6. Greyish.
7. Blue in Grey.
8. Red.
9. Muddy Colour.
10. Black Mansfield, having Imprints of Fishes.
11. Black, containing Twigs of Trees, like the Olive Branch.
12. Black Andegrave, used for the Roofs and Walls of Houses, and also for Tables, Counters, etc.
13. Black Rhenish, of which Towers, Steeples, and Gables are built.
SARA GRAVIDA ~ Heavy Rocks.
1. Hard Grey Rocks, in which Sea Shells are imbedded and petrified.
2. Grey, in which Bivalves are found in the Sands of Lusatia.
3. White, Sandy, containing Mussel Shells.
SARA QUADRANGULA ~ Hewn Stone Blocks; Square Stones.
SAXUM ~ Foundation Stone.
SAXUM INVERSUM ~ An Inverted Stone.
SAXI SPECIES ~ Fast Rock, Shelf, Lattice Work.
SAXUM TERMINALE ~ Sandstone.
SAXA TINCTA AB EHALATIONIBUS ~ Rocks coloured by Exhalations.
1. Rock coloured Red by the action of damp.
2. Iron-coloured.
3. Yellow.
4. Brown.
5. Black.
SAXA VILIA ~ Common Composite Rock.
SAXIFRAGIS ~ Pallid Crystal, a Herb.
SAXIFRAGIA ~ Anything which expels Sand and Gravel from the Body.

SAXIFRAGIUM — A Stone which is supposed to produce the above result.
SBESTEN — That is Calx Viva, or Living Calx.
SCACURCULAI — Spirit extracted from the Bones of a Stag's Heart.
SCAIOLAE — are Spiritual Powers of the Mind, its properties and virtues, which are fourfold, according to the number of the elements, and the four wheels of fire which were part of the Chariot in which Elias was taken up to Heaven. They emanate from the soul in man. Fancy, imagination, speculative faculty, etc., are included under the term. It also embraces, in a special sense, the Articles of our Christian Faith in Jesus Christ, Baptism, partaking of the Eucharist, Charity towards our neighbour, manifesting the perfect Fruits of Faith, whereby we attain not merely prolonged but eternal life.
SCALE EXCOCTORUM — A Miner's Balance.
SCIDEN — White Lead.
SCIRONA — Autumn Dew, a Herb.
SCHEHENDENEGI — The Herb Cannabis, or its Seed.
SCHISTUM — of the kind we treat here-is a Precious Stone, of the Hematite order, and is included among this genus by Pliny. However, it differs from true Hematite, being paler, crocus-like in colour, friable, and eminently scissile. It is full of Veins which resemble Sal Ammoniac, whereas Hematite has red veins like blood. Nevertheless, the properties of the two things are similar, although Schist is less powerful. As far as I know, we have no genuine Schist. But we have a substance that resembles it. Dioscorides states that it is native in Iberia. Pliny mentions an African species. Evax, in his Lapidary, states that it is dark or pale red, with long feathery streaks like fissile alum, and that it is a strong astringent. Such a Stone occurs in the Iron Mines of

Salvedia, but its astringent power is slight. Consult Pliny as to the burning of Schist with Iron.

SCOSS — Alkali.
SCOBES — Refuse of any Metal.
SCORAX — Gum of the Olive Tree.
SCOPIA STILLA — An Exudation.
SCORITH — Sulphur.
SCORIA — Slag, Refuse, the Coarse Matter which is separated from the rest of the composition. Also the foundation of Mercury.
SCORPIUS CONSTRICTUS — Prepared Iron.
SCRIBA FODINARUM — Clerk of the Works.
SCUMA — Iron or other Metallic Scale.
SCUTA TABESI — A Tortoise.
SCHWELEN — A species of Rock.
SES — Gold, or Alum. Also called Salt.
SEB IMMUTATI COLORIS — Scabious.
SEBEL — A Poisoned Swelling of the Eye.
SECARE IN PARTES — Gradual Drying.
SECERNERE METALLA — To Separate Metals.
SECRETOR — Separator of Ore and Metal.
SECUR — Gold.
SEDAFF — A Marine Shell.
SEDATIVA, etc. — Medical Preparations given to allay pain; they are also curative and health-giving.
SEDEN — The Cask.
SEDENEGI — Hemp Seed.
SEDHE — i.e., Cinnabar.
SEDILIA FOLLIUM — The lower part of the Bellows.
SEDINA or **SEDEN** — Dragons' Blood.
SEDMA or **SCEDUNE** — Hematite.
SEGAX — Dragons' Blood.
SEGITH, SERNECH, or **SAGITH** — i.e., Vitriol.

SEGREGATIO — Separation of a Composite Substance into its Elements. It is also Distraction and Extraction. By this process the resolved or separated portions remain intact one from another, and do not flow together as in the operation of melting.
SEL — A Military Engine used in Sieges (Sambucus).
SELATUS — Called also Satir, Saic, and Solat — i.e., Quicksilver.
SEGREGATIO — is the Dissolution of a Whole into its Parts.
SELINITIS or **MOONSTONE** — Is a Transparent Stone of the Mica Genus, as we stated in dealing with the Arabian Stone, which we then affirmed to be properly transparent, especially that species which Pliny says is similar to Ivory, and is the Spotted Ivory of Dioscorides. But my own opinion is as follows If Selenite be a transparent stone, the extremely white quality, of which windows are made, is the true species. For Moonstone has many species. Thus I maintain that White Moonstone is true Selenite, and the ivorine variety is — Arabian Stone. Dioscorides calls Selenite Aphroselium, because at night it reflects the moon. This is true of the white stone, for the moon in her splendour is reflected therein as in a mirror. Whether it waxes and wanes with the moon I know not. The stone itself seems a solidified moisture. See Pliny, who differs slightly from Dioscorides, and writes fables according to his wont. See also Solinus in his Polyhistory. Albertus appears to confuse Selenite with Chelonite.
SELLA — A Block of Brass.
SELLA AENEA — A Saddle of Brass.
SELSAS or **SILIX** — A Fern.
SEMAFOR or **SEMAR** — A kind of Fig.
SEMEN VENERIS — Scale of Copper.
SEMPERVIVO — Winter Green, the herb Pyrola.

SENDANEGUM or **SENDANEGI** — i.e., Hematite.

SEPARATORIUM — An oblong Vessel for transmitting liquid in a uniform manner. It has an open mouth, the bore being the size of the little finger; through this the matter is passed. The base narrows off like a needle, and through this the matter is again removed.

SEPARATIO ELEMENTORUM — Much has been said about the Separation of the Elements, yet no such thing takes place. There is simply an alteration which separates the pure from the impure, as when an Alkol is constructed, and the pure Essence is preserved. Then the Separation of the Elements has been accomplished.

SEPARATIO PER ABSCESSUM — Separation by Removal is when parts of diverse nature mutually break away from their conjunction, and depart in opposite directions. It is either a discession or dilution.

SEPARATIO PER ABSTRACTIONEM — Separation by Abstraction is when heterogeneous parts are separated mutually one from another. It is either Ablation or Subduction, accordingly as the matter is liquid or solid.

SEPARATIO PER DILATIONEM — Separation by Dilation at one side is accomplished by means of a trough with a low edge. The trough is oblong, and narrows off on one side to a point, by which it can be turned in the hands, and shaken in various directions. It is called a Running Basin by the Germans.

SEPARATIO PER DILUTIONEM — Separation by Dilution is when the earth is drenched to such an extent that the parts are separated, so that the heavy ones sink and the light float, while those of medium weight occupy a middle place. In the case of muddy, earthy matters, or others reduced to consistency by means of pulverisation, calcination, and kindred processes, this manner of washing was called by the ancients Geopelusia. Abstraction, depletion, occasionally filtration, and similar operations, contribute to separation by dilation. The matters, being dissolved, stirred up, and dilated to their places, are poured through a sieve, as otherwise they will again conjoin.

SEPES — A Sloping Fence, Frame-work of Wood, Balcony.
SEPHIROS — A Hard, Dry, Imposthumous Sore.
SEPTIMEN — Gum-arabic.
SEPTENTRIO — The German Vort, Aqua Fortis.
SEPTUM — A Sluice.
SERAPHIN — A Vast Chorus or Host of the Angelical Powers of Heaven.
SEREX — Sour Milk.
SERICON — Minium.
SERICIACUM — Arsenic.
SERITIS or **SIDERITIS** — The Herb whose Sap is called Dragons' Blood.
SERAPINUS — Gum-arabic.
SERPENS — Serpent, Spirit of Chastity, Mercury.
SERPENTINA — A Powerful Herb for Healing Wounds.
SERPHETA — A Medicine which Dissolves Stone.
SERVUS FUGITIVUS — The Runaway Slave, Mercury. Hermes gives it this name on account of the escaping moisture.
SEULO — Lead.
SIBAR — Quicksilver.
SIBEDATA HIRUNDINARIA — Swallows' Root. Also a Miner's Braying or Pounding Hammer.
SICCARE — To Dry.
SIDIA — A Scale.
SIFANTIS or **SIMPHUS** — Silver Earth.
SIDIA — Liquid Storax.
SIGILLIREN — To Seal Up.

SIGILLUM HERMETIS — A. The mouth of the glass is melted by the heat of a coal fire, and is so sealed. Some make this the Seal of Hermes.

B. To whiten Venetian Glass. Triturate. Have a glass stopper at hand, placed upon the chemical vessel, so that there is no fear of it falling off. Strew powder thereupon to the thickness of a knife. Bury the vessel in the earth, so that it protrudes only to the extent of two fingers' breadth. Make a ring of fire round it. Raise gradually till the powder begins to glow, when the stopper will descend. Remove the coals quickly. Clap a glowing pan upon it. Let it grow cold, or make another, accordingly as it may please you. There is also the ordinary process.

SIGNO IN SAXUM INCISO PUGNARE TERMINOS — To Cut Out Steps in a Flint.

SILEX LAPIS — The German Pebble-stone, commonly used to obtain fire. Hence it is called Silex, because flame springs forth from it. Its general name is Fire stone, though the latter suits Pyrites, as already shown, and with Pliny Pyrites is not a species but a genus; it is indeed every stone from which fire can be struck. Therefore with him a Flint is a Pyrites on account of this property. True Silex is of two kinds:

1. A Pebble, so called by the Germans. It is found by riversides, on banks of sand, in torrents, etc. It is sometimes white in colour. It is employed for other purposes besides producing fire. Sometimes it is of an impure yellow, sometimes of crocus colour, sometimes very gracefully ornamented with white lines.

2. The Horned Rock or Stone of the Germans, called HornBtone on account of its colour, or perhaps of its hard quality. It is indeed so close grained that its parts cannot be distinguished, though there are varieties which differ in this point, the component parts of the stone being distinct even to the eye. This also is called a Firestone by the Germans,

and is used as such. It is found in mines, by rivers like the Elbe, and in the fields of Saxony.

The species are various:
1. Of a white colour.
2. Of a black colour.
3. Of a blue colour.
4. Of a red colour.
5. Of a purple colour.
6. Like Horn in colour.
7. Yellow.
8. Crocus colour.
9. Of livid appearance.
10. White externally and black

The varieties, moreover, have inside different dimensions: long, broad, large, small, forked like coral, etc. Some have the shape of horns. I myself found a flint of this appearance along the Elbe. It was like the head of a serpent, having a serpent's mouth, fangs, eyes, and crown. I also found another like a fortified citadel with towers, and yet a third, which was like a mountain. Natural objects also make impressions on these stones in spite of their hardness. I came across a flint in the same place whereon appeared the impress of a wolf or lion in alto relievo on the surface, looking like the work of a skilled artist. Sometimes faces or limbs of other animals appear, also stars and letters are visible, so far is Nature from idleness. There are, moreover, opaque flints.

1. Metallic, white, Marieburg, combined with white Mica.
2. Found in the river of Treves, containing white fluors within it, and tinged with the hue of Amethyst.
3. Containing a kind of Clay or Chalk.
4. Like Polished Horn.
5. Honey-coloured.
6. Like Purple Jasper.

7. Black with a White Cross.
8. Black with many White Lines.
9. A Small Stone about the size of a Nut, marked with innumerable lines.
10. A variety from Misnia, having lines like an amphitheatre.
11. Another from the same place — Cynocephalous Flints, large and small.
12. Cheese-like.
13. Like a Dutch Cheese, divided down the middle. The surface is of the colour of Cheese; in the middle there are solid Fluors.
14. A poor quality, native in Persia.
15. Of chestnut colour, round, having the appearance of a Calf's Liver.
16. White, from which Glass is manufactured.
SILICES PELLUCIDI — Transparent Flints: —
1. White Transparent Flint.
2. Honey-coloured Transparent Flint.
3. Sand-coloured Transparent Flint.
SILO — Earth.
SILIPIT — Copper.
SILIQUA — A Pod or Husk; a weight of Five Grains. .
SIMMITIUM — Ceruse.
SIMILITUDINES — Similitudes, heavenly Figures which correspond with things that are visible.
SIMUS — A kind of Clay.
SINAPISIS — An Armenian Bolus.
SINOIVIA — A Fatty Substance surrounding the joints of the Body.
SINOPIS — Minium from the City of Sinope.
SINOPIDA — Sinople.
SIPHONS — Pumps.
SIPHINCULUS ORICHALCUS — A Brazen Fire-engine.
SIRA — Orpiment.

SIRICON DE PLUMBO ~ Burnt Recrement, or Cinders, of Lead.
SIRONES ~ Scabby, Irritant Pimples, generally appearing on the hands.
SIRINGAE ~ Lime.
SIRZA, ESCHARA ~ An Edge, or Parapet, of Walls.
SITULA ~ Pails or Water-cans.
SMARAGDUS ~ The Emerald. It holds the third place among Gems, and does so for many reasons, among others because of its pleasing negative colour. It has a Green Tint which surpasses every Herb and Leaf. It is the only Gem which completely absorbs the ocular rays. It refreshes the sight when this has been obscured by looking at other objects. Pliny and Solinus distinguish twelve species.
1. The Scythian Stone, moat excellent of all, the least subject to imperfections, and the hardest, for nothing can cause a flaw in it. It is said to be guarded by Griffins.
2. The Bactrian, deposited in fissures and seams of rocks by the Etesian winds. They are also found on the sea-shore when the sand has been disturbed by the wind.
3. The Egyptian, mined on the Hills and Rocks of the Thebaid.
4. Cyprian, Variegated and Bluish Grey.
5. Attic, more brilliant than others at a distance. Found also in Silver
Mines.
6. Ethiopian, of which there are several varieties.
7. Medicinal ~ Very Green, found in Silver Mines.
8. Carchedonius ~ Called also Chalcedony and Smaragdites.
9. A Species from Tanos.
10. A Flinty Species.
11. Laconian Flinty.
12. Chalcosmaragdus ~ From Cyprian Copper Veins. There are also false specimens. Sometimes we find a Stone which is

half Emerald and half jasper. It is in course of transformation. Emeralds are also made from Crystal by washing in undiluted Acid Wine and soaking in Green Oil. There are certain genera of Emeralds which are found in our own Copper Mines. Albertus states that the Stone exists in Scotland and Britain ; it is produced in Veins of Copper, and sometimes in Submarine Rocks. There are, moreover, dull or blind Emeralds, and others of an opaque quality. Some are clouded ; others have capillary markings, and various flaws and blemishes. The most excellent quality does not alter either in light or shade. The virtue of the Emerald is to counteract poison. They say that if a venomous animal should look at it, it will become blinded. The gem also acts as a preservative against epilepsy ; it cures leprosy, strengthens sight and memory, checks copulation, during which act it will break, if worn at the time on the finger. The old astronomers dedicated the Emerald to Mercury. Chrysoprase, which has golden spots, and Prase, which sometimes has red and white spots, are said to be the mother or palace of the Emerald. But Pliny and Solinus regard Chrysoprase as a species of Beryl.

SMIRIUS or **SANDARCITAS** — The Smyris Stone. Extremely hard and rough. Called by the Germans Emery. The makers of rings, and other artificers, split Stones by concussion against it. Dioscorides enumerates several of its useful qualities. It is a good dentrifice, and heals ulcerated gums.

SOL — The Sun, i.e., Gold; Sonir is another name. It also stands for a day. Lastly, it is the Sun in man, an invisible fiery influence from the celestial Sun, nourishing the innate fire of man.

SOLARIUM — A Gallery.
SOLATER — Quicksilver.
SOLEAE — Sandals.

SOLELASAR ~ Alkali.

SOLUTUM ~ Dissolved.

SOLUTIO DIAKRISIS ~ The first part of Practical Chemistry, whereby the bonds of coagulated substances are dissolved and attenuated. There are several distinct species, but among artists the term is applied more commonly to one process. Sometimes each particular species takes the generic name. Solution is of two kinds: Melting or Liquation, and Segregation or Separation, otherwise, Calcination and Dissolution.

SOLSEQUIUM ~ Sulphur.

SOMNIA ~ Dreams; Operations taking place during sleep, and proceeding from the stars.

SOPHIA ~ Golden Wisdom, whether on account of its Flowers or its Virtues. The noblest of our solidified substances. It is most common among the Illyrians and Liburnians. If a leaf of it be eaten, it causes contraction of the lips. It may be bruised and torn, yet it will reconstruct itself. It abounds in the most excellent sweetness and balm.

SORORES ~ Sister and Brother, Sun and Moon.

SORTILEGIUM ~ A Prophecy of Spirits.

SORUS or **SORY** ~ is of the same genus as Melanteria, and almost of the same colour as Black Atrament. Hence the ancients believed that Sory and Melanteria were the same, and that each became the Copperas Water used by Fullers. But Sory contains so strong a venom that it produces nausea, while Melanteria has no such effect. Dioscorides says that it is found in Egypt, Lybia, Spain, and Cyprus, but the best is Egyptian. This appears blacker when rubbed. It is full of holes, is slightly coarse, astringent, and yields a strong odour when smelt or tasted. But because, when rubbed, it does not emit sparks like Misy, we must reckon it of another genus. Dioscorides also enumerates its potencies and the manner of burning it. See also Pliny. Consult Paulus on

Burnt Sory, and on the Fleshy Growth upon the Toes and Fingers. Almost all these substances are produced when Pyrites is generated, and the raw substances are superior to those which have been completely burnt, while Salt, Wine-lees, Nitre, Lime, etc., profit by the operation of fire. In the ruined Copper Mines of Thuringia, near Obernitz, where dwells the noble family of Thun, with its immense genealogy, a nauseating substance is found, which, in my judgment, is certainly a species of Sory.

SPAGIRIA — The Spagyric Art, is that which treats of the separation of the pure from the impure, so that after the refuse matter has been rejected, the virtue which remains can operate. It is the Art of Distilling and Separating.

SPAGIRUS — Any man who can separate the true from the false, set the good apart from the bad, and the pure from the impure, rejecting duality and cleaving to unity.

SPARA — The Mineral Virtue of the first substance from Ilech, i.e., from the greater minerals.

SPARALLIUM — Uterine Bag.

SPATHA — Any Instrument for Pounding.

SPATHA EXCISORIA — A Scrapel, Scraper.

SPATA LIGNEA — A Wooden Paddle for Melted Substances.

SPATULA — A Broad Instrument used in compound furnaces for increasing and diminishing heat.

SPAUL — Blood.

SPECIFICUM FORMALE — That which restores a species by means of its formal properties. Should it then possess the material virtues as well, it is excellent, and such specifics are sought above all for developing processes. There is both a Tincture and an Oil.

SPECULUM CITRINUM — Citrine Arsenic.

SPECULUM ALBUM — Precipitated Arsenic.

SPECULUM INDICUM — Iron Scaling.

SPECULAR — According to some it is Moonstone, since it is called Affroselenum, or Moon-froth. Others say it is Talc or Gypsum.

SPERMA AQUAE FORTIS — The Sperm of Aqua Fortis.

SPERNIOLUM or **SPERNIOLA** — Blood, Moisture, or Spawn of a Frog, a Slimy and Mucilaginous Matter in Congealed Water — Tadpoles' Poringles.

SPHIERA SOLIS, etc. — According to Senior, it is the Mixed Matter of Two Seeds, out of which the Stone is made. According to Theophrastus, it is Heaven or the Quintessence.

SPINAE — Thorns of four kinds, like Foam or Spume.

SPIRITUS — A Solvent Water produced from a simple and acrid substance, having the nature of a fiery breath, which is the chief part, though it is combined with a gaseous substance. It acquires an aqueous consistence, and possesses a specific virtue. The spirit fluctuates between an aqueous and oleaginous state, and is nearer to the aqueous. In the case of minerals especially, it is sometimes called an Oil. Some spirits are more oleaginous, some more aqueous than others. Their exhalations are also called Spirits, as, e.g., Metallic Smoke, Antimony, Tin, Flower of Salt, Wine, etc.

1. *Clangor Buccinae* says: Spirit is the name of the internal power wherein the powers of Metals lie hidden-the first and highest matter, the Mediator, a vaporous product from Mercury and Sulphur which becomes as tears. Therein lies the Essence.

2. It is a warmth which gives life to and tinges the earth, which is moistened with it and becomes like the coarse part of wood. That which remains in the Ash, and is fixed, is called Mercurial Water, Wind, Life and Soul, Water and Blood, Collars of Gold, Red Gum, Olives, the Cock, the Ox, Crocus, Burnt Ore, the Composite.

3. The Spirit draws the Mercury from the earth, and is still a solid ; when it is fluid, it is called a Spirit. Subsequently, it is called a Body.

4. It is of two kinds-preparatory and tinging. The first prepares, dissolves, and purifies the bodies. This is the Egyptian physician of the parable, and it is derived from Minerals. That which tinges is the Mercury of the Philosophers, extracted from the perfect Body. This is the Alexandrian physic which the Alchemists conceal.

5. Mineral Spirits are of no use for the true Tincture, but only for Sophistication.

6. The Spirit is in the water. It drives and conducts the philosophical clouds as the wind drives clouds and rain. Without the air everything is dead and corrupt. Therefore must the Spirit return to the bodies, and therefore Hermes says the wind bears it in its belly. The hidden air, which dwells in water, takes it along and conducts the water through the Alembic. This cannot take place without the Spirit.

7. The air bears our Stone out, and improves it by ascent and descent, just as the common air improves and nourishes all things, conducting the clouds, and preparing dews and rain, the fire being concealed therein, which the rain has received from the earth and from the shining of the sun during his ascent in the heavens.

If the Spirit were not restored to its body, the body would not return to strength and life.

SPIRITUS CHYMICAE — The Spirits of Chemistry are seven in number:

1. Black Quicksilver.
2. Red Sulphur.
3. Yellow Orpiment.
4 Green Sal Ammoniac.

These four are living as they come from the ore, or dead when they are melted. Marcasite, Bismuth, and Tutty (out of Venus and Mercury) complete the list, and are called Spirits, because they admit of elevation, and because they escape fire.

SPIRITUS ANIMALIS — An Animal Spirit is the Strength of the Soul, by means of which it approaches the Body, having acquired a likeness to the corresponding and stable symmetry of the Heavens.

SPIRITUS FOETENS — Stinking Spirit, that is, Sulphur.

SPODIUS — A species of Tutty; also called Succudus, i.e., Sappy, Juicy.

SPODION — Rust of Copper; also Ios.

SPODIUM — Ash of Gold, Stone of Gold.

SPODUS: —

1. Ash-coloured Soot, heavier than Pompholix. A greyish-black, Crystalline Arsenic.
2. Yellow Crystalline Arsenic, from the refining furnaces of metals.
3. Subterranean Smoke.
4. Black Subterranean Smoke.
5. Green Subterranean Smoke.

SPONGIA or **MARINE FUNGUS** — Attracts and Absorbs Water. It is a Zoophyte, neither Animal nor Vegetable, but having a third nature which is composed of both. Avicenna defines it as a marine body of loose, yielding texture, holding firmly to the matter it adheres to. It is warm in the first, and dry in the second grade. Dioscorides defines a masculine and feminine genus. The first has strong but thin internal pores, of white colour, while the feminine usually has large pores. Some writers add a third species, containing hard stones internally. According to Avicenna, these stones are not so warm as the Sponge itself. Pliny terms them Cystic, or Bladder Stones, because they are good for this urinary

complaint. Certain Nuclei are also found in masculine and feminine Sponges. They are like an almond deprived of its husk, and are most important in medicine, especially for worms in children. Concerning the calcination of Sponges, and their medicinal value, as well as the process of their albification, consult Dioscorides and others. Serapion affirms that Sponges are found at Affengara. Pliny enumerates three genera of Sponges:
1. Thick, very hard, and rough.
2. Less thick and softer; these are called Nanos, from a Greek word, which signifies Necklace.
3. Thin and compact, called Achilleum, the name of a Cake of fine Barley. Serapion says that all Sponges are generated in rocks, in dead shells, small fishes' lime, etc. They are also said to have a certain rational quality, because they contract at the approach of the tide, resist being removed from their places, etc. Pliny seeks to prove that they are nourished by eating shells, that when torn from their rocks they give forth bloody moisture, and that they can be reproduced from the root.

There is the marine and there is the ordinary Sponge which shopkeepers exhibit for sale.
1. Male.
2. Female, which contains Nuclei.
3. The German Sponge, partly marine and partly nourished by the moisture of the meadows. It is called Pofist.

SPONSUS — Mercury.

SPONTUM — Ashes Sprinkled with Water and strewed at the bottom of the Furnace.

SPUMA — Ashes.

SPUMA ARGENTI — Silver Litharge.

SPUMA — Sea Foam or Halcyon. There are five species.

SPUMA NITRI — A kind of coarse Soda or Potass-Affronitum-in Arabic, Baurach.

SPUTA MARI ~ Sea Spittle.
SPUTA BOLETORUM ~ Spittle of Mushrooms.
SPUTUM ~ A Confection of Sulphur and Magnesia. Also called Thickened Gold, and Sulphur Water.
STAG or **STOAC** ~ Coagulation, Solidification.
STAKTI ~ Sputum, Spittle, Spodos.
STANNUM ~ Tin, which differs from White Lead. Many chemists state that Tin is a white metallic substance, not pure, livid, having something of an earthy nature, the product of a pure Quicksilver (fixed or not), clear and white, and of a Red Sulphur, of slight fixity, not pure, and unable to prevail over the Quicksilver. But what they thus predicate of Tin should be referred to White Lead. Stannum, according to Serapion, is mined in the earth, whence it is obtained in lumps. White Lead, on the other hand, is not mined, it is produced from Galena, Pyrites, etc. Pliny states plainly that Stannum is the first liquid to flow in furnaces, and that White Lead is smelted from Black Stones with White Markings. He says also that Stannum is adulterated with White Lead. Stannum among the Arabs is doubtless a more precious metal than White Lead.
STANNUM or **ASEBUM** ~ The Pure Body. Called also Sand.
STANNUM DIVES ~ Rich Lead.
STANNUM MEDIOCRE ~ Raw, Workable Lead.
STANNUM PAUPER ~ Uncalcined Lead.
STARMAR ~ The Mother of the Metals-a hidden smoke whence they are generated.
STIBIUM: ~

1. Roman-Soft, Black, Crustaceous, like a Magnet. Roman Antimony.
2. Mined, Friable, like Polished Iron, from Ilea, an island in the Tyrrhenian Sea.
3. Bohemian, in a White Flint.

4. From Stolberg, containing White, Cubical, Transparent Fluors.
5. Isfeldian, inheres in a White Flint by means of its angular points.
6. Hungarian, containing Gold and Black Lead.
7. Vein of Antimony, like Barren Galena.
8. Silver-coloured, in a Stone, like a hard Pyrites.
9. Found in Ironstone.
10. From Friberg in Misnia, found near a Schist Stone.
11. Steel Wire.
12. Recrement of Steel.
13. Steel Needles.

STELLIO, ADUSTUS, or CINNOBRIUM — The Burnt Lizard, i.e., Pulverised Cinnabar, or Calcined Vitriol.
STELLA OCCIDENS — Sal Ammoniac.
STELLA TERRAE — Talc.
STERCORUM EZEFF — Lltharge
STRATUM SUPER STRATUM, NOTUM CHYMICIS — Layer Superposed upon Layer.
STRIDOR — Preparation, Friction, Rattling of Machinery.
SQUAMA FERRI — Iron Scales.
SQUILLA FIXA — Officinal Squill.
SQUILLINUM AZIZA — Horse Dung.
SQUINANTIA — An Abscess on the Neck.
STUPIO or CALDIDA — Tin.
SUBCISIVUM — A Remainder.
SUBDUCTION — A Downward Abstraction, which is of two kinds, by the Filter and the Clepsydria.
SUBLIMATION — is of two kinds — one is effected by means of Distance, the other by means of Surface. Sublimation does not always denote an ascension, but also a process by which substances become more precious, splendid, and excellent -yet is it true that the vapour ascends. Sublimation means improvement of quality and virtue, as

when Sol is made out of Luna, and is called that which is elevated, that which is above on the heights; but that which is improved may be the highest or the lowest, for they are one.

SUBSOLANUS ~ The East Wind.

SUBTILATIO, SUBTILATION ~ A dissolving or separating of the subtle parts from the gross. There are two kinds ~ long and short ~ the first when the bodies are dissolved for a prolonged time; the second when they are dissolved in a short space.

SUBVESPERUS ~ The South-west Wind.

SUCCU ALBUS ~ Quicksilver.

SUCCUTERE ~ To Trickle, to Extract.

SUCCUS ~ Sap, an Essence having almost the consistency of an extract. Hence the sap is more akin to the magistery, and it carries some corporeity with it, so that if it be compared therewith it is a body, although it is insufficiently elaborated. It is coarser than an essence. It contains some moisture, more or less according to circumstances. As it is reducible to gas, it can easily be obtained. A somewhat liquid sap can be gradually thickened by digestion so as to solidify. It is then Concreted Sap. It is the Apochalismata of the ancients, Rob, Syrup, Must, New Wine, from the fermentation of which is produced a potential extract.

SUCCUBUS ~ A Nocturnal Female Visitant, who causes sleeping men to fancy they
are enjoying the embraces of Venus. Incubus is the Male who plagues women.
These are nightmares, black nocturnal lemures, were wolves, etc.

SUCCINA GRAVIDA ~Solid Succinum.
1. Of a Yellow Colour, in which is a White Butterfly.
2. Of the same colour, in which is a Water Spider.
3. Of the same colour, wherein are Flies.

4. Of the same colour, containing Gnats.
5. Of the same colour, containing Ants.
6. Of the same colour, containing, as it were, a regular swarm of Gnats.
7. Of a Honey Colour, wherein is a Centipede.

SUCCINA LIQUINA -- Liquid or Transparent Succinum: --

1. Falernian Succinum -- White, Clear Amber.
2. Falernian-colour, or White Amber, resembling Moonstone.
3. A Green Amber, mixed with White.
4. A Light Yellow Amber.
5. A Pale Yellow Amber.
6. Yellow Amber.
7. Like a Topaz -- Golden Yellow.
8. An Orange-coloured Amber.
9. Like a Hyacinth.
10. Saffron-colour.
11. Like a Chrysolite-Fire-colour.
12. Red, like Cornelian.
13. Like a Carbuncle-Red, Granite-colour.

SUCCINUM PRUSSICUM -- Very White, Precious Opaque, Prussian Succinum: --

1. Whitest and Best Amber or Hornstone.
2. White.
3. Dull White.
4. Whitish Yellow.
5. Pale Yellow.
6. Yellow.
7. Wax-colour.
8. Yellow, having White Lines.
9. Honey-colour.
10. Orange-colour.
11. Dark Honey-colour.

SUCCINA MIXTA ~ Succinum mixed with other Saps:
1. Succinum of Honey-colour, combined with Atrament which continually.
2. Of a Honey-colour, containing fragments of Wood and Bark.
3. Of a mixed Ashen and Honey-colour.
4. Mixed with many colours ~ a newly-found variety.
5. An Adulterated Species from the Brandenburg Marsh, consolidated from Resin and sold for Myrrh. It does not differ in colour from true Succinum, and has the same smell when burnt.
6. Called Oriental Falernian by the Prussians, because, when burnt, it does not yield the odour of Succinum, but a sweet and aromatic odour like Mastic. An Oriental Succinum, clear as water.
7. Oil of Succinum is a powerful remedy in Epilepsy.
8. The Dross of Succinum.
9. The Salt of Succinum.
10. Native Manufactured Amber.
SUDOR ~ Permanent Water.
SUFFO ~ A Pig Nut.
SULPHUR ~ In Arabic Chibur, Albusao, is a part of the Stone of the Philosophers, warm and dry in the fourth grade. It is the fat of the earth, thickened by a moderate cooking, until hardened and made dry. Rightly considered, it is produced from the purest, driest earth, wherein fire altogether prevails. It is a sort of warm and dry vapour, the cause and father of metals. To sum up, Sulphur is Earth Cooked by Heat, and changed by the watery, fiery, and earthy matters passing through it.

Sulphur is obtained in Germany from mountain mines and marshes. The latter is Apyron, or unforged Sulphur, because it has not come in contact with fire. This is also the simple, natural Sulphur, called, vulgarly, living Sulphur, because it

produces Metals, and is one of their elements. Dioscorides praises Apyron, because it shines brilliantly, and is not stony. It abounds at Melon and Lipara. Its nature is heating, exciting, cooking. The species of Sulphur are as follows:
1. A Sulphur which solidifies into a cloddy earth. This is properly called living; it is the only genus employed by physicians; it is transparent, brilliant, compact, excellent.
2. Exceptionally fine.
3. Like to Goslarian Mica. Concerning all these, consult Pliny, Avicenna, and others. There is great affinity between Sulphur and Bitumen. In the Eolian Isles it is collected, and very readily kindles the fire. It is found in great abundance, and is exported to Italy, and thence to us. Concerning its sublimation, solution, and melting, consult the chemists, for these exceed my purpose.

Manufactured Sulphur is that prepared and perfected by art, that which has been treated by fire, burning Sulphur, the substance used everywhere. It comes imperfect from the mines. There are three species — Gleba, used by fullers; Ezula, employed in dyeing wool; while the third is Elychina. Sulphur is a formative principle, partly gaseous, partly fiery, partaking of an ethereal nature; it is that whence strength proceeds, and life inheres in things. Hence it is called the Balm of Nature — Sal Terminator, Sulphur Informator — possessing plastic virtue. Mercury is an unctuous vapour. As for the essential form of Sulphur, chemists leave this to physicists. Although Mercury is a living, active, spiritual principle, which can be rarefied, it is a dry, acidulating, preservative Salt. Sulphur is strong-smelling, warm, and very pure. Note the peculiar significance of the term Mercury; it cannot be compared with liquid Quicksilver. The life of these elements is not Galenian or Aristotelian, but chemical. Consult Paracelsus.

Sulphur is the seed of the stone, and is of two kinds — an external, whereby the internal is born in Mercury, which, being earthy, combustible, useless, is removed as menstrual water from a child. The internal Sulphur is the power which makes and prepares the body and cannot be separated from it, because it is inherent, congenital in its very heart and substance. It is originally white, becomes red by means of heat, just as food in the belly by means of the liver, and is the form of the matter, the soul and ferment of the stone, the husband, king, and bridegroom — Red Arsenic, Burnt Ashes, our Gold, Philosophical Gold, Dry, Stony Water, Fire, Earth, Red Stone, Coagula, Mercury, Tincture. Ordinary Sulphur, by whatever name we may call it, remains an enemy of all metals; consumes, blackens, and destroys; but Philosophical Sulphur is life-giving, matures, makes black, but destroys not, and is called Sulphur because it is never found in the perfect body.

Tercusculus in his *Epistles* says: Among metals there are two kinds of Sulphur — one can be separated, the other cannot just as in man there are two kinds of blood — one that becomes flesh, and another which departs by means of perspiration. Essential Sulphur is a real working of the air and of fire, which digests and cooks its proportioned and cognate earth and warm waters in a Mercury. The Mercurial Water is a Dissolved Gold; a Vitalising Water, Incombustible, Philosophic Gold, found in Sol and Luna.

SULPHUR RUBEUM — Arsenic.

SULPHUR — one of the three principles of which all substances are composed of an Oily and Inflammable Matter.

The general species of Sulphur are as follows :

1. White Liquid Sulphur, not unmixed with Alum, obtained at certain seasons during the overflow or inundation of a

lake, and deposited on the surface of the earth. From this Sulphur there is a Natural Oil extracted.

2. Clay-like Neapolitan, from the Forum Vulcanium, as Pliny terms the
place, naturally concreted into a fibrous or capillary mass.

3. Pure, Native, Neapolitan, Clay-like Sulphur, not tried by fire.

4. Fossile Neapolitan, of the natural colour, but combined with a Greyish
Earth.

5. Clay-like, Neapolitan, Living Sulphur, in a Hard, Grey Atrament.

6. Living, Grey, Cloddy, Native Sulphur, in a White Earth.

7. Grey, Living, Native Sulphur, having a Grey, Petrine Cortex.

8. Living, Grey Sulphur, in a Grizzly-coloured Cortex.

9. Black, Living Sulphur, combined with a Soft and White Sulphur.

10. Black, Manufactured Sulphur, of poor quality.

11. Oil of Sulphur, similar to Liquid Bitumen, derived from Liquid Sulphur.

12. Oil of Sulphur, derived from Native Sulphur.

13. Elychnia — a Preparation of Sulphur, by Clarifying or Straining.

14. Sulphureous Neapolitan Earth, from which Sulphur is excocted in large
quantities.

15. A Stone of a Black and Ruddy Colour, which is the Parent of Sulphur. Sulphur-stone.

16. Sulphur, of Blue Colour, known to the people of Ausonia, and perchance to those of Spain.

SUCCI EFFLORESCENTES SEU EXTRACTI — Extracted Or Exuding Saps:

1. Goslarian Pyrites, from which all species of Atrament are derived.
2. Radberg Pyrites, from which Misy, Melanteria, and thin White Atrament exude.
3. A Hard Vein of Silver-coloured Pyrites, vulgarly called Aquatic, like Sibana; when exposed in an open and sunny place, a thin, White Atrament and Alum exude. When exposure to the air continues too long, it degenerates into a crumbling and earthy condition.
4. Pyrites, native in that substance which is called Dryita, namely, the Wood of Oaks hardened into Stone. Atrament and Misy exude from these Pyrites.

Five species of Sulphur are excocted from Pyrites at Dresden:
1. Of the colour of Rude, Red, Transparent Silver — Red Sulphur — Red Golden Earth.
1a. Of the colour of Red, Transparent Quicksilver.
2. Of the colour of Quicksilver.
3. Of the colour of Native Sandarac.
4. Like that Mercury which is termed Sublimated and Pulverised.
5. Of black colour, like Black Pebbles, out of which White Lead is excocted. The four following species are derived from Moravian Pyrites, and are of a heavy and loathsome smell:
1. Green, having Lighter Green Zones.
2. Ochrine, like English Plumbaria.
3. Of various colours, having White, Black, Waxen, Yellow, and Honey
colour Zones; also frequently like to the Plumage of the Peacock.
4. Citrine, containing Honey-coloured Sulphur, like a Rude, Red Silver;
smooth on the outside.
Also: —

1. Friberg Pyrites, combined with Sterile Plumbago, out of which Sulphur is
obtained, mined in large quantities at Scharfenberg.
2. Radberg Pyrites, from which various species of Sulphur are excocted, as
indeed is possible with all Pyrites, but the smell is more hurtful than
that of Native Sulphur, and quickly induces cold in the head.
3. Burnt Tartar.
4. Oil of Tartar.
5. Tartar from Wine Lees, the Bitter Recrement or Earthy Sediment which is found in the bottom and at the sides of jars or Flagons.

SULPHURIS AQUA, ATHICTES ~ Alum made from Sulphur.

SULPHUR INCOMBUSTIBILE ~ Incombustible Sulphur, the perfect work of Gold and Mercurial Water of the Perfect Body, the Soul of the Metals, which operates in the Mercury, and the masculine seed which has in itself the property of all Metals, and is their key. But it cannot tincture of itself without the spirit. It is an essential fire which surpasses the flames; it does not destroy the Mercury, but changes the lowest part of it with its qualities. When it is like a gum, it is called Mercury; when it is hard and white, it is called Sulphur. The Sulphur of Metals is Quintessence.

SULPHUR VITRIOLATUM ~ Sulphur derived from Vitriol by decoction in water, upon which it floats.

SULPHUR VIVUM ~ Unstrained Sulphur.

SUMA ~ Tartar.

SUMBI ~ Sour; also Saffron.

SUMMA OPERATIO SIDERUM IN HOMINE ~ That Influence of the Stars on Man which descends during sleep in the night.

SUPERNUS ~ North-east.
SUPERFICIES ~ White of Egg.
SUPERNA MEDICINA CUM DURUM AB IMPURO ~ Essential Virtue Separated from Substance.
SUPREMI PANES ~ The top part of roasted ore.
SYDIA ~ The Moon.
SYLO ~ The Universal World.
SYLPHES ~ Pigmies, Little Men.
SYLVESTRES or **SYLVANS** ~Are Men of the Air, Spirits of the Air, Aerial Spirits, which inhabit the woods and deserted places in the solitudes of the same. They are also called Fauns, and are much taller than ourselves, and also stronger, but they are incapable of speech. One such was captured by German traders, but was not treated in a severe manner, for they placed food and drink before him. He, however, refused all nourishment, and struck with a great fear, and being in a continual dread, he died on the third day. This race is said to be unable to live longer among men, being a monstrosity, unnaturally produced among natural animals.
SYMAR ~Verdigris.
SYNOPIS PONTICA ~Moisture. ? Pontic Water.
SYPHITA PRAVA ~St. Vitus's Dance.
SYPHITA STRICTA ~Somnambulism.
SYRENES ~ Marine Monsters Born of Nymphs.

TABAISIR ~ i.e., Ashes, Orpine; an Arabic term.
TABALLA ET TABIELLA TRANSVERSA ~ A Transverse Counter.
TABELLAE ~ Crossed Boards.
TABERGETA ~ i.e., Bleaching.
TABULA ~ A Screen.
TABULA FERREA ~ is a Hemispheric Instrument with Furrows or Cavities for receiving the Overflow in Testing and Assaying.
TABULATA FOLLIUM ~ The Boards of the Bellows.
TAL ~ Peacocks' Slime, Alkali.
TALCUM or **TALC** ~ A Transparent Material, Brilliant; similar to those Pearls called Unio, or to the Onion, as it is composed of many layers, and is of flaky nature. There are four species-white, yellow, black, and red.
TALC ~ Cocted Wine.
TALK ~ is White like Gypsum, and is therefore called Spar-plaster, Mortar, Magnesian Limestone, etc.

TALPA or **TULAXIS** — A Mole, Rat.
TARITH or **RUSCIA** — is Mercury.
TARO — i.e., the Resin or Oil called Lentiscum.
TARGAR — i.e., Oil of Juniper.
TAIN — Armenian Bolus, which see.
TARTAR — i.e., Tartarum.
TARTARUS — is Calculus of Wine, called Wine-stone by similitude, the stone, or deposit, which cleaves to the sides of vessels. Paracelsus uses it for stone in the bladder or kidneys, or the albuminous deposit in the other members which causes gout.
TALCUM — is believed to be a word of Arabic origin, signifying little sparkling Stars, and it is given by metallurgists to the stone which is composed of layers or flakes, and which is always impervious to fire. Some of these stones are white, dense, and fragile, like Selenite or Moonstone; some have a green light, and are flexible, though very dense. Such are found in the mines of Misnia. There are other species which seem to consist of sparkling Scales, and can be dissolved in water. These are Catsilver or Talc.
TASSUS — i.e., A Worm in the Entrails.
TEFRA or **KONIS** — Ash.
TEGULA — A Mufle [chemical term].
TEGULA FORNICATA — is an Earthen Vessel; vessel of oblong shape, designed as a cover for other vessels to protect the matter, and through which ventilation is also secured. There are several variations in the details of its construction.
TELON — As it were, a Dart of Fire.
TEMPERATURA — A Flux.
TEMPERATURA PRIMA — The First Degree of Heat.
TEMPERATURA SECUNDA — The Second Degree of Heat.
TEMPERATURA TERTIA — The Third Degree of Heat.

TEMPERAMENTUM — is anything which softens the inherent nature of a substance, and puts a curb thereon, by admitting another nature, as Burnt Wine, Ardent Water, etc.

TENACITAS GLUTINIS — A Mineral Resin or Balsam, as that of the Terebinth is a Tree Resin.

TENTA — A Plug of Lint that is put into wounds; a small Spiral Cylinder of Scraped Linen, Rags for Moistening, a Cylinder of Split Lint.

TENUM — A Substance used by Cobblers. ? Cobblers' Wax.

TERAGOLINIEM — i.e., Composed by the Hand:

1. White, Slimy Earth, which contains Petrified Shells.
2. White, Soapy Earth, Fuller's Earth.
3. Very White Earth of Milos, celebrated by the ancients.
4. White Lemnian Earth or Stamped Earth. Ours is adulterated. The genuine is from Lemnos.
5. Grey, Slimy Earth.
6. Greasy, Soft, Ash-like Julian Earth.
7. Ashy Ultramarine Earth of Eretria, used in Medicine.
8. Earth of Patavina, containing Lazuli; clods of it are found in fields. When broken, there is a very white, soft, crumbling earth in the centre, which soon changes colour under the influence of the air, and turns blue.
9. Grey Spanish Earth, out of which Melting Vessels are made.
10. Grey Irish, avoided by all venomous animals. There is said to be a specimen in Suevia.
11. Very rare Giselan, Grey, of which Vessels are made, which exude new Wine and other liquids.
12. Thick, Greyish Waldenberg, of which they made Vases, which do not absorb moisture, and are used to hold Aquafortis.
13. Grey, Hard, and Crustaceous, of which they make Kettles, etc., in Italy.

14. Grey Anneberg, mixed with Potters' Rubrica.
15. Crumbling, Violet-brown, Juliacensis.
16. Manufactured Saponaceous, used for Washing Clothes.
17. Green Saponaceous of Thuringia, near Biehlingum.
18. Yellow, Slatey Earth.
19. Like Ochre, from which Lead is smelted, at Ilmena.
20. Tripoli Earth.
21. Alana, from the country of the Alani, now called Valachi.
22. Red, Sandy, Metallic, in Aldenberg; the slightest touch stains the hands.
23. Hard, Red, in the Copper Mines of Islebia, and called Red, etc.
24. The same, Red and Crumbling.
25. Red, Soft, Scissile, Waldenberg, not unlike a vein of minium.
26. Red, Stony, Rodicensian, with which Marl is cut out.
27. Earth in which a species of Mined Cadmia is found.
28. Soft, Greasy, Dull red Juliacensian, with which Bolus is dug out.
29. Black Bituminous Earth.
30. Terra Ampelitis, used by doctors and vine dressers.
31. Pacodian Earth, also medicinal.
32. Crumbling, similar to Scales, and out of which Iron is Smelted.
33. Lemnian or Stamped, the most medically celebrated of all Earths.
34. Earth from which Tiles are made.
35. Nitrous Thuringian Earth, which in many places occurs on the surface of the land.
36. Aluminous Misnensian, of various colours, but chiefly Ochrine and Ferruginous.
37. Grey Aluminous Misnensian, which shines like Pyrites in a few instances.

38. Atramental or Cuprine Earth.
39. Sulphureous Earth.
40. Carbonaceous from the Belgian and Misnensian Turfs, which are used in place of Coal. In Antwerp it is called Durff; in Misnensia, Dorpte; it is useful in places where wood is scarce, and in some operations of smelting.

TEREHINTHIA — i.e., Resin.

TERENIABIN — The Fat of Manna, Wild Honey, approaching black, a deposit from the Air, and not from bees; it is found upon grass, trees, and herbs, and it is as sweet as true honey. It is found largely during the summer months-June, July, August. The ancients call it Threr.

TERDINE — The Herb Angelica.

TERRA MELIA — This is the Terra Melina of Pliny, a kind of natural white colour, of which the best quality was found at Melos. Because at the present day it is brought from Tripoli of Syria, it is called the Stone of Tripoli. There is also an oil, an unguent, a species of quince, and an herb, called Apiastrum, to which the term Melinus is applied. It is found at Hildesheim in Saxony, and gives forth a smoke or vapour when touched. It has little of the quality of a stone, for it is soft, crumbling, and easily dissolved.

TERRA AMPELITUS — A kind of Resinous Earth, found at Seleucia in Syria, and very similar to Bitumen. Pliny (1. 35, c. 16) tells us that it was the custom to cover vines with it for the destruction of vermin, and hence its name. It has affinity with coal, and uniform brilliance, is dissolved by oil, and has a cooling and dispersing quality in medicine. The black is commended by Pliny and Dioscorides, who disparage the grey and white varieties, which do not dissolve in moisture. It is called by the Germans Black Chalk.

TERRAE — There are certain earths which are found in mines, which from their colour seem a species of clay, but are distinguished therefrom by their dryness. Some qualities are white, some black, some are like Pnigitis, others like a slime, others again are ochrine in colour, others reddish, purple, or like Sandarac. There are green, grey, and blue varieties. White Earth bears various names, according to its specific nature and the place where it is found. It seldom occurs in metallic mines, but is found in mines of its own. There is, however, as it were, a marrow, or pith, of rock which is found in mines, and is of white colour. It is called by the Germans Lithomarge, and is like the marrow in the bones of animals. It is not so moist as clay, nor of such a stick fatness or greasiness. It is sometimes found hard and dry. It is found at Jena in Thuringia, and Hercynia ; there it is white, crumbly, and hardened. It is used as a powder by boys to dry blots in writing. There is a variety in Saxony which is similar to Alabaster.

TERRA LEMNIA-- Under the heading of Rubrics, we have already made extended reference to this earth, which in fact is a species of Rubrica, in colour similar to Minium. It is also the Sigillated Earth of Avicenna, which was stamped by the priests of Diana with the image of Diana, and was sacred to her. It was stamped also with the image of a goat, as we have already said, and was sprinkled with goats' blood. Thus sprinkled, as we may learn from Galen, it was supposed to possess the highest medicinal qualities. Scarcely any true Lemnian Earth now reaches us because of the jealousy of the Turks, to whom Lemnia is now subject. Cretan Earth is used largely as a substitute. There is also an adulterated material from Italy which is sold as an antidote to poison. The Emperor of the Turks holds the mines of Lemnos, and sends some of it by his ambassadors with great ceremony to our own Emperor as a protection against poison and plague. It is supposed to abound especially at the base of that mountain in Lemnos where Vulcan was said to have his forge. Nicander informs us that it is a special antidote to lethal poisons. Galenus, Pliny, Serapion, Paulus and Avicenna may all be consulted as to its nature and virtues. Platearius calls it Aromatic Calx, Argent Earth, and Saracenic Earth. He also warns his readers that it can be easily sophisticated. But every kind of pastille which I have beheld is of a pallid quality because of its combination with earth, and I have not seen any that correspond in appearance to Minium, as Pliny affirms. It is a fitting thing that man, who was created by God out of a red earth, should find in a red earth his best antidote for poison.

There is also the white and red Sigillated Earth of His Majesty the Emperor, which is stamped with the impression of a scorpion, and is composed by our own Lord, but must yield in the matter of its virtues to the Turkish Lemnian Earth.

TERRA ERE TRIADES — Dioscorides enumerates two species, White and Grey. It is Earth of Eretria in the island of Eubcea, and was used in medicines and painting. The grey was considered to be the finer quality. Its species, its qualities, its appearance, and the methods of its preparation are described by Pliny (l. 35, c. 16). It is found in the potteries of Saxony, and on the banks of such rivers as the Elbe.

TERRA SAMIA — was also duplex according to Dioscorides. It is an Earth of that island of the Ionian Sea, which is very near Ionia, and opposite Ephesus. This earth was very good, and very celebrated. It had the highest healing qualities, and was equally excellent for the manufacture of vases, which were made in great numbers at Samos. They were so hard that they could be used for cutting other substances. The two species of Saurian Earth were:

1. White, Light, adhering like a gluten to the tongue when touched by it. Soft, Sappy, and Crumbling. Some call it Collyrion.

2. Hard, Crustaceous, very dense and close. We ourselves have a species of Samian Earth which is obtained from potteries in the neighbourhood of Hierichunt, not far from the Elbe.

TERRA CHIA — is White and Crustaceous; it is like Samian Earth, both in appearance and quality, as Dioscorides and Pliny inform us. It is exceedingly good for the skin, and may be used as a detergent substitute for Nitre in baths. Women are supposed to be especially benefited by it. This earth is found in many parts of Saxony, particularly in the mines near the town of Belzick.

TERRA SELINUSIA — has the same nature as the two preceding earths, especially the Brilliant, White, or Milky, and Crumbling species. This is on the authority of Pliny and Dioscorides. It is used as a plaster or whitewash for walls.

TERRA CIMOLIA — Of this there are two species, according to Dioscorides — one white, the other approaching transparency. The best has an inherent greasiness, and is cold to the touch. It has a cooling, restraining, and expelling quality. This earth was formerly well known not only to doctors but to basketmakers and silver smelters. It is called Argent Earth. Celsus praises it, and says it is of subcerulean colour. Consult Serapion. Under the name of Tenchi rrzolea there seem to have been several varieties of earths included, and the opinions concerning them have varied. There is a Spanish variety which is black; there is also one of greenish colour, and some suppose it to have been that sandstone on which swords were sharpened. But here, as elsewhere, when we have no actual knowledge, we presume to speak nothing that is definite.

TERRA RUBEA — Armenian Bolus.

TERRA AURI — Gold Litharge.
TERRA ARGENTI — Silver Litharge.
TERRA FIDELIS, TERRA COELESTIS, COELUM TERRESTRE — i.e., Silver.
TERRA HISPANICA — i.e., Vitriol.
TERRA FOETIDA — i.e., Sulphur.
TERRA CLIVULI — i.e., Step cut in the Rock.
TERRA FERRUGINEA — Earth containing Iron.
TERRA FERE LUTEA — Slimy Earth.
TERRA SIGILLATA — Red-coloured Earth.
TERRA FIGULA — Potters' Earth.
TERRA RUBEA — i.e., Orpiment.
TERRA FOLIATA — Leaves, Mecurial Water, wherein Gold is sown. Mirerius says that it is Mercury which collects in the Aludel, in order that water may be again poured upon it. Therefore, says Hermes, sow thy Gold in Terra Foliata. It is the spiritual water. The white Terra Foliata is the crown of victory spiritual water extracted from ashes of other bodies.
TESTA — Bloom (metallurgic term).
TESTA — any Baked Earthen Vessel.
TESTUDO — Sea Spume, Meerschaum.
TESTUDO — A Slug or Snail.
THAMATICA — An Art by which those Machines are Invented which are driven by Air or Water-power.
THAPHNEUS — A Cleansed and Purged Medicine, a Preparation of Arsenic (?).
THEBAYCO — Copper.
THEMYANTHUS — Gold.
THERIACA — Poison, Ferment, Matter of the Stone.
THIMIA — The Vessel by which we make a Descending Distillation.
THISMIA — The Bearing or Direction of the Vein.
THRACIAS — North-west.
THUCIA — Calamine.

THUCIOSI ~ Living Sulphur.

THYITES ~ A Stone which takes its name from mortars, now unknown. Dioscorides says that it is of semi-green colour, and comes from Ethiopia. He cites little from other authors about it. Some say that it is the Stone Lyncis, which see.

TIFACOUM ~ Quicksilver.

TIGILLA RUDIA INFIMIE PUTEI PARTI SUPER IMPOSITA ~ A Pent House, or Roof in a Pit.

TIGILLA ~ Lining Timbering.

TIGILLA TERETIA ~ Stakes over props of platforms.

TIGILLA TRANSVERSARIA ~ Grain of the Wood.

TIGILLA TRANSVERSORIA ~ A Cross-beam.

TIGILLA ALLIIS TIGILLIS IN TERRA DEFOSSIS IMMISSA ~ Pile-driving, Stakes set one over the other in the Earth.

TIGNA ~ A Drawing Cage [mining term].

TIGNA IN FRONTE ET TERGO PUTEI COLLOCATA ~ A Windlass Tree, used for Wells.

TIGNA IN TERRA DEFOSSA ~ Seats for Workmen.

TIGNA LONGISSIMA ~ A Stringing Plank.

TIGNA OBLIQUE DESCENDENTIA ~ Tiebands, Stripe, Hoop.

TIGNA STATUTA ~ Baluster.

TIGNORUM SPECIES ~ Struts.

TIGNUM ~ A Column.

TIGNUM CUJUS FORAMEN PENETRAT AXICULUS DUPLEX ~ A Swipe, Swape, or Drawing Beam.

TIGNUM MOBILE ~ A movable Column.

TIGNA PER INTERVALLA LOCATA ~ Props for supporting the perpendicular beams in mines.

TIGNA HUMI STRATA ~ Stakes Set in the Ground.

TIGNUM BREVE ~ A kind of Wedge.

TIN, TIFATUM ~ Sulphur.

TINCKAR — i.e., Band of Gold, i.e., Borax.
TINGERE — To Tinge is to Change the Nature.
TINGIREN — Tinging and Transmuting.
TINKAR — is the Green of the Ore, or Water made out of Salt.
TILETTEN — Iron Plates.
TINCTURA — That which Penetrates and Permeates Bodies with its Colour, as Saffron does Water.
TINCTURA — Tincture is a Specific Arcanum, having a certain essence, qualities, and forms, and also a colour, which it can impart, and so, as it were, infuse its own appearance into a substance. If this Tincture be properly developed, it will have the consistency and perspicuity of a most tenuous nature, just as the air is perspicuous, pure, and coloured in a certain way, transparency not interfering with the possession of colour. So also it can exist a long time without depositing a sediment. When so developed, it will impart an unchanging and persisting quality to a thing in proportion to its capacity for receiving it. And so in medicine, it conduces, above all, to the restoration of health, and the confirmation and strengthening thereof. By its high potency, it may be fitly said to be a renovator, acting upon every member, the blood, the spirit, and the vital heat. Tincture is of two kinds — open and brought out. The first spontaneously manifests on the surface, and frequently takes place in metals.

That which is brought out is produced from the centre to the surface, and is extracted. There is in many substances a latent virtue or colour, which is called potential, and is to be developed by processes of exaltation, before it is extracted. Most noble are the tinctures of metals, and there are those also which are found in the investigation of vegetable natures.

TIPSARIA — i.e., Water of Barley.

TITAR — Unknown.
TITANOS — i.e., Calx from Gypsum.
TOPASIUS: —
1. Topaz.
2. A Dark Topaz.
TOPAZION — A Gem, first found in the Arabian Island of Chitus, when certain pirates, pressed by hunger and driven by tempest, dug up herbs and roots therein. Or it is named after the cloudy island of the Red Sea, which navigators gators sought so often, and which they therefore called Topazion, which signifies to seek in the tongue of the Troglodytes. From this island, on the testimony of Pliny, was the Topaz first brought by the Egyptian queen, Berenice. But some say that it was found originally in the Thebaid. A pallid species exists in Hungary. There are also certain fluors in our mines, of a mud-colour, which are not unlike Topaz. Pliny distinguishes two species of Topaz: the Prazoin and the Chrysepteron, like to the Chrysopras. Albertus, Evax, and others, speak of a Golden variety, which even exceeds Gold in the depth of its colour. It is said to check lust, and to make men chaste and full of life.
TOPHI ET PUMICES: —
1. Grey-white Pumice Stone.
2. Theophus, which is rarer.
3. Thuringian, which is found in the Helba, and is thrown up abundantly on the banks. It is used as a cement for walls, and is of grey colour.
4. Stones which are found in the beds of thermal springs, similar to Thophis (unknown).
5. Stones found in channels of aqueducts, more solid than Thophis.
6. A kind of Stalactite Stone.
7. White Misnian Rabschicius, from which calx is burnt.
8. White, fistulous Stone of Misenus.

9. The same, but like grapes on the surface.
10. White Crustaceous Misenian.
11. White Misenian, full of shells.
12. White Misenian, with impressions of oak and alder leaves.
13. Very hard, chestnut-coloured, from the warm springs of the Carolines.
14. Yellow, also from the channels of warm springs.
15. The same, but found pendent like stalactite.
16. A deposit on everything that is left in water.
17. Yellow-coloured, pallid, globular Stones from the thermal springs of the Carolines.
18. Smooth, yellow, and so perfectly round that they would seem to have been made by art.
19. Orange.
20. Purple.
21. Chestnut brown.
22. Green.
23. Yellow, with a smooth surface.
24. Like pulse in size, shape, and colour; found in the springs of the Carolines.
25. Very like Coriander Seed.

TORREFACTOR — A Roaster.
TORUSCULA — is an Erudition of Resin from the Pine Tree.
TRACHSAR — is every Metal in its own Ore.
TRAHE SIVE CAPSA — A Sledge.
TRAHA CUI IMPOSITA EST CAPSA — A kind of Truck.
TRANSUDATIO — If in descending distillation an essence drawn forth should sweat out, it is received by drops into a proper vessel. The focus is above, round the ergastulum, whence it is said to be acted on by a circular fire. It is performed in a descending furnace, with a descending bath, etc.

TRANSVERSUM — Cross-wise.

TRARARMES — The Acts of Shades and Spectres who are invisible, but can nevertheless be heard.

TRICA or **TICA** — Good.

TRICOR — Gold.

TRIFERTES — Spirits Inhabiting the Element of Fire.

TRIGIAS — i.e., Tartarum Trigia, i.e., Refuse.

TRIGONUM — is the Fourfold Transmutation of Astral Spirits, according to the number of the four elements; each reigns for two hundred years. When an igneous trigonum begins for a superior planet its conjunction takes place in a fiery sign, so long as this igneous trigonum endures, and so for the rest.

TRIPES — An Iron Vessel for the reception of a Matter when Heated.

TRIPUS — A Three-legged Stool.

TRITORIUM — The ordinary Funnel, a Transmitting Vessel, broad at the top, and having a handle attached to it.

TROCHLEA — A Pulley.

TRONUS and **TRONOSIA** — Celestial Dew, born of Air, very sweet, thick, tenacious, good smelling, generated in whiteness out of the Mercury of a middle region, separated from all Salt and Sulphur; it falls in spring and summer, and is found sticking to the leaves of trees.

TRULLA — A Trowel.

TRUPHAT — That Mineral Virtue which brings every Metal to its own stage of development.

TUBEL — is the Scale or part given off in hammering from any metal on the anvil.

TUBULI — Little Tubes.

TUMBABA, TIMPABAR, CAPAPIUM, THION — Names of Living Sulphur.

TUMBALUM — i.e., Rubel. ? Red, or a kind of Vine.

TUMBIL — i.e., Earth.

TURBA MAGNA — is the Innumerable Multitude of the Stars of the Firmament of Heaven; a Presage of all those things which are done in the worlds of the four elements.
TURBITH MINERALS — is Mercury without any Corrosive, precipitated in a sweet state.
TURPETHUM — is a Specific Fixed Coagulate, whence all impurities have been extracted; also whatever is endowed with an unconquerable volatility; it is found separated in the bottom of the vessel, and is obtained chiefly from minerals. The term appears to be of Arabic origin, and signified either the Cortex or Bark of the herb Fennel-green or Southern-wood, or else the Root thereof. It was afterwards applied to Medicine prepared from herbs of the genus Tithymalus, which includes Spurge or Sea-lettuce. But in the present connection, the term is applied not in things vegetable, but in the mineral kingdom.
TURSIET — Armenian Salt.
TUTIA — Calamine, Katimia.
TYMPANUM — A Basket.
TYMPANUM QUOD EX FUSIS CONSTAT — Machine-work, Motive-power, Gear.

ULCUS AESTIOMENUM ~ A Cancerous Abscess.
ULPHI, UFFI, INSI ~ A Specimen of the Stone. See Morien, fol. 34.
ULPHA, LAPSATURA ~ Ore left unbaked by the Furnace.
ULRACH ~ Dragon's Blood.
ULYSSIPONA ~ The Herb Serpentaria; most serviceable in Colic.
UMBILICUS VENERIS ~ is a Stone or Gem, sometimes of a dull-red, sometimes white or purple. It is called the Navel of Venus, being flat on one side, while the other is rounded after the manner of the belly of a beautiful girl, and has lines like the snail-shell encircling it. The Germans, having regard to its shape, which is like that of the horse-bean, and to the place whence it comes, denominate it Sea-bean, for it is found among shells on the sea-shore. It is said to conciliate the favour of girls; it improves their figure, increases their beauty, wins love for them, and is serviceable in their special complaints.

UMBRA ~ Shadow, Red Earth.
UMBRAGINES ~ Pygmies.
UMBRATILES, or **UMBRATILIA CORPORA** ~ Phantasmal Apparitions which appear to men under a changing guise, by means of the hidden stellar potencies. Such are the lemures, etc. Phantoms of this kind are the production of magical power.
UNCAM ~ Quicksilver.
UNCIA ~ An Ounce.
UNDAE ~ Aerial or Terrene Spirits.
UNGOSA ~ The Excrements of Men and Cattle.
UNGUENTUM CROCEUM ~ The Elixir.
UNGULA ~ A Disease of the Eye.
UNITAS TRITHEMII ~ The Reduction of the Triad into the Monad by the Subtraction of the Duad. It is supernatural and spagyrical, the foundation of the search into abstruse things. From this ultimate division of philosophy transition is accomplished to the primal division by the mediation of moral philosophy.
UNTERRAUCHSTEIN ~ A Species of Rock.
UNTERSCHWELLEN ~ Another Species of Rock.
URINA ~ Resolved Salt, generated in the liver, and expelled through its proper outlet; the superfluous Saline Excrement naturally expelled.
URINA PUERORUM ~ Mercury.
URINA TEXI ~ Tartar Water.
URINA VINI ~ Vinegar, but the term is also applied to the Urine of persons who are incessant wine-drinkers.
URITUR ~ Cinnabar.
USFIDA ~ Scoria of Gold.
USIFUR ~ Cinnabar from Sulphur and Mercury.
USIFUR or **VAFUR** ~ Some say that it is Minium.
USRUB, URSUB, UZURUP ~ Saturn, i.e., Lead.
USURAT ~ Tin

UTRES ~ Leathern Bottles.
UVA QUERCINA ~ A Substance of much importance, yet unknown to the ancients. It is a certain concretion, in the form of a bunch of grapes, which forms in spring under the earth at the roots of oak-trees, originating perchance from a superfluous moisture of the roots. It has a stiptic taste, is outwardly of purple colour, but is white inwardly, and, as it were, milky. In the winter it becomes wood; it should be collected in spring, dried in the shade, and then pulverised. The powder is most efficacious in dysentery; the most desperate cases have I cured with one of these Uva.
UVAE HERMETIS ~ Philosophical Water, Distillation, Solution, Sublimation, Calcination, Fixation.
UZIFUR or **UZUFAR** ~ Cinnabar.

VALRAT or **ULCAT** ~ A Leaf.
VAMAS ~ The Vinegar of the Philosophers.
VAPOR ~ Smoke, Smoke of Mercury.
VAS CRUDUM ~ A New Vessel.
VAS FICTILE ~ A Potter's Vessel.
VAS METALLICUM ~ A Metallic Vessel used in Sublimation ; a Bronze Vessel or Vesica, i.e., Bladder.
VAS MINUS ~ A Kobel in which Mined Substances are Extracted.
VASA FUSORIA ~ Fusing Vessels, those which contain the matter itself, by the aid of which minerals are melted ~ as, for example, a cupel or a crucible.
VECTARII ~ Men Working on the Windlass.
VECTES RECTI ~ Lines laid for the Truck to travel on.
VECTIS ~ A Handle.
VECTIS ~ Hooked Handle.
VECTIS ~ A Sleeper for a Rail.

VECTORES ~ Truck Boys who stand upon the Lines for the Truck.
VEHICULUM ~ A Small Wagon.
VENA ~ A Seam. A Vein of Metal, or Horizontal Stratum.
VENA CUMULATA ~ Mixed Gangues. A Flat Bed.
VENA CONTINUA COHERENS ~ An Uninterrupted Vein.
VENA TRANSVERSA ~ A Cross-way. A Crossing Vein
VENA USTA ~ Roasted Ore.
VENA VENERIS ~ Vervain.
VENA PRINCIPALIS ~ Champion Lode, Main Lode.
VENA SOLIDA ~ A Pure Vein.
VENAE CAPUT ~ The Beginning of the Vein.
VENAE CORIO NUDARE, ET VENAM APERIRE ~ The Opening Up of a Vein.
VENAE DURISSIMAE NONUS ~ A Knot of very hard Ore, Mispickel, possibly also Arsenical Pyrites.
VENAE TECTUM ~ The Bed over a Horizontal Stratum.
VENAE URERE ~ To Roast the Ore.
VENAM, QUA PARTS ABUNDAT METALLO, LUTO OBLINTRE ~ The Concealment of the rich part of the Vein with mud, earth or stones.
VENAM TECTI VEL FUNDAMENTI SAXIS ABRUMPERE ~ The Separation of the Vein from the Rocks which surround it.
VENARUM FRAGMENTA ~ Large Pieces of Ore.
VENENUM ~ Venom, Mercurial Stone; the soul kills the king, but because she rises again it is also called Theriaca. Mercury is the poison of all metals; it alters and changes.
VENER ~ Mercury, St. Jacob's Pecten.
VENTER EQUI ~ Horse Dung.
VENTI ~ Spirit.
VENTUS ALBUS ~ Mercury.
VENTUS CITRINUS ~ Sulphur.

VENTUS RUBEUS ~ Red Orpiment.

VENULA ~ A Small Vein, or Fissure, which may be empty or filled with deads.

VENULA FIBRA ~ Fissures.

VENUS, or **MURPUR** ~ Copper.

VENUS ~ The Impure Stone, the Matter.

VERMICULUM ~ Elixir, Tincture.

VERMILION ~ Cinnabar, Minium; it may also denote any red colour.

VERNICE ~ Dry Varnish.

VERTO ~ The Fourth Part of a Pound.

VESICA ~A Metallic Vessel, generally of Copper, having the form of a bladder or egg; it is two or three feet in height, and of corresponding breadth; it has an opening at the top for the reception of an alembic corresponding to its capacity, for the alembic must so exactly fit the orifice of the vessel as to completely close it up, preventing any escape of air. There must be a cover on the top, and from the said cover a tube must project to the height of two or three feet, over which there must be another covering in connection with an ahenum containing cold water, whereby the spirits in the alembic may be elevated, congealed, and condensed. From this cover there must be another tube carried to send down the condensed vapours into a vessel beneath. The use of this bladder in operations upon vegetable substances is by no means to be neglected.

VIA RECREMENTORUM ~ Operation upon Refuse.

VICARIUS DOMINI ~ The Representative of the Master of the Mine.

VINUM CORRECTUM ~ Rectified Wine, Alcohol of Wine.

VINUM ESSATUM ~ That which Attracts the Essences of Herbs, and other Substances, upon which it is poured.

VILTRUM PHILOSOPHORUM ~ The Alembic; it is entirely covered up in a woollen sleeve, like that of Hippocrates, or like the lingula through which liquids are clarified.
VIRIDE AERIS ~ Greek, or Spanish, Green, i.e., Verdigris.
VIRIDITAS SALIS ~ Liquor, or Oil of Salt.
VIRGULA FURCATA ~ A Forked Stick, a Divining Rod, by which some imagine that they can discover where a vein exists.
VISCALEUS, or **VISCUS ARBORIS** ~ Mistletoe, Corylinus.
VISCUS ~ Properly Pitch, decocted from the Exuditions of Fissures in Trees.
VISCUS SECUNDIE GENERATIONIS ~ A Kind of Blood derived from Salts. Visio-This term is applied to the Supernatural Apparition of Spirits, in some manner or other made visible to human eyes.
VISMAT ~ Rude Leprous, Intractible Tin.
VITELLUM POLI ~ Alum.
VITRI SEL ~ Glass Gall.
VITRIFICATIO ~ The Burning of Lime and Cinders into Transparent Glass.
VITRIOLUM ALBUM ~ The Same.
VITRIOLUM LIQUEFACTUM or **VITRIOLATUM** ~ Melted Vitriol, is either Liquid Chalcanthum derived from Minera, and needing no further coagulation, or Chalcanthum derived from the Minera of Copper.
VITRIOLUM NOVUM ~ White Vitriol; White Galitzen Stone.
VITRIOLUM ROMANUM ~ Roman Vitriol, Green Atrament.
VITRUM ~ Glass, Sieve, Riddle for Distillation, Grave, Churchyard, because the Stone lies hidden therein, and is driven up and down; also a Prison, because the Bride and

Bridegroom are shut in there by force. Therefore it is called the Old Green Lion, because he uses violence.

VITRUM: ~

1. Among European Glass, the best is that of Murana, called Venetian, and compared to Crystal.
2. The most costly Glass of Asia was that of Sareptana, called Sidonian, and compared to Amber by Lucian.
3. Green Recrement of Glass on a White Ground.
4. Red Recrement of Glass.
5. Glass for the Colouring of Metals, Enamel.

VITRUM NIGRUM ~ Black Glass, Black Enamel.

VOLANS, or **UNQUASI** ~ Quicksilver.

VOLATILE ~ In general, any substance that is very light and ascends easily, like Ash, Dust, etc.

VOMITIVUM ~ Any Medicament which purges by means of sickness; an Emetic.

VULCANII or **VULCANICI** ~ The name given to the men who are at work continually by the fire, engaged upon smelting and liquefaction.

VULSELLA ~ Fire.

VULTURNUS ~ South-East.

XENECHTUM --- is a preservative against pestilence, fastened to the neck, as, for example, Quicksilver Enclosed in a Nut, and the like; another authority regards it as the first Menstrua of a Virgin.

XENECHDON ~ According to Paracelsus, is a Tablet of Arsenic, or Arsenic prepared as a Preservative against the Pestilence. Although this composition not only contains Arsenic, but also Toads, Ditany, and other Substances.

XENI NEPHIDEI ~ are Spirits who delight to reveal to men the hidden properties of nature.

XISSUM ~ is Vinegar.

XISTON ~ That is Scraped off Rust.

YARIN, MARIA, or **IARIA** — The Flower of Copper.
YDRARGYROS — that is, Quicksilver.
YDROCECUM, YDRICIIJM, YDENS, or **YDRARGYROS** — that Is, Quicksilver.
YELION, YALOS — Glass.
YC, or **YO** — that is, Good.
YGROPISSOS — that is, Bitumen, or Liquid Pitch, Thin Pitch.
YOMO, YOS, or **YN** — that is, Verdigris.
YRIDIS, or **PRIDE** — that is, Orpiment.
YRIS — Iron.
YRIUS, LAGIDES, DASYPUS, GEORICHUS, LEBERIS — Male Pigmy. If he be fed on diaphoretic diet, his blood will soften or melt glass and flint. The unlearned ascribe this property to the goat. .
YSOPUS — Theophrastus in his work, Concerning Nature, states: They formerly designated it Ysopus and Ysopaica, an art of smelting and fusing, with which the world cannot

easily dispense, since hence proceed all good medicine, art, handicraft, etc.
YSIR ~ Every Colour.
YSPAR ~ The Same.
YXIR ~ Good Medicine.
YSIR ~ Powder, the Dry Stone, to be drunk with the Mercurial Water. It is the blackness on the floor.
YCAR ~ is Medicine.

ZAFRAN ~ that is, the Garden Crocus.
ZAFFABEN ~ Puttea Putta.
ZAFFRAN ~ that is, Yellow Ochre.
ZAOCEL ~ Yew Tree.
ZAIBAC, ZEIDA, ZAIBACH, ZAIBAR, ZERACHAR, or **ZIBATUM** ~ that is, Quicksilver.
ZAIBAR ~Mercury.
ZAIDIR ~ Venus, or Verdigris.
ZAUHIRON ~ that is, the Oriental Crocus.
ZARAS ~ that is, Gold.
ZARFA ~ that is, Tin.
ZANDICK ~ Foliated Water.
ZARNEC ~Eggs with Fire, Sulphur.
ZARNICH ~ that is, Orpiment, called also Zarnec, Zarneck, and Zarne.
ZATANEA ~ that is, the Flower of the Pure Lamb, called also Zuccar and Zuccaiar.
ZAUN ~A species of Hedge.

ZEBEB, or **CHARA** — that is, Dung.
ZEBD — Butter.
ZEC — that is, Draganthum.
ZEFR — that is, Pitch.
ZEGI, ZET, ZEZI — that is, Vitriol.
ZEHERECH ALCKAS — Flower of Copper.
ZEITRABRA — Fluxional.
ZEMECH — Lapis Lazuli.
ZERCI — Vitriol.
ZERTUCK — The White.
ZENGIFUR, or **ZEMASARUM** — that is, Cinnabar.
ZINGAR — that is, Verdigris, or Flower of Copper.
ZEO — that is, I Boil.
ZENIUM, ZENII — Pestles, might also be Hairs, Javelins.
ZEPHENI — are Small Circles about the extremities of the ears and lips and other parts.
ZECHSTEIN — A kind of Stone, Limestone.
ZERICUM — that is, a kind of Arsenic.
ZERIFARI — that is, Curdled Milk.
ZONCO — A Cord, Snare, Spring.
ZONNETTI — Are the Phantastic Bodies of Gnomes.
ZORABA — that is, Vitriol.
ZERNA — is an Ulcerated Complaint of the Skin called Impetigo.
ZINIAR — is Verdigris.
ZINIAT — is Dough.
ZINC — is a Metallic Marcasite, a certain composition from four imperfect metals, in which copper predominates.
ZIMAR PHILOSOPHICUM — Philosophic Zimar, made from Copper.
ZIMEX — Vitriol from Copper Ore.
ZUITTER, or **ZITTER** — From Marcasite.
ZUB, or **ZUSN** — that is, Crude Butter.
ZWITTER — Ore that has been roasted once.

ZYMAR — that is, Verdigris.
ZYNSER — The same as Zymar.

A Supplement To The Alchemical Lexicon of Martinus Rulandus, Containing The Terms Of The Philosophers And The Veils Of The Great Mystery

ABBREVIATION ~ A word which in its literal sense means to gain time is used by the philosophers, for they say that " The Stone tolerates no abbreviation," meaning that the artist must not weary over long labour, nor endeavour to speed the operation by increasing the fire, since by so doing he will destroy his process.
ABSEMIR ~ One of the names which have been given by Philosophers to the matter of the art.
ACARTUM ~ One of the names of Minium. Others call it Azimar.
ACALACH ~ Salt-according to the terminology of the Spagyric Philosophers.
ACATE ~ Soot.
ACONOR ~ An Earthen Pot, pierced with a number of holes at the sides and bottom.
ACETUM ACERRIMUM ~ The Mercurial Water of the Sages.

ACHACHI — Water of Light-is the Mercury of the Philosophers, so called because its active virtue purifies the Laton, and causes it to pass from the Black colour to the White, which they term Light.

ADAM — is a Name which the Philosophers have given to their Magisterium when it has attained the perfection of the Red, because their matter, being the Quintessence of the Universe and the First Matter of all individuals in Nature, has a perfect correspondence with that original Adam, in whom God united the most pure substance of all beings, and, otherwise, because the word Adam signifies Red, and thus expresses at once the colour and the quality of the Magisterium — that is, Red Earth, Mercury of the Sages, Sulphur, Soul, Fire of Nature.

ADAMITE — A kind of white tartar, or foliated earth, which the Hermetic Philosophers have named Adamic Earth, Tartar, Virgin Earth, Adamita, etc.

ADAPTATION — This process of the Philosophers occurs when the projection of the Elixir to the white or to the red is made upon a metal that has been melted upon or reduced to its mercurial form, so long as it is of the same nature, and for this reason is in harmony and agreement with the Elixir. Thus, Adaptation means Harmony, or Natural Likeness, or Affinity, or a capacity for entering into these conditions. In effect, should any one endeavour to project the white or the red upon any substance other than metallic, he will produce neither gold nor silver, because the matter upon which he is projecting has no affinity with the Elixir.

ADDITION — This process is mainly concerned with Philosophical Gold, or Citrine Sulphur. It is the Rubification or Tincture of Mercury, which of itself adds nothing to the work, because it inheres to the Mercury. Sometimes, by the addition of Philosophical Gold, we understand the projection of the Elixir upon a suitable liquefied or heated matter.

ADHEBE — Has the same meaning as Adhaec.

ADHIEC — A Spirit which Conserves Life and Motion in Animals. In Man the Hermetic Philosophers distinguish three constituents which make up his humanity — namely, Soul, Spirit, and Body. The Soul is immortal and spiritual, and derives its nourishment and its life from God, being a kind of extension of the Deity, to make use of an expression which occurs in the Asclepius of Hermes. The Spirit occupies a middle position between the Soul and the Body; it unites them together, and has its nourishment from all that is most subtle in Nature, and from the quintessence of the elements, which it absorbs by means of respiration. Lastly, there is the gross and terrene body, which is nourished by the earth and water of which it is itself composed.

ADIRLAPIS — Sal Ammoniac.

ADULPHUR — Ash or Sand.

ADUMA — The Stone of the Philosophers arrived at the Red before it has become Elixir.

AFFLICTION — This term refers to the Grief of the Artist, who has permitted his spirits to escape or evaporate, when his vessels are broken by excessive heat, etc.

AFFAX, or **AFFARIS** — Every kind of Scum.

AFFEMICUM — This name is given by chemists to the Soul of Things.

AGAR — Lime.

AGAZOPH — See Adulphur.

AHALCABOR, ALCHONAR, ALASTROB, ALOMBA, AGAR-ALGIT, ALGERIT — Are all names of Calx.

ALARTA — Burnt Copper.

ALBUSIE — The Sulphur of the Sages. Some chemists have given the same name to Common Sulphur.

ALCADY — Vitriol, White Atrament, White Salt of the Sages.

ALCALHAL — The Vinegar of Vulgar Chemical Philosophy, but this Vinegar is not that of the Philosophers, which is nothing else but their Pontic Water, or Dissolving Mercury.

ALCES UNGULA — The Hoof of the Elk, is used by physicians as a medicine for the nerves. What is called specific hoof is celebrated for its efficacy against epilepsy, both as a preventive and a cure. It is used externally and internally, the powder thereof being administered in the latter fashion. Externally a particle is placed in a ring, which is worn on what is commonly called the ring finger, next to the little finger, and so as to face the hand. Or, it is worn opposite to that finger in a ring purposely turned to it. It is also placed on the wrist, applied to the pulse, put into the left ear, suspended from the neck, so as to touch the skin, etc. It is said to be recognised by its smell, for it yields a pleasant odour in fumigation.

ALCHAZANON — A Slime which falls off Millstones, and of which an excellent mastic is made.

ALCHEMY — A word composed of the Arabic article Al and of Chymia.

ALCHEMY — According to George Ripley, the Universal Matter of all Metals is Mercury, which set over the fire, together with the purest Sulphur, will become Gold. But if either of these constituents be sick or leprous — that is to say, infected with any impurity — some other metal will be produced instead of gold.

He adds that as mercury and sulphur are sufficient for the making of all metals, so of these may be composed a universal medicine, or metal, for curing all the sick; which some by an error have understood as a universal metal, efficacious in all the diseases of the human body.

ALCHEMY ~ Authorities therein: Among later writings on the Hermetic science, there is a French Catechism of Alchemy which, as it is founded directly on a unique Ms. of Paracelsus, is of very high authority. It says that to obtain a knowledge of the mysteries of the art, it is necessary to be acquainted with all the works of Hermes, which should be first studied, and their lessons put to heart. The disciple should then proceed in the following order with his reading:
1. *The Passage of the Red Sea.*
2. *The Entrance Into the Land of Promise.*
3. Paracelsus, especially his *Manual.*
4. Raymund Lully, particularly his *Vade Mecum, Lignum Vitae, Testament,* and *Codicil.*
5. *The Turba Philosophorum.*
6. Denis Zachaire.
7. Trevisan.
8. Roger Bacon.
9. D'Espagnet.

ALCHITURA ~ Liquid Pitch.

ALCOOLIZATION ~ Reduction of a Body into its smallest parts. According to the Spagyric Philosophers, it is the same thing as Philosophic Calcination. Indeed, the terms are used interchangeably, and express the same process. But Alcoolization should not be confounded with ordinary chemical calcination, for in hermetic science the latter term has only a symbolical significance.

ALCOFIL NIGRA ~ One of the names which the Alchemists give to Antimony. It is also called Alophjt.

ALCUR ~ Sulphur.

ALETH ~ The Jupiter of the Philosophers, and the Tin of the Chemists.

ALLEGORY ~ A Greek Term which signifies that words should be understood in another than their natural sense ~ that is, when one thing is said, and another meant.

ALERNET ~ Orpiment.

ALLOR ~ Burnt Copper.

ALLUTEL ~ A Vessel designed for the Sublimation of Liquefied Matter.

ALMAGRA ~ Chemists of the vulgar school give this name to Bolus, to Copper, and to Laton, but the philosophers understand by it the Matter of their Stone. According to Morien, it is Laton, named Red Earth, that is, Philosophical Sulphur.

ALMAKIST ~ Lltharge.

ALMAT ~ Ceruse, or Rust of Lead.

ALMAT KASITE ~ Quicksilver.

ALMA ~ Philosophical Water.

ALOE ~ An Elk.

ANABISI, or **ADEBEZI** ~ A Term of the Spagyric philosophers, which signifies the Shell, Bark, or Rind, which encloses the true matter of the Mercury of the Philosophers. It signifies the climbing Tendril of a Vine and also a Tortoise.

ANDROGYNE, or **HERMAPHRODITE** ~ That is to say, Bisexual Water ~ a name which the Philosophers have given to the purified matter of their Stone after Conjunction. It is properly their Mercury, which they call male and female.

ANGELS ~ The chemical Philosophers sometimes give this name to the Volatile Matter of their Stone. They then say that their body is spiritualized, and that one will never succeed in performing the Grand Work unless one corporifies spirits, and spiritualizes bodies. This operations is philosophical sublimation, and it is certain that the fixed never becomes sublimated without the assistance of the volatile.

ANGLE ~ The thing which has three angles ~ a term of Hermetic science-The Philosophers say that their matter, or the Philosophical Mercury, is a substance having three angles as regards the substance of which it is composed, of four as regards its virtue, and of two in respect of its matter, while in its root it is one. These three angles are salt, sulphur, and mercury; the four are the elements; the two are the fixed and the volatile, and the one is the remote matter, or the chaos from which all has been produced.

ANIMAL — The Philosophers have bestowed this name upon their matter after it has passed through putrefaction. It is so called because it grows in sublimation, and Chas a soul of blood colour, namely, the invisible spirit of vitriol.

ANIMATION — This term of Hermetic science signifies the endowment of Mercury with a metallic spirit, which vivifies it, so to speak, and fits it for the production of philosophical sulphur. Philalethes and Bernard Trevisan have written much about this animation. The latter calls it Double Mercury.

ANRIC — Sulphur.

ANTIMUM — Spring Honey.

APHORISMUS — A General Rule in Medicine.

APHIDEGI — Ceruse.

APPOSITION — The Philosophers say that one — must begin by the apposition of citrine red Mercury in order to pass from the white to the red. It is a philosophical figure of speech. The truth is that nothing is added, for the matter contains within itself all that is required. The matter is simply cooked, augmenting the necessary fire. Those who understand this figure of speech literally, and introduce a citrine red Mercury fall into a serious error.

AQUA OLVES — Distilled Vinegar. Some chemists use the same term to signify Aquafortis.

AQUALA — Philosophical Arsenic.

AQUILEGIA — Theophrastus calls the yellow-flowered plant Genista by this name.

AQUILENA — The plant Larkspur.

ARACAB — The Eagle of the Philosophers.
ARACEUM — A Slime for Sealing Vessels.
ARAXOS — Soot.
ARCHILAT — A Weight of Three Grains.
AROP — The Matter of which the Stone is formed — at least, it is the Matter of which the Magisterium is composed, which also contains but one thing.
ARSAG — Arsenic.
ARSAVEILE — Sublimed Arsenic. Called also Arcanec and Artanec.
ARSENIC OF THE PHILOSOPHERS — The Mercury of the Wise — otherwise, the matter from which this Mercury is extracted. It is also the Hermetic Matter when it has reached the black stage, and the Sulphur or active and masculine seed. Some also understand by this term that Salt, which is the bond between Sulphur and Mercury, and is one of the three principles of Nature, and of all composites.
ARSENIC — Incombustible Arsenic of the Philosophers — the Hermetic Stone perfected to the white degree.
ARUNCULA MAJOR — The Matter of the Philosopher's Stone.
ASABON — In Hermetic science, the Azoth of the Philosophers, with which they whiten their Laton.
ASABUM — Tin; the Jupiter of the Philosophers.
ASERIT — Living Sulphur.
ASMON — Sal Ammoniac.
ASMUM — Weights for weighing — such as the pound, ounce, etc.
ASROB — The Matter of the Philosophers in Putrefaction — their Head of the Raven, Saturn, etc.
ASSA FOETIDA — The Hermetic Philosophers have applied this name to the Mercury of Ripley, because it has the smell of this substance, when newly extracted from the mineral ore. This odour, according to Raymund Lully, is of

the strongest kind, but it is changed by circulation into a quintessence of a most sweet and pleasant savour.

ASSALA ~ An Arabic term which signifies Alum.

ASSUGAR ~ Verdigris.

ASTRUM EX IGNE ~ The Archetypal Form of Fire.

ATALANTA ~ According to the Spagyric Philosophers is the Volatile Matter of the Magnum Opus which can only be arrested by the fixed matter, symbolically represented as the Golden Apples, since there is nothing more fixed than the radical matter of gold. When a fountain is said to be caused to burst forth from a rock, it means that the philosophical stone produces water, of which earth is made, and then again water. It is also said that Atalanta sleeps in the temple of her mother with Hippomenes, because the fixed and the volatile are placed together in the same vessel, and this is the chemical marriage which is so much talked of by philosophers.

ATIMAD ~ Antimony.

ATTENUATION ~ Reduction into Powder; Pulverised Matter or Substance, separated from all terrene particles, or otherwise subtilised.

ALTAR ~ Some adepts have assigned this name to their Mercury and to their Matter, when operated on in the vessel.

AUTUMN ~ The period when the artist obtains the reward of his labours. It is of a dry and cold complexion. It must ever be remembered that dissolution takes place in winter, coction in spring, coagulation in summer, and the garnering of the fruits in autumn-that is, the imparting of the tincture.

AYBORZAT ~ Galbanum.

AZECI ~ Philosophical Vitriol.

AZINARBAN ~ A term by which the Spagyric Philosophers signified the Feces, or that impurity which is separated from the pure matter of the sages.

ARIES ~ The Sulphur of the Philosophers when perfect at the Red stage. It derives this name from its warm and dry quality, which is characteristic of the Sign Aries. The adepts say that they extract their steel from the belly of Aries, and they call their steel Magnet by this name. But when the Cosmopolite and Philalethes so express themselves, they speak of the actual matter of the work, of which their sulphur is formed.

ATTEMPER ~ This is the same as Coction, and it is in this sense that Raymund Lully says that our iron attempers sharp and bitter substances.

APOCALYPSE ~ While the adepts of Hermetic science claim that the secret sense of the Book of Genesis is concerned with their mysteries, they regard the Apocalypse as especially alchemical in its interior meaning. It is, in fact, nothing less than a poem in praise of Alchemy.

BAGEDIA ~ A Weight of One Ounce, or a Pound according to the measure of medicine.

BALM ~ Universal Balm of Nature ~ is the Elixir perfected to the white or red stages, abounding in marvels and astonishing powers in the three kingdoms of Nature-vegetable, animal and mineral-for it educes their latent perfections, and is a most rare and little understood Medicine; it is an infallible and sovereign remedy of all diseases and can even resuscitate the dead.

BALSAM ~ The Universal Balsam, or The Elixir of Life. According to Bernard Trevisan, the Universal Catholicon is nothing else than the reduction of the Philosophical Stone into Mercurial Water. It is also called Potable Gold. It cures every species of disease, and prolongs life even beyond the common limits of humanity. According to the same authority, the Perfect Elixir at the Red changes copper, lead, iron, and all metals into purer gold than can be produced from any mines. The Perfect Elixir at the White, which is also called Oil of Talc, changes all metals into the finest silver.

Among the many recipes for a Balsam or Elixir of Life, the following may be cited in this place. Take eight pounds of Mercurial Sap, two pounds of the Sap of Borage, using leaves and stems for the extract; twelve pounds of Narbonne or other honey, the best that can be found in the country; boil them altogether and skim. Filter and clarify. For the space of twenty-four hours set apart for infusion over hot cinders four ounces of sliced gentian root, infused in three half-pints of white wine. Stir occasionally. Pass the wine through a linen bag without squeezing it. Add this concoction to the saps and honey; boil the whole gently till it reaches the consistence of syrup. Turn it, to cool, into a glazed earthenware pan; then put it into bottles, which must be stored in a warm place. One spoonful should be taken every morning. This syrup prolongs life, confirms health against all manner of maladies, even gout, and moderates heat in the bowels. It is good for sciatica, vertigo, and generally for all internal complaints.

BALSAM — The Sovereign Medicine, regarded from the standpoint of the Metallic Kingdom, is said to be made by taking the Stone, grinding it, powdering it, separating its terrestrial nature by the secret fire, subliming it, dissolving it in the Water of the Sea of the Wise, and then proceeding by the way of decoction. The Water of the Sea of the Philosophers is of the same nature as the Stone, because all that is comprised under the mineral and metallic nature was formed and nourished of that very same water in the bowels of the earth, whither it penetrates along with the influence of the stars.

BALSAM — The Philosophical Stone, which is simply the Elixir of Life in another form, and under another phase, while the Elixir of Life is in like manner another phase and form of the Philosophical Stone, is the pledge not only of incalculable riches, of health ever blooming, but even, as some affirm, of immortality. The person who possesses it will find no one able to withstand him.

The philosophical theory of the Metallic Elixir is thus stated: Those Philosophers who experimented by the dry path have succeeded in rendering a part of their gold volatile, and reducing it into a sublimate, white as snow and shining like crystal. The remaining portion they have converted into a fixed salt, and from the conjunction of the volatile and the fixed, they have made their Elixir. Other Philosophers, subsequently, after another method, which is the humid way, have extracted from the interior of Mercury an igneous spirit, which is mineral, vegetable, and reproductive. In the humid concavity of this spirit is concealed the primitive Mercury, or universal quintessence. By the means of this spirit, they have attracted the spiritual seed contained in gold, and have thus obtained their sulphur, and that Mercury of the Philosophers which is neither solid as a Metal, nor of fluid-like Quicksilver, but has a medial condition between them.

BARNA -- A Glass Vessel.

BASILISK -- The Chemical Philosophers have sometimes given this name to their Mercury, because it dissolves everything. Some understand it to refer to the Stone at the White Stage, others to the Stone at the Red Stage, because just as the ancients said that the basilisk slew by the mere glance of its eye all those upon whom it fell, so also the powder of projection made of the stone at the white or the red stage, and projected upon Mercury or other metals, kills them, so to speak, by fixing them (as the eye of the basilisk killed also by fixing its victims) and transmutes them into silver or gold.

BASZIAL -- Beans.

BATH OF THE PHILOSOPHERS — That which the alchemists term the Bath is a matter reduced into a liquid or aqueous form; thus when it is required to perform projection on a metal, that metal must be melted, and this is called the Bath, or reduction in to the mercurial form, where the King and Queen come to Bathe — that is, the Sun and Moon-because it is liquid water.

BATH OF THE PHILOSOPHERS — is when operations of circulation take place in the egg. The philosophers say that the King and Queen bathe in the fountain as many times as it will naturally contain them. Reference is also implied to the time when the distillation of the philosophical Mercury takes place.

BATHE — To put in a Bath. The Philosophers say that they prepare a bath for the Sun and the Moon, for the King and the Queen, etc. In the symbolic pictures of Abraham the Jew, preserved by Flamel, there is a king so-called, armed with a great cutlass, who causes a large number of children to be slain in his presence by soldiers, while their mothers wail at the feet of the merciless military. The blood which flows from the victims is subsequently collected into a large vessel, wherein the Sun and Moon of the heaven come down to bathe themselves. This fountain is solely for the use of the king of the country. Sometimes the alchemists understand by the term Bathing the Coction of the Matter, and its Circulation in the Philosophical Egg.

BATHE — Remark that Calcination, Tinging, Washing, Whitening and Bathing signify one operation, and that all these words signify the Coction of the Matter until it has attained its perfection.

BDELLERUM — Saintfoin.

BDOLA — Sulphur.

BEAST — The Venomous Beast of the Sages and their Serpent. This is the Philosophical Stone when it is sublimated, and this by similitude as much as because the serpent glides along insensibly, and slays by means of its venom. In like manner the Stone, being perfect, enters and penetrates the metal, which is imperfect, and kills it-that is to say, annihilates its first imperfect being, together with its volatility, and tinges and fixes it at the perfect white or red.

BELISIS ~ The Coral of the Philosophers.

BEMBEL ~ is the Philosophical Mercury, and sometimes the operation of the Stone of the Sages ~ one is often taken for the other.

BERINBRUCH ~ A Stone found in the neighbourhood of Ephesus. The inhabitants of Darmstadt on the Rhine have applied this name to it on account of the effects it produces. The physicians term it Otea Colla.

BESEC ~ Mercury of the Sages.

BHACTA ~ Red Earth.

BLACINA ~ Several Metals melted or fused together.

BOLUS, JUDAIC BOLUS ~ The Marshmallow.

BOLESIS ~ See Belisis.

BULESON ~ Balm.

BORAX ~ The Stone of the Philosophers at the white stage.

BORIN ~ Vinegar, Terebinth, or Alkali.

BORITIS ~ The Philosophers apply this name to their Mercury when it has reached the black stage, and is indeed very black as well as very thick. It is, otherwise the Laton which must be rendered white.

BOTHRACHIUM ~ The Ash of Sardaigre, called by the botanists Apium Risus. Bozix ~ Turpentine, or the Balsam which is artificially extracted therefrom.

BLAS CARDIS ~ A Vital Spirit, and, consequently, a kindler of heat. The spirit is animated, and becomes the mother of the heat.

BLAS REGIMINIS ~ Acts around the effluvium of the body when the moon disturbs the sea.

BRETAN ~ Brefil Wood.

BRUMAZAR ~ A name which some Philosophers have bestowed on their Mercury. It is a Fatty and Unctuous Vapour which the author of Clangor Buccinae refers to in the following terms: Bread which has been fermented and baked occupies, so far as it is perfect in itself, the same position as gold when it is purified by fire; it is a fixed body, susceptible of no further fermentation, unless it is mixed with Brumazar, that is, the First Matter of metals, wherein a becomes resolved into this First Matter. Take therefore this matter of which gold is composed, and by means of our art make the philosophical ferment, etc.

BRAY ~ In chemical language this signifies the Coction of the Matter, and not its pounding in a mortar or otherwise.

BURN ~ In chemical language this term is equivalent to assaying; it is not to be interpreted as calcination or submitting actually to the fire. It is simply the Coction of the Matter in its own vase by a moderate fire.

C C C

CAB ~ Philosophical Gold.

CABALA ~ The Science of the Philosophical Stone, or of Hermetic Philosophy, forms part of the Cabala, or Kabbalah, and is only orally taught.

CABET ~ Iron Scales, or Filings of Iron.

CACOCHYLA ~ An Injurious Sap found in certain Bodies.

CADMIA AURI ~ Litharge of Gold.

CADMIA ~ One of the names which the Hermetic Philosophers have given to the matter of their Stone. Some have also given the name of Cadmia to the heterogeneous parts of this matter which must not be permitted to enter into the work. It is correctly the stone in the red stage.

CADUCEUS ~ The Chemical Philosophers have given to their dissolvent the name of the Caduceus of Mercury, because they affirm that the makers of the classical fable in question intended to indicate the dissolvent by the symbol of the Caduceus. The Caduceus is composed of three parts -- of the golden stem, or rod, surmounted by an iron apple, and of two serpents which seem to be on the point of devouring it. One of these serpents represents the volatile portion of the matter of the Philosophers, the other signifies the fixed part, and these strive with one another in the vessel. They are united, equilibrated, and restrained in the poise of fixation by the philosophical gold, typified in the stem or rod, and thus they are inseparably united in one body.

CAGASTRUM -- A term which Paracelsus invented, the image, or representation, or simulacrum of a real thing, or something which in itself has no reality. It is the antithesis of Yliastrum. He says that Cagastrum is what nitrous salt is to the first matter of all things, or what the flesh of man is to the first matter of that flesh. The flesh of man became Cagastrum after the fall -- a mere image of what it was in the primal state. In like manner, there are two kinds of life -- one according to Yliaster, or that of the spirit, the other Cagastric, or that of the animal nature. Consult Paracelsus in Azoth.

CAIN -- A name which the Philosophers have applied to their Matter in putrefaction and when it has reached the black stage, possibly on account of the malediction which God pronounced upon the son of Adam when he murdered his brother Abel, or because the flagitious lives of his descendants necessitated the deluge which destroyed almost the whole of the human race. This deluge is represented by the Dissolution of the Matter, and its effect by putrefaction.

CAL -- Philosophical Arsenic, or the Matter of the Chemists, not only during the period of its dissolution, when it is a virulent poison, but also when it has arrived at the white state.

CALAMBAC ~ Aloes.

CALCADIN ~ Colcotar, or the Matter of the Philosophers arrived at the red state.

CALCICOS ~ Copper.

CALCITHOS ~ Green Copper.

CALCITARI ~ Alkaline Salt, Alkael.

CALDAR ~ Tin.

CALERUTH ~ A sign of a tendency or desire to return to the perpetual principle, as when substance desires to return to the first matter whence it proceeded.

CALIDITY or **CALOR** ~ A quality of the Fixed Matter of the Philosophers. They have given this name to their male, or the Fixed-which is also called Sulphur, Living Silver, Frigidity, Humidity, etc.

CALIX CHYMICUS ~ Glass of Antimony.

CALLENA ~ Saltpetre.

CALMET ~ The Antimony of the Philosophers.

CALUFAL ~ Indian oil.

CALYFUR ~ An Arabic word which some chemists make use of to signify cloves.

CAMBAR ~ The Matter of the Sages arrived at the white stage.

CAMBIA ~ An exudation, gum, etc.

CAMBILE ~ The Red Earth of the Philosophers.

CAMERETH ~ The Fixed or Red Mercury of the Philosophers, or the Sulphur of the Sages.

CAMES or **CAMET** ~ Silver, or the Philosophical Matter arrived at the white stage.

CANCER ~ The Stone of the Philosophers fixed at the red stage, and so named on account of its warm and dry quality, and of its igneous virtue, which has also caused it to be designated the Stone of Fire and Mineral of Celestial Fire.

CANICULUM ~ The Fire of the Caniculum. Some Hermetic Philosophers have applied this name to their Third Fire or Fire of the Third Grade, which is compared to the warmth of the Caniculum or the Dog-Star, which is supposed to be the most extreme or fierce of the whole year. This does not, however, mean that we are to augment the fire up to the third degree, for we are told that it must be equal and continuous throughout the whole course of the work. The augmentation in question refers to the interior fire.

CAPE ~ Mineral Earth which forms bodies and composes the metallic stones which are combined with metal but are not themselves metallic. It is the petrine matter which occasions the operations of extracting alloy from metals in order to obtain them in a pure state.

CAPITELLUM ~ Water of Soap, also Caput Mortuum, or Feces.

CAPITELLUM ~ Some Philosophers have applied this name to Lye and Water of Soap.

CAPITELLUM OF ALAMBAT ~ This name has also been given to the Matter of the Work when it has reached the black stage.

CAPRICORNUS ~ According to Mangetus some Philosophers have applied this name to Lead. He would have been correct if he had said that they applied it to the Lead of the Philosophers, or their Saturn. The name in question was given to this substance because Capricornus signifies the winter solstice, corresponding to the matter of the work in its black stage, for the Saturn of the Philosophers is also the Winter of the Philosophers.

CARAB ~ Vegetable Salt [?].

CARAHA ~ A name which the Chemical Philosophers have given to one of their Philosophical Bulls. It is the first of these; the second is called Aludel.

CARDEL ~ Mustard.
CARDIS ~ Jupiter or Tin.
CARUMFEL ~ The Giraffe.
CARSUFLE ~ Same as Corsufle.
CASIBO ~ The Cypress.
CASMET ~ Antimony.
CASPA ~ The Philosophical Matter at the white stage.
CATILIA, or **CORTILIA** ~ A Weight of Nine Ounces.
CENTRAL FIRE ~ This is the Sulphur of Matter ~ the Universal Fire of Nature which informs all things. Mercury also, according to Espagnet, manifests itself by the gentle heat of Nature.
CENTRE OF THE WORLD ~ This is the Matter of the Stone of the Philosophers, and the Stone itself when it is in its perfection. The Philosophers have so named it, because they say that all the properties of the universe are united and meet therein.
CERAUNO ~ Fulminating Gold.
CERDAC ~ Mercury.
CEXIM ~ Vinegar.
CHAIA ~ Matter of the Philosophers when it has arrived at the white colour.
CHALCOS ~ Copper.
CHANDEL ~ Coloquintha.
CHANQUE ~ Nitre of the Philosophers.
CHAOS ~ In order to attain to the knowledge and the execution of the physical work, the Philosopher must follow the same route that the Great Architect of the universe employed at the creation of the world, by observing how the chaos was disentangled. The chaos could have consisted of no other substance but a moist vapour, for water only is the true receptacle of forms. An illustration may be found in ordinary seeds, which always change into a certain humour. Now, this humour is their particular chaos, whence the

whole form of the plant is extracted, as it were, by irradiation. The Philosopher will therefore see that from the confused mass whence the world was formed, the Sovereign Artist began by an extraction of the light, which at the same instant dissipated the darkness covering the surface of the earth, to serve as a universal form to matter. He will thence conclude easily that in the generation of all composite bodies a species of irradiation takes place, a separation of the light from the darkness, in which Nature is continually the imitator of her Creator. The Philosopher will equally understand that by the action of this light there was formed that firmament which separated the waters from the waters. The sky was afterwards adorned with luminous bodies, but things superior being too remote from things inferior, it was necessary to make the moon, as an intermediate torch between the above and the below. So the moon, when it has received the celestial influences, communicates them to the earth. Here it should be noted that there is properly but one heaven, which separates the waters from the waters. Three, nevertheless, are admitted. The first is beyond the region of the clouds, and there the rarified waters are returned towards the fixed stars. In this place are the planets and the wandering lights. The second is the abode of the fixed stars themselves. The third is the home of the celestial waters. Having separated the waters of heaven and earth, the Creator, to give a field for generation, produced a light particularly destined to this end, which he placed in the central fire, tempering that fire by the humidity of water and the coldness of earth, in order to restrain its action, and to conform its heat to the design of its author. The central fire acts continually upon the humid matter which is nearest, whence it causes a vapour to rise. This vapour is the Mercury of Nature and the First Matter of the Three Kingdoms. By the double action, or, rather, the reaction of the central fire upon the mercurial vapour, the Sulphur of Nature was afterwards formed.

Now, a truly wise Philosopher, once he has understood the foundation and order of nature which the Great Architect of the Universe observed for the construction of what exists in Nature should, so far as he is able, be a faithful imitator of his Creator. In his physical labour he should make his chaos such as it actually was, he should separate the light from the darkness, he should form his firmament to divide the waters from the waters; and, in a word, accomplish perfectly, following the path indicated, the whole work of creation.

CHAOS ~ The Philosophers have given by comparison the name of Chaos to the Matter of the Work in a state of putrefaction, because then the Elements or Principles of the Stone are in such confusion that they cannot be distinguished. This chaos is developed by volatilisation; the abyss of water leaves the earth visible little by little in proportion as the humidity is sublimed and rises to the summit of the vase. It is for this reason the Hermetic Chemists have compared their work to the development of the universe out of the primeval chaos.

CHAOS, CAHOS, or **CAHAS** ~ This is sometimes termed Water of the Dew of the Equinox, and also Menstruum of the World, or, simply, Menstruum. The Cosmopolite says in his *Enigma* that it is found in the belly of Aries, and in his *Epilogue* that the Pontic Water is congealed in the Sun and Moon, and is extracted from both by means of the Steel of the Philosophers. Both these methods of speaking have reference to the same thing.

CHARIOT OF PHAETON ~ One of the designations which the Philosophers have given to the Grand Work.

CHARON ~ The son of Erebus and of Night. The chemists, however, regard Charon as the symbol of the colour grey, which is intermediate between black and white. The three rivers of the fable signifies the putrefaction which takes place in the three operations of the work. These operations are termed by Gebir the Medicines of the first, second, and third order. In each the matter must be dissolved and undergo putrefaction; it must also reach the black colour, to which grey succeeds, and this grey is the mythological Charon. It is for this reason that he is called the Son of Erebus and of Night. During the course of the grey colour, the matter becomes volatile, and the philosophical Laton whitens. This is the passage of souls through or over the three rivers of the mythos, so as to arrive at the Elysian fields represented by the white stage.

CHEF D'OEUVRE — This is the Stone of the Philosophers, the Elixir perfect at the Red Stage. Those chemists have done well who have given it this name, for it is the most excellent thing which man can possibly imagine for the realisation of his well-being.

CHELOPA — Jalop.

CHESEP — The Air we breathe, also that of the Philosophers. According to Avicenna and Aristotle, you will not succeed in the work unless you extract water from air, earth from water, and fire from earth.

CHIBUR or **CHIBUT** — The Sulphur of the Sages when it has attained to the colour Red.

CHIMERA — The ignorant crowd has ever regarded the search for the Philosophers' Stone as a chimera. The Adepts say that this is by a just judgment of God, who does not permit so precious a secret to be possessed by the wicked and unwise.

CHISIR — The Sulphur principle of Metals.

CHYLE — Matter in putrefaction.

CICEBRUM — The Water of the Philosophers.

CIDMIA — Litharge.

CIMMERIANS ~ The Bubbles which Ascend in the Philosophical Vessel during Putrefaction.

CIRCLE ~ In the terms of Hermetic Science, this signifies the Circulation of the Matter in the Egg of the Philosophers. It is in this sense that they call their operation the Movement, or Revolution, of the Heavens, the Circular Revolution of the Elements, and that they also name the Grand Work the Quadrature of the Physical Circle. Moreover, they divide the practice of the Philosophical Stone into seven circles or operations, each of which consists, nevertheless, of solution and coagulation. The first circle is the reduction of the matter into water. The second is the coagulation of this water into fixed earth. The third is the digestion of the matter, which is performed very slowly, for which reason the Philosophers say that the revolutions of this circle shall take place in the secret furnace. It cooks the nourishment for the Child of the Sages, and converts it into homogeneous parts, after the same way that the stomach prepares the aliment and turns it into substance for the body. The adept Espagnet recognises only three circles, by the repetition of which there may be performed, he tells us, the reduction of water into earth, the reconciliation of the enemies ~ that is, of the volatile, and the fixed, the moist and the dry, water and fire.

CLANCHEDEST ~ Steel.

CLEARNESS ~ In the terminology of Hermetic Science, this signifies the Whiteness which succeeds the Blackness of the Matter in putrefaction.

COAL ~ Almost all the Philosophers have said that their fire is not a fire of coal. When the regimen of the fire is concerned, that of the philosophical fire must be understood, and not that of a coal fire. Philalethes and several others, as, for example, Denis Zachaire, speak of a fire of coal as necessary to the work. According to

Philalethes, a hundred measures of coal are required for the three entire years. Espagnet says that there will be few causes of expense for him who has the materials prepared and suitable, but that coal is needful.

COCK ~ Sulphur, perfect in the Red Stage.

COCK ~ The Fire of the Philosophers.

COLOUR ~ The colour of things, and more especially of flowers, has its principle based in the sulphur and mercurial salt existing in coloured substances. There are three colours which follow one upon another in a harmonious sequence, which is, however, interrupted by intermediate colours of a transitory and evanescent nature. The first is the colour Black, which should make its appearance on or after the forty-second day. Next comes the White, to which Citrine succeeds, and this the philosophers call their Gold. Finally, the colour Red appears, and this is the Flower of their Gold, and their Royal Crown. Should the red colour be produced before the black, that is the sign of an extreme violence in the fire. The operation must be undertaken anew. The colour black is an indication of putrefaction and of the complete dissolution of the Medicine. The white indicates fixation of an advanced stage in the Matter. The red is a sign of perfect fixation. All these colours must reappear in the work of multiplication, but they are not of such long duration.

COMBUSTION ~ An old term found in the works of some chemists to signify the too violent action of fire upon the matter.

COMERISSON ~ One of the names of the Stone of the Sages when it has reached the white stage.

COMMIXTURE ~ Some Philosophers have substituted this term in place of those of Conjunction, Marriage, Union. It is performed during putrefaction, because the fixed and the volatile then mingle to be no further separated.

COMPANION ~ Philosophical Mercury Vitalised by Sulphur, and educed to the white stage.

COMPAR ~ By this term the Adepts understand the fixed and the volatile Mercury and Gold of the Sages which act successively in the work. The Mercury, or the female principle, prevails first up to the end of the stage of putrefaction, at which point the matter begins to be dessicated and to whiten. Then the Gold of the Sages predominates. Afterwards, they work harmoniously together to accomplish the perfection of the work.

COMPOST ~ This signifies in the philosophical vocabulary the Matter of the Stone in the Black Stage, because then the four elements are, as it were, united.

CONTRITION ~ In the terms of Hermetic Chemistry this means Reduction into Powder, but only as regards the evaporation of humidity in the matter by the regimen of fire. It does not mean pounding, or braying, in a mortar.

CORPUSCULE ~ The whole of the great and sublime operation of the Philosophers is performed with a single corpuscule or little body, which contains, so to speak, only feces, dross, abominations, and from which there is extracted a certain dark and mercurial moisture, which includes in itself all that is necessary to the Philosopher. For he seeks only the true Mercury. The Mercury which he should use is not that which is found in the earth, but that which is extracted from bodies. Common Mercury does not contain a sufficient quantity of Sulphur, and, consequently, we must work upon a body created by nature, in which Sulphur and Mercury are united, that is, the male and female principles, which the artist should separate. He should then purify them and afterwards join them anew. The resulting substance is the Rude Stone, Chaos, Iliaster, Hyle.

COMPOSITES ~ In each Composite Substance there are three Humids:
1. The Elementary, which is properly only the vase of the other elements.
2. The Radical, which is properly the Oil or Balm, wherein resides all the virtue of the subject.
3. The Alimentary, which is the true dissolvent of Nature, exciting the internal fire, causing corruption and blackening, and informing and nourishing the subject.

CONCEPTION ~ The Marriage or Union which is effected between the volatile and the fixed portions of the matter of the Philosophers during the state of putrefaction. Hermetic chemists say that the conception of the Son of the Sun, and of the Young King takes place also at this period. The term in question has been employed with analogical reference to the birth of a man or of an animal.

CONFECTION ~ A Combination of Several Substances, as, for example, of the Mercury and Sulphur of the Philosophers. Flamel says that the Philosophical Egg is a matrix of glass in the form of an escritoire, and it is full of the confection of art, that is, of the Waters of the Red Sea, and of the Breath of the Mercurial Wind.

CONFECTION ~ The Elixir of the Philosophers, at once a species of Stone and a Medicine for purging, curing, and transmuting all bodies into the true Luna.

CONFORMANCE, or **ADAPTABILITY** ~ This is when projection takes place upon a metal in a state of fusion, or reduced into a liquid form, or mercurial form. It is then said that the metal has a similitude with, or is conformed to (in its Nature) the Elixir which is composed of the Mercury of the Sages. The Philosophers also recommend for the work the selection of a matter which has some conformance with the metal, because a bull is not to be produced from a tree nor from a metal.

CONGEAL — To fix the volatile Matter of the Work of the Sages.

CONVERSION OF THE ELEMENTS — Those who interpret the language of the Hermetic Philosophers in a literal sense imagine that the Elements of the Sages are actually four distinct and separate things, which must be extracted from one matter, and must be subsequently converted into one another-thus, for example, Oil must be made from Water, Earth from Fire, Fire from Air, etc. By the processes of common chemistry four things are extracted from composite substances — a Spirit, a Phlegmatic Water, an Oil, and an Earth, called Caput Mortuum, or Death's Head. By others these substances have been termed a Salt, a Sulphur, a Mercury, and a Recremental, Condemned, Relegate, or Useless Earth. Those who believe themselves to have arrived at the Magistery of the Philosophers by these operations of vulgar chemistry have given the name of Air to the Oil, of Fire to the Spirit, of Water to the Phlegmatic Water, and of Earth in some cases to the Salt, and in others to the Recremental Earth. But the Elements of the Philosophers differ altogether from these substances; their operations are those of Nature and not of ordinary chemistry; their fire is enclosed in their earth, and in no case separates therefrom; their air also is contained in their water. There are therefore but two visible elements with which conversion has to be accomplished; that is to say, their water changes into their earth, in its liquid nature of water, and afterwards the entire composition which has become water must become earth. In becoming water, all becomes volatile, and, in like manner, when reduced into earth, all is fixed. Thus, when they speak of the cold and the humid, they refer to their water, and when they speak of the warm and the dry, we must understand it as concerned with their earth.

CONVERT — To Convert the Elements. This expression of Hermetic Chemistry signifies to Dissolve and to Coagulate; to change body into spirit and spirit into body; to volatilize that which is fixed, and to fix that which is volatile. All these terms refer to one only operation, which Nature, assisted by art, performs in one vessel, which is the Vase of the Philosophers, by the same process continuously persisted in, when the matter has been thoroughly purified and sealed in the Hermetic Egg. It is then simply a question of the conduct of fire.
COPHER — Bitumen or Asphalt.
COPULATION — Combination, or Union, of the Fixed and the Volatile, which the Philosophers call Male and Female.
CORAL — Red Coral. One of the names which the Philosophers have applied to their Stone when it is fixed at the red stage, which is the apex of its perfection.
CORBATUM — Copper.
CORBIN — I'he Work of the Stone of the Philosophers.
CORDUMENI — The Seed called Cardanom.
CORRECTUM — Distilled Vinegar.
CORSUFLE or **CARSUFLE** — The Sulphur of the Philosophers fixed at the Red Stage.
COSMAI — Tincture or Water of Saffron.
COSMEC or **CASMET** — The Antimony of the Philosophers and of Vulgar Chemistry.
COSMETIC — A name generally applied to all Medicaments used for healing the skin.
COSUMET — See Cosmec.
COTONORIUM — Liqueur.
CROWN — The Celestial Crown. This signifies in alchemical terminology the Spirit of Wine. But when Raymund Lully and other Philosophers speak of Spirit of White Wine and of Red Wine, they must not be taken

literally, for they are making veiled reference to the Red and White Mercury which are made use of in the Grand Work.

CROWN ~ Royal Crown. This is the Perfect Stone at the Red Stage, and qualified to compose the Stone of Projection.

CROWN OF VICTORY ~ Same as the Royal Crown. Nevertheless, some Philosophers have applied the name to their matter when it has begun to issue from the stage of putrefaction and from the Black colour.

CUT ~ The Operation of Cutting with Scissors or with any other instrument, signifies chemically the coction or digestion of the matter, without opening or removing the vase.

DABESTIS ~ Tortoise.

DAIMOGORGAN ~ By this term the Hermetic Philosophers understand that principle which animates the whole of Nature, and, in particular, the innate and vivifying spirit of the earth of the sages, which acts in all the stages of the operation of the great work.

DAMATAU ~ The Gum of the Philosophers.

DATEL or **ETDATEL** ~ Stramonium, Thorn Apple, Greater Nightshade.

DAUGHTER OF THE GRAND SECRET ~ That is, the Stone of the Philosophers, according to one authority.

DAVERIDON ~ Oil.

DEALBATION ~ A term of the Hermetic science. It is the Coction of the Matter until it has lost its blackness, and becomes white as snow. It is also called Lotion and Lavation. It is in this sense that we must understand the philosophical term of Washing the Laton until all its obscurity has been removed.

DECEMBER — The Magisterium in the Black Stage-the Lime of the Putrefaction of the Matter-so called because the Philosophers give the name of winter to this operation, and because the month of December is the beginning of that season when Nature seems idle, entranced, and asleep. On this account also December in some cases signifies the Magisterium in the White Stage, because snow falls commonly during this month, and the matter in the white stage is like snow, and has indeed received the latter name on the part of certain Adepts.

DECOCTION — In Hermetic chemistry signifies the Action of Digestion, the Circulation of the Matter in the Vessel, without the addition of any foreign matter whatever.

DECOMPOSITION — The separation of the constituents of a composite for the discovery of its prime principles. It is properly Analysis, but, as regards the Hermetic philosophy, it signifies nothing else but the reduction of the body of the gold of the Sages to its first matter, which is done by dissolution through the mediation of the Mercury of the Philosophers.

DISENGAGEMENT — signifies the Hen, which stands for Heat-namely, that degree of warmth which the bird in question imparts to her eggs in brooding. It is the normal and natural warmth of the given substance. Therefore when the Philosophers recommend imparting to the regimen of the fire of the work, the degree of heat which is diffused by a brooding fowl, they are not counseling the making of an artificial fire of that grade, but are, in reality, directing that Nature should be left to act with the innate implanted heat which belongs to the Matter, and is no less natural in the mineral order than is that of the Hen in the animal.

DEGREES OF THE FIRE — See Inspissation.

DELEGI — Azfur, is Mirabolans.

DELUGE — By this term the Philosophers understood the Distillation of their Matter, which, after it has ascended in the form of vapours to the summit of the vessel, returns upon the earth like a rain which completely inundates it.

DEMOGORGON — See Daimogorgon.

DENUR — Dust..

DEPOSIT — A term of chemistry which refers to a Liquid in which Heterogeneous Matter is infused-which matter is separated and precipitated to the bottom of the vessel in which the liquor is contained. The matter precipitated is termed a Sediment.

DERAUT — Urine.

DESENI — Mirabolans.

DESSICATION — Coagulation or Fixation of the Mercurial Humidity.

DESTRUCTION — In the terminology of Hermetic science, this term signifies the Radical Dissolution of Bodies in the Philosophical Mercury, or the Reduction of Metals into their First Matter, which is the Mercury of the Sages. Destruction signifies also the blackness and putrefaction of the Matter.

DETONATION — A kind of noise or hissing which is heard when the volatile parts of any compound are expelled with violence, or are fixed with the help of a strong fire. This hissing also takes place, according to the philosophers at the moment of projection upon the metal.

DEVENDEN — Oil of Nard or of Lavender.

DIACELTATESSON — A Species for Fevers discovered by Paracelsus.

DIADEM — The Red Colour which obtains in the Matter of the Stone at the close of each process or operation. Despise not the cinder for the diadem of our King is hidden there.

DIAMETER — Spagyric Diameter-the Equilibrium or Temperament of the Elements in the stone.

DIAMOND — The Stone arrived at the White Stage.

DIANA — This is properly the Matter when it has attained the White Colour, which appears previously to the red in the Work. The red colour is called Apollo. Then is Diana wholly unveiled. When the Philosophers apply the name of the Moon, they understand their Mercurial Water. Espagnet says that the yoke of Diana is alone capable of containing the ferocity of the philosophical Dragon. Philalethes calls this yoke the Doves of Diana.

DICALEGI — The Tin or Jupiter of the Philosophers.

DICTE — The Cavern in which Jupiter is born. It is the Philosophical Vase.

DIGESTION — That action by which a liquid body and a fluidic body are united, either wholly or in part, to extract their tincture, to modify them, to prepare them for dissolution or putrefaction, to cause them to circulate, and thus to volatilize the fixed and to fix the volatile by means of proportioned heat. Almost all the operations of the Great Work may be reduced to that of digestion, which the Philosophers call by various names, according to the phenomena which they have remarked in the vessel at the various stages of the operation. Thus when they make use of the terms Distillation, Sublimation, Imbibition, Ceration, Inspissation, Descension, Solution, Emission, Coagulation, etc., they understand one only operation, or digestion repeated in the medicines of the first, second and third order.

DIKALEGI — The Tin of the Philosophers.

DIMENSIONS — The Adepts declare that their stone has the three dimensions of other bodies, namely, height, length and depth.

DIRT or **SLIME** — The Philosophers have sometimes given this name to their Matter, which has led many chemists into error, for they have set to work upon mud, sediment, etc.

But Philalethes informs us that the term can only be applied to the Matter when it is in putrefaction.

DISPOSITION — A Philosophical Confection so-called by Maria, but Trevisan terms it Weight or Proportion, and others name it Composition. It is a synthesis of the three principles philosophically combined. In his *Vade Mecum*, Philalethes says that we must take one part of the red or the white body, which answer to the male, two or three parts of arsenic, which fulfils the office of the female; and four parts or more, up to twelve, of the sea-water of the Sages; the whole, being well mixed, must be placed in the vase, which must be well sealed, and the vase placed in the athanor, where it must be subjected to the required regimen.

DISSOLUTION — By this term the Chemical Philosophers do not understand the reduction of a solid body into a liquid state, but the reduction of a body into its first matter-that is to say, into those elementary principles which are its ultimate constituents. They never pretend to reduce gold, for example, into air, water, earth and fire, but into mercury composed of its four elements, albeit this mercury partakes more of water and earth than of the two others, as indeed is the case in the whole mineral kingdom.

DISSOLVENT — The Hermetic Philosophers give the name of Universal Dissolvent to their Mercury, and the same name was applied by Paracelsus and Van Helmont to their Alkaest. The anonymous writer known under the name of Pantaleon, says that the Alkaest can and does derive from the same mineral matter as the Mercury of the Sages. But it is obtained by a different method of manipulation, and furthermore the Alkaest never mixes with the body that it dissolves, while the Mercury of the Sages combines so intimately therewith that separation cannot be subsequently performed by any artifice whatever.

DITALEM — Jupiter of the Philosophers.

DIVISION ~ When the Philosophers speak of Division or Separation into two or more parts, it must not be supposed that they refer to a manual operation, but to that which is performed in the vessel by the help of fire ~ in fact, they refer to Putrefaction.

DOG OF ARMENIA ~ One of the names which the Hermetic Philosophers have given to their Sulphur, or to the Masculine Sperm of their Stone.

DOG OF CORUSCENE ~ One of the names which the Chemical Philosophers have given to their Mercury, or Feminine Seed of their Stone.

DOVERTAILUM ~ Generation of Composite Substances by the combination of constituting Elements.

DRAGON APPEASED ~ Sweet Mercury.

DRAGON WITH THREE TAILS ~ Mercury when animated, for then it contains the three chemical principles -~ Salt, Sulphur, and Mercury.

DRAGON WITH WINGS ~ Mercury or Feminine Sperm, the Volatile part of the Matter, which strives with the fixed part, and must subsequently become fixed like that.

DRAGON WITHOUT WINGS ~ The Masculine Sperm, the Sulphur or fixed part.

DRIFF ~ Van Helmont has applied this name to Sand and to Virgin Earth.

DRY ~ To Dry; the Coction of the Matter, its Fixation, by means of circulation, up to the point of the perfection of the Sulphur of the Stone.

DUDAMI ~ Mandragore.

DUE MATTER ~ The due, requisite, and veritable matter. Trevisan tells us that he laboured for forty years upon innumerable substances, but could not succeed because he had not the "due matter".

DUZAMA ~ The Work of the Stone.

DYAMASSIEN or **DIAMASCIEN** ~ Flower of Copper.

EBDANIC ~ Mars, or Iron.

EBISEMET ~ Randeric.

EBISEMETH ~ The Matter of the Hermetic Chemists during its period of putrefaction.

ECHEL ~ The Matter of the Philosophical Egg when it is in a very black state, or imperfect putrefaction.

ECHINEIS ~ A small, slug-shaped Fish. Some Philosophers have applied the name to their Matter when fixed, because it fixes that which is volatile, by rejoining therewith in an inseparable manner, being henceforth one body.

EDULCERATE ~ To Wash a Saline Substance, until all the salt has been removed. This term, understood in its vulgar sense, also signifies moderation of the acidity and corrosive quality of salts, spirit, or other substances. Raymond Lully employs it more than once to express, or symbolize, the coction or digestion of the Mercury of the Philosophers to the point of fixation.

EFFERVESCENCE -- A physical term which means the action of two composite substances which by interpretation produce, or generate, heat, as takes place in almost every combination of acids and alkalis, as well as in most mineral dissolutions.

EFFUSION -- The First Purification of the Stone of the Philosophers, or the Medicine of the First Order.

ELEISIR -- Philosophical Elixir when arrived at the white stage.

ELKALEI -- Marsh, Pond, or Sea of the Sages.

ELMANTES -- Earthenware Glasses, Goblets, or Phials.

ELPOSILINGI -- Scum or Scale of Iron.

ELQUALITER -- Green Vitriol.

ELZARON -- This is the Salt of the Sages, which they call their Body and their Gum. "Take", says a certain alchemical writer, "The clear body which is obtained upon the small protuberances which are not the result of putrefaction but of movement only. Broil this gum with the gum that is called Elzaron and with the two smokes. For the gum Elzaron is the body which shall be the spirit".

EMBLEGI -- That is, Mirabolans (?).

EMBRYO -- The Chemical Philosophers have also given this name among others to their Mercury before it has been extracted from its ore, and to their Sulphur before it has been rendered manifest. Michael Maier in his Chemical Symbols represents them under the form of a child placed on the navel of a man, who has his arms extended, and fire emanating from his fingers and hair amidst a great cloud of smoke. Beneath are these words: "The wind has carried it in its belly". In another emblem, a woman has a globe in place of a stomach, with two breasts above, by ones of which she suckles a child, whom she is holding in her right hand. The following words are underneath: "The Earth is its nurse; the Sun. is its father, and the Moon is its mother".

EMERALD OF THE PHILOSOPHERS ~ A name which has been given to the Flos Coeli, and sometimes to the Dew of May and of September. The last is looked upon as masculine because it is more cocted and digested by the warmth of the summer. The other is considered female because it is colder, cruder, and more akin to winter in its quality. Some chemists, understanding these words literally, have imagined that dew was the matter from which the Philosophers extracted their mercury, because they often say in their books that mercury is male and female. So they have deemed that the union of the Dew of May with that of September would constitute that marriage so recommended by true chemists. But they should have noticed that the matter of their mercury must be mineral because the ox will produce but the ox, the apple an apple only, and it is an egregious blunder to suppose that any metal can ever be produced from a tree or a plant.

EPHESUS, or **THE BATH** ~ The Second Operation of the Stone, wherein the dry fire is dissolved by the humid fire.

EPHODOBUTIS ~ Some chemists have given this name to their Stone when it is perfect at the red, on account of the purple colour of the vestment which formerly bore this name.

EPOSILINGI ~ Scoria.

ETHEB ~ A term of Hermetic science which signifies Perfect. Thus, when the Philosophers say that their powder converts so many parts of lead, tin, etc., into Etheb, they understand Gold or Silver, which they regarded as perfect metals.

EVAPORATION ~ Separation of the Spirits, or spirituous matter of bodies, by the action of air on fire. The Mercury of the Sages has two original sins, says Espagnet; the first is an impure earth and sulphureous, which is separated from it by the humid bath; the second is a superfluous humidity which must be evaporated not by the dry bath of fire, but of the mild and benign fire of Nature.

EVE ~ The Magisterium of the Sages when it has attained whiteness.

EXTREMES ~ The Extremes of the Work are the Radical Elements of All Things, and Gold, the Perfection of the Work. We must neither take the elements for the matter of the work, nor yet Gold, but another matter, which participates in the principiating elements, or secondary matter of metallic compounds. In the same way that to make bread, we do not take baked bread, but the flour of wheat, so do we proceed in the operations of our art.

EXTREMITIES OF THE STONE ~ Philalethes terms them the Dimensions, and says that Mercury is one of them, while the complete Elixir is the other. The middle substances are the bodies or the imperfect philosophical metals. The two extremities in the work are the excessive crudity of the matter before it is prepared, and its perfect fixation~in other words, crude Mercury and the Powder of Projection.

EYEB or **EZEPH** ~ The Sun of the Philosophers.

EZIMAR~ Flowers of Brass.

FACCA DE MALACCA ~ Molucca Bean.
FADA ~ The Matter of the Work when arrived at the White Stage.
FAUFEL ~ Cashou.
FEBLECH ~ Iron or Steel of the Philosophers.
FELDA ~ Lung, or Silver of the Philosophers.
FIDEUM ~ Saffron.
FIDHE ~ Luna of the Alchemists.
FLUX ~ That which helps towards the fusion of those substances with which they are combined. In the language of Hermetic science, flux means anything which enters readily into the condition of fusion. One of the signs of the perfection of the Elixir of Philosophy, and of the Powder of Projection, is that they will flow like wax when brought into proximity with fire, and can be liquefied into all kinds of liquids.

FLUX OF THE ART — Some assign this name to the Prepared Mercury of the Philosophers, others to the Matter when arrived at the White Stage.

FOG, MIST, etc. — There is a thick vapour resembling Fog or Mist which rises from the Matter and Condenses in the Philosophical Air, whence it again descends to moisten, purify, and fructify the Philosophical Earth.

FORCE — Another term of the Hermetic science, which must be understood as much of the Mercury of the Philosophers as of the Spirit which it encloses. When it is said that all its power is converted into earth, this means that it has really become a fixed white earth, which will successfully resist all tests. To "lay hold of the power of things superior and inferior", is to perform the extraction of Mercury, and to put it, when thoroughly purified, into a state of digestion, to prepare it for circulation, and finally fix it in the form of earth at the bottom of the vase.

FORCE OF ALL FORCES — By this expression, we must understand the Elixir when perfect at the Red, or the Powder of Projection, when it has vanquished all the diseases of the three kingdoms, however persistent they may be.

FOREST — When the Philosophers say that their Matter is found in the Forests, the assertion must not be understood literally, nor must one actually seek that Matter in the woods. But, as it is everywhere, and not in the Forests more than in other places, the term signifies the terrestrial Matter in which the true First Matter is confused, and whence it must be extracted, as from a chaos where it is well hidden from vulgar eyes, and where the Philosophers alone can perceive it, albeit an innumerable multitude of persons make common use of it, sell it publicly at a small price, for indeed it costs really nothing at all, and is found everywhere. This terrestrial and superfluous Matter, from which the true

Matter must be disengaged, is that which has been termed by Philosophers, both ancient and modern, their Forests, their dark, umbrageous, obscure, and cavernous places. It is also on the same principle that they say: Make manifest that which is hidden.

FORM ～ The Human Form ～ The Sulphur of the Philosophers when perfect at the Red Stage. This name has been applied to it because man in his masculine quality gives the human form to the seed which produces the child in the womb of its mother, even as does the Philosophical Sulphur in respect of the Feminine Mercury of the Sages. The Philosophical Mercury is, moreover, termed Microcosm as well as Man.

FORM ～ The Female Form-The Stone at the White Stage. By this term Dry Mercurial Water is sometimes understood, and at other times the Luna of the Philosophers.

FRIDANUS ～ Dissolving Mercury of the Sages.

FRUIT ～ The Magisterium at the Red Stage, so called because it is in all truth the fruit of the labour of the artist.

FRUIT ～ with Two Breasts ～ The Stone when perfect at the White and the Red, which both proceed from the same root, that is, from the Mercury of the Sages.

FRUIT ～ Solar and Lunar ～ The same as above, or White and Red Sulphur, produced by the Lunar and Solar Trees, of which the Cosmopolite speaks in his Enigma for the Children of Science.

FURFIR ～ The Red Colour which appears in the Matter of the work as the result of coction only.

FUSIBILITY ～ A Quality of Melting under Heat possessed by certain Bodies. The term is scarcely applicable to anything but metals. The quality in question is due to the Mercury of the Bodies ～ those which have more Mercury being more fusible, while those which have less are harder and offer more resistance to fire. Many chemists, misled by common experience, have attributed fusibility to Sulphur, but, as Becher points out, it only accelerates fusion by absorbing the Acid Spirits and Salt.

FYADA ~ This term signifies, in the terminology of Secret Chemistry, the White Smoke of the Philosophers.

GABERTIN ~ The Fixed Part of the Matter of the Magnum Opus. The volatile part is called Beza.
GABRIENIS ~ The Sulphur of the Philosophers.
GABRIUS ~ See Gabertin.
GAME ~ A Game for Children. The Philosophers have given this name to the Work of the Stone after the preparation of the Mercury, because there nature takes up the work, and it is requisite only to maintain the fire, following the rules of a certain definite procedure.
GANNANA ~ Peruvian Bark.
GARDEN ~ The Garden of the Philosophers is the Vessel which contains the Matter of the Magnum Opus.
GARMENT ~ Dark Garment. Another of the multitudinous names by which the Adepts have described the black colour which possesses the Matter of the work during the period of putrefaction.
GAZAR ~ Galbanum.
GAZARD ~ The Laurel Tree.

GELAPO ~ Jalap.
GELSEMIN ~ The Plant Jasmin.
GELUTA ~ A Plant mentioned by Paracelsus. It is the Carline Thistle.
GENTARUM ~ Succinum or Amber.
GEPSIN ~ A Plaster.
GERM ~ The Mercury of the Philosophers, the principle and the seed of all metals, without being actually itself a metal, though potentially it is, of course, metallic.
GERSA ~ White Lead.
GIALAPPA ~ Jalap or Marvel of Peru.
GLASS OF MARY ~ Talc and Arabian Stone.
GLESSUM ~ Succinum or Amber.
GOLD ~ Its Artificial Production. It is not only by the common operations of mining and digging in the profundities of the earth that it is possible to obtain Gold. It is quite within the powers of Art to imitate Nature in this matter, for Art perfects Nature in this as in many other things. We propose to provide in this place an account of a formal experiment, the worth of which has been tested over and over again, and has in fact become little less than familiar among operators in the pursuit of the Grand Work. In order to perform it a large crucible must be provided, and it must be of such a quality as will be able to resist the action of intense heat. This crucible must be set over a burning furnace, and at the bottom of the vessel there must be strewn Powder of Colophony (a kind of resin) to about the thickness of the little finger. Above this undermost layer there must be another layer of Fine Powder of Iron -that is, the Finest Iron Filings ~ which shall be of the same thickness. Subsequently, the filings must be covered with a little Red Sulphur. Then the fire in the furnace must be increased till the iron filings have passed into a liquid condition. The next operation is to throw in Borax ~ that

kind which is made use of by goldsmiths for melting gold. To this must be added a like quantity of Red Arsenic, and as much Pure Silver as will be equivalent to the weight of the Iron Filings. Let the entire composition undergo coction by driving the furnace, taking care at the same time not to inhale the steam, on account of the arsenic in the vessel. Take then another crucible into which, by inclining the first vessel, you must pour the cocted matter, having previously stirred it effectually with an iron spatula. Proceed in such a manner that the composition will flow into the second crucible in a purified state, and devoid of recremental matter. By means of the Water of Separation, the Gold will be precipitated to the bottom. When it has been collected, let it be melted in a crucible, and the result will be good Gold, which will repay all pains and expense which have been devoted to its production. This chemical secret is contained in the "Hermetic Cabinet", and the facility with which the experiment can be performed has led many persons to undertake it. The authority cited in support of it is no less than that of the most learned Basil Valentine, who also affirms that the operation of the Grand Work of the Philosophers can be performed in less than three or four days, that the cost should not exceed three or four florins, and a few earthen vessels are sufficient for the whole experiment.

GOLD — Its Artificial Production. It is said that all roads lead to Rome, and the student of the Adepts and their followers will sometimes be tempted to conclude from the immense variety of methods that are described in the works of the Philosophers that there are as many processes which may result in the manufacture of Artificial Gold, as there are paths leading to the Eternal City. There is no doubt that a very considerable proportion of these must be discounted, some as the subterfuges resorted to by veritable initiates to conceal their arcanum from the vulgar crowd of fortune-hunters and dealers in the curious, but many more as the spurious devices of impostors who traded in the name of Alchemy at a period when it was possible to do so. Over and above these, there is a certain proportion of neglected and unknown experiment which has no authority to recommend it, and must be taken for what it is worth. An example of this class is the Process of Caravana, a Spanish-American of the early colonial period. It runs in the following manner: Take Living Sulphur, Salt of Nitre, and Saltpetre — the same quantity of each, that is to say, about four ounces. Having reduced the whole to powder, place it in a well-sealed glass vessel, and plaster it over thoroughly with an adhesive clay. Set it by a slow fire for the space of two hours. At the end of this time augment the fire until it burns without emitting any smoke-that is, until it is a clear glowing fire-then let a clear flame play round the neck and along the sides of the vessel, and when it is expended the Sulphur will be found precipitated at the bottom of the vase, and it will be of a white colour and a fixed consistence. Let it be removed, and having added thereto a like quantity of Sal Ammoniac, the whole must be well pounded and pulverised, and afterwards sublimed over a fire which shall be slow at the beginning, but shall be gradually increased for the space of four hours. All the sublimed matter must then be taken from the vase, including the lees at the bottom. The whole must be incorporated together, again sublimed, and this operation is to continue up to the sixth time, after which the Sulphur will be again found at the bottom, must be again collected, and again pounded, this time on a marble slab in a moist locality. It will then be changed into an oil, six drops of which must be poured upon a Ducat of Gold that has been melted in a crucible. From this another oil will result, which will congeal upon a slab of marble. One part of this oil poured upon fifty parts of prepared and purged Mercury will produce a most excellent Sol.

GOLD — A process for its manufacture, attributed to Raymond Lully. Perfect Coction is the one thing needful in the great work of the Philosophers. To ensure this Perfect Coction, proceed in the following manner: Prepare an Ash, composed of the Wood of the Vine, and the Bones of a Horse or an Ox, well burned and calcined, until they are exceedingly white. Pulverise this Ash, place it in a Vessel of Glazed Clay, filled with forge-water, and add thereto as much Quick Lime as there is of Ash. Boil the whole together until the water is reduced by half. Then add four ounces of Fine Silver, previously beaten into thin plates of about the weight of a halfpenny. Let there be twelve of these plates. Cast them into the vessel which contains the Decocted Ash, and continue boiling until the water is again reduced by half. Then extract the twelve Silver plates; clean them at once with a white linen cloth, and leave the composition in the vessel to settle. A species of Salt will be found upon the surface, after the manner of crystals, and this must be skimmed off by means of a pewter spatula. Throw a little more forge-water into the vessel, and again boil. Then let it cool, and skim off the crystals of Salt. Continue this process until no more Salt can be obtained. Add to this Philosophical Salt four times the quantity of what is called Vegetable Salt, which is composed of Sulphur, Saltpetre and Tartar, in such a manner as good artists know how to combine them, and as indeed it may be obtained from all good apothecaries. Over and above this, take four ounces of Cement of Tiles, the reddest that can be obtained. Reduce them to a very fine powder. Then beat out as many small plates of Ducat Gold as you have already prepared of Silver, both being of the same weight. Use the best quality of crucible that you can obtain, and place at the bottom thereof a layer of your Salts, and your cement of Red Earth, with a little goldsmith's Borax. On the top of this layer place a plate of Gold. Cover it with a second layer of the Salts and Cement, and on this place a second plate of Gold. Continue this arrangement up to the twelfth time, and let the twelfth plate of Gold be covered with a final layer of Salts and Cement. Cover the crucible, seal it with adhesive clay, and set it in a burning fire, for such time as you shall judge will be required to melt your Gold, and precipitate it to the bottom of the crucible. This being done, take another vessel, shaped like a horn, and having a top which will shut or open, as required, when it is in the furnace. Transfer your Gold to this vessel, with a little Borax to melt it. When you judge that the Gold is melted, pass one of your prepared plates of Silver through the mouth into the vessel, so that the Gold may assimilate and be nourished thereby. Do this every twelve hours, till you have exhausted all your plates of Silver. Then extinguish your fire, allow your vessel to cool, and therein you shall find nearly double the quantity of Gold that you have placed therein; it will, moreover, furnish you with an excellent menstruum for augmenting Gold, if you follow the directions that have been given. It can be multiplied a million times.

GOLD — Precipitated Gold or Gold of Life. Take two ounces of Quicksilver, which has been purged and cleansed by means of Salt and Vinegar. Add one drachm of fine Oriental Gold reduced to powder. Knead them well together in a glazed earthenware dish, which must be slightly warmed until they are thoroughly mixed. Such a composition is usually termed an Amalgam. Turn this Amalgam into cold water. Should there be a small quantity of Quicksilver which has not become incorporated with the Gold, it must be again cocted and purified, after which it must be reunited to the Amalgam, and the latter must be washed with Distilled

Salt and Vinegar, till all recremented matter disappears. Should the Quicksilver become diminished by these processes, it must be augmented. For one drachm of Gold, there must be eight drachms of the Mercury. Place the Amalgam in an alembic of strong glass, well luted, and sealed with adhesive earth, taking care to add two ounces of Aquafortis, and distil the composition by a sand fire. Return to the alembic what has passed into the recipient. Repeat this process five times, after which you will find a fine powder at the bottom of the alembic. Place this powder in an earthenware vessel which will withstand a violent heat. Moisten the powder with good rose-water. Close the vessel so effectually that nothing can possibly escape; place it in the furnace; raise the fire till the vessel becomes red-hot; let it cool in the same furnace; and then you will be in possession of your Precipitated Gold.

This Precipitated Gold has the power of curing the plague, the pox, leprosy, dropsy, and other maladies which resist the healing art. It is a sovereign remedy for obstructions; it will be serviceable in the case of persons who have drunk poison, or have partaken of poisoned food; it will cure severe ulcers, poisonous erysipelas, etc., whether taken in a liquid form or mixed with ointment. Half-a-penny weight ~ old French style ~ must alone be taken in two spoonfuls of good capillary syrup, in the case of women and children. Adult males may take one penny-weight in half a glass of good old wine.

GOLD ~ To Dissolve Gold. The Blood of a Stag is an excellent dissolvent of Gold. Take two pounds weight from the veins of a stag that has just been killed. Distil it five times in the Bath of Mary by means of Cohobation, always returning the product of each distillation to the sediment which remains in the alembic. After the fifth time, place it in a strong glass phial, and this quintessence is so good, and so simple a dissolvent of Gold that you can make the experiment upon the naked hand without fear of the consequences.

GOLD — Another Dissolvent. Take two ounces of Saltpetre, half an ounce of very dry Saw-dust of Walnut-wood. Reduce the whole into an impalpable powder. Fill a large nut-shell as full as it will hold with this powder, and thereon [that is, upon the powder] place a small plate of fine Gold, so as to cover it completely. Cover the plate with another layer of powder about the thickness of a finger; and then you will see by experience that the plate will melt and go down to the bottom of the shell, without the shell being burnt. The same experiment may be made with other metals.

GOLD — To change Lead into Fine Gold. There are many persons, says the book on natural secrets which is called Albertus Parvus Lucii Libellus, who reject as uncertain the method of the learned chemist Falopius for the transmutation of Lead into Fine Gold, because it appears too easy for an operation of such importance. Nevertheless, he is by no means alone among the recognised Philosophers, many of whom have expressed themselves in similar terms. Basil Valentine and Odomarus say nearly the same thing. However this may be, the receipt of Falopius is as follows: Infuse one pound of Cyprus Copperas in one pound of forge water which has been well clarified by filtration. The infusion must continue for twenty-four hours in such a way that the Copperas shall be completely liquefied and incorporated with the water. Then distil it by filtration through very clean felt, and afterwards by means of an alembic and sand furnace. Preserve the result of the distillation in a globular bottle of strong glass, well corked. Then place one ounce of good Quicksilver in the crucible, which must be covered to prevent evaporation, and when you judge that it is boiling, or, rather, at boiling point, add one ounce weight of Fine and Good Gold Leaves, at once removing the crucible from the fire. This being done, take one pound of Fine Lead, well purified after a manner that shall be hereinafter set forth. Melt this Lead; incorporate it with the composition of Gold and Quicksilver; mix the three substances well together over the fire with an iron spit; then add one ounce of the Copperas Water; and let the whole digest over the fire for a time. When the composition has become cold, you will find that it is good Gold.

The method of the preparation and purification of the Lead is as follows. In order to obtain one pound of pure metal, take four ounces over that quantity to allow for recrement and for evaporation. Melt it, then plunge it in good, strong, clarified Vinegar; again melt, and plunge in the sap or juice of the Celandine (?); continue the melting process, and plunge in salt water; melt it for the last time, and extinguish in strong Vinegar, in which Quicklime has been plunged. It will then be effectually purified.

GOPHRITH — The Magisterium when arrived at the Red Stage.

GOTNE — Cotton.

GRASSALE — A Pottinger.

GREAT SECRET OF ARISTEUS — The Albertus *Parvus Lucii Libellus* has the following account of a process which is attributed to this celebrated artist. If the great name of Aristeus had not become celebrated among those of Adepts in the high operations of philosophy, it would be difficult to give credit to the writing which he has addressed to his son by election, as an instruction for the undertaking of the great philosophical work. It will be discerned amidst the obscurities of the document that Aristeus considered the mysterious Stone of the Philosophers to be composed of condensed air, artificially rendered palpable. And this is how he instructs his son upon the all-important subject:

My son, after having imparted to thee a knowledge of all things, and after having taught thee how to live, after what manner to regulate thy conduct by the maxims of a most excellent wisdom, and after having also enlightened thee in that which concerns the order and the nature of the monarchy of the universe, it only remains for me to communicate those Keys of Nature which hitherto I have so carefully held back. Among all these Keys, that which is most closely allied to the highest spirits of the universe deserves to take the first rank, and there is no one who questions that it is very specially endowed with an altogether divine property. When one is in possession of this Key, the rich become miserable in our eyes, inasmuch as there is no treasure which can possibly be compared to it. In effect, what is the use of wealth, when one is liable to be afflicted with human infirmities? Where is the advantage of treasures, when death is about to destroy us? There is no earthly abundance which we are not bound to abandon upon the threshold of the tomb. But it is no longer thus when I am possessed of this Key, for then I behold death from afar, and I am convinced that I have within my hands a secret which extinguishes all fear of misfortunes in this life. Wealth is ever at my command, and I no longer want for treasures; weakness flees away from me; and I can ward off the approach of the destroyer while I own this Golden Key of the Grand Work. My son, it is of this Key that I propose to make thee the inheritor; but I conjure thee, by the name of God, and by the Holy Place wherein He dwelleth, to lock it up in the cabinet of thy heart, under the seal of silence. If thou knowest how to make use of it, it will overwhelm thee with good things, and when thou shalt be old or ill, it will rejuvenate, console, and cure thee; for it has the special virtue of curing all diseases, of transfigurating metals, and of making happy those who possess it. It is that Key to which our fathers have often exhorted us under the bond of an inviolable oath. Learn, then, to know it, cease not to do good to the poor, to the widow, to the orphan, and learn its seal of me, and its true character.

Know that all beings which are under heaven, each after its own kind, derives origin from the same principle, and it is, as a fact, unto Air that all owe their birth as to a common principle. The nourishment of each existence makes evident the nature of its principle, for that which sustains the life is that which gives the being. The fish joys in the water; the child sucks from its mother. The tree no longer bears fruit when its trunk is deprived of humidity. It is by the life that we discern the principle of things; the life of things is the Air, and by consequence Air is their principle. It is for this reason that Air corrupts all things, and even as it gives life, so also it takes it away. Wood, iron, stones, are consumed by fire, and fire cannot subsist but by Air. Now, that which is the cause of corruption is also the cause of generation. When, by reason of divers corruptions, it comes to pass that creatures fall sick and do suffer, either through length of days or by mischance, the Air coming to their succour cures them, whether they be imperfect or languishing. The earth, the tree, the herb languish under the heat of excessive drought; but all things are recuperated by the dew of the Air. But, nevertheless, as no creature can be restored and re-established except by its own nature, Air being the fountain and original source of all things, it is in like manner the universal source. It is manifestly certain that the seed, the death, the sickness, and the remedy of all things are all alike in the Air.

There has Nature stored up all her treasures, establishing therein the principles of the generation and corruption of all things, and concealing them as behind special and secret doors. To know how to open these doors with sufficient

facility so as to draw upon the radical Air of the Air, is to possess in truth the golden Keys, and to be in ignorance thereof precludes all possibility of acquiring that which cures all maladies and recreates or preserves the life of men.
If thou desirest then, O my Son, to chase away all thine infirmities, thou must seek the means in the primal and universal source. Nature produces like from like alone, and that only which is in correspondence or conformity with Nature can effect good to her. Learn then, my Son, to make use of Air, learn to conserve the Key of Nature. It is truly a secret which transcends the possibilities of the vulgar man, but not those of the sage, this knowledge of the Extraction of Air, the Celestial Aerial Substance, from Air; for Air may be familiar to all beings, but he who would truly avail himself thereof must possess the secret Key of Nature. It is a great secret to understand the virtue which Nature has imprinted in substances. For natures are attracted by their like; a fish is attracted by a fish — a bird by a bird-and air by another air, as with a gentle allurement. Snow and ice are an air that has been congealed by cold; Nature has endowed them with the qualities which are requisite to attract air. Place thou, therefore, one of these two things in an earthen or metallic vessel, well closed, well sealed, and take thou the Air which congeals round this vessel when it is warm. Receive that which is distilled in a deep vessel with a narrow neck, neat and strong, so that thou canst use it at thy pleasure, and adapt to the rays of the Sun and Moon — that is, Silver and Gold. When thou hast filled a vessel cork it well, so that the heavenly scintillation concentrated therein shall not escape into the air. Fill as many vases as thou wilt with liquid; then hearken to thy next task, and keep silent. Build a furnace, place a small vessel therein, half full of the Liquid Air which thou hast collected; seal and lute the said vessel effectually. Light thy fire in such a manner that the

thinner portion of the smoke may rise frequently above. Thus shall Nature perform that which is continually accomplished by the central fire in the bowels of the earth, where it agitates the vapours of the air by an unceasing circulation. The fire must be light, mild, and moist, like that of a hen brooding over her eggs, and it must be sustained in such a manner that it will cook without burning the aerial fruits, which, having been for a long time agitated by a movement, shall rest at the bottom of the vessel in a state of perfect coction.

Add next unto this Cocted Air a fresh air, not in great quantity, but as much as may be necessary; that is to say, a little less than on the first occasion. Continue this process until there shall be no more than half a bowl of Liquid Air uncooked. Proceed in such wise that the cooked portion shall gently liquefy by fermentation in a warm dunghill, and shall in like manner blacken, harden, amalgamate, become fixed, and grow red. Finally, the pure part being separated from the impure by means of a legitimate fire, and by a wholly divine artifice, thou shalt take one part of pure crude Air and one part of pure hardened Air, taking care that the whole is dissolved and united together till it becomes moderately black, more white, and finally perfectly red. Here is the end of the work, and then hast thou composed that elixir which produces all the wonders that our Sages aforetime have with reason held so precious; and thou dost possess in this wise the Golden Key of the most inestimable secret of Nature — the true Potable Gold and the Universal Medicine. I bequeath unto thee a small sample, the quality and virtues of which are attested by the perfect health which I enjoy, being aged over one hundred and eight years. Do thou work, and thou shaft achieve as I have done. So be it in the name and by the power of the great Architect of the Universe.

Such skilful artists of the Great Work as have pondered deeply on the principles confided to the son of Aristeus, have concluded that it would be no vain operation to make an Amalgam with the veritable Balm of Mercury, and this is the way in which they claim to produce this Balm:

Take one pound of the best Mercury that can be obtained; purge it three times through a skin, and once by calcined Montpellier Tartar. Place it in a glass horn, which shall be strong enough to resist a fierce heat. With it combine Vitriol, Salt of Nitre, Rock Alum, and eight ounces of good Spirit of Wine. Having hermetically sealed the horn, so that nothing can evaporate, place it for digestion in a warm dung-hill during a space of fifteen days. At the end of this time the composition will be transformed into a phlegmatic grease; it must then be exposed to a sand fire, and the fire must be raised gradually to an extreme point, till a white, milky humour exudes from the substance and falls into the recipient. Let it then be replaced in the horn to be rectified, and for the consumption of the phlegm. This second distillation will cause a sweet, white oil to exude; this oil will be devoid of corrosive qualities; it will surpass all other metallic oils in excellence; and there is no doubt that, combined with the Elixir of Aristeus, it will be possible to perform such marvels as might be expected from so admirable an experiment.

GREAT WORK, THE ~ One of the names which Chemical Philosophers have given to their Art because of the difficulty of succeeding therein, and on account also of its two great objects ~ the confection of a universal medicine for the treating of all maladies in the three kingdoms of Nature, and, in particular, the transmutation of imperfect metals into Gold purer than even that of the mines.

GRENARD ~ The Stone when it has reached the Red Stage.

GUININA — The Magisterium at the White Stage.
GUM OF THE SUN — The Matter of the Work when it has arrived at the White Stage.

HABITATION OF THE FOWL ~ The Hermetic Vessel.
HABRAS ~ A Plant known under the name of Staphis Agria, or Flea's Bane.
HACUMIA ~ Same as Endica, according to Morien. See Endica in Rulandus.
HAC ~ The Stone at the White.
HAGER ALIENDI ~ Judaic Stone.
HAGER ARCHTAMACH ~ Eagle Stone.
HAGER ALZARNAD ~ The Mercury of the Sages digested and cooked till it has attained the red colour of the Poppy.
HALCAL ~ Vinegar.
HALEREON ~ The Eagle of the Philosophers.
HALIACMON ~ A River of Macedonia which has the property of whitening the fleece of the sheep that drink from it-supposing naturally that their fleece is not already white. See Pliny (l. 34, c. 2). Hence the expression which occurs in Hermetic Terminology, that the Philosophic Dragon and Eagle must be made to drink of the river Haliacmon,

meaning that the Laton must be made white, or that the Matter of the Work must proceed from the Black to the White Stage. The word cited is also written Aliacmon.

HALLS — Glue.

HANDEL, or **HANDAL** — Colocinth.

HARMALA — Wild Rue.

HATCHET — The Fire of the Philosophers. To strike with the hatchet or axe is to cook the matter.

HEBRIT — Red Sulphur of the Philosophers.

HEDELTABATENI — Turpentine.

HEIGHT — The Allegorical and Mysterious Dimension of the Stone of the Sages. If we are to believe Philalethes, the Height is nothing else than the Matter of the Philosophers as it is manifested to our eyes during the time of its preparation. For example, the Body of the Matter of our Art, he tells us in his treatise on the True Composition of the Philosophical Stone, is black during its first decomposition which takes place by means of putrefaction. This blackness which strikes our eyes, and is called Cold and Moist, is that which is manifested to our sight, and it is this quality, state, or disposition, that we term the Height of our Body.

HELSATON — Salt that has lost its Savour.

HELSEBON — Common Prepared Salt.

HEMIOBOLON — The Twelfth Part of a Drachm.

HEMIOLIUM — Some understand by this term a Weight of Half-an-Ounce, others a Weight of an Ounce and a Half.

HENRY — Red Colestar.

HERB — The White Herb — A Plant which grows on small hills. In the terminology of the Great Art, it means the Matter when cooked and perfect at the White. Some understand it of the Mercury of the Sages, some of the Ore whence it is extracted, but the circumstances under which it is used in the Dialogue of Mary and of Aros show that it is really applied to the Matter at the White, because the philosophers sometimes represent their vase and their furnace by the expression small hills.

HERB ~ Philosophic Herb ~ Saturnian Herb ~ Medicinal Herb ~ All these terms of the Great Art signify the same thing ~ that is to say, the Mercury of the Sages, and sometimes the Ore whence this Mercury is extracted.

HERB ~ The Triumphant Herb ~ Mineral Matter, forming part of the Composition of the Philosophers. It is that which they call their Sieve.

HERB ~ Potherb, etc. ~ The Stone at the White.

HERB ~ Saturnian Herb or Saturnia ~ A Vegetable Matter from which the Hermetic Philosophers know how to extract their Mercury.

HERMES ~ The name which some chemists have given to Nitre. It is also one of the names, and, in fact, it is the true and proper name of the Mercury of the Philosophers, because it is actually the Mercury of Bodies, and particularly that of all the members of the Mineral Kingdom.

HERMETICS ~ The Art or Science of the Hermetic Philosophers. Hermetic Physics are a part of this science which regards all beings of the sublunary world as formed from three principles ~ Salt, Sulphur, and Mercury, while it ascribes all maladies to a want of proper equilibrium in their action. The second object of the Art is to compose what is called the Elixir at the White or at the Red, which they also term Powder of Projection and Philosophical Stone. It is also claimed that by means of the Elixir at the White, it is possible to transmute metals into Silver,, and by means of the Elixir at the Red into Gold.

HERNEC ~ The Orpiment of the Philosophers.

HESPERIS ~ A species of the Aloe Tree.

HEXAGIUM ~ According to some, a Weight of Four Scruples; according to others, a Drachm and a Half.

HIDROS ~ Sweat.

HILLA — The Jejunum (an Intestine).
HIN — Assafoetida.
HIPPURIS — The Plant called Horse-tail.
HOLCE — A Drachm.
HOREUM — Honey extracted from the Hive during Summer.
HORIZONTIS — Potable Gold.
HUMATION — An action by which the Matter of the Stone of the Sages is placed in the Vase to be there subjected to putrefaction. Some chemists have compared this action to the Sepulchre of Jesus Christ. But albeit Humation in the terms of Hermetic Science signifies properly the Putrefaction of the Matter, yet the term is sometimes applied to its fixation, because the fixation of the volatile is one species of death, and that which was water during dissolution becomes water after fixing.
HUMECTATION — That Process by which Humidity is imparted to the Stone, when it is perfect, and when it is desired to multiply it.
HUMIDITY — Ignited Mercury of the Sages animated by its Sulphur. Sometimes the Philosophers understand by this term the matter of the work when it has arrived at the Black Stage.
HUMIDITY OF THE STONE — This is also the Mercury, for the Mercury is a dry water which does not wet the hands, and attaches or clings only to that which is of its own nature. To impart its Humidity to the Stone is to perform the work of Imbibition; that is to say, to continue the regimen of the Philosophical Fire, which sublimes this Humidity to the summit of the Vase, whence Imbibition is performed of itself, the same Humidity returning upon the earth at the bottom.
HYDOTODES VINUM — Wine mingled with Water.

IBERIS — A Species of Water-cress or Cardamom (a Medicinal Seed), or Lepidium, which is called Sidymbrium by Dioscorides.

IBIGA — Chamaepytis.

IBIS — The Egyptians employed the figure of this Bird in their hieroglyphics, to signify in the first place, a part of the Matter of the Grand Work. The Ibis in fact became a symbol of the volatile part which dissolves and volatilizes the fixed part, frequently typified by Serpents. Sometimes the White Ibis signified the Matter at the White, and the Black Ibis the Matter in Putrefaction.

ILLEIAS — The First Matter of all things.

ILLEIDOS — Elementary Air which nourishes the life of all things.

INDIVISIBLE — The Chemists call their Mercury the sole Indivisible thing known to the Sages.

IMPASTATION — When the Matter of the Work succumbs into Putrefaction in the Philosophical Egg, and has become black, it thickens or congeals into the consistency of molten Black Pitch. It is then like a paste or a sediment, and hence the name of the operation.

IMPREGNATION — There is no Impregnation without Conjunction says Morien, that is to say, if there be no marriage between the male and the female, or, what is the same thing, between the Fixed and the Volatile, one cannot act on the other and produce a third body which participates in the nature of both. The philosophical Impregnation is performed during the period when the Volatile and the Fixed are in a condition of complete dissolution, because then interpenetration takes place between them even to the inmost of their natures, and they are, so to speak, confounded together, and that in so complete a manner that after having circulated they become inseparable. The term Impregnation is also used in Chemistry to signify the communication of the properties of one composite substance to another, in what manner soever it may be accomplished. For example, when the emetic quality of Antimony is communicated to Tartar, which is then called Stibium Tartar.

INCOMBUSTIBLE — The hermetic chemists give the name of Incombustible to their Sulphurs, because they are so fixed that they can withstand the most assaults of fire.

INFINITE — This name is given to the Sulphur of the Philosophers, because it can be infinitely multiplied.

INFANT — The Hermetic Chemists frequently apply this term to their Sulphur, and sometimes to their Mercury. The Four Infants of Nature are the Four Elements of which she makes use in the formation of all sublunary beings. The alchemists say that two of these Elements are male and female, two are heavy and two are light. The Chemical Philosophers find their Infant ready formed by Nature, and their whole secret consists in the extraction of its Matrix or

Ore. Subsequently, they nourish it with a milk which is proper thereto.

INGRESS — The Philosophers Say that their Stone is piercing, tinging, and penetrating, or that it has Ingress-that is to say, that although a body, it enters into the inmost marrow of other bodies.

INGRESSION — That action by which substances combine in such a manner that they cannot afterwards be separated. Putrefaction operates this change during the period of perfect dissolution, and when the Matter is in the Black State.

INGROSSATION — That action by which the Volatile and the Fixed Parts of the Matter of the Sages combine and unite intimately after having contended together for a long time.

INSIPID or **TASTELESS SUBSTANCE** — The Magisterium at the White.

INSPIRE — To join the Soul with its Body. Also to Whiten the Matter, which is accomplished by means of a single substance in its proper and sole vase without any operation of the hands.

INSPISSATION — An operation which follows that of the Dissolution of Bodies, and which, nevertheless, is really the same process, since the body does not dissolve or become spiritualised unless the spirit corporifies. Inspissation is performed by means of a fire of the second grade. On this subject, it should be remarked that when the Philosophers speak of degrees in their fire which should be administered to their matter, the expression must not be interpreted to mean that the fire is to be exalted and diminished, as the vulgar chemists are accustomed to do in their furnaces, by means of registers or dampers, or of a varying quantity of coal, but that the secret fire of Nature must be augmented by digestion. In proportion, as the matter becomes more fixed, its fire increases by degrees, and these degrees are measured by the colours which it assumes.

INTERMEDIATE ~ The Third Matter which is added to the two others in chemical or mechanical operations, either to unite them, to separate them, or to set them in action. Salts which differ among themselves never unite together so well as by the means of a terrene intermediary. The Philosophers give the name of intermediary to their Mercury, and also call it Philtre, or Beverage of Love, the bond and the proper means of joining Tinctures inseparably together.

INTUBUM, or **INTUBUS** ~ Endive, a species of Chicory.

ISCHAS ~ The Dried Fig.

ISIR ~ The author of the Hermetic Dictionary says that the Philosophers understand by this term the Elixir at the White, and that the Sages have so named it when it is desired to multiply it. But the Philosophers also make use of it to signify the same thing that they express under the term Iris, which see.

ISIS ~ The Hermetic Philosophers subsequent to Hermes who have made use of this name understand this goddess to signify the Volatile, Humid, Cold, Passive, and Feminine Portion of the Hermetic or Sacerdotal Art.

JABORA ~ Mandragore.

JANUS ~ The two Visages of the Classical God signify, according to the alchemists, the Matter of the Stone Philosophical, which they call Rebris, because it consists of two things.

JONI ~ To assemble ~ mix ~ unite one thing with another. See Inspire.

JOURDANI ~ In Hermetic Science this is a name which the Philosophers have given to their Dissolvent Mercury, because this Mercury must wash the soluble body seven times in order to purify it.

JOY OF THE PHILOSOPHERS ~ When the Stone or the Matter of the Philosophers has arrived at the perfect White Stage, which is the philosophical White Gold, or White Sulphur, or Endica of Morien, or the Swan, then all the philosophers say that this is the time of joy, because they behold Diana unveiled, and they have avoided all the rocks and dangers of the sea. The Code of Truth remarks: Whiten the Laton, and then destroy your books, for then have they become useless unto you, and will serve only as an incumbrance, a source of doubt and disquietude, when you should experience nothing but joy. When the Matter has arrived at the White State nothing but clumsiness can prevent the success of the work, and its eduction towards the perfection of the Red State, since all the volatile portion is then fixed in such a manner that it can withstand the most active and violent fire.

JUDGMENT ~ Raymond Lully has given this name to the Projection of the Hermetic Powder upon imperfect Metals, because it is on this occasion that the artist has to be the judge of the operation, and by his success or his failure he judges whether he has operated well or badly, and he is recompensed according to his works.

KANECH — Dew.
KEIRI, or **KEIRIM** — According to some, the Narcissus, according to others, the Violet or the Yellow Gilliflower. It is also written Cheiri.
KIMENNA — A Large Bottle.
KIMIT — White Cinnabar.
KIRATH — A Weight of Four Grains.
KIST — Oppoponax. This term also signifies a Weight of Fifteen Grains, or, as some say, of Four Pounds. It also signifies Two Measures of Wine.
KUKUL — See Kuhul, in Rulandus.

LABOS BALSAMAM ~ The Water in which a Red-hot Metal has been Plunged.
LACHANUM ~ Herbages, Vegetables.
LACINIAS ~ A Woollen Strainer.
LAMATI ~ Gum Arabic.
LAMER ~ Living Sulphur.
LAMP ~ When the Philosophers speak of the fire of a Lamp as of their fire, they are not to be understood as referring to a lamp that is fed with oil or spirit of wine. Their Lamp-fire is that of their Matter.
LAMPACOS ~ Lampatan China.
LANDINVA ~ Lingwort or Angelica.
LANGUAGE ~ In the writings of Hermetic Science, the Philosophers never express the true significance of their thoughts in the vulgar tongue, and they must not be interpreted according to the literal sense of the expressions. The sense which is presented on the surface is not the true sense. They discourse in enigmas, metaphors, allegories,

fables, similitudes, and each Philosopher adapts them after his own manner. A chemical Adept explains his philosophical operations in terms borrowed from the operations of common chemistry, speaking of distillation, sublimation, etc., of furnaces, of vases, of fires in use among chemists, as Gebir, Paracelsus, and others invariably do. An alchemical soldier like Denis Zacharie borrows his imagery from battles and from sieges. A churchman like Basil Valentine speaks in the terminology of moral philosophy and theology, as in his work upon Azoth. In a word, they have spoken so obscurely, in terms so different, in styles so various, that one must indeed be well versed in their mysteries to understand their meaning, and one Philosopher is frequently considerably embarrassed to explain another in any complete and intelligible manner. Some vary the names and reverse the operations; others begin their books in the middle of their practice; others again at the end; while not a few intermingle sophistic experiments, omit something that is important, and add something that is superfluous. One directs the student to make use of a certain ingredient, others advise him to avoid it. Rupecissa maintains that Roman Vitriol is the true Matter of the Philosophers, and the very writers who would maintain that Rupecissa was a veritable Adept recommend you to have nothing to do either with Roman or any other vitriol. All these manners of expression constitute a language which is exceedingly difficult to understand, but some Philosophers, the better to veil their practice, have had recourse to the Enigma. The Cosmopolite, among others, adds a very long one at the end of his Twelve Treatises. The ancients commonly made use of fables, and those of the Egyptians and Greeks were devised only in view of the Great Work, if we are to believe the Philosophers who frequently refer to them in their works. It was by following their ideas in this respect that Pernety devised a complete system of Hermetic mythology in his work upon The Egyptian and Greek Fables Unveiled. Some Philosophers have had recourse to a mute language by which to speak to the eyes of the spirit. They have presented by means of symbols and hieroglyphics, after the manner of the Egyptians, at one time the materials required for the work, the various necessary preparations, and even the demonstrative signs or the colours which appear in the Matter during the various stages of the process, because it is by these signs that the artist knows whether he has operated well or badly. Some Philosophers have added a discourse to their hieroglyphics, but the apparent explanation is invariably more difficult to understand than is the symbol itself. Such, for example, are those of Nicholas Flamel, Senior, Basil Valentine, and Michael Maier, although D'Espagnet says that those of the last-mentioned writer are a species of lunettes which discover clearly enough the truth which the Philosophers have concealed.

LAPPAGO — Burdock.
LARON — The Mercury of the Sages.
LARUSUS — The Plant Mouse-Ear.
LASER — Benzoin, an Aromatic Gum or Medicinal Resin.
LATERIUM — Lye or Capitel.
LATHYRIS — Spurge.
LATHYRUS — A species of Pulse called Gerces.
LATRO — Mercury of the Philosophers.
LAUNDRY — The Yeoman of Laundry. A name which the Philosophers have given to Jupiter when the period of its rule is at its zenith, during the operations of the Stone. It is the Circulation of the Matter in the Vase. It rises in vapour to the summit of the Philosophical Egg; then it condenses and falls back like a dew upon the Matter, which remains at the bottom. This dew or rain whitens the Matter, removing the black colour which prevailed during

the period of Saturn. It is the Washing of the Philosophers, and what they term Whitening the Leton or Laton.

LAUDANUM ~ A name which Paracelsus gives to a Composition of Gold, Corals, Pearls, etc. It was a Specific for Fevers.

LAUM ~ Bitter Almond.

LASCA CYMOLEA ~ A Salt which forms upon Stones.

LEPHANTE ~ First Tartar or Bolus, occupying a middle place between Stone and Slime.

LEPROSY ~ Heterogeneous Parts, Terrestrial Impurities, which Metals contract in the mine, and which the mere Powder of Projection is incapable of curing. Gebir and some other chemists have described the vices of imperfect metals. There are two kinds-the first being termed Original; and this is regarded as almost incurable, arising as it does from the first combination of the elements in Quicksilver or Mercury, which is their principle. The second is found in the union of Sulphur and of Mercury. The more that the elements are purified, the more they are proportionally mixed and homogeneous, the more have they of weight, malleability, capacity for fusion, extension, fulgidity, and permanent incorruptibility. The second malady, which comes from a more or less impure Sulphur, constitutes the imperfection of metals, to wit, the leprosy of Saturn, the jaundice of Venus, the lachrymosity of Jupiter, the dropsy of Mercury, and the scab of Mars. The dropsy of Mercury is caused by its excessive aquosity and crudity, which results from the frigidity of its matrix. This vice is an original sin, which it communicates and transmits to all metals that are engendered from it. Although the Philosophers have named Mercury a Quintessence, composed by Nature, it is, nevertheless, so aqueous, and so cold, that it can only be cured by a most potent Sulphur. The internal Sulphur, predominating in Mercury, cooks, digests, thickens, and fixes it into a perfect body; and the external, adustible, and separable Sulphur of the true substance of metals, suffocates the internal, deprives it of its activity, and mingles the impurities with those of the Mercury, which produces the imperfect metals. The causes of these maladies are the terrenity, aquosity, combustibility, and aerosity of the elements combined in them. The first prevents the union of substances, the second makes them crude, the third inflammable, and the fourth volatile. The first prevents penetration and ingress, the second is an obstacle to digestion and sublimation of the Matter, the third interferes with incorruptibility, and the fourth is opposed to fixation.

LETA — Red Colour.

LEUCELECTRUM — White Amber.

LEUCCENUS — White Wine.

LEUCOLACANUM — White Valerian.

LEUCOPHAGUM — A Ragout said to be a Remedy for Consumption.

LEUCOSIS — That Operation by which the Laton is Whitened. It is performed by the circulation of Azoth in the Vase of the Philosophers.

LEVIGATE — The Reduction of a Hard and Solid Body into an Impalpable Powder.

LIAB — Vinegar.

LIBANOTIS — Rosemary.

LIGAMENT — That Unctuosity of Bodies which binds the parts together, reunites the fixed with the volatile, prevents the evaporation of spirit, and forms the composition of sublunary beings.

LIGAMENT OF TINCTURES — The Mercury of the Philosophers, called the Medium Conjugendi.

LIGAMENT OF QUICKSILVER — This is Philosophical Gold, or the Fixation of Mercury, which happens when the Matter of the Work has arrived at the colour Red.

LIGHT ~ The Hermetic Chemists give this name to Mercury when it whitens after putrefaction, and it is then that a separation is made between the darkness and the light. They also term Light the Powder of Projection, because it seems to illustrate the imperfect metals when it transmutes them into Gold or Silver. The Philosophers have also occasionally given this name to their Red Sulphur, because otherwise they call it the Sun, and the sun transmits light to our planet.

LIQUIDITY ~ That State of a Body in which the Constituent Parts do not adhere together. There are two kinds of Liquidity; one, like that of water, which wets the hands, and one which does not wet them. Such is that of common Mercury and of the metals. This latter species of Fluidity is owing to the presence of terrestial particles insinuated into the pores of the metals in an excessive quantity.

LOTION ~ Circulation of the Matter in the Vase of the Philosophers. It ascends in vapour and returns in rain upon the terrestial portion at the bottom, whitening and purifying it, like a shower upon new linen at the fullers. The Lotion of the Philosophers is only a term applied by similitude. They wash with fire even as they burn with water. Their Lotion is but a purification made by the Philosophical Fire. Let no one be therefore deceived by the author who says " Go and look at the women who are employed over the washing and fulling of linen; see what they do, and do thou even as they are doing ". He simply means to say: cleanse the Matter of its impurities, and that by the Philosophical Fire or the Fire of the Matter itself, for another author assures us that it dissolves, purifies, congeals, blackens, whitens, and reddens of itself; that, as a fact, nothing is taken away and nothing is added save that which is indispensable to the success of the work.

LUMINARIES ~ The two grand luminaries of the Sages are the Gold and Silver of the Philosophers, that is to say, the matter of the Work arrived at the White Colour, which they term the Moon, and the Magisterium at the Red, which they name the Sun.
LUNARY ~ The Sulphur of Nature.
LUPINUS ~ A Weight of Half-a-drachm. Fernel understands it to be Six Grains and Agricola Eight.
LUPULUS ~ The Plant called Hops.
LYCOCTONUM ~ Aconite.
LYE ~ The Azoth of the Philosophers, so named because it whitens the Laton of the Sages.

MACERATION — The Attenuation of a Composite Substance by means of its own, or otherwise, in some foreign menstruum. Maceration precedes putrefaction, and there adapts the Composite.

MACHINOR — The Material with which Clay Vessels are Varnished.

MAGALE — A Latin term by which Paracelsus understands every species of Perfume made from minerals.

MAGI — The Philosophers, Priests, and Offerers of Sacrifice in Persia, persons who were renowned informer times for their knowledge and for their wisdom. Their doctrine was identical with that of the priests of Egypt, who were the successors of Hermes; it was identical also with that of the Brahmins of India, the Greek philosophers, etc. Philo informs us that the end of their science was the knowledge of Nature and of her Author, and so intimate did this knowledge become, that they could perform the most surprising and wonderful works. They were able to avail themselves of all the resources of Nature, and of the mutual interaction of her forces, the achievements that resulted being taken for miracles in their time. The Magi believed in the resurrection of the body, and in the immortality of the soul. They also professed Magic, but it was that sublime Magic, as it were, a celestial art, which was practised by the greatest men of antiquity, and to which, at a later date, the name of Theurgy was applied, to distinguish it from the superstitious and detestable art, which has its essence in the abuse of holy things, and is concerned with the invocation of evil spirits. The essence of Theurgy, on the other hand, is to be found in the knowledge and the practice of the most curious and least known secrets of Nature.

MAGIC AND CHEMISTRY — The transformations of Magic and of Hermetic Chemistry are both nothing more — marvellous as they may seem — than the artificial development of natural germs. No one actually makes gold; it is Nature who is assisted to make it. The problem resolved by the Magic of Hermes is briefly this: To accumulate and to fix in an artificial body the latent Caloric, in such a manner as to change the molecular polarisation of natural substances by their amalgamation with an artificial substance. On the other hand, the problem which Thaumaturgic Magic seeks to deal with should be thus formulated: To control or to exalt the principle that governs form manifestations in such a manner as to change appearances. By this definition it is plain that the prodigies of magical fascination are in effect nothing but prestige. To make use of illusions without being their dupe is therefore the great secret of this kind of magic. He who creates illusions without being subject to them commands all vertigo and all perdition. He who is victimised by illusion is carried away by vertigo.

MAGNETISM — Human Magnetism — This must be regarded as one of the active principles of the Great Work.

As a fact the man who himself is perfectly equilibrated becomes an equilibrating centre for the things with which he deals, and rectitude in thinking gives exactitude in operation. Now, the operations of science are so delicate that they demand minds emancipated from all passions and all species of cupidity.

MAGOREUM — Medicaments which perform their office without our being able to discover the physical cause. Such is the Sympathetic Powder and the Unguent of Paracelsus.

MALADORAM — Sal Gemmae. See Rulandus.

MALARIBIO — Opium.

MALE — The Magisterium at the Red Stage. In reading the works of the philosophers, particular note should be taken of the point at which their work begins — that is to say, of what part of the operation they first speak. A large number of writers have omitted all reference to the Magisterium, supposing it to have been already accomplished. It is on this understanding that they say Take the male, and unite it to the female. The reference here is to the Perfect Magisterium at the Red Stage.

MALCHORUM or **MALEHORUM** — Sal Gemmae.

MALICORIUM — Orange Peel.

MALINATHALIA — Cypress.

MALTACODE — A Medicament into which Wax enters as one of the ingredients.

MAMOLARIA — The Plant called Acanthus.

MANIS NOSTER — The Dew of the Philosophers and the Magnet of the Sages.

MANUS CHRISTI — The Hand of Christ — that is, Pearled Syrup.

MARATHRUM — Fennel Seed.

MARGA — A certain Fatty and Unctuous Matter which is found in some species of Stones, whence it has been called the Marrow of Pebbles.

MARIS ~ A Weight of Eighty-three Pounds Three Ounces.
MARMORARIA ~ Same as Mamolaria, which see.
MARRIAGE ~ There is no term in more frequent use among the philosophers than is the word Marriage. They say that the Sun and the Moon must be joined in marriage together, that Gabertin must be united with Beza, the Mother with the Son, the Brother with the Sister, and all these expressions have reference exclusively to the union between the Fixed and the Volatile, which takes place in the Vase by the intermediation of Fire. All seasons are fitting for the celebration of this Marriage, but the Philosophers especially recommend spring as that period when Nature is most impelled to generation. Basil Valentine says that the Bride and the Bridegroom must be stripped of all their vestures, and must be well washed and purified before entering into the nuptial bed. D'Espagnet and others assert that the work will by no means succeed if the male and female are not so purified that no heterogeneous particle remains in them. In this purification the whole secret of the purification of Mercury consists. The ferment or leaven must also be perfectly pure, if we desire the Son born of this Marriage to possess such a degree of perfection that he can transmit his own high quality to his brethren and his subjects.
MARTHETO ~ By this term some writers describe the Stone at the Red Stage, the Ferment of the Work; but it is said in the Code of Truth, Take Martheto and whiten it. This refers to the Laton or the Matter at the Black Stage.
MASAL ~ A term employed in some chemical works to signify Sour Milk.
MASARDEGI ~ Lead.
MASAREA ~ Creeping Mouse-Ear.
MASSERIUM ~ Hermetic Mercury.

MASTACH — A Preparation of Opium much in use among the Turks.

MATER SYLVA — Honeysuckle.

MATTER — The First Matter of the Philosophers. The true and primal matter of metals is of double essence, or is dual in itself. One of these essences without the concurrence of the other will not create a metal. The first and the chief essence is a moisture of air, mixed with a warm air in the form of an oily water, which indifferently adheres to everything, pure or impure. This moisture is called the Mercury of the Philosophers — that is, the Universal Dissolvent. It is governed by the rays of the Sun and Moon. The second essence is the heat of the earth; it is that dry heat which the Philosophers call Sulphur.

The First Matter of things is begotten by Nature without the help of any seed. That is, Nature receives the matter from the elements, and from it she afterwards engenders seed. Speaking absolutely, the seed in a body is nothings else but a congealed air, or a moist vapour, which, if not resolved by a warm vapour, becomes quite useless. By the artifice of Archeus, the four elements, in the first generation of Nature, distil at the centre of the earth a vapour of heavy water, which is the seed of metals, and is called Mercury, not on account of its essence, but of its fluidity and facile adherence to everything. The vapour itself is compared to Sulphur because of its internal heat. After its congelation, the seed becomes the moist radical of the Matter. Metals are composed of the Mercury of the Philosophers, and of no common Mercury, which cannot be a seed, having its own seed within it, like the other metals. The Subject of our Matter is the seed only, or fixed grain, and not the entire body, which is divided into Living Male — that is, Sulphur — and Living Female — that is, Mercury. These should be joined together in order that they may produce a germ, whence they will procreate a fruit according to their nature. In this operation the artist has only to separate what is subtle from what is gross. Therefore, all the philosophical combination is reduced to making one of two and of two one. There is nothing beyond this.

MATTER OF THE PHILOSOPHERS — The First Matter of the Sages is to be found in ourselves. We all indifferently possess it, from the beggar to the king; and could our ingenious chemists but find a process for extracting it, their labours would be more than well paid. But we cannot draw or extract the secret Matter of the Stone out of ourselves by any common means. Nevertheless, it can be drawn into very action, and that not only by a most simple means, but in such a manner that the attainment of the Philosopher's Stone would very soon follow it. Look into thyself, and endeavour to find out in what part of thy composition is the Prima Materia of the Lapis Philosophorum, or out of what part of thy substance can the First Matter of the Stone be drawn. Thou sayest: It must be either in the hair, sweat, or excrement, but in none of these shalt thou ever be able to find it and yet thou shalt find it in thyself. In us is the power of all wonderful things, which the Supreme Creator has, of His infinite mercy, implanted in our souls. Out of these is to be extracted the First Matter, the true Argent vif, the Living Silver, the Mercury of the Philosophers, the true ens of Sol — namely, a Spiritual Living Gold, or Waterish Mercury, or First Matter, which by being maturated is capable of transmuting a thousand parts of impure metal into good and perfect gold which shall endure fire, test, and cupel. Our soul has the power, when the body is free of any pollution, the heart void of malice and offence, to act spiritually and magically upon any matter whatsoever. Therefore the First Matter is in the Soul, and the extracting of it is to bring the dormant power of the pure, living, breathing spirit and eternal soul into act. The expense which is involved is a trifle. All the necessary instruments are three in number — a crucible, a philosophical egg, and a retort with its receiver. Put thou fine gold, in weight about five pennyweights, fill it up, place it in the philosophical egg, pour upon it twice its weight of the best Hungarian Mercury, close up the egg with an hermetic seal, put it for three months in horse-dung. Take it out at the end of that time, and see what kind of form the gold and mercury has assumed. Then remove it from the egg, pour on it half its weight of good spirit of sal ammoniac, and set them in a pot full of sand over the fire in the retort. Let them distil into a pure essence. Add to one part of this Mercury two parts of thy Water of Life, or First Matter; put them into thy philosophical egg, and set them again into horse-dung for another three months. Then take them out, and see what thou hast — a pure ethereal essence, which is the Living Gold. Pour this pure spiritual liquor upon a drachm of molten fine gold, and then shalt thou find that which shall satisfy thy hunger and thy thirsting after this secret, for the increase of thy gold will seem to thee nothing less than miraculous, as indeed it is. Take it to a jeweller's or a goldsmith's; let him try it in thy presence, and thou wilt have reason to bless God for His mercy unto thee.

MAZA — Macaroons or Mecal — a Weight.

MECERI — Opium.

MEDICAL MAN OF THE PLANETS — This is not the Mercury of the Philosophers, it is the Philosopher himself who employs the Mercury of the Sages to heal the imperfections of metals, which are termed Planets. The Medicine cures and the Physician administers. The Stone of the Philosophers or the Powder of Projection constitutes this Medicine, which makes perfect metals, and cures the diseases that afflict the three kingdoms of Nature.

MEDICINE — The Unique Medicine. The Stone at the White.

MEDICINE — Paracelsus reduces the whole art of healing into principles which are very simple, both as regards theory and practice, and so did his cures eclipse anything achieved by the doctors of his age. Had he written his books in a more intelligible manner, possibly justice would be done to him at the present day, whereas now it is refused. He has made a mystery of everything; he has employed bizarre names to describe known things; and it is he who has suffered in consequence, for the successes that he promised have not resulted to those who have followed his experiments, and thence it has been concluded that he was nothing more than a charlatan. The proper and only method of removing these obstacles to his reputation would be to publish the process of what he terms the Universal Medicine, but those who pass for being acquainted with it, and having practised it, declare that the result of so doing would be extremely prejudicial to society on account of the abuse which would be made of it by the wicked. They have thus forborne to treat of it in their works except in an enigmatical, allegorical, and metaphorical manner, in order, as they say, that it may be understood by those only to whom God wills that it should be made known. The Philosophers distinguish several species of Medicine, though all have the same object, namely, the healing of diseases which attack the members of any of the three kingdoms of Nature. They term their Elixir the Medicine of the Superior Order when it is perfected for the cure of the maladies of the human body, and for the transmutation of the imperfect metals into Gold. But they have also made occasional use of the same name when their Stone is only perfect at the White. Their Medicine of the Inferior Order is their Elixir projected upon an imperfect metal, which becomes perfect by means of this

Elixir, and can so be put in use, after coction, that is, adapted for projection upon other imperfect metals. This Medicine is by no means adapted for the treatment of human diseases. That of the Superior Order cures them by an operation of comforting and reinforcing. Medea made use of it in the case of the father of Jason. The Medicine which is obtained from the apothecaries is wholly opposite in its effect; it weakens by evacuating; it ruins the temperament, and hastens the sufferer towards the tomb. The Philosophers also apply the name of Physic or Medicine to the different operations of the Great Work. It is for this reason that they enumerate three sorts. The Medicine of the First Order is, according to Paracelsus, the preparation of the Stone, which is preliminary to the operation of the perfect preparation. It is properly called the Separation of the Elements, and the adaptation of each by each. The Medicine of the Second Order is that operation which immediately follows the first. It is termed perfect preparation and Fixation. The Medicine of the Third Order is the preparation of the Stone, which the Philosophers speak of as multiplication.

MEDIMNUS — A Measure containing One Hundred and Eight Pounds, or Six Bushels.

MELANCHOLY — This state signifies, alchemically, the Putrefaction of the Matter. The philosophers also term it Calcination, Incineration, Pregnation. The name has been also applied to the Matter in the Black Stage, doubtless, because that colour has a certain aspect of sadness, and that the humour which in humanity is called Melancholy, is attributed to a Black Bile, which causes heavy and depressing vapours to permeate the frame.

MELANZANA — Love Apple [Tomato].

MELEAGRIS — The Plant called Frittany or Imperial Crown; so-called possibly because the flowers are speckled like the plumage of that bird which in Latin is called Melagris.

MELGA ~ Salamander.

MELIA ~ Ash Tree.

MELICRATUM ~ Hydromel, which is composed of one part of Honey to eight parts of Water.

MELOCARPUS ~ A kind of Birth Mark or Wart.

MELON ~ Poppy.

MEMBRANE OF THE EARTH ~ The Matter from which the Philosophers extract their Mercury.

MENALOPIPER ~ The Black Pear.

MEDICINE ~ Raymund Lully is the first known author who considered alchemy expressly with a view to the Universal Medicine.

MENSTRUUM ~ The Menstruum of the Philosophers is properly their Mercury. Nevertheless, they often use this name to designate the Matter from which they extract their Mercury. Water is the Menstruum which contains the seed of things, and carries that seed into the earth by insinuating itself through the pores of the earth. Now, the earth serves as the matrix of the seed, which it hatches and digests-as much by the heat proper to the sperm as by the aid of the celestial fire ~ and manifests at last the individuals which must come therefore according to the determined species of the sperm. The sperm differs from the Menstruum in that the latter is but the receptacle of the former.

MERCURY ~ Our Mercury is double-fixed and volatile ~ in regard to its nature. In regard to its movement it is also dual, for it has one of ascension and one of descension. Having regard to that of descent, it is the influence of plants by which it rekindles the fire of slumbering Nature, and this is its first office before congelation. By the ascensional movement it rises to purify itself, and as this is by congelation it is considered as the radical moisture of all things, which under vile scoria still preserves the nobility of its first origin.

The Mercury of the Philosophers may be considered under four aspects. The Mercury of Bodies, which is the Hidden Seed; the Mercury of Nature, which is the Bath or Vase of the Philosophers, otherwise called the Radical Moisture; the Mercury of the Philosophers, because it is found in their laboratory and in their mineral storehouse. It is the Sphere of Saturn; it is their Diana; it is the true Salt of Metals. After its acquisition the philosophical work begins. In the fourth place, it is called Common Mercury, not the vulgar Mercury, but the true air of the Philosophers; the true middle substance, the true, secret, hidden Fire, called Common Fire because it is common to all minerals, since the substance of metals consists of it, and their quantity and quality are drawn from it.

MERCURY and **LIGHT** — A French chemist, Monsieur Homberg, is said to have made Gold out of Mercury by introducing Light into its pores, but at such trouble and expense that no one would undertake the experiment for profit. By this juncture of Light and Mercury both bodies became fixed and produced a third different from either — to wit, real Gold. Consult the Memoirs of the French Academy of Sciences concerning the genuineness of this experiment which goes to prove that Gold is only a mass of Mercury, penetrated and cemented by the substance of Light, the particles of these bodies attracting and fixing each other. This seems to have been not altogether unknown to former philosophers. Marcilius Ficinus, the Platonist, in his Commentary on the first book of the Second Ennead of Plotinus, and others likewise before him, regarded Mercury as the Mother and Sulphur as the Father of Metals, while Plato himself in his Timczus described Gold to be a dense fluid with a shining yellow light, which well suits a composition of Gold and Mercury.

METALLIC SEED — Seed of Metals. The Seeds of Metals are contained in the four elements, and whatever the Philosopher produces he must produce from the germ of the said thing, which is the Elixir, or Superlative Quintessence thereof. It is more useful to the artist than is Nature herself. So soon as the Philosopher has obtained this Seed or Germ, Nature will be ready to perform her duty and assist him. The Germ, or Seed, of anything is the most finished and perfect decoction of the thing itself, or, rather, it is the Balm of Sulphur, which is the same as the Radical Moisture. Now, the Radical Moisture is the Mercury of the Philosophers, according to some authorities, and this Mercury is the foundation of every species in the three Kingdoms of Nature, but more especially is it the Seed and Base of Metals when it is prepared philosophically. The philosophical preparation consists in extracting what is superfluous and adding what is wanting.

The Seed or Germ of Metals is produced by the Four Elements through the will of the Supreme Being and the Imagination of Nature. These elements operate by an indefatigable and continual movement, each one, according to its quality, projecting its seed to the centre of the earth, where it is received and digested, and is finally forced outward by the laws of motion. The centre of the earth here referred to is a certain void place conceived by the Philosophers, wherein nothing can repose; according to one authority it is the Matter of the Stone of the Philosophers and also the Stone itself in the state of perfection. It is so called because all the essential qualities which go to compose the universe are supposed to be united therein as in a centre. The four elements deposit their seed in the ex-centre, or margin and circumference of the centre, which, when it has appropriated a part, rejects what remains and casts it out. Hence come excrements and scoria, even the stones of the natural world. When it has been deposited by the four elements in the centre the Seed contracts different modifications, because it passes through different places; thus each thing is produced according to the diversity of places.

METALLIC SEED — How engendered. In order to understand how the elements engender this Seed we must note that two elements are heavy and two light; two are exceedingly dry and two exceedingly moist. They are, moreover, masculine and feminine. Each of these is most prompt to produce things like itself within its own sphere. Note also that the four elements never rest, but act continually on each other, and each one develops by itself and of itself that which is most subtle within it. Their general gathering-place is at the centre, and in the centre even of the Archeus, that servant of Nature — the Universal Agent, which puts all Nature in motion, disposing the germs and the seeds of all sublunary things to the production and multiplication of their species.

The eight-hundredth part of any substance — that which reposes at the very centre of the substance — can alone be converted into seed. Relatively to this seed, the whole body of a substance is but an envelope which serves as a preservative against excessive heat, cold, moisture, or dryness, and generally against all hurtful intemperateness. To obtain this seed, the artist must separate all impurities from the substance. Such impurities exist even in the purest metals. He should also direct his attention to the end of Nature, and this he should not seek in the vulgar metals, in which it does not exist, for such metals — and Gold especially — are absolutely dead, while our own are absolutely living, and possess a spirit. The life of metals is fire, while they are still buried in the mines. Their death and their life are according to the same principle, for they die by a fire of fusion. Every metal which has undergone fusion loses its life through the tyranny of fire. The Living Gold, to which reference has been made above, is the fixed grain, or the principle of fixation, which animates the Mercury of the Sages, and the Matter of the Stone — that is, the radical moisture of metals, the most digested portion of the unctuous and mineral vapour which composes them. Another authority adds that it takes the name of Living Gold more properly when it has become the Sulphur of the Philosophers, or the Red Magistery.

The metals are thus engendered in the bowels of the earth: After the Four Elements have produced their power or their virtue in the centre of the earth, and have deposited their seed, the Archeus of Nature, in distilling them, sublimises them on the surface by the heat and action of a perpetual movement. The Wind, which, according to Raymund Lully, seems to be the Mercury of the Philosophers, by distilling itself through the pores of the earth, results in a water, wherein all things have birth. It is then no longer anything but a moist vapour, from which the essential principle and archetype of each thing is afterwards formed. This serves as the First Matter of the Philosophers that is, the essential principle and primordial form of things is the First Matter of the Children of Knowledge, and this same Matter, when it has been once conceived, can suffer no mutation of form. Saturn, Jupiter, Mars, Venus, the Sun, the Moon, etc., have each the same seed. The locality of their birth is the cause of their difference, the more so as Nature achieves her work far sooner in the procreation of Silver than in that of Gold. When the vapour which we have said is sublimated at the centre of the earth, passes through warm and pure places, where a certain grease of Sulphur adheres to the sides, then this vapour, which the Philosophers have called their Mercury, accommodates and joins itself to this grease, and coming afterwards to sublimate itself in other places, which have been cleansed by the preceding vapour, and in which the earth is subtle, pure and moist, it fills the pores of the earth, joins itself thereto, and thus Gold is produced. When the same unctuousness or grease enters into totally impure and cold places, the result is Lead. Venus is engendered where the earth is pure, but is mingled with impure Sulphur. This vapour at the centre of the earth has the power of invariably sublimating, by its continued progress, all that is crude and impure, attracting to itself continually what is pure.

The seed and life of metals is properly water, which is the centre and core of every mineral.

No seed is of any value unless it shall have been placed, either by Art or Nature, in a suitable matrix, where it may receive life in the corruption of the germ, and the congelation of the pure particle, or fixed grain. The seed is nourished and preserved by the heat of its body. In the mineral kingdom, the artist accomplishes what Nature could not finish on account of the crudity of the air, which by its violence has filled the pores of every body, not in the bowels of the earth but on the surface.

METALS — These are composed or generated of a Viscous Water, or aqueous Living Silver.

METALS AND THEIR CORRESPONDENCES — To understand properly the correspondence which exists between metals, we must consider the position of the planets, and notice that Saturn is higher than all, to whom Jupiter succeeds, then Mars, then the Sun, Venus, Mercury, and, lastly, the Moon. The virtues of these planets do not ascend, but descend, and experience teaches that Mars is easily converted into Venus, not Venus into Mars, and so on with the other planets, the Sun, however, excepted, for Sol enters into all, but is never ameliorated by its inferiors.

METALS AND THEIR FORMATION ~ Before all things it is necessary that the amateur should understand the formation of metals in the bowels of the earth. This should be his first study. Without this, and the faithful imitation of Nature, he will never achieve anything successful. Nature composes all metals of Sulphur and Mercury, and forms them by their double vapours. Mercurial vapours are united to sulphureous vapours in a cavernous place, where a saline water is found. This serves as their matrix. There is first the Vitriol of Nature. From this, by the strife of the elements, there rises a new vapour, which is neither mercurial nor sulphureous, but is allied to both. It rises in places where the Grease of Sulphur adheres; it unites thereto; from this union there results a glutinous substance, or an unformed mass. On this mass the vapour, spread through these cavernous regions, acts by means of the Sulphur it contains. If the place and the vapour are pure, perfect metals result, if impure, then imperfect metals. Note that metals are termed perfect or imperfect according as they have or have not received a complete coction.

The vapour of which we are speaking contains a spirit of light of fire; being of the nature of the celestial bodies. This spirit should be properly considered as the form of the universe. The vapour thus impregnated by the Universal Spirit accurately represents the primeval chaos, wherein was enclosed all that was necessary for the creation, that is, universal matter and universal form.

METALS AND THEIR TRANSMUTATION ~ According to the Clavicle or Little Key of Raymund Lully, metals cannot be transmuted unless they are reduced into their First Matter, i.e., into Mercury, not volatile, but fixed. But this is not to be understood of Common Mercury, for no preparation of art can change Vulgar Mercury into the Mercury of the Philosophers. Common Mercury cannot be detained in the fire except by the help of another Mercury which is hot and dry — that is, more fixed. When the Mercury of the Philosophers is mixed with the current or running Mercury, they are united in the bond of love and never part. The Mercury of the Philosophers mixes actually with the other, drying up its phlegmatic humidity, and taking away the coldness from the body, making it black as a coal, which afterwards it turneth into powder. It possesses of itself the heat of Nature, and changes the Vulgar Mercury into its own temperate quality, afterwards transmuting it into pure metal, into Sol and Luna-one or other according as it is extended. It changes also the Vulgar Mercury into Medicine, which Medicine can transmute Imperfect Metals into Perfect, while it turns the Vulgar Mercury into true Sol and Luna, better than those of the Mines. This Sophic Mercury is the secret of the Philosophers.

METHODS OF INTERPRETATION — The symbols and allegorical language made use of by the hermetic philosophers lend themselves readily to interpretations which have no connection with physical chemistry. Under this treatment the Philosopher's Stone assumes a purely moral or spiritual significance. One writer explains it as follows: He who can dive into the depths of his own soul and penetrate to its centre, avoiding the monsters of the deep (the passions) which guard the mystery, and the water-nymphs (the desires) who endeavour to distract his attention, will find at that centre the jewel of priceless value, the Philosopher's Stone, or Wisdom Revealed, before whose touch the portals of the mysterious temple will open, and he will behold things which no tongue can describe, and hear words which it is "not lawful for man to utter". He will find the seed out of which grows the tree of life, and having eaten of the fruits of that tree, he will die no more, for he will be one with Christ, and will be rendered immortal in Him.

MORNING — The Magisterium at the Red, so called by the Philosophers because its colour is rosy like the dawn before it attains the perfect Red.

MOTHER — The Spagyric Philosophers sometimes apply the name of Mother to the Vase which contains the Matter of the Great Work, but they more commonly say that the Sun is the Father of the Stone, and that the Moon is its Mother, because, in their opinion, the Matter of the Stone, as of every other substance, is engendered by the Four Elements, mingled and combined by the action of these two luminaries, and not, it should be noted, because ordinary Gold, which they also call Sun, and vulgar Silver, which they call Moon after the same manner, must be made use of for the achievement of the Great Work.

MOTHER — The Mother has Drowned her Child. This allegorical expression is used by some Philosophers to mean that the philosophical earth has absorbed all the water that originally issued from it. It is the same process as Cohobation.

MOTHER OF THE STONE — Matter of the Stone when arrived at the White Stage. But the name also applies, and that indeed more exactly, to Mercurial Water, since it is of that the Matter of the Stone is formed.

MOTHER OF THE ELEMENTS — The Chaos Or Hyle. The First Matter of which the Elements and all things are composed.

MARVEL OF MARVELS — This is the true name of the Perfect Elixir, because there is no greater wonder upon earth. It is for this reason that the majority of Philosophers call the Great Work the Work of Divine Wisdom.

MARVEL OF THE WORLD — The Mercury of the Philosophers,

MESSENGER OF THE GODS ~ The Universal Spirit which permeates all Nature, or the Mercury of the Philosophers, which is formed from it.

MESTUDAR ~ Sal Ammoniac.

METALS ~ When the Sages speak of Metals, they do not in most cases refer to those which are used in ordinary life and in the commercial world. Their metals are nothing else but the several states of their Mercury during operation of the Magisterium. Just as there are seven planets, so are these states seven in number, and so also we speak commonly of seven metals. For the same reason, the Philosophers ascribe the regime of their work to the planets, which they say, dominate each state, each dominion being characterised by its special colour. The bellows-blowers and vulgar chemists, when they set to work upon ordinary metals, deceive themselves equally in this as in other matters, for they will never accomplish the Magisterium by such means.

METOPIUM ~ Galbanum.

METROS ~ The Stone at the Red Stage.

MEZEREUM ~ A species of Plant which belongs to the genus Laurel.

MICLETA ~ A Medicament for stopping Haemorrhage.

MIGMA ~ A Combination of several Simples, which is used as a Medicament.

MILCONDAT ~ Dragon's Blood.

MILITARIS, or **STRATIOTIS** ~ An Aquatic Plant which stops bleeding of wounds. The same name has been given to another plant called Milfoil, or Garrow.

MINE ~ The Matter out of which metals or minerals are formed in the bowels of the earth. According to the principles of Hermetic Philosophy, this Matter in its original state is nothing but a vapour put in motion by the elements together with air and water in the interior of the earth. The central fire sublimes towards the surface. It digests and cooks, combining with the Sulphur it meets with, and according to the degree of purity which exists in the combination, more or less perfect metals result.

MINE OF CELESTIAL FIRE ~ The Magisterium at the Red Stage, or the Sulphur of the Philosophers.

MINERAL ~ A Combination or Composite Substance participating of the principle of metals. Metallic minerals are composed of very simple and homogeneous parts, which make the composition extremely fixed, and almost incapable of corruption. The Vase of the Philosophers is an unctuous and vitrifiable earth, and as it does not possess the reproductive organs of vegetables and animals, it forms by simple accretion, and all its genera possess a similar form or, more correctly, they have none of them any determinate form, such as is possessed by every species in the two other kingdoms of Nature. Nevertheless, the metals possess a seed, but it is the same in all; it does not consist of a conglomeration of different parts, but is a very simple subject to which are conjoined and do adhere many other parts constituting its outward or apparent form. Three ingredients enter into the compositions of a mineral, namely, a seed, an unctuous moisture attaching to it, and, finally, an unctuous humidity which augments and nourishes it.

MINIERE ~ The Philosophers apply this term to several things, as, for example, to that Matter out of which they extract their Mercury by the proper process learned of experiment and of experience. This also they call the Miniere of their Mercury, or the Miniere of Metals. Then again they designate their Animated Mercury by this name, or ~ which is the same thing ~ their Matter after Putrefaction in the Medicine of the First Order, because it is in Putrefaction that the reunion between body and spirit takes place. Philalethes says that the Steel of the Sages is the

Miniere of their Gold, and that their Magnet is the Miniere of their Steel. Once more, a number of Adepts have given the same name to their Sulphur, because this red body is the principle and the beginning of their tincture, as it is also of their metals. Their White Miniere is their Magisterium at the White Stage, and their Red Miniere is their Stone at the Red in the operation of the First Work.

MIRACLE OF ART — The Powder of Projection at the White and at the Red, so called because Art can accomplish nothing more perfect in the efficacity of the influence that it exercises over the health of the human body, or more potent for the transmutation of Metals into Gold.

MISSADAM — Mercury or Quicksilver.

MIXED BODY — An Assemblage of several Homogeneous or Heterogeneous Substances. It is possible to reduce all mixed or composite substances into three classes on the theory that all things are composed of air and water. The first of these classes contains those composites which consist of water and water, the second of those which are constituted of earth and earth, the third of those which have earth and water for their principles. The individual composites comprised in each of these three kingdoms differ also among themselves according to the different proportions in which the constituting elements are combined. The melange which forms the bodies of animals consists in union, that of vegetables in coagulation, and that of minerals in fixation.

MOLHORODAN — Sal Gemmae. See Rulandus.

MOLLIFICATION — Identical with Solution, Trituration, and Putrefaction.

MORTAR — The Dissolving Mercury of the Philosophers.

MORTIFICATION — In chemical terminology, this process is a species of Pulverisation which disposes the mortified body towards a new generation, such as that of the seeds of vegetables. The name of Mortification has been given to this species of corruption, because this kind of putrefaction takes place slowly, and the seed appears to die. In Mortification, the Radical Moisture of earth in vegetables, and that of the seed in animals, governs for a time the innate and vivifying heat, but at the end of a given time this igneous spirit, assisted by external heat, reassumes its active powers, and dominating the Radical Moisture in its turn, achieves generation.

MOSARDEGI -- Lead.

MOSEL -- Pewter; but according to some chemists it signifies Mercury.

MOOT -- The same as Endica.

MOUNTAIN -- The Philosophers have analogically given this name to Metals.

MOZ -- Myrrh.

MUCAGO -- Mucilage.

MUCARUM -- Syrup and Infusion of Roses.

MURPHUR -- Copper or Venus.

MOON -- This term is understood in a variety of senses. By it the Philosophers sometimes understand their Mercury in its simple state, sometimes their Matter at the White Stage, and occasionally common Silver. When they say that their Stone is made with the Sun and the Moon, we must understand that the reference is to the Volatile Matter for the Moon, and to the Fixed Matter for the Sun. They also call their White Sulphur or White Gold by the same name. The dominion of the Moon in the operations begins when the Matter, after putrefaction, changes its colour of grey into that of white. When the sages speak of their Moon in this state they call it Diana Unveiled, and they say that happy is the man who has beheld Diana naked, that is to say, the Matter at the perfect White Stage. He is happy as a fact because the perfection of the Red Sulphur, or of

Philosophical Gold, depends only, when once this point is reached, upon the sustenance of the fire.

MOON OF THE PHILOSOPHERS ~ The Matter of the Philosophers, not isolated, but making part of a Composite. It is not Common Silver nor Mercury extracted therefrom. It is the Vegetable Saturn, the Daughter of Saturn, called by some Venus, and by others Diana, because she has a forest which is consecrated unto her. Common Silver performs the office of the male in the operations of the Great Work, and the Moon of the Philosophers performs the office of female. An infinite number of names have been applied to it, some of which appear to exclude one another, but it must be always borne in mind that such designations are relative only, either to the operations or else to the colours of the work, or again to the qualities of this Matter. At times they have termed it Water, and at times Earth. In respect of perfect bodies it is a Pure Spirit, and relatively to mineral water it is a Body, but a Hermaphrodite Body. Having regard to Gold and Silver, it is a Living Mercury, a Fugitive Water. In comparison with Mercury it appears to be an Earth, but an Adamic Earth, a Chaos. It is the true Proteus.

MOON ~ Horned Moon. The chemists apply this name to Calx of Silver made by aquafortis in the manner following: Dissolve one ounce of fine silver in two ounces of aquafortis. When the dissolution has taken place add spirit of common salt, which will precipitate the silver to the bottom. When this calx has been subsequently edulcorated the resultant is called the Horned Moon.

MOON ~ The Moon Compressed. Cupellated Silver. But when the chemists speak of their Luna Compacts the reference is to the Philosophical Luna, or the Matter of the Work arrived at the White State, which is also called White Gold and the Mother of the Stone.

MUD — Mud, Lute, or Slime, is properly a species of Mortar, composed of different substances, which artists make use of to harden or encrust glass vessels, so that they may the better resist the action of fire. Lute also serves to join the orifices of two vessels, or their communicating beaks, to prevent the spirits when passing from one to another, or therein circulating, from escaping and becoming dissipated in the air.

MULTIPLICATION — An operation of the Great Work by means of which the Powder of Projection is multiplied, either in quantity or quality, to infinity, according to the good pleasure of the artist. In consists in recommencing the operation which has been already performed, but with exalted and perfected matters, and not with crude substances as in the previous case. The whole secret, says one Philosopher, is a physical dissolution in Mercury and a reduction into its First Matter. With this end in view the Philosophers take the Matter, as prepared and cocted by Nature, and reduce it into its First Matter, into the Philosophical Mercury from which it has been extracted. In order to attain to a full acquaintance with this operation five points must be observed:

1. That the Adepts reduce years into months, months into weeks, weeks into days, days into hours, etc.
2. It is an axiom among the Philosophers that all dry matters absorb greedily their proper moistures.
3. That then the dry matter acts more rapidly upon its humid part than it did previously.
4. That the greater, the proportion of earth, and the less that of water, the sooner does solution take place.
5. That every solution is made according to expediency, and that every matter which dissolves the Moon dissolves also the Sun.

NAMPHORA ~ Oil of Stone.
NAPORAN ~ A Sea-shell whence the colour Purple is obtained. The Adepts have occasionally applied this name to their Sulphur because it possesses this colour.
NASSE ~ Furnace.
NEAGULA ~ New Milk.
NECTAR ~ The Beverage of the Gods. It is the Medicine of the Philosophers. The philological meaning makes it equivalent to a drink which preserves youth. The Hermetic Philosophers attribute the same property to their Medicine. In the course of the operation of the Work, they give the name of Nectar to their Mercury or Azoth, because it drinks the Matter which remains at the bottom of the vessel, which they term Saturn, Jupiter, Venus.
NESTUDAR ~ Sal Ammoniac.
NEPSU ~ Pewter; an Alloy of Tin and Lead.
NEUSI ~ The Magisterium at the Red.

NEST OF THE FOWL ~ The Mercury of the Sages. It is also sometimes the Vase containing the Matter, or the Triadic Vessel which Flamel calls the Domicile of the Fowl.

NUCLEUS ~ The Mercury of the Philosophers, so called because it must be extracted from its Ore by separation from the terrestrial parts, the aqueous parts, and the heterogeneous parts in which it is imbedded like the kernel of a nut in the shell.

NUCHT ~ Brass.

NURSE ~ The Philosophers apply this name to their Mini2re or Ore; that is, to their Matter from which they extract their Mercury and their Sulphur. This must be understood as referring to the condition which antecedes the first preparation and also during the course of the second. Michael Maier represents the Philosophical Child by an emblem in which is depicted a woman having a terrestrial globe about the middle of her belly. From this globe two breasts issue, which are sucked by a child whom she carries. Above there are these words, which are taken from the Emerald Table of Hermes ~ *Nutrix ejus est Terra* ~ The Earth is its Nurse. But when the Nurses of the Gods are referred to, the reference is usually to the volatile portions of the Matter, or the Mercurial Water of the Philosophers.

NYSAE ~ Sal Ammoniac.

O ~ The letter O taken simply is a chemical character which signifies Alum. When it is horizontally divided in the middle, or in the direction of its diameter, it indicates Common Salt. It is identical with the circle which stands for the most precious of all the metals, as also for its philosophical antitype, the Gold of the Sages. If this circle be perpendicularly divided, it then represents Nitre. The circle also enters into the symbols which represent the following substances:

Iron, or Steel. Alum. Antimony. Mercury. Arsenic. Wax. Cinnabar. Copper, Venus. Calcined Copper. Spirit. Wheel of Fire. Oil. Day. Nitre. Night. Gold, or Sol. Orpiment. Powder. Purifying Agent. Realgar. Mars. Salt of Alkali. Sal Gemmae. See Ruland. Black Sulphur. Sublimating Agent. Sal Ammoniac. Glass. Verdegris.

The above enumeration by no means exhausts the list.

OBAC ~ Sal Ammoniac.

OBJECT OF THE ALCHEMISTS — The end of the research of philosophers is to attain the art of perfecting what Nature has left imperfect in the mineral genera, and to arrive at the treasure of the Philosopher's Stone. This stone is nothing else but the radical moisture of the elements, perfectly purified and brought to a sovereign fixity, which causes it to operate those great things for life and health that dwell alone in the radical moisture. The secret for performing this admirable work consists in a knowledge of the true process for extracting and educing from potentiality into activity the inner or latent heat which dwells in the radical moisture, and is called the Fire of Nature. The precautions which must be taken to prevent failure are mainly centred in an exceeding carefulness over the extraction of excrement from the matter, and in seeking only for the nucleus, or middle point, which contains all the virtue of composite substances. The Medicine here treated of has the power of curing every kind of disease, not on account of the variety of its qualities, but simply because it so powerfully fortifies the natural warmth of the body, by a gentle and moderate elevation or excitement thereof, whereas other remedies irritate it by an over-violent action.
OCCULT — This term sometimes stands for the Sun of the Philosophers concealed in the belly of the Magisterium. We do honour to the Sun, says Philalethes, because without him our Arcanum could not be separated from its imperfections. This Sun, however, is not Vulgar Gold; only the sages behold, perceive and know it. Nor can this Sun of itself make our tincture perfect; it has need of the assistance of the Moon, which makes it ethereal and volatile, by purifying it of its imperfections. This Moon is the Mother and the Field in which our Gold must be sown.
To make the occult manifest is to extract the Mercury from the Ore; it is also the coction of the Matter in Putrefaction

until the manifestation of the colour white, and of the other colours which succeed it.

To make that which is manifest occult and that which is occult manifest This expression means nothing else but the dissolution of the Fixed into Mercurial Water, with its subsequent volatilisation in view.

OCCUPATION ~ A Commingling, by means of weight and measure, of a perfect body with the matter of which it is composed. It is performed in a suitable vessel, and at a philosophical fire.

OCHEMA ~ The Entire Liquor, or the vehicle with which Medicaments are mixed together.

OCHRUS ~ A Vegetable Nature.

ODOUR ~ The philosophers say that they recognise their Matter by its smell, which is that of Assafoetida, that of the tombs and that of the sepulchres. But this must not be understood of the crude Matter, considered before its entrance into the state of putrefaction. Nicholas Flamel teaches us that the artist does not become acquainted with this evil odour unless he breaks his vessels, whence it is to be concluded that he refers to the Matter in putrefaction. He further refers to the Matter, when in this state, as a thing that is dead, and as a dead body in its grave. Morien also speaks of it as possessing the smell of a corpse. Raymund Lully also describes it in similar terms, but he adds that the bad odour is succeeded by one so pleasant and delicious that it attracts all the birds in the neighbourhood to the house where the process is being carried out. In other words, the Matter passes into a volatile state after its putrefaction, and ascends to the top of the vase, to fall afterwards into the Sea of the Philosophers.

OLEANDER ~ The plant Bears' Breech.

OLIVE ~ The Magisterium at the Red. Called also Everlasting Olive.
OLLUS ~ The Matter at the Black Stage.
ONITIS ~ A species of Wild Marjoram.
ONOBRYCHIS ~ Sainfoin.
ONOLOSAT ~ A Weight of Half a Scruple.
ONOMEL ~ Wine mingled with honey.
ONOOLOEUM ~ A Mixture of Oil and Wine.
OPEN ~ To Open is to Dissolve the Matter, to render Bodies Fluidic. According to Flamel, the Philosophers, anxious to protect their secret, have never spoken of the mystery of multiplication except under the veil of common names ~ such as to open, to shut, to bind, to loose. Opening and loosing is the reduction of a body into a fluid state, like water. Binding and closing is coagulation by a stronger decoction.
OPERATION ~ There is but one Operation in our work, and that is, according to Gebir, the Elevation of the Dry Substance by means of Fire, with adherence to its proper vase.
OPERATION ~ A Philosopher may risk the performance of the work when he knows how to extract from a dissolved body, by means of a crude spirit, a digested spirit, which he must then reunite to the vital oil.
OPERATION [a further view] ~ When the Philosopher shall know how by means of a vegetable menstruum, united to a mineral menstruum, to accomplish the dissolution of a third essential, having united which together, he must wash the earth, and then exalt it into a celestial quintessence for the composition of the sulphureous thunder, which in a moment shall penetrate bodies, and destroy their excrements, then may he commence his work.
OPOCHRISMA ~ An Unguent or a Sympathetic Balm which Cures Hurts and Sores by the unusual method of

rubbing the instrument which inflicted them. It is also called Unguentum Armarcum.

OPRIMETHIOLIM ~ A Mineral Spirit which assists in the formation of Metals and Minerals.

OREPIS ~ A Fiery Vapour of Tartar.

ORIZONTIS ~ Tincture of Gold.

ORNUS ~ The Wild Ash.

OSATIS ~ Wood, Dyer's Wood, Pastel.

OSCIEUM ~ The Plant Api or Smallage.

OSEMUTUM ~ Iron Wire.

OSMUNDA ~ A Species of Fern-the Fern Royal.

OSYRIS ~ A Plant known by the name of Purging Flax.

OTAP ~ Sal Ammoniac Tinged Red by Water of Colestar.

OUBELCOR ~ A Cucurbit.

OXELEUM ~ Vinegar Beaten up with Oil.

OXOS ~ Vinegar.

OXYACANTHA ~ Barberry.

OXYCROCEUM ~ A Medicament composed of Vinegar, Saffron, and some other drugs.

OXYDERCICA ~ Remedies adapted for Strengthening the Sight. Eye-salve.

OXYGALA ~ Sour Milk.

OXYLAPATHUM ~ A sort of Sorrel or Dock.

OXYTRIPYLLUM ~ The Sour or Acid Trefoil; so called, firstly, on account of its flavour, and, secondly, because it has three leaflets like common trefoil.

P. AE, PAR, PART AEQ ~ Abbreviations for Equal Parts.
PACHUNTICA ~ Ingredients used for Thickening, or for giving Consistence to a Medicament. Some Philosophers have applied this name to the Sulphur of the Sages, because it coagulates and fixes their Mercury.
PAJON ~ Bezoar, Animal Concretion, Medicinal Stone, Antidote.
PANACEA ~ The Universal Panacea is one of the results of the Hermetic Work, and the only one which the philosophers of ancient times proposed as their end in view. [Note that this view is in contradiction with what has been previously cited from another source.] It is probable that the transmutation of metals was in no sense their main object, and that it was only by a consideration of the virtue and the qualities of their Medicine that they were led to apply it to the achievement of this end, which succeeded according to their hopes.
PANCHYMAGOGUM ~ Sweet Sublimate.

PANDATIEA ~ Solid Electuary.

PARADISE (Grain of) ~ Cardamon.

PARDALIANCHES ~ Aconite.

PAREGORIC ~ A Medicament with the assuaging properties of Anodyne, Soothing and Tranquilzing Pain.

PARONYCHIA ~ A small Plant, which is good for Sores in the neighbourhood of the Nails.

PART WITH PART ~ Amalgam of Gold and Silver.

PASSIVE ~ The Inactive Condition of Substance; that which is acted on by an agent. It is interchangeable with the term Patient.

PATIENT ~ A Substance acted on by another Substance to accomplish the generation of a composite. Mercury is the Patient in the Work of the Stone, while Sulphur combined with Fire, are the Agents.

PAULADADA ~ A species of Sigillated Earth, found in Italy.

PEARL OF THE CHEMISTS ~ The Dew of the Spring Season. It is so called, because it condenses into drops which resemble these precious Stones. Some chemists have regarded it as the veritable Matter of the Hermetic Work, and as the Philosophers affirm that there are two indispensable Matters ~ the one Male and the other Female ~ they have given the name of the Male to the Dew of the Autumn period, or that of the month of September, and the name of Female to the Dew of the month of May. This is because they say that springtime dew partakes more of the winter cold which has preceded, and the other of the heat and geniality of the summer.

PELLICULE ~ The Matter of the Work during the period in which it is in Putrefaction; so named, because it has the form of a Pellicule upon its surface; it is also polished, and like Black Pitch.

PENTAMYRON — An Unguent, composed of five ingredients — to wit, Styrax, Calamite, Mastic, Opobalsamum, Wax, and Nardic Ointment.

PEPANSIS — A process of Cooking or Dressing, which is adapted to giving perfection to a thing.

PEPANTINQUE — The First Heat that is requisite in the digestion of the Matter of the Work, and for disposing it towards that putrefaction which is preliminary to a fresh generation.

PIERCE — To Pierce with the Lance, or with an Arrow, or a Javelin; the coction of the Matter of the Work by means of the Philosophical Fire, which is called the Lance or javelin.

PERYCLYMENUM — Honeysuckle or Woodbine.

PERIMINEL — An operation by which a Substance is reduced to Cinders. Reduction to ashes or fine dust is sometimes called Adulphurs. The two processes in conjunction are termed Agasoph.

PERIPLOCA — A species of Convolvulus.

PHACE — The Vegetable called Lentil.

PHELLODRIS — Cork.

PHILADELPHUS — A Species of Gluten.

PHILOSOPHER — The Lover of Wisdom who is instructed in the secret operations of Nature, and who takes pattern by her procedure for the production of more perfect things than she has herself evolved. The name of Philosopher has been given from time immemorial to all those who are duly initiated into the operations of the Great Work, which they term also Hermetic Science or Philosophy, because Hermes Trismegistus is regarded as the first who became illustrious therein. It is further claimed that the proficients in this achievement do alone really deserve the title of Philosophers, because it is they only who know Nature in her inmost depths, and because by means of this knowledge they have arrived at the knowledge of the Creator, unto whom they pay worship and adoration in all love, fidelity, and respect. They affirm further that it is precisely this love of God that is the first step which educes towards wisdom, and they never weary of impressing on their disciples, whom they call the children of Science, the necessity of this love.

PHILTRATION or **FILTRATION** -- That Action whereby a Liquor is Clarified and Purified. The subtle part is separated from the gross, thick, and terrestrial part. It is generally performed by passing the liquid through a linen cloth, or by some similar means.

PHILTRE -- In Vulgar Chemistry this is a piece of some kind of stuff, cut to a convenient size, and shaped like an inverted cone. Liquids are passed through it with a view to clarify them. It is also performed by means of a funnel of prepared paper, and in other ways. But in the terminology of the Hermetic Science the Philtre signifies the Azoth of the Sages, because it is by means of Azoth that the pure is separated from the impure. Philtre represents further in symbolic language that Azoph of the Wise which whitens the Laton, otherwise the unclean body, and strips it of its impurities.

PHIONITA -- Natural Hostility or Antipathy, such as one animal or composite of any kind entertains towards another, as for example, the antipathy of the cat for the mouse, of one pole of the magnet for the other. The Philosophers say that their Dragon has this quality in respect of water, and that it must be forced to drink thereof, and to bathe therein, so that it may be relieved of its old skin or impure cortex.

PHISON -- Sulphur of the Philosophers, or Magisterium at the Red.

PHLEGM -- A Water or Vapour which rises up from the Matter of the Work, and which whitens itself in distilling. It is by reason of this quality that the Philosophers have given the name of Phlegm to the Mercury and to the Stone when they have attained the White State.

PHLOGISTIC — Fixed Fire which has become a Principle of Bodies. It is the Inflammable Matter or Primal Sulphur. The phlogistic virtue in metals ' accomplishes the union of their parts, a fact which is evident because when deprived of this fire they are reduced into Lime, but can be brought back to their former condition by the addition of phlogistic substance. It is by ascertaining the quantity of this substance that is present in any metal or by ascertaining the degree of cohesion among its principles that their relative value can be appraised, independently of any value which opinion may attribute to them, for the more these substances resist fire the greater is their solidity in proportion, and the more brilliant is their sparkling. The preciousness of metals depends therefore on their power of resistance, and not upon any question of their comparative scarcity or their abundance. Thus Gold, which fire cannot overcome, and which seems to have the least phlogistic quality which is possible consistently with the cohesion of its parts, is regarded as chief among the metals. Silver, which fire can permeate or penetrate, it is true, but only with the greatest difficulty, unless Lead or Borax be added to it, or some Alkaline Salt, follows immediately upon Gold. Then ensue Copper, Iron, Pewter, Lead, Bismuth, and Zinc. For the rest this resistance must not be interpreted as that opposition which the metals in question offer to fusion, but the constancy with which they persist in their fused state, with less or more evaporation and waste, or, alternatively, the more or less great difficulty which is experienced in converting them into scoria and cinder. Independently of this, one would attribute a greater virtue to Iron than to Silver or to Copper, because it resists fusion much better than the two latter metals. The excess of the Phlogistic element produces in metals the same result as its deficiency. Both make the substance impregnable to fire. The Phlogistic element is found in all species of Nature. In the animal it preponderates in the oily or unctuous parts, which are the most open to inflammation. This fire was known to the ancients as it is now familiar to the moderns, more especially to the Hermetic Philosophers, who have almost invariably spoken of it in allegories or under the veil of metaphors, and have in almost every case assigned it some name borrowed from the different fires of vulgar chemistry.

PHLOGIUM — A species of Violet, so named because the blossoms, or flowers, have a certain fire-coloured aspect.

PHOSPHORUS — One of the names which the Philosophers have applied to the small white circle which forms upon the Matter of the Work when it enters upon the White Stage. They have thus named it because it is the herald of this White State, which in its turn is denominated Light.

PHTORTICUM — A Medicament adapted to Dissolving or Softening Flesh and producing Suppuration.

PHU or **PHY** — Valerian.

PHYLLUM — A species of Herb.

PHYSALOS — The Toad.

PHYTEUMA — A Plant.

PIMING — The Areca.

PISO — Mortar.

PISSASPHALTOS — Asphalt, Indian Bitumen.

PISSALCON — Pitch.

PITYSA — Esula.

PLECMUM — Lead.

PLELYOPHTHALMON — Antimony.

PLERES ARCHONTICUM — Cephalic Powder.

PLOMA — White Bouillon.

POINT ~ The philosophers apply the name of point or puncture to their Magisterium at the White, because the whole work depends thereon. Hence they have said: Whiten the Laton, and burn your books. For once you have reached this stage, success depends solely on continuing the regimen of the fire.

POLISH (To) ~ The Coction or Digestion of the Matter, in order to lead it on to perfection.

POLYOPPORA ~ Wine or any other Intoxicating Liquor.

POLYNEURON ~ Plantain.

POMAMBRA ~ A Pastil or composition of several Odoriferous Substances, among which Amber is particularly prominent. The name itself is equivalent to Apple of Amber.

POPPY OF THE PHILOSOPHERS ~ The Stone when perfect at the Red Stage; so called because it has the vivid colour of this field flower.

PORRONITRI ~ Fusible Salt.

POSCA ~ Oxycrat.

POT OF THE PHILOSOPHERS ~ The vessel which contains the Matter of the Philosophers or of the Work.

POWDER ~ Black Powder ~ The Matter of the Sages in the condition of Putrefaction.

POWDER ~ White Powder ~ The Matter of the Work fixed at the White Stage.

POWDER ~ Discontinuous ~ The Matter of the Sages when it has issued from the state of Putrefaction and manifests in the colour of the white state.

POWDER OF PROJECTION ~ The Outcome of the Hermetic Work, which being projected upon metals, transforms them into Gold or into Silver, according as the work has been developed to the white or to the red stage.

PULVERISE ~ To Dissolve the Gold of the Philosophers. Flamel says that such Dissolution reduces the said Gold or Sulphur into a powder so fine that it may be fittingly compared with the atoms which are visible in a ray of sunlight.

POUST — Opium.

PRATUM VIRIDE — Flowers of Copper.

PRECIPITATE PHILOSOPHICAL — Mercury Precipitated by the Internal Fire of Gold or Gold essentialized.

PRECIPITATION — A Failing which is charged by the Philosophers against those who grow weary of the length of the Work.

PREGNATION — The period of the Putrefaction of the Matter. It is so-called because corruption is an indispensable forerunner of generation, and there is no conception which has not been preceded by Putrefaction.

PREPARATION — That action or process, by means of which Superfluous Substances are removed from the Matter, and that which is wanting to it is added. There are three kinds of preparation in the Work or Confection of the Magisterium. The first is Manual and not Philosophical; it is for this reason that it has been omitted in the writings of the philosophers, though success depends thereon. The second is the Philosophical Preparation of the Agents, which the Philosophers call the First Preparation, and Philalethes, the Imperfect Preparation. The third is the Preparation of the Elixir, or the Complete and Perfect Preparation. But the successive philosophical preparations are only one operation repeated, so at least is the declaration of Morien, who terms them Dispositions.

PRESMUCHIM, PRESMUCHUM and **PRESMUKIS** — Are all significant of one substance, and that is Ceruse.

PRISON — The Philosophers use this term in several senses. They apply it firstly to the more gross and heterogeneous matters, in which their Mercury and their Gold are shut up as in a Prison, and from which it is necessary to set them free. They apply it, secondly, to the Vase, in which the Matter of the Work is placed, in order to work upon it with a view to the Magisterium. It is in this sense that we must understand Aristeus, when he says that the King of the Sea Coasts imprisons it in a narrow dungeon, wherein he retains it for forty days and more, and does not set it free till it has given up to him his son Gabertin. Trevisan also uses the word in the same sense. Thirdly, the Philosophers apply it to the Mercury, which, dissolving the Fixed Part, holds it, as it were, in Prison, during the entire period of the Black State. The terms, Sepulchre and Tomb, are made to serve as equivalent for Prison in this connection. It is applied, fourthly, in reference to the Fixation of the Mercury, and it is in the three senses last enumerated that we must interpret the Prison of which Basil Valentine speaks in the preface to his Twelve Keys.

PROCESSES — Operation, Method, Manner of Proceeding, etc. The Processes of the Hermetic Art in the composition of the Stone of the Sages are an imitation of those which Nature employs in the production of Mixed Substances.

PROCESSION — Nicholas Flamel, in his hieroglyphic figures, has employed the symbol of a procession, at which many persons assist, clothed in different colours, as much to indicate the successive ascensions and descensions of the Matter by means of circulation in the Vase, as to signify the colours which develop in the operation of the Great Work.

PROJECTION — It is to be noticed that in the operation of Projection, all the Metal upon which the Powder is projected does not transform into Gold or Silver unless it has been well purified before fusion. There is an exception in the case of Mercury because it has naturally a smaller proportion of impure and heterogeneous matters, and possesses also much closer analogy with gold. To make projection upon Mercury, it is sufficient to warm it slightly, and the powder must be projected before it begins to give off smoke. The powder is wrapped in a little wax, and the pellet thus formed is cast upon the metal in fusion. The crucible is covered over, and the powder is left to act for the space of a quarter of an hour or thereabouts. The Matter is then allowed to get cold, and is then taken out of the vessel. If cracked or broken, it must be projected upon a small quantity of the same metal in fusion, for it is a proof that too much powder has been used.

PROPOLIS, or **PROPOLIX** ~ A species of Cement or unctuous Wax, of a somewhat bitter taste and blackish colour. It is that substance with which bees coat over the clefts of their hives, and even the entrance, when the approach of winter impels them to close quarters. Planoscampi terms it Virgin Wax, others Sacred Wax. When placed upon burning coals, it exhales an odour which is very similar to aloes. One writer says that this matter is a species of reddish or yellow mastic.

PROPOMA ~ A Beverage composed of Wine and Honey, or of Wine and Sugar.

PROPORTION ~ Combination of the Weights, or by Weight, of the Principal Materials in the Composition of the Hermetic Work.

PSAMMODEA ~ A Sandy Sediment.

PSILOTHRON ~ A name which is given to certain Unguents used to remove Superfluous Hair.

PSORICA ~ A Medicament for the Cure of the Itch.

PSORICUM ~ A Composition of Two Parts of Chalcitis and one of Cadmia or Refuse of Silver, pulverised and mixed together by means of Vinegar (White Vinegar). The whole is placed in a Vase which is well sealed, and then set in horse-dung (warm) for the space of forty days. The matter is subsequently dried over live coals until it assumes a red colour.

PTERIS ~ Fern.

PTERNA ~ Cinders.

PUCHO ~ Tenesmus.

PURITY OF DEATH ~ The Matter of the Philosophers when it has arrived at the White Stage. It is so called because the Black colour occasioned by Putrefaction is called Death and the Impurity of Death, while the colour White, being of itself the symbol of purity succeeds the Black. When it is in this latter state it is said that the Laton must be washed and made pure. When it has been washed it is pure.

PYRE OF THE SUN ~ Philosophical Sulphur.

QUATARUM ~ Identical with Quadrans. It signifies also a Measure containing Five Ounces of Wine, or Four and a Half Ounces of Oil.
QUEBOLIA ~ The Indian Plum, used as a Purgative.
QUERCOLA ~ A Little Oak.
QUERN ~ Mercurial Water of the Philosophers, so called because they have applied the term King to their Sulphur, and this Sulphur must be married to Mercurial Water.
QUIAMOS ~ Copperas.
QUIRIS ~ A Stone found in the Nest of the Lapwing.

R ~ Signifies, in Chemistry, Take or Place, etc.
RAAN ~ Sal Ammoniac.
RAARI ~ Sal Ammoniac.
RABEBOYA ~ Some have applied this name to the Luna, or Female of the Sages.
RABRIC ~ Sulphur of the Philosophers.
RACARI ~ Sal Ammoniac.
RADIRA ~ Tin; Jupiter.
RAIB ~ Any species of Stone.
RAMED ~ Rhubarb.
RAMICH ~ Gall Nut.
RANDERIC ~ Matter of the Work, or Rebis, before it has attained the white stage.
RASTIS ~ The Chemical Jupiter.
RAVED ~ Rhubarb. Seni ~ Oriental Rhubarb.
RAXAD ~ Sal Ammoniac.
RAYB ~ Same as Raib.

REBUS — See Ruland. But, according to another authority, it is the Matter of the Sages in the first operation of the Work. The crude Mineral Spirit which is like water, says the good Trevisan, mingles with its body in the first decoction, and dissolves the same. This is why it is called Rebus, because it is made of two things — to wit, Male and Female; in other words, the Dissolvant and the Dissolved Body, though at the bottom these are but one and the same thing, and one matter. The Philosophers have also given the name of Rebus to the Matter of the Work when it has arrived at the White Stage, because it is then a Mercury, animated by its Sulphur, and these two things have issued from one only root, and from one homogeneous substance.

RECEIPT — Uninstructed performers of experiments allow themselves to be duped by imposters, who proffer them false receipts, and demand gold to make gold. If they had studied the works of the true Philosophers they would have seen that the Matter is one which is vile and common, and that he who has a sufficient quantity of this Matter has more need of patience and of diligence than of extensive resources — that the work is not performed in the multiplication of things — and that there is only one Nature, one Vase, and one Furnace. If the Philosophers do occasionally furnish receipts, they take pains to warn their readers that they are not to be literally understood. For example, when they say: Take this or, Add that, they by no means intend that some foreign substance is really to be added to something that is already in the vase; but that the regimen must be continued to procure a change in the colour of the Matter, and to develop it from an imperfect state to a very high degree of perfection. They must not therefore be understood literally when they say Take or Add, except indeed in so far that the Matter has to be placed in the vase first of all, to compose the Mercury, and afterwards the Sulphur. From this Sulphur and this Mercury the Rebus has to be formed, so that in the end the Stone may be composed, and lastly from this Stone, combined with the Mercury, there must be obtained the great Elixir. This is the whole work.

RECFAGE ~ Dissolution of Bodies by means of a Humid and Igneous Spirit.

RECONCILIATION OF FOES ~ A Hermetic expression which signifies the reunion of the Fixed with the Volatile by means of the Mercury of Vulcan.

RECTIFICATION ~ A Fresh Depuration of a Body or of a Chemical Spirit by means of reiterated distillation, or by some other operation which is adapted to this end. In the terminology of Hermetic Chemistry, it is identical with Sublimation or Exaltation of the Matter of the Work.

RECTIFY ~ To Impart a Greater Degree of Perfection.

RED ~ A term of the Hermetic Art which signifies the Sulphur of the Philosophers.

RED ~ Blood Red ~ The Magisterium when it has reached, under the process of coction, the colour of Purple.

REDDEN, To ~ To Cook and Digest the Matter of the Work until it has attained the colour of Purple.

REEZON ~ The Sulphur of the Philosophers when perfect at the Red Stage.

REFACTION ~ Identical with Conversion of Elements.

REFECTIVUM ~ A Medicament which restores the exhausted energies.

REGIMEN, or RULE ~ The Philosophers say that everything consists in the Regimen of Fire. Here again one must guard against going astray over the literal sense of the words. The reference is not only to the conduct of the External Fire, which preserves the Matter from the influences of the cold air, it must also be understood of the Philosophical Fire ~ that is to say, of the Fire of Nature, and of the Fire which is against Nature, in order that from these two well combined there may be gotten a third, which the philosophers term Unnatural Fire.

REGULUS ~ This is a generic term which is much in use among chemists to describe the mass which remains at the bottom of the Crucible when Mineral or Metallic Ore has been melted therein. The name of Regulus is most commonly given to Calot of Antimony, and when it is combined with other metals it is called also by the name of the metal in question. Thus Martial Regulus is that in which there is a proportion of Iron or Mars. Many chemists have looked upon the last-mentioned Regulus as being the Matter of the Great Work, but they have misinterpreted a passage of Philalethes.

REGULIFY ~ To Reduce a Metal into Regulus.

REILLI ~ Acid Salt, or Vinegar.

REMIRUDATION ~ Retrogradation.

REINCRUDATE ~ To Reduce a Body into its First Principles. Artephius says that it signifies Decoction, the Mollifying of a Body until it is deprived of its hard and dry consistence. No one can succeed in the Work without performing the incrudation of the perfect body, and reducing it to its First Matter.

REITERATION OF DESTRUCTION ~ This is performed in the second disposition for the Composing of the Stone, after the Sulphur has been made. Morien says that this disposition, or second operation, is a repetition of the first.

REMORE ~ This is, firstly, the name of a small kind of Fish. But, secondly, it has been applied by the Philosophers to the Fixed Part of the matter of the Work by allusion to the supposed property possessed by this fish ~ namely, that it can arrest a ship in its course.

RESTORE ~ To Restore the Soul. This is the Restoration of the Soul to the Stone after having removed it thence. The expression signifies the Imbibition of the Volatile Matter upon the Fixed.

REPAST ~ The Delicious Repast of the Philosophers. This expression is used to signify the discovery by the Sages of something which was previously unknown.

RESERVOIR OF THE UPPER AND NETHER WATERS ~ The Mercury of the Sages. It has received this name because it is the abridgment, epitome, or synthesis of the Little World or Microcosmos, and it is, as it were, the Quintessence of the Elements.

RESIDENCE ~ The Magisterium at the Red Stage, so called because therein is to be found everything which is needed to animate the Mercury, of which it is itself the residue or the resultant. When all these things have been united together, modified, and adapted, they constitute a whole substance which is capable of remaining for ever in the fire, and of resisting its fiercest attacks.

RESIN CARDIC ~ A Gum or Extract, obtained from the Root of the Herb Angelica.

RESIN ~ To drink Resin from the Earth. Sublimated Sulphur reduced to a Liquor, and called the Oil or Balm of Sulphur.

RESURRECTION ~ The Hermetic Philosophers apply this name to the passage from the Black to the White in the operation of the Great Work, because the Black marks the stage of Putrefaction, which is a Sign of Death. They also give the same name to the Transmutation of Imperfect Metals into Gold, for, according to them, Lead, Iron, etc., are dead metals which cannot be resuscitated and glorified, except by becoming Gold, which is the highest degree of their perfection.

REVIVIFICATION ~ That Action by which a Composite Substance is brought back into its First State, before it was corrupted by combination.

REVIVIFY, To — The Return of a Mixed and Disguised Substance to its First State, received from Nature. Thus Mercury is Revivified from Cinnabar and other preparations that are combined with it to make it flow. Metals are Revivified by reducing them into Cinders by means of Calcination, or, otherwise, by the use of Aqua Fortis. In the terminology of Hermetic Science to Revivify is to reinfuse life, that is, to return the soul to its body.
RHA — Rhapontic.
RHIZOTOMUM — A Specific Medicament for radically Curing a Disease.
RHODELAEUM — Red Oil.
RHODOMEL — Honey.
RHODOSTAGMA — Rose Water.
RHOE — Sumach.
RHOCAS — The Wild Red Poppy.
RIASTEL — Salt.
RILLUS — A vessel used in the fusing of metals.
RISIGALLUM — A Species of Orpiment of a Reddish Colour.
RIVER — The Philosophers have frequently personified Rivers, so as to make them Symbols of the Mercurial Water of the Sages.
RIVER — Alkalised River. Chemists have applied this name to Rivers, the waters of which are charged with an Alkaline Salt, and they say that the water becomes impregnated with these Salts when passing among Stones which are calcined naturally in the earth.
ROBE — This is one of the names which the Philosophers have applied to the successive colours which appear in the Matter during the course of the operations. Thence it is that they say their King and Queen change their garments according to the seasons.

ROBE ~ The White Robe is the White Colour which follows the Black.

ROBE ~ The Dark Robe is one of the colours which appear, or, at least, should appear, in the course of the philosophical operations. In the first preparation of the Crude Matter these colours should not be expected.

ROBE OF PURPLE ~ This is the Red Colour of the Sulphur when perfectly fixed. It should also be noted that the Philosophers apply the name of Robe to the terrestrial and gross matters, wherein are concealed the Living Gold of the Sages and their Mercury. Consequently, they say that the vestments and robes of their King must be stripped off, as also those of their Queen, and that they must be well cleaned before they are put into the nuptial bed, because they must enter therein both pure and naked, so that they may give forth Venus to the world.

ROBUB ~ A Conserve of Flowers or of Fruits.

ROCK ~ The Philosophers have given the name of Rock to their Vase, because their Metals are formed therein after the same manner that the Ordinary or the Vulgar Metals, and Gold more especially, are deposited or formed in the rocks and in the bosom of the stony earth.

ROHEL ~ The Blood of the Philosophical Dragon.

ROSCOD ~ Vinegar.

ROSE ~ This Symbol is sometimes understood to signify Tartar, but it has many and most profound meanings not only in Alchemy, but in all branches of the Hermetic Mystery, as well as in the Symbolism of Universal Mythology.

ROSE OF LIFE ~ According to Mangetus, this is a Liquor which is composed of Brandy and of a most pure tincture of Gold, extracted by Spirit of Salt, the whole being subsequently combined by means of the Salt of Pearls.

RUBELLA — A certain Spirituous Liquor possessing dissolving properties, adapted for the extraction of the tincture of bodies. Such are the Spirit of Venus, and the Alkaest of Paracelsus and of Van Helmont, and these rank higher than all other dissolving menstrua.

RUBIFICATION — The Continuation of the Hermetic Regimen, or of that process by means of which the Matter of the Work of the Philosophers is passed from the colour White to that of Red.

RUETORIUM — Caustic or the Infernal Stone.

RUM — The Magisterium at the Perfection of the Red.

RUSANGI — Copper.

RUSCIAS — Mercury.

SABRE ~ The Fire of the Philosophers.
SACUL ~ Succinum.
SAGITH, or **SEGITH** ~ Vitriol.
SAHAB ~ Mercury.
SAIL ~ Quicksilver.
SAL ANDERON ~ Nitre.
SALINUCAR ~ Lavender.
SALT ~ Fusile Salt, that is, Salt which has lost its savour, and is only fit for the fire. Some understand the term as an equivalent for Sal Gemmae.
SALT OF TABAR ~ Sal Alembroth.
SAMBAC ~ Jasmine.
SARCION ~ The Ruddy Stone.
SARCOTICUM ~ An Unguent with qualities that are adapted for renewing the flesh.
SATIR ~ The Saline Water of the Philosophers.
SATURN ~ Though according to vulgar chemists this term signifies Lead only, the Hermetic Philosophers apply it to a

number of things. In the first place, it is the Black Colour, or the Matter when it has arrived thereat under the operation of dissolution and of putrefaction; it is again the Adrop of the Sages, or the Azoqueated Vitriol of Raymund Lully; it is ordinary Copper which the Mirror of Alchemy by the illustrious Arnold de Villanova denominates the First of Metals. Fourthly, it is Vulgar Lead, which is the most imperfect of metallic natures, and for the same reason is that which is furthest removed from the Matter of the Great Work. In the fifth and final place, it is the philosophical preparation of Philosophical Copper by means of the Vegetable Menstruum, from which it has received the name of the Vegetable Saturnian Plant, to distinguish it from Unprepared Copper. But this Vegetable Menstruum is also the Philosophical Menstruum.

SATURN — Horned Saturn — A name which chemists have applied to Lead when dissolved in Aquafortis and precipitated with Spirit of Salt.

SATURNIAN — The Mercury of the Philosophers.

SAURE — Fresh Water-cress.

SAVOUR — That sensation which Sulphureous, Mercurial, and Saline Spirits occasion in the organs of taste. The varieties of Salt in themselves possess no savour, and their sharp or acrid nature is to be attributed to the igneous quality which is communicated to them by a Volatile and Mercurial Sulphur which is invariably combined with them, and is exceedingly difficult to separate. The different savours must be entirely attributed to the proportion in which the said Sulphur combines with the Salts; it is bitter, sweet, or acid, in strict correspondence with this proportion; the more penetrating the savour the greater is the quantity of Mercurial Sulphur.

SAYRSA — A name of Mars — i.e., of Iron.

SCAOPTEZE — Flame.

SCARELLUM — Feathery Alum.
SCARTEA — The plant Orval, or Clery.
SCHONAM — Salt of the Philosophers.
SCIRPUS — A Reed.
SCOLYMUS — Artichoke.
SCORODON — Garlic.
SCORPION — A term which certain chemists have applied to the Stone of the Philosophers.
SCRIPTULUM — A Scruple, a Weight used in Medicine; it is the Third Part of a Drachm.
SCYTHE OF SATURN — An expression made use of by the Philosophers in reference to the Fixed Part of the Matter of the Work which fixes the volatility of the Mercury of the Sages.
SCYTICA RADIX — Liquorice.
SEASONS — The Philosophers have their four Seasons, corresponding to the four divisions of the vulgar year, but they differ materially from these. They understand by the term Seasons the different states through which the Matter of the Art passes during the course of the operations, and these Seasons are renewed throughout each philosophical year-that is to say, each time that an operation is reiterated to arrive at the perfection of the Work. Their Winter is the period of Dissolution and of Putrefaction. Spring succeeds, and it endures from the time that the Black colour begins to vanish until the moment when the White has become perfect. The period of the White Colour and of the Saffron which follows it constitutes the Summer of the Work, while the ensuing Red colour is the Autumn of the Sages. It is for this reason that they say Winter is the first season of the year, and the Work must be begun in the Winter. Those who recommend beginning in Spring have in view only the Matter with which the Work must be performed, and not

the commencement of the labour of the Artist, since he can perform that during any of the vulgar seasons.
SEBLEINDE — The Matter of the Work.
SECRET OF THE SCHOOL — This expression possesses a special application to the true and intimate Matter of the Work, and to its first preparation.
SEDEN, or **SEDINA** — Dragon's Blood.
SEMEN, or **SEED** — When simply so called, signifies, in the terminology of Alchemy, the Sulphur of the Philosophers. But when they speak of the seed of metals the reference is made to their Mercury, and sometimes to their Magistery when it has attained to the Red Stage. When, however, the Adepts discourse in a more general manner of the Seed of Metals, i.e., of the vulgar metals, and when they give instruction as to the manner of its formation in the bowels of the earth, the Seed of which they then speak is a Vapour formed by the union of the elements, carried down into the earth by the air and water, but afterwards sublimed back again to the surface by the operation of the central fire. This vapour becomes corporified, and either of an unctuous or viscous quality; it adheres in its sublimations to the Sulphur which it carries away with it, and forms more or less perfect metals according to the greater or lesser purity of the Sulphur and the Matter.
SIEVE OF NATURE — The Air.
SIEVE OF THE SAGES — Hermetic Mercury.
SIEVE (Hermetic) — Mercurial Water.
SIMILITUDES — Celestial Appearances.
SOW — To Sow is to Cook, i.e., to Continue the Regimen of the Fire. The Philosophers say: Sow your Gold in a white and foliated earth which has been well prepared — that is to say, Elaborate your Matter from the White to the Red colour.
SEMINALIS — Knob-grass, Centinodia.

SEMIS — For which S is commonly used as a sign or symbol, signifies a Half-ounce, a Half-pound, etc.
SENTISSIS — The same as Semis.
SEMMOCIA — A Half-ounce.
SENCO — Lead.
SEVEN — This is the Mysterious Number of Holy Scripture, and it is that also of the Great Work. The Philosophers speak of Seven Planets, Seven Kingdoms, Seven Operations, Seven Circles, Seven Metals. They say that their work resembles the creation of the world, which was accomplished in seven days. St. Thomas Aquinas in his Epistle to Brother Raynang, his friend, says that the work is performed in three times seven days and one day.
SEPULCHRE — This name has been applied by one of the Adepts to the Glass Vase which contains the Compost or Matter of the Work; but the same name has been applied by others to a certain Matter which contains another Matter as if entombed in its breast. It is also given to the Black colour which appears during the period of putrefaction, because corruption is a sign of death, and black is a symbol of mourning. Sometimes the term Sepulchre has been used to signify the Dissolvent of the Sages.
SERAPIAS ORCHIS — A Species of Ragwort, the Flowers of which resemble some very fertile Insect.
SERAPINUS — Gum Arabic.
SERAPINUS — Syrup.
SERF — The Mercury of the Philosophers. Vide Servus Fugitivus in Rulandus. The term is significant of the Volatile Quality.
SERINECH — The Magistery at the White Stage.
SERIOLA or **SERIS** — Endive.
SERNEC — Vitriol.
SERPENT of MARS — The Mercury of the Philosophers.
SERPIGO — Moss.

SERRIOLA — Endive.
SERTULA CAMPANA — Sweet Trefoil.
SERVANT — This name is applied by the Philosophers to their Matters because they work according to the desires of the Adepts and yield obedience to their will. But in addition to this generic term, they at the same time make use of other epithets by which the Matters are severally distinguished.
SERVANT — The Red Servant. The Matter from which the Philosophers extract their Mercury.
SENTLOMALACH — Some have understood this term to signify Beet, some Spinach, and others Mallow.
SEXTARIO — A Weight of Two Ounces.
SEXTULO — Four Scruples.
SEXUNX — Six Ounces, or Half-a-pound, according to the old method of computing the Pound in Medicine, which consisted of Twelve Ounces.
SEZUR or **SFACTE** — Marine Oil.
SICILIUS or **SICILIUM** — The Name of a Weight equal to Half an Ounce, but some understand it to be the Fourth Part of an Ounce.
SICYOS — Cucumber.
SIEF ALBUM — Dry Collyrium.
SIGIA — Storax.
SION or **SIUM** — Water-cress, according to some explanations.
SIPAR — Quicksilver.
SMALTERNIUM — Succinnum.
SISTER — The Magistery at the White Stage.
SOLIDITY — This condition is in opposition to the liquid state, and three kinds are distinguished. The first is that form of consistence in which the component parts of bodies are brought together and adhere to one another in the manner of a jelly; in this consistence the fluid state has just been passed, but the process of melting can be easily

accomplished by the two ordinary solving agents, i.e., Fire and Water. The second species of Solidity is that of bodies which are termed Coagulated. The third is the fixation which takes place when the component parts are very intimately united in a compact manner, as we see in Metals and Stones. The first species is that of the soft parts of Animals; the second is that of Vegetables; the third is of Minerals.

SKIN — The Human Skin — Some Philosophers have given this name to their Dissolvent Mercury, and there have been artists in consequence who have regarded human hair and skin as the Matters of the Great Work. Doubtless these persons had never read the treatise of Trevisan on the Philosophy of Metals, who enumerates hair and skin among the substances which are excluded from the Work, as indeed are all substances which are derived from animals.

SPAIRIA — Commonly understood as another name for Alchemy.

SPAITIUM — A species of Broom; it is adapted for the Manufacture of Bonds, etc.

SPATULA OF IRON OR STONE — The Matter of the Philosophers in Putrefaction and when arrived at the Black colour.

SPERM — The Seed of Individuals in the three kingdoms, Animal, Vegetable, and Mineral. In the first, it is a white, humid, unctuous substance, and is composed of the purest parts of the blood. In vegetables, it is the seed itself, composed of oleaginous and unctuous substances, whence the name of Sulphur has been given to it by chemists. But that which is properly called Sulphur is the Sperm of Metals. According to Aristotle, it is a Vapour, but this must be understood of an unctuous, sulphureous, and mercurial Vapour, the Ethereated Liquor of the Philosophers — a Mineral Sulphur which penetrates metallic stones and is fixed therein. The remote principle of this vapour is common Sulphur. Mineral Sulphur is an unctuous, incombustible Humour, which the Hermetic Philosophers term their Sun and their Masculine Seed. The Sperm must not be confounded with the Seed; the one is the vehicle of the other. The Sperm is the Generative Grain and the principle of the substance to which it belongs. It is for this reason that the Philosophers have given the name of Sperm of Metals to Sulphur and Seed of Metals to Mercury. The germ within the seed of vegetables is the Sperm.

SPERM OF MERCURY — The True Mercury of the Sages.

SPRING — The Matter at the White Stage, or the Regimen of the Fire of the Third Degree. Its complexion is igneous. The third degree fixes the Mercury, and it must be continued till the development of the Red Stage.

SWEAT OF THE SUN — Mercury of the Sages. The same name has been given to the Philosophical Matter in Putrefaction.

SUPERFLUOUS — Gebir, and other Philosophers who have followed his leading, have affirmed that there exists in their Matter a certain Superfluous Portion which must be eliminated. Such words are very generally interpreted after a literal fashion, and it is concluded that the operator must separate something from the Matter in the Medicine of the Second Order, etc. But the veritable sages assure us that such elimination takes place of itself in the Medicine, and that the superfluity is very useful in the Work. It is an Oil or a species of Slime originating in the body, and it comes floating to the surface of the Menstruum after the body is dissolved. The said slime is absolutely indispensable to the conversion of the body into oil, and such a conversion is, on the other hand, so essential that success is impossible to the Work without it, because it is impossible to obtain the principles of the Art.

SUPPRESSION ~ The Fire of Suppression is that which is made above or within the Vase.
SUTTER ~ Sugar.
SOOT OF METALS ~ Arsenic.
SYCAMINOS ~ The Mulberry Tree.
SYCE ~ Fig.
SYNACTICUM ~ An Astringent Medicament.
SYNCRITICUM ~ Antispasmodic.
SYRUP OF GRANADA ~ The Stone at the Red Stage.

TABLETS OF THE PHILOSOPHERS ~ These are their Books, their Allegories, their Hieroglyphics, etc.

TAGETES ~ Tanesy.

TAIL ~ The White Tail of the Dragon, Oil of the Mercury, or the Stone at the White. It is so called because the Black colour is termed the Dragon, and it is succeeded by the White.

TAIL ~ The Red Tail of the Dragon ~ This is the Magistery of the Red, or the Red Sulphur of the Philosophers.

TAIL OF THE DRAGON ~ According to Hermes, the Mercury of the Philosophers in putrefaction.

TAIL OF THE PEACOCK ~ The Colours of the Rainbow which manifest upon the Matter in the operations of the Stone. To indicate the colours which pass in succession over this Matter, Basil Valentin and many other Philosophers have employed a defined sequence of symbolism. The Raven signifies the Black colour, the Peacock the several hues of

the Rainbow, the Swan the colour White, while the Phoenix stands for the Red.
TAIL OF THE RED FOX ~ Minium.
TAMUE ~ The Matter of the Work prepared and cooked to the Red colour of the Poppy.
TAMUS, or **TANUS** ~ Snake-weed, or Bryony.
TANECH ~ Pumice Stone.
TARAGUAS ~ Bezoar.
TARGAR ~ Oil of Juniper.
TARTAR ~ White Tartar, or the Salt of Tartar of the Sages, is their Magistery arrived at the White Colour.
TARTAR OF MARBLE ~ The Stones which form in the human body. They are so called on account of the terrestrial or tartaric substance of which they are composed.
TELESME ~ End, Perfection, Complement.
TEMEYNCHUM ~ The Gold of the Philosophers or their Magistery at the Red Stage.
TERENGIBIL ~ Marina.
TERSA ~ Mustard.
TETRAPHARMICUM ~ A Medicament composed of Four Ingredients.
TETRABOLON ~ A Weight of Four Drachms.
TEVOS ~ The Matter of the Work arrived at the White Stage.
THABRITIS ~ The Jupiter of the Philosophers.
THAMAR ~ The Fruit of the Palm-tree.
THELIMA ~ The Stone elaborated to the perfection of the Red Stage.
THELYPTERIS ~ Fern.
THERMUS ~ The Bath. Some Philosophers have given this name to their Mercurial Water.
THERMOMETER ~ The Philosophical Thermometer is the Natural Warmth of Composites.
THIMI VENETIANI ~ Absynth.

THITA — The Magistery of the Sages in its Fixation at the Purple colour.

THUNDERBOLT OF JUPITER — The Fire of the Philosophers, which by its dissolving property reduces the imperfect bodies of the Work into a state of solution, and after by its fixing quality converts them into a powder or ash which can suffer nothing further from the assault of the most potent fire.

TICALIBAR — Sea Foam or Scum — That Red Scum of the sea of which Flamel speaks when he enigmatically indicates the Matter of the Work.

TIERCELET — A French term, signifying Tassel, and standing for a certain composition once in vogue among charlatans who pretended that they were Adepts in Hermetic art. By means of the composition in question they imposed upon those who were so credulous as to part with their money to them.

TIFACUM — The Mercury of the Philosophers.

TIFARUM — Hermetic Sulphur.

TINCTURE — In the terminology of the Hermetic science to tinge or tincture signifies to Conduct the Regimen of the Fire, to administer it to the Matter for its digestion and coction in such a manner that the latter shall assume the successive different colours which are enumerated by the Philosophers, and are called by them demonstrative signs.

TINCTURE — Living Tincture — The Stone at the Red Stage.

TINCTURE — The Red or Purple is the same as the Illuminating Tincture.

TINCTURE — The Illuminating Tincture of Bodies — This is the same thing as the Powder of Projection. Some, nevertheless, understand this expression to signify the Stone at the Red Stage, or the Auriferous Sulphur of the Philosophers, because they call it the Sun, and the Sun is, so to speak, the principle or the distributor of Light. Vainly do the chemists endeavour to extract the Tincture from Gold of the vulgar order for the rehabiliment of the rest of the metals. The true Tincture of Gold consists in its Radical Sulphur, which is inseparable from the very body of Gold, according to Espagnet. Moreover, were the thing otherwise to be regarded as possible, such a tincture could never give more than it possesses; in other words, it could never tinge a larger weight of Silver than that of the Gold from which it was derived; while, on the contrary, a single grain of the Philosophical Tincture, when elaborated to the utmost perfection of which its nature is possible, will tinge a million times its own volume of any metal whatsoever.

TINGENT — A necessary property of the Stone of the Philosophers, or of their Powder of Projection. It was required that it should be capable of tingeing that is to say, that it should be able to impart to the imperfect metals the fixed and permanent colour of Gold or Silver, according to the degree of perfection to which it had been elaborated.

TIME — The Philosophers do not seem to be in agreement with one another as to the duration of the operations or processes which are necessary for the attainment of the end of the Hermetic Work. Some say that it requires three years, others seven, and there are again some who extend the experiment to twelve. There are those also who reduce its duration to the space of eighteen months. Raymund Lully is satisfied with fifteen months. But these are so many manners of expressions which are only contradictory in appearance; it is actually the same period of time calculated upon a variety of methods. Their months and their seasons are not of the vulgar kind. A year must elapse, says Ripley, before we can enjoy the fruits that we expect from our labours. An anonymous writer explains the different periods in the following manner. Even as we call by the name of day that interval of time which the Sun takes to travel through the sky from the east to the west, so do the philosophers apply the same term to the period required by their coction. Those who say that a month alone is necessary, make reference to the course of the Sun through each celestial sign, while those who speak of a year have in view the four principal colours which successively manifest in the Matter, because these four colours are the four philosophical seasons.

TIRFIAT, or TIRSIAT — Sal Ammoniac.

TERRELATI — Corporeal Spirits living on the earth.

THIRD PRINCIPLE AND COLOUR — The Sulphur of the Philosophers, digested and cooked till it attains the Red Colour. It is called third because Red is the third of the chief colours assumed by the Matter in the course of the Hermetic operation.

THIRTEENTH — The Sulphur of the Sages attained to the Red Stage.

TIN — Calcined Tin is a name of the Stone when it has been elaborated to the White Stage, which is also termed Cinders of Tin, Tin Ashes, the Full Moon, Diana Unveiled, etc.

TIN OF THE PHILOSOPHERS, or WHITE LEAD OF THE PHILOSOPHERS — Their Mercury stripped of its blackness, but before it has arrived at the perfect White.

TIE — To Tie, in its general philological sense, is to Reunite, to bind together, to make the separated parts of a body cleave one to another. But in the terminology of Hermetic Philosophy, it is to coagulate and to fix, just as to untie or unbind are equivalent to dissolve and volatilize.

TIE — That Unctuosity of Bodies which Binds their Component Parts together, which reunites the volatile with the fixed, prevents evaporation of the spirits, and forms the composing quality of sublunary things.

TIE OF QUICKSILVER — Philosophical Gold or the Fixation of Mercury; it takes place when the Matter of the Work has arrived at the Red Stage.

TIE OF TINCTURES — The Mercury of the Philosophers.

TMETICUM — An Attenuating or Reducing Medicament.

TOMB — The Philosophers have often made use of the symbolism of the tomb to contrive allegories concerning the putrefaction of the Matter of the Work.

TOPIC — A Medicament which is applied to the Skin after the manner of a Plaster.

TORDYLIUDS — Cretan Sefeli.

TORTOISE — The Philosophers have employed the Tortoise as an emblem of the Matter of their Art.

TOTHUS — A White Gypsum-like Substance, resembling Dead Ashes. It is that Matter which forms about the joints of the bones in those persons who are subject to violent attacks of Gout.

TOWER — Certain Philosophers have given this name to their Furnace.

TOWER — The Transparent Tower is the Glass Vase in which the Matter for the performance of the Great Work is enclosed.

TOXICUM — Poison or Venom. It is one of the names given to the Matter of the Great Work because before its preparation it is literally a most dangerous poison, while after preparation it becomes a remedy for all evils. The name has also been applied to the Mercurial Water of the Sages, because it dissolves the Philosophical Metals, and reduces them to their First Matter, which is the Philosophical Killing and Burying.

TRANSMUTATION — The Changing or the Alteration of the Form of Bodies in such a way that they no longer have any resemblance to that which they previously were, but have acquired another manner of being both inwardly and outwardly, even another colour, a new virtue, a diverse property, as when a metal is converted into glass by the power of fire, wood into coal, clay into brick, hide into glue, rag into paper. Every Transmutation is performed by degrees or stages, of which it is commonly computed that there are seven. The others which are referred to by chemists can be reduced to this number, all, that is to say, are resolvable into Calcination, Sublimation, Solution, Putrefaction, Distillation, Coagulation and Tincture. The Metempsychosis of the ancient Philosophers was nothing else but the Transmutations of Nature understood in their physical sense.

TREASURE BEYOND COMPARISON -- This is the Powder of Projection, the source of all blessings, since it produces infinite riches. Some Philosophers have termed the Magistery at the White an Incomparable Treasure, as also Sulphur when it is perfect at the Red Stage.

TRICALILIBAR -- Sea-Foam or the Matter of the Stone of the Philosophers.

TRICEUM -- Wild or Autumn Honey.

TRIDENT -- The Hermetic Philosophers say that their Trident is the symbol of the three principles of the Great Work, which principles are found in the Mercury of the Sages from the first moment of its birth.

TRIENS -- A Weight of Four Ounces.

TRIOBOLAM -- A Weight of Half-a-drachm.

TRIPATER -- The Matter of the Sages, composed of the Three Principles.

TRIPOLIUM -- Marine Asparagus.

TRITURATION -- An Operation by Which Bodies are reduced into Powder. When the Philosophers affirm that bodies must be Tirturated, they do not mean by the process of the Mortar or the Marble Slab, but they refer to the dissolution of the parts of the Matter of the Magistery, which takes place of itself in the Vase by the aid of hire and of Putrefaction.

TRUNGIBIN ~ Manna.

TUMBABA ~ Living Sulphur.

TURN ~ To Turn in a Circle is to cause the Matter to circulate in the Vessel.

TURSES ~ Sal Ammoniac.

TUSIASI ~ Living Sulphur.

TUBEROSA ~ Oriental Hyacinth.

TURIONES ~ New shoot of trees.

TWENTY-ONE ~ No one but an Adept can understand for what reason the Philosophers have given the name of Twenty-One to their Magistery at the White. To explain it here would be a partial violation of that secrecy which is so solemnly enjoined. They make no explanation themselves in their writings, and Philalethes is contented to inform us by a condescension that the enigmatical term in question signifies the same thing as Sulphur, the Root of the Art, or the Salt of Metals. This refers it to their Matter when cooked and digested at the perfect White.

TYPHA ~ A Reed; also a Mass of Gum.

TYRIAN ~ This Colour or Dye, derived from certain Marine Shells on the Coast of Tyre, has been utilised by the adepts as an emblem of the Red State of their Magistery. Compare Theriaca in Rulandus.

UBIDRUGEL ~ Matter in Perfect Putrefaction.
UFFITUFFE ~ The Odour of the Mercury of the Sages, which is as strong and disagreeable as that of graves and charnel-houses.
ULRACH ~ Dragon's Blood.
ULVA ~ Sea Weed.
UMO ~ Tin.
UNDYING LAMPS ~ The search for an unquenchable and ever-burning fire must be included among the quests, and if we are to believe what so many of them have affirmed, amongst the discoveries of the alchemists. Many marvelous accounts are related concerning the existence of everlasting lamps by the hundred and seventy authors who are said to have written on this subject. The discovery of the inextinguishable and enduring fire, like most of the transcendent secrets of alchemy and magic, is attributed to the ancient Egyptians, who hung lamps in the sepulchres of rich and noble persons. Many medieval writers affirm that

on the opening of Egyptian and Roman tombs, which occurred occasionally in their own days, these lamps were found still burning but were at once extinguished on the admission of fresh air. The golden lamp wrought by Callimachus for the Athenian Temple of Minerva was replenished but once a year; another in the Temple of Jupiter Ammon is described Plutarch, whom the priests assured that it had burnt continually for years, and though it stood in the open air, neither wind nor water could extinguish it. Baptista Porta describes the discovery of a Roman sepulchre of marble, situated in a small island of the Bay of Naples. On opening it, a lamp was discovered diffusing a brilliant light, which dazzled and overwhelmed the beholders. It was extinguished instantaneously by the wind, but the inscription proved it to have been placed there before the birth of Christ. During the Papacy of Paul III a sepulchre was opened in the Appian Way, and there was found the entire body of a young girl, swimming in a bright liquor, which had so well preserved it that the face was beautiful, and like life itself. At her feet burned a lamp, but the flame vanished upon opening the tomb. This was supposed to be the body of Tullia, Cicero's daughter. Some years previously a similar lamp was unearthed by a labourer, who, while digging in a field near Atteste, came upon an urn containing another urn, in which last there was deposited one of these miraculous lamps, the most wonderful of all those described in medieval treatises. The aliment of this lamp, says a writer who has treated of the subject, appeared to be a very exquisite crystal liquor, by the ever-during powers of which it continued to shine Mercury. It is at least certain that common substances were adapted in such a manner by the initiates that their natural imperfections were eliminated, and their concealed potencies developed to a high point of manifestation and activity. The erudite Jesuit,

Kircher, affirms that asbestos possesses the marvelous properties attributed by those who have recorded this experiment. He himself possessed a tablet of the substance in question which he used for writing purposes, and was accustomed to clean it by placing it in the fire, out of which it emerged white and shining. What is more to the purpose, he was acquainted with an asbestos lamp which burned for two years uninterruptedly, and was then stolen. He believed the extraordinary petrine substance to be composed of a species of talc, and a material akin to aluminium. The oil extracted from it was said to be a perpetual fuel, but later chemistry has failed to perform this operation; it has equally failed to extract the essential Oil of Gold, which was regarded as the fittest pabulum for the mystic flame, because of all metals gold wastes least when either heated or melted. Incombustible wicks were also made from the loadstone, which was supposed to burn in oil without being consumed, and the mysterious stone Carystios was endowed with the same properties. Another writer has attributed the alleged perpetuity of these flames to the consummate tenacity of the unctuous matter in which they were maintained, and to the exquisitely perfect balance between this and the strength of the flame.

Baptista Porta, having contemptuously noticed numerous experiments for extracting an inconsumable oil from metals, juniper-wood, magnets, etc., propounds as follows his own theory: If a flame were shut up in a glass and all vent-holes stopped close, if it could last one moment it would last continually, and could not be possibly put out. But how the flame should be lighted within a glass hermetically sealed is worth the while to know. Sometimes the old chemical writers give instructions for producing a light which, though not perpetual, has sufficiently extraordinary properties, as for example: Take four ounces of the herb Serpentinet, place them in a sealed vase, and cover them with warm horse manure for the space of fifteen days, when the matter will be transformed into small red worms, from which an oil must be extracted according to the transcendent principles of the Hermetic Art. With this oil a lamp may be trimmed, which, set to burn in any room, will cast all within it into a slumber so profound that no power can awaken them so long as the lamp continues burning.

UNICORN — The Mineral Unicorn is Red Sigillated Earth.

UNION — Volatilization of the body and copulation of the spirit, performed by the same operation. It has been termed the union of earth and water by the Philosophers, and is accomplished by the agency of putrefaction. Then are the elements confounded; the water contains air and the earth fire, while the two make one thing, namely, Hyle, or Chaos. This union of earth and water is achieved also by the fixation of the Volatile.

UNION OF ENEMIES — The fixation of the volatile Mercurial Water by the fixed Sulphur of the Sages.

UNION OF SPIRITS — Dry Water.

UNIQUE — The Unique Substance is the Mercury of the Sages.

UNION OF ELEMENTS — The Coction of the Matter.

UNIVERSAL MEDICINE — The renewal of youth by the processes of alchemy and the communication of the arcane vitality and renovating potencies of the Universal Medicine must be distinguished from natural or ordinary longevity. There are many authors who treat of the regimen of long life and the way to preserve health, but these have nothing to do with alchemy, and their authors are not alchemists, or followers of our secret science of great Hermes. A robust constitution, life sober, life active, passed amidst an air that is keen, bracing, and pure, as in so many of our northern countries, will frequently enable the individual to subsist beyond the ordinary limits of the span of physical being. In isolated cases, perhaps insufficiently substantiated, many lustrums are said to have been added to an entire century of healthy existence. The facts of ordinary longevity substantiate the claim of the disciples of our art by exhibiting the possibilities of unassisted Nature. Our science steps in where Nature fails and falls short, completes what she has begun, makes perfect that which passes defective from her hands. It does not do violence to Nature; it is rather her extension and her supplement. The theory and the practice of the Universal Medicine repose upon natural law as a firm and immovable basis, and they achieve their end by reason of a development of natural potencies. The works which treat of this subject by no means ignore the curious facts of ordinary longevity either in men or animals, but regard them as a point of departure whence they develop their own principles. The philosophical theory and practice of the Universal Medicine is thus elaborated.

Man, made in the image of God, and by a special act of the creative power, so that he is regarded by theology as having come forth out of the hands of Omnipotence in a manner which cannot be postulated for the rest of the physical universe, was endowed from the moment of his creation with the high crown of immortality. But this immortality depended on his condition being immutably preserved in the innocence of the unfallen state. The Tree of Life in the centre of the terrestrial paradise was like a Universal Medicine or Reparative Elixir, of which he was privileged to partake, and he required no other food. Moreover, his primeval form of subsistence was devoid of all those contrary qualities which do now encompass his destruction. Amidst continual youth he enjoyed all the powers of maturity without any fear of lapsing into the infirmity of age. He was guided by the adequate illumination of a supreme reason by which a perfect knowledge was imparted to him without any need of study. He was equally innocent in body and in mind. His interior and exterior nature were therefore combined in harmony, and acted in the concert which is indispensable to perfect human felicity. The Tree of Life united soul and body so intimately by its celestial food that no separation could happen between them till man fell from the first standard of excellence. It was by sin only that he was ultimately rendered subject to mortality and entered into the power of death. Then his eyes were opened to his misfortune; guilt made him conscious of nakedness; he was stripped of the privilege of immortality; he was deprived of the Tree of Life.

Thus, eternal youth and strength were not inherent in primeval Adam. He was sustained in innocence by a perfect regimen, and this was the Arbor Vitae. The Elixir, the Grand Quintessence, the Universal Medicine, sustained him, that gift of God which has never been attained by any one except through the favour of God. Thus also, the Desire of the Wise after the Balm which is the consolation of philosophy, is an aspiration after the Tree of Life, and he who would compose the Universal Medicine must first enter into Paradise. But he only can enter into Paradise who has returned into the first condition of innocence. Now, the Philosophers from time immemorial have taught that the Stone is obtained by a Divine light entering the mind of the artist, and that a blameless, prayerful, charitable, studious, perfect life is an indispensable condition of success. Be ye, therefore, perfect like Adam, be ye enlightened by the rational light of the Edenic state, and ye shall not fail of the Grand Elixir.

It is a doctrine of the Adepts that fallen man has not lost the capacity for immortality, but simply the food or regimen of eternal life. The possibility is indestructible in his nature.

They are also persuaded that the human body conceals the inexhaustible fountain of a Sovereign Balsam by which this life, under given circumstances, may yet be recovered. It is alike in blood and milk, grease and bone, brain and marrow; in a word, it sustains his physical nature at all points. Man has, therefore, within him the materials of a medicine which surpasses the healing properties of any herb or stone, as well as of any extract of other animal natures. This is the virtue of the food of the Tree of Life which once sustained Adam, and still persists in all his descendants. Extract it, and thou hast found the treasure. The essence is in thy hands; thou hast no need to seek outside thyself for that which is so abundantly within thee. Man is the monarch of Nature; his soul is his noblest part, which remains immortal and in its essence like unto the angels; it communicates to his fallen body the majesty which illuminates the countenance. But that body has still a thousand virtues which are the remains of his primal prerogatives, and, above all, a principle of life which it is still possible to develop.

Had Adam persisted in his first estate, his body would not always have remained upon earth. God placed him in the Garden of Delights to cultivate it and to nourish it. Then would he have laboured in sanctification by fidelity and adoration; then confirmed in his innocence and penetrated by the longing for a full possession of God, dome gentle ecstasy would have ravished him to heaven. In that brilliant form of subsistence which our understanding now cannot realize, the body would have been glorified in the soul's glory, as the soul herself would have been transfigured by the light and joy of God. This is the transport of Enoch and Elias, and it is the supreme desire of the Adepts, as their writings testify, and as their great hidden labours do proclaim to those who know.

A certain shadow of the primeval state of immortality is afforded by those who are instances of ordinary longevity. Now, as then, the way of innocence is the way of strength, health, and long life. Temperance has ever been regarded as a chief aid towards duration in years. It is a Divine inclination, agreeable to God, friendly to Nature, the daughter of reason, the mother of virtues, the companions of chastity; it is full of peace and happiness. It purifies the senses, fortifies the body, illuminates the mind, strengthens memory, embellishes the soul. It disengages slowly from the bonds which too securely bind us to the earth, exalts us above ourself, and makes us new men in proportion as it ensures us new days wherein we can work to merit ultimately the new life of immortality.

The Adepts assure us that it is possible not only to prolong life, but also to renew youth. To renew youth is to enter once again into that beautiful season when the forces of our being were at the spring and freshness of early power. Paracelsus, by means of his celebrated Mercury of Life, claimed to metamorphose an old into a young man, as well as change iron into gold. Arnold de Villa Nova, that great physician of France who lived towards the close of the thirteenth century, also invented a method to accomplish this most desirable object, and bequeathed it as a treasure to his disciples. This admirable operation must be renewed once in every seven years upon bodies that are naturally healthy and well organized. On the first day of the process, and during sleep,, a plaster must be placed upon the heart, consisting of one ounce of Oriental saffron, half-an-ounce of red roses, two drachms of red santal, one drachm of aloe wood, and the same quantity of good amber. These drugs must be well ground, and combined with half-a-pound of white wax, kneaded together by a sufficient quantity of oil of roses. At the moment of waking, this plaster should be removed, rolled up, and placed in a leaden box, to be again made use of on the following night. The next point in the process consists in a diet of chickens prepared after a prescribed manner. For sanguine temperaments it should be continued sixteen days, twenty-five for phlegmatic, and for melancholic dispositions as long as thirty days. A special brood of chickens must be bred for the purpose, the number thereof being regulated by the days computed for the special temperament; they must be kept in a spacious run where the air is clear and pure, and where there is no kind of herbage to tempt them from the food on which they must be reared. Their nourishment is to consist of as many fine vipers as there are fowls in the poultry-run. The reptiles must be placed in a cask in such a manner that their heads and tails can be cut off at once; they must then be flayed, steeped in vinegar, and salt must be rubbed into them with a rough cloth. Subsequently, they must be cut up in pieces and placed in a large kettle, with half-a-pound of flowers of rosemary, fennel, calamanth, and anise, in equal proportions, to which should be added half-a-pound of the African herb cumin. The kettle must be two-thirds full of clear water, and the whole must be gently boiled until the vipers are cooked. A quantity of well-cleansed corn, sufficient for the maintenance of the chickens during the required period must then be added, and again the whole must be boiled, until the corn has become saturated with the virtue of the reptiles. The better, to insure this end, the kettle should be kept covered, and should be suspended over the fire on a tripod, being subjected to an equable and gentle heat, till the whole mass is thickened. Water, when necessary, may be added to the contents of the kettle to make up for the evaporation by steam. When this operation is finished, the kettle must be removed from the fire, the corn must be spread out to dry in some well-ventilated place to prevent it putrefying, and when still warm it should be administered to the fowls, kneaded into little balls by means of bran soaked in the liquor of the stew. In this manner, the fowls must be fattened for the space of two months, one of the birds being eaten daily by the person who is undertaking the experiment with a view to renew youth. It must be cooked after one manner only, in a quantity of water which will be sufficient to make two plates of broth, which must be made with some bread of pure wheaten flour, well baked and two days old. At supper, as at dinner, one plate of the broth must be taken, and the remaining half of the fowl, or two or three fresh eggs, boiled in water, eaten with a little of the bread, and washed down with white wine or claret. This operation answers most successfully during the months of April or May, when all Nature is itself undergoing the grand process of renewal. When the prescribed period has been accomplished, a clear warm water bath must be taken three times a week, or every other day. In the water must be poured a decoction of rosemary flowers, elder, the two cassidonies, or French lavender, camomile, sweet trefoil, red roses, and water-lily — of each one pound. The roots of snake-weed, briony, alder, the plant patience, and iris — of each one handful, cleansed and pounded, the whole being placed in a linen bag and boiled in a large caldron of river water. The bath must be taken fasting and immersed to the neck, seated on the bag of flowers for at least one hour. The same bag will answer for two or three baths. On issuing from the water a drachm of good theriaca must be swallowed in six spoonfuls of wine infused with flowers of rosemary and cumin. The patient must then retire to bed for the purpose of repose and sleep. Should sweating take place, it may be regarded as a favourable sign, and on awaking a moderate repast may be takes according to appetite. As a conclusion of the operation, for at least twelve days, the following confection must be taken after the bath.

Rx — Four ounces of calx of gold, philosophically dissolved, aloe-wood, sandalwood, seeds of pearl, sapphire, hyacinth, emeralds, rubies, topazes, white and red coral, purest balm, raspings of ivory, the bones of a stag's heart, of each half-a-drachm, together with six grains of best amber and musk. Pulverise the whole in such a manner that it shall become an impalpable powder; combine it with conserves of citron, borage and rosemary — of each one ounce. Add one pound of sugar of the finest quality, together with sugar of roses in sufficient quantity to make a confection which must be placed in a porcelain or earthenware vase, which must be well covered. Every morning, on an empty stomach, and every evening, before retiring to rest, about half a spoonful must be taken of this syrup, and in a very short time the patient will feel the value of this rare quintessence for the reparation of caducity and of decrepitude.

This marvelous arcanum for the rehabilitation of Nature is not to be found in the folio volume of the works of the celebrated Arnold de Villa Nova, printed at Lyons and Basle in the fifteenth century. It is extracted from an ancient Latin manuscript which, in the seventeenth century, came into the hands of M. de Poirier, physician-in-chief to the general hospital at Tours.

UNIVERSAL MEDICINE — Substances which contribute to the prolongation of life. The best among these are quintessences, extracted from animals, minerals, and vegetables. The perfection of these quintessences consists in their preparation. So much does this vary that it would sometimes seem almost impossible that these essences are extracted from one and the same principle.

The Essence of Vipers preserves health for a number of years, providing it is operated on according to the true principles of art. This essence is more health-giving than is even the Powder of Vipers, because the latter contains their terrestrial matter.

The Essence of the Myrtle preserves everything, including that which is inanimate from corruption.

The Balsamic Oil of Sulphur, according to Paracelsus, preserves all things, whether dead or living, from corruption; it always does good and never evil, according to Fioramenti. When the Philosophical Salt is extracted, and the Essential Oil and Tincture of this Sulphur, the eduction of its Balsamic Oil is then performed.

The Oil of Mars, or of Vitriol, extracted from its Salt and Oil, rectified and cocted together, produces the fixed Oil of Mars, the virtues of which are concealed from the greater part of the world.

Among other quintessences which officiate in the prolongation of life may be enumerated:

(a) The true Tincture of Coral, extracted by the rays of the Sun and Celestial Brandy, or by the juice of the Citron.

(b) The Quintessence of Pearls, so useful in the fortifying of the life principle against poisons.

(c) The Quintessence of Ambergris, used medicinally and not as a perfume, which augments, without inflaming, our natural heat, and foments without dissolving it. It recuperates the depleted energies of the old by means of the Universal Spirit with which it abounds.

(d) The Quintessence of Sugar, which was discovered by Isaac the Hollander, is so favourable to every form of temperament that he regarded it as a sovereign remedy for dropsy, pthisis and consumption, as well as in epilepsy and confinements.

(e) The Quintessence of Honey, composed of flowers and dew, which contains a truly Heavenly Spirit.

(f) The Tincture of Natural Gold, the metal being reduced by spagyric operation into a true Oil or Tincture of Gold. Of all these essences or tinctures there may be ultimately composed what occult chemistry has termed the DIAPHORON, a transcendant quintessence which has power over every kind of disease. It is referred to by Bartholomew Korodorfer in the following terms: It would be difficult to explain the virtue exercised by the Diaphoron upon all species of malady. When combined in doses with an aureated water, the person who takes it will enjoy most vigorous health. It is the Balm of Life, and it performs miracles. By its means a certain Gentile monarch extended his life to the age of three hundred years. I have re-established my own thereby, and that also of a friend eighty-nine years old, and we became as it were twenty years of age. I have administered half-a-spoonful to dying people, and they have returned to life and health.

UNIVERSAL MEDICINE — Its Composition — The auriferous Tincture of Antimony, which is primal ens of Gold, is so homogeneous to the body of man that it has been made the foundation of a Universal Medicine.
Take refined Salt of Nitre; melt it slowly in an iron vessel; being melted, add a small quantity of charcoal, made of some sweet wood like the willow, which has been well pounded. This charcoal will burn quickly, and fresh must therefore be added, till the Salt of Nitre shall become fixed after detonation, and attain a greenish colour. When this point has been reached, pour the melted Salt of Nitre into a very warm marble mortar. When it has grown cold, it will be like a white stone, and as brittle as glass. Pound it at once, and spread the powder upon an earthenware plate; having covered it to preserve it from dust, expose it slightly to the air by inclining the plate, but let this be in a place where neither sun, rain, nor dew can penetrate. Place an earthen

vessel underneath to receive the oleaginous liquid which will flow from it, for the humidity of the air, resolving the Salt of Nitre in a few days, will produce twice the weight of oil in comparison with the salt, providing the operation be performed in a mild, temperate, and humid time. This oil, when rectified, is a most powerful dissolvent for the extraction of all kinds of mixed essences.

Rx ~ Four or five parts of this rectified oil, combined with one part of the best Antimony, which may be distinguished by the redness which it obtains from gold in the mine where it is deposited. When the Antimony has been reduced to very fine powder on a marble slab, place it in a large glass vial, and pour in the Oil of Nitre above it. Two-thirds of the vial must remain empty, and the vessel must be so effectually sealed that nothing can possibly evaporate. Place it for the digestion of the matter in a mild and equable fire, or expose it to the heat of a lamp until the oil, which floats over the Antimony, appears to be of a gold or a ruby colour. Then extract your oil, filter it through paper, pour it into a long-necked glass vessel. Fill up with good and well-rectified Spirit of Wine, but, at the same time, let the vessel be two-thirds empty. Seal it carefully, place it for digestion by a gentle heat during a period of several days, until the Spirit of Wine has extracted all the colour of the oil in the Tincture of Antimony, but in such a manner that the Oil of Nitre shall remain at the bottom very clear and white, with the Spirit of Wine floating over it. They must be separated by decanting. The Oil of Nitre will always serve for subsequent operations in the extraction of the Essence of Antimony. Place the Spirit of Wine in a glass alembic; let it be distilled slowly till there shall remain at the bottom only the fifth part, which will retain the Tincture of Antimony; or, alternatively, distil the whole of the Spirit of Wine, and leave only the Essence of Antimony at the bottom. You will then possess the

Universal Medicine in a liquid form, and it will cure and preserve against every form of disease. The dose is five or six drops either in wine or broth, according to the nature of the complaint. A stronger dose will not, however, prove harmful. Commonly, the disease will be cured when it has been taken three times, but, if obstinate, the dose must be doubled. It should be taken three times a week. It will cure both internal and external disorders, including wounds and gangrene. In external diseases it should be applied in the form of a balm. It strengthens head and stomach, and is a veritable potable Gold. It operates by an insensible perspiration or sweat, as also by the passage of water, but seldom in any other way. Its effect is natural and void of violence, so that it can be used at any age, by all temperaments, and at any time.

UNIVERSAL MEDICINE — The admirable master and adept, Denis Zachaire, assures us that the Philosophical Stone, internally received, becomes the most precious of all medicaments. In the Natural Philosophy of Metals he lays down the true method of using the Divine Work to heal the diseases and woes of physical humanity: In applying our Great King for the recovery of health, a grain's weight must be taken and dissolved in a silver vessel with good white wine, which will thus be converted into a citrine colour. The patient must drink it a little after midnight, and he will be healed in one day if the disease has endured for a month, in twelve days if it should have lasted a year, but if he has been a confirmed sufferer, the cure will be accomplished in a month, during which period the medicine must be administered nightly. To ensure permanent good health, the same must be taken at the beginning of autumn and spring in the form of an electuary confection. By this means shall a man be ever fortified and established in perfect health even unto the very end of the days which the good God hath appointed him, as the Philosophers do testify in their writings.

UNIVERSAL SPIRITUAL MEDICINE -- Not only does the Blessed Stone of the Wise Adepts convert all metals indifferently into Gold or Silver, not only does it heal the diseases and remove the infirmities of the body of man; it is also an interior panacea, a great medicine of the mind. Those who are so fortunate as to have attained to the possession of this high inestimable treasure of the whole world, however evil and vicious they may previously have been, experience a change of disposition, and become persons of good act and deportment. They are transmuted in intention and exalted in aspiration; they no longer regard any earthly matters as worthy of their desire or their affection, and having nothing left that they can wish for in this world, they thirst henceforth after God only, and after the beatitudes of eternity, and they exclaim with the prophet: Lord, now only do I need the possession of Thy glory for the attainment of my entire satisfaction. So also the most pious Nicholas Flamel affirms that when any one has perfected the Stone, all that is bad within him is changed into good; the radix of sin is uprooted; he becomes liberal, mild, pious, religious, God-fearing; how bad soever he may have once been, he is henceforth ravished by the great grace and mercy which he has obtained from God, and by the contemplation of the height and depth of His divine and admirable works. The illustrious Cosmopolite, whose high achievements are among the glories of Hermetic history, also declares that the Philosophical Stone is nothing else but a mirror in which may be perceived the three divisions of the wisdom of the world. He who possesses it is wise as Aristotle or Avicenna. So also Thomas Norton, the English alchemist, testifies, in his Confession of Faith, that the Stone of the Philosophers is a help to its possessor in all his needs, of whatsoever kind they may be; it strips him of all vain-glory, and equally of hope and fear; it annihilates ambition and the violence or excess of desire; it sweetens and softens the most severe forms of adversity. God ranks the Adepts of our art next to the saints of His religion. Hence it was concluded that the ancient sages must have been in enjoyment of the Philosophical Stone, that Adam received it from the hands of God Himself, that the Hebrew patriarchs and King Solomon were initiated into the secrets of Alchemy, and that the same inestimable treasure has been promised to all good Christians by that passage in the Apocalypse: To him that overcometh I will give a White Stone.

The consideration of these benefits and blessings which accrue from the possession of the Grand Treasure of Philosophy must account for the tabulated comparisons between the mysteries of Alchemy and of religion which have been undertaken with so much profit to our art and with no detriment to that pious reverence with which the teachings of Christ should be regarded by all faithful members of the Church, whether proficient in the admirable secrets of the true knowledge or uninstructed disciples rich only in the humility of the faith. Thus, the resurrection is regarded as a veritable operation of Alchemy and a transmutation of the superior order. Our science indeed abounds in the most magnificent comparisons between metallic processes, the resurrection of the dead, and the Last Judgment. Nor are suggestive analogies wanting between our processes and the most central dogmas of the Christian religion. In his Allegory of the Holy Trinity and the Philosophical Stone Basil Valentin thus expresses himself: Dear Christian, Lover of the Blessed Art, after how brilliant and marvelous a manner has the Holy Trinity created the Philosophical Stone! For God the Father is a spirit, and He appears, nevertheless, under the form of a man, as we learn in the Book of Genesis. Of God the Father is begotten Jesus Christ His Son, who is at once God and man, and is without sin. He had no need to die, but He died voluntarily, and then rose from the dead to give eternal life to all His brothers and sisters who do also keep themselves unspotted from the world. So is Gold without stain, fixed, glorious, and able to withstand all tests, but it dies for the sake of its imperfect and disease-stricken brothers and sisters. Then, with all speed, doth it rise up glorious to deliver them and to tinge them for life eternal. It establishes them perfectly in the state of pure Gold.

UNIVERSAL MEDICINE OF METALS AND OF MAN ~ The method of preparing the Quintessence is delineated as follows by George Ripley: The operation must be begun at sunset, when the Red Bridegroom and the White Bride unite in the spirit of life to live and love in tranquility, by the exact proportion between water and earth. From the West shalt thou advance through the darkness to the North; thou shalt modify and dissolve husband and wife between winter and spring; change water into black earth; exalt thyself through many colours towards the East where the full Moon rises. After the purgatory appears the Sun, and he is white and radiant. It is now summer after winter, day after night. Earth and water are transformed into air, the shadows and the darkness are dispersed, light is manifested. The West is the beginning of this; practice, the East the beginning of the theory, and the principle of destruction is comprised between East and West.

UNQUASI ~ Quicksilver.

URINE ~ A Measure of the Ancients. It is equivalent to forty pounds of Wine, or thirty-five pounds of Oil.

URINE ~ Mercury of the Philosophers, according to Artephius.

URINE OF THE PERICARDIUM ~ Water Enclosed in a Membrane round the Heart.

VAPOUR ~ The Philosophers testify that the First Matter of Metals is a Vapour which solidifies and becomes specialised into a given metallic substance by the action of the Sulphur with which it combines in the bowels of the earth. And as they have called the Magisterium at the White the First Matter of their Metals, so also have they applied to it the name of Vapour. But by the same term they at times designate their Mercury during the period of its volatilisation, because it is then sublimed into a vapour which again falls down in the form of a dew or rain upon that earth which is at the bottom of the vase, that it may whiten as well as fertilise it.
VASE ~ The Philosophers have often given this name to their Dissolvent, which they have also termed the Vessel of the Sages.
VASE ~ The Double Vase is that of Art and Nature.
VASE ~ The Triple Vase is the Secret Furnace of the Philosophers. Some understand it to be the furnace which

contains the Vase, which, literally interpreting Flamel, they affirm to be triple. They appeal also to the authority of Trevisan.

VASE, or **VESSEL DIPLOMA** ~ A Double, or Extra Thick, Glass Vessel.

VASE ~ That Vessel which receives the Matter of the Work to be cooked or digested therein, and to be elaborated to its perfection. This Vessel must be of glass, as this substance is most adapted to retain the subtle, volatile, and metallic spirits of the philosophical compost. It is not of this Vessel that the Philosophers have made any mystery. Their secret Vase is their Water or Mercury, and not the Vessel which holds the Matter of the Work. It is in this sense that we must understand them when they say that if the Philosophers had disregarded the quality and quantity of the Vase, they would never have reached the end of the Hermetic labour. Our Water, says Philalethes, is our Fire, and in it is the whole secret of our Vase, while the structure of our arcane furnace is based on the composition of our Water. Our regimens, our weights, and our fires do all lie hidden therein.

VASE ~ Philalethes and many others distinguish two kinds, the one containing and the other contained, but the latter is also containing; it is indeed properly the Philosophical Vase; it is the receptacle of all tinctures; it is the unvarnished, earthen Aludel.

VASE OF HERMES ~ Mary the Prophetess says that this Vessel is nothing but the grade of the Philosophic Fire.

VASE OF NATURE ~ In its primary meaning, this term is referred to the Air, which receives fire, and transmits it to water. In the second place, it is that Water which is the receptacle of seeds, and carries them down into the earth. Thirdly, it is the earth which is the matrix wherein seeds corporify and develop. When the special formation of metals is the subject in hand, the Rock is the Vase or the Matrix. But when the Great Work is to be understood, the Vase is sometimes the Matter which contains the Mercury, and sometimes the Mercury itself.

VASTRIER ~ Saffron.

VAU ~ Red Sulphur of the Sages.

VEGETABLE ~ When the philosophers make use of this term they do not actually refer to any plant or vegetable substance, and in this connection we must be careful to avoid confusion. It must be noted, for example, that Saturn is described as vegetal, not as a vegetable, and it is so called, according to a number of Hermetic explanations, because it possesses a vegetative soul, which cooks, digests, and conducts it to perfection. The Sages, moreover, carefully advise their disciples to avoid operating upon vegetable matters with a view to the Great Work. The allusion would appear to be made exclusively to the colour green which manifests at a certain period in the subject that is under operation. This is the Green Lion, a symbol so frequently recurring in alchemical works. Nevertheless, Raymund Lully says that that the Mercury of the Sages must have its activity and its penetrating power augmented by the help of vegetables, and gives a list of some that will be useful, including Celandine. But even here we must not understand him in a literal manner, for he says elsewhere: When you shall have extracted your Matter from the earth, add unto it neither powder, nor water, nor any foreign substance. Now, every one knows that things of a vegetable nature are foreign to those that are of a metallic or mineral nature. However, the Philosophers have occasionally conferred on wine the title of the Grand Vegetable; but the White Wine and the Red Wine of Raymund Lully are the Menstrua of the Sages, and not the beverages which are commonly understood by these terms.

VENOM ~ The Hermetic Philosophers say that their Stone is a deadly Venom and Poison. This is not to be understood of the Perfect Stone, for that they affirm to be a Universal Medicine. The reference is to the Matter out of which the Stone is formed, and especially at the Black Stage, the corruption which then manifests being indeed a deadly poison. The name of Venom is also applied by some Philosophers to their Mercury, because it dissolves all substances with which it is combined in digestion. They say further that this Mercury is a violent poison before it has been prepared, but that after preparation it is theriacal, or an antidote to poison.

VENOM OF THE LIVING ~ The Mercury of the Sages, so called because it slays and reduces to putrefaction the Philosophical Metals which are termed Living to distinguish them from the Vulgar Metals.

VENUS ~ Step or Grade of Venus ~ The Mildness and Sweetness of Nature, the Life of Verdure.

VESTURE ~ The Matter of the Work during the Black Stage.

VIAND ~ Viand of the Heart ~ The Mercury of the Philosophers, the Principle and the Nourishment of all Metals, more especially, and in a more eminent manner, of the Hermetic Metals, because it nourishes them in the Vase, imparts strength to them, and develops them to the point of their perfection.

VIANDS OF THE DEAD ~ which also effect resuscitation ~ ~ The Mercury of the Sages. It kills the living and gives life to the dead ~ that is to say, it dissolves and induces putrefaction in the philosophical metals and gives life to those which otherwise are void of life, in other words, to the common metals.

VICTORY ~ To Gain the Victory is to Cook the Matter of the Work until it shall have acquired the White Colour.

VICTORY ~ To Chant the Victory is to Continue the Coction up to the Purple Colour.

VICUNIRAS ~ Bezoar.

VINE OF THE SAGES ~ That Matter from which the Hermetic Chemists extract their Mercury.

VINEGAR ~ Antimonial or Saturnian Vinegar ~ The Matter of the Magistery prepared for introduction and digestion in the Vase, according to the philosophical regimen. Artephius says: Take Crude Gold, beat it into leaves, or let it be calcined by Mercury; steep it in Antimonial Saturnian Vinegar and Sal Ammoniac; then place the whole into a glass vessel.

VINEGAR ~ Very Sour or Rectified Vinegar ~ is, according to the chemists, that Vinegar which has been distilled several times, and each time has been cohobated upon its feces. It becomes so potent and of so igneous a nature, that it is even affirmed to dissolve stones and metals. But this is not a radical dissolution like that of the Mercury of the Philosophers. It has a similar quality to Aquafortes which do not separate component parts, nor reduce metals to their First Principle. This, however, is accomplished by that most acrid Vinegar of the Philosophers which is their Mercury.

VIPER ~ The Matter of the. Philosophers in Putrefaction, because it is then one of the most violent and active poisons in the world. Philalethes advises the most extreme caution during operation thereon, more especially the protection of the eyes, ears, and nose.

VIPER OF REXA ~ The Matter of the Work when it has arrived at the Black Colour. The alchemists say: Take the Viper of Rexa and behead it ~ that is to say, adds Flamel, deprive it of its blackness.

VIRGIN ~ The Moon or Mercurial Water of the Sages, after it has been purified from the unclean and Arsenical Sulphurs with which it has been combined in the mines.

The author of the Secret Work of Hermetical Philosophy says that, without sacrificing her virginity, she contracts a spiritual union before she is joined in wedlock with her brother Gabritius.

VIRTUE — First Virtue — The Hermetic Chemists have given this name to their Mercury — not to the common Mercury — because theirs contains the virtues of things superior and things inferior, and is the vessel and the principle of both.

VIRTUE OF HEAVEN — Fire implanted in, and inseparable from, the Matter of the Work, which, put into activity by another fire, produces the Sulphur of the Philosophers, called the Minera of the Heavenly Fire.

VISIT OF THINGS HIDDEN — The Dissolvent of the Sages, which penetrates the most obdurate substances and extracts the tincture which they conceal.

VISQUALENS — Mistletoe.

VITRIOL — The Green of the Philosophers is their Crude Matter.

VITRIOL — Red Vitriol is the Colcotar, or Perfect Sulphur, of the Philosophers at the Red Stage.

VITRIOL — Metallic Vitriols are the Salts of Metals.

VITRIOLATUM — Liquid Vitriol.

VOARCHADUMIA — A liberal art gifted with the virtue of occult science. It is what formerly was known as the Kabbalistic Science of Metals. It is thus defined Voarchadumia is that art of auriferous metallic veins which furnishes a substance abounding in extractive metallic virtue. This art also explains the intrinsic fixed form and the natural yellow colour of gold; it distinguishes its heterogeneous, combustible, volatile parts, and exhibits how the same may be conducted to the point of perfection. It defines, lastly, the Matter of the Work — a heavy, corporeal, fixed fusible, ductile, tinged, rarefied, and arcane substance of Quicksilver and Mercury, and of an incombustible Metallic Sulphur, reduced and transmitted into true Gold by means of cementation.

VOLATILISE — To exalt a Solid Body into a rarefied state. The whole art consists in the Volatilization of the Fixed and the Fixation of the Volatile.

VOMIT — The Matter of the Philosophers at the Black Stage, because it is then in putrefaction, which separates the good from the bad, and manifests the concealed properties.

VEGETABLE WORK — Many alchemists recommend operation upon vegetable substance with a view to the transmutation of metals. Greek writers celebrated in this connection the sap of the plant Celandine, whereof the juice, the flower, and the root have alike the yellow colour of Gold. Primrose and Rhubarb were prescribed by Democritus, or by the adept who assumes his name Raymund Lully indicates the sap of Lunaria Major and Lunaria Minor for the conversion of metals into Silver. Of these the Provencal alchemist Delis pretended that he manufactured his powder of projection. Hortulanus, the philosophical gardener, gives the following singular process for the preparation of the Stone by the Vegetable Way: For the space of twelve days let the sap of reprimand, purslain, and celandine be digested in dung. Then distill it and a red liquor will be obtained. Place it again in the dung. Worms will then be brought forth which will devour one another till only one will remain. This must be nourished on the plants already mentioned until it has grown to large size; it must be then burnt and reduced to ashes. The powder that obtained is mixed with Oil of Vitriol, and this is the quintessence. It hay been indicated already that the Vegetable Way is not to be literally understood.

VISIONS — The allegorical and symbolical method adopted by the Philosophers to impart a veiled instruction upon the processes of Hermetic Science has led many of them to enclose their secrets in visions or parables. Such is the *Allegory of the Fountain*, by Bernard Trevisan, introduced into his *Natural Philosophy of Metals*, and said to contain the whole of the practice in a parabolic form. I wandered, he says, through the meadows in a mood of contemplation, being weary with much study. As the night fell, I came to a little fountain, very beautiful and clear, surrounded by a fine stone on all sides, and the said stone was beneath an old hollow oak. It was altogether encircled by walls, so that no cattle, nor indeed birds, could by any means bathe therein. I felt straightway a strong desire to sleep, and I seated myself above the said fountain, whereupon I perceived that it was covered underneath, and sealed up. In a little time a priest of great age passed by, and I demanded why this fountain was thus enclosed both above and below, and also on every side. He received my inquiry in a gracious mood, and began to speak to me in this wise: Sir, it is true that this fountain possesses a terrific virtue, above any other which can be found in all the world. It is reserved solely for the King of the country, they being well known to one another, and never does the said King pass by this fountain without being drawn hereto, so that he remains in it, bathing, for the space of eighty-two days. Then is the King renewed in youth and strength in such a manner that no one can overcome him. Straightway I besought of him to tell me if he had beheld the King, and he replied that he had seen him enter, but since then the fountain had been closed by his body-guard, nor could any one now look on him till one hundred and thirty days had elapsed, when he would begin to issue forth and to shine resplendently. The porter who is his guard continually heats the water so as to preserve his natural vital warmth. Thereupon I inquired what was the colour of the King, and he told me that he was vested in cloth of gold, that he had a black doublet, that his shirt was white as snow, while his flesh was red as blood. I then asked whether, when the monarch came to the fountain, he brought a great company with him. He answered, smiling in an amiable manner, that the King was invariably by himself, that no one otherwise approached the fountain save only the porter, who was a person of simple mind. When the monarch is within the precincts, he first of all removes his vestment of fine cloth of gold, beaten into the thinnest leaves, and delivers it to his first man, whom he calls Saturn. Saturn receives it, and has charge of it for forty or forty-two days at most. Afterwards the monarch delivers his black doublet to his second man, who is Jupiter, and he has charge of it for twenty full days. Then Jupiter, by command of his royal master, surrenders it to Luna, who is the third attendant, beautiful and resplendent to see, and she also has charge of it for twenty days. Then is the King in his clean shirt only, white as snow, with fine flowers of florid salt. This he ultimately hands over to Mars, who, in like manner, has charge of it for forty and sometimes for forty-two days. After this period, Mars, by the will of God, delivers it to the yellow and clouded Sun, who also guards it for the space of forty days. Then cometh the most bright and clear Sun, who in turn hath charge of it. Then said I unto him: Do no physicians come ever to this fountain? None, he answered me; there cometh only the porter who maintains below a continual vaporous warmth. Has this porter much work to perform? I asked. Then said the ancient priest: He has more labour at the end than at the beginning, for the fountain bursts into flame. Have many folks beheld this marvel? I inquired. It is before the eyes of the whole world, he made answer, but nothing is known thereof.

Then I said unto him: What do they after? If they desire it, he replied, they can purge the King in the fountain, circulating and containing the place in the contained of the contained containing, returning to him his doublet on the first day, his shirt on the second, and his blood-red flesh upon the third.

I cried unto him: What is this? And he answered me: God maketh one and ten hundred and a thousand and a hundred thousand, and then ten times doth he multiply the same.

I replied: I understand not at all. Then said he unto me: I shall tell thee no more, for I am weary. And I looked at him, and beheld that he was weary. But I also was weary, for I desired to sleep, having much studied on the preceding day.

In similar enigmatical and symbolical terms the same writer describes the preparation of the Magisterium in the *Vision of Verdure*:

I was buried in a most profound slumber when meseemed that I beheld a statue of about fifteen feet in height, representing a venerable and ancient man, very handsome, and beautifully proportioned in all the members of his body; he had long silver-coloured hair, falling in waves upon his shoulders; his eyes were like fine turquoises, set with carbuncles in the middle, and the radiation thereof was so brilliant that I could not support the light. His lips were of gold, his teeth of Oriental pearls, and the rest of his body was a most brilliant ruby. His left foot rested on a terrestrial globe which seemed to support him. With his right arm uplifted and outstretched, he seemed to be poising above his head a celestial globe at the end of his finger; his left hand held a key made of a large rough diamond.

This man approached me, and said: I am the Genius of the Sages; fear not to follow where I lead. Then, taking me by the hair with the hand which held the key, he raised me up, carried me away, and caused me to traverse the three regions of the air, the fire, and the heaven of all the planets. Beyond even these did he transport me; then, having enveloped me in a whirlwind, he disappeared, and I found myself on an island floating in a sea of blood. Surprised at finding myself in so remote a region, I walked along the bank or shore, and contemplating the said sea with profound attention, I remarked that the blood of which it was composed was all warm and living. I remarked also that a very gentle wind, which continually agitated it, maintained the heat thereof, and did excite in this sea a bubbling and movement which caused the whole sea to vibrate with a scarcely perceptible motion.

Ravished with admiration in that I was gazing on things so passing strange, I was reflecting on all these marvels, when I looked up, and lo! many persons standing by my side! I apprehended at first that they would seek to molest me, and I passed quickly into a bush of jasmine to conceal myself; but the odour of the said flowers did so speedily cast me into a sleep that they found and took possession of me. The tallest of the gang, who seemed to command the others, required of me in a haughty tone what had made me so rash as to enter from the Low Country into this most exalted empire. I described to him after what manner I had been transported thither. The personage did then immediately change his deportment, manners, and accent, and he said unto me: Be thou welcome, O stranger, who hast been here led by our most high and powerful Genius! He thereupon saluted me, as also did all the others, after the fashion of their land, which is first of all to lie flat upon the back, then in like way upon the belly, and so rise. I returned their salutation after the custom of my own country. After this ceremony, the commander notified unto me that he would present me to Hagacestaur, who is their emperor. He solicited me that I would excuse him in that he had no carriage by which he might transport me to the town, from which we were distant one league. He entertained me by the way with an account of the power and grandeur of the said Hagacestaur, telling me that his dominion extended over seven kingdoms, and that he had chosen that which was in the middle of the other six to establish his ordinary residence.

As he remarked that I found it difficult to walk upon the lilies, roses, jasmines, carnations, tuberoses, and a prodigious variety of other flowers, most beautiful and curious to behold, which blossomed even upon the road, he inquired, with a smile, if I feared to harm those plants. I answered that I was well aware they were devoid of a sensitive soul, but, seeing they were most rare in my own country, I shrank from trampling them under foot. Then, noticing that the whole land seemed to be nothing but flowers and fruits, I asked him where grain was sown therein. He replied that they sowed nothing of the kind, but the sterile portion of the Kingdom abounded in grain, and that Hagacestaur caused the greater portion to be thrown down into the Low Country to give us pleasure. As for the rest, it was devoured by the beasts. For themselves, they made their bread of the most beautiful flowers, kneading it with dew, and baking it by the rays of the sun. As I beheld everywhere an abounding quantity of the finest fruits, I had the curiosity to gather some pears that I might taste their flavour, but they would have prevented me, saying that these also were only eaten by animals. I, nevertheless, found that they were of delicious quality. The commander presently offered me some peaches, melons, and figs, nor ever has Provence, nor yet all Italy, nor Greece itself, produced fruits of such surpassing excellence. He swore unto me by royal Hagacestaur that the said fruits grew wild, that they did nothing to cultivate them, and that they ate nothing else with their bread. I inquired of him after what manner they preserved their flowers and fruits during the winter season, but he answered me that they knew no winter, that their years had three seasons only, to wit, spring and summer, and that of these two there was formed a third, which was autumn. The latter contained in the bodies of the fruits both the spirit of spring and the soul of summer, at which time they harvested the grape and the pomegranate, these being the choicest of their fruits.

This personage manifested an extreme astonishment when I informed him that we ate beef and mutton, game, fish, and other animals. He told me that we must possess but a gross or clouded understanding, since we made use of such coarse nourishments. I experienced no fatigue or distraction while listening to his curious and wonderful information, which I heard with great attention. But being counseled to take note of the appearance of the tower from which we were now distant only two hundred paces, I had no soon; raised my eyes to look at it than I beheld nothing, for I had become sudden: blind. At this my conductor fell a laughing, and all his company with him. The vexation of finding all these gentlemen making merry over my ill-chance caused me more chagrin than the misfortune itself. Seeing that their behavior displeased me, he who had taken such pains to entertain me consoled me t commending me to a little patience, for I should see clearly in a moment. He then went in search of an herb which he rubbed over my eyes, and I straightway beheld the light and glittering of this superb town, whereof the houses we built of purest crystal, while the sun illuminated it continually, for in the island no night or darkness did ever fall. On no account would they permit me to enter any of these houses, but I was allowed to look upon what was passing therein through the transparent medium of the walls. I examined the first of these mansions, which were all built on the same model. I remarked that they

consisted of one storey only, divided into three apartments, having several chambers and cabinets on the same floor. The first apartment was a dining-room, ornamented with hangings of gold lace, bordered by a fringe of the same precious material. The ground colour of this stuff was variable between red and green, enriched with finest silver, the whole being covered with white gauze. There were also some cabinet garnished with gems of different colours. Next I discovered a chamber entirely furnished with the richest black velvet, laced with very black and very glossy bands of satin, the whole being relieved by embroidery of jet, which had also a most brilliant and iridescent blackness. In the second apartment there was a chamber hung with white watered silk, enriched ar relieved by a broidery of very fine Oriental pearls. There were also several cabinets furnished in various colourings, such as blue satin, violet damask, citrine mohair, and carnation glazed silk. In the third apartment was a chamber draped with an eminently resplendent material, purple on a gold ground, beyond all comparison more beautiful and more rich than all the other fabrics I had seen. I inquired where were the master and mistress of this dwelling-place, and learned that they were concealed at the further end of this chamber, and that they must pass to one which was remoter still, and was separated from this one by certain communicating cabinets. The furniture of these cabinets was all of different colours, some yellow, some citrine, some purest and finest gold-brocade. I could not see the fourth apartment, but was told that it consisted of a single chamber, the furniture being covered with a tissue of solar rays, the purest and the most concentrated, on a ground of the purple fabric which I had previously remarked.
After having beheld all these curious things, I was informed after what manner marriages took place among the

inhabitants of this island. The royal Hagacestaur, having a most perfect knowledge of men and of his subjects' dispositions, from the smallest even to the greatest, assembled the nearest relatives, and placed a young, unspotted maiden with a strong, healthy, and excellent old man. Then he purged and purified the girl, washed and cleansed the old man, who presented his hand to the maiden, and the maiden took the hand of the old man. Thereupon they were conducted to one of these lodgings, the door being sealed with the same substance of which the house itself was built. Thus shut up, they were destined to remain together for a period of nine months, during which time they made all the beautiful furniture and appointments which I had so much admired. At the end of the prescribed time they came forth joined in one and the same body, possessing but one soul, the power whereof is of singular greatness on the earth. Of this Hagacestaur makes use to convert all wicked persons in his kingdoms.

They promised me that I should enter into the palace of Hagacestaur, and should behold the apartments therein, among others a saloon in which there are four statues as old as the world, that in the centre being the most powerful Seganisseged, who had transported me into this island. The three others, which form a triangle about him, are three women — to wit, Ellugat, Linemalor, and Tripsarecopsen. It was also promised me that I should behold the temple wherein is the image of their divinity, whom they call Elesel Vassergusin; but by this time the cocks had begun to crow, the shepherds were already leading their flocks to pasture, and the husbandmen, yoking their oxen to ploughs, made such a clatter that I awoke, and my dream was altogether dissipated. All that I had seen was but nothing in comparison with what they had promised to reveal me. Nevertheless, I have found abundant consolation when I have reflected on that other and heavenly empire where the Most Migh is seen seated on His throne, surrounded with glory, and acct partied by angels, archangels, cherubim, seraphim, thrones, and dominatic: There shall we behold what eye hath never seen, shall hear what ear hath never heard, since it is in that place we shall partake of eternal felicity, which God bath promised to all those who seek to make themselves worthy of it, having been created to participate in this glory. Let us then do our best to merit it. God be praised!

VULTURE — The Vulture which Flies without Wings is the Mercury of the Philosophers.

WASH ~ When the Hermetic Philosophers make use of the term To Wash, to describe an operation of their work when the Matter is in the Philosophical Egg, we must not understand that the Matter is to be extracted from the Vase and washed in water or any other liquid, but simply that the grade of the fire is to be maintained or increased, for substances are purified by fire better than by any aqueous substance. Therefore, when the Adepts say: When the artist shall behold the blackness floating over the top of the Matter, this blackness is an earth which is fetid, sulphureous, corrupting, and it must be separated from that which is pure by frequent washing in fresh water, till the Matter becomes wholly white, this signifies that the fire must be maintained at the same grade until the whitening of the Matter.
WATER ~ Purified Water. The Magistery at the White.
WATER ~ Venomous Water. The Moon of the Sages.

WATER — Arsenical Water. The Green Lion of the Philosophers.

WATER — Dead Water. The Water of Sulphur which is known to the Philosophers.

WATER — Dry Water which does not wet the hands. It must be remembered in this connection that those Adepts who give this name to their Mercury are followers of the Dry Way in the operation of the Magisterium; those who, like Paracelsus, Basil Valentine, etc., are operators of the Humid Way, apply to the same substance the appellation of Virgin's Milk, because it is a white liquor which does wet the hands, while the other is a fluid Mercury of the nature of Vulgar Quicksilver.

WATER — Purified, of the Earth — So-called because the Mercury is the purest portion thereof. But this name is more particularly applied when the Matter has become perfect at the White.

WATER — Mineral Water — Is so-called because it is obtained from the mineral kingdom, and possesses a metallic quality.

WATER — Pontic Water — Is again one of the many names which have been given to the Mercury of the Sages; in this case, the reference is to that Pontic quality which has otherwise obtained for it the appellation of a most sharp Vinegar.

WATER — Sweet Water — So called because it has the power to dissolve Gold and Silver without corrosion.

WATER — Secondary Water — So called because Mercury is a species of Aquafortis, but of a mild quality, dissolving, without corroding, metallic natures.

WATER — Antimonial, Mercurial, and Saturnian Water — So called because Antimony participates to a large degree in that Lead which is called Saturn of the Philosophers, while Mercury is called the Grandson of Saturn.

WATER ~ Bleaching Water ~ The Azoth of the Adepts, with which they say that the Laton must be whitened, and its darkness removed.

WATER ~ Aureated Water ~ Mercury when it is Perfect at the Red.

WATER ~ Radical Water of Metals ~ So called because it is their root and principle.

WATER ~ Vegetable Water ~ Brandy or Rectified Spirit of Wine.

WATER ~ Thickened or Solidified Water. The Mercury of the Philosophers in that state wherein the spirit is conjoined with the body, or in that during which they say that Mercury contains all that is desired by the Wise. When spirits and body have united to compose this Mercury, they are no longer distinguished by separate names, but are known under the one name of Mercury, because it is then properly Animated Mercury, or Mercury of the Sages.

WATER ~ Ladies' or Tinsel Water. A Liquid which softens, whitens, and gives a fresh tint to the skin. See Mynsicht, p. 189.

WATER OF HEAVEN ~ See Aqua Coelestina in Rulandus.

WATER OF THE PHILOSOPHERS ~ Some chemists have erroneously considered this to be Distilled Vinegar, others Brandy made from Wine, others again Rectified Spirit of Wine, following a statement of Raymund Lully, that the Quintessence is extracted from Wine, and is sometimes called Wine by the same writer. They would have seen their mistake had they remembered that Lully himself gives warning that this is not to be literally understood, and that when he says the Mercury of the Philosophers is obtained from Wine, he is speaking by similitude only, and that this Mercury or Philosophical Water is actually derived from the Red Sea of the Philosophers.

WATER OF SEPARATION — Aqua Fortis.

WATER OF CELESTIAL GRACE — So-called because the science which teaches the extraction of this Mercury from its mineral source is a gift of God and a heavenly favour.

WATER OF WATERS — So-called because it is actually an Aqueous Principle which contains the substance of the four elements.

WATER OF LIFE OF THE SAGES — Called also the Perfect Elixir; in that state which is requisite that it should attain before it can be used as a medicine, whether for the human body or for imperfect metals.

WATER OF FIRE — Igneous Water — So called because the Mercury contains the Fire of Nature when it is animated, and has then all that is needful for coction and digestion, as well as for the eventual communication of that multiplying virtue to Gold which of itself it does not possess.

WATER OF THE MICROCOSMOS — Spirit of Nitre.

WATER OF THE EQUINOXES — This is properly the Dew of Spring and Autumn, which possesses admirable properties for the cure of many diseases when it has been treated by an operator who is skilful in the spagyric art. The Philosophers have, however, applied the same term to their Mercury, with the intention of confusing the unenlightened, some of whom, taking such expressions literally, have concluded that the Mercury of the Sages can be extracted from equinoctial dew, and have lost both their labour and their money.

WATER WHICH BLEACHES THE INDIAN STONE — The Magisterium at the White.

WATER OF THE WORLD — Mercury in the operation of the Medicine of the First Order, or the First Preparation for the Magistery. Other names for the Mercury at this stage are as follow: Elevated Water, Exalted Water, Water of Art, Burning Water, Water of the Fountain, Purifying Water, the

First Water, Simple Water, Water of Blood, etc. When the philosophers have given the name of Water to this Mercury during the period of the Second Preparation, or the Medicine of the Second Order, they term it: Dense Water, Water of Talc, Water of Life, Water of Urine, Stony Water, Foliated Water, Azothic Water, Metallic Water of Life, Ponderous Water, Water of the Styx. In the operations of the Medicine of the Third Order it is called: Sulphureous Water, Divine Water, Water from the Clouds, Venomous Water, Water of Gold, Water of Phlegeton, Alchemical Preparation of Tartar.

WATER OF CHASTITY — An Artificial Water, made use of by persons who are anxious to safeguard chastity. The receipt may be found in the work of Adrian Mynsicht, p. 286.

WATER OF LOVE — An Extract of Human Blood, so-called by Beguin in his work on chemistry; by its means he pretended that he could compose a philter for the preservation of love between married people.

WATER OF HEALTH — A Water Distilled from Human Blood, the Flowers of the Celandine, Virgin Honey, and a number of Aromatics. Paracelsus calls it the Balm which is above every Balm, and strongly recommends it in medicine.

WATER BEARER — Aquarius. This sign of the Zodiac has been adopted by Hermetic Philosophers as a symbol of Dissolution and of Distillation.

WHEEL — The Sequence of Operations in the Hermetic Work.

WHEEL — To turn the Wheel is to observe the regimen of the Fire.

WHEEL — To make the Wheel revolve is to recommence operations, either for the confection of the Stone or for the multiplication of its virtue.

WHEEL ~ The Elementary Wheel of the Sages is the conversion of the Philosophical Elements; that is to say, it is the Transformation of Earth into Water, and then of Water into Earth. The Water contains Air, and the Earth contains Fire.

WIDTH ~ The philosophers suppose Three Dimensions in their Matter, just as Geometers assume in ordinary bodies. The Philosophical Length is the preparation of the Matter, by means of which they compose a Medicine. The Philosophical Height is its manifest part, while the Width or Breadth is the method which they employ to educe what is concealed therein. Height was regarded as cold and moist, and Width succeeded by a change of disposition, namely, to dry and cold, because the manifest always conceals its opposite.

WILL ~ The Sulphur of the Sages, or their Living Gold.

WIND OF THE STOMACH ~ Soma chemists suppose this to signify the Matter in Putrefaction; others say that it is Sulphur.

WIND OF THE WEST ~ The Stone at the Red Stage.

WIND OF THE NORTH ~ The Philosophers say that this Wind is opposed to the extraction of the Universal Menstruum. The allusion is to the dew of May and September, which falls only when the North Wind blows.

WINTER ~ The sages have sometimes applied this name to their Mercury, but they use it commonly in an allegorical sense to signify the commencement of their Work, or the time which precedes putrefaction. Thus, they say that the operation must be begun in winter and completed in autumn.

WORK ~ The philosophers enumerate various Works, but there is properly only one Work, and that may be divided into three parts. The first, which they term Simple Work, is the Medicine of the First Order, or that preparation of the

Matter which precedes the Perfect Preparation, is the Work of Nature. The second part, called the Middle Work or the Mean Work, is the perfect preparation, the Medicine of the Second Order, the Elixir, and the Work of Art. The third is Multiplication, and the Work both of Art and Nature. The First Preparation purges, purifies bodies, and tinges them in outward appearance, but the tincture will not resist the test of the Coppel. The second preparation, or the Medicine of the Second Order, still further cleanses and imparts a permanent tincture to bodies, but without much profit. The Medicine of the Third Order is properly the Grand Work. It requires more sagacity and industry, and with much profit doth perfectly tinge bodies, because a single grain converts into Gold or Silver even millions of grains of the imperfect metals. Philalethes affirms that he has most clearly explained both the work and its regimen in his treatise entitled *Enarratio Methodica Trium Gebri Medicarum, seu de Vera Confectione Lapidis Philosophi*, and he adds at the end of the book that everything is enclosed in the four following numbers: 448, 344, 256, 224. It is even impossible to succeed without the knowledge of these numbers. All the operations together constitute what may be properly said to be the Grand Work, the Work of the Sages, so called on account of the excellence by which it transcends all other productions of Art. Morien testifies that it is the Secret of Secrets which God revealed to the holy prophets whose souls are in His heavenly Paradise. Therefore does the Grand Work hold the first rank among desirable things; Nature without Art cannot achieve it, and Art apart from Nature undertakes the experiment in vain. The potency of both is needed for the accomplishment of such a chef d'oeuvre. Its effects are so miraculous that the health which it procures, the perfection which it develops in all composites of the natural world, and the great wealth which it produces, are not among its greatest marvels. If it purifies bodies, it also illumines minds; if it elaborates composites to the apex of their possible perfection, it elevates understanding to the greatest of all knowledge. Many Philosophers have regarded it as a perfect emblem of the Christian religion; they have called it the Saviour of Humanity and of all beings in the great world, because the Universal Medicine, which is one of its consequences, cures all diseases in the three kingdoms of Nature, and repairs the disorder of their disposition by the great power of its virtue. It must follow that the Magnum Opus is very easy to accomplish, because the Philosophers have all set themselves to conceal it, while at the same time they termed it a pastime for women and a game for children. But when they have spoken of it as a work of women, they refer often to the conception of man in the womb of his mother, because, according to Morien, the Work of the Stone is parallel to the creation of man. It requires, in the first place, a conjunction of male and female, in the second place, conception, thirdly, birth, then nourishment and education. The Great Work is also called the Stormy Sea, whereon those who embark are perpetually exposed to shipwreck on account of the extreme difficulties which are in the way of complete success.

WORK OF PATIENCE — The Great Work is so called because it is extremely protracted. For this reason, the Philosophers commend patience to all, and the necessity to avoid being rebuffed by the length of the time required. All precipitation comes from the demon. Nature has her weights, her measures, and her fixed periods in order to attain her ends.

WORK OF THE WOMAN — The Great Work; a term used, as we have seen, on account of the facility with which the Stone may be composed by those who are instructed in the proper method of operation.

X. ~ In some alchemical writings this letter is used to signify a Weight of One Ounce.
XEROMIRUM ~ An Unguent used in Medicine, and said to possess a desiccating quality.
XIPHIDIUM ~ Corn Flag.
XIR ~ The Matter of the Great Work when it has reached the Black Colour, and is thus in the state of Putrefaction.
XOLOCH COPALLI ~ The Gum Copal.
XYLAGIUM ~ Holy Wood.
XYLOALOES ~ Wood of the Aloe Tree.
XYLOBALSAMUM ~ Wood of that Tree on which Balm grows.
XYLOCASSIA ~ Wood of the Cinnamon Tree.

YARIA — A Name of Verdegris.
YDENS — Mercury.
YEAR — The philosophers, as we have previously exhibited, have a method of computation in time which differs from that of the Vulgar Calendar. Their years, months, weeks, and days must not be interpreted in any ordinary fashion. Their year is the time requisite for the perfect eduction of the Work, and it is so called because the operation is divided into four chief grades, even as the common year is distinguished by four seasons.
YELDIA — The Matter of the Hermetic Work. The same term has occasionally been used to signify Mercury.
YERCIA — Otherwise, the Black Pear, that is, the Matter of the Work during the period of Putrefaction.
YESIR — The Earth of the Sages. The adepts advise their disciples to beware against feeding the Philosophical Earth with too much Mercury during the process of Imbibition. It is simply to be coated or overlaid therewith; the Mercury

must not float above it to the depth of two or three fingers, for then it will be overwhelmed and submerged thereby. When the Yeser has moderately imbibed, it is to be placed in the Vase, which must be hermetically sealed.

YHARIT ~ The Matter of the Work when it has reached that White Colour which the Philosophers term their Silver.

YLIASTRUM ~ The Iliaster of Rulandus and other Philosophers, which see.

YN, YOMS, YOS ~ Names of Verdegris.

YOUTH ~ The Magistery of the Philosophers when it is Perfect at the Red Stage.

Z. ~ This letter was formerly accepted as the symbol of a Weight of Half-an-ounce, but by some it was understood to signify A.

ZAAPH ~ The Stone of the Philosophers, or their Sulphur, at the Red Stage. It was so-called on account of its warm and dry quality.

ZADDAH ~ Antimony.

ZAFARAM ~ Iron Scaling Burnt in a Copper Vessel.

ZAHAU ~ The Magistery at the Red.

ZANCRES ~ Orpiment.

ZANDARITH ~ A Substance which participates in equal proportion of Body and Spirit, that is, of the Fixed and the Volatile. Artephius explains that it refers to the Magistery at the White, and he affirms that it is identical with Corsufle and Cambar.

ZANERE ~ Orpiment.

ZANTIRON ~ Oriental Saffron.

ZARCA ~ Tin.

ZARUS — This signifies Gold.
ZAZAR — Sugar.
ZEBLICIUM — A Species of Stone having marks like the Skin of a Serpent.
ZECO — The Gum called Tragacanth.
ZEIDA — Mercury.
ZELOTUM — Petrine Mercury.
ZEMASARUM — Cinnabar.
ZENIC — The Mercury of the Philosophers.
ZENIFARI — Whey.
ZEPHYR — The Stone at the White Stage.
ZERNA — Moss.
ZERACHAR — Mercury.
ZERICUM — Arsenic.
ZERNIC — The Orpiment of the Philosophers.
ZEROBILEM — Bell Nut.
ZERSRABAR — Quicksilver.
ZERUS — Gold.
ZIBACH — The Magistery at the White.
ZIBUTUM — Mercury.
ZIMEN — Vitriol.
ZINGAR — Verdigris.
ZINGIFUR — Cinnabar.
ZIPAR — Rhubarb.
ZIT — The Red Sulphur of the Philosophers.
ZITHUM — Beer.
ZIVA — The Stone of the Sages at the White.
ZIZIPHA — A Berry.
ZOPISSA — The Pear.
ZORABA — Vitriol.
ZOTICON — The Magistery of the Philosophers elaborated to the Perfect White.
ZUMEC — The Sulphur of the Philosophers elaborated to the Perfect Red.

ZUMELAZULI ~ The Magistery of the Philosophers when it has attained to the colour of the Red Poppy.
ZUNITER ~ Marcasite
ZUNZIFAR ~ Cinnabar.

www.ingramcontent.com/pod-product-compliance
Lightning Source LLC
Chambersburg PA
CBHW071429300426
44114CB00013B/1358